Study Guide to accompany

ECONOMICS

Principles, Problems, and Policies

FOURTH CANADIAN EDITION

ALSO AVAILABLE FROM McGRAW-HILL RYERSON:

ECONOMICS: Principles, Problems, and Policies, Fourth Canadian Edition
by Campbell R. McConnell and William Henry Pope
ISBN 0-07-549174-5

MICROECONOMICS, Fourth Canadian Edition
by Campbell R. McConnell and William Henry Pope
ISBN 0-07-549175-3

MACROECONOMICS, Fourth Canadian Edition
by Campbell R. McConnell and William Henry Pope
ISBN 0-07-549176-1

ECONOMIC CONCEPTS: A Programmed Approach, Second Canadian Edition
by R.C. Bingham and William Henry Pope
ISBN 0-07-548921-X

Study Guide to accompany
ECONOMICS
Principles, Problems, and Policies

FOURTH CANADIAN EDITION

ROBERT C. BINGHAM
Professor Emeritus
Department of Economics
Kent State University

WILLIAM HENRY POPE
Department of Economics
Ryerson Polytechnic Institute

McGRAW-HILL RYERSON LIMITED
Toronto   Montreal   New York   Auckland   Bogotá   Cairo   Hamburg
Lisbon   London   Madrid   Mexico   Milan   New Delhi   Panama   Paris
San Juan   São Paulo   Singapore   Sydney   Tokyo

Study Guide to accompany
ECONOMICS: Principles, Problems, and Policies,
Fourth Canadian Edition

ISBN 0-07-549177-X

Printed and bound in Canada

3 4 5 6 7 8 9 10 AP 6 5 4 3 2 1 0 9 8

Care has been taken to trace ownership of copyright material contained in this text. The publishers will gladly take any information that will enable them to rectify any reference or credit in subsequent editions.

Canadian Cataloguing in Publication Data

Bingham, Robert C.
   Study guide to accompany Economics: principles, problems, and policies, fourth Canadian edition

Supplement to McConnell, Campbell R. Economics: principles, problems, and policies. 4th Canadian ed.
ISBN 0-07-549177-X

1. Economics — Problems, exercises, etc.
2. Economics. 3. Canada — Economic conditions — 1971- .* I. Pope, W.H. (William Henry), date. II. McConnell, Campbell R. Economics: principles, problems, and policies. 4th Canadian ed. III. Title.

HB171.5.M223   1987   330   C87-093389-2

ABOUT THE AUTHORS

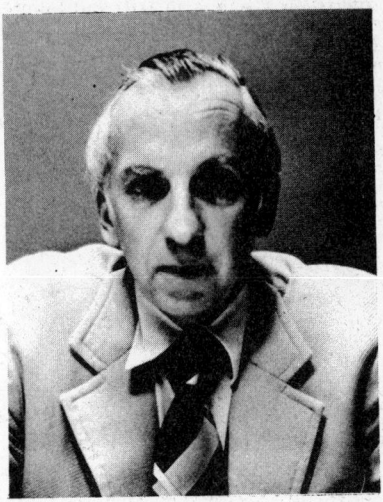

Robert C. Bingham

A week before Bob Bingham was to complete his work on the tenth (U.S.) edition of this study guide we learned that he had suffered a fatal heart attack. The following day the publishers received in their express mail the final batch of manuscript, including the following author's biography.

Robert C. Bingham was an undergraduate student at DePauw University and obtained M.A. and Ph.D. degrees from Northwestern University. He taught at the University of Nebraska—Lincoln where he was a colleague of Professor McConnell before coming to Kent State University from which he retired in 1985. He is the author of several other study guides and supplements for the principles of economics courses. Now that he is retired he teaches only one semester a year; works harder than he did before he retired; and has only a little time left for bridge, military history, and golf.

As he did for every edition, Bob not only met the writing schedules set by his editors, he met his schedules with manuscript written with his love and his skill for teaching to others the things he learned throughout his life.

William Henry Pope

Back in 1961 when Harry Pope's article "On Bomarcs, Bombs . . . and Bears" was published in the second (and last) issue of *Exchange*, its editor, Stephen Vizinczey of *In Praise of Older Women* fame, wrote that "Major W.H. Pope is a remarkable exception to the trend towards overspecialization." Vizinczey based his judgment on the author's service in action as an infantry soldier with the Royal 22e Régiment in Italy, Holland, and Korea; his tour as an aide-de-camp to the Governor General; two years as adjutant of Fort Churchill; graduation from the Army Staff College; taking a spare-time degree in philosophy and political science; heading the General Staff in Quebec City; resigning from the Army in 1959 in thorough disagreement with NATO's then (and now) limited nuclear war strategy; being elected president of the Social Democratic Party of Quebec; and working as executive assistant to the leaders of the CCF/NDP in the House of Commons. It was this last experience that convinced the author to become even less overspecialized, with the result that he has been studying economics for the past twenty-five years and writing on it and teaching it for twenty—usually in criticism of economic policies that can countenance 10% unemployment and a current account $10 billion in the hole . . . and, what's worse, seemingly without noticing the connection between them.

CONTENTS

HOW TO USE THE STUDY GUIDE TO LEARN ECONOMICS

This *Study Guide* was designed to help you read and understand Campbell R. McConnell/ W.H. Pope's textbook, *Economics: Principles, Problems, and Policies,* Fourth Canadian Edition. If used properly, a guide can be a great aid to you in what is probably your first course in economics.

No one pretends that the study of economics is easy, but it can be made easier. Of course, a study guide will not do your work for you, and its use is no substitute for reading the text. You must be willing to read the text, spend time on the subject, and work at learning if you wish to understand economics.

Many students do read their text and work hard on their economics course and still fail to learn the subject. This is because principles of economics is a new subject for them, and they have had no previous experience in learning economics. They want to learn but do not know just how to go about it. Here is where the *Study Guide* can come to their assistance. Let us first see what the *Study Guide* contains; then we will look at how to use it.

WHAT THE STUDY GUIDE IS

The *Study Guide* contains thirty-four chapters—one for each chapter in the text—an answer section, and a glossary. Each of the chapters has eight parts.

1. An *introduction* explains what is in the chapter of the text and how its subject matter is related to material in earlier and later chapters. It points out topics to which you should give special attention, and re-emphasizes difficult or important principles and facts.

2. A *check list* tells you the things you should be able to do when you have finished the chapter.

3. A *chapter outline* shows how the chapter is organized and summarizes briefly the essential points made in the chapter.

4. A list of the *important terms* found in the chapter points out what you must be able to define in order to understand the material in the chapter. A definition of each of these terms and concepts will be found in the glossary at the end of the *Study Guide*.

5. *Fill-in questions* (short-answer and list questions) help you to learn and remember the crucial and important generalizations and facts in the chapter.

6. *Problems and projects* assist you in learning and understanding economic relationships and ask you to think about certain economic problems.

7. *Objective questions* (true-false and multiple-choice) can be used to test yourself on the material in the chapter.

8. *Discussion questions* can be used to test yourself, to identify important questions in the chapter, and to prepare for examinations.

HOW TO STUDY AND LEARN WITH THE HELP OF THE STUDY GUIDE

For best results, quickly read the introduction, outline, list of terms and concepts, and check list in the *Study Guide* before you read the chapter in the text. Then read the chapter in the text slowly, and keep one eye on the outline and the list of terms and concepts. Always read with pencil in hand and use your textbook as though you expected to sell it for wastepaper at the end of the year. The outline in the *Study Guide* contains only the major points in the chapter. Outline the chapter as you read it by identifying the major *and the minor* points and by placing appropriate numbers or letters (such as I or *A* or 1 or *a*) in the margins. It is also wise to underline the major and minor points in the chapter and to circle important terms and concepts. When you have completed the chapter, you will have the chapter outlined and your underlining will give you a set of notes on the chapter. It is not necessary to keep a separate notebook for textbook notes or outlines. Be careful to underline only the really important or summary statements.

After you have read the chapter in the text through once, turn again to the introduction, outline, and list of terms and concepts in the *Study Guide*. Reread the introduction and outline. Does everything there make sense? If not, return to the text and reread the topics that you do not remember well or that still confuse you. Look at the outline. Try to recall each of the minor topics or points that were contained in the text under each of the major points in the outline. When you come to the list of terms, go over them one by one. Define or explain each to yourself and then look for the definition of the term either in the text chapter or in the glossary. Compare your own definition or explanation with that in the text or glossary. The quick way to find the definition of a term in the text is to look in the index of the text for the page or pages on which that term is mentioned. Make any correction or change in your own definition or explanation that is necessary.

When you have done all this, you will have a pretty fair general idea of what is in the text chapter. Now take a look at the short-answer (fill-in) questions, the problems and projects, and the objective questions. Tackle each of these three sections one at a time using the following procedure. (1) Answer as many questions as you can without looking in the text or in the answer section. (2) Check the text for whatever help you need. It is a good idea to do more than merely look for answers in the text: reread any section for

which you were not able to answer questions. (3) Then consult the answer section for the correct answers and reread any section of the text for which you missed answers.

The questions in these three sections are not all of equal difficulty. Do not expect to get them all right the first time. Some are designed to pinpoint things of importance, which you will probably miss the first time you read the text, and to get you to read about them again. None of the questions is unimportant. Even those that have no definite answers will bring you to grips with many important economic questions and increase your understanding of economic principles and problems.

In answering the discussion questions—for which no answers are given—it is not necessary to write out answers. All you need to do is mentally outline your answer. For the more difficult questions you may want to write out a brief outline of the answer or a full answer. Do not avoid the difficult questions just because they are more work. Answering these questions is often the most valuable work a student can do toward acquiring an understanding of economic relationships and principles.

Before you turn to the next chapter in the text and *Study Guide*, return to the check list. If you cannot honestly check off each of the items in the list, you have not learned what the authors of the text and of this *Study Guide* hoped you would learn.

SOME FINAL WORDS

Perhaps the method of using the *Study Guide* outlined above seems like a lot of work. It is. Study and learning necessarily entail work on your part. This is a fact you must accept if you are to learn economics.

After you have used the *Study Guide* to study three or four chapters, you will find that some sections are of more value to you than others. Let your own experience determine how you will use it. But do not stop using the *Study Guide* after three or four chapters merely because you are not sure whether it is helping you. Stick with it.

In addition to the material in the *Study Guide,* there are questions at the end of each chapter in the text. Some of these questions are similar to questions in the *Study Guide,* but none is identical. It will be worthwhile for you to examine all the questions at the end of each chapter and to work out or outline answers for them. Students who have trouble with the problems in the *Study Guide* will find the end-of-chapter problems useful in determining whether they have actually mastered their difficulties. All students will find many of the end-of-chapter questions more thought-provoking than the discussion questions in the *Study Guide.*

For those of you who either have trouble with or wish to learn more rapidly the sec-tions of the text containing explanations of economic theory (or principles), *Economic Concepts: A Programmed Approach* is recommended. As with the *Study Guide,* its Canadian editions have also been prepared by the Canadian co-author.

A programmed book is a learning device that speeds and increases comprehension. Its use will greatly expand your understanding of economics.

This revision is dedicated to the memory of Robert C. Bingham. Bing's suggestions and criticisms over the years were critical to the success of *Economics.* As principal author of this and the previous editions of the *Study Guide* and of *Economic Concepts,* as a colleague, and as a friend, he will be sorely missed.

Campbell R. McConnell   *W.H. Pope*

1

THE NATURE AND METHOD OF ECONOMICS

Chapter 1 introduces you to the study of economics. Its aim is to explain the subject matter of economics and the methods economists employ in the study of this subject matter.

While this chapter indicates the value to be derived from the study of economics and the importance of economic questions and problems to every individual, the heart of the chapter is the discussion of economic principles. Economic principles are generalizations based on facts; but, because economists cannot employ laboratory experiments to test their generalizations, these principles are always imprecise and subject to exceptions. Economics is a science, but it is not an exact science.

If the study of economics is to be of any worth to you, it is necessary to understand from the very beginning that economic principles are simplifications—approximations—of a very complex real world, and that both the formulation and application of these principles present many opportunities for the making of serious mistakes. Economic principles are not the answers to economic questions but are tools—intellectual tools—for analysing economic problems and finding policies to solve these problems. Selection of the economic policies to follow depends not only upon economic principles but also upon the value judgments of society—that is, upon the goals of the economy.

Pages 13 to 15 of the textbook outline a few of the many errors of commission and omission of which the beginner in economics ought to beware. The study of economics is difficult enough without compounding the difficulty with emotional, logical, and semantical errors.

CHECKLIST

When you have studied this chapter you should be able to

☐ Write the formal definition of economics.

☐ Give two (allegedly) good reasons for studying economics.

☐ Define descriptive economics.

☐ Explain what an economic principle is and how economic principles are obtained.

☐ List the two important characteristics of every economic principle and explain each of these characteristics.

☐ Explain what the "other things equal" (*ceteris paribus*) assumption is and why this assumption is employed in economics.

☐ Accurately construct a graph of two variables based on numerical data presented to you.

☐ Explain what an economic policy is.

☐ Identify the five economic goals.

☐ Recognize the "pitfalls to straight thinking" when confronted with examples of them.

CHAPTER OUTLINE

1 Economics is concerned with efficiently utilizing limited productive resources to achieve the maximum satisfaction of human material wants.

2 Citizens in a democracy must understand elementary economics in order to understand the present-day problems of their society and to make intelligent decisions when they vote. Economics is an academic rather than vocational subject, but a knowledge of it is valuable to business executives, consumers, and workers.

3 Economists gather relevant facts to obtain economic principles that may be used to formulate policies which will solve economic problems.

a. Descriptive economics is the gathering of relevant facts about the production, exchange, and consumption of goods and services.

b. Economic theory is the analysis of the facts and the derivation of economic principles.

(1) Economic principles are also called laws, theories, and models.

(2) Each of these principles is a generalization.

(3) Economists employ the *ceteris paribus* (or "other things equal") assumption to obtain these generalizations.

(4) These principles are also abstractions from reality.

(5) To obtain and test their principles economists use both the inductive and the deductive method.

(6) Economists express their principles or models not only with words, tables, and equations but with graphs.

(7) Economic models can be quite useful; but there are at least three dangers in building and using them.

c. Policy economics is the combination of economic principles and economic values (or goals) to control economic events.

(1) Values are the judgments people make about what is desirable (good, just) and what is undesirable (bad, unjust).

(2) Canada appears to have at least five major economic goals; but several of these goals may be mutually exclusive.

(3) There are three steps in creating a policy designed to achieve an economic goal.

d. To recapitulate, finding a public policy that will lead to the solution of a particular social problem requires that economists develop principles based on facts found in the world of reality.

4 Straight thinking in the study and use of economic principles requires strict application of the rules of logic in which personal emotions are irrelevant, if not detrimental. The pitfalls encountered by beginning students in studying and applying economic principles include:

a. bias or preconceived beliefs not warranted by facts;

b. loaded terminology or the use of terms in a way that appeals to emotions and leads to a non-objective analysis of the issues;

c. the definition by economists of terms in ways that may not be the same as the ways in which these terms are more commonly used;

d. the fallacy of composition or the assumption that what is true of the part is necessarily true of the whole;

e. the belief that what is true or valid during a depression is, therefore, true or valid during a period of prosperity (and *vice versa*); and

f. the *post hoc* fallacy, or the mistaken belief that when one event precedes another, the first event is the cause of the second.

IMPORTANT TERMS

Descriptive economics	Directly related
Economic principle (law)	Inversely related
	Induction
Economic theory (analysis)	Deduction
Generalization	Applied (policy) economics
Economic model	Economic policy
Abstraction	Value judgment
"Other things equal" assumption (*ceteris paribus*)	Mutually exclusive goals

Loaded terminology
Fallacy of composition
Macroeconomics
Microeconomics

Post hoc, ergo propter hoc fallacy
Correlation
Causation

FILL-IN QUESTIONS

1 Economics as a subject

a. is, first of all, the study of the _____ ,

_____ ,

and _____

of the material goods and services that satisfy human wants;

b. but, more formally, it is concerned with

the efficient utilization of _____

productive resources to achieve the _____ satisfaction of these wants.

2 An understanding of economics is essential if we are to be well-informed _____ and it has many personal applications even

though it is an academic and not a _____

_____ subject.

3 Economics, like other sciences, begins with the facts found in the world around us. The gathering of relevant economic facts is

the part of economics called _____ economics.

4 The economic principles (often called theories, laws, or models) derived from facts

are all _____ about human economic behaviour and, as such,

necessarily involve _____ from reality.

5 Economists know that the amount consumers spend for goods and services in any year depends upon their after-tax income in that year, and several factors other than their income. To look at the relationship between

the spending and income of consumers, economists often assume that these other factors are constant and do not change; and when economists do this they make the

_____ assumption.

6 What three dangers are inherent in the construction and application of economic models?

a. _____

b. _____

c. _____

7 Economic principles enable the economist to predict the result of a certain economic act or of certain economic behaviour; this ability to predict is valuable because it

makes it possible frequently to _____

_____ economic events or, at least to

_____ for them.

8 Five widely accepted economic goals in Canada are:

a. _____

b. _____

c. _____

d. _____

e. _____

9 The three steps involved in the formulation of economic policy are:

a. _____

b. _____

c. _____

10 Macroeconomics is concerned with the

_____

output of the economy and the _____ level of prices, while microeconomics is

concerned with output in a(n)_____

and the price of a(n)_____

_____ .

PROBLEMS AND PROJECTS

1 "In 1983, the Russian demand for wheat from Canada increased and caused the price of wheat throughout Canada to rise." This is a *specific* instance of a more *general* economic principle. Of which economic *generalization* is this a particular example? _____

_____

_____

2 Below are four statements. Each of them is an example of one of the pitfalls frequently encountered in the study of economics. Indicate, in the space following each statement, the type of pitfall involved.

a. "Thrift (or saving) promotes the welfare

of the economy." _____

b. "An unemployed worker can find a job if he or she looks diligently and conscientiously for employment; therefore, all unemployed workers can find employment if they are diligent and conscientious in looking for a

job." _____

_____

c. Right-of-centre: "Regulation of public utilities in Canada is an immoral and unconscionable interference with the God-given right of private property and, as you know, there is no private property in the communist states." Left-of-centre: "It is far from that. You know perfectly well that it is an attempt to limit the unmitigated avarice of mammoth corporations in order to promote the general welfare of a democratic Canada."

_____

_____

d. "The stock market crash of 1929 was followed by and resulted in ten years of

depression." _____

3 Below are three exercises in making graphs. On the graphs, plot the economic relationships contained in each exercise. Be sure to label each axis of the graph and to indicate the unit of measurement and scale used on each axis.

a.

National Income, billions of dollars	Consumption expenditures, billions of dollars
$600	$600
650	645
700	685
750	720
800	750
850	775
900	800

Graph national income on the horizontal axis and consumption expenditures on the vertical axis; connect the seven points and label the curve "Consumption Schedule."

The relationship between national income and consumption expenditures is a(n)

(direct, inverse) _____

one and the Consumption Schedule a(n)

(up-, down-) _____ sloping curve.

0

b.

Rate of interest, %	Investment expenditures, billions of dollars
8	$22
7	28
6	33
5	37
4	40
3	42
2	43

Graph investment expenditures on the horizontal axis and the rate of interest on the vertical axis; connect the seven points and label the curve "Investment Schedule."

The relationship between the rate of interest and investment expenditures is a(n) ____ one and the Investment Schedule is a(n)

_____ sloping curve.

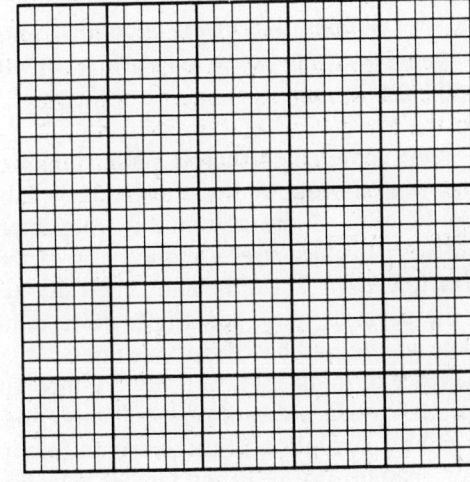

0

c.

Average Salary, Canadian University Professors	Annual Per Capita Rye Whisky Consumption in Canada (litres)
$42,000	15
43,000	16
44,000	17
45,000	18
46,000	19
47,000	20
48,000	21

Graph average salary on the horizontal axis and whisky consumption on the vertical axis; connect the seven points.

(1) The average salary of a university professor and whisky consumption (are, are not)

_____ *correlated*; and the higher average salary (is, is not) _____ the *cause* of the greater consumption of whisky.

(2) The relationship between the two variables may be purely _____ ; or, as is more likely, both the higher salaries and the greater consumption of whisky may

be the result of the higher _____ in the Canadian economy.

0

SELF-TEST

Circle T if the statement is true, F if it is false.

1 Economics deals with the activities by which people earn their living and improve their standard of living.   **T F**

2 Economics is academic and of little value because it does not teach the student how to earn a living.   **T F**

3 Gathering the relevant economic facts from which economic principles are derived is the part of economics called economic analysis. **T F**

4 In economics, the terms "law," "principle," "theory," and "model" mean essentially the same thing. **T F**

5 The "other things equal" or *ceteris paribus* assumption is made in order to simplify the reasoning process. **T F**

6 The deductive method is the scientific method, and the method used to derive economic principles from economic facts. **T F**

7 Economic principles enable us to predict the economic consequences of many human actions *and* to control (or prepare for) the occurrence of undesirable events. **T F**

8 One of the widely (though not universally) accepted economic goals of Canadians is an equal distribution of income. **T F**

9 The first step in the formulation of an economic policy, the statement of the goal or desired result, may be an occasion for disagreement because different prople may have different and conflicting goals. **T F**

10 Once a single goal or end has been determined as the sole objective of economic policy, there is seldom any question of which policy to adopt to achieve that goal. **T F**

11 If you speak of "capital" to the average person, he or she understands you to be referring to money. The economist, therefore, is obligated to use the term "capital" to mean money.

T F

12 If it is true that an increase in government spending during a period of prosperity will be inflationary, an equal increase in government spending during a depression must also be inflationary. **T F**

Circle the letter that corresponds to the best answer.

1 Which of the following terms is *not* found in a sophisticated definition of economics? (*a*) efficient utilization; (*b*) unlimited productive resources; (*c*) maximum satisfaction; (*d*) human material wants.

2 Economics is a practical field of study in several ways. Which one of the following is *not* an element of its practicality? (*a*) every person affects and is affected by the operation of the economy; (*b*) every person has to earn a living in some manner, and economics develops skills and trains the student in the art of making a living; (*c*) every person in a democracy is confronted with its political problems and many of them are economic in nature; (*d*) every person who understands the overall operation of the economy is in a better position to solve personal economic problems.

3 One economic principle states the lower the price of a commodity, the greater will be the quantity of the commodity consumers will wish to purchase. On the basis of this principle *alone*, it can be concluded that (*a*) if the price of mink coats falls more mink coats will be purchased by consumers; (*b*) if the price of mink coats falls, Mrs. James will purchase two instead of one; (*c*) if the price of mink coats falls and there are no important changes in the other factors affecting their demand, the public will probably purchase a greater quantity of mink coats than it did at the higher price; (*d*) if more mink coats are purchased this month than last month, it is because the price of mink coats has fallen.

4 An economic model is *not* (*a*) an ideal type of economy or an economic policy for which we ought to work; (*b*) a tool economists employ to enable them to predict; (*c*) one or a collection of economic principles;

(*d*) an explanation of how the economy or a part of the economy functions in its essential details.

5 Which of the following is *not* a danger to be encountered in the construction or application of economic models? (*a*) it may contain irrelevant facts and omit more relevant data; (*b*) it may come to be accepted as "what ought to be" rather than as "what is"; (*c*) it may be overly simplified and so be a very poor approximation of the reality it explains; (*d*) it may result in a conclusion that is unacceptable to the citizens or the government of a nation.

6 Knowing that as the price of a commodity rises the quantity of the commodity sold decreases, and that the imposition of a higher tax on a commodity increases its price, the economist concludes that if a government increases the tax on gasoline, less gasoline will be sold. This is an example of (*a*) prediction; (*b*) control; (*c*) policy; (*d*) the fallacy of composition.

7 Which of the following economic goals is subject to reasonably accurate measurement? (*a*) economic security; (*b*) full employment; (*c*) a viable balance of payments; (*d*) an equitable distribution of income.

8 To say that two economic goals are mutually exclusive means that (*a*) it is not possible to achieve both goals; (*b*) these goals are not accepted as goals in the USSR; (*c*) the achievement of one of the goals results in the achievement of the other; (*d*) it is possible to quantify both goals.

9 Which of the following would be studied in *micro*economics? (*a*) the output of the entire economy; (*b*) the total number of workers employed in Canada; (*c*) the general level of prices in the Canadian economy; (*d*) the output and price of wheat in Canada.

10 During World War II, Canada employed price controls to prevent inflation; this was referred to as "a fascist and arbitrary restriction of economic freedom" by some and as "a necessary and democratic means of preventing ruinous inflation" by others. Both labels are examples of (*a*) economic bias; (*b*) the fallacy of composition; (*c*) the misuse of common-sense definitions; (*d*) loaded terminology.

11 If an individual determines to save a larger percentage of his or her income, he or she will no doubt be able to save more. To reason, therefore, that if all individuals determine to save a larger percentage of their incomes they will be able to save more is an example of (*a*) the *post hoc, ergo propter hoc* fallacy; (*b*) the fallacy of composition; (*c*) a generalization that is true during a depression but untrue during prosperity; (*d*) using loaded terminology.

12 The government increases its expenditures for road-construction equipment and later the average price of this equipment falls. To reason that the lower price was due to the increase in government expenditures may be an example of (*a*) the *post hoc, ergo propter hoc* fallacy; (*b*) the fallacy of composition; (*c*) a generalization that is true during a depression but untrue during prosperity; (*d*) using loaded terminology.

DISCUSSION QUESTIONS

1 Define economics in both a less and a more sophisticated way. In your second definition, explain the meaning of "resources" and "wants."

2 What are the principal reasons for studying economics?

3 What is the relationship between facts and theory?

4 Define and explain the relationships between descriptive economics, economic theory, and applied economics.

5 What is a "laboratory experiment under controlled conditions"? Does the science of economics have any kind of laboratory? Why do economists employ the "other things equal" assumption?

6 Why are economic principles and models necessarily generalizations and abstract?

7 In what ways are the construction and application of economic models dangerous?

8 What does it mean to say that economic principles can be used for prediction and control?

9 Of the five economic goals of the Canadian economy listed in the text, which one would you *rank* first, second, third, and so on? Would you add any other goals to this list? If economic goals 2 and 3 were mutually exclusive, which goal would you prefer? Why? If goals 2 and 5 were mutually exclusive, which would you prefer? Why?

10 What procedure should be followed in formulating sound economic policies?

11 Explain each of the following: (*a*) fallacy of composition; (*b*) loaded terminology; (*c*) the *post hoc, ergo propter hoc* fallacy.

12 Explain briefly the difference between (*a*) macroeconomics and microeconomics; (*b*) deduction and induction; and (*c*) correlation and causation.

2

AN INTRODUCTION TO THE ECONOMIZING PROBLEM

The aim of Chapter 2 is to explain the central problem of economics and the Five Fundamental Questions into which this central problem can be divided.

The central problem of economics is that resources—the ultimate means of satisfying material wants—are scarce *relative* to the insatiable wants of society. Economics as a science is the study of the various aspects of the behaviour of society in its effort to allocate the scarce resources—land, labour, capital, and entrepreneurial ability—in order to satisfy, as best it can, its unlimited desire for consumption. This basic problem becomes, in reality, five problems or questions that must be answered: The level at which resources will be utilized; what will be produced; how it will be produced; how the output will be distributed; and how the economic system can be made to accommodate changes.

The production-possibilities table and curve are used in this chapter to illustrate the meaning of the scarcity of resources and of increasing costs. It is both an illustrative device that will help you to understand several economic concepts and problems and a tool that has many applications in the real world.

Every economy is faced with the problem of scarce resources and has to find answers to the Five Fundamental Questions. But no economy arrives at answers to its fundamental economic questions in the same way that another economy does. Between the extremes of pure (or *laissez-faire*) capitalism and the command economy (or commu-

nism) are various economic systems; all of these systems are different devices—different methods of organization—for finding answers to the Five Fundamental Questions.

The three practices of all modern economies are: the employment of large amounts of capital; extensive specialization; and the use of money. Economies use capital and engage in specialization because it is a more efficient use of their resources: it results in a larger total output and the greater satisfaction of wants. But when workers, business firms, and regions within an economy specialize, they become dependent on each other for the goods and services they do not produce for themselves. To obtain these goods and services, they must engage in trade. Trade is made more convenient by using money as a medium of exchange.

The circular-flow-of-income model (or diagram) is a device that illustrates, for a capitalistic economy, the relation between households and businesses, the flow of money and economic goods and services between households and businesses, their dual role as buyers and sellers, and the two basic types of markets essential to the capitalistic process.

Understand these essentials of the economic skeleton first; then a little flesh—a little more reality, a little more detail—can be added to the bones. Understanding the skeleton makes it much easier to understand the whole body and its functioning.

In Chapter 2 of the textbook are a number of economic definitions and classifications. It would be well for you to learn these definitions and classifications *now*. They will be used later on and it will be necessary for you to know and understand them if you are to understand what follows.

CHECK LIST

When you have studied this chapter you should be able to

☐ Write a definition of economics that incorporates the relationship between resources and wants.

☐ Identify the four economic resources and the type of income associated with each.

☐ State the four assumptions made when a production-possibilities table or curve is constructed.

☐ Construct a production-possibilities curve when you are given the appropriate data.

☐ Define opportunity cost and utilize a production-possiblities curve to explain the concept.

☐ State the law of increasing costs and, in as few words as possible, present the economic rationale for this law.

☐ Use a production-possibilities curve to illustrate economic growth, underemployment of resources, and increasing costs.

☐ Identify the Five Fundamental Questions.

☐ List the two major characteristics of pure capitalism and the command economy.

☐ Name and explain the three characteristics of all modern economies.

☐ Draw the circular flow diagram; and correctly label the real and money flows and the two major types of markets.

CHAPTER OUTLINE

1   The bases upon which the study of economics rests are two facts.

a.   Society's material wants are unlimited.

b.   The economic resources that are the ultimate means of satisfying these wants are scarce in relation to the wants.

(1) Economic resources are classified as land, capital, labour, and entrepreneurial ability.

(2) The payments received by those who provide the economy with these four resources are rental income, interest income, wages, and profits, respectively.

(3) Because these resources are scarce (or limited), the output the economy is able to produce is also limited.

2   Economics, then, is the study of how society's scarce resources are used (administered) to obtain the greatest satisfaction of its material wants.

a.   To be efficient in the use of its resources, an economy must achieve both full employment and full production.

b.   The production-possibilities table indicates the alternative combinations of goods and services an economy is capable of producing when it has achieved full employment and full production.

(1) Four assumptions are made when a production possibilities table is constructed.

(2) The table illustrates the fundamental choice every society must make: what quantity of each product it wants produced.

c.   The data contained in the production possibilities table can be plotted on a graph to obtain a production-possibilities curve.

d.   Which of these alternative combinations society chooses—which product-mix it selects—depends upon the preferences of that society; and preferences are subjective and non-scientific.

e.   The opportunity cost of producing an additional unit of one product is the amounts of other products that are sacrificed; and the law of increasing costs is that the opportunity cost of producing additional units of a product increases as more of that product is produced.

(1) The law of increasing cost results in a production possibilities curve that is concave (from the origin).

(2) The opportunity cost of producing additional units of a product increases as more of the product is produced because resources are not completely adaptable to alternative uses.

(3) The production possibilities curve illustrates the concepts of scarcity, choice, opportunity cost, and increasing costs.

3 The following modifications make the production-possibilities concept more realistic.

a. The failure to achieve full employment and full production reduces the output of the economy.

b. Improvements in technology and increased amounts of resources expand the output the economy is capable of producing.

c. The combination of goods and services an economy chooses to produce today helps to determine its production possibilities in the future.

d. There are many real-world applications of the production-possibilities curve and table.

4 Faced with unlimited wants and scarce resources, every economy must find answers for Five Fundamental Economic Questions: the level of resource use; what goods and services to produce; how to organize the production of these goods and services; how to divide this output among the citizens of the society; and how to accommodate changes in tastes, resources, and technology.

5 Different economic systems employ different methods to obtain answers to these Five Fundamental Questions.

a. At one extreme is pure capitalism, which relies upon the private ownership of its economic resources and the market system to answer the questions.

b. At the other extreme, the command economy uses public ownership of its resources and central planning.

c. Economies in the real world lie between these two extremes and are hybrid systems.

d. Some underdeveloped nations have traditional (or customary) economies, in which the answers to the Fundamental Economic Questions are provided by the customs and traditions of the society.

6 In common with other advanced economies of the world, the Canadian economy has three major characteristics.

a. It employs complicated and advanced methods of production and large amounts of capital equipment to produce goods and services efficiently.

b. It is a highly specialized economy, and this specialization increases the productive efficiency of the economy.

c. It also uses money extensively to facilitate trade and specialization.

7 The circular flow model is a device used to clarify the relationships between households and business firms in a purely capitalistic economy.

a. In resource markets, households supply and firms demand resources, and in product markets, the firms supply, and households demand, products. Households use the incomes they obtain from supplying resources to purchase the goods and services produced by the firms; and in the economy there is a real flow of resources and products and a money flow of incomes and expenditures.

b. The circular flow model has at least four limitations.

IMPORTANT TERMS

The economizing problem	Capital goods
	Real capital
Unlimited wants	Money (financial) capital
Scarce resources	
Land, capital, labour, and entrepreneurial ability	Rental income, interest income, wages, and profit
Investment	Factors of production
Consumer goods	Economics

Economic efficiency

Full employment

Full production

Production-
possibilities table

Production-
possibilities curve

Optimum product-mix

Opportunity cost

Law of increasing
costs

Unemployment

Underemployment

Economic growth

Five Fundamental
Economic Questions

Pure (*laissez-faire*)
capitalism

Command economy
(communism)

Authoritarian
capitalism

Market socialism

Traditional
(customary)
economy

Roundabout
production

Specialization

Division of labour

Money

Medium of exchange

Barter

Coincidence of wants

Circular flow model

Household

Resource market

Product market

FILL-IN QUESTIONS

1 The two fundamental facts that provide
the foundation of economics are

a. _____

b. _____

2 Complete the following classification of
resources.

a. _____

(1) _____

(2) _____

b. _____

(1) _____

(2) _____

3 Both consumer goods and capital goods
satisfy human wants. The consumer goods
satisfy these wants (directly, indirectly)

_____, and the capital
goods satisfy them_____ .

4 The incomes of individuals are received
from supplying resources. Four types of incomes are

_____

_____

_____

and _____ .

5 Economics can be defined as _____

_____

_____ .

6 Economic efficiency requires that there

be both full _____

of resources and full _____ .

7 When a production-possibilities table or
curve is constructed, four assumptions are
made. These assumptions are

a. _____

b. _____

c. _____

d. _____

8 Following is a production-possibilities
curve for tractors and suits of clothing.
a. If the economy moves from point *A* to

point *B* it will produce (more, fewer) ____

tractors and (more, fewer) _____
suits of clothing.
b. If the economy is producing at point *X*,
some of the resources of the economy are

either _____ or_____ .
c. If the economy moves from point *X* to

point *B* (more, fewer) _____

tractors and (more, fewer) _____
suits will be produced.

d. If the economy is to produce at point *Y*, it must either _____ or_____ .

Tractors

9 All the combinations of products shown in the production-possibilities table (or on the curve) can be achieved only if there are both full employment and full production in the economy; the best combination of products depends upon the (values, resources, technology) _____ of that society and is a (scientific, non-scientific) _____ matter.

10 The quantity of other goods and services an economy must go without in order to produce more low-cost housing is the _____ of producing the additional low-cost housing.

11 The cost of producing a commodity tends to increase as more of the commodity is produced because _____ _____ .

12 The more an economy consumes of its current production, the (more, less) _____

it will be capable of producing in future years if other things are equal.

13 List the Five Fundamental Questions that every economy must answer.

a. _____

b. _____

c. _____

d. _____

e. _____

14 The changes that occur almost continuously in modern industrial economies, and that these economies must accommodate if they are to be efficient, are changes in

a. _____

b. _____

c. _____

15 In
a. pure capitalism, property resources are (publicly, privately) _____ owned and the means employed to direct and co-ordinate economic activity is the _____ system;
b. a command economy, the property resources are _____ owned and the co-ordinating device is central _____ .

16 The three practices or institutions common to all modern economies are _____ _____ , _____ , and _____ .

17 Modern economies make extensive use of capital goods and engage in roundabout production because it is more _____ than direct production.

18 If an economy engages in extensive specialization, the individuals living in the economy are extremely _____ and if these individuals are to enjoy the benefits of specialization there must be _____ among them.

19 Modern economies practise specialization and the division of labour because the self-sufficient producer or worker tends to be a(n) _____ one.

20 In modern economies, money functions chiefly as a _____ .

21 Barter between two individuals will take place only if there is a _____ .

22 For an item to be "money," it must be _____ .

23 In the circular flow model,
a. households are demanders and businesses are suppliers in the _____ markets; and businesses are demanders and households are suppliers in the _____ markets of the economy;

b. the two flows are called the _____ flow and the _____ flow;

c. the expenditures made by businesses are a _____ to them and become the _____ of households.

PROBLEMS AND PROJECTS

1 Below is a list of resources. Indicate in the space to the right of each whether the resource is land (L_d), capital (K), labour (L), entrepreneurial ability (EA), or some combinations of these.

a. Fishing grounds in the North Atlantic ____

b. A cash register in a retail store ____

c. Uranium deposits in the Northwest Territories ____

d. An irrigation ditch in Saskatchewan ____

e. The work performed by the late Henry Ford ____

f. The oxygen breathed by human beings ____

g. The Steel Company of Canada plant in Hamilton, Ontario ____

h. The goods on the shelf of a retail store ____

i. The work done by a welder on an assembly line ____

j. The tasks accomplished in perfecting colour television for commercial sales ____

2 A production-possibilities table for two commodities—wheat and automobiles—is shown below. The table is constructed employing the usual assumptions, Wheat is measured in units of 100,000 bushels and automobiles in units of 100,000.

Combination	Wheat	Automobiles
A	0	7
B	7	6
C	13	5
D	18	4
E	22	3
F	25	2
G	27	1
H	28	0

a. Following the general rules for making graphs (Chapter 1), plot the data in the table on the graph below to obtain a production possibilities curve. Place wheat on the vertical axis and automobiles on the horizontal axis.

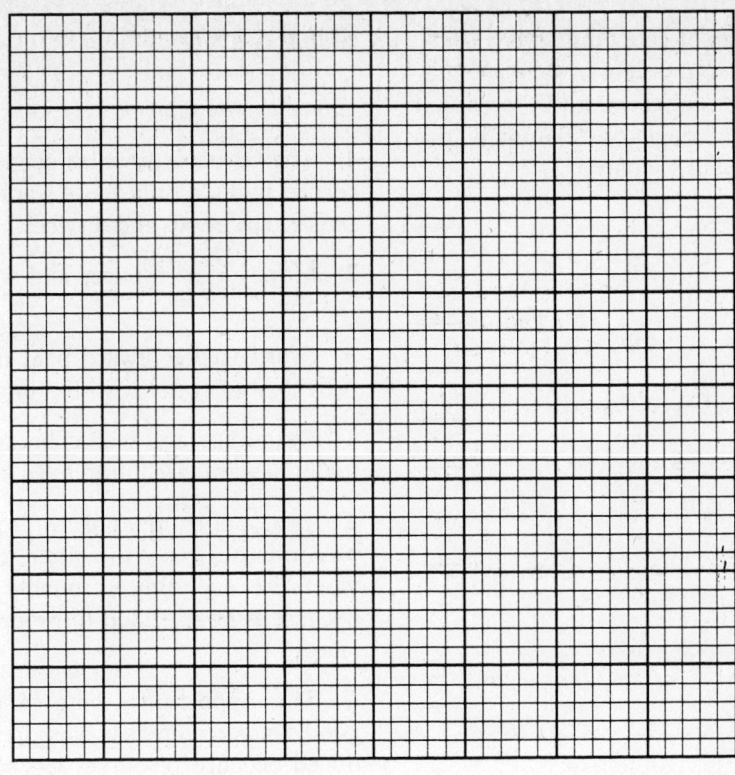

0

b. Fill in the table below, showing the *opportunity cost per unit* of producing the first to the seventh automobile.

Automobiles	Cost of production
1st	_____
2nd	_____
3rd	_____
4th	_____
5th	_____
6th	_____
7th	_____

3 In the next column is a production-possibilities curve.
Draw on this graph
a. a production-possibilities curve that indicates greater efficiency in the production of good *A*;

b. a production-possibilities curve that indicates greater efficiency in the production of good *B*;
c. a production-possibilities curve that indicates an increase in the resources available to the economy.

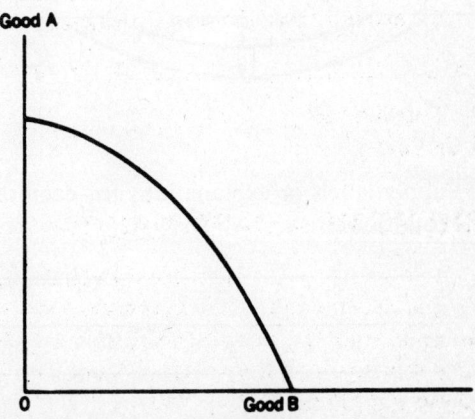

4 Below is a list of economic goods. Indicate in the space to the right of each whether the good is a consumer food (*C*), a capital good (*K*), or that it depends (*D*) upon who is using it and for what purpose.

a. An automobile   ____

b. A tractor   ____

c. A taxicab   ____

d. A house   ____

e. A factory building   ____

f. An office building   ____

g. An ironing board   ____

h. A refrigerator   ____

i. A telephone   ____

j. A bottle of Scotch whisky   ____

k. A cash register   ____

l. A screwdriver   ____

5 In the circular flow diagram below, the upper pair of flows (*a* and *b*) represents the product market and the lower pair (*c* and *d*) the resource market.

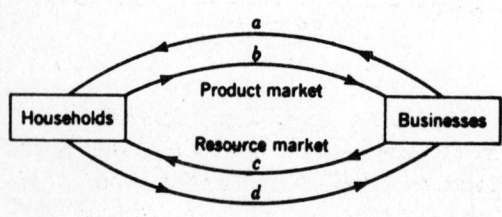

Supply labels or explanations for each of the four flows.

a. _____

b. _____

c. _____

d. _____

SELF-TEST

Circle T if the statement is true, F is it is false.

1 The wants with which economics is concerned include only those wants that can be satisfied by goods and services. **T F**

2 Money is a resource and is classified as "capital." **T F**

3 Profit is the reward paid to those who provide the economy with capital. **T F**

4 Resources are scarce because society's material wants are unlimited. **T F**

5 The opportunity cost of producing anti-pollution devices is the other goods and services the economy is unable to produce because it has decided to produce these devices. **T F**

6 The opportunity cost of producing a good tends to increase as more of it is produced because resources less suitable to its production must be employed. **T F**

7 Drawing a production-possibilities curve concave to the origin is the geometric way of stating the law of increasing costs. **T F**

8 It is not possible for an economy capable of producing just two goods to increase its production of both. **T F**

9 Economic growth means an increase in the ability of an economy to produce goods and services; this is shown by a movement of the production-possibilities curve to the right. **T F**

10 The more capital goods an economy produces today, the greater will be the total output of all goods it can produce in the future, other things being equal. **T F**

11 It is economically desirable for a nation to have unemployed resources at the outset of a war, because it can increase its production of military goods without having to decrease its production of civilian goods. **T F**

12 In the economic system called authoritarian capitalism, most property is publicly owned but the market system is used to coordinate economic activity.   **T   F**

13 Prices are not employed in communistic and socialistic economies.   **T   F**

14 The employment of capital to produce goods and services requires that there be "roundabout production" but it is more efficient than "direct" production.   **T   F**

15 Increasing the amount of specialization in an economy generally leads to more efficient use of its resources.   **T   F**

16 Money is a device for facilitating the exchange of goods and services.   **T   F**

17 "Coincidence of wants" means that two persons desire to acquire the same good or service.   **T   F**

18 Cigarettes may serve as money if sellers are generally willing to accept them as money.   **T   F**

19 In the circular flow model, the household functions on the demand side of the resource and product markets.   **T   F**

Circle the letter that corresponds to the best answer.

1 An "innovator" is defined as an entrepreneur who (*a*) makes basic policy decisions in a business firm; (*b*) combines factors of production to produce a good or service; (*c*) invents a new product or process for producing a product; (*d*) introduces new products on the market or employs a new method to produce a product.

2 An economy is efficient when it has achieved (*a*) full employment; (*b*) full production; (*c*) either full employment or full production; (*d*) both full employment and full production.

3 When a production-possibilities schedule is written (or a production-possibilities curve is drawn), four assumptions are made. Which of the following is *not* one of those assumptions? (*a*) only two productions are produced; (*b*) the nation is not at war; (*c*) the economy has both full employment and full production; (*d*) the quantities of all resources available to the economy are fixed.

4 At point *A* on the production-possibilities curve in the illustration below, (*a*) more wheat than tractors is being produced; (*b*) more tractors than wheat are being produced; (*c*) the economy is employing all its resources; (*d*) the economy is not employing all its resources.

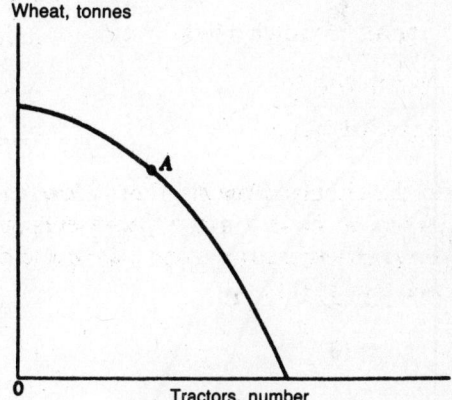

5 In a society's production-possibilities table, the combination of products that is its optimum product-mix depends upon that society's (*a*) resources; (*b*) technology; (*c*) level of employment; (*d*) values.

6 The production-possibilities curve, when viewed from the origin, is (*a*) concave; (*b*) convex; (*c*) linear; (*d*) positive.

7 A farmer who produces crops by inefficient methods is (*a*) an employed worker; (*b*) an underemployed worker; (*c*) a fully employed worker; (*d*) an apparently unemployed worker.

8 If there is an increase in the resources available within the economy, (a) more goods and services will be produced in the economy; (b) the economy will be capable of producing more goods and services; (c) the standard of living in the economy will rise; (d) the technological efficiency of the economy will improve.

9 If the production-possibilities curve on the graph below moves from position A to position B, then (a) the economy has increased the efficiency with which it produces wheat; (b) the economy has increased the efficiency with which it produces tractors; (c) the economy has put previously idle resources to work; (d) the economy has gone from full employment to less than full employment.

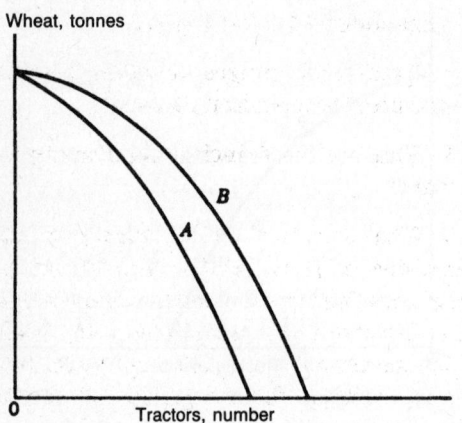

10 Which one of the following is *not* one of the Five Fundamental Questions every economy must answer? (a) what level of resource-use to have; (b) what goods and services to produce; (c) how to distribute the output of the economy; (d) how to enforce the law of increasing costs.

11 The private ownership of property resources and use of the market system to direct and co-ordinate economic activity is characteristic of (a) pure capitalism; (b) the command economy; (c) market socialism; (d) the traditional economy.

12 The public ownership of property resources and use of a market system to direct and co-ordinate economic activity is characteristic of (a) pure capitalism; (b) the command economy; (c) market socialism; (d) authoritarian capitalism.

13 To decide how to use its scarce resources to satisfy human wants, pure capitalism relies on (a) central planning; (b) roundabout production; (c) a price system; (d) the coincidence of wants.

14 In pure capitalism, the role of government is best described as (a) non-existent; (b) limited; (c) significant; (d) extensive.

15 Which of the following is *not* a necessary consequence of specialization? (a) people will use money; (b) people will engage in trade; (c) people will be dependent upon each other; (d) people will produce more of some things than they would produce in the absence of specialization.

16 In an economy in which there are full employment and full production, constant amounts of resources, and unchanging technology (a) to increase the production of capital goods requires an increase in the production of consumer goods; (b) to decrease the production of capital goods necessitates a decrease in the production of consumer goods; (c) to increase the production of capital goods is impossible; (d) to increase the production of capital goods a decrease in the production of consumer goods is needed.

17 Which of the following is *not* a characteristic of competition as the economist sees it? (a) the widespread diffusion of economic power; (b) a large number of buyers in product markets; (c) several sellers of all products; (d) the relatively easy entry into and exit of producers from industries.

18 The two kinds of market found in the circular flow model are (a) the real and the money markets; (b) the real and the product markets; (c) the money and the resource markets; (d) the product and the resource markets.

19 In the circular flow model, businesses (a) demand both products and resources; (b) supply both products and resources; (c) demand products and supply resources; (d) supply products and demand resources.

20 One of the limitations of the circular flow model found in this chapter is that (a) no mention is made of the role of government; (b) it is assumed households save some of their income; (c) too much attention is paid to how resource and product prices are determined; (d) it "ensnares the view in a maze of detail."

DISCUSSION QUESTIONS

1 Explain what is meant by the "economizing problem." Why are resources scarce?

2 In what sense are wants satiable, and in what sense are they insatiable?

3 What are the four economic resources? How is each of these resources defined? What is the income earned by each of them called?

4 When is a society economically efficient? What is meant by "full production," and how does it differ from "full employment"?

5 What four assumptions are made in drawing a production-possibilities curve or schedule? How do technological advance and an increased supply of resources in the economy affect the curve or schedule?

6 Why cannot an economist determine which of the combinations in the production-possibilities table is "best"? What determines the optimum product-mix?

7 What is opportunity cost? What is the law of increasing cost? Why do costs increase?

8 What is the important relationship between the *composition* of the economy's current output and the *location* of future production-possibilities curves?

9 What are the Five Fundamental Economic Questions?

10 Pure capitalism and the command economy differ in two important ways. Compare these two economic systems with each other and with authoritarian capitalism and market socialism.

11 What are the advantages of "indirect" or "roundabout" production?

12 How does an economy benefit from specialization and the division of labour?

13 What disadvantages are there to specialization and the division of labour?

14 What are the principal disadvantages of barter?

15 What is money? What important function does it perform? Explain how money performs this function and how it overcomes the disadvantages associated with barter. Why are people willing to accept paper money in exchange for the goods and services they have to sell?

16 In the circular-flow-of-income model: (a) What two markets are involved? (b) What roles do households play in each of these markets? (c) What roles do businesses play in each of these markets? (d) What two income flows are pictured in money terms? In real terms? (e) What two expenditures flows are pictured in money terms? In real terms?

17 What are the four shortcomings of the circular-flow-of-income model?

3

DEMAND, SUPPLY, AND ELASTICITY

Chapter 3 is an introduction to the most fundamental tools of economic analysis: demand and supply. If you are to progress successfully to an understanding of elasticity in the latter part of this chapters, it is essential that you understand what is meant by demand and supply and how to use these powerful tools.

Demand and supply are simply "boxes" or categories into which all the forces and factors that affect the price and the quantity of a good bought and sold in a competitive market can conveniently be placed. Demand and supply determine price and quantity exchanged, and it is necessary to see *why* and *how* they do this.

Many students never do understand demand and supply because they never learn to *define* demand and supply *exactly* and because they never learn (1) what is meant by an increase or decrease in demand or supply, (2) the important distinctions between "demand" and "quantity demanded" and between "supply" and "quantity supplied," (3) the equally important distinctions between an increase (or decrease) in demand and an increase (or decrease) in quantity demanded and between an increase (or decrease) in supply and an increase (or decrease) in quantity supplied.

Having learned these, however, it is no great trick to comprehend the so called "law of supply and demand." The equilibrium price—that is, the price that will tend to prevail in the market as long as demand and supply do not change—is simply the price at which *quantity demanded and quantity supplied* are equal. The quantity bought and sold in the market (the equilibrium quantity) is the quantity demanded and supplied at the equilibrium price. If you can determine the equilibrium price and quantity under one set of demand and supply conditions, you can determine them under any other set and so will be able to analyse for yourself the effects of changes in demand and supply upon equilibrium price and quantity.

The chapter includes a brief examination of the factors that influence demand and supply and of the ways in which changes in these influences will affect and cause changes in demand and supply. A graphic method is employed in this analysis, in order to facilitate an understanding of demand and supply, equilibrium price and quantity, changes in demand and supply, and the resulting changes in equilibrium price and quantity. In addition to understanding the *precise* definitions of demand and supply, it is necessary to understand the two counterparts of demand and supply: the demand *curve* and the supply *curve*. These are simply graphic (or geometric) representations of the same data contained in the schedules of demand and supply.

Of particular importance and value in studying much of the material found in the remainder of the text is the concept of elasticity, to which the second half of Chapter 3 is devoted.

With respect to the concept of elasticity of demand, it is essential for you to understand (1) what elasticity measures; (2) how the price-elasticity formula is applied to measure the elasticity of demand; (3) the difference between elastic, inelastic, and unitary elastic demand; (4) how total revenue varies in each of these three cases; and (5) the meaning of perfect elasticity and perfect inelasticity.

When you have become throughly acquainted with the elasticity-of-demand concept, you will find you have very little trouble understanding the elasticity of *supply* and that the transition requires no more than the substitution of the words "quantity supplied" for the words "quantity demanded." Here attention should be concentrated upon the meaning of elasticity of supply, its measurement, and its principal determinant.

In the final section of the chapter, two topics are discussed. The first of these topics is price ceilings and supports. You should note that these ceilings and supports prevent supply and demand from determining the equilibrium price of a commodity and from determining the quantity of the commodity that will be bought and sold in the market. The consequences will be shortages or surpluses of the commodity.

The incidence of a sales excise tax is the second topic. Incidence means "who ends up paying the tax." The most important thing you will learn is that the elasticities of demand *and* of supply determine how much of the tax will be paid by buyers and how much of it will be paid by sellers. you should be especially careful to learn and to understand how the two elasticities affect the incidence of a tax.

Demand and supply and elasticity are the foundation of the rest of Part 2 and Parts 3 and 4 of the text. If you master these topics now, you will be able to understand the material in these chapters. Demand and supply have so many applications that they are the most important single tool in economics. You will employ this tool over and over again. It will turn out to be as important to you as jet propulsion is to the pilot of a DC-10. You can't get off the ground without it.

CHECK LIST

When you have studied this chapter you should be able to

☐ Define a market.

☐ Define demand, quantity demanded, supply, and quantity supplied.

☐ Graph demand and supply when you are given demand and supply schedules.

☐ State the law of demand and the law of supply.

☐ List the major determinants of demand and of supply.

☐ Determine, when you are given the demand for and the supply of a good, what the equilibrium price and the equilibrium quantity will be.

☐ Explain why the price of a good and the amount of the good bought and sold in competitive market will be the equilibrium price and the equilibrium quantity, respectively.

☐ Predict the effects of changes in demand and supply on equilibrium price and equilibrium quantity; and on the prices of substitute and complementary goods.

☐ Explain the meaning of the rationing function of prices.

☐ Define elasticity of demand and compute the coefficient of elasticity when you are given the demand data.

☐ Explain the meaning of elastic, inelastic, and unitary elastic demand; apply the total-revenue test to determine whether demand is elastic, inelastic, or unitary elastic.

☐ List the four major determinants of the elasticity of demand; explain how each of these affects elasticity.

☐ Define elasticity of supply; compute the coefficient of the elasticity of supply from data; explain how time affects the elasticity of supply.

☐ Explain the economic consequences of price supports and price ceilings.

☐ State the relationship between the elasticities of demand and supply and the incidence of an excise tax.

CHAPTER OUTLINE

1 A market is any institution or mechanism that brings together the buyers and the sell-

ers of a particular good or service; and in this chapter it is assumed that markets are perfectly competitive.

2 Demand is a schedule of prices and the quantities that buyers will purchase at each of these prices during some period of time.

a. As price rises, buyers will purchase smaller quantities, and as price falls they will purchase larger quantities; this is the law of demand.

b. The demand curve is a graphic representation of demand and the law of demand.

c. Market (or total) demand for a good is a summation of the demands of all individuals in the market for that good.

d. Demand for a good depends upon the tastes, income, and expectations of buyers; the number of buyers in the market; and the prices of related goods.

e. A change (either an increase or a decrease) in demand is caused by a change in any of the factors (in *d*) that determine demand, and means that the demand schedule and demand curve have changed.

f. A change in demand and a change in the quantity demanded are *not* the same thing.

3 Supply is a schedule of prices and the quantities sellers will sell at each of these prices during some period of time.

a. The law of supply states that, as the price of the good rises, larger quantities will be offered for sale, and that, as the price of the good falls, smaller quantities will be offered for sale.

b. The supply curve is a graphic representation of supply and the law of supply; the market supply of a good is the sum of the supplies of all sellers of the good.

c. The supply of a good depends upon the techniques used to produce it, the prices of the resources employed in its production, the extent to which it is taxed or subsidized, the prices of other goods that might be produced, price expectations of sellers, and the number of sellers of the product.

d. Supply will change when any of these de-terminants of supply changes; a change in supply is a change in the entire supply schedule or curve.

e. A change in supply must be distinguished from a change in quantity supplied.

4 The market or equilibrium price of a commodity is that price at which quantity demanded and quantity supplied are equal; and the quantity exchanged in the market (the equilibrium quantity) is equal to the quantity demanded and supplied at the equilibrium price.

a. The rationing function of price is the elimination of shortages and surpluses of the commodity.

b. A change in demand, supply, or both, changes both the equilibrium price and the equilibrium quantity in specific ways.

c. In resource markets, suppliers are households and demanders are business firms, and in product markets, suppliers are business firms and demanders are households; and supply and demand are useful in the analysis of prices and quantities exchanged in both types of markets.

d. When demand and supply schedules (or curves) are drawn up, it is assumed that all the non-price determinants of demand and supply remain unchanged.

5 Price elasticity of demand is a measure of the sensitivity of quantity demanded to changes in the price of the product; and when quantity demanded is relatively sensitive (insensitive) to a price change demand is said to be elastic (inelastic).

a. The exact degree of elasticity can be measured by using a formula to compute the elasticity coefficient.

(1) The changes in quantity demanded and in price are measured in percentages so that the elasticity coefficient is not affected by the choice of units employed to measure price and quantity.

(2) Because price and quantity demanded are inversely related to each other, the price elasticity of demand coefficient is a negative

number; but economists ignore the minus sign in front of the coefficient and focus their attention on its absolute value.

(3) Demand is elastic (inelastic, unit elastic) when the percentage change in quantity is greater than (less than, equal to) 1.

b. In measuring the percentage changes in quantity and in price, the average of the two quantities and the average of the two prices are used as the reference points.

c. The way in which total revenue changes (increases, decreases, or remains constant) when price changes is a test of the elasticity of demand for a product.

d. It is important to note that the elasticity of demand

(1) is not the same at all prices and that demand is typically elastic at higher and inelastic at lower prices; and

(2) cannot be judged from the slope of the demand curve.

e. The price elasticity of demand for a product depends upon the number of good substitutes the product has, its relative importance in the consumer's budget, whether it is a necessity or a luxury, and the period of time under consideration.

f. Price elasticity of demand is of practical importance in matters of public policy and in the setting of prices by the individual business firm.

g. Price elasticity of supply is measure of the sensitivity of quantity supplied to changes in the price of the product; while there is no total-revenue test, the formula used to measure elasticity of demand can also be used to measure elasticity of supply. The elasticity of supply depends primarily upon the amount of time sellers have to adjust to a price change.

6. Supply and demand analysis and the elasticity concepts have many important applications.

a. Price ceilings and price supports set by government prevent price from performing its rationing function.

(1) A price ceiling results in a shortage of the commodity, may bring about formal rationing by government and a black market, and causes a misallocation of resources.

(2) A price support creates a surplus of the commodity, and may induce government to undertake measures either to increase the demand for or to decrease the supply of the commodity.

b. The price elasticities of demand and supply determine the incidence of a sales or excise tax.

(1) The imposition of such tax on a commodity decreases the supply of the commodity and increases its price. The amount of the price increase is the portion of the tax paid by the buyer; the seller pays the rest.

(2) The price elasticities of demand and supply affect the portions paid by buyers and sellers.

(i) The more elastic (inelastic) the demand for the commodity, the greater (smaller) is the portion paid by the seller.

(ii) The more elastic (inelastic) the supply of the commodity, the greater (smaller) is the portion paid by the buyer.

(3) In addition to these conclusions, it is possible to discover who benefits from the subsidization of the production of a product and how taxes and subsidies may be used to improve the allocation of resources whenever spillover costs or benefits are present.

IMPORTANT TERMS

Demand schedule

Quantity demanded

Law of demand

Diminishing marginal utility

Income effect

Substitution effect

Demand curve

Individual demand

Total or market demand

Non-price determinant of demand

Increase (or decrease) in demand

Normal (superior) good

Inferior good

Substitute (competing) goods

Complementary goods

Independent goods

Supply schedule

Quantity supplied

Law of supply

Supply curve

Non-price
  determinant
  of supply

Increase (or decrease)
  in supply

Equilibrium price

Equilibrium quantity

Rationing function of
  prices

Price-increasing
  (-decreasing) effect

Quantity-increasing
  (-decreasing) effect

Price elasticity of
  demand

Elastic demand

Inelastic demand

Total-revenue test

Elasticity coefficient

Elasticity formula

Unitary elasticity

Perfect inelasticity of
  demand

Perfect elasticity of
  demand

Price elasticity of
  supply

Elastic supply

Inelastic supply

Market period

Short run

Long run

Increasing-cost
  industry

Constant-cost industry

Price ceiling

Price support

Tax incidence

FILL-IN QUESTIONS

1 A market is the institution or mechanism that brings together the _____ and the _____ of a particular good or service.

a. In resource markets, prices are determined by the demand decisions of (business firms, households) _____ and the supply decisions of _____ .

b. In product markets they are determined by _____ and _____ .

2 When demand or supply is graphed, price is placed on the (horizontal, vertical) _____ axis and quantity on the _____ axis.

3 The relationship between price and quantity in the demand schedule is a(n) (direct, inverse) _____ relationship; in the supply schedule the relationship is a(n) _____ one.

4. The added satisfaction or pleasure obtained by a consumer from additional units of a product decreases as her or his consumption of the product increases. This phenomenon is called _____ .

5 A consumer tends to buy more of a product as its price falls because

a. the purchasing power of the consumer is increased and the consumer tends to buy more of this product (and of other products); this is called the (income, substitution) _____ effect.

b. the product becomes less expensive relative to similar products and the consumer tends to buy more of this and less of the similar products; and this is called the _____ effect.

6 When a consumer demand schedule or curve is drawn up, it is assumed that five factors that determine demand are fixed and constant. These five determinants of consumer demand are

a. _____

b. _____

c. _____

d. _____

e. _____

7 A decrease in demand means that consumers will buy (larger, smaller) _____ quantities at every price or will pay (more, less) _____ for the same quantities.

8 A change in income or in the price of another product will result in a change in the (demand for, quantity demanded of)

the given product, while a change in the price of the given product will result in ____

_____ .

9 The fundamental factors that determine the supply of any commodity in the product market are

a. _____

b. _____

c. _____

d. _____

e. _____

f. _____

10 The equilibrium price of a commodity is the price at which _____

_____ .

11 If quantity demanded exceeds quantity supplied, price is (above, below) _____ the equilibrium price; and the (shortage, surplus) _____ will cause the price to (rise, fall) _____.

12 In the spaces below each of the following, indicate the effect [*increase* (+), *decrease* (-), or *indeterminate* (?)] upon the equilibrium price *and* equilibrium quantity of each of these changes in demand and/or supply.

a. Increase in demand, supply constant

____ ____

b. Increase in supply, demand constant

____ ____

c. Decrease in demand, supply constant

____ ____

d. Decrease in supply, demand constant

____ ____

e. Increase in demand, increase in supply

____ ____

f. Increase in demand, decrease in supply

____ ____

g. Decrease in demand, decrease in supply

____ ____

h. Decrease in demand, increase in supply

____ ____

13 If supply and demand establish a price for a good such that there is no shortage or surplus of the good, then price is successfully performing its _____ function.

14 To assume that all the non-price determinants of demand and supply do not change is to employ the _____ _____ assumption.

15 If a relatively large change in price results in a relatively small change in quantity demanded, demand is _____; if a relatively small change in price results in a relatively large change in quantity demanded, demand is _____.

16 If demand is elastic, price and total revenue are (directly, inversely) _____ related; if demand is inelastic, they are _____ related.

17 Complete the summary table.

If demand is	The elasticity coefficient is	If price rises, total revenue will	If price falls, total revenue will
Elastic	____	____	____
Inelastic	____	____	____
Of unitary elasticity	____	____	____

18 If a change in price causes no change in quantity demanded, demand is perfectly (elastic, inelastic) _____ and the demand curve is (horizontal, vertical)

_____ ; if an extremely small change in price results in an extremely large change in quantity demanded, demand is _____

_____

and the demand curve is _____

_____ .

19 If the price of a commodity declines,
a. when demand is inelastic, the loss of revenue due to the lower price is _____ the gain in revenue due to the greater quantity demanded;
b. when demand is elastic, the loss of revenue due to the lower price is _____ the gain in revenue due to the greater quantity demanded;
c. when demand is of unitary elasticity, the loss of revenue due to the lower price is _____ the gain in revenue due to the greater quantity demanded.

20 List four determinants of the price elasticity of demand.
a. _____
b. _____
c. _____
d. _____

21 The most important factor affecting the price elasticity of supply is _____ .

22 If the demand and supply schedules for a certain product are those given in the table, answer the following questions.

Quantity demanded	Price	Quantity supplied
12,000	$10	18,000
13,000	9	17,000
14,000	8	16,000
15,000	7	15,000
16,000	6	14,000
17,000	5	13,000
18,000	4	12,000

a. The equilibrium price of the product is $ _____ and the equilibrium quantity is _____ .
b. If the government imposes a price ceiling of $5 on this product, there would be a (shortage, surplus) _____ of _____ units.
c. If the government supports a price of $8, there would be a _____ of _____ units.

23 Price ceilings imposed by the Canadian government have usually occurred during _____ periods; they result in _____ of the commodities, and require that the government institute _____ .

24 A mimimum price imposed by the government on a commodity causes a _____ of the commodity and requires that the government either _____ or _____ to eliminate this.

25 The two most common examples of government-imposed minimum prices are

_____

and _____ .

26 Price ceilings and price supports prevent prices from performing their _____ function.

27 When a sales or excise tax is levied on a

commodity, the amount of the tax borne by buyers of the commodity is equal to

_____ .

The incidence of such a tax depends on the elasticity of demand and supply.

a. The buyer's portion of the tax is larger the (more, less) _____ elastic the demand and the _____ elastic the supply.

b. The seller's portion of the tax is larger the _____ elastic the demand and the _____ elastic the supply.

PROBLEMS AND PROJECTS

1 Using the demand schedule below, plot the demand curve on the graph below. Label the axes and indicate for each axis the units being used to measure price and quantity.

Price	Quantity demanded, 1,000 bushels of soybeans
$7.20	10
7.00	15
6.80	20
6.60	25
6.40	30
6.20	35

a. Plot the following supply schedule on the same graph.

Price	Quantity supplied, 1,000 bushels of soybeans
$7.20	40
7.00	35
6.80	30
6.60	25
6.40	20
6.20	15

b. The equilibrium price of soybeans will be

$ _____.

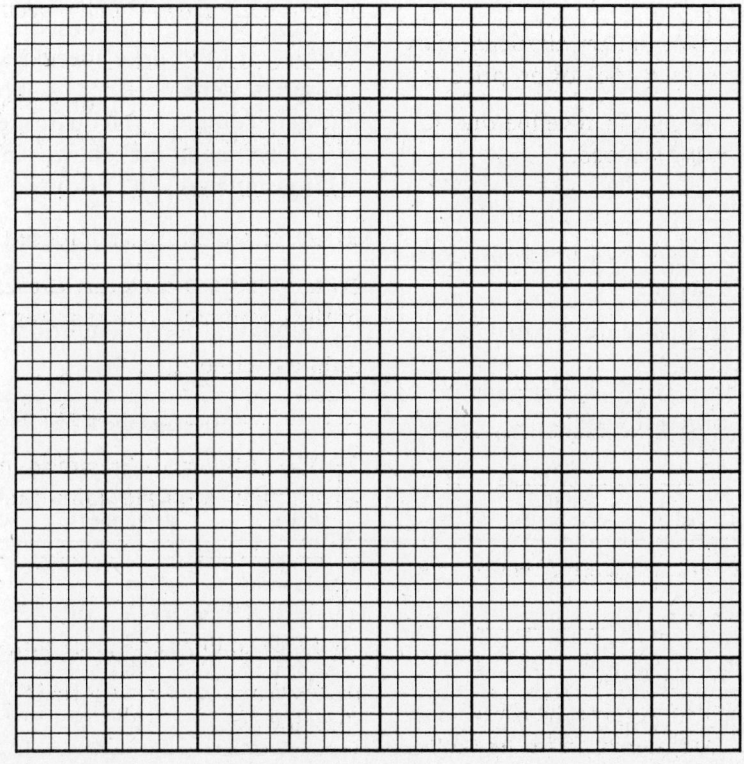

0

c. _____
thousand bushels of soybeans will be exchanged at this price.

d. Indicate clearly on the graph the equilibrium price and quantity by drawing lines from the intersection of the supply and demand curves to the price and quantity axes.

e. If the federal government supported a price of $7 per bushel there would be a

(shortage, surplus) _____

of _____ bushels of soybeans.

2 The demand schedules of three individuals (Robert, Charles, And Lynn) for loaves of bread are shown below. Assuming there are only three buyers of bread, draw up the total or market demand schedule for bread.

Price	Quantity demanded, loaves of bread			Total
	Robert	Charles	Lynn	
$1.15	1	4	0	_____
1.10	3	5	1	_____
1.05	6	6	5	_____
1.00	10	7	10	_____
0.95	15	8	16	_____

3 Below is a demand schedule for bushels of apples. In columns 3 and 4, insert *any* new figures for quantity that represent in column

3 an increase in demand, and in column 4 a decrease in demand.

(1) Price	(2) Quantity demanded	(3) Demand increases	(4) Demand decreases
$16.00	400	_____	
15.90	500	_____	_____
15.80	600	_____	_____
15.70	700	_____	_____
15.60	800	_____	_____

4 Assume that O'Rourke has, when his income is $300 a week, the demand schedule for good A shown in columns 1 and 2 of the table below and the demand schedule for good B shown in columns 4 and 5. Asssume that the prices of A and B are $.80 and $5, respectively.

a. How much A will O'Rourke buy?

_____ How much B? _____

b. Suppose that, as a consequence of a $30 increase in O'Rourke's weekly income, the quantities demanded of A become those shown in column 3 and quantities demanded of B become those shown in column 6. (1) How much A will O'Rourke now buy?

_____

How much B?_____

(2) Good A is (normal, inferior) _____ .

Demand for A (per week)			Demand for B (per week)		
(1) Price	(2) Quantity demanded	(3) Quantity demanded	(4) Price	(5) Quantity demanded	(6) Quantity demanded
$.90	10	0	$5.00	4	7
.85	20	10	4.50	5	8
.80	30	20	4.00	6	9
.75	40	30	3.50	7	10
.70	50	40	3.00	8	11
.65	60	50	2.50	9	12
.60	70	60	2.00	10	13

(3) Good B is _____ .

5 The market demand for good X shown in columns 1 and 2 of the table below. Assume the price of X to be $2 and constant.

(1) Price	(2) Quantity demanded	(3) Quantity demanded	(4) Quantity demanded
$2.40	1,600	1,500	1,700
2.30	1,650	1,550	1,750
2.20	1,750	1,650	1,850
2.10	1,900	1,800	2,000
2.00	2,100	2,000	2,200
1.90	2,350	2,250	2,450
1.80	2,650	2,550	2,750

a. If, as the price of good Y rises from $1.25 to $1.35, the quantities demanded of good X become those shown in column 3, it can be concluded that X and Y are (substitute, complementary) _____ goods.

b. If, as the price of good Y rises from $1.25 to $1.35, the quantities demanded of good X become those shown in column 4, it can be concluded that X and Y are _____ goods.

6 In a local market for hamburger on a given date, each of 300 sellers of hamburger has the following supply schedule.

(1) Price	(2) Quantity supplied– one seller, kg.	(3) Quantity supplied– all sellers, kg.
$4.10	150	_____
4.00	110	_____
3.90	75	_____
3.80	45	_____
3.70	20	_____
3.60	0	_____

a. In column 3 construct the market supply schedule for hamburger.

b. Below is the market demand schedule for hamburger on the same date and in the same local market as that given above.

Price	Quantity demanded, kg.
$4.10	28,000
4.00	31,000
3.90	36,000
3.80	42,000
3.70	49,000
3.60	57,000

c. If the federal government set a ceiling price on hamburger at $3.80 a kilogram, the result would be a (shortage, surplus) _____ of _____ kilograms of hamburger in this market.

7 Each of the following events would tend to increase or decrease either the demand for or the supply of video games, and thus increase or decrease the price of these games. In the first blank, indicate the effect upon demand or supply and in the second, whether price would rise or fall.

a. It becomes known that a local department store is going to have a sale on these games three months from now. _____ ;
_____ .

b. The workers who produce the games go on strike for more than two months. _____ ;
_____ .

c. The workers in the industry receive a ninety-cent-an-hour wage increase. _____ ;
_____ .

d. The average price of movie tickets increases. _____ ; _____ .

e. The firms producing the games undertake to produce a large volume of antitank missile components for the Department of National Defence. _____ ;
_____ .

f. It is announced by a private research institute that children who have taken to playing video games also improve their grades in school. _____; _____ .

g. Because of the use of mass-production techniques, the amount of labour necessary to produce a game decreases. _____ ;

_____ .

h. The price of stereos decreases. _____ ;

_____ .

i. The average consumer believes that a shortage of games is developing in the economy. _____; _____ .

j. The federal govenment imposes a $5 per game tax upon the manufacturers of video games. _____; _____ .

8 In the following table, using the demand data given, complete the table by computing total revenue at each of the seven prices and the six price elasticity coefficients between each of the seven prices, and indicate whether demand is elastic, inelastic, or of unitary elasticity between each of the seven prices.

Price	Quantity demanded	Total revenue	Elasticity coefficient	Character of demand
$1.00	300	$_____	_____	_____
.90	400	_____	_____	_____
.80	500	_____	_____	_____
.70	600	_____	_____	_____
.60	700	_____	_____	_____
.50	800	_____	_____	_____
.40	900	_____	_____	_____

9 Using the supply data in the schedule below, complete the table by computing the six price elasticity-of-supply coefficients between each of the seven prices, and indicate whether the supply is elastic, inelastic, or of unitary elasticity.

Price	Quantity supplied	Elasticity coefficient	Character of supply
$1.00	800	$_____	_____
.90	700	_____	_____
.80	600	_____	_____
.70	500	_____	_____
.60	400	_____	_____
.50	300	_____	_____
.40	200	_____	_____

10 On the following graph are three different supply curves (S_1, S_2, S_3) for a product bought and sold in a competitive market.

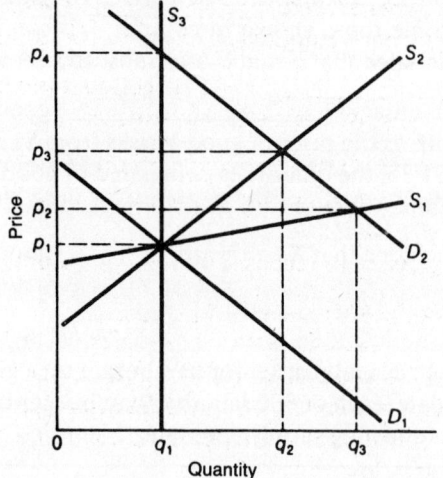

a. The supply curve for the

(1) market period is the one labelled _____ ;

(2) short run is the one labelled _____ ;

(3) long run is the one labelled _____ .

b. No matter what the period of time under consideration, if the demand for the product were D_1, the equilibrium price of the product would be _____ and the equilibrium quantity would be_____ .

c. Were demand to increase from D_1 to D_2,

(1) in the market period, the equilibrium price would increase to _____

and the equilibrium quantity would _____

_____ ;
(2) in the short run, the price of the product

would increase to _____ and the

quantity would increase to _____ ;
(3) in the long run, the price of the product

would be _____ and the

quantity would be _____.
d. The longer the period of time allowed to
sellers to adjust their outputs, the (more,

less) _____ elastic is the supply of
their product.
e. The more elastic the supply of a product,

the (greater, less) _____ is the effect on equilibrium price, and the

_____ is the effect on equilibrium quantity of an increase in demand.

11 In the table below are the demand and
supply schedules for copra in the New Hebrides Islands.
a. Before a tax is imposed on copra, its

equilibrium price is $ _____.
b. The government of the New Hebrides
now imposes an excise tax of $.60 per kilo-
gram on copra. Complete the after-tax supply schedule in the right-hand column of the
table below.

c. After the imposition of the tax, the equi-

librium price of copra is $ _____.
d. Of the $.60 tax, the amount borne by

(1) the buyer is $_____ or _____%;

(2) the seller is $_____ or _____%.

12 Two graphs follow.
a. On the first graph, draw a perfectly elastic demand curve and a normal upsloping
supply curve for a commodity.
(1) Now impose an excise tax on the commodity, and draw the new supply curve that
would result.
(2) As a consequence of the tax, the price of

the commodity has _____.
(3) It can be concluded that, when demand is

perfectly elastic, the buyer bears _____

_____ of the tax and the seller

bears _____ of the tax.
(4) Thus the *more* elastic the demand, the

_____ is the portion of the tax

borne by the buyer and the _____ is
the portion borne by the seller.
(5) But the *less* elastic the demand, the

_____ is the portion borne by

the buyer and the _____ is the portion borne by the seller.

Quantity demanded (kilograms)	Price (per kilogram)	Before-tax quantity supplied (kilograms)	After-tax quantity supplied (kilograms)
150	$4.60	900	_____
200	4.40	800	_____
250	4.20	700	_____
300	4.00	600	_____
350	3.80	500	_____
400	3.60	400	_____
450	3.40	300	0
500	3.20	200	0
550	3.00	100	0

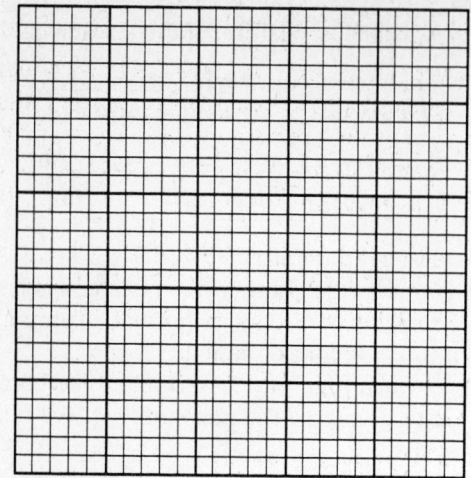

0

b. On the second graph, draw a perfectly elastic supply curve and a normal downsloping demand curve.

(1) Again impose an excise tax on the commodity and draw the new supply curve.

(2) As a result of the tax, the price of the commodity has _____.

(3) From this it can be concluded that when supply is perfectly elastic, the buyer bears _____ of the tax and the seller bears _____ of the tax.

(4) Thus the *more* elastic the supply, the _____ is the portion of the tax borne by the buyer and the _____ is the portion borne by the seller.

(5) But the *less* elastic the supply, the _____ is the portion borne by the buyer and the _____ is the portion borne by the seller.

SELF-TEST

Circle T if the statement is true, F if it is false.

1 A market is any arrangement that brings the buyers and sellers of a particular good or service together. **T F**

2 Demand is the amount of a commodity or service a buyer will purchase at a particular price. **T F**

3 The law of demand states that as price increases, the quantity of the product demanded increases. **T F**

4. In graphing supply and demand schedules, supply is put on the horizontal axis and demand on the vertical axis. **T F**

5 If price falls, there will be an increase in demand. **T F**

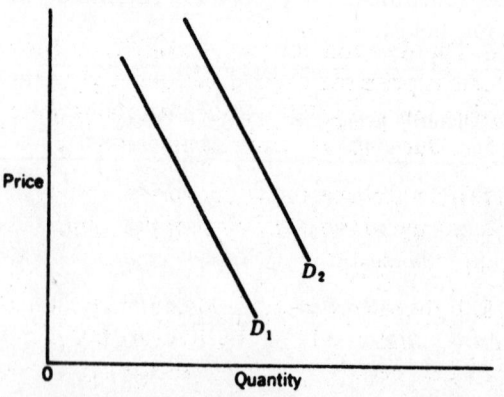

6 If the demand curve moves from D_1 to D_2 in the graph above, demand has increased. **T F**

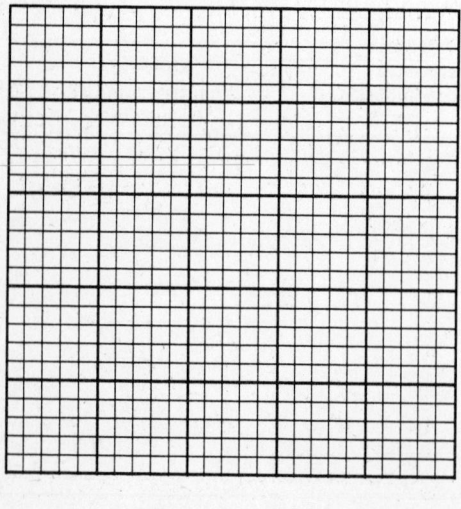

0

7 A fall in the price of a good will cause the demand for goods that are substitutes for it to increase.　　　**T F**

8 If two goods are complementary, an increase in the price of one will cause the demand for the other to increase.　　**T F**

9 If the market price of a commodity is for a time below its equilibrium price, the market price will tend to rise because demand will decrease and supply will increase. **T F**

10 The equilibrium price of a good is the price at which the demand and the supply of the good are equal.　　　　　**T F**

11 The rationing function of prices is the elimination of shortages and surpluses. **T F**

12 Demand tends to be inelastic at higher prices and elastic at lower prices.　　**T F**

13 Total revenue will not change when price changes if the price elasticity of demand is unitary.　　　　　　　**T F**

14 If the relative change in price is greater than the relative change in quantity demanded, the price elasticity coefficient is greater than one.　　　　　　　**T F**

15 Price elasticity of demand and the slope of the demand curve are two different things.　　　　　　　　　**T F**

16 The demand for most agricultural products is price inelastic. Consequently, an increase in supply will reduce the total income of producers of agricultural products. **T F**

17 If an increase in product prices results in no change in the quantity supplied, supply is perfectly elastic.　　　　　**T F**

18 If the government imposes a price ceiling above what would be the free-market price of a commodity, a shortage of the commodity would develop.　　　　**T F**

19 A provincial government seeking to increase its excise-tax revenues is more likely to increase the tax rate on a restaurant meals

than on automobile tires.　　　**T F**

20 When an excise tax is placed on a product bought and sold in a competitive market, the portion of the tax borne by the seller equals the amount of the tax less the rise in the price of the product due to the tax.　　**T F**

21 The more price elastic the demand for a good, the greater will be the portion of an excise tax on the good borne by the seller. **T F**

Circle the letter that corresponds to the best answer.

1 The markets examined in this chapter are (*a*) perfectly competitive markets; (*b*) markets for goods and services; (*c*) markets for products and resources; (*d*) all of the above.

2 Which of the following could cause a decrease in consumer demand for a product X? (*a*) a decrease in consumer income; (*b*) an increase in the prices of goods that are good substitutes for product X; (*c*) an increase in the price that consumers expect will prevail for a product X in the future; (*d*) a decrease in the supply of product X.

3 If two goods are substitutes for each other, an increase in the price of one will necessarily (*a*) decrease the demand for the other; (*b*) increase the demand for the other; (*c*) decrease the quantity demanded of the other; (*d*) increase the quantity demanded of the other.

4 The income of a consumer decreases and he or she increases demand for a particular good. It can be concluded that the good is (*a*) normal; (*b*) inferior; (*c*) a substitute; (*d*) a complement.

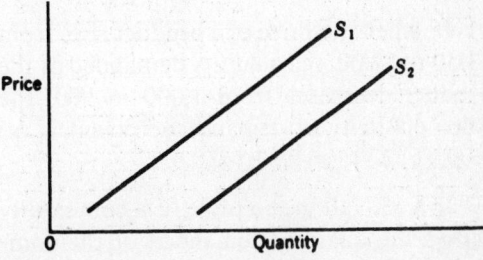

5 If the supply curve moves from S_1 to S_2 on the previous graph, there has been (a) an increase in supply; (b) a decrease in supply; (c) an increase in quantity supplied; (d) a decrease in quantity supplied.

6 An increase in demand and a decrease in supply will (a) increase price and increase the quantity exchanged; (b) decrease price and decrease the quantity exchanged; (c) increase price and the effect upon quantity exchanged will be indeterminate; (d) decrease price and the effect upon quantity exchanged will be indeterminate.

7 An increase in supply and an increase in demand will (a) increase price and increase the quantity exchanged; (b) decrease price and increase the quantity exchanged; (c) affect price in an indeterminate way and decrease the quantity exchanged; (d) affect price in an indeterminate way and increase the quantity exchanged.

8 Which of the following could *not* cause an increase in supply of wheat; (a) an increase in the price of wheat; (b) improvements in the art of producing wheat; (c) a decrease in the price of the machinery employed in wheat production; (d) a decrease in the price of oats.

9 The law of supply states that as price increases, (a) supply increases; (b) supply decreases; (c) quantity supplied increases; (d) quantity supplied decreases.

10 Demand and supply may be employed to explain how price is determined in (a) product markets; (b) resource markets; (c) markets for foreign currency; (d) all of the above markets.

11 If, when the price of a product rises from $1.50 to $2.00, the quantity demanded of the product decreases from 1,000 to 900, the price elasticity of demand coefficient is (a) 3.00; (b) 2.71; (c) 0.37; (d) 0.33.

12 If a 1% fall in the price of a commodity causes the quantity demanded of the commodity to increase 2%, demand is (a) inelastic; (b) elastic; (c) of unitary elasticity; (d) perfectly elastic.

13 Which of the following is *not* a characteristic of a commodity the demand for which is elastic? (a) the price elasticity coefficient is less than unity; (b) total revenue decreases if price rises; (c) buyers are relatively sensitive to price changes; (d) the relative change on quantity is greater than the relative change in price.

14 Which of the following is *not* characteristic of a good the demand for which is price inelastic? (a) there are a large number of good substitutes for the good; (b) the buyer spends a small percentage of his total income on the good; (c) the good is regarded by consumers as a necessity; (d) the period of time for which demand is given is very short.

15 If a 5% fall in the price of a commodity causes quantity supplied to decrease by 8%, supply is: (a) inelastic; (b) of unitary elasticity; (c) elastic; (d) perfectly inelastic.

16 If supply is inelastic and demand decreases, the total revenue of sellers will (a) increase; (b) decrease; (c) decrease only if demand is elastic; (d) increase only if demand is inelastic.

17 The chief determinant of the price elasticity of supply of a product is (a) the number of good substitutes the product has; (b) the length of time sellers have to adjust to a change in price; (c) whether the product is a luxury or a necessity; (d) whether the product is a durable or a non-durable good.

18 If the government sets a minimum price for a commodity and this minimum price is less than the equilibrium price of the commodity, the result will be (a) a shortage of the commodity; (b) a surplus of the commodity; (c) neither a shortage nor a surplus of the commodity; (d) an increase in total receipts from the sale of the commodity if demand is inelastic.

19 In a competitive market, the portion of an excise tax borne by a buyer is equal to (*a*) the amount the price of the product rises as a result of the tax; (*b*) the amount of the tax; (*c*) the amount of the tax less the amount the price of the products rises as a result of the tax; (*d*) the amount of the tax plus the amount the price of the product rises as a result of the tax.

20 Which of the following statements is correct? (*a*) The more elastic the supply, the greater the portion of an excise tax borne by the seller. (*b*) The more elastic the demand, the greater the portion of an excise tax borne by the buyer. (*c*) The more inelastic the supply, the greater the portion of an excise tax borne by the buyer. (*d*) The more inelastic the demand, the greater the portion of an excise tax borne by the seller.

21 When the government places a ceiling on the price of a good and that ceiling is below the equilibrium price, the result will be (*a*) a surplus of the good; (*b*) a shortage of the good; (*c*) an increase in the demand for the good. (*d*) a decrease in the supply of the good.

DISCUSSION QUESTIONS

1 How is a market defined?

2 Carefully define demand and state the law of demand. Now define supply and state the law of supply.

3 Several years ago, the price of coffee in Canada rose as a result of bad weather in coffee-producing regions. Employ the income-effect and the substitution-effect concepts to explain why the quantity of coffee demanded in Canada declined. A few years later, when the weather became normal, the price of coffee fell. Use the diminishing marginal-utility notion to explain why the quantity of coffee demanded rose.

4 Explain the difference between an increase in demand and an increase in quantity demanded, and between a decrease in supply and a decrease in quantity supplied.

5 Neither demand nor supply remains constant for long because the factors that determine demand and supply do not long remain constant. What are these factors? How do changes in them affect demand and supply?

6 How are normal, inferior, substitute, complementary, and independent goods defined? How can these concepts be used to predict the way in which a change in income or in the price of another good will affect the demand for a given good?

7 Given the demand for and the supply of a commodity, what price will be the equilibrium price of this commodity? Explain why this price wil tend to prevail in the market and why higher (lower) prices, if they do exist temporarily, will tend to fall (rise).

8 Analyse the following quotation and explain the fallacies contained in it. "An increase in demand will cause price to rise; with a rise in price, supply will increase and the increase in supply will push price down. Therefore, an increase in demand results in little change in price because supply will increase also."

9 What is the difference between individual and market demand? What is the relationship between these two types of demand? Does this distinction and relationship also apply to individual and market supply?

10 Suppose homemakers, because of higher meat prices, decide to boycott meat. What effect will the boycott, as long as it lasts, have upon the demand for meat and the price of meat? After the homemakers end their boycott, what will happen to the demand for and the price of meat?

11 The interest rates received by those who lend money have in recent years been higher in the United States than in most other countries. This has led many non-Americans to increase their purchases of American dollars (which they pay for with their own money) and to lend these dollars in the United States. The price non-Americans have to pay to obtain an American dollar is the exchange rate for the dollar. What do you think has been the effect of higher interest rates in the United States on the exchange rate for the dollar — has it risen or fallen?

12 Define and explain the price elasticity of demand concept in terms of each of the following: (a) the relative sensitiveness of quantity demanded to changes in price; (b) the behaviour of total revenue when price changes; (c) the elasticity coefficient; (d) the relationship between the relative (percentage) change in quantity demanded and the relative (percentage) change in price.

13 What is meant by perfectly elastic demand? By perfectly inelastic demand? What does the demand curve look like when demand is perfectly elastic? When it is perfectly inelastic?

14 In computing the price elasticity coefficient it usually makes a considerable difference whether the higher price and lower quantity or the lower price and higher quantity are used as a point of reference. What have economists done to eliminate confusion that would arise if the elasticity-of-demand coefficient varied and depended upon whether a price rise or price fall were being considered?

15 When the price of a commodity declines, the quantity demanded of it increases. When the demand is elastic, total revenue is greater at the lower price; but when demand is inelastic, total revenue is smaller. Explain why total revenue will sometimes increase and why it will sometimes decrease.

16 Demand seldom has the same elasticity at all prices. What is the relationship between the price of most commodities and the price elasticity of demand for them?

17 What is the relationship, if there is a relationship, between the elasticity of demand

and the slope of the demand curve?

18 What are the factors that together determine the price elasticity of demand for a product?

19 Of what practical importance is the price elasticity of demand? Cite examples of its importance to business firms, workers, farmers, and governments.

20 Explain what determines the elasticity of supply of an economic good or service.

21 Why does the government impose price ceilings and minimum prices on certain goods and services from time to time? What are the consequences of these ceilings and minimums if they are not set at the price that would prevail in the free market?

22 Explain the effect that the imposition of an excise tax has upon the supply of a commodity bought and sold in a competitive market. How do you find what part of the tax is passed on to the buyer and what part is borne by the seller? What determines the division of the tax between buyer and seller?

23 What is the relationship between the elasticity of demand for a commodity and the portion of an excise tax on a commodity borne by the buyer and by the seller? What is the relationship between the price elasticity of supply and the incidence of the tax?

24 The interest rate is a price. It is the price paid by borrowers for the use of money and the price received by the lenders of the money. Unless government interferes, the demand for borrowed money and the supply of loanable money determine the interest rate. What would be the effect of (a) a government imposed interest-rate ceiling on this money market; (b) the deduction of interest expenses from the taxable incomes of borrowers on the demand for borrowed money and the rate of interest; and (c) the exclusion of interest incomes from the taxable incomes of lenders on the supply of loanable money and the rate of interest?

4

FURTHER TOPICS IN THE THEORY OF CONSUMER DEMAND

In Chapter 3 it was pointed out that consumers typically buy more of a product as its price decreases and less of it as its price increases. Chapter 4 looks behind this law of demand to explain why consumers behave this way. Two explanations are presented. One, developed in terms of the income effect and the substitution effect, is a general and simple explanation. The other, developed in terms of the concept of marginal utility, is a more detailed explanation and is more difficult to understand. (A third explanation employs indifference curves to explain consumer demand; it is a newer and in many ways better explanation of consumer behaviour; and is found in the appendix to this chapter).

The marginal-utility explanation requires that you first understand the concepts and asssumptions upon which this theory of consumer behaviour rests; second, you must do some rigorous reasoning using these concepts and assumptions. It is an exercise in logic, but be sure that you follow the reasoning. To aid you, several problems are provided so that you can work things out for yourself.

Of course, no one believes that consumers actually perform these mental gymnastics before they spend their incomes or make a purchase. But the marginal-utility approach to consumer behaviour is studied because consumers behave "as if" their purchases on the basis of very fine calculations. Thus, this approach explains what we do in fact observe, and make it possible for us to predict, with a good deal of precision, how consumers will react to changes in their incomes and in the prices of products.

The consumption of any good or service requires that the consumer use scarce and valuable time. The final section of the chapter will show you how the value of the time required for the consumption of a product can be put into the marginal-utility theory, and what the implications of this modification of the theory are.

CHECK LIST

When you have studied this chapter you should be able to

☐ Define and distinguish between the income and the substitution effects of a price change; use the two effects to explain why a consumer will buy more (less) of a commodity when its price falls (rises).

☐ Define marginal utility; state the law of diminishing marginal utility.

☐ List the four assumptions made in the theory of consumer behaviour.

☐ State the utility-maximizing rule.

☐ Use the utility-maximizing rule to determine how the consumer would spend his or her fixed income when you are given the utility and price data.

☐ Derive a consumer's demand for a product from utility, income, and price data.

☐ Explain how the value of time is incorporated in the theory of consumer behaviour; explain several of the implications of this modification of the theory.

CHAPTER OUTLINE

1 The law of consumer demand can be explained by employing either the income-effect and substitution-effect concepts, or the concept of marginal utility.

a. Consumers buy more of a commodity when its price falls because their money income will go further (the income effect) and because the commodity is now less expensive relative to other commodities (the substitution effect).

b. The essential assumption made in the alternative explanation is that the more the consumer buys of any commodity, the smaller becomes the marginal (extra) utility obtained from it.

2 The assumption (or law) of diminishing marginal utility is the basis of the theory that explains how a consumer will spend his or her income.

a. The typical consumer, it is assumed, is rational, knows his or her marginal-utility schedule for the various goods available, has a limited money income to spend, and must pay a price to acquire each of the goods that yield utility.

b. Given these assumptions, the consumer maximizes the total utility obtained when the marginal utility of the last dollar spent on a commodity is the same for all commodities.

c. Algebraically, total utility is a maximum when the marginal utility of the last unit of a commodity purchased divided by its price is the same for all commodities.

3 To find a consumer's demand for a product, the utility-maximizing rule is applied to determine the amount of the product the consumer will purchase at different prices, assuming income, tastes, and the prices of other products remain constant.

4 The marginal-utility theory includes the fact that consumption takes time, and time is a scarce resource.

a. The full price of any consumer good or service is equal to its market price plus the value of the time taken to consume it (the income the consumer could have earned had that time been used for work).

b. The inclusion of the value of consumption-time in the theory of consumer behaviour has several significant implications.

IMPORTANT TERMS

Income effect	Rational
Substitution effect	Budget restraint
Utility	Utility-maximizing rule
Marginal utility	
Law of diminishing marginal utility	

FILL-IN QUESTIONS

1 A fall in the price of a product tends to (increase, decrease) _____ the *real* income of a consumer, and rise in its price tends to _____ real income. This is called the_____ effect.

2 When the price of a product increases, the product becomes relatively (more, less) _____ expensive than it was and the prices of other products become relatively (higher, lower) _____ than they were; the consumer will, therefore, buy (less, more) _____ of the product in question and _____ of the other products. This is called the _____ effect.

3 The law of diminishing marginal utility is that marginal utility will (increase, decrease) _____ as the consumer increases the consumption of a particular commodity.

4 The marginal-utility theory of consumer behaviour assumes that the consumer is _____ and that the consumer has certain _____ for various goods.

5 A consumer can not buy all he or she wishes of every good and service because income is _____ and goods and services have _____; these two facts are called the _____ .

6 When the consumer is maximizing the utility got from income, the _____ _____ _____ is the same for all the products bought.

7 If the marginal utility of the last dollar spent on one product is greater than the marginal utility of the last dollar spent on another product, the consumer should (increase, decrease) _____ purchases of the first and _____ purchases of the second.

8 Assume there are only two products, X an Y, a consumer can purchase with a fixed income. The consumer is maximizing utility algebraically when

(a) $\dfrac{\rule{2cm}{0.4pt}}{\rule{2cm}{0.4pt}}$ = (c) $\dfrac{\rule{2cm}{0.4pt}}{\rule{2cm}{0.4pt}}$

(b) _____   (d) _____

9 In deriving a consumer's demand for a particular product, the two factors (other than the tastes of the consumer) that are held constant are

a. _____

b. _____

10 The consumption of any product requires _____ .
a. This is a valuable economic resource because it is _____.
b. Its value is equal to _____ _____ .
c. And the full price to the consumer of any product is, therefore, _____ plus _____ .

PROBLEMS AND PROJECTS

1 Suppose that when the price of bread is $1 per loaf, the Robertson family buys six loaves of bread in a week.
a. When the price of bread falls to 80 cents, the Robertson family will increase bread consumption to seven loaves.
(1) Measured in terms of bread, the fall in the price of bread will _____ their real income by _____ loaves (*Hint:* How many loaves of bread *could* they now buy without changing the amount they spend on bread?)
(2) Is the Robertsons' demand for bread elastic or inelastic? _____
b. When the price of bread rises from $1.00 to $1.20 per loaf, the Robertson family will decrease their bread consumption to four loaves.
(1) Measured in terms of bread, this rise in the price of bread will _____ their real income by _____ loaf of bread.
(2) Is the Robertsons' demand for bread elastic or inelastic? _____

2 Assume that Palmer finds that only three goods, A, B and C are for sale; and that the amounts of utility their consumption will yield are as shown in the table below.

Compute the marginal utilities for successive units of A, B and C, and enter them in the appropriate columns.

Good A			Good B			Good C		
Quantity	Utility	Marginal utility	Quantity	Utility	Marginal utility	Quantity	Utility	Marginal utility
1	21	_____	1	7	_____	1	23	_____
2	41	_____	2	13	_____	2	40	_____
3	59	_____	3	18	_____	3	52	_____
4	74	_____	4	22	_____	4	60	_____
5	85	_____	5	25	_____	5	65	_____
6	91	_____	6	27	_____	6	68	_____
7	91	_____	7	28.2	_____	7	70	_____

3 Using the marginal-utility data for goods A, B, and C, which you obtained in problem 2, assume that the prices of A, B, and C are $5, $1, and $4, respectively, and that Palmer has an income of $37 to spend.

a. Complete the table below by computing the *marginal utility* per dollar for successive units of A, B, and C.

b. Palmer would *not* buy 4 units of A, 1 unit of B, and 4 units of C because _____

_____ .

c. Palmer would *not* buy 6 units of A, 7 units of B, and 4 units of C because _____

_____ .

d. To maximize utility, Palmer will buy (1) _____ units of A, (2) _____ units of B, (3) _____ units of C; Palmer's total utility will be _____ and the marginal utility of the last dollar spent on each good will be

_____ .

e. If Palmer's income increased by $1, it would be spent on good _____ assuming Palmer can buy fractions of a unit of a good, because _____

_____ .

Good A		Good B		Good C	
Quantity	Marginal utility per dollar	Quantity	Marginal utility per dollar	Quantity	Marginal utility per dollar
1	_____	1	_____	1	_____
2	_____	2	_____	2	_____
3	_____	3	_____	3	_____
4	_____	4	_____	4	_____
5	_____	5	_____	5	_____
6	_____	6	_____	6	_____
7	_____	7	_____	7	_____

| | Good D | | | | | | Good E | |
Quantity	MU	MU/$6	MU/$4	MU/$3	MU/$2	MU/$1.50	MU	MU/$4
1	45	7.5	11.25	15	22.5	30	40	10
2	30	5	7.5	10	15	20	36	9
3	20	3.33	5	6.67	10	13.33	32	8
4	15	2.5	3.75	5	7.5	10	28	7
5	12	2	3	4	6	8	24	6
6	10	1.67	2.5	3.33	5	6.67	20	5
7	9	1.5	2.25	3	4.5	6	16	4
8	7.5	1.25	1.88	2.5	3.75	5	12	3

4 Ms. Thompson has an income of $36 to spend each week. The only two goods she is interested in purchasing are D and E. The marginal-utility schedules for these two goods are shown in the table above.

The price of E does not change from week to week, and is $4. The marginal-utility per dollar from Good E is also shown in the table.

But the price of D varies from one week to the next. The marginal-utility per dollar from Good D when the price of D is $6.00, $4.00, $3.00, $2.00, and $1.50 is shown in the table.

a. Complete the next table to show how much of Good D Ms. Thompson will buy each week at each of the five possible prices of D.

Price of D	Quantity of D demanded
$6.00	_____
4.00	_____
3.00	_____
2.00	_____
1.00	_____

b. What is the table you completed in *a.* above called? _____

5 Assume that a consumer can purchase only two goods. These two goods are R (recreation) and M (material goods). The market price of R is $2 and the market price of M is $1. The consumer spends all the income in such a way that the marginal utility

of the last unit of R bought is 12 and the marginal utility of the last unit of M bought is 6.

a. If we ignore the time it takes to consume R and M, is the consumer maximizing the total utility obtained from the two goods?

_____

b. Suppose it takes 4 hours to consume each unit of R and 1 hour to consume each unit of M; and the consumer can earn $2 an hour by working.

(1) The full price of a unit of R is $ _____.

(2) The full price of a unit of M is $ _____.

c. If we can take into account the full price of each of the commodities, is the consumer maximizing total utility? _____

How do you know this? _____

_____

d. If the consumer is not maximizing utility, should consumption of R or of M be increased? _____ Why should the consumer do this? _____

e. Will the consumer then use more or less time for consuming R? _____

SELF-TEST

Circle T if the statement is true, F if it is false.

1 An increase in the real income of a consumer will result from an increase in the price of a product that the consumer is buying. **T F**

2 Utility and usefulness are not synonymous. **T F**

3 All consumers are subject to the budget restraint. **T F**

4 When a consumer is maximizing total utility, the marginal utilities of the last unit of every product bought are identical. **T F**

5 Because utility cannot actually be measured, the marginal-utility theory cannot really explain how consumers will behave. **T F**

6 To find a consumer's demand for a product, the price of the product is varied while his or her tastes and income and the prices of other products remain unchanged. **T F**

7 A consumer can earn $10 an hour when working. It takes 5 hours to consume a product. The value of the time required for the consumption of the product is $5. **T F**

Circle the letter that corresponds to the best answer.

1 The reason the substitution effect works to encourage a consumer to buy more of a product when its price decreases is (a) the real income of the consumer has been increased; (b) the real income of the consumer has been decreased; (c) the product is now relatively less expensive than it was; (d) other products are now relatively less expensive than they were.

2 Which of the following best expresses the law of diminishing marginal utility? (a) the more a person consumes of a product, the smaller becomes the utility received from its consumption; (b) the more a person consumes of a product, the smaller becomes the utility received as a result of consuming an additional unit of the product; (c) the less a person consumes of a product, the smaller becomes the utility received from its consumption; (d) the less a person consumes of a product, the smaller becomes the utility received as a result of consuming an additional

unit of the product.

3 Which of the following is *not* an essential assumption of the marginal-utility theory of consumer behaviour? (a) the consumer has a small income; (b) the consumer is rational; (c) goods and services are not free; (d) goods and services yield decreasing amounts of marginal-utility as the consumer buys more of them.

4 Assume that the consumer has the marginal-utility schedules for goods X and Y given below, that the prices of X and Y are $1 and $2, respectively, and that the income of the consumer is $9. When total utility is being maximized, the consumer will buy (a) 7X and 1Y; (b) 5X and 2Y; (c) 3X and 3Y; (d) 1X and 4Y.

Good X		Good Y	
Quantity	MU	Quantity	MU
1	8	1	10
2	7	2	8
3	6	3	6
4	5	4	4
5	4	5	3
6	3	6	2
7	2	7	1

5 When the consumer in multiple-choice question 4 above purchases the combination of X and Y that maximizes total utility, utility is (a) 36; (b) 45; (c) 48; (d) 52.

6 Suppose that the prices of A and B are $3 and $2, respectively; that the consumer is spending his or her entire income and buying 4 units of A and 6 units of B; and that the marginal utility of both the 4th unit of A and the 6th unit of B is 6. It can be concluded that (a) the consumer is in equilibrium; (b) the consumer should buy more of A and less of B; (c) the consumer should buy less of A and more of B; (d) the consumer should buy less of both A and B.

7 The full price of a product to a consumer is (a) its market price; (b) its market price plus the value of its consumption time; (c) its market price less the value of its consumption time; (d) the value of its consumption time less its market price.

DISCUSSION QUESTIONS

1 Explain, employing the income-effect and substitution-effect concepts, the reasons consumers buy more of a product at a lower price than at a higher price, and *vice versa*.

2 Why is utility a "subjective concept"? How does the subjective nature of rationality limit the practical usefulness of the marginal-utility theory of consumer behaviour?

3 What essential assumptions are made about consumers and the nature of goods and services in developing the marginal-utility theory of consumer behaviour? What is meant by "budget restraint"?

4 When is the consumer in equilibrium and maximizing total utility? Explain why any deviation from this equilibrium will decrease the consumer's total utility.

5 Using the marginal-utility theory of consumer behaviour, explain how an individual's demand schedule for a particular consumer good can be obtained. Why does a demand schedule obtained in this fashion almost invariably result in an inverse or negative relationship between price and quantity demanded?

6 Explain how a consumer might determine the value of his or her time. How does the value of time affect the full price the consumer pays for a good or service?

7 What does taking time into account explain that the traditional approach to consumer behaviour does not explain?

APPENDIX TO CHAPTER 4: INDIFFERENCE CURVE ANALYSIS

This brief appendix contains the third explanation or approach to the theory of consumer behaviour. You are introduced first to the budget line and then to the indifference curve. These two geometrical concepts are next combined to explain *when* a consumer is purchasing the combination of two products that maximizes the total utility obtainable with his or her income. The last step is to vary the price of one of the products to find the consumer's demand (schedule or curve) for the product.

CHECK LIST

When you have studied this appendix you should be able to

☐ Define the budget line; state how to measure its slope and what determines its location.

☐ Define an indifference curve; state the two characteristics of an individual indifference curve.

☐ Explain what an indifference map is; determine which indifference curves on a map bring a consumer more and less total utility.

☐ State, employing the indifference curve approach, which combination of two products maximizes the total utility of a consumer; explain why this is the utility maximizing combination.

☐ Explain how to use the indifference curve approach to derive a consumer's demand for a particular product.

☐ Contrast the assumptions regarding the measurability of utility made in the marginal-utility and the indifference-curve approaches to consumer behaviour.

APPENDIX OUTLINE

1   A budget line shows, graphically, the different combinations of two products a consumer can purchase with a particular money income; it has a negative slope.

a. An increase (decrease) in the money income of the consumer will shift the budget line to the right (left) without affecting its slope.

b. An increase (decrease) in the prices of both products shifts the budget line to the left (right); but an increase (decrease) in the price of the product the quantity of which is measured horizontally (price of the other product remaining constant) pivots the budget line around a fixed point on the vertical axis in a clockwise (counter-clockwise) direction.

2   An indifference curve shows, graphically, the different combinations of two products that bring a consumer the same total utility.

a. An indifference curve is downsloping; if utility is to remain the same when the quantity of one product increases, the quantity of the other product must decrease.

b. An indifference curve is also convex to the origin: the more a consumer has of one product, the smaller is the quantity of a second product he or she is willing to give up to obtain an additional unit of the first product.

c. The consumer has an indifference curve for every level of total utility; the nearer (farther) a curve is from the origin in this indifference map, the smaller (larger) is the utility of the combinations on that curve.

3 The consumer is in equilibrium and purchasing the combination of two products from which maximum utility is derived when the budget line is tangent to an indifference curve.

4 In the marginal-utility approach to consumer behaviour, it is assumed that utility is measurable; but in the indifference curve approach, it need only be assumed that a consumer can say whether a combination of products has more, less, or the same amount of utility as another combination.

6 The demand schedule, or curve, for one of the products is derived by varying the price of that product and shifting the budget line, holding the price of the other product and the consumer's income constant, and finding the quantity of the product the consumer will purchase at each price when in equilibrium.

IMPORTANT TERMS

Budget line   Indifference map
Indifference curve   Equilibrium position

FILL-IN QUESTIONS

1 A budget line shows the various combinations of two products that can be purchased with a given _____ and, when quantities of *X* are measured horizontally and quantities of *Y* vertically, it has a slope equal to the ratio of _____ to the _____.

2 When
a. a consumer's income increases, the budget line moves to the (right, left) _____

b. quantities of *E* are measured horizontally and quantities of *F* vertically, an increase in the price of *E* will fan the budget line (outward, inward) _____ around a fixed point on the _____ axis.

3 An indifference curve shows the various combinations of two products that give a consumer the same _____.
a. An indifference curve slopes (upward, downward) _____; and the slope of an indifference curve is equal to the marginal _____ of _____ .

b. It is (concave, convex) _____ to the origin.

4 The more a consumer has of one product, the (greater, smaller) _____ is the quantity of a second product he or she will give up to obtain an additional unit of the first product; as a result the marginal rate of substitution of the first for the second product (increases, decreases) _____ as a consumer moves from left to right (or downward) along an indifference curve.

5 The farther from the origin an indifference curve lies, the (greater, smaller) _____ is the total utility obtained from the combinations of products on that curve.

6 A consumer obtains the greatest obtainable total utility or satisfaction when he or she purchases that combination of two products at which his or her budget line is

_____

_____. At this point the marginal rate of substitution is equal to

_____

_____

_____ .

7 Were a consumer to purchase a combination of two products that lies on his or her budget line, and at which the budget line is steeper than the indifference curve intersecting that point, he or she could increase satisfaction by trading (down, up) _____ the budget line.

8 The marginal-utility approach to consumer behaviour requires that we assume utility (is, is not) _____ numerically measurable; and the indifference curve approach (does, does not) _____ require that we make this assumption.

9 When quantities of product X are measured along the horizontal axis, a decrease in the price of X

a. fans the budget line (inward, outward) _____ and to the (right, left) _____;

b. puts the consumer, when in equilibrium, on a (higher, lower) _____ indifference curve;

c. and normally induces the consumer to purchase (more, less) _____ of product X.

10 Using indifference curves and different budget lines to determinate how much of a particular product an individual consumer will purchase at different prices makes it possible to derive that consumer's _____ curve or schedule for that product.

PROBLEMS AND PROJECTS

1 Following are the schedules for three indifference curves.

a. Measure quantities of A along the horizontal axis (from 0 to 9) and quantities of B along the vertical axis (from 0 to 45). On the graph on the next page:

Indifference Schedule 1		Indifference Schedule 2		Indifference Schedule 3	
A	B	A	B	A	B
0	28	0	36	0	45
1	21	1	28	1	36
2	15	2	21	2	28
3	10	3	15	3	21
4	6	4	10	4	15
5	3	5	6	5	10
6	1	6	3	6	6
7	0	7	2	7	3
		8	0	8	1
				9	0

(1) Plot the 8 combinations of A and B from Indifference Schedule 1, and draw through the 8 points a curve that is in no place a straight line. Label this curve IC # 1.

(2) Do the same for the 9 points in Indifference Schedule 2, and label it IC # 2.

(3) Repeat the process for the 10 points in Indifference Schedule 3, and label the curve IC # 3.

b. Assume the price of A is $12.00, and the price of B is $2.40; assume also that a consumer has an income of $72.00.

(1) Complete the following table to show the quantities of A and B this consumer is able to purchase.

A	B
0	_____
1	_____
2	_____
3	_____
4	_____
5	_____
6	_____

(2) Plot this budget line on the graph you completed in part *a* above.

(3) This budget line has a slope equal to _____.

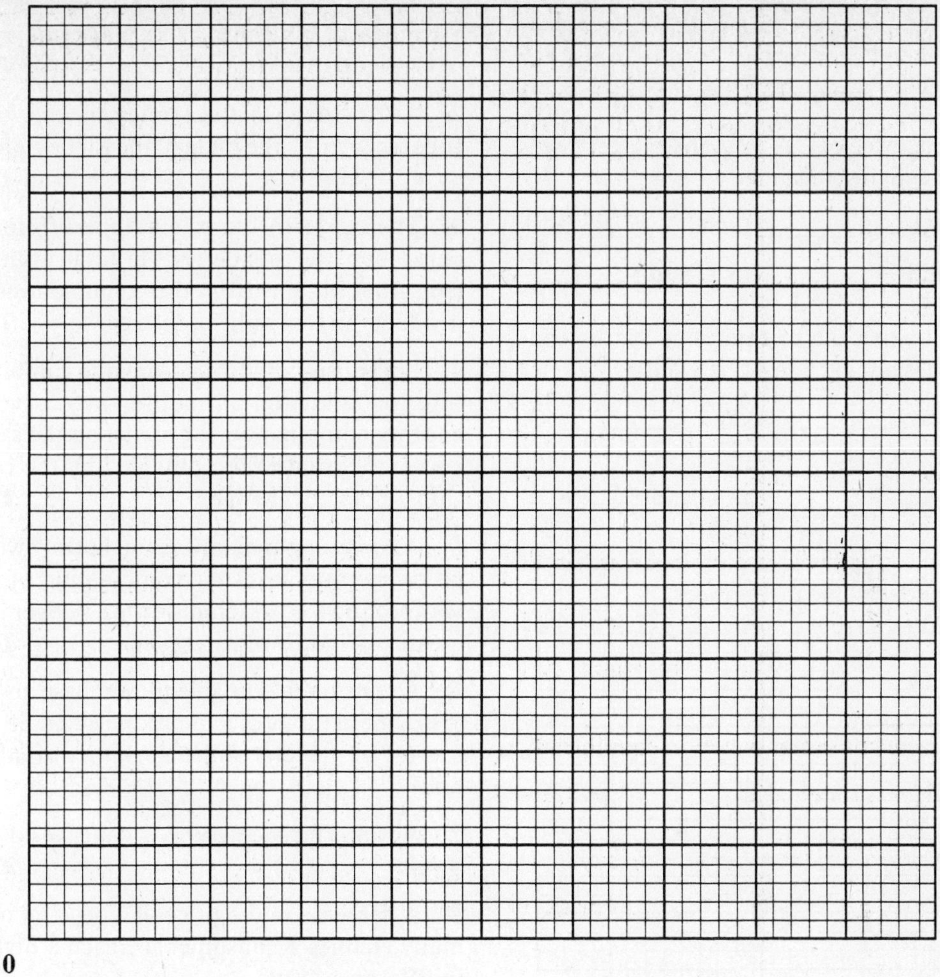

0

c. To obtain the greatest satisfaction or utility from an income of $72, this consumer will

(1) purchase _____ units of A and _____ of B;

(2) and spend $ _____ on A and $ _____ on B.

2 Following is a graph with three indifference curves and three budget lines. This consumer has an income of $100, and the price of D remains constant at $5.

a. When the price of C is $10, the consumer's budget line is BL #1 and the consumer

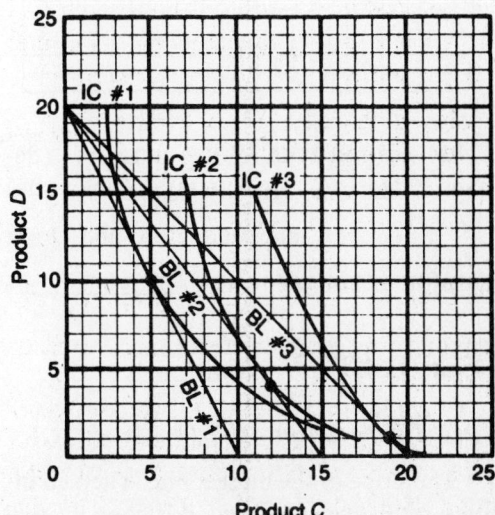

(1) purchases _____ C and _____ D;

(2) spends $ _____ on C and $_____ for D.

b. If the price of C is $6 $^2/_3$ the budget line is BL # 2 and the consumer

(1) purchases _____ C and _____ D;

(2) spends $ _____ for C and $ _____ for D.

c. And when the price of C is $5, the consumer has budget line BL # 3 and

(1) buys _____ C and _____ D; and

(2) spends $ _____ on C and $ _____ on D.

d. on the graph below, plot the quantities of C demanded at the three prices.

0

e. Between $10 and $5, this consumer's demand for C is (elastic, inelastic) _____, and products C and D are (substitutes, complements)_____ .

SELF-TEST

Circle T if the statement is true, F it is false.

1 The slope of the budget line, when quantities of F are measured horizontally and quantities of G vertically, is equal to the price of G divided by the price of F.　　　**T F**

2 An increase in the money income of a consumer shifts the budget line to the right.　　　**T F**

3 The closer to the origin an indifference curve lies, the smaller is the total utility a consumer obtains from the combinations of products on that indifference curve.　　**T F**

4 If a consumer moves from one combination (or point) on an indifference curve to another combination (or point) on the same curve, the total utility obtained by the consumer does not change.　　　**T F**

5 A consumer maximizes total utility when he or she purchases the combination of the two products at which his or her budget line crosses an indifference curve.　　**T F**

6 A consumer is unable to purchase any of the combinations of two products that lie below (or to the left) of the consumer's budget line).　　　**T F**

7 An indifference curve is concave to the origin.　　　**T F**

8 A decrease in the price of a product normally enables a consumer to reach a higher indifference curve.　　　**T F**

9 It is assumed, in the marginal-utility approach to consumer behaviour, that utility is numerically measurable.　　　**T F**

10 In both the marginal-utility and indifference-curve approaches to consumer behaviour, it is assumed that a consumer is able to say whether the total utility obtained from combination A is greater than, equal to, or less than the total utility obtained from combination B.　　　**T F**

Circle the letter that corresponds to the best answer.

1 Suppose a consumer has an income of $8; suppose the price of R is $1, and the price of S is $0.50. Which of the following combinations is on the consumer's budget line? (*a*) 8R and 1S; (*b*) 7R and 1S; (*c*) 6R and 6S; (*d*) 5R and 6S.

2 If a consumer has an income of $100, if the price of U is $10, and if the price of V is $20, the maximum quantity of U the consumer is able to purchase is (*a*) 5; (*b*) 10; (*c*) 20; (*d*) 30.

3 When the income of a consumer is $20, the price of T is $5, the price of Z is $2, and the quantity of T is measured horizontally, the slope of the budget line is (*a*) $^2/_5$; (*b*) $2\,^1/_2$; (*c*) 4; (*d*) 10.

4 An indifference curve is a curve that shows the different combinations of two products that (*a*) give a consumer equal marginal utilities; (*b*) give a consumer equal total utilities; (*c*) cost a consumer equal amounts; (*d*) have the same prices.

5 In the schedule for an indifference curve below, how much of G is the consumer willing to give up to obtain the third unit of H? (*a*) 3; (*b*) 4; (*c*) 5 (*d*) 6.

Quantity of G	Quantity of H
18	1
12	2
7	3
3	4
0	5

Use the first diagram in the next column to answer multiple-choice questions 6 and 7.

6 Which combination of I and J will the consumer purchase? (*a*) A; (*b*) B; (*c*) C; (*d*) D.

7 Suppose the price of I decreases. The budget line will fan (*a*) inward around a point on the J axis; (*b*) outward around a point on the J axis; (*c*) inward around a point on the I axis; (*d*) outward around a point on the I axis.

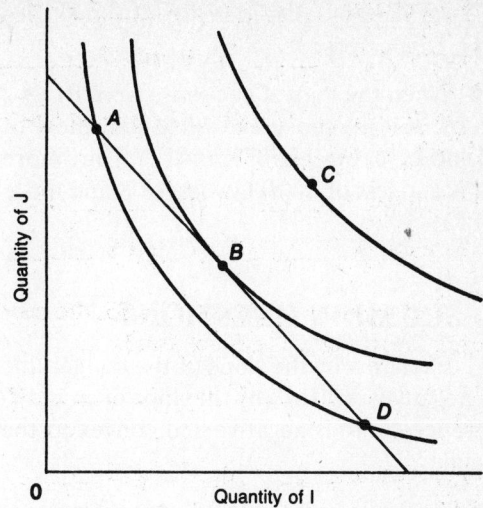

8 To derive the demand for product K, the price of K is varied. Held constant is (*a*) the money income of the consumer; (*b*) the price of another product, L; (*c*) the consumer's preferences; (*d*) all of the above.

Use the following diagram to answer multiple choice questions 9 and 10.

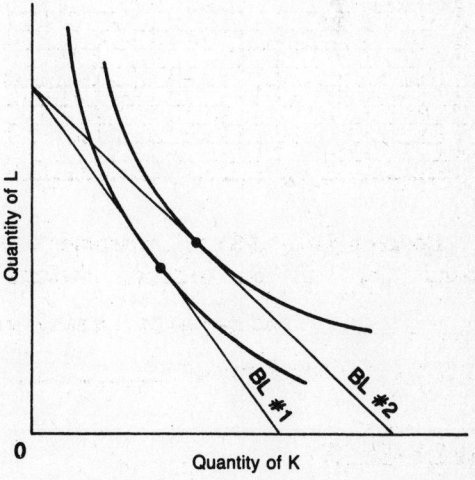

9 If the budget line shifts from BL #1 to BL #2, it is because (*a*) the price of K has increased; (*b*) the price of K has decreased;

(c) the price of L has increased; (d) the price of L has decreased.

10 When the budget line shifts from BL #2 to BL #1, the consumer will (a) buy more of K and L; (b) buy less of K and L; (c) buy more of K and less of L; (d) buy less of K and more of L.

DISCUSSION QUESTIONS

1 Explain why the slope of the budget line is negative; explain why the slope of an indifference curve is negative and convex to the origin.

2 How will each of the following events affect the budget line? (a) a decrease in the money income of the consumer; (b) an increase in the prices of both products; (c) a decrease in the price of one of the products.

3 Explain why the budget line can be called "objective" and an indifference curve "subjective."

4 Suppose a consumer purchases a combination of two products that is on his or her budget line, but that budget line is not tangent to an indifference curve at that point. Of which product should the consumer buy more and of which should he or she buy less? Why?

5 What is the "important difference between the marginal utility theory and the indifference curve theory of consumer demand"?

6 Explain how the indifference map of a consumer and the budget lines are utilized to derive the consumer's demand for one of the products. In deriving demand, what is varied and what is held constant?

5

CAPITALISM, ITS MARKET STRUCTURES, AND CANADIAN BUSINESS

Chapter 5 has four principal aims: to outline six ideological and institutional characteristics of pure capitalism; to list the characteristics of the four basic market models (which are analysed in Chapters 7 to 10); to list the determinants of these market structures; and to describe briefly the actual structure of Canadian business.

The resources of a purely capitalistic economy are owned by its citizens, who are free to use them as they wish in their own self-interest; prices and markets serve to express the self-interest of resource owners, consumers, and business firms; and competition serves to regulate self-interest—to prevent the self-interest of any person or any group from working to the disadvantage of the economy as a whole and to make self-interest work for the benefit of the entire economy.

Not all product markets, however, are perfectly competitive. Most are imperfectly competitive. But even in these markets, the cost of producing the product (along with demand) will determine the price of the product and the amount of the product produced and sold. The way in which the costs of production and demand together determine price and output depends upon the characteristics of the market in which the product is sold—upon the amount of competition in that market.

Thus the second section focuses attention upon the different characteristics or structures of markets in which products are sold. Table 5-1 lists the five major character-

istics of each of the four market situations. Most of the analysis in later chapters is based on an understanding of these categories and their characteristics. Five general determinants are suggested as causes for the actual development of a market into one of the four categories.

The brief third section of the chapter describes four market situations from the buyers' side of the market. Each of these situations is defined solely in terms of the number of buyers—one, few, fairly many, or very many—and they are, therefore, quite easy to learn and remember.

The latter part of the chapter is concerned with the business firms of Canada. It is apparent that what most characterizes Canadian business is the differences among firms insofar as their size and legal form are concerned, as well as in the products they produce. You should note the distinction between a proprietorship, a partnership, and a corporation, and the advantages and disadvantages of each.

In the last section of the chapter, you will find that the Canadian economy can be divided into eleven sectors or industry classes. The privately owned business firms are found in ten of these industry classes.

These ten sectors are not equal in terms of the number of firms in the class nor in the contribution to gross domestic product made by the industry class. These facts serve as an introduction to two major observations. In the manufacturing sector of the economy, a relatively few firms produce a relatively large part of the output of that sector. And in this sector are to be found many specific industries in which the four largest firms produce a high percentage of the output of that industry. These two observations indicate that big business is an important characteristic of the Canadian economy. The corollary of these observations is that the Canadian economy also has a large number of small business firms. But the problems created by big business and the ways in which government deals with these problems are topics examined later in the text.

CHECK LIST

When you have studied this chapter you should be able to

☐ Identify and explain the six important institutional characteristics of capitalism.

☐ Name the four basic market models on the sellers' side of the market and list the *five* characteristics of *each*.

☐ List the five major determinants of market structure and describe how each of them influences the structure of a market.

☐ Name the four market models on the buyers' side of the market and define each in terms of its single characteristic.

☐ Explain the difference between a plant, a firm, and an industry; and between limited and unlimited liability.

☐ State the advantages and disadvantages of the three legal forms of business enterprise.

☐ Report the relative importance of each of the legal forms of business enterprise in the Canadian economy.

☐ Cite evidence to indicate that large corporations dominate some major Canadian industries; and indicate in which industry classes big business is and is not a dominant force.

CHAPTER OUTLINE

1 The Canadian economy is not pure capitalism, but is a fairly close approximation of pure capitalism. Pure capitalism has the following six pecularities that distinguish it from other economic systems:

a. Private individuals and organizations own and control its property resources by means of the institution of private property.

b. These individuals and organizations possess both the freedom of enterprise and the freedom of choice.

c. Each of them is motivated largely by self-interest.

d. Competition entails large numbers of buyers and sellers and freedom of entry and exit.

e. Markets and prices (the price system) are used to communicate and co-ordinate the decisions of buyers and sellers.

f. And the role of govenment is limited in a competitive and capitalistic economy.

2 On the sellers' side of the market, markets fall into one of four catergories. The distinction between market categories depends upon the number of sellers, the type of product, the degree of control that one seller has over price, the ease of entry into the market, and the extent of non-price competition.

a. In pure competition, a very large number of firms sell a standardized product; no firm has any control over the price of the product; entry is easy; and there is no non-price competition.

b. In pure monopoly, one firm sells a unique product and has considerable control over its price; entry is blocked; and the firm may engage in (a public relations kind of) advertising and sales-promotion activity.

c. In monopolistic competition, a fairly large number of firms sell a differentiated product; each firm has some control over the price of its product; entry is relatively easy; and there is considerable non-price competition.

d. In oligopoly, a few firms sell either a standardized or differentiated product; each firm's control over the price of its product is limited by mutual interdependence; entry is difficult; and the more differentiated the product, the greater is the extent of the non-price competition.

3   The type of market that develops for the exchange of any good or service is determined by such things as the government's laws, regulations, and policies; the practices and behaviour of the firms in the market; the technology employed in producing the product; the institutions of the capitalistic economy; and foreign direct investment.

4   On the buyer's side of the market, the distinction between the four market categories depends solely upon the number of buyers; in pure competition there are a very large number, in pure monopsony there is one, in oligopsony there are a few, and in monopsonistic competition there are a fairly large number of buyers.

5   The three principal legal forms of organization of firms are the proprietorship, the partnership, and the corporation; each form has special characteristics, advantages, and disadvantages. The form of organization that any business firm should adopt depends primarily upon the amount of money capital it will require to carry on its business. Although the proprietorship is numerically dominant in Canada, the corporation accounts for the major portion of the economy's output.

6   The business population of the Canadian economy consists of many imperfectly defined and overlapping industries; business firms that operate one or more plants and produce one or more products are the components of these industries.

7   An examination of the eleven industry classes found in the Canadian economy leads to the conclusion that large firms are a characteristic of the Canadian economy and that many of its industries are dominated by big business.

IMPORTANT TERMS

Private property	Oligopsony
Freedom of enterprise	Bilateral monopoly
Freedom of choice	Plant
Self-interest	Firm
Competition	Industry
Pure competition	Horizontal combination
Pure monopoly	
Monopolistic competition	Vertical combination
Oligopoly	Conglomerate combination
Standardized product	Sole proprietorship
Non-price competition	Partnership
Product differentiation	Corporation
Price-taker	Unlimited liability
Price-maker	Limited liability
Imperfect competition	Double taxation
Monopsony	Separation of ownership and control
Monopsonistic competition	

FILL-IN QUESTIONS

1   The ownership of property resources by private individuals and organizations is the institution of _____ .

2   Two basic freedoms encountered in a capitalistic economy are the freedoms of _____ and _____ .

3   Self-interest means that each economic unit attempts to _____ ; this self-interest might work to the disadvantage of the economy as a whole if it were not regulated and constrained by _____ .

4 According to the economist, competition is present if two conditions prevail; these two conditions are

a. _____ ;

b. _____ .

5 The competitive price system is a mechanism for both _____ the decisions of producers and households and _____ these decisions.

6 In a capitalistic economy, individual buyers communicate their demands and individual sellers communicate their supplies in the _____ of the economy; and their decisions are co-ordinated by the _____ determined there by demand and supply.

7 In the ideology of pure capitalism government is assigned (no, a limited, an extensive) _____ role.

8 List the five characteristics of pure competition.

a. _____

b. _____

c. _____

d. _____

e. _____

9 Oligopoly is a market model viewed from the (buyers', sellers') _____ side of the market, and monopsonistic competition is a model viewed from the _____ side.

10 The products produced by purely competitive firms are (standardized, differentiated) _____ while those produced by monopolistically competitive firms are _____ ; the product produced by the pure monopolist has no _____ .

11 A pure monopolist has no close rivals or competitors because there are _____ to entry into the industry.

12 The advertising done by a pure monopolist tends to be of a _____ or _____ nature.

13 Monopolistic competition is like pure competition because there are a (small, large) _____ number of sellers and entry into the industry is fairly (easy, difficult) _____ ; but like pure monopoly because each firm has (no, some) _____ control over the price of its product.

14 List five characteristics of pure monopoly.

a. _____

b. _____

c. _____

d. _____

e. _____

15 In order for the number of firms in a monopolistically competitive industry to be considered "large," it is necessary that each firm produces a fairly (small, large) _____ share of the total output of the industry.

16 List the five characteristics of monopolistic competition.

a. _____

b. _____

c. _____

d. _____

e. _____

17 Pure competition and monopolistic competition differ chiefly because

_____

_____ .

18 The product produced by the firms in an oligopoly may be either _____ or _____ .

19 Oligopolistic firms that produce a standardized product are typically found in those industries that produce either _____ materials or (finished, semifinished) _____ goods and those that produce differentiated products are apt to produce (finished, semifinished) _____ (consumer, producer) _____ goods.

20 The number of firms in an oligopoly is (few, many) _____ and each firm supplies a (small, significant) _____ percentage of the total market supply.

21 The ability of a single oligopolist to control the price at which it sells its product is limited by the mutual _____ found in oligopolies.

22 The five factors that have been important determinants of market structures in Canada are

a. _____

b. _____

c. _____

d. _____

e. _____

23 In column (1) of the table below, list the four market models viewed from the buyers' side of the market. In column (2) opposite each of the four market models, list its distinguishing characteristic.

(1) Market model	(2) Distinguishing characteristic
_____	_____
_____	_____
_____	_____
_____	_____

24 There are today about _____ million business firms in Canada. The legal form of the great majority of these firms is the _____ ; and the legal form that produces more than one-half the output of the Canadian economy is the _____ .

25 The liabilities of a sole proprietor and of partners are _____ but the liabilities of stockholders in a corporation are _____ .

26 Indicate, in the spaces to the right of each of the following, whether these business characteristics are associated with the proprietorship (PRO), partnership (PART), corporation (CORP), two of these, or all three of these legal forms.

a. Much red tape and legal expense in beginning the firm _____

b. Unlimited liability _____

c. No specialized management _____

d. Has a life independent of its owner(s)

_____

e. Modest tax advantage if its profits are large _____

f. Greatest ability to acquire funds for the expansion of the firm _____
g. Permits some but not a great degree of specialized management _____
h. Possibility of an unresolved disagreement among owners over courses of action _____
i. Makes it possible for a businessperson to avoid responsibility for illegal actions _____

27 Goods production makes up _____% of Canadian Gross Domestic Product and services make up the remaining _____%.

28 Of the eleven industry classes in which firms are found, two that make the largest contribution to gross domestic product are _____ and _____.

29 Agriculture produces roughly _____% of Canada's gross domestic product.

30 Canada is often called a big-business economy because a relatively _____ firms produce a relatively _____ part of the output of the economy and of some industries.

PROBLEMS AND PROJECTS

1 Employing the following set of terms, complete the table at the foot of the page by inserting the appropriate letter or letters in the blanks.

a. one
b. few
c. many
d. a very large number
e. standardized
f. differentiated

g. some
h. considerable
i. very easy
j. blocked
k. fairly easy
l. fairly difficult
m. none

2 Listed below are several firms or types of firms. In the blanks, indicate (1) into what market type—from the sellers' side of the market—this firm falls and (2) the chief reason(s) for placing it in this classification.

a. A local dry-cleaning firm _____ _____

b. A manufacturer of toothpaste _____ _____

c. A farmer raising pigs _____ _____

d. The Ford Motor Company _____ _____

e. A used-car dealer _____ _____

f. A steel producer _____ _____

Market characteristics	Market situation			
	Pure competition	Pure monopoly	Monopolistic competition	Oligopoly
Number of firms	_____	_____	_____	_____
Type of product	_____	_____	_____	_____
Control over price	_____	_____	_____	_____
Entry	_____	_____	_____	_____
Non-price competition	_____	_____	_____	_____

3 Indicate, for each of the following industries, whether its firms compete in any significant way with firms in other industries, and what the competing industries are.

a. Airlines _____

b. Silk _____

c. Plastics _____

d. Television sets _____

e. Copper _____

4 Indicate, to the best of your ability, what you would call the industries in which the following firms operate:
a. Eaton's
b. The Canadian General Electric Company
c. A used-car dealer in your town
d. Woolco
e. Your local gas or electric company
f. A new-car dealer
g. General Foods
h. Alcan Aluminium
i. Inco
j. Dominion Textile

5 Are any of the firms in question 4 in industries that Table 10-1 of the text lists as highly concentrated manufacturing industries?

SELF-TEST

Circle T if the statement is true, F if it is false.

1 The Canadian economy can correctly be called "pure capitalism." **T F**

2 In Canada, there are legal limits to the right of private property. **T F**

3 The freedom of business firms to produce a particular consumer good is always limited by the desires of consumers for that good. **T F**

4 In a purely capitalistic economy, it is consumers who ultimately decide what goods and services the economy will produce. **T F**

5 Every industry in the Canadian economy falls clearly into one of the four market models. **T F**

6 A large number of sellers does not necessarily mean that the industry is purely competitive. **T F**

7 Only in a purely competitive industry do individuals firms have no control over the price of their product. **T F**

8 Because it is the sole supplier of a product, the pure monopolist cannot affect the market price of its product. **T F**

9 Insofar as pure monopoly is concerned, the industry and the firm are one and the same. **T F**

10 There are no substitutes for the product produced by the pure monopolist. **T F**

11 The monopolistic competitor has only a limited amount of control over the price of its product. **T F**

12 Entry into the monopolistically competitive industry is usually quite difficult. **T F**

13 If an oligopolistic firm is producing a differentiated product, it is more likely to engage in advertising and sales promotion than a firm producing a standardized product. **T F**

14 Imperfectly competitive markets are all markets except those that are purely competitive. **T F**

15 The policies of the federal government have been consistently directed at preventing or eliminating monopoly and at encouraging competition. **T F**

16 The existence of just two sellers in a market is called "bilateral monopoly." **T F**

17 A plant is defined as a group of firms under a single management. **T F**

18 An industry is a group of firms that pro-

duce the same or nearly the same products.
T   F

19 The corporate form of organization is the least used by business in Canada.   **T   F**

20 The corporation in Canada today often has a tax advantage over other legal forms of business organization.   **T   F**

21 Whether a business firm should incorporate or not depends chiefly upon the amount of money capital it must have to finance the enterprise.   **T   F**

22 The wholesale and retail trade and the service industries contain a relatively large number of firms but are insignificant sources of income and employment in the Canadian economy.   **T   F**

23 Corporations produce more than one half of the total output produced by business firms in Canada.   **T   F**

Circle the letter that corresponds to the best answer.

1 Which of the following is *not* one of the six characteristics of capitalism? (*a*) competition (*b*) central economic planning; (*c*) private property; (*d*) freedom of enterprise and choice.

2 Maximization of the profits appears to be in the self-interest of (*a*) business firms; (*b*) land owners; (*c*) workers; (*d*) consumers.

3 The competitive price system is a method of (*a*) communicating the decisions of consumers, producers, and resource suppliers; (*b*) synchronizing these decisions; (*c*) communicating and synchronizing these decisions; (*e*) neither communicating nor synchronizing the decisions.

4 Which of the following is *not* one of the four market models, as viewed from the sellers' side of the market? (*a*) pure competition; (*b*) monopoly; (*c*) monopolistic competition; (*d*) oligopsony.

5 Which of the following is characteristic of monopolistic competition? (*a*) standardized product; (*b*) very few firms; (*c*) fairly easy entry; (*d*) very little non-price competition.

6 Which of the following is *not* characteristic of pure competition? (*a*) large number of sellers; (*b*) differentiated product; (*c*) easy entry; (*d*) no advertising.

7 If the product produced by an industry is standardized, the market structure can be (*a*) pure competition or monopolistic competition; (*b*) pure competition or oligopoly; (*c*) monopolistic competition or oligopoly; (*d*) pure competition, monopolistic competition, or oligopoly.

8 Into which of the following industries is entry least difficult? (*a*) pure competition; (*b*) pure monopoly; (*c*) monopolistic competition; (*d*) oligopoly.

9 Which of the following industries comes *closest* to being purely competitive? (*a*) corn; (*b*) shoes; (*c*) retailing; (*d*) farm implements.

10 Which of the following is the *best* example of pure monopoly? (*a*) the local taxi company; (*b*) the local water company; (*c*) Alcan Aluminium; (*d*) The Steel Company of Canada.

11 With respect to which of the following characteristics are purely competitive industries and monopolistically competitive industries most similar? (*a*) type of product; (*b*) number of firms; (*c*) difficulty of entry; (*c*) extent of non-price competition.

12 Which of the following industry classifications encompasses the greatest number of actual market situations in the Canadian economy? (*a*) pure competition; (*b*) monopoly; (*c*) monopolistic competition; (*d*) oligopoly.

13 Which of the following is an example of an oligopoly producing a differentiated product? (*a*) automobiles; (*b*) sugar; (*c*) shoes; (d) women's dresses.

14 Mutual interdependence is characteristic of (a) pure competition; (b) pure monopoly; (c) monopolistic competition; (d) oligopoly.

15 Which of the following is one of the four market models as viewed from the buyers' side of the market? (a) pure competition; (b) monopoly; (c) monopolistic competition; (d) oligopoly.

16 From the buyers' side of the market, the market for automobile workers in Oshawa would be (a) purely competitive; (b) monopsonistic; (c) monopsonistically competitive; (d) oligopsonistic.

17 In which of the following market models is the individual seller of a product a "price-taker" (a) pure competition; (b) pure monopoly; (c) monopolistic competition; (d) oligopoly.

18 If we include self-employed farmers and professional people, there are approximately how many million business firms in Canada? (a) $\frac{1}{4}$; (b) $\frac{1}{2}$; (c) 1; (d) 2.

19 A group of three plants that is owned and operated by a single firm and consists of a farm growing wheat, a flour-milling plant, and a plant that bakes and sells bakery products, is an example of (a) a horizontal combination; (b) a vertical combination; (c) a conglomerate combination; (d) a corporation.

20 Limited liability is associated with (a) only proprietorships; (b) only partnerships; (c) both proprietorships and partnerships; (d) only corporations.

21 Which of the following forms of business organization can most effectively raise money capital? (a) corporation; (b) partnership; (c) proprietorship; (d) vertical combination.

22 Which of the following industry classes contributes the most to Gross Domestic Product? (a) finance, insurance and real estate; (b) community, business, and personal service; (c) trade; (d) construction.

23 About what percentage of the gross domestic product of Canada is produced by mines, quarries, and oil wells? (a) 1; (b) $2\frac{1}{2}$; (c) 8; (d) 12.

24 The contribution to sales of big business (firms that have sales greater than $20 million a year) is (a) 8%; (b) 18%; (c) 28%; (d) 61%.

DISCUSSION QUESTIONS

1 Explain the several elements—institutions and assumptions—embodied in pure capitalism.

2 What do each of the following seek if they pursue their own self-interest? Consumers, resource owners, and business firms.

3 In what way does the desire of entrepreneurs to obtain economic profits and to avoid losses make consumer sovereignty effective?

4 If the basic economic decisions are not made in a capitalistic economy by a central authority, how are they made?

5 What are the four market models as seen from the buyers' side of the market and their distinguishing characteristics?

6 What factors are important in determining the type of market or industry a particular group of firms will become?

7 How has the federal government contributed to the formation of monopolies? In what ways has it attempted to limit their formation or to regulate them?

8 Why is it dangerous to employ just four market models—from the sellers' side of the market—in classifying and analysing Canadian industries?

9 What is the difference between a plant and a firm? Between a firm and an industry? Which of these three concepts is the most difficult to apply in practice? Why? Distinguish between a horizontal, a vertical, and a conglomerate combination.

10 What are the principal advantages and disadvantages of each of the three legal forms of business organization? Which of the disadvantages of the proprietorship and partnership account for the employment of the corporate form among the big businesses of the Canadian economy?

11 Explain what "separation of ownership and control" of the modern corporation means. What problems does this separation create for stockholders and the economy?

12 Is the Canadian economy and manufacturing in Canada dominated by big business? What evidence do you use to reach this conclusion?

6

THE COSTS OF PRODUCTION

In previous chapters, the factors that influence the demand for a product purchased by consumers were examined in some detail. Chapter 6 turns to the other side of the market and begins the investigation of the forces that determine the amount of a particular product a business firm will produce and the price it will charge for that product. In addition to the demand for the product, the factors that determine the output of a firm and the price of the product are the costs of producing the product *and* the structure of the market in which the product is sold. These market structures were briefly described in Chapter 5. In the following four chapters you will find an explanation of how costs and demand determine price and output in the four different kinds of product markets.

Chapter 6 is an examination of the way in which the costs of the firm change as the output of the firm changes. This chapter is extremely important if the chapters that follow it are to be understood. For this reason it is necessary for you to master the material dealing with the costs of the firm.

You will probably find that you have some difficulty with the new terms and concepts. Particular attention, therefore, should be given to them. These terms and concepts, which are listed below, are used in the explanation of the costs of the firm; they will be used over and over again in later chapters. If you will try to learn them in the order in which you encounter them, you will have little difficulty because the later terms build on the earlier ones.

After the new terms and concepts are well fixed in your mind, understanding the generalizations made about the relationships between costs and output will be much simpler. Here the important things to note are (1) that the statements made about the behaviour of costs are *generalizations* (they do not apply to any particular firm or enterprise, but are more or less applicable to every business firm); and (2) that the generalizations made about the relationships between particular types of cost and the output of the firm are fairly precise generalizations. When attempting to learn these generalizations, you will find it worthwhile to draw rough graphs (with cost on the vertical and output on the horizontal axis) that describe the cost relationships. Try it especially with the following types of costs: *short-run* fixed, variable, total, average fixed, average variable, average total, and marginal costs; and *long-run* average cost.

One last cue: in addition to learning *how* the costs of the firms vary as its output varies, be sure to understand *why* the costs vary the way they do. In this connection, note that the behaviour of short-run costs is the result of the law of diminishing returns and that the behaviour of long-run costs is the consequence of economies and diseconomies of scale.

CHECK LIST

When you have studied this chapter you should be able to

☐ Define economic cost and distinguish between an explicit and an implicit cost.

☐ Explain the difference between normal profit and economic profit; explain why the former *is* a cost and the latter *is not* a cost.

☐ State the law of diminishing returns.

☐ Compute the marginal and average product when you are given the necessary data; explain the relationship between marginal and average product.

☐ Explain the difference between a fixed cost and a variable cost, and between average cost and marginal cost.

☐ Compute and graph average fixed cost, average variable cost, average total cost, and marginal cost when you are given total cost data.

☐ State the relationship between average product and average variable cost, and between marginal product and marginal cost.

☐ Explain the difference between the short run and the long run, and between short-run costs and long-run costs.

☐ State why the long-run average cost curve is expected to be U-shaped; list the causes of the economies and the diseconomies of scale.

☐ Indicate the relationship between long-run average costs and the structure and competitiveness of an industry.

CHAPTER OUTLINE

1 Because resources are scarce and may be employed to produce many different products, the economic cost of using resources to produce any one of these products is an opportunity cost: the amount of other products that cannot be produced.

a. In money terms, the costs of employing resources to produce a product is also an opportunity cost: the payments a firm must make to the owners of resources to attract these resources away from their best alternative opportunities for earning incomes; and these costs may be either explicit or implicit.

b. Normal profit is an implicit cost and is the minimum payment that entrepreneurs must receive for performing the entrepreneurial functions for the firm.

c. Economic, or pure, profit is the revenue a firm receives in excess of all its explicit and implicit economic (opportunity) costs. (The

firm's accounting profit is its revenue less only its *explicit* costs.)

d. The firm's economic costs vary as the firm's output varies; and the way in which costs vary with output depends upon whether the firm is able to make short-run or long-run changes in the amount of resources it employs. The firm's plant is a fixed resource in the short run and a variable resource in the long run.

2 In the short run the firm cannot change the size of its plant and can vary its output only by changing the quantities of the variable resources it employs.

a. The law of diminishing returns determines the manner in which the costs of the firm change as it changes its output in the short run.

b. The total short-run costs of a firm are the sum of its fixed and variable costs. As output increases,

(1) the fixed costs do not change;

(2) the variable costs increase at first at a decreasing and then at an increasing rate; and

(3) total costs at first increase at a decreasing and then at an increasing rate.

c. Average fixed, variable, and total cost are equal, respectively, to the firm's fixed, variable and total cost divided by the output of the firm. As output increases,

(1) average fixed cost decreases;

(2) average variable cost at first decreases and then increases; and

(3) average total cost also decreases at first an then increases.

d. Marginal cost is the extra cost incurred in producing one additional unit of output.

(1) Because the marginal product of the variable resources increases and then decreases (as more of the variable resource is employed to increase output), marginal cost decreases and then increases as output increases.

(2) At the output at which average variable cost is a minimum, average variable cost and marginal cost are equal; and at the output at which average total cost is a minimum, aver-

age total cost and marginal cost are equal.

3 In the long run all the resources employed by the firm are variable resources, and all its costs, therefore, are variable costs.
a. As the firm expands its output by increasing the size of its plant, average cost tends to fall at first because of the economies of large-scale production; but as this expansion continues, sooner or later, average cost begins to rise because of the diseconomies of large-scale production.
b. The economies and diseconomies encountered in the production of different goods are important factors influencing the structure and competitiveness of various industries.

IMPORTANT TERMS

Economic cost	Variable resource
Opportunity cost	Fixed cost
Explicit cost	Variable cost
Implicit cost	Total cost
Normal profit	Average fixed cost
Economic (pure) profit	Average variable cost
	Average (total) cost
Short run	Marginal cost
Long run	Economies of (large) scale
Law of diminishing returns	Diseconomies of (large) scale
Total product	
Marginal product	Minimum efficient scale (MES)
Average product	Natural monopoly
Fixed resource	

FILL-IN QUESTIONS

1 The cost of producing a particular product is the quantity of _____ products that cannot be produced. The value or worth of any resource is what it can earn in its best alternative use and is called the (out-of-pocket, opportunity) _____ cost of that resource.

2 The money cost of producing a product is the amount of money the firm must pay to resource owners to _____ these resources away from alternative employments in the economy; and these costs may be either _____ or _____costs.

3 Normal profit is a cost because it is the payment that the firm must make to obtain the services of the _____ ;
a. economic profit is not a cost and is equal to the firm's total _____ less its total _____ ;
b. accounting profit is equal to the firm's total revenue less its (explicit, implicit) _____ costs.

4 In the short run the firm can change its output by changing the quantity of the (fixed, variable) _____ resources it employs; but it cannot change the quantity of the _____ resources. This means that the firm's plant capacity is fixed in the (short, long) _____ run and variable in the _____ run.

5 The law of diminishing returns is that as successive units of a (fixed, variable) _____ resource are added to a _____ resource beyond some point the (total, marginal) _____ product of the former resource will decrease.

6 When the marginal product of any input
a. exceeeds its average product the average product is (rising, falling) _____;
b. is less than its average product the average product is _____;
c. equal to its average product the average product is a (minimum, maximum) _____.

7 On the following graph sketch the way in which the average product and the marginal product of a resource change as the firm increases its employment of that resource.

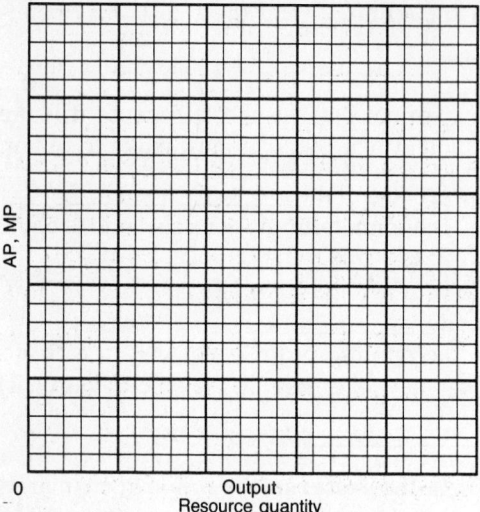

8 The short-run costs of a firm are either _____ costs or _____ costs, but in the long run, all costs are _____ costs.

9 On the following graph, sketch the manner in which fixed cost, variable cost, and total cost change as the output the firm produces in the short run changes.

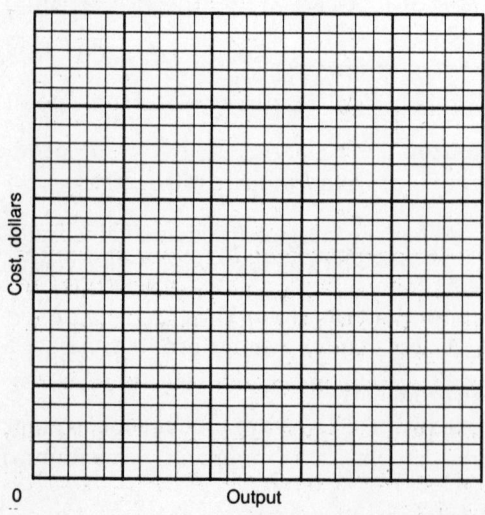

10 The law of diminishing returns causes a firm's _____ cost, _____ cost, and _____ cost to decrease at first, and then to increase as the output of the firm increases. On the following graph, sketch these three cost curves in such a way that their proper relationship to each other is shown.

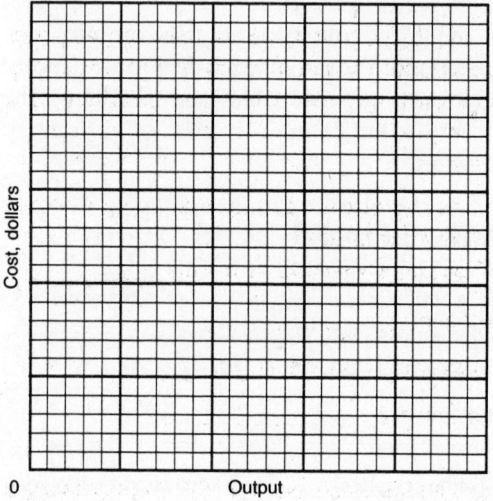

11 Marginal cost is the increase in either

_____

cost or _____ that occurs when the firm increases its output by one unit.

12 If marginal cost is less than average variable cost, average variable cost will be

(rising, falling, constant) _____ , but if the average variable cost is less than marginal cost, average variable cost will be

_____ .

13 Assume that labour is the only variable input in the short run and that the wage rate paid to labour is constant.
a. When the marginal product of labour is rising, the marginal cost of producing a

product is (rising, falling) _____.

b. When the average variable cost of producing a product is falling, the average product of labour is _____.

c. At the output at which marginal product is a minimum, the marginal product of labour is a (minimum, maximum) _____.

d. At the output at which the average product of labour is a maximum, the average variable cost of producing the product is a _____ .

e. At the output at which average variable cost is a minimum,
(1) average variable cost and _____ cost are _____;
(2) average product and _____ product are _____.

14 The long-run average cost of producing a product is equal to the lowest of the short-run cost of producing that product after the firm has had all the time it requires to make the appropriate adjustments in the size of its _____ .

15 Below are the short-run and average cost curves of producing a product with three different sizes of plants: plant 1, plant 2, and plant 3. Draw this firm's long-run average cost curve on this graph.

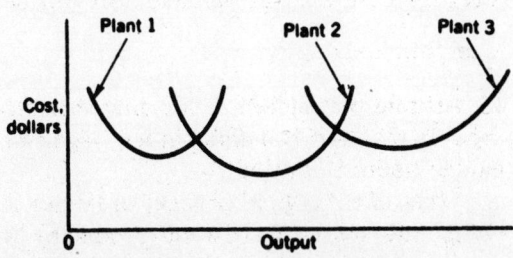

16 List below four important types of economy of large scale.

a. _____

b. _____

c. _____

d. _____

17 The factor that gives rise to diseconomies of large scale is _____ .

18 Economies and diseconomies of scale are significant in the Canadian economy because they affect the _____ and the _____ of a particular industry.

PROBLEMS AND PROJECTS

1 The table below shows the total production of a firm as the quantity of labour employed increases. The quantities of all other resources employed are constant.

Units of labour	Total production	Marginal product of labour	Average product of labour
0	0		
1	80	_____	_____
2	200	_____	_____
3	330	_____	_____
4	400	_____	_____
5	450	_____	_____
6	480	_____	_____
7	490	_____	_____
8	480	_____	_____

a. Compute the marginal products of the first to the eighth unit of labour and enter them in the table.
b. There are increasing returns to labour from the first to the _____ unit of labour, and decreasing returns from the _____ to the eighth unit.

c. When total production is increasing, marginal product is (positive, negative) _____, and when total production is decreasing, marginal product is _____ .

d. Now compute the average products of the various quantities of labour, and enter them in the table.

2 Assume that a firm has a plant of fixed size and that it can vary it output only by varying the amount of labour it employs. The table below shows the relationships between the amount of labour employed, the output of the firm, the marginal product of labour, and the average product of labour.

a. Assume each unit of labour costs the firm $10. Compute the cost of labour for each quantity of labour the firm might employ, and enter these figures in the table.

b. Now determine the marginal cost of the firm's product as the firm increases its output. Divide the *increase* in total labour cost by the *increase in total output* to find the marginal cost. Enter these figures in the table.

c. When the marginal product of labour (1) increases, the marginal cost of the firm's product (increases, decreases) _____; (2) decreases, the marginal cost of the firm's product _____.

d. If labour is the only variable output, the total labour cost and the total variable cost are equal. Find the average variable cost of the firm's product (by dividing total labour cost by total output) and enter these figures in the table.

e. When the average product of labour (1) increases, the average variable cost (increases, decreases) _____; (2) decreases, the average variable cost _____ .

3 In the first table on the next page, you will find a schedule of a firm's fixed cost and variable cost.

Quantity of labour employed	Total output	Marginal product of labour	Average product of labour	Total labour cost	Marginal cost	Average variable cost
0	0	—	—	$_____	—	—
1	5	5	5	_____	$_____	$_____
2	11	6	$5^1/_2$	_____	_____	_____
3	18	7	6	_____	_____	_____
4	24	6	6	_____	_____	_____
5	29	5	$5^4/_5$	_____	_____	_____
6	33	4	$5^1/_2$	_____	_____	_____
7	36	3	$5^1/_7$	_____	_____	_____
8	38	2	$4^3/_4$	_____	_____	_____
9	39	1	$4^1/_3$	_____	_____	_____
10	39	0	$3^9/_{10}$	_____		_____

Output	Fixed cost	Variable cost	Total cost	Average fixed cost	Average variable cost	Average total cost	Marginal cost
$ 0	$200	$ 0	$_____				
1	200	50	_____	$_____	$50.00	$_____	$_____
2	200	90	_____	_____	45.00	_____	_____
3	200	120	_____	_____	40.00	_____	_____
4	200	160	_____	_____	40.00	_____	_____
5	200	220	_____	_____	44.00	_____	_____
6	200	300	_____	_____	50.00	_____	_____
7	200	400	_____	_____	57.14	_____	_____
8	200	520	_____	_____	65.00	_____	_____
9	200	670	_____	_____	74.44	_____	_____
10	200	900	_____	_____	90.00	_____	_____

a. Complete the table by computing total cost, average fixed cost, average total cost, and marginal cost.

b. On the small graph below, plot and label fixed cost, variable cost, and total cost.

c. On the large graph on the next page, plot average fixed cost, average variable cost, average total cost, and marginal cost; label the four curves.

4 Below are the short-run average-total-cost schedules for three plants of different size that a firm might build to produce its product. Assume that these are the only possible sizes of plants the firm might build.

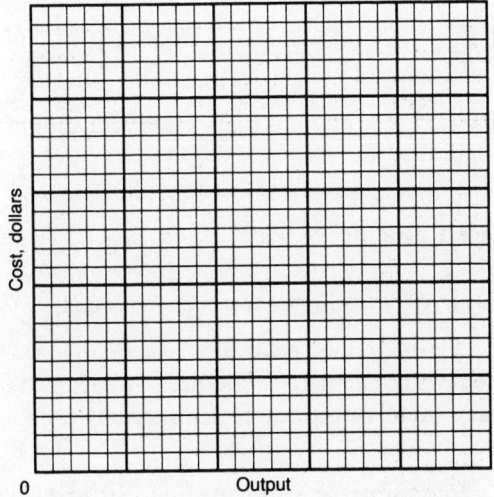

Plant size A		Plant size B		Plant size C	
Output	ATC	Output	ATC	Output	ATC
10	$ 7	10	$17	10	$53
20	6	20	13	20	44
30	5	30	9	30	35
40	4	40	6	40	27
50	5	50	4	50	20
60	7	60	3	60	14
70	10	70	4	70	11
80	14	80	5	80	8
90	19	90	7	90	6
100	25	100	10	100	5
110	32	110	16	110	7
120	40	120	25	120	10

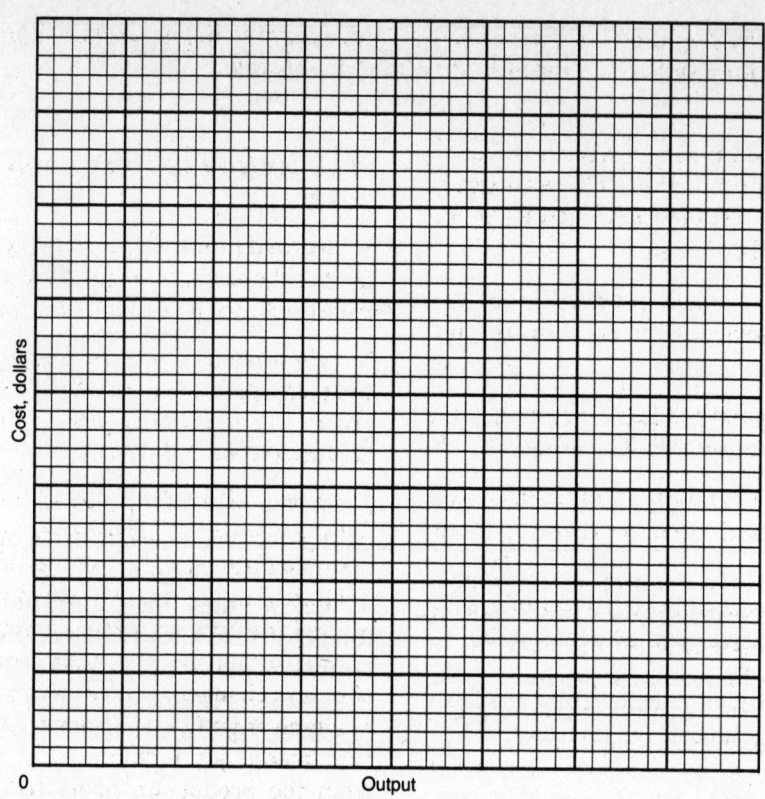

Cost, dollars

0   Output

a. Complete the following *long-run* average-cost schedule for the firm.

Output	Average cost
10	$_____
20	_____
30	_____
40	_____
50	_____
60	_____
70	_____
80	_____
90	_____
100	_____
110	_____
120	_____

b. For outputs between

(1) _____ and _____ , the firm should build plant A;

(2) _____ and _____ , the firm should build plant B;

(3) _____ and _____ , the firm should build plant C.

SELF-TEST

Circle T if the statement is true, F it is false.

1 The economic costs of a firm are the payments it must make to resource owners to attract their resources from alternative employments.   **T F**

2 Economic or pure profit is an explicit cost, while normal profit is an implicit cost.   **T F**

3 In the short run the size (or capacity) of a firm's plant is fixed.   **T F**

4 The resources employed by a firm are all variable in the long run and all fixed in the short run. **T F**

5 The law of diminishing returns is that as successive amounts of a variable resource are added to a fixed resource, beyond some point total output will diminish. **T F**

6 When the average product is falling, marginal product is greater than average product. **T F**

7 When marginal product is negative, total production (or output) is decreasing. **T F**

8 The larger the output of a firm, the smaller is the fixed cost of the firm. **T F**

9 If the fixed cost of a firm increases from one year to the next (because the premium it must pay for insurance on the buildings it owns has been increased) while its variable cost schedule remains unchanged, its marginal cost schedule will also remain unchanged. **T F**

10 Marginal cost is equal to average variable cost at the output at which average variable cost is a minimum. **T F**

11 When the marginal product of a variable resource increases, the marginal cost of producing the product will decrease; and when marginal product decreases, marginal cost will increase. **T F**

12 One of the explanations of why the long-run average-cost curve of a firm rises after some level of output has been reached is the law of diminishing returns. **T F**

13 A firm can avoid the diseconomies of large scale by becoming a multiplant firm. **T F**

14 If a firm has constant returns to scale in the long run the total costs of producing its product do not change when it expands or contracts its output. **T F**

15 Many firms appear to be larger than is necessary for them to achieve the minimum efficient scale. **T F**

Circle the letter that corresponds to the best answer.

1 Normal profit is defined as the cost of obtaining the services of (a) management; (b) entrepreneurs; (c) capital; (d) land.

2 The revenues of a firm less its explicit costs are defined as the firm's (a) normal profit; (b) accounting profit; (c) economic profit; (d) economic rent.

3 Which of the following is most likely to be a long-run adjustment for a firm that manufactures jet fighter planes on an assembly line basis? (a) an increase in the amount of steel the firm buys; (b) a reduction in the number of shifts of workers from three to two; (c) a changeover from the production of one type of jet fighter to the production of a later-model jet fighter; (d) a changeover from the production of jet fighters to the production of sports cars.

4 Assume that the only variable resource is labour and that as the amount of labour employed by a firm increases, the output of the firm increases in the way shown in the table below. The marginal product of the fourth unit of labour is (a) 3 units of output; (b) $3^3/_4$ units of output; (c) 4 units of output; (d) 15 units of output.

Amount of labour	Amount of output
1	3
2	8
3	12
4	15
5	17
6	18

5 Employing the schedule in the previous question, when the firm hires four units of labour, the average product of labour is (a) 3 units of output; (b) $3^3/_4$ units of output; (c) 4 units of output; (d) 15 units of output.

6 Because the average product of a variable resource initially increases and later decreases as a firm increases its output, (*a*) average variable cost decreases at first and then increases; (*b*) average fixed cost declines as the output of the firm expands; (*c*) variable cost at first increases by increasing amounts and then increases by decreasing amounts; (*d*) marginal cost at first increases and then decreases.

7 Because the marginal product of a resource at first increases and then decreases as the output of the firm increases, (*a*) average fixed cost declines as the output of the firm increases; (*b*) average variable cost at first increases and then decreases; (*c*) variable cost at first increases by increasing amounts and then increases by decreasing amonts; (*d*) total cost at first increases by decreasing amounts and then increases by increasing amounts.

For questions 8, 9, and 10 use the data given in the table below. The fixed cost of the firm is $500, and the firm's variable cost is indicated in the table.

Output	Variable Cost
1	$ 200
2	360
3	500
4	700
5	1,000
6	1,800

8 The average variable cost of the firm when 4 units of output are being produced is (*a*) $175; (*b*) $200; (*c*) $300; (*d*) $700.

9 The average total cost of the firm when 4 units of output are being produced is (*a*) $175; (*b*) $200; (*c*) $300; (*d*) $700.

10 The marginal cost of the sixth unit of output is (*a*) $200; (*b*) $300; (*c*) $700; (*d*) $800.

11 Marginal cost and average variable cost are equal at the output at which (*a*) marginal cost is a minimum; (*b*) marginal product is a

maximum; (*c*) average product is a maximum; (*d*) average variable cost is a maximum.

12 In the table below, three short-run cost schedules are given for three plants of different sizes that a firm might build in the long-run. What is the *long run* average cost of producing 40 units of output? (*a*) $7; (*b*) $8; (*c*) $9; (*d*) $10.

Plant 1		Plant 2		Plant 3	
Output	ATC	Output	ATC	Output	ATC
10	$10	10	$15	10	$20
20	9	20	10	20	15
30	8	30	7	30	10
40	9	40	10	40	8
50	10	50	14	50	9

13 Using the data given for question 12, at what output is long-run average cost at a minimum? (*a*) 20; (*b*) 30; (*c*) 40; (*d*) 50.

14 Which of the following is *not* a factor that results in economies of scale? (*a*) more efficient utilization of the firm's plant; (*b*) increased specialization in the use of labour; (*c*) greater specialization and division of labour in the management of the firm; (*d*) utilization of more efficient equipment.

15 The long-run average costs of producing a particular product is one of the factors that determines (*a*) the competition among the firms producing the product; (*b*) the number of firms in the industry producing the product; (*c*) the size of each of the firms in the industry producing the product; (*d*) all of the above.

DISCUSSION QUESTIONS

1 Explain the meaning of the opportunity cost of producing a product, and the difference between an explicit and an implicit cost. How would you determine the implicit cost of a resource?

2 What is the difference between normal and economic profit? Why is the former an economic cost? How do you define accounting profit?

3 What type of adjustments can a firm make in the long run that it cannot make in the short run? What adjustments can it make in the short run? How long is the short run?

4 Why is the distinction between the short run and the long run important?

5 State precisely the law of diminishing returns. Exactly what is it that diminishes, and why does it diminish?

6 Distinguish between a fixed cost and a variable cost. Why are short-run total costs partly fixed and partly variable costs, and why are long-run costs entirely variable?

7 Why do short-run variable costs increase at first by decreasing amounts and later increase by increasing amounts? How does the behaviour of short-run variable costs influence the behaviour of short-run total costs?

8 Describe the way in which short-run average fixed cost, average variable cost, average total cost, and marginal cost vary as the output of the firm increases.

9 What is the connection between marginal product and marginal cost and between average product and average variable cost? How will marginal cost behave as marginal product decreases and increases? How will average variable cost change as average product rises and falls?

10 What is the precise relationship between marginal cost and minimum average variable cost? Between marginal cost and minimum average total cost? Why are these relationships necessarily true?

11 What does the long-run average cost curve of a firm show? What relationship is there between long-run average cost and the short-run average total-cost schedules of the different-sized plants a firm might build?

12 Why is the long-run average-cost curve of a firm U-shaped?

13 What is meant by an economy of large scale? What are some of the more important types of such an economy?

14 What is meant by and what causes diseconomies of large scale?

15 Why are the economies and diseconomies of scale of great significance? How do they influence the size of firms in an industry and the number of firms in an industry?

7

PRICE AND OUTPUT DETERMINATION: PURE COMPETITION

Chapter 7 is the first of four chapters that bring together the demand for a product and the production costs studied in Chapter 6. Each of the four chapters combines demand and production costs in a *different* market structure, and analyses and draws conclusions for that particular kind of product market. The questions analysed, and for which *both short-run and long-run* answers are sought, are the following. Given the costs of the firm, what output will it produce; what will be the market price of the good; what will be the output of the entire industry; what will be the profit received by the firm; and what relationships will exist between price, average total cost, and marginal cost.

In addition to finding the answers to these questions, you should learn *why* the questions are answered the way they are in each of the market models; you should know in what way the answers obtained in one model *differ* from those obtained in the other models.

Actually, the answers are obtained by applying logic to different sets of assumptions. It is important, therefore, to note specifically how the assumptions made in one model differ from those of other models. Each model assumes that every firm is guided in making its decisions solely by the desire to maximize its profits, and that the costs of the firm are not materially affected by the type of market in which it *sells* its output. The important differences in the models, which account for the differing answers, involve (1) such characteristics of the market as the number of sellers, the ease of entry into and exodus from the industry, and the kind of product (standardized or differentiated) produced; and (2) the way in which the *individual firm* sees the demand for *its* output.

Chapter 7 begins by noting that there are several good reasons for studying pure competition. Not the least of these reasons is that, in the long run, pure competition—subject to certain exceptions—results in an ideal or perfect allocation of resources. After obtaining the answers to the questions listed in the first paragraph, we return, at the end of the chapter, to explain in what sense competitive resource allocation is ideal and in what cases it may be less than ideal. In Chapters 8 and 9, which concern monopoly and monopolistic competition repectively, it will be found that in these market situations, resource allocation is less than ideal. You, therefore, should pay special attention, in Chapter 7, to what is meant by an ideal allocation of resources and to why perfect competition results in this perfect allocation.

CHECK LIST

When you have studied this chapter you should be able to

☐ List the conditions that must be fulfilled if an industry is to be purely competitive.

☐ Explain why a purely competitive firm is a "price taker" and the way in which it sees the demand for its product and the marginal revenue from the sale of an additional unit of its product.

☐ Compute average, total, and marginal revenue when you are given the demand schedule faced by a purely competitive firm.

☐ Use both the total-revenue—total-cost and the marginal-revenue—marginal-cost approaches to determine the output the purely competitive firm will produce in the short run; explain *why* the firm will produce this output.

☐ Explain how to find the *firm's* short-run supply curve; construct its short-run supply schedule when you are given its short-run cost schedules.

☐ Explain how to find the *industry's* short-run supply curve (or schedule).

☐ Determine the price at which the product will sell, the output of the industry, and the output of the individual firm in the short run.

☐ Determine the price that will be charged and the output of the individual firm and of the industry when the industry is in long-run equilibrium; explain how the entry and exit of firms assure this result.

☐ Define a constant-cost and an increasing-cost industry; explain how to obtain the long-run industry curve in both of these industries.

☐ Explain how a competitive price system determines what will be produced.

☐ Predict what will happen to the price charged by and the output of a prosperous and an unprosperous industry; and explain why these events will occur.

☐ Explain how production is organized in a competitive system.

☐ Find the least-cost combination of resources when you are given the technological data and the prices of the resources.

☐ Explain the significance of P = AC = MC; and distinguish between productive and allocative efficiency.

☐ List the three kinds of change to which an economy must be able to adapt itself if it is to remain efficient; and explain how a competitive price system both adjusts to and initiates desirable changes.

☐ Explain how a competitive price system determines the distribution of total output.

☐ Present the case for and the case against the price system.

☐ Identify the two basic differences between an ideal price system and the price system found in Canada.

☐ Define a spillover cost and a spillover benefit; explain why a competitive market fails to allocate resources efficiently when there are spillovers; and list the things government may do to reduce spillovers and improve the allocation of resources.

☐ Define a public good and a private good and explain how government goes about reallocating resources from the production of private to the production of public goods.

CHAPTER OUTLINE

1 Pure competition is a situation in which a large number of independent firms, no one of which is able by itself to influence market price, sell a standarized product in a market that firms are free to enter and to leave in the long run. Although pure competition is rare in practice, there are at least three good reasons for studying this "laboratory case."

2 A firm selling its product in a purely competitive industry cannot influence the price at which the product sells; such a firm is a price-taker.
a. The demand for its product is, therefore, perfectly elastic.
b. Average revenue (or price) and marginal revenue are equal and constant at the fixed market price; total revenue increases at a constant rate as the firm increases its output.
c. The demand (average revenue) and marginal revenue curves faced by the firm are horizontal and identical at the market price; the total revenue curve has a constant, positive slope.

3 There are two complementary approaches to the analysis of the output that the purely competitive firm will produce in the short run.

a. Employing the total-revenue–total-cost approach, the firm will produce the output at which total economic profit is the greatest or total loss is the least, provided that the loss is less than the firm's fixed costs (that is, provided that total revenue is greater than total variable cost). If the firm's loss is greater than its fixed cost, it will lessen its loss by producing no output.

b. Employing the marginal-revenue–marginal-cost approach, the firm will produce the output at which marginal revenue (or price) and marginal cost are equal, provided price is greater than average variable cost. If price is less than average variable cost, the firm will shut down to minimize its loss. The short-run supply curve of the individual firm is that part of its short-run—marginal-cost curve that is above average variable cost.

c. Table 7-7 in the text summarizes the principles that the competitive firm follows when it decides what output to produce in the short run.

d. The short-run supply curve of the industry (which is the sum of the supply curves of the individual firms) and the total demand for the product determine the short-run equilibrium price and equilibrium output of the industry; and the firms in the industry may be either prosperous or unprosperous in the short run.

4 In the long run, the price of a product produced under conditions of pure competition will equal the minimum average total cost, and firms in the industry will neither receive economic profits nor suffer losses.

a. If economic profits are being received in the industry in the short run, firms will enter the industry in the long run (attracted by the profits), increase total supply, and thereby force price down to the minimum average cost.

b. If losses are being suffered in the industry during the short run, firms will leave the industry in the long run (seeking to avoid losses), reduce total supply, and thereby

force price up to the minimum average total cost.

c. If an industry is a constant-cost industry, the entry of new firms will not affect the average-total-cost schedules or curves of firms in the industry. An increase in demand, therefore, will result in no increase in the long-run equilibrium price, and the industry will be able to supply larger outputs at a constant price.

d. If an industry is an increasing-cost industry, the entry of new firms will raise the average-total-cost schedules or curves of firms in the industry. An increase in demand, therefore, will result in an increase in the long-run equilibrium price, and the industry will supply larger quantities only at higher prices.

5 In the long run, each purely competitive firm is compelled by competition to produce that output at which price (or marginal revenue), average cost, and marginal cost are equal and average cost is a minimum.

6 The system of prices and markets and the choices of households and business firms furnish the economy with answers to four of the five Fundamental Questions (all except the level of resource use).

a. The demands of consumers for products and the desires of business firms to maximize their profits determine what and how much of each product is produced (and its price).

b. The desires of business firms to maximize profits by keeping their costs of production as low as possible guide them to employ the most efficient techniques of production and determine their demands for and prices of the various resources; competition forces them to use the most efficient techniques and assures that only the most efficient will be able to stay in business.

c. Implicit in *b.* is adaptation to change.

d. Output is distributed according to contribution to production.

7 An economy in which all industries were purely competitive would use its resources efficiently.

a. Goods are efficiently produced when the average cost of producing them is at a minimum; and buyers benefit most from this efficiency when they are charged a price just equal to minimum average cost.

b. Resources are efficiently allocated when goods are produced in such quantities that the total satisfaction obtained from the economy's resources is a maximum; or when the price of each good is equal to its marginal cost.

8 Competitive pricing has been praised and damned because it has both merits and faults.

a. The major merits of the system are
(1) It is able to accommodate itself to changes in consumer tastes, technology, and resource supplies.
(2) The desires of business firms for maximum profits and competition lead the economy to make the appropriate adjustments in the way it uses its resources.
(3) Competition and the desire to increase profits promote both better techniques of production and capital accumulation.
(4) Competition in the economy compels firms seeking to promote their own interests to promote (as though guided by an "invisible hand") the best interest of society as a whole: an allocation of resources appropriate to consumer wants, production by the most efficient means, and the lowest possible prices.

b. The chief faults are
(1) The income distribution problem: with resource prices determined, the money income of each household is determined; and with product prices determined, the quantity of goods and services that these money incomes will buy is determined.
(2) The competitive pricing system cannot account for externalities or provide public goods and services, which are not subject to the exclusion principle.

IMPORTANT TERMS

Total revenue
Average revenue
Marginal revenue
Total-receipts—total-cost approach
Marginal-revenue—marginal-cost approach
The profit-maximizing case
Break-even point
The loss-minimizing case
The close-down case
MR = MC rule
P = MC rule
The firm's short-run supply curve (schedule)
The competitive industry's short-run supply curve (schedule)
Short-run competitive equilibrium
Long-run competitive equilibrium

Constant-cost industry
Increasing-cost industry
Long-run supply
Productive efficiency
Least-cost production
Allocative efficiency
Consumer sovereignty
Dollar votes
Guiding function of prices
Invisible hand
Derived demand
Market failure
Spillover (externality)
Spillover cost
Spillover benefit
Subsidy
Public (social) good
Private good
Exclusion principle
Quasi-public good
Free-rider problem

FILL-IN QUESTIONS

1 What are the four specific conditions that characterize pure competition?

a. _____

b. _____

c. _____

d. _____

2 The individual firm in a purely competitive industry finds that the demand for its product is perfectly (elastic, inelastic) _____ and that marginal revenue is (less than, greater than, equal to)

_____ the price of the product.

3 Economic profit is equal to _____

_____ .

4 The two approaches that may be used to determine the most profitable output for any firm are the _____

approach and the_____
approach.

5 A firm should produce in the short run

only if it can obtain a _____ or suffer

a loss no greater than its _____ .
Provided it produces any output at all
a. it will produce that output at which its profit is a (maximum, minimum)

_____ or its loss is a

_____ ;
b. or, said another way, the output at which

marginal _____ and marginal

_____ are equal.

6 A firm is willing to produce at a loss in the short run if the price it receives is greater than its average (fixed, variable, total)

_____ cost.

7 In the short run, the individual firm's

supply curve is _____ ;
the short-run market supply curve is

_____ .

8 The short-run equilibrium price for a product produced by a purely competitive

industry is the price at which _____

_____

and _____
are equal; the equilibrium quantity is

_____ .

9 In a purely competitive industry in the short run the number of firms in the industry

and the size of their plants are (fixed, variable) _____ ; but in the long run they

are _____ .

10 When a purely competitive industry is in long-run equilibrium, the price that the firm is paid for its product is equal not only to marginal revenue but to long-run

_____ cost and to long-run

_____ cost; and long-run average cost is a (maximum, minimum, neither)

_____ .

11 Firms tend to enter industry in the long

run if _____

and leave it if _____ .

12 If the entry of new firms into an industry tends to raise the costs of all firms in the industry, the industry is said to be a(n) (constant-, increasing-, decreasing-)

_____ cost industry; and its long-run supply curve is (horizontal,

downsloping, upsloping) _____ .

13 If an economy is to make the best use of its scarce resources it is necessary that it

achieve both _____ and

_____ efficiency.

14 Business firms tend to produce those products from which they can obtain

a. at least a (pure, normal) _____
profit; and

b. the maximum _____
profit.

15 If firms in an industry are obtaining economic profits, firms will (enter, leave)

_____ the industry, the price of the

industry's product will (rise, fall) _____ ,
the industry will employ (more, fewer)

_____ resources, produce a (larger, smaller) _____ output, and the industry's economic profits will (increase, decrease) _____ until they are equal to _____ .

16 Because firms are interested in obtaining the largest economic profits possible, the technique they select to produce a product is the one that enables them to produce that product in the least _____ly way.

17 Consumers

a. vote with their _____ for the production of a good or service when they buy that good or service;

b. are said, because firms are motivated by their desire for profits to produce the goods and services consumers vote for in this way, to be (dependent, sovereign) _____ ;

c. (restrict, expand) _____ the freedom of firms and resource suppliers.

18 The purely competitive economy achieves productive efficiency in the long run because price and _____ cost are equal and the latter is a (maximum, minimum) _____ .

19 In the long run the purely competitive economy is allocatively efficient because price and _____ cost are equal.

20 In determining how the total output of the economy will be divided among its households, the price system is involved in two ways:

a. it determines the money _____ each of the households receives; and

b. it determines the _____ they have to pay for each of the goods and services produced.

21 In industrial economies

a. the changes that occur almost continuously are changes in consumer _____, in _____, and in the supplies of _____ ;

b. to make the adjustments in the way it uses its resources that are appropriate to these changes, a market economy allows price to perform its _____ function.

22 The competitive price system tends to foster technological change.

a. The incentive for a firm to be the first to employ a new and improved technique of production or to produce a new and better product is a greater economic _____ ;

b. and the incentive for other firms to follow its lead is the avoidance of _____ .

23 If the price system is competitive, there is an identity of _____ interests and the _____ interest: firms seem to be guided by a(n) _____ to allocate the economy's resources efficiently.

24 The chief economic advantage of the price system, it is said, is that _____ _____ ; its chief non-economic advantage is that _____ .

25 Government frequently reallocates resources when it finds instances of _____ _____ failure; and the two major cases of such failure occur when the competitive price system either

a. _____ or

b. _____.

26 Competitive markets bring about an optimum allocation of resources only if there are no _____ costs or benefits in the consumption and production of the good or service.

27 There is a spillover whenever some of the costs of producing a product or some of the benefits from consuming it accrue to __

_____ .

28 Whenever, in a competitive market, there are
a. spillover costs, the result is an (over-, under-) _____ allocation of resources to the production of the good or service;
b. spillover benefits, the result is an _____ allocation of resources to the production of the good or service.

29 What two things can government do to
a. make the market reflect spillover costs?

(1) _____

(2) _____
b. make the market reflect spillover benefits?

(1) _____

(2) _____

30 Public (social) goods tend to be goods that are not subject to the _____ principle and which are (divisible, indivisible) _____. Quasi-public goods are goods that could be subjected to the exclusion principle but which are provided by government because they have large spillover _____ .

31 To reallocate resources from the production of private to the production of public goods, government reduces the demand for private goods by _____ consumers and firms and then _____ public goods.

PROBLEMS AND PROJECTS

1 Below is the demand schedule facing an individual firm.

Price	Quantity demanded	Average revenue	Total revenue	Marginal revenue
$10	0		$_____	
10	1	$_____	_____	$_____
10	2	_____	_____	_____
10	3	_____	_____	_____
10	4	_____	_____	_____
10	5	_____	_____	_____
10	6	_____	_____	_____

a. Complete the table by computing average revenue, total revenue, and marginal revenue.
b. Is this firm operating in a market that is purely competitive? _____
How can you tell? _____

_____

c. On the following graph plot the demand schedule, average revenue, total revenue, and marginal revenue; label each of these curves. (*Note:* Plot marginal revenue at $^1/_2$, $1^1/_2$, and $2^1/_2$, units of output, and so on, rather than 1, 2, 3, and so on.)
d. The coefficient of the price elasticity of demand is the same between every pair of quantities demanded. How much is it?

_____

e. What relationship exists between average revenue and marginal revenue?____

_____

2 Assume that a purely competitive firm has the schedule of costs given in Table 1 on the next page.
a. Complete Table 2 on p. 80 to show the total revenue and total profit of the firm at each level of output the firm might produce. Assume market prices of $55, $120, and $200.

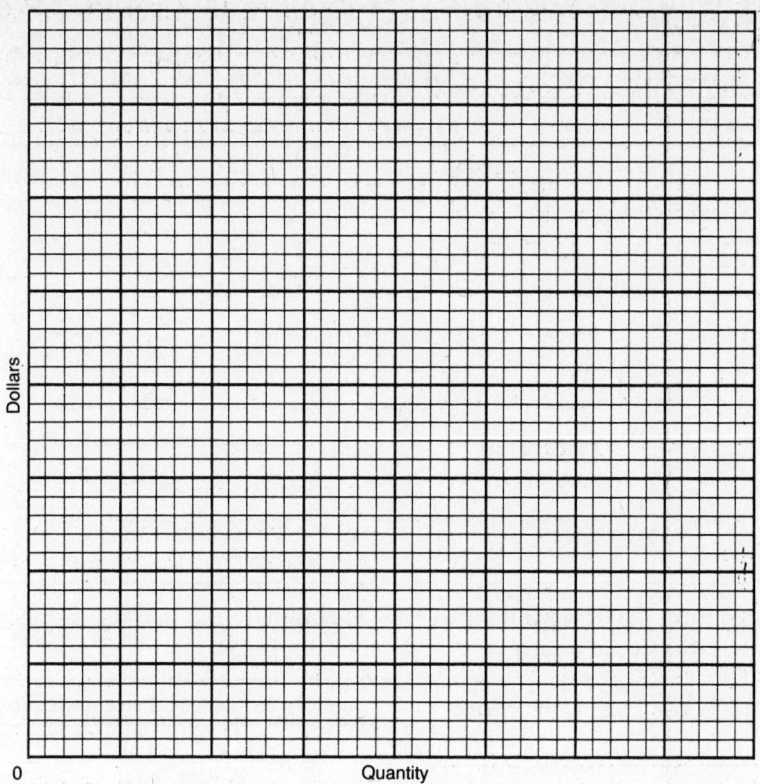

TABLE 1

Output	TFC	TVC	TC	AFC	AVC	ATC	MC
0	$300	$ 0	$ 300				
1	300	100	400	$300	$100	$400	$100
2	300	150	450	150	75	225	50
3	300	210	510	100	70	170	60
4	300	290	590	75	73	148	80
5	300	400	700	60	80	140	110
6	300	540	840	50	90	140	140
7	300	720	1,020	43	103	146	180
8	300	950	1,250	38	119	156	230
9	300	1,240	1,540	33	138	171	290
10	300	1,600	1,900	30	160	190	360

TABLE 2

Output	Market price = $55		Market price = $120		Market price = $200	
	Revenue	Profit	Revenue	Profit	Revenue	Profit
0	$_____	$_____	$_____	$_____	$_____	$_____
1	_____	_____	_____	_____	_____	_____
2	_____	_____	_____	_____	_____	_____
3	_____	_____	_____	_____	_____	_____
4	_____	_____	_____	_____	_____	_____
5	_____	_____	_____	_____	_____	_____
6	_____	_____	_____	_____	_____	_____
7	_____	_____	_____	_____	_____	_____
8	_____	_____	_____	_____	_____	_____
9	_____	_____	_____	_____	_____	_____
10	_____	_____	_____	_____	_____	_____

b. Indicate what output the firm would produce and what its profits would be at a

(1) price of $55: output of _____

and profit of _____ ;

(2) price of $120: output of _____

and profit of _____ ;

(3) price of $200: output of _____

and profit of _____ .

c. Complete the supply schedule of a firm in the next table and indicate what the profit of the firm will be at each price.

Price	Quantity supplied	Profit
$360	$_____	$_____
290	_____	_____
230	_____	_____
180	_____	_____
140	_____	_____
110	_____	_____
80	_____	_____
60	_____	_____

d. If there are 100 firms in the industry and all have the same cost schedule,

(1) complete the market supply schedule in the table below.

Quantity demanded	Price	Quantity supplied
400	$360	_____
500	290	_____
600	230	_____
700	180	_____
800	140	_____
900	110	_____
1,000	80	_____

(2) Using the demand schedule given in question (1): (a) what will the market price of the product be? $_____; (b) what quantity will the individual firm produce?

_____ ; (c) how large will the firm's profit be? $_____; (d) will firms tend to enter or leave the industry in the long run?

_____. Why? _____

3 If the total costs assumed for the individual firm in problem 2 were long-run total costs, and if the industry were a constant-cost industry,

a. what would be the market price of the

product in the long run? $_____

b. what output would each firm produce when the industry was in long-run equilibrium? _____

c. approximately how many firms would there be in the industry in the long run, given the present demand for the product?

_____

d. if the following were the market demand schedule for the product, how many firms would there be in the long run in the industry? _____

Price	Quantity demanded
$360	500
290	600
230	700
180	800
140	900
110	1,000
80	1,100

e. On the graph below, draw the long-run supply curve of
(1) a constant-cost industry
(2) an increasing-cost industry

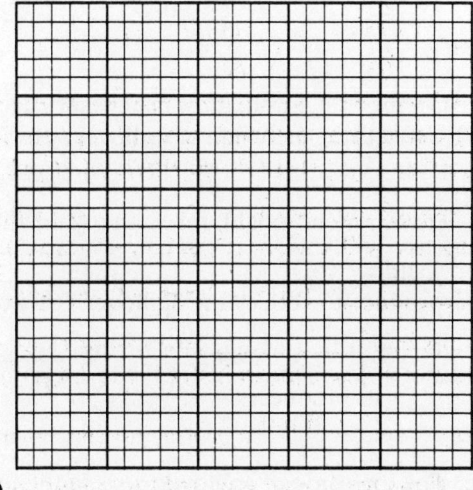

0

4 Assume that a firm can produce *either* product A, product B, or product C with the resources it currently employs. These resources *cost* the firm a total of $50 per week. Assume, for the purposes of the problem, that the firm's employment of resources cannot be changed. The market prices and the quantities of A, B, and C these resources will produce per week are given below. Compute the firm's profit when it produces A, B, or C; enter these profits in the table below.

Product	Market price	Output	Economic profit
A	$7.00	8	$_____
B	4.50	10	$_____
C	.25	240	$_____

a. Which product will the firm produce? __

b. If the price of A rose to $8, the firm would _____ .
(*Hint:* You will have to recompute the firm's profit from the production of A.)

c. If the firm were producing A and selling it at a price of $8, what would tend to happen to the number of firms producing A?

_____

5 Suppose that a firm can produce 100 units of product X by combining labour, land, capital, and entrepreneurial ability in three different ways. If it can hire labour at $2 per unit, land at $3 per unit, capital at $5 per unit, and entrepreneurship at $10 per unit: and if the amounts of the resources required by the three methods of producing 100 units of product X are indicated in the table, answer the questions following it.

Resource	Method		
	1	2	3
Labour	8	13	10
Land	4	3	3
Capital	4	2	4
Entrepreneurship	1	1	1

a. Which method is the least expensive way of producing 100 units of X? _____

b. If X sells for 70 cents per unit, what is the

economic profit of the firm? $_____

c. If the price of labour should rise from $2 to $3 per unit and if the price of X is 70 cents, (1) the firm's use of

labour would change from ___ to _____ ,

land would change from ___ to _____ ,

capital would change from ___ to _____ ,

entrepreneurship would not change; (2) the firm's economic profit would change

from $_____ to $_____ .

6 On the graph are the demand and supply curves for a product bought and sold in a competitive market. Assume that there are no spillover benefits or costs.

a. Were this market to produce an output of Q_1, there would be an (optimum, under, over) _____ allocation of resources to the production of this product.
b. Were this market to produce Q_3, there would be an _____ allocation of resources to this product.

c. The equilibrium output is _____ , and at this output there is an _____ allocation of resources.

7 On the two graphs that follow are product demand and supply curves that do *not* reflect either the spillover costs of producing the product or the spillover benefits obtained from its consumption.

a. On the first graph, draw in another curve that reflects the inclusion of spillover *costs.*

(1) Government might force the (demand for, supply of) _____ the product to reflect the spillover costs of producing it by (taxing, subsidizing) _____ _____ its producers.

(2) The inclusion of spillover costs in the total cost of producing the product (increases, decreases) _____ the output of the product and _____ its price.

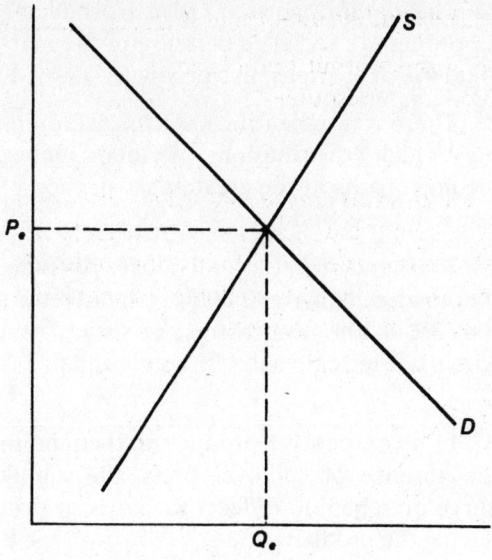

b. On the second graph, draw in a curve that reflects the inclusion of spillover *benefits*.

(1) Indicate on the graph the output that is optimum when spillover benefits are included.

(2) To bring about the production of this optimum output, government might (tax, subsidize) _____ the producers of this product and this would (raise, lower) _____ the supply curve for the product.

(3) Draw on the graph this new supply curve. It should cross the original demand curve at the optimum output determined in (1) above.

(4) This optimum output is (greater than, less than, equal to) _____ Q_e, and the price of the product is (above, below, equal to)_____ P_e.

SELF-TEST

Circle T if the statement is true, F if it is false.

1 One of the reasons for studying the pure competition model is that many industries are almost purely competitive.   **T F**

2 The purely competitive firm views an average-revenue schedule that is identical to its marginal-revenue schedule.   **T F**

3 When a market is competitive, the individual sellers of the commodity are unable to reduce the supply of the commodity enough to drive its price upward.   **T F**

4 Although no individual purely competitive firm is able to influence the market price of the product it produces, the total supply of all the firms in a purely competitive industry does influence the market price.   **T F**

5 A firm will produce, in the short run, the output at which marginal cost and marginal revenue are equal provided that the price of the product is greater than its average variable cost of production.   **T F**

6 If a purely competitive firm is producing an output less than its profit-maximizing output, marginal revenue is greater than marginal cost at that output.   **T F**

7 The short-run supply curve of a purely competitive firm tends to slope upward from left to right because of the law of diminishing returns.   **T F**

8 A firm wishing to maximize its profits will *always* produce that output at which marginal cost and marginal revenue are equal.   **T F**

9 When firms in an industry are earning profits that are less than normal, the supply of the product will tend to decrease in the long run.   **T F**

10 Given the short-run costs of firms in a purely competitive industry, the profits of these firms in the short run depend solely upon the level of the total demand for the product.   **T F**

11 Pure competition, if it could be achieved in all industries in the economy, would result

in the most efficient allocation of resources.
T F

12 Under conditions of pure competition, firms are forced to employ the most efficient production methods available to them if they are to earn no less than normal profits. **T F**

13 Business firms try to maximize their normal profits. **T F**

14 Industries in which economic profits are earned by the firms in the industry will attract the entry of new firms into the industry. **T F**

15 If firms have sufficient time to enter and leave industries, the economic profits of an industry will tend to disappear. **T F**

16 Business firms are really only free to produce whatever they want in any way they wish *if* they do *not* want to maximize profits or to minimize losses. **T F**

17 To say that the demand for a resource is a derived demand means that it depends upon the demands for the products the resource is used to produce. **T F**

18 Resources will tend to be used in those industries capable of earning normal or economic profits. **T F**

19 Economic efficiency requires that a given output of a good or service be produced in the least costly way. **T F**

20 If the market price of a resource A increases, firms will tend to employ smaller quantities of resource A. **T F**

21 Changes in the tastes of consumers are reflected in changes in consumer demand for products. **T F**

22 The incentive that the price system provides to induce technological improvement is the opportunity for economic profits. **T F**

23 In a capitalistic economy, it is from the entrepreneur that the demand for capital goods arises. **T F**

24 The marginal costs of a firm in producing a product are society's measure of the marginal worth of alternative products. **T F**

25 There is no scientific basis for determining which distribution of total money income results in the greatest satisfaction of wants in the economy. **T F**

26 The tendency for individuals pursuing their own self-interests to bring about results that are in the best interest of society as a whole is often called the "invisible hand." **T F**

27 In a competitive product market and in the absence of spillover costs, the supply curve or schedule reflects the costs of producing the product. **T F**

28 If demand and supply reflected all the benefits and costs of a product, the equilibrium output of a competitive market would be identical with its optimum output. **T F**

The following graph should be used to answer true–false question 29 and multiple-choice question 21.

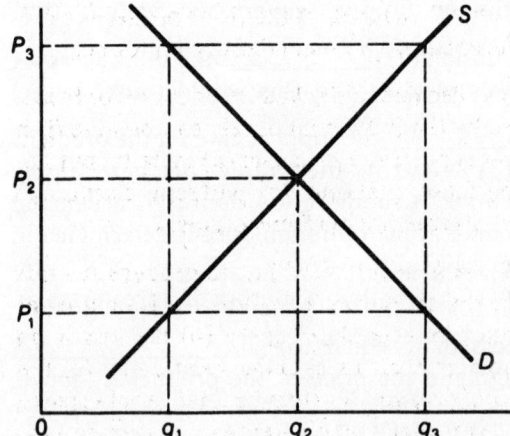

29 Assuming there are no spillover costs or benefits, the production of q_1 units of this product would result in an overallocation of resources to the production of the product. **T F**

30 The inclusion of the spillover benefits by subsidizing consumers would increase the demand for a product.　　　　**T F**

31 When there are spillover costs involved in the production of a product, more resources are allocated to the production of that product and more of the product is produced than is optimal or most efficient.　**T F**

32 Subsidizing the firms producing goods that provide spillover benefits will usually result in a better allocation of resources.　**T F**

33 The economies of mass production and the role of research in the development of new products and techniques of production generally lead to an increase in the number of firms in an industry and a decrease in the size of these firms.　　　　**T F**

Circle the letter that corresponds to the best answer.

1 In a purely competitive industry, (a) each of the firms will engage in various forms of non-price competition; (b) new firms find no obstacles to entering the industry in the short run; (c) individual firms do not have a "price policy"; (d) each of the firms produces a differentiated (non-standardized) product.

2 The demand schedule or curve confronted by the individual purely competitive firm is (a) perfectly inelastic; (b) inelastic but not perfectly inelastic; (c) perfectly elastic; (d) elastic but not perfectly elastic.

3 A firm will be willing to produce at a loss in the short run if (a) the loss is no greater than its total fixed costs; (b) the loss is no greater than its average fixed costs; (c) the loss is no greater than its total variable costs; (d) the loss is no greater than its average variable cost.

4 The individual firm's short-run supply curve is that part of its marginal-cost curve lying above its (a) average-total-cost curve; (b) average-variable-cost curve; (c) average-fixed-cost curve; (d) average-revenue- curve.

5 If a single purely competitive firm's most profitable output, in the short run, were an output at which the firm was neither receiving a profit nor suffering a loss, one of the following would *not* be true. Which one? (a) marginal cost and average total cost are equal; (b) marginal cost and average variable cost are equal; (c) marginal cost and marginal revenue are equal; (d) marginal cost and average revenue are equal.

6 Which one of the following statements is true of a purely competitive industry in short-run equilibrium? (a) price is equal to average total cost; (b) total quantity demanded is equal to total quantity supplied; (c) profits in the industry are equal to zero; (d) output is equal to the output at which average total cost is a minimum.

7 When a purely competitive industry is in long-run equilibrium, one of the following statements is *not* true. Which one? (a) firms in the industry are earning normal profits; (b) price and long-run average total cost are equal to each other; (c) long-run marginal cost is at its minimum level; (d) long-run marginal cost is equal to marginal revenue.

8 Increasing-cost industries find that their costs rise as a consequence of an increased demand for the product because of (a) the diseconomies of scale; (b) diminishing returns; (c) higher resource prices; (d) a decreased supply of the product.

9 Which one of the following is *most* likely to be a constant-cost industry? (a) agricultural and extractive industries; (b) an industry in the early stages of its development; (c) an industry that employs a significant portion of the total supply of some resource; (d) the steel and oil industries.

10 It is contended that which of the following triple identities results in the most efficient use of resources? (a) $P = AC = MC$; (b) $P = AR = MR$; (c) $P = MR = MC$; (d) $AC = MR = MR$.

11 An economy is producing the goods most wanted by society when, for each and every good, its (a) price and average cost are equal; (b) price and marginal cost are equal; (c) marginal revenue and marginal cost are equal; (d) price and marginal revenue are equal.

12 If less than normal profits are being earned by the firms in an industry, the consequences will be that (a) lower-priced resources will be drawn into the industry; (b) firms will leave the industry, causing the price of the industry's product to fall; (c) the price of the industry's product will rise and fewer resources will be employed by the industry; (d) the price of the industry's product will fall and thereby cause the demand for the product to increase.

13 Which of the following would *not* necessarily result, sooner or later, from a decrease in consumer demand for a product? (a) a decrease in the profits of the industry producing the product; (b) a decrease in the output of the industry; (c) a decrease in the supply of the product; (d) an increase in the prices of resources employed by the firms in the industry.

14 If firm A does not employ the most "efficient" or least costly method of production, which of the following will *not* be a consequence? (a) firm A will fail to earn the greatest profit possible; (b) other firms in the industry will be able to sell the product at lower prices than A; (c) new firms will enter the industry and sell the product at a lower price than that at which firm A now sells it; (d) firm A will be spending less on resources and hiring fewer resources than it otherwise would.

15 If an increase in the demand for a product and the resulting rise in the price of the product cause the supply of the product, the size of the industry producing the product, and the amounts of resources devoted to its production to expand, price is successfully performing its (a) guiding function; (b) rationing function; (c) medium-of-exchange function; (d) standard-of-value function.

16 In a capitalistic economy characterized by competition, if one firm introduces a new and better method of production, other firms will be forced to adopt the improved technique (a) to avoid less than normal profits; (b) to obtain economic profits; (c) to prevent the price of the product from falling; (d) to prevent the price of the product from rising.

17 Which of the following would be an indication that competition does not exist in an industry? (a) less than normal profits in the industry; (b) inability of the firms in the industry to expand; (c) inability of firms to enter the industry; (d) wages lower than the average wage in the economy paid to workers in the industry.

18 Economic criticism of the price system is widespread and has pointed out many of the failures of the system. However, the chief economic virtue of the system remains that of (a) allowing extensive personal freedom; (b) efficiently allocating resources; (c) providing an equitable distribution of income; (d) eliminating the need for decision making.

19 Which one of the following is *not* a part of the case *against* the price system? (a) with the passage of time, competition becomes excessive; (b) it distributes income unequally; (c) spillover costs and benefits are not registered in the market place; (d) it does not guarantee either full employment or price stability.

20 The operation of a competitive price system accurately measures (a) both spillover costs and spillover benefits; (b) spillover costs but not spillover benefits; (c) spillover benefits but not spillover costs; (d) neither spillover costs nor spillover benefits.

Use the graph on page 84 to answer the following question.

21 If there are neither spillover costs nor spillover benefits, the output that results in the optimum allocation of resources to the production of this product is (a) q_1; (b) q_2; (c) q_3; (d) none of these outputs.

22 When the production and consumption of a product entail *both* spillover costs and benefits, a competitive product market results in (a) an underallocation of resources to the product; (b) an overallocation of resources to the product; (c) an optimum allocation of resources to the product; (d) an allocation of resources that may or may not be optimum.

23 Which of the following is the best example of a good or service providing the economy with spillover benefits? (a) an automobile; (b) a drill press; (c) a high-school education; (d) an operation for appendicitis.

24 In the Canadian economy, the reallocation of resources needed to provide for the production of public goods is accomplished mainly by means of (a) government subsidies to the producers of public goods; (b) government purchases of public goods from producers; (c) direct control of producers of both private and public goods; (d) direct control of producers of public goods only.

25 Which of the following is characteristic of public goods? (a) they are indivisible; (b) they are sold in competitive markets; (c) they are subject to the exclusion principle; (d) they can be produced only if large spillover costs are incurred.

26 Quasi-public goods are goods and services (a) to which the exclusion principle could not be applied; (b) that have large spillover benefits; (c) that would not be produced by private producers through the market system; (d) that are indivisible.

DISCUSSION QUESTIONS

1 Explain exactly what the economist means by pure competition.

2 If pure competition is so rare in practice, why are students of economics asked to study it?

3 Explain how the firm in a purely competitive industry sees the demand for the product it produces in terms of (a) the price elasticity of demand; (b) the relation of average to marginal revenue; and (c) the behaviour of total, average, and marginal revenue as the output of the firm increases.

4 Why is the firm willing to produce at a loss in the short run if the loss is no greater than the fixed costs of the firm?

5 Explain how the short-run supply of an individual firm and of the purely competitive industry are determined.

6 What determines the equilibrium price and output of a purely competitive industry in the short run? Will economic profits in the industry be positive or negative?

7 Why do the MC = MR rule and the MC = P rule mean the same thing under conditions of pure competition?

8 What are the important distinctions between the short run and long run? Between equilibrium in the short run and in the long run in a competitive industry?

9 When is the purely competitive industry in long-run equilibrium? What forces the purely competitive firm into this position?

10 What is a constant-cost industry? What is an increasing-cost industry? Under what economic conditions is each likely to be found? What will be the nature of the long-run supply curve in each of these industries?

11 When has an economy achieved the most efficient use of its scarce resources? What two kinds of efficiency are necessary if the economy is to make the most efficient use of its resources?

12 Why is the ability of firms to enter industries that are prosperous important to the effective functioning of competition?

13 Explain *in detail* how an increase in the consumer demand for a product will result in more of the product being produced and in more resources being allocated to its production.

14 To what extent are firms "free" to produce what they wish by methods they choose? Do resource owners have freedom to use their resources as they wish?

15 What are the two important functions of prices? Explain the difference between these two functions.

16 Households use the dollars obtained by selling resource services to "vote" for the production of consumer goods and services. Who "votes" for the production of capital goods? Why do they "vote" for capital-goods production? Where do they obtain the dollars needed to cast these "votes"?

17 Why is it said that a purely competitive economy is an efficient economy?

18 What did Adam Smith mean when he said that self-interest and competition bring about results that are in the best interest of the economy as a whole without government regulation or interference?

19 Even if an economy is purely competitive, the allocation of resources may not be ideal. Why?

20 Does pure competition *always* promote both the use of the most efficient technological methods of production and the development of better methods?

21 Explain what economists mean by competition. Why is it important in an economy whose members are motivated by self-interest?

22 What is meant when it is said that competition is the mechanism that "con-

trols" the price-market system? How does competition do this? What do critics of the price system argue tends to happen to this controlling mechanism as time passes, and why do they so argue?

23 "An invisible hand operates to identify private and public interests." What are private interests and what is the public interest? What is it that leads the economy to operate as if it were directed by an invisible hand?

24 What five arguments do critics of the price system advance to refute the contention that the price system allocates resources efficiently?

25 Why does the market system provide some people with lower incomes than it provides others?

26 What is "market failure"? What are the two major kinds of such a failure?

27 What is meant by a spillover in general? By spillover cost and spillover benefit in particular? How does the existence of such costs and benefits affect the allocation of resources and the prices of products? If a market could be required to take these costs and benefits into account, how would the allocation of resources and the price of the product bought and sold in that market be changed?

28 What methods do governments employ to (*a*) redistribute income; (*b*) reallocate resources to take account of spillover costs; (*c*) reallocate resources to take account of spillover benefits?

29 Distinguish between a private and a public good. Include in your answer an explanation of the "exclusion principle" and the distinction between divisible and indivisible goods.

30 What basic method does government employ in Canada to reallocate resources away from the production of private goods and towards the production of public goods?

8

PRICE AND OUTPUT DETERMINATION: PURE MONOPOLY

Chapter 8 is the second of the four chapters that deal with specific market models; it is concerned with what economists call pure monopoly. Like pure competition, pure monopoly is rarely found in the Canadian economy. But there are industries that are very close to being pure monopolies, and an understanding of pure monopoly is helpful in understanding the more realistic situation of oligopoly.

It is only possible for pure monopoly, approximations of pure monopoly, and oligopoly to exist if firms are prevented, in some way, from entering an industry in the long run. Anything that tends to prevent entry is referred to as a "barrier to entry." After describing the characteristics of pure monopoly, the first part of Chapter 8 is devoted to a description of the more important types of barriers to entry. Remember that barriers to entry not only make it possible for monopoly to exist in the economy, but also explain why so many markets are oligopolies (which you will study in Chapter 10).

Like the preceding chapter, this chapter tries to answer certain questions about the firm. These are: what output will the firm produce? what price will it charge? what will be the profit received by the firm? and what will be the relationship between price and average cost and between price and marginal cost? In answering these questions for the monopoly firm, and in comparing pure competition and pure monopoly, note the following:

1. Both the competitive and monopoly firm try to maximize profits by producing that output at which marginal cost and marginal revenue are equal.

2. The individual competitor sees a perfectly elastic demand for its product at the going market price because it is only one of many firms in the industry; but the monopolist sees the market demand schedule that is less than perfectly elastic because the monopolist *is* the industry. The former, therefore, has *only* an output policy, and is a price-taker; the latter is able to determine the price at which it will sell its product and is a price maker.

3. When demand is perfectly elastic, price is equal to marginal revenue and is constant; but when demand is less than perfectly elastic, marginal revenue is less than price and both decrease as the ouput of the firm increases.

4. Because entry is blocked in the long run, firms cannot enter a monopolistic industry to compete away profits as they can under conditions of pure competition.

In addition to determining the price the monopolist will charge, the quantity of its product it will produce, and the size of its profits, Chapter 8 has three other goals. It appraises resource allocation under monopoly conditions by comparing it with resource allocation under purely competitive conditions. Chapter 8 also explains what is meant by price discrimination, the conditions that must prevail if a monopolist is to engage in price discrimination, and the two economic consequences of discrimination. The final section of Chapter 8 introduces you to the problem a government agency faces when it must determine the maximum price a public utility—a natural mono-poly—will be allowed to charge for its prod-uct.

CHECK LIST

When you have studied this chapter you should be able to
- [ ] Define pure monopoly.
- [ ] List the five characteristics of pure monopoly.
- [ ] List the six barriers to entry and explain how each of them would prevent or deter the entry of new firms into an industry.
- [ ] Describe the demand curve or schedule for the product produced by a pure monopo-list.
- [ ] Define marginal revenue and compute marginal revenue when you are given the de-mand for the monopolist's product.
- [ ] Explain the relationship between the price the monopolist charges and the mar-ginal revenue from the sale of an additional unit of product and between the monopo-list's demand and marginal revenue schedule (curve).
- [ ] State the principle that explains what output the monopolist will produce and the price that will be set; determine this output and price when you are given the demand and cost data.
- [ ] Describe the effects of pure monopoly on the price of the product, the quantity of the product produced, and the allocation of the economy's resources.
- [ ] Explain how and why significant economies of scale and X-inefficiency are apt to affect the costs of purely competitive and monopolistic firms.
- [ ] Define technological progress (or dy-namic efficiency) and compare technologi-cal progress in the competitive and monopolistic models.
- [ ] Describe the effects of monopoly on the distribution of income in the economy.
- [ ] Define price discrimination, list the three conditions that must exist before there can be price discrimination, and explain the two economic consequences of price dis-crimination.
- [ ] Identify, for the regulated monopoly (a public utility), the socially optimum and the fair-return price; and explain the dilemma the regulatory agency encounters.

CHAPTER OUTLINE

1 Pure monopoly is a market situation in which a single firm sells a product for which there are no close substitutes. While it is rare in practice, the study of monopoly provides an understanding of firms that are "almost" monopolies, and is useful in understanding monopolistic competition and oligopoly.

2 Pure monopoly (and oligopoly) can exist in the long run only if potential competitors find there are barriers that prevent their en-try into the industry. There are at least six types of entry barriers, but they are seldom perfect in preventing the entry of new firms. Efficient production may, in some cases, re-quire that firms be prevented from entering an industry.

3 The pure monopolist employs cost and demand data to determine the most profit-able output and the price to charge.
a. Unlike the pure competitor, the monop-olist has a price policy. Because it is the sole supplier, the price charged will determine the amount of product sold (or the amount produced and sold will determine the price at which it can be sold). Consequently, price is greater than marginal revenue (and both de-crease as the output of the monopolist in-creases); and the firm is a price maker.
b. Monopoly power in the sale of a product does not necessarily affect the prices the mo-nopolist pays or the costs of production.
c. The monopolist produces that output at which the marginal cost and marginal rev-enue are equal, and charges the price at which this profit-maximizing output can be sold.

d. It is not true that a monopolist charges as high a price as is possible, and it is not true that profit per unit is as large as it might be; and a monopoly may not be profitable at all.

4 The existence of pure monopoly has significant effects on the economy as a whole.
a. Because it produces smaller outputs and charges higher prices than would result under conditions of pure competition and because price is greater than both average total and marginal cost, monopoly misallocates resources (results in neither productive nor allocative efficiency).
b. A monopolist may, however, have lower or higher average costs than a pure competitor producing the same product would have.
(1) if there are economies of scale in the production of the product, the monopolist is able to produce the good or service at a lower long-run average cost than a large number of small pure competitors could produce it.
(2) But if a monopolist is more susceptible to X-inefficiency than a purely competitive firm, its long-run average costs at every level of output are higher than what those of a purely competitive firm would be.
c. A monopolist may also be more or less efficient over time than pure competitors in developing new lower-cost techniques of producing existing products and in developing new products.
d. Monopoly contributes to income inequality in the economy.

5 To increase profits, a pure monopolist may engage in price discrimination by charging different prices to different buyers of the same product (when the price differences do not represent differences in the costs of producing the product).
a. To discriminate, the seller must have some monopoly power; be capable of separating buyers into groups that have different elasticities of demand; and be able to prevent the resale of the product.
b. The seller charges each group the highest price that group would be willing to pay for the product rather than go without it. Discrimination increases not only the profits but also the output of the monopolist.
c. Price discrimination is common in the Canadian economy.

6 The prices charged by monopolists are often regulated by governments to reduce the misallocation of resources.
a. A ceiling price determined by the intersection of the marginal-cost and demand schedules is the socially optimum price, and it improves the allocation of resources.
b. This ceiling price may force the firm to produce at a loss, and so government may set the ceiling at a level determined by the intersection of the average-cost and demand schedules to allow the monopolist a fair return.
c. The dilemma of regulation is that the socially optimum price may cause losses for the monopolist, and that a fair-return price results in a less efficient allocation of resources.

IMPORTANT TERMS

Pure monopoly	Dynamic efficiency
Barrier to entry	Price discrimination
Natural monopoly	Socially optimum
Unfair competition	price
The economies of	Fair-return price
being established	Dilemma of regulation
X-inefficiency	

FILL-IN QUESTIONS

1 Pure monopoly is an industry in which a single firm is the sole producer of a product for which there are no (substitutes, close substitutes) _____ and into which entry in the long run is (easy, difficult, blocked) _____ .

2 What are the six most important types of barriers to entry?

a. _____

b. _____

c. _____

d. _____

e. _____

f. _____

3 If there are substantial economies of scale in the production of a product, a small-scale firm will find it difficult to enter into and survive in an industry because its average costs will be (greater, less) _____ than those of the established firms; and a firm will find it difficult to start out on a large scale because it will be nearly impossible to acquire the needed (labour, money capital) _____ .

4 Public utility companies tend to be ____ _____ monopolies, and they receive their franchises from and are _____ by governments.

5 The demand schedule confronting the pure monopolist is _____ perfectly elastic; this means that marginal revenue is (greater, less) _____ than average revenue (or price) and that both marginal revenue and average revenue (increase, decrease)_____ as output increases.

6 When the profits of a monopolist are being maximized _____ and _____ are equal; and price (or average revenue) is (greater, less) _____ than marginal cost.

7 Three common fallacies about pure monopoly are that

a. it charges the _____ price;

b. its average (or per unit) profit is _____ _____ ;

c. it alway receives a _____ .

8 The output produced by a monopolist is inefficiently *produced* because the average total cost of producing the product is not __ _____ and resources are not efficiently *allocated* because _____ is not equal to _____ .

9 Resources can be said to be more efficiently allocated by pure competition than by pure monopoly only if the purely competitive firm and the monopoly have the same _____ and they will not be the same if the monopolist,
a. by virtue of being a large firm enjoys economies of _____ not available to a pure competitor; or

b. is more susceptible to _____ _____ than pure competitors.

10 Monopolists are more dynamically efficient than pure competitors if they improve the _____ of producing existing products (and thereby lower the _____ of producing them) and develop new _____ over time more rapidly than pure competitors.

11 Monopoly seems to result in a greater inequality in the distribution of income because the owners of monopolies are largely in the (upper, middle, lower) _____ income groups.

12 There is price discrimination whenever a product is sold at different _____ and these differences are not equal to the differences in the _____ of producing the product.

13 Price discrimination is possible only when the following three conditions are found.

a. _____

b. _____

c. _____

14 The two economic consequences of a monopolist's engagement in price discrimination are a(n) (increase, decrease) _____ in the profits and a(n) _____ in the output of the monopolist.

15 The misallocation of resources that results from monopoly can be *eliminated* if a ceiling price for the monopolist's product is set equal to _____ ; such a price is, however, usually less than

_____ .

16 If a regulated monopolist is allowed to earn a fair return, the ceiling price for the product is set equal to _____ ; such a price reduces but does not eliminate the _____ of resources caused by monopoly.

PROBLEMS AND PROJECTS

1 The demand schedule for the product produced by a monopolist is given in the table following.

a. Complete the table by computing total revenue at each of the eleven prices and the ten marginal revenue figures.

b. Regardless of the cost of producing this product the monopolist will never produce an output greater than 7 because beyond 7 units the demand for the product is _____

Price	Quantity demanded	Total revenue	Marginal revenue
$700	0	$_____	$_____
650	1	_____	_____
600	2	_____	_____
550	3	_____	_____
500	4	_____	_____
450	5	_____	_____
400	6	_____	_____
350	7	_____	_____
300	8	_____	
250	9	_____	
200	10	_____	

c. Using the table of costs given in problem 2 of Chapter 7:

(1) What output will the monopolist produce?

_____

(2) What price will the monopolist charge?

$ _____

(3) What total profit will the monopolist receive? $ _____

d. Assume this monopolist is able to engage in price discrimination and to sell each unit of the product at a price equal to the maximum price the buyer of that unit of the product would be willing to pay.

(1) Complete the table following by computing total revenue at each of the eleven quantities and the marginal revenue this discriminating monopolist obtains for each additional unit sold.

(2) From the table it can be seen that the marginal revenue which the discriminating monopolist obtains from the sale of an additional unit is equal to the _____ .

Quantity demanded	Price	Total revenue	Marginal revenue
0	$700	$_____	
1	650	_____	$_____
2	600	_____	_____
3	550	_____	_____
4	500	_____	_____
5	450	_____	_____
6	400	_____	_____
7	350	_____	_____
8	300	_____	_____
9	250	_____	_____
10	200	_____	_____

(3) Using the same table of costs, the discriminating monopolist would produce ____ units of the product, charge the buyer of the last unit of product produced a price of $_____, and obtain a total economic profit of $_____.

(4) If the pure monopolist is able to engage in price discrimination its profits will be (larger, smaller, the same) _____ and it will produce an output that is (larger, smaller, the same) _____ .

2 In the following table are cost and demand data for a pure monopolist.

Quantity demanded	Price	Marginal revenue	Average cost	Marginal cost
0	$17.50			
1	16.00	$16.00	$24.00	$24.00
2	14.50	13.00	15.00	6.00
3	13.00	10.00	11.67	5.00
4	11.50	7.00	10.50	7.00
5	10.00	4.00	10.00	8.00
6	8.50	1.00	9.75	8.50
7	7.00	-2.00	9.64	9.00
8	5.50	-5.00	9.34	9.25
9	4.00	-8.00	9.36	9.50

a. An unregulated monopolist would produce _____ units of a product, sell it at a price of _____, and receive a total profit of _____.

b. If this monopolist were regulated and the maximum price it could charge were set equal to marginal cost, it would produce _____ units of a product, sell it at a price of _____, and receive a total profit of _____. Such regulation would either _____ the firm or require that the regulating government _____ the firm.

c. If the monopolist were not regulated and were allowed to engage in price discrimination by charging the maximum price it could obtain for each unit sold, it would produce 6 units (because the marginal revenue from the 6th unit and marginal cost of the 6th unit would both be $8.50). Its total revenue would be $_____, its total costs would be $_____, and its total profit would be $_____.

d. If the monopolist were regulated and allowed to charge a fair-return price, it would produce _____ units of a product, charge a price of _____, and receive a profit of _____.

e. From which situation — *a*, *b*, or *d* — does the most efficient allocation of resources result? _____ From which situation does the least efficient allocation result? _____ In practice, government would probably select situation _____.

SELF-TEST

Circle T if the statement is true, F if it is false.

1 The pure monopolist produces a product for which there are no substitutes. **T F**

2 The weaker the barriers to entry into an industry, the more competition there will be in the industry, other things being equal.
T F

3 Monopoly is always undesirable unless it is regulated by government.
T F

4 The monopolist can increase the sale of its product if it charges a lower price.
T F

5 As a monopolist increases its output, it finds that its total revenue at first decreases, and that after some output level is reached, its total revenue begins to increase.
T F

6 A purely competitive firm is a price-taker but a monopolist is a price maker.
T F

7 A monopolist will not voluntarily sell at a price at which the demand for its product is inelastic.
T F

8 The monopolist determines profit-maximizing output by producing that output at which marginal cost and marginal revenue are equal, and sets the product price equal to marginal cost and marginal revenue at that output.
T F

9 When a monopolist is maximizing its total profit, it is also producing that output at which its per unit (or average) profit is a maximum.
T F

10 Resources are misallocated by a monopolist because price is not equal to marginal cost.
T F

11 When there are substantial economies of scale in the production of a product, the monopolist may charge a price that is lower than the price that would prevail if the product were produced by a purely competitive industry.
T F

12 The purely competitive firm is more likely to be affected by X-inefficiency than a monopolist.
T F

13 Economists are agreed that monopolies are less dynamically efficient than competitive firms.
T F

14 In a society in which technology is not changing and the economies of scale can be employed by both pure competitors and monopolists, the purely competitive firm will use the more efficient methods of production.
T F

15 One of the economic effects of monopoly is less income inequality.
T F

16 If a monopolist engages in price discrimination rather than charging all buyers the same price, its profits are greater and its output is smaller.
T F

17 The dilemma of monopoly regulation is that the production by a monopolist of an output that causes no misallocation of resources may force the monopolist to suffer an economic loss.
T F

Circle the letter that corresponds to the best answer.

1 Which of the following is the *best* example of a pure monopoly? (*a*) your neighbourhood grocer; (*b*) the telephone company in your community; (*c*) the manufacturer of a particular brand of toothpaste; (*d*) the only airline furnishing passenger service between two major cities.

2 Which of the following is *not* an important characteristic of a natural monopoly? (*a*) substantial economies of scale are available; (*b*) very heavy fixed costs; (*c*) essential natural resources controls; (*d*) competition is impractical and/or would be very expensive for the consumer.

3 Monopoly can probably exist over a long period of time only if (*a*) it is based on the control of raw materials; (*b*) it controls the patents on the product; (*c*) cut-throat competition is employed to eliminate rivals; (*d*) government assists the monopoly and prevents the establishment of rival firms.

4 Which of the following is *not* true with respect to the demand data confronting a monopolist? (*a*) marginal revenue is greater than average revenue; (*b*) marginal revenue decreases as average revenue decreases; (*c*) demand is less than perfectly elastic; (*d*) average revenue (or price) decreases as the output of the firm increases.

5 Assume the cost and demand data for a pure monopolist as given in the table below. How many units of output will the firm produce? (*a*) 1; (*b*) 2; (*c*) 3; (*d*) 4.

Output	Total cost	Price
0	$ 500	$1,000
1	520	600
2	580	500
3	700	400
4	1,000	300
5	1,500	200

6 The monopolist in question 5 above would set its price at (*a*) $120; (*b*) $200; (*c*) $233; (*d*) $400.

7 If the monopolist for whom cost and demand data are given in question 5 above were forced to produce the socially optimum output by the imposition of a ceiling price, the ceiling price would have to be (*a*) $200; (*b*) $300; (*c*) $400; (*d*) $500.

8 When the monopolist is maximizing total profits *or* minimizing losses, (*a*) total revenue is greater than total cost; (*b*) average revenue is greater than average total cost; (*c*) average revenue is greater than marginal cost; (*d*) average total cost is less than marginal cost.

9 A monopolist does not *produce* the product as efficiently as is possible because (*a*) the average total cost of producing it is not a minimum; (*b*) the marginal cost of producing the last unit is less than its price; (*c*) it is earning a profit; (*d*) average revenue is great-

er than the cost of producing an extra unit of output.

10 X-inefficiency means that a firm fails to (*a*) produce an output at the lowest average cost possible; (*b*) produce an output at the lowest total cost possible; (*c*) employ resources in their least-cost combination to produce an output; (*d*) do all of the above.

11 Dynamic efficiency refers to (*a*) the achievement of economies of scale in producing products; (*b*) the development over time of more efficient (less costly) techniques of producing products and the improvement of these products; (*c*) the avoidance of X-inefficiency; (*d*) the avoidance of allocative inefficiency.

12 Over time, monopoly *may* result in greater technological improvement than would be forthcoming under conditions of pure competition for several reasons. Which of the following is *not* one of these reasons? (*a*) technological advance will lower the costs and enhance the profits of the monopolist, and these increased profits will not have to be shared with rivals; (*b*) technological advance will act as a barrier to entry and thus allow the monopolist to continue to be a monopolist; (*c*) technological advance requires research and experimentation, and the monopolist is in a position to finance them out of profits; (*d*) technological advance is apt to make existing capital equipment obsolete, and the monopolist can reduce costs by speeding up the rate at which its capital becomes obsolete.

13 Which of the following is *not* one of the conditions that must be realized before a seller finds price discrimination is workable? (*a*) the buyer must be unable to resell the product; (*b*) the product must be a service; (*c*) the seller must have some degree of monopoly power; (*d*) the seller must be able to segment the market.

14 If a monopolist engages in price discrimination rather than charging all buyers the same price, its (a) profits and its output are greater; (b) profits and its ouput are smaller; (c) profits are greater and its output is smaller; (d) profits are smaller and its output is greater.

15 Look at the demand data in question 5 above. If the monopolist could sell each unit of the product at the maximum price the buyer of that unit would be willing to pay for it, and if the monopolist sold 4 units, total revenue would be (a) $1,200; (b) $1,800; (c) $2,000; (d) $2,800.

16 A monopolist who is limited by the imposition of a ceiling price to a fair return sells the product at a price equal to (a) average total cost; (b) average variable cost; (c) marginal cost; (d) average fixed cost.

DISCUSSION QUESTIONS

1 What is pure monopoly? Why is it studied if it is so rare in practice?

2 What is meant by a barrier to entry? What kinds of such barriers are there? How important are they in pure competition, pure monopoly, monopolistic competition, and oligopoly?

3 Why are the economies of scale a barrier to entry?

4 Why are most natural monopolies also public utilities? What does government hope to achieve by granting exclusive franchises to and regulating such natural monopolies?

5 How do patent laws contribute to the growth of monopoly power? (In your answer, mention patent pools and tying agreements.)

6 What advantage does the going, established firm have over the new, immature firm in an industry?

7 Compare the pure monopolist and the individual pure competitor with respect to (a) the demand schedule; (b) the marginal-revenue schedule; (c) the relationship between marginal revenue and the average revenue; (d) price policy; (e) the ability to administer (or set) price.

8 Explain why marginal revenue is always less than average revenue when demand is less than perfectly elastic.

9 Suppose a pure monopolist discovered it was producing and selling an output at which the demand for its product was inelastic. Explain why a decrease in its output would increase its economic profits.

10 What output will the monopolist produce? What price will it charge?

11 Why does the monopolist not charge the highest possible price for the product? Why does the monopolist not set the price for the product in such a way that average profit is a maximum? Why are some monopolies unprofitable?

12 In what sense is resource allocation and production more efficient under conditions of pure competition than under monopoly conditions?

13 What are the two complications that may result in a monopolist having lower or higher average costs than a competitive firm? How does each of these complications affect the average costs of a monopolist and what evidence is there to support the belief that these two complications lower or raise the average costs of a monopolist?

14 Does monopoly, when compared with pure competition, result in more or less dynamic efficiency (technological progress)? What are the arguments on *both* sides of this question? What evidence is there to support the two views?

15 How does monopoly allegedly affect the distribution of income in the economy, and why does monopoly seemingly have this effect on income distribution in the Canadian economy?

16 What is meant by price discrimination, and what conditions must be realized before it is workable? Explain how a monopolist who discriminates would determine what price to charge for each unit of the product sold (or to charge each group of buyers) and how discrimination would affect the profits and the output of the monopolist.

17 How do public utility regulatory agencies attempt to eliminate the misallocation of resources that results from monopoly? Explain the dilemma that almost invariably confronts the agency in this endeavour; explain also why a fair-return price only reduces but does not eliminate the misallocation.

9

PRICE AND OUTPUT DETERMINATION: MONOPOLISTIC COMPETITION

Chapter 9 is the third of the four chapters that deal with specific market situations. As its name implies, monopolistic competition is a blend of pure competition and pure monopoly; one of the reasons for studying those relatively unrealistic market situations was to prepare you for this more realistic study of monopolistic competition. Monopolistic competition is not a realistic description of all markets, but the study of it will help you to understand the many markets that are nearly monopolistically competitive. It will also help you to understand why oligopoly is prevalent in the Canadian economy, and how oligopoly differs from monopolistic competition.

The first task is to learn exactly what is meant by monopolistic competition. Next you should examine the demand curve the monopolistically competitive firm sees for its product, and note how and why it differs from the demand curves faced by the purely competitive firm and by the monopolist. In this connection, it is also important to understand that as the individual firm changes the character of the product it produces or changes the extent to which it promotes the sale of its product, both the costs of the firm and the demand for its product will change. A firm confronts a different demand curve every time it alters its product or its promotion of that product.

With the product and promotional campaign of the firm *given*, the price-output analysis of the monopolistic competitor is relatively simple. In the short run, this analysis is identical with the analysis of the price-output decision of the pure monopolist in the short run. It is only in the long run that the competition element makes itself apparent: the entry (or exit) of firms forces the price the firm charges down (up) *towards* the level of average cost. This price is not equal either to *minimum* average cost or to marginal cost; and consequently monopolistic competition, on these two scores, can be said to be less efficient than pure competition.

A relatively large part of Chapter 9 is devoted to a discussion of non-price competition. This is done for very good reasons. In monopolistically competitive industries, a part of the competitive effort of individual firms is given over to product differentiation, product development, and product advertising. Each firm has three things to manipulate—price, product, and advertising—in trying to maximize its profits. While monopolistic competition may not be so economically efficient as pure competition in terms of a *given* product and the promotion of it, when all the economic effects—good and bad—of differentiation, development, and advertising are considered, this shortcoming may or may not be offset. Whether it is actually offset is an unanswerable question. If Chapter 9 has one central idea, it is this: monopolistic competition cannot be compared with pure competition solely on the basis of prices charged at any given time; it must also be judged in terms of whether it results in better products, in a wider variety of products, in better-informed consumers, in lower-priced radio and television programs, magazines, and newspapers, and the other redeeming features.

In short, the study of monopolistic competition is a realistic study and for that reason it is a difficult study. Many factors have to be considered in explaining how such a group of firms behaves and in appraising the efficiency with which such an industry allocates scarce resources.

CHECK LIST

When you have studied this chapter you should be able to

☐ List the characteristics of monopolistic competition.

☐ Determine the output of and the price charged by a monopolistic competitor (producing a given product and engaged in a given amount of sales promotion) in the short run when you are given the cost and demand data.

☐ Explain why the price charged by a monopolistic competitor (producing a given product and engaged in a given amount of sales promotion) will, in the long run, tend to equal average cost.

☐ Identify the "wastes of monopolistic competition" and explain why product differentiation may "offset" these wastes.

☐ Enumerate the three principal types of non-price competition.

☐ Present the major arguments in the cases for and against advertising.

CHAPTER OUTLINE

1 A monopolistically competitive industry is one in which a fairly large number of independent firms produce differentiated products, in which both price and various forms of non-price competition occur, and into which entry is relatively easy in the long run.

Many Canadian industries approximate monopolistic competition.

2 Assume that the products the firms in the industry produce and the amounts of promotional activity in which they engage are given.

a. The demand curve confronting each firm will be highly but not perfectly elastic because each firm has many competitors that produce close but not perfect substitutes for the product it produces.

b. In the short run, the individual firm will produce the output at which marginal cost and marginal revenue are equal and charge the price at which that output can be sold; either profits or losses may result in the short run.

c. In the long run, the entry and exodus of firms will *tend* to change the demand for the product of the individual firm in such a way that profits are eliminated (price and average cost are made equal to each other).

3 Monopolistic competition among firms producing a *given* product and engaged in a *given* amount of promotional activity results in less economic efficiency and more waste than does pure competition. Although the average cost of each firm is equal to its price, the industry does not realize allocative efficiency (because output is smaller than the output at which marginal cost and price are equal); and it does not realize productive efficiency (because the output is smaller than the output at which average cost is a minimum).

4 In addition to setting its price and output so that its profit is maximized, each individual firm also attempts to differentiate its product and to promote (advertise) it in order to increase the firm's profit; these additional activities give rise to non-price competition among firms.

a. Product differentiation and product development, as devices firms employ in the hope of increasing their profit, may offset the wastes of monopolistic competition to the extent that they result in a wider variety and better quality of products for consumers.

b. Whether the advertising of differentiated products results in economic waste or in greater economic efficiency is debatable; there are good arguments on both sides of this question and there is no clear answer to it.

c. Empirical evidence on the economic effects of advertising shows that it leads to less competition and a misallocation of resources in some cases, and to more competition and lower prices in other cases.

d. The monopolistically competitive firm tries to adjust its price, its product, and its promotion of the product so that the amount by which the firm's total revenue exceeds the total cost of producing and promoting its product is at a maximum.

IMPORTANT TERMS

Monopolistic
  competition
Product
  differentiation

Non-price competition
Wastes of
  monopolistic
  competition

FILL-IN QUESTIONS

1 In a monopolistically competitive market, a (few, relatively large number of) _____ producers sell (standardized, differentiated) _____ products; these producers (do, do not) _____ collude; and they engage in both _____ and _____ competition. In the long run, entry into the industry is (difficult, fairly easy) _____ .

2 Because monopolistically competitive firms sell differentiated products each firm has (no, limited, complete) _____ control over the price of its product, and there is _____ between the firms.

3 Given the product being produced and the extent to which that product is being promoted, in the *short run*,

a. the demand curve confronting the monopolistically competitive firm will be (more, less) _____ elastic than that facing a monopolist and _____ elastic than that facing a pure competitor;

b. the elasticity of this demand curve will depend upon _____ and _____ ;

c. the firm will produce the output at which _____ and _____ are equal.

4 In the long run, the *entry* of new firms into a monopolistically competitive industry will (expand, reduce) _____ the demand for the product produced by each firm in the industry and (increase, decrease) _____ the elasticity of that demand.

5 In the long run, *given* the product and the amount of product promotion, the price charged by the individual firm will tend to equal _____, its economic profits will tend to equal _____, and its average cost will be _____ than the minimum average cost of producing and promoting the product.

6 Given the product and the extent of product promotion, monopolistic competition is wasteful because _____ and because _____ .

7 In the long run, the monopolistic competitor cannot protect and increase profits by varying the product's price or output, but it can try to protect and increase profits by

_____

and _____ .

8 Product differentiation and product development tend to result in the consumer being offered a wider _____ of goods at any given time and an improved _____ of goods over a period of time.

9 The different case studies of the economic effects of advertising indicate that in North America it is (competitive, anticompetitive, both) _____ .

10 In attempting to maximize profits, the monopolistic competitor will vary the price, the _____ , and the _____ of the product until the firm feels no further change in these three variables will result in greater profits.

PROBLEMS AND PROJECTS

1 Listed below are several industries. Indicate, in the space to the right of each, whether you believe it is monopolistically competitive (MC) or not monopolistically competitive (N). If you indicate the latter, explain why you think the industry is not a monopolistically competitive one.

a. The production of automobiles in Canada. _____

_____

b. The retail distribution of automobiles in Canada. _____

_____

c. Grocery supermarkets in a city of

500,000 people. _____

_____

d. The retail sale of gasoline in a city of 500,000 people. _____

_____

e. The production of low-priced shoes in Canada. _____

_____

f. The mail-order sale of men's clothes.

_____

_____

2 Assume that the short-run cost and demand data given in the table on the next page confront a monopolistic competitor selling a given product and engaged in a given amount of product promotion.
a. Compute the marginal cost and marginal revenue of each unit of output and enter these figures in the table.
b. In the short run, the firm will (1) produce _____ units of output, (2) sell its product at a price of $ _____, and (3) have a total economic profit of $ _____.
c. In the long run, (1) the demand for the firm's product will _____, (2) until the price of the product equals _____, and (3) the total economic profits of the firm are _____.

SELF-TEST

Circle T if the statement is true, F if it is false.

1 Monopolistic competitors have no control over the price of their products. **T F**

2 The publisher of McConnell/Pope's *Economics* and this *Study Guide* is a monopolistic competitor. **T F**

Output	Total cost	Marginal cost	Quantity demanded	Price	Marginal revenue
0	$ 50		0	$120	
1	80	$_____	1	110	$_____
2	90	_____	2	100	_____
3	110	_____	3	90	_____
4	140	_____	4	80	_____
5	180	_____	5	70	_____
6	230	_____	6	60	_____
7	290	_____	7	50	_____
8	360	_____	8	40	_____
9	440	_____	9	30	_____
10	530	_____	10	20	_____

3 The smaller the number of firms in an industry and the greater the extent of product differentiation, the greater will be the elasticity of the individual seller's demand curve. **T F**

4 One reason why monopolistic competition is wasteful, given the products the firms produce and the extent to which they promote them, is that the average cost of producing the product is greater than the minimum average cost at which the product could be produced. **T F**

5 The wider the range of differentiated products offered to consumers by a monopolistically competitive industry, the less excess capacity there will be in that industry. **T F**

6 A firm will improve the quality of its product only if it expects that the additional revenue it will receive will be greater than the extra costs involved. **T F**

7 If advertising expenditures fluctuate directly (or positively) with total spending in the economy, they will be counter-cyclical and lead to greater stability in employment and the price level. **T F**

8 Those who contend that advertising contributes to the growth of monopoly in the economy argue that the advertising by established firms creates barriers to the entry of new firms into an industry. **T F**

9 There tends to be rather general agreement among both critics and defenders of advertising that advertising increases the average cost of producing and promoting the product. **T F**

10 Empirical evidence clearly indicates that advertising reduces competition and leads to a misallocation of the economy's resources. **T F**

Circle the letter that corresponds to the best answer.

1 Which of the following is *not* characteristic of monopolistic competition? (*a*) product differentiation; (*b*) a relatively large number of firms; (*c*) a feeling of interdependence among the firms; (*d*) relatively easy entry in the long run.

2 Given the following short-run demand and cost schedules for a monopolistic competitor, what output will the firm produce? (*a*) 2; (*b*) 3; (*c*) 4; (*d*) 5.

Price	Quantity demanded	Total cost	Output
$10	1	$14	1
9	2	17	2
8	3	22	3
7	4	29	4
6	5	38	5
5	6	49	6

3 Assuming the short-run demand and cost data in question 2 above, *in the long run* the number of firms in the industry (*a*) will be less than in the short run; (*b*) will be the same as in the short run; (*c*) will be greater than in the short run; (*d*) cannot be determined from the available information.

4 In the short run a monopolistically competitive firm (*a*) obtains an economic profit; (*b*) breaks even; (*c*) suffers an economic loss; (*d*) may have an economic profit or loss or break even.

5 Given the product the firm is producing and the extent to which the firm is promoting it, *in the long run* (*a*) the firm will produce that output at which marginal cost and price are equal; (*b*) the elasticity of demand for the firm's product will be less than it was in the short run; (*c*) the number of firms in the industry will be greater than it was in the short run; (*d*) the economic profits being earned by the firms in the industry will tend to equal zero.

6 Which of the following is *not* one of the features of monopolistic competition that may offset the wastes associated with such a market structure? (*a*) a wider variety of products is offered to consumers; (*b*) much advertising is self-cancelling; (*c*) the quality of products improves over time; (*d*) consumers are better informed of the availability of products.

7 If an industry is to be economically efficient, it is necessary that (*a*) price equal average cost; (*b*) price equal marginal cost; (*c*) average cost equal marginal cost; (*d*) all of the above.

8 Were a monopolistically competitive industry in long-run equilibrium, a firm in that industry might be able to increase its economics profits by (*a*) increasing the price of its product; (*b*) increasing the amounts it spends to advertise its product; (*c*) decreasing the price of its product; (*d*) decreasing the output of its product.

9 Which of the following can be fairly concluded with respect to the economic effects of advertising? (*a*) advertising helps to maintain a high level of aggregate spending in the economy; (*b*) consumers benefit less from advertising expenditures than they do from expenditures for product development; (*c*) advertising in the Canadian economy leads almost invariably to higher product prices; (*d*) lower unit costs and lower prices result when a firm advertises, because advertising increases the size of the firm's market and promotes economies of scale.

10 In seeking to maximize its profits the three variables that the monopolistically competitive firm must consider are (*a*) price, product and promotion; (*b*) price, publicity, and promotion; (*c*) price, product, and publicity; (*d*) product, publicity, and promotion.

DISCUSSION QUESTIONS

1 What are the chief characteristics of a monopolistically competitive market? In what sense is there competition and in what sense is there monopoly in such a market?

2 What is meant by product differentiation? By what methods can products be differentiated? How does product differentiation affect the kind of competition in, and inject an element of monopoly into, markets?

3 Comment on the elasticity of the demand curve faced by the monopolistically competitive firm in the short run. Assume that the firm is producing a given product and is engaged in a given amount of promotional activity. What two factors determine just how elastic that demand curve will be?

4 What output will the monopolistic competitor produce in the short run, and what price will it charge for its product? What determines whether the firm will earn profits or suffer losses in the short run?

5 In the long run, what level of economic profits will the individual monopolistically competitive firm *tend* to receive? Why is this just a tendency? What forces economic profits towards this level, and why will the firm produce a long-run output smaller than the most "efficient" output? (Again assume, in answering this question, that the firm is producing a given product and selling it with a given amount of promotional activity).

6 In what two senses is monopolistic competition wasteful or a misallocation of resources?

7 What methods, other than price cutting, can an individual monopolistic competitor employ to attempt to protect and increase its profits in the long run?

8 To what extent, and how, do product differentiation and product development offset the "wastes" associated with monopolistic competition?

9 Does advertising result in a waste of resources, or does it promote a more efficient utilization of resources? What arguments can be presented to support the contention that it is wasteful and detrimental, and what claims are made to support the view that it is beneficial to the economy? What empirical evidence is there?

10 When is a monopolistic competitor in long-run equilibrium not only with respect to the price it is charging but also with respect to the product it is producing and the extent to which it is promoting its product?

10

PRICE AND OUTPUT DETERMINATION: OLIGOPOLY

This last of the four chapters dealing with specific market situations is, in a way, the most difficult. Oligopoly is one of those areas of economic study where economists have found it impossible to reach definite conclusions. Under conditions of pure competition, pure monopoly, and monopolistic competition, fairly definite conclusions regarding market prices and the outputs of individual firms are reached, but such conclusions are not easily drawn from an analysis of oligopoly. This is why the study of oligopoly is difficult—the generalizations are few in number—and this is unfortunate but also unavoidable.

Oligopoly is probably the most realistic market situation you will examine, and many economists believe it is the type of market most prevalent—or at least, most important—in the Canadian economy. Because it is so realistic, its study is all the more difficult. Chapter 10 is little more than an introduction to this very complex market situation. There are, however, certain things you can and should learn about it.

What oligopoly *is* is fairly simple to understand. The *consequences* of "fewness" and the "mutual interdependence" and feeling of uncertainty to which it gives rise are not quite so easy to grasp, but they are of the greatest importance. For these reasons, you should make every attempt to learn exactly *what is meant* by mutual interdependence and *why it exists* in an oligopoly. If you can do this, you will be well on the road to understanding why specific and definite conclusions cannot be reached concerning market

prices and the outputs of individual firms. You will also see why oligopolists are loath to engage in price competition and why they frequently resort to collusion to set prices and to non-price competition to determine market shares.

Because oligopoly is a number of different (though similar) market structures, in Chapter 10 we analyse four variants of oligopoly for you. The kinked demand-curve model is the first of these variants. It explains why, in the absence of collusion, oligopolists will not raise or lower their prices even when their costs change. But the kinked demand curve does not explain what price oligopolists will set; it only explains why price, once set, will be relatively inflexible. To set price, oligopolists often resort to some form of collusion.

Cartels and gentlemen's agreements are the most overt forms of collusion, and the second variant of oligopoly analysed. The third variant is the tacit collusion that is found when price leadership exists. Cost-plus pricing is the final variant of oligopoly discussed in Chapter 10.

Whether oligopoly is socially efficient (and, therefore, desirable) is a debatable question. Both the traditional and Schumpeter-Galbraith viewpoints are presented; and the question of whether large firms lead to rapid technological progress is examined by looking at the sources of major inventions.

In the mid-section of the chapter, the North American automobile industry is examined to illustrate a real-world oligopoly in action. Here you will see that three firms dominated an industry characterized by high barriers to entry, price-leadership, and non-price competition in the three decades following World War II. But you will also discover that the North American automobile industry needed government assistance in the early 1980s to regain its profitability in the face of greatly increased foreign competition. It is possible that the market structure of this oligopoly has been changed forever.

Part of the second half of Chapter 10 is devoted to an examination of the ways in which the federal government has attempted to prevent the formation of business monopolies and to limit the use of monopoly power. In addition, the chapter examines the ways in which this same government has—either intentionally or unintentionally—promoted and fostered monopoly. In these sections, you will find a discussion of the Combines Investigation Act and its succesor, the Competition Act.

If you are to understand how government has restricted and promoted monopoly, you should know (1) what the aims and/or results of this legislation have been; and (2) what the main provisions of the law are.

Another question students often raise with respect to the anti-combines law is "What good is there in knowing it anyway?" In examining any important current problem, it is important to know how the problem arose, what steps have already been taken to solve it, how successful the attempts were, and why the problem is still not solved. A more general answer to the same question is that an informed citizenry is necessary if a democracy is to solve its problems. And the anti-combines law, however named, continues in force and is enforced; many of you will work for business firms that are subject to its provisions.

Two more things need to be said about this chapter. First, in addition to restricting and fostering monopoly, the federal government has also undertaken to regulate industries that appeared to be natural monopolies; but this regulation by agencies and commissions has at least two serious shortcomings. Second, beginning in the early 1960s, a host of new agencies and commissions began to engage in regulation of the prices charged by and the services offered by specific industries; and its critics contend that the economy is now overregulated to such an extent that, on balance, this new regulation has been harmful to the economy.

Anti-combines and regulation, you should conclude when you have finished this chapter, is a trouble spot in the economy because important questions and issues remain to be answered; how we answer them will affect how well or poorly the economy will perform and how good or bad our lives will be in the future.

CHECK LIST

When you have studied this chapter you should be able to

□ Define oligopoly and distinguish between homogeneous and differentiated oligopolies.

□ Identify the three most significant causes of oligopoly and explain how each of these tends to result in oligopolistic industries.

□ Explain why it is difficult to predict what price will be charged and what output will be produced by an oligopolist.

□ Employ the kinked demand curve to explain why oligopoly prices tend to be inflexible.

□ State the three principal advantages of collusion to oligopolists, at least three forms such collusion may take, and five obstacles to this collusion.

□ Explain what price colluding oligopolists with identical cost and demand curves and producing a homogeneous product would set and what output each would produce.

□ Describe how a firm (such as General Motors) employs cost-plus pricing to determine the prices it will charge for its products.

□ Explain the role played by non-price competition in oligopolistic industries, the three principal forms of such competition, and two reasons oligopolists emphasize non-price competition.

□ Compare the Schumpeter-Galbraith view with the traditional view of oligopoly; explain whether the empirical evidence does or does not support the former viewpoint.

□ Describe the North American automobile industry in terms of the number of sellers and their market shares, the height and kinds of barriers to entry, the method employed to set prices, the types of non-price competition, the level of profits, and the rate of technological progress; and explain how foreign competition and "hard times" have changed the industry in recent years.

□ Explain how the term monopoly is used in the second half of this chapter.

□ Outline the major provisions of the Combines Investigation Act as it existed before mid-1986.

□ Outline those major changes brought about by the Competition Act in 1986.

□ List the groups that are exempt from the provisions of the Competition Act; and the laws that tend to restrict competition and promote monopoly in Canada.

□ Define a natural monopoly.

□ State the three problems that have been encountered in the economic regulation of industries by agencies and commissions.

□ Distinguish between the public interest and legal cartel theories of regulation.

□ Describe the principal economic effects of the deregulation of the airline industry in the United States; and compare these effects with the effects predicted by the critics of deregulation.

□ Contrast industrial (or economic) regulation with social regulation; state the three principal distinguishing features of the latter.

□ Present the case against social regulation made by its critics; state the three implications of overregulation.

CHAPTER OUTLINE

1 Oligopoly is an industry structure frequently encountered in the Canadian economy.
a. It is composed of a few firms that sell either a standardized or a differentiated product; and the concentration ratio, despite its several shortcomings, is a measure of the extent to which "fewness" prevails in a particular industry.
b. The existence of an oligopoly is usually the result of economies of scale, other barriers to entry, and the advantages of merger.
c. The firms in the industry are mutually interdependent because they are few in number.

2 The economic analysis of oligopoly is difficult for two reasons: the term "oligopoly" actually covers many different market situations; and the individual oligopolist, because of the uncertainty that accompanies mutual interdependence, is seldom able to estimate its own demand curve. Important characteristics of oligopoly are inflexible prices and simultaneous price changes.

3 An examination of four oligopoly models will help to explain the pricing practices of oligopolists.
a. In the kinked demand-curve model, oligopolists do not collude.
(1) Each firm believes that when it lowers its price its rivals will lower their prices, and when it increases its price, its rivals will not increase their prices.
(2) The firm is, therefore, reluctant to change its price for fear of decreasing its profits.
(3) But this model has at least two shortcomings.

b. The uncertainties and disadvantages of non-collusive oligopoly may induce firms to collude.

(1) Firms that collude tend to set their price and joint output at the same level at which a pure monopolist would set them.

(2) The method of collusion employed by the firms may be one of several forms that include the cartel and the gentlemen's agreement.

(3) At least five obstacles make it difficult for firms to collude.

c. Price leadership is the third model, and a frequent form of tacit collusion, in which one firm initiates price changes and the other firms in the industry follow its lead.

d. In the cost-plus pricing model, a firm determines its price by adding a percentage markup to its average cost of production.

4 Oligopolistic firms avoid price competition but engage in non-price competition to determine each firm's market share (sales).

5 To compare the efficiency of an oligopolist with that of a pure competitor is difficult.

a. It has been traditionally believed that oligopoly has much the same result as monopoly; but Schumpeter and Galbraith believe that oligopoly is needed if there is to be rapid technological progress (dynamic efficiency).

b. While the evidence is not conclusive, it appears that most of the important inventions have not been made by large firms; and the structure of the industry may not affect its technological progress.

6 The automobile industry in North America is an example of an oligopoly in which are found a few large firms; substantial barriers to entry, price leadership; styling competition among the sellers; and significant competition from foreign producers.

7 The term "monopoly" as used in the second half of this chapter means a situation in which a small number of firms control all or a substantial percentage of the total output of a major industry. Business firms may be large in either an absolute or a relative sense, and in many cases they are large in both senses. Chapter 10 is concerned with firms large in both senses.

8 Government policies toward business monopoly have not been clear and consistent; legislation and policy, however, have, for the most part, been aimed at restricting monopoly and promoting competition.

a. In the 1880s, the slow expansion of the Canadian economy brought with it the creation of combines (or business monopolies) in some industries.

b. Canadian anti-combines legislation began in 1889. This law and its successor, the Combines Investigation Act, have attempted to restrain the growth and use of monopoly power.

9 The effectiveness of the anti-combines law in preventing monopoly and maintaining competition has depended upon the zeal with which the federal government has enforced the law, and the interpretation of the law by the courts.

10 The Competition Act, designed to tighten the rules for corporate behaviour, replaced the Combines Investigation Act in mid-1986.

11 Government in Canada has also promoted monopoly and restricted competition in several ways.

a. It has exempted Canadian exporters, labour unions, agricultural marketing boards, credit unions, and (at the local and provincial levels) certain occupational groups from the provisions of the anti-combines law.

b. The patent laws give monopoly power to the producers of patented goods.

c. Tariffs and other barriers to international trade protect Canadian producers from competition.

12 In addition to the enactment of the anti-combines law, government has undertaken to regulate natural monopolies.

a. If a single producer can provide a good or service at a lower average cost (because of economies of scale) than several producers and competition is, therefore, not economical, a natural monopoly exists; and government may either produce the good or service or (following the public interest theory) regulate private producers of the product for the benefit of the public.

b. The effectiveness of the regulation of business firms by regulatory agencies has been criticized for two principal reasons.

(1) Regulation, it is argued, increases costs and leads to an inefficient allocation of resources and higher prices.

(2) The regulatory agencies, it is also contended, have been "captured" by the regulated industries and protect them rather than the public.

(3) And some of the regulated industries, it can be argued, are not natural monopolies and would be competitive if they were not regulated.

c. The legal cartel theory of regulation is that potentially competitive industries want and support the regulation of their industries in order to increase the profits of the firms in the industries by limiting competition among them.

13 The three criticisms of the regulation of industries and the legal cartel theory of regulation led during the 1970s and 1980s to the deregulation of a number of industries in the United States; and the deregulation of the airlines is a case study of the effects of deregulation on air fares, on air services, on competition in the industry, and on the firms and workers in the industry. Canada is tending to follow the United States' example.

14 Beginning in the early 1960s, a "new" social regulation developed rapidly and resulted in the creation of additional regulatory agencies.

a. This regulation differed in several ways from the older regulation of specific industries and aimed to improve the quality of life in Canada.

b. While the objectives of the new regulation are desirable, the costs to the economy are high; and critics argue that the marginal costs of this regulation exceed its marginal benefits and it is, therefore, inefficient.

c. This overregulation, they argue, is inflationary, slows the rate of innovation, and lessens competition.

d. The defenders of the new regulation contend that it is needed to fight serious and neglected problems and that the social benefits will over time exceed the costs.

IMPORTANT TERMS

Oligopoly

Fewness

Homogeneous oligopoly

Differentiated oligopoly

Concentration ratio

Interindustry competition

Mutual interdependence

Non-collusive oligopoly

Kinked demand curve

Price war

Collusive oligopoly

Cartel

Gentlemen's agreement

Price leadership

Cost-plus pricing

Traditional view (of oligopoly)

Schumpeter-Galbraith view (of oligopoly)

Big business

Regulatory agency

Combines Investigation Act

Tied selling

Exclusive dealing

Price discrimination

Predatory pricing

Bid-rigging

Competition Act

Natural monopoly

Public utility

Public interest theory of regulation

Legal cartel theory of regulation

Industrial (economic) regulation

Social regulation

FILL-IN QUESTIONS

1 In an oligopoly a _____

firms produce either a _____

or a _____
product, and entry into such an industry is

_____ .

2 The three major underlying causes of oligopoly are _____ ;

_____ ; and

_____ .

3 Because oligopoly consists of a small number of firms, they are necessarily ____

_____ ;
this means that when setting the price of its product each firm must consider _____

_____ ; the
monopolist does not face this problem because it has _____ rivals, and the pure and monopolistic competitors do not

face it because each has _____ rivals.

4 Formal economic analysis cannot be easily used to explain the prices and outputs of oligopolists because oligopoly is in fact

(one, a small number of, many) _____
specific market situation(s); and when firms are mutually interdependent each firm is

(certain, uncertain) _____
about how its rivals will react when it changes the price of its product.

5 Oligopoly prices tend to be (flexible,

inflexible) _____ ,
and oligopolists tend to change their prices

(independently, simultaneously) _____ .

6 The kinked demand curve that the individual non-colluding oligopolist sees for its product is highly (elastic, inelastic)

_____ at prices above the
current or going price, and tends to be only

slightly _____

or _____

below that price.

7 The kinked demand curve for a non-colluding oligopolist is drawn on the assumption that if the oligopolist raises its

prices, its rivals will _____ ,

and if it lowers its price its rivals will ____

_____ .

8 Because the oligopolist confronting a kinked demand curve finds that there is a

_____ in its marginal-
revenue curve, small changes in the

marginal-cost curve do not change the____

_____ .

9 When oligopolists collude, the price they set and their combined ouput tend to be the same as would be set (in a purely competitive

industry, by a pure monopolist)_____

_____ .

10 A cartel is a formal agreement among

sellers in which the _____ and the total

_____ of the product and each

seller's_____ of the market are
specified.

11 A gentlemen's agreement is (a formal, an

informal) _____ agreement on

_____ ; each firm's share of the market

is determined by _____

_____ .

12 Five obstacles to collusion among oligopolists are

a. _____ ;

b. _____ ;

c. _____ ;

d. _____ ;

e. _____ .

13 When one firm in an oligopoly is almost always the first to change its price and the other firms change their prices after it has changed its price there is a type of (overt, tacit) _____ collusion called _____
_____ .

14 When a firm employs a cost-plus formula to determine the price it will charge for a product it adds a percentage _____ to the _____ cost of producing the product.

15 There tends to be very little (price, non-price) _____ competition among oligopolists and a great deal of _____ , competition which they use to determine each firm's _____
_____ .

The two reasons for the emphasis on this kind of competition are

a. _____ ;

b. _____ .

16 The traditional view of oligopoly is that it results in (lower, higher) _____ prices and profits, _____ outputs, and a rate of technological progress that is (slower, faster) _____ than would be found if the industry were more competitive.

17 In the Schumpeter-Galbraith view of oligopoly,
a. only oligopolists have both the _____ and the _____ to be technologically progressive;
b. over time oligopolies will bring about a more rapid rate of _____ ,

lower _____ and _____ , and perhaps greater _____ and _____ than the same industry competitively organized.

18 The empirical evidence seems to indicate that the large oligopolists (have, have not)_____ been the major source of technological progress.

19 As used in the second half of this chapter, monopoly means that (one firm, a few firms) _____ control(s) all or a substantial portion of the ouput of a major industry; and this chapter is concerned with firms that are large (absolutely, relatively, both absolutely and relatively) _____ .

20 Federal legislation and policies have mostly attempted to maintain (competition, monopoly) _____ , but at times they have fostered the development of _____
_____ .

21 Under the Competition Act, mergers and monopolies are offences only where they are likely to be, or to operate, to the detriment or against the interest of _____ .

22 In its 1969 report,
a. the Economic Council of Canada did *not* recommend barriers be placed in the way of a company achieving dominance through
_____ ;
b. the Council's whole approach was based on the goal of _____ ;
c. the Council also recommended that competition policy be extended to _____ .

23 Government promotes the growth of monopoly and restricts competition when it exempts certain industries or practices from the provisions of the _____ laws.

a. Subject to limitations, the following are exempt from anti-combines law: _____ , _____ , _____ , and _____ ; moreover, legislation and policy have attempted to provide some measure of monopolistic power for _____ .

b. The _____ laws have the effect of granting inventors legal monopolies on their products; and _____ and other barriers to trade shelter Canadian producers from foreign competition.

24 When a single firm is able to supply the entire market at a lower average cost than a number of competing firms, there is a _____ monopoly. In Canada, many of these monopolies are controlled by regulatory _____ or _____ .

25 The three major criticisms of regulation of industries by an agency or commission are
a. the regulated firms have no incentive to reduce their _____ s because the commission will then require them to lower their prices; and, because the prices they are allowed to charge are based on the value of their capital equipment, firms tend to make uneconomical substitutions of (labour, capital) _____ for _____ ;

b. the regulatory commission has been "captured" or is controlled by_____ _____ ;

c. regulation has been applied to industries that are not _____ monopolies and which in the absence of regulation would be _____ .

26 The public-interest theory of regulation assumes that the objective of regulating an industry is to protect society from abuses of _____ power; but an alternative theory assumes that the firms wish to be regulated because it enables them to form, and the commission helps them to create, a profitable and legal _____ .

27 The basic reason for the "new" social regulation and the creation and growth of the new regulatory agencies has been the desire to improve the (quantity, quality) _____ of life in Canada.
a. It is concerned with the _____ under which goods and services are produced, the impact of their production upon _____ , and the physical _____ of the goods.
b. And it differs in several ways from the "old" regulation, which is labelled_____ or _____ regulation.

28 Critics of "new" social regulation contend
a. that its marginal costs are (greater, less) _____ than its marginal benefits; and
b. that its results are (recession, inflation) _____ , a (slower, more rapid) _____ rate of innovation, and (more, less) _____ competition in the economy.

PROBLEMS AND PROJECTS

1 The kinked demand schedule that an oligopolist believes confronts it is given in the following table.
a. Compute the oligopolist's total revenue at each of the nine prices, and enter these figures in the table.

Price	Quantity demanded	Total revenue	Marginal revenue
$2.90	100	$____	
2.80	200	____	$____
2.70	300	____	____
2.60	400	____	____
2.50	500	____	____
2.40	525	____	____
2.30	550	____	____
2.20	575	____	____
2.10	600	____	____

b. Also compute marginal revenue between the nine prices, and enter these figures in the table.

c. What is the current, or going, price for the oligopolist's product? $ _____

How much is it selling?_____

d. On the graph below plot the oligopolist's demand curve and marginal-revenue curve. Connect the demand points and the marginal-revenue points with as straight a line as possible. *Be sure* to plot the marginal-revenue figures at the average of the two quantities involved, that is, at 150, 250, 350, 450, $512\frac{1}{2}$, $537\frac{1}{2}$, $562\frac{1}{2}$, and $587\frac{1}{2}$.

e. Assume that the marginal-cost schedule of the oligopolist is given in columns (1) and (2) of the table following. Plot the marginal-cost curve on the graph on which demand and marginal revenue are plotted.

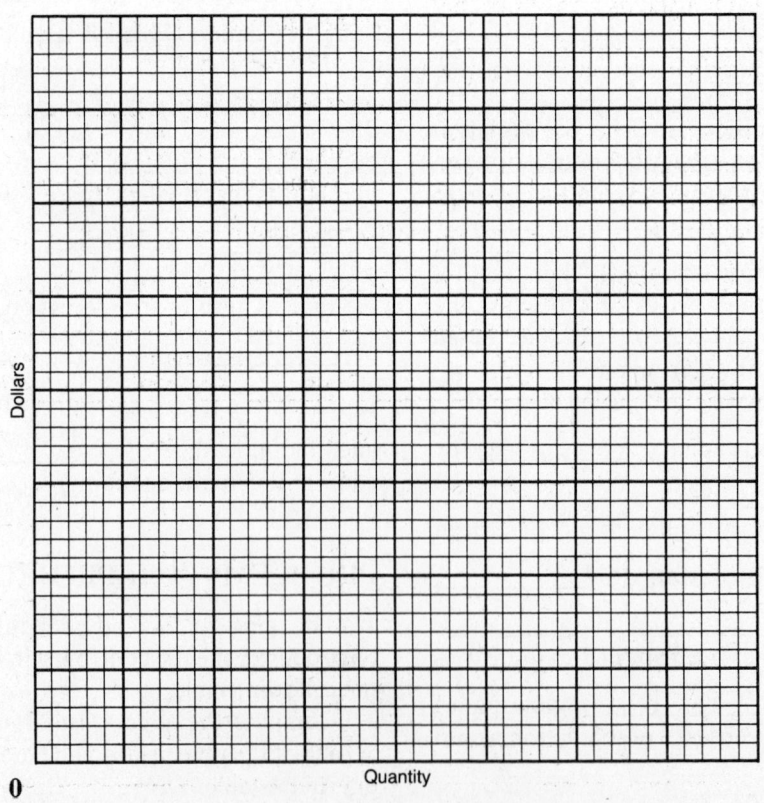

Dollars

0   Quantity

(1) Output	(2) MC	(3) MC'	(4) MC"
150	$1.40	$1.90	$.40
250	1.30	1.80	.30
350	1.40	1.90	.40
450	1.50	2.00	.50
512$\frac{1}{2}$	1.60	2.10	.60
537$\frac{1}{2}$	1.70	2.20	.70
562$\frac{1}{2}$	1.80	2.30	.80
587$\frac{1}{2}$	1.90	2.40	.90

(1) Given demand and marginal cost, what price should the oligopolist charge to maximize profits? $ _____ How many units of product will it sell at this price?

_____

(2) If the marginal-cost schedule changed from that shown in columns (1) and (2) to that shown in columns (1) and (3), what price should it charge? $ _____ What level of output will it produce? _____
How have profits changed as a result of the change in costs? _____
Plot the new marginal-cost curve on the graph.
(3) If the marginal-cost schedule changed from that shown in columns (1) and (2) to that shown in columns (1) and (4), what price should it charge? $ _____ What level of output will it produce? _____

How have profits changed as a result of the change in costs? _____
Plot the new marginal-cost curve on the graph.

2 An oligopoly producing a homogeneous product is composed of three firms. Assume that these firms have identical cost schedules. Assume also that if any one of these firms sets a price for the product, the other two firms charge the same price. As long as they all charge the same price, they will share the market equally and the quantity demanded of each will be the same.

Following is the total-cost schedule of one of these firms and the demand schedule that confronts it when the other two firms charge the same price as this firm.

a. Complete the marginal-cost and marginal-revenue schedules facing the firm.

b. What price would this firm set if it wished to maximize its profit? $ _____

c. How much would

(1) it sell at this price? _____

(2) its profits be at this price? $ _____

d. What would be the industry's

(1) total output at this price? _____

(2) joint profits at this price? $ _____

Output	Total cost	Marginal cost	Price	Quantity demanded	Marginal revenue
0	$ 0		$140	0	
1	30	$_____	130	1	$_____
2	50	_____	120	2	_____
3	80	_____	110	3	_____
4	120	_____	100	4	_____
5	170	_____	90	5	_____
6	230	_____	80	6	_____
7	300	_____	70	7	_____
8	380	_____	60	8	_____

e. Is there any other price this firm can set, assuming that the other two firms will charge the same price, which would result in a greater joint profit for them? _____ If so what is that price? $ _____

f. If these three firms colluded in order to maximize their joint profit, what price would they charge?$ _____

3   A firm producing automobiles has $4 billion invested in capital and its average-total-cost schedule is shown below.

Output (cars per year)	Average total cost
1,100,000	$14,000
1,200,000	10,000
1,300,000	8,000
1,400,000	7,000
1,500,000	6,500
1,600,000	6,250
1,700,000	6,600
1,800,000	7,200

a. If the objective of the firm is to have an annual return *after* taxes equal to 10% of its invested capital it must earn $ _____ million after taxes each year.

b. To earn this amount after taxes when its earnings are taxed at a 50% rate it must earn $ _____ million *before* taxes.

c. When the firm estimates that its most likely annual output (its "standard volume") is 1,500,000 automobiles,

(1) To achieve its objective of a 10% after-tax return on its investment it must earn

$ _____ per automobile; (*Hint:* Divide the required return before taxes by its annual output.)

(2) to earn this amount per automobile it must set the price of an automobile at

$ _____ ;

(3) the markup is approximately _____ %.

4   Below is a series of years. Following this is a series of facts concerning Canada's anti-

monopoly law. Match each year with the appropriate fact by placing the appropriate letter after each of the facts.

A. 1889
B. 1910
C. 1952
D. 1969
E. 1976
F. 1971
G. 1981
H. 1986

a. First enactment of the Combines Investigation Act.

b. Setting up of two separate agencies: Director of Investigation and Research and Restrictive Trade Practices Commission.

c. Enactment of Competition Act.

d. Initial introduction of the Bill that led to the Competition Act.

e. Canada's first anti-combines legislation.

f. Economic Council of Canada reported that the provisions of the Combines Investigation Act making mergers and monopolies criminal offences were "all but inoperative."

g. Combines Investigation Act became applicable to pure services.

SELF-TEST

Circle T if the statement is true, F if it is false.

1   The products produced by the firms in an oligopolistic industry may be either homogeneous (standardized) or differentiated. **T F**

2   Concentration ratios are low in those industries that are oligopolies.   **T F**

3   The uncertainty that exists in oligopolies is the uncertainty faced by each firm on how its rivals will react if it changes its price. **T F**

4   The kinked demand curve is an economic tool that can be used to explain how the current market price of a product is determined.   **T F**

5   A cartel is usually a written agreement among firms; it sets the price of the products and determines each firm's share of the market. **T   F**

6   The practice of price leadership is almost always based on a formal written or oral agreement. **T   F**

7   An oligopolist utilizing a cost-plus pricing formula typically adds a percentage markup to what its unit cost would be if it operated at full capacity. **T   F**

8   Price competition between firms is an important characteristic of oligopoly. **T   F**

9   Non-price competition is the typical method of determining each oligopolist's share of the total market. **T   F**

10   It is often argued that oligopolists typically possess both the means and the incentives to technological progress, and that the means are the substantial profits received by them. **T   F**

11   Almost all the important technological advances between 1880 and 1965 can be attributed to the research and development activities of large business firms. **T   F**

12   The North American automobile industry is a fairly good example of a differentiated oligopoly. **T   F**

13   The term "monopoly" in the second half of this chapter is taken to mean a situation in which a single firm produces a unique product and entry into the industry is blocked. **T   F**

14   It is clear that on balance, oligopoly is detrimental to the functioning of the Canadian economy. **T   F**

15   Those who defend oligopolies contend that they are technologically more progressive than smaller firms. **T   F**

16   The federal government has consistently passed legislation and pursued policies designed to maintain competition. **T   F**

17   The courts are the final authority in interpreting the anti-combines law. **T   F**

18   Since 1910, several thousand convictions have been obtained under the Combines Investigation Act. **T   F**

19   A natural monopoly exists when the *minimum* average cost of producing a good or service of one firm is less than the *minimum* average cost of any other firm. **T   F**

20   Public ownership rather than public regulation has been overwhelmingly the means utilized in Canada to ensure that the behaviour of monopolists is socially acceptable. **T   F**

21   Natural monopolies tend to have relatively large fixed and relatively small variable costs. **T   F**

22   The rationale underlying the public interest theory of regulation of natural monopolies is to allow the consumers of their goods or services to benefit from the economies of scale and to prevent the abuse of the market power of the monopolist by allowing it to charge a price no greater than the marginal cost of producing the good or service. **T   F**

23   Because the prices they are allowed to charge are set to enable them to earn a "fair" return over their costs, regulated firms have a strong incentive to reduce their costs. **T   F**

24   While painful for the firms and the workers in the industry, the deregulation of airlines in the United States has been generally beneficial to consumers of airline services. **T   F**

25   Those who favour the "new" social regulation believe that it is needed in order to improve the quality of life in Canada. **T   F**

26   Critics of the "new" social regulation argue that it has resulted in the overregulation of the economy and that its marginal costs exceed its marginal benefits. **T   F**

Circle the letter that corresponds to the best answer.

1 The number of firms in an oligopolistic industry is (*a*) one; (*b*) a few; (*c*) many; (*d*) very many.

2 Concentration ratios take into account (*a*) interindustry competition; (*b*) import competition; (*c*) the existence of separate local markets for products; (*d*) none of the above.

3 Which of the following does *not* contribute to the existence of oligopoly? (*a*) the economies of large-scale production; (*b*) the gains in profits that result from mergers; (*c*) high barriers to entry into an industry; (*d*) standardized products.

4 Mutual interdependence is only characteristic of (*a*) pure and monopolistic competition; (*b*) monopolistic competition and oligopoly; (*c*) pure competition and oligopoly; (*d*) oligopoly.

5 Mutual interdependence means that: (*a*) each firm produces a product similar but not identical to the products produced by its rivals; (*b*) each firm produces a product identical to the products produced by its rivals; (*c*) each firm must consider the reactions of its rivals when it determines its price policy; (*d*) each firm faces a perfectly elastic demand for its product.

6 The prices of products produced by oligopolies tend to be (*a*) relatively flexible and when firms change prices they are apt to change them at the same time; (*b*) relatively inflexible and when firms change prices they are not apt to change them at the same time; (*c*) relatively inflexible and when firms change prices they are apt to change them at the same time; (*d*) relatively flexible and when firms change prices they are not apt to change them at the same time.

7 The demand curve confronting an oligopolist tends to be (*a*) elastic; (*b*) of unitary elasticity; (*c*) inelastic; (*d*) one that depends upon the prices charged by its rivals.

8 If an individual oligopolist's demand curve is "kinked," it is necessarily (*a*) inelastic below the going price; (*b*) inelastic above the going price; (*c*) elastic above the going price; (*d*) of unitary elasticity at the going price.

9 Below is the demand schedule confronting an oligopolist.

Price	Quantity demanded
$5.00	10
4.50	20
4.00	30
3.50	40
3.00	42
2.50	44
2.00	46
1.00	48

Which one of the eight prices seems to be the "going" price of the product produced by the firm? (*a*) $4.50; (*b*) $4; (*c*) $3.50; (*d*) $3.

10 Which of the following is *not* a means of colluding? (*a*) a cartel; (*b*) a kinked demand curve; (*c*) a gentlemen's agreement; (*d*) price leadership.

11 Oligopolists tend to collude because collusive control over the price they charge permits them to (*a*) increase their profits; (*b*) decrease their uncertainties; (*c*) deter the entry of new firms into their industry; (*d*) do all of the above.

12 When oligopolists collude, the results are generally (*a*) greater output and higher price; (*b*) greater output and lower price; (*c*) smaller output and lower price; (*d*) smaller output and higher price.

13 Which of the following constitutes an obstacle to collusion among oligopolists? (*a*) a general business recession; (*b*) a small number of firms in the industry; (*c*) a homogeneous product; (*d*) the patent laws.

14 It is the belief of Schumpeter and Galbraith that an industry organized oligopolistically, when compared with the same industry organized competitively, would, over time, (*a*) foster more rapid improvement in the quality of the good or service produced; (*b*) bring about a greater reduction in the average cost of producing the product; (*c*) lower the price of the product by a larger percentage; (*d*) all of the above.

15 "Big business" in the second half of this chapter refers to which one of the following? (*a*) firms that are absolutely large; (*b*) firms that are relatively large; (*c*) firms that are either absolutely or relatively large; (*d*) firms that are both absolutely and relatively large.

16 As described in the Combines Investigation Act, "price discrimination" is an illegal trade practice, which consists in (*a*) selling in different parts of the country at different prices *not* justified by different costs; (*b*) giving a trade purchaser an unfair advantage over his competitors by selling to him at a lower price; (*c*) charging different consumers different prices; (*d*) exporting at lower prices.

17 As described in the Combines Investigation Act, "predatory pricing" is an illegal practice, which consists in (*a*) charging what the market will bear; (*b*) selling at prices unreasonably low with a view to eliminating competition; (*c*) selling above marginal and average cost; (*d*) price-setting by oligopolists.

18 As described in the Combines Investigation Act, "bid rigging" is an illegal action of (*a*) stock promoters who bid up share prices to create an inflated market before unloading their holdings; (*b*) oligopolists who agree either not to bid on tenders or on what bids they will make; (*c*) a monopolist who tells buyers what bids are acceptable; (*d*) a monopsonist who tells sellers what bids to make.

19 Which of the following have *not* been exempted from the anti-combines law? (*a*) chartered banks; (*b*) labour unions; (*c*) credit unions; (*d*) agricultural marketing boards.

20 All but one of the following have tended to reduce competition. Which one has not? (*a*) occupational licensing; (*b*) the patent laws; (*c*) protective tariffs; (*d*) the Competition Act.

21 Those who oppose the regulation of industry by regulatory agencies contend that (*a*) many of the regulated industries are not natural monopolies; (*b*) the regulatory agencies have been "captured" by the firms they are supposed to regulate; (*c*) regulation results in higher costs and reduced efficiency in the production of the good or service produced by the regulated industry; (*d*) all of the above are true.

22 The legal cartel theory of regulating natural monopolies (*a*) would allow the forces of demand and supply to determine the rates (prices) of the good or service; (*b*) would attempt to protect the public from abuses of monopoly power; (*c*) assumes that the regulated industry wishes to be regulated and government officials provide the regulation in return for public support; (*d*) assumes that both the demand for and supply of the good or service produced by the regulated industry are perfectly inelastic.

23 Critics of the deregulation of industry argue that (among other things) deregulation will lead to (*a*) higher prices for the products produced by the industry; (*b*) the monopolization of the industry by a few large firms; (*c*) a decline in the quantity or the quality of the product produced by the industry; (*d*) all of the above.

24 Deregulation of airlines in the United States has so far resulted in (*a*) higher air fares; (*b*) the monopolization of the airline industry by two large firms; (*c*) a reduction in the availability of air services in the smaller communities; (*d*) lower wage rates for airline employees.

25 Which of the following is *not* a concern of the "new" social regulation? (*a*) the prices charged for goods; (*b*) the physical characteristics of goods produced; (*c*) the conditions under which goods are manufactured; (*d*) the impact upon society of the production of goods.

26 Which of the following is *not* one of the criticisms levelled against the "new" social regulation by its opponents? (*a*) it contributes to inflation; (*b*) it will require too long a time for it to achieve its objectives; (*c*) it will slow the rate of innovation in the economy; (*d*) it is anti-competitive.

DISCUSSION QUESTIONS

1 What are the essential characteristics of an oligopoly? How does it differ from monopolistic competition?

2 Explain how the concentration ratio in a particular industry is computed. What is the relationship between this ratio and fewness?

3 What are the shortcomings of the concentration ratio as a measure of the extent of competition in an industry?

4 What are the underlying causes of oligopoly?

5 What do "mutual interdependence" and "uncertainty" mean with respect to oligopoly? Why are they special characteristics of oligopoly?

6 Why is it difficult to employ formal economic analysis to explain the prices charged by and the outputs of oligopolists?

7 Explain what the kinked demand curve is, state its most important characteristics, the assumptions upon which it is based, and the kind of marginal-revenue curve to which it gives rise. How can the kinked demand curve be used to explain why oligopoly prices are relatively inflexible? Under what conditions will oligopolists acting independently raise or lower their prices even though their demand curves may be kinked?

8 Why do oligopolists find it advantageous to collude? What are the obstacles to collusion?

9 Suppose a small number of firms produce a homogeneous product, have identical cost curves, and charge the same price. How will the price they set, their combined output of the product, and their joint profit compare with what would be found in the same industry if it were a pure monopoly with several plants?

10 Explain (*a*) a cartel, (*b*) a gentlemen's agreement, (*c*) price leadership, (*d*) cost-plus pricing.

11 Why do oligopolists engage in little price competition and in extensive non-price competition?

12 Contrast the Schumpeter-Galbraith view on the dynamic economic efficiency of oligopoly with the traditional view.

13 What does the empirical evidence have to say about sources of technological progress in industrialized countries?

14 Using the following criteria, describe the North American automobile industry, (1) the number of firms and their market shares; (2) the barriers to entry; (3) the means used to establish the prices of automobiles; (4) the role of non-price competition; (5) profits; (6) technological progress.

15 Explain the causes of and the effects of foreign competition on the North American automobile industry during the past ten or so years. How has competition in the market for automobiles in Canada been affected?

16 Explain the difference between the way the term "monopoly" is used in the second half of this chapter and the way it is used in Chapter 8. How can "big business" be defined? How is the expression used in this chapter?

17 Why has it been so difficult to obtain a conviction under the Combines Investigation Act for forming a monopoly or a merger?

18 In what ways has the federal government fostered the growth of monopoly? How have the various protective tariffs fostered monopoly?

19 What is a natural monopoly? What are the two alternative ways that can be used to ensure that it behaves in a socially acceptable fashion?

20 Explain the three major criticisms levelled against public interest regulation as it is practised by commissions and agencies in Canada.

21 What is the legal cartel theory of regulation? Contrast it with the public interest theory of regulation.

22 How does the new social regulation differ from the older industrial (or economic) regulation? What is the objective of this type of regulation, its three principal concerns, and its three distinguishing features?

23 The critics of the new social regulation argue that it has resulted in overregulation of the economy. What does this mean? If there is overregulation, what are its more important implications?

11

PRODUCTION AND THE DEMAND FOR ECONOMIC RESOURCES

Chapter 11 is the first of a group of three chapters that examine the markets for resources. Resource markets are markets in which employers of resources and the owners of these resources determine the prices at which resources will be employed and the quantities of these resources that will be hired. (These resources—you should recall—are labour, land, capital, and entrepreneurial ability. The prices of resources have particular names. The price paid for labour is called a wage, the price paid for the use of land is rent, the price paid for the use of capital is interest, and the price paid for entrepreneurial ability is profit.)

The employers of resources are business firms, which use resources to produce their products. When the number of employers *and* the number of owners of a resource are large, the market for that resource is a competitive market; and—as you already know—the demand for and the supply of that resource will determine its price and the total quantity of it that will be employed. Chapter 11 begins the examination of resource markets by looking at the business firm and the demand (or employer) side of the resource market. The material in this chapter is *not* an explanation of what determines the demand for a *particular* resource; but it is an explanation of what determines the demand for *any* resource. In Chapters 12 and 13, the other sides of the resource markets and particular resources are examined in detail.

The list of important terms for Chapter 11

is relatively short, but included in the list are two very important concepts—marginal revenue product and marginal resource cost—that you must grasp if you are to understand how much of a resource a firm will hire. These two concepts are similar to but not identical with the marginal-revenue and marginal-cost concepts employed in the study of product markets and in the explanation of how large an output a firm will produce. Marginal revenue and marginal cost are, respectively, the change in the firm's total revenue and the change in the firm's total cost when it produces and sells an additional unit of *output*; marginal revenue product and marginal resource cost are, respectively, the change in the firm's total revenue and the change in the firm's total cost when it hires an additional unit of an *input*. (Note: the two new concepts deal with changes in revenue and costs as a consequence of hiring more of a *resource*.)

When a firm wishes to maximize its profits, it produces that *output* at which marginal revenue and marginal cost are equal. But how much of each resource does it hire if it wishes to maximize its profits? It hires that amount of each *resource* at which the marginal revenue product and the marginal resource cost of that resource are equal. And a firm that employs the amount of each resource that maximizes its profits *also* produces the output that maximizes its profits. (If you doubt this statement, see footnote number 5 in the text.)

There is still another similarity between

the output and the input markets insofar as the firm is concerned. You will recall that the competitive firm's *supply* curve is a portion of its *marginal cost* curve. The competitive firm's demand curve for a resource is a portion of its *marginal revenue product* curve. Just as cost is the important determinant of supply, the revenue derived from the use of a resource is the important factor determining the demand for that resource.

CHECK LIST

When you have studied this chapter you should be able to

☐ Present four reasons for studying resource pricing.

☐ Define marginal revenue product.

☐ Determine the marginal revenue product schedule of a resource used to produce a product that is sold in a purely competitive market when you are given the relevant data.

☐ Find the marginal revenue product schedule of a resource used to produce a product that is sold in an imperfectly competitive market when you are given the necessary data.

☐ Define marginal resource cost.

☐ State the principle employed by a profit-maximizing firm to determine how much of a resource it will employ, and, when you are given data, apply this principle to find the quantity of a resource a firm will hire.

☐ Explain why the marginal revenue product schedule of a resource is the firm's demand for the resource.

☐ List the three factors that would change a firm's demand for a resource; predict the effect of an increase or decrease in each of these factors upon the demand of a firm for a resource.

☐ Enumerate the four determinants of the price-elasticity of demand for a resource; state precisely how a change in each of these

four determinants would affect the price-elasticity of demand for a resource.

☐ State the rule employed by a firm to determine the least-cost combination of resources; utilize this rule to find the least-cost combination when you are given the needed data.

☐ State the rule employed by a profit-maximizing firm to determine how much of each of several resources to employ; when you are given the necessary data, apply this rule to find the quantity of each resource the firm will hire.

☐ Explain what is meant by the "marginal productivity theory of income distribution." State the reason it is said to result in "a fair and equitable distribution of income"; list the two major criticisms of this theory.

CHAPTER OUTLINE

1 The study of what determines the prices of resources is important because resource prices influence the size of individual incomes and the distribution of income; allocate scarce resources; affect the way in which firms combine resources to produce their products; and raise ethical questions about the distribution of income.

2 Economists generally agree upon the basic principles of resource pricing, but the complexities of different resources markets make these principles difficult to apply.

3 The demand for a single resource depends upon (or is derived from) the demand for the goods and services it can produce.

a. Because resource demand is a derived demand, the demand for a single resource depends upon the marginal productivity of the resource and the market price of the good or service it is used to produce.

b. Marginal revenue product combines these two factors—the marginal physical product of a resource and the market price of the product it produces—into a single useful tool.

c. A firm will hire a resource up to the quantity at which the marginal revenue product of the resource is equal to its marginal resource cost.

d. The firm's marginal revenue product schedule for a resource is that firm's demand schedule for the resource.

e. If a firm sells its output in an imperfectly competitive market, the more the firm sells the lower becomes the price of the product. This causes the firm's marginal revenue product (resource demand) schedule to be less elastic than it would be if the firm sold its output in a purely competitive market.

f. The market (or total) demand for a resource is the sum of the demand schedules of all firms employing the resource.

4 Changes in the demand for the product being produced, changes in the productivity of the resource, and changes in the prices of other resources will tend to change the demand for a resource.

a. A change in the demand for a product produced by a resource such as labour will change the demand of a firm for labour in the same direction.

b. A change in the productivity of resource such as labour will change the demand of a firm for the resource in the same direction.

c. A change in the price of a

(1) *substitute* resource will change the demand for a resource such as labour in the same direction if the substitution effect outweighs the output effect, and in the opposite direction if the output effect outweighs the substitution effect.

(2) *complementary* resource will change the demand for a resource such as labour in the opposite direction.

5 The elasticity of the demand for a particular resource depends upon the rate at which the marginal physical product of that resource declines, the extent to which other resources can be substituted for the particular resource, the elasticity of demand for the product being produced, and the ratio of the cost of the resource to the total costs of the firm.

6 Firms typically employ more than one resource in producing a product.

a. The firm employing resources in perfectly competitive markets is hiring resources in the least-cost combination when the ratio of the marginal physical product of a resource to its price is the same for all the resources the firm hires.

b. The firm is hiring resources in the most profitable combination if it hires resources in a competitive market when the marginal revenue product of each resource is equal to the price of that resource.

c. A numerical example illustrates the least-cost and profit-maximizing rules for a firm that employs resources in perfectly competitive markets.

d. If the firm employs resources in imperfectly competitive markets, it is hiring resources in the least-cost combination when the ratio of the marginal physical product of a resource to its marginal resource cost is the same for all resources; and it is hiring resources in the most profitable combination when the marginal revenue product of each resource is equal to its marginal resource cost.

7 The marginal productivity theory seems to result in an equitable distribution of income because each unit of a resource receives a payment equal to its marginal contribution to the firm's revenue; but the theory has at least two serious faults.

a. The distribution of income will be unequal because resources are unequally distributed among individuals in the economy.

b. The income of those who supply resources will not be based on their marginal productivities if there is monopsony or monopoly in the resource markets of the economy.

IMPORTANT TERMS

Derived demand

Marginal revenue
product

Marginal resource
cost

MRP = MRC rule

Substitution effect

Output effect

Least-cost rule
(combination)

Profit-maximizing
rule (combination)

Marginal productivity
theory of income
distribution

FILL-IN QUESTIONS

1 Resource prices allocate _____
and are one of the factors that determine the

(incomes, costs) _____ of households; they are also one of the determinants

of the _____
of business firms.

2 The demand for a resource is a _____

demand and depends upon the _____

of the resource and the _____
of the product produced from the resource.

3 A firm will find it profitable to hire units
of a resource up to the quantity at which the

_____

and the _____
of the resource are equal; and if the firm
hires the resource in a purely competitive

market, the _____

and the _____
of the resource will be equal.

4 A firm's demand schedule for a resource

is the firm's _____
schedule for that resource because both
indicate the quantities of the resource the

firm will employ at various resource _____ .

5 A producer that sells its product in an
imperfectly competitive market finds that
the more of a resource it hires, the (higher,

lower) _____ becomes the price at
which it can sell its product. As a
consequence, the marginal revenue product
(or demand) schedule for the resource is

(more, less) _____ elastic than it
would be if the output were sold in a purely
competitive market.

6 The market demand curve for a resource

is obtained by _____

_____ .

7 The demand for a resource will change if

the demand for the _____

changes, if the _____

of the resource changes, or if the _____
of other resources change.

8 In the space to the right of each of the
following, indicate whether the change
would tend to increase (+), decrease (−), or
have an uncertain effect (?) upon a firm's
demand for a particular resource.
a. An increase in the price of the firm's

product.   ____
b. A decrease in the amounts of all other

resources the firm employs.   ____
c. An increase in the productivity of the

resource.   ____
d. An increase in the price of a substitute
resource when the output effect is greater

than the substitution effect.   ____
e. A decrease in the price of a com-

plementary resource.   ____

9 The output of the firm being constant, a
decrease in the price of resource A will
induce the firm to hire (more, less)

_____ of resource A and _____ of
other resources; this is called the

_____ effect. But if the decrease in
the price of A results in lower total costs and
an increase in output, the firm may hire

_____ of both resources; this is called the _____ effect.

10 Four determinants of the price-elasticity of demand for a resource are the rate at which the _____ of the resource decreases, the ease with which other resources can be _____ for the resource, the _____ of demand for the product which it is used to produce, and the _____

_____ .

11 Suppose a firm employs resources in purely competitive markets. If the firm wishes to produce any given amount of its product in the least costly way, the ratio of the _____ of each resource to its _____ must be the same for all resources.

12 A firm that hires resources in purely competitive markets is employing the combination of resources that will result in maximum profits for the firm when the

_____

of every resource is equal to its _____ .

13 When the marginal revenue product of a resource is equal to the price of that resource, the marginal revenue product of the resource divided by its price is equal to

_____ .

14 Assume that a firm employs resources in imperfectly competitive markets. The firm is
a. employing the combination of resources that enables it to produce any given output in the least costly way when the _____

_____ of every re-

source divided by its _____ is the same for all resources;
b. employing the combination of resources that maximizes its profits when the

_____ of every resource

is equal to its _____

(or when the _____ of

each resource divided by its _____

_____ is equal to _____).

15 In the marginal productivity theory, the distribution of income is an equitable one because each unit of each resource is paid an amount equal to its _____

_____ .

PROBLEMS AND PROJECTS

1 Table 1-1 on the next page shows the total product a firm will be able to obtain if it employs varying amounts of resource A while the amounts of the other resources the firm employs remain constant.
a. Compute the marginal physical product of each of the seven units of resource A and enter these figures in the table.
b. Assume the product the firm produces sells in the market for $1.50 per unit. Compute the total revenue of the firm at each of the eight levels of output and the marginal revenue product of each of the seven units of resource A. Enter these figures in Table 1-1.
c. On the basis of your computations, complete the firm's demand schedule for resource A in Table 1-2 by indicating how many units of resource A the firm would employ at the given prices.

TABLE 1-1

Quantity of resource A employed	Total product	Marginal physical product of A	Total revenue	Marginal revenue product of A
0	0		$_____	
1	12	_____	_____	$_____
2	22	_____	_____	_____
3	30	_____	_____	_____
4	36	_____	_____	_____
5	40	_____	_____	_____
6	42	_____	_____	_____
7	43	_____	_____	_____

TABLE 1-2

Price of A	Quantity of A demanded
$21	_____
18	_____
15	_____
12	_____
9	_____
6	_____
3	_____
1.50	_____

(1) Total revenue for each of the seven quantities of B employed.
(2) The marginal revenue product of each of the seven units of resource B.
c. How many units of B would the firm employ if the market price of B were

(1) $25: _____

(2) $20: _____

(3) $15: _____

(4) $9: _____

(5) $5: _____

(6) $1: _____

2 In Table 2-1 on the next page you will find the marginal physical product data for resource B. Assume that the quantities of other resources employed by the firm remain constant.
a. Compute the total product (output) of the firm for each of the seven quantities of resource B employed and enter these figures in the table.
b. Assume that the firm sells its output in an imperfectly competitive market, and that the prices at which it can sell its product are those given in the table. Compute and enter in the table:

3 In Table 3-1 are the marginal physical product and marginal revenue product schedules for resource C and resource D. Both resources are variable and are employed in purely competitive markets. The price of C is $2 and the price of D is $3.
a. The least-cost combination of C and D that would enable the firm to produce

(1) 64 units of its product is _____ C

and _____ D;

(2) 99 units of its product is _____ C

and _____ D.

TABLE 2-1

Quantity of resource B employed	Marginal physical product of B	Total product	Product price	Total revenue	Marginal revenue product of B
0		0		$ 0.00	
1	22	_____	$1.00	_____	$_____
2	21	_____	.90	_____	_____
3	19	_____	.80	_____	_____
4	16	_____	.70	_____	_____
5	12	_____	.60	_____	_____
6	7	_____	.50	_____	_____
7	1	_____	.40	_____	_____

TABLE 3-1

Quantity of resource C employed	Marginal physical product of C	Marginal revenue product of C	Quantity of resource D employed	Marginal physical product of D	Marginal revenue product of D
1	10	$5.00	1	21	$10.50
2	8	4.00	2	18	9.00
3	6	3.00	3	15	7.50
4	5	2.50	4	12	6.00
5	4	2.00	5	9	4.50
6	3	1.50	6	6	3.00
7	2	1.00	7	3	1.50

b. The profit-maximizing combination of C and D is _____ C and _____ D.

c. When the firm employs the profit-maximizing combination of C and D, it is also employing C and D in the least-cost combination because _____ equals _____ .

d. Examination of the figures in the table reveals that the firm sells its product in a _____ competitive market at a price of $ _____ .

e. Employing the profit-maximizing combination of C and D, the firm's

(1) total output is _____ ;

(2) total revenue is $_____ ;

(3) total cost is $ _____ ;

(4) total profit is $_____ .

SELF-TEST

Circle T if the statement is true, F if it is false.

1 In the resource markets of the economy, resources are demanded by business firms and supplied by households. **T F**

2 The prices of resources are an important factor in the determination of the supply of a product. **T F**

3 A resource that is highly productive will always be in great demand. **T F**

4 A firm's demand schedule for a resource

is the firm's marginal-revenue-product schedule for the resource.   T F

5 A firm's demand schedule for a resource will be more elastic if it sells its product in a purely competitive market than it would be if it sold the product in an imperfectly competitive market.   T F

6 The market demand for a particular resource is the sum of the individual demands of all firms that employ that resource.   T F

7 When two resources are substitutes for each other, both the substitution effect and the output effect of a decrease in the price of one of these resources operate to increase the quantity of the other resource employed by the firm.   T F

8 The output effect of an increase in the price of a resource is to increase the quantity demanded of that resource.   T F

9 If two resources are complementary, an increase in the price of one of them will reduce the demand for the other.   T F

10 An increase in the price of a resource will cause the demand for the resource to decrease.   T F

Use the following information as the basis for answering questions 11 and 12. The marginal revenue product and price of resource A are $12 and a constant $2, respectively; and the marginal revenue product and price of resource B are $25 and a constant $5, respectively. The firm sells its product at a constant price of $1.

11 The firm should decrease the amount of A and increase the amount of B it employs if it wishes to decrease its total cost without affecting its total output.   T F

12 If the firm wishes to maximize its profits, it should increase it employment of both A and B until their marginal revenue products fall to $2 and $5, repectively.   T F

13 When a firm hires a resource in an imperfectly competitive market, it finds that the price of the resource is greater than its marginal resource cost.   T F

14 As long as the markets in an economy are competitive, the marginal productivity theory of income distribution results in an equal distribution of the economy's income among its households.   T F

15 The marginal productivity theory of income distribution results in an equitable distribution only if resource markets are perfectly competitive.   T F

Circle the letter that corresponds to the best answer.

1 The price paid for resources affect (a) the money incomes of households in the economy; (b) the allocation of resources among different firms and industries in the economy; (c) the quantities of different resources employed to produce a particular product; (d) all of the above.

2 The study of the pricing of resources tends to be complex because (a) supply and demand do not determine resource prices; (b) economists do not agree on the basic principles of resource pricing; (c) the basic principles of resource pricing must be varied and adjusted when applied to particular resource markets; (d) resource pricing is essentially an ethical question.

3 The demand for a resource is *derived* from (a) the marginal productivity of the resource and price of the good or service produced from it; (b) the marginal productivity of the resource and the price of the resource; (c) the price of the resource and the price of the good or service produced from it; (d) the price of the resource and the quantity of the resource demanded.

4 As a firm that sells its product in an imperfectly competitive market increases the quantity of a resource it employs, the

marginal revenue product of that resource falls because (a) the price paid by the firm for the resource falls; (b) the marginal physical product of the resource falls; (c) the price at which the firm sells its product falls; (d) both the marginal physical product and the price at which the firm sells its product fall.

Use the total product and marginal physical product schedules for a resource, below, to answer questions 5, 6, and 7. Assume that the quantities of other resources the firm employs remain constant.

Units of resource	Total product	MPP
1	8	8
2	14	6
3	18	4
4	21	3
5	23	2

5 If the product the firm produces sells for a constant $3 per unit, the marginal revenue product of the 4th unit of the resource is (a) $3; (b) $6; (c) $9; (d) $12.

6 If the firm's product sells for a constant $3 per unit and the price of the resource is a constant $15, the firm will employ how many units of the resource? (a) 2; (b) 3; (c) 4; (d) 5.

7 If the firm can sell 14 units of output at a price of $1 per unit and 18 units of output at a price of $0.90 per unit, the marginal revenue product of the third unit of the resource is (a) $4; (b) $3.60; (c) $2.20; (d) $0.40.

8 Which of the following would increase a firm's demand for a particular resource? (a) an increase in the prices of complementary resources used by the firm; (b) a decrease in the demand for the firm's product; (c) an increase in the productivity of the resource; (d) a decrease in the price of the particular resource.

9 In finding the substitution effect of a change in the price of a particular resource, which of the following is assumed to be constant? (a) the total output of the firm; (b) the total expenditures of the firm; (c) the employment of all other resources; (d) the MPPs of all resources.

10 Suppose resource A and resource B are substitutes and the price of A increases. If the output effect is greater than the substitution effect, (a) the quantity of A employed by the firm will increase and the quantity of B employed will decrease; (b) the quantity of both A and B employed by the firm will decrease; (c) the quantity of both A and B employed will decrease; (d) the quantity of A employed will decrease and the quantity of B employed will increase.

11 Which of the following would result in an increase in the elasticity of demand for a particular resource? (a) an increase in the rate at which the marginal physical product of that resource declines; (b) a decrease in the elasticity of demand for the product that the resource helps to produce; (c) an increase in the percentage of the firm's total costs accounted for by the resource; (d) a decrease in the number of other resources that are good substitutes for the particular resource.

12 A firm is allocating its expenditure for resources in a way that will result in the least total cost of producing any given output when (a) the amount the firm spends on each resource is the same; (b) the marginal revenue product of each resource is the same; (c) the marginal physical product of each resource is the same; (d) the marginal physical product per dollar spent on the last unit of each resource is the same.

13 A firm that hires resources in competitive markets is *not necessarily* maximizing its profits when (a) the marginal revenue product of every resource is equal to 1; (b) the marginal revenue product of every resource is equal to its price; (c) the ratio of the marginal revenue product of every resource to its price is equal to 1; (d) the ratio of the price of every resource to its marginal revenue product is equal to 1.

14 If a firm employs resources in imperfectly competitive markets, to maximize its profits the marginal revenue product of each resource must equal (a) its marginal physical product; (b) its marginal resource cost; (c) its price; (d) one.

15 In the marginal productivity theory of income distribution, when all markets are purely competitive, each unit of each resource receives a money payment equal to (a) its marginal physical product; (b) its marginal revenue product; (c) the needs of the resource owner; (d) the payments received by each of the units of the other resources in the economy.

DISCUSSION QUESTIONS

1 Why is it important to study resource pricing?

2 Why is resource demand a derived demand, and upon what two factors does the strength of this derived demand depend?

3 Explain why firms that wish to maximize their profits follow the MRP = MRC rule.

4 What constitutes a firm's demand schedule for a resource? Why? What determines the total, or market, demand for a resource?

5 Why is the demand schedule for a resource less elastic when the firm sells its product in an imperfectly competitive market than when it sells it in a purely competitive market?

6 Explain what will cause the demand for a resource to increase and what will cause it to decrease.

7 Explain the difference between the "substitution effect" and the "output effect."

8 What determines the elasticity of the demand for a resource? Explain the exact relationship between each of these four determinants and elasticity.

9 Asssuming a firm employs resources in purely competitive markets, when is it spending money on resources in such a way that it can produce a given output for the least total cost?

10 When is a firm that employs resources in purely competitive markets utilizing these resources in amounts that will maximize the profits of the firm?

11 Were a firm to employ resources in *imperfectly* competitive markets, what would your answers to questions 9 and 10 be?

12 What *is* the marginal productivity theory of income distribution? What ethical proposition must be accepted if this distribution is to be fair and equitable? What are the two major shortcomings of the theory?

12

THE PRICING AND EMPLOYMENT OF RESOURCES: WAGE DETERMINATION

In the preceding chapter, the text defined marginal revenue product and marginal resource cost. It also explained what determines the demand for *any* resource. Chapter 12 builds upon these explanations and applies them to the study of a particular resource—labour—and to the price paid for labour—the wage rate.

But as you learned in Chapters 7 to 10, it requires more than an understanding of supply and demand to explain the prices of a product and the output of a firm and an industry. An understanding of the competitivenesss of the market in which the product is sold is also required. It was for this reason that purely competitive, monopolistic, monopolistically competitive, and oligopolistic markets were examined in detail. The same is true of labour markets. The competitiveness of labour markets must be examined if the factors that determine wages rates and the quantity of labour employed are to be understood.

Following comments on the meanings of certain terms, the general level of wages, and the reasons for the high and increasing general wage level in Canada, Chapter 12 explains how wage rates are determined in particular types of labour markets. Six kinds of labour markets are studied: (1) the competitive market, in which the number of employers is large and labour is non-unionized; (2) the monopsony market, in which a single employer hires labour under competitive (non-union) conditions; (3) a market in which a union controls the supply of labour, the number of employers is large, and the union attempts to increase the total demand for labour; (4) a similar market, in which the union attempts to reduce the total supply of labour; (5) another similar market, in which the union attempts to obtain a wage rate that is above the competitive-equilibrium level by threatening to strike; and (6) the bilateral monopoly market, in which a single employer faces a labour supply controlled by a single union.

It is, of course, important for you to learn the characteristics of and the differences between each of these labour markets. It is also important that you study each of them carefully to see *how* the characteristics of the market affect the wage rate that will be paid in these markets. In the first two types of market, the wage rate that will be paid is quite definite, and here you should learn exactly what level of wages and employment will prevail.

When unions control the supply of labour, wage and employment levels are less definite. If the demand for labour is competitive, the wage rate and the amount of employment will depend upon how successful the union is in increasing the demand for labour, in restricting the supply of labour, or in setting a wage rate that employers will accept. If there is but a single employer, wages and employment will fall within certain limits; exactly where they occur within these limits will depend upon the bargaining strength of the union and of the firm. You should, however, know what the limits are.

The sections explaining wages in particular labour markets are the more important parts of the chapter. But the sections that examine the effect of minimum wage laws on employment and wage rates, the effect of unionization upon wage rates in Canada, the reasons different workers receive different wage rates, and the effect of investment in human capital are also important. You should, therefore, pay attention to (1) the case against, the case for, and the real-world effects of the minimum wage; (2) the two generalizations that emerge from studies of the effects of unions upon wages; (3) the several causes of wage differentials, especially between men and women; (4) the crowding hypothesis; and (5) the theory of human capital and the criticisms of that theory.

CHECK LIST

When you have studied this chapter you should be able to

☐ Define wages (or the wage rate), and distinguish between money and real wages.

☐ List the several factors that have led to the high and rising general level of real wages in Canada.

☐ Explain, using graphs, what determines the wage rate and the level of employment in competitive labour markets and in monopsonistic labour markets; and be able, when given numerical data, to find the equilibrium wage rate and employment level in each of these models.

☐ List three techniques labour unions use to increase the demand for labour.

☐ Enumerate the devices used by the labour movement and by craft unions to decrease the supply of labour; and explain the effects of these devices upon wage rates and the employment of labour.

☐ Explain, using a graph, how the organization of workers by an industrial union in a previously competitive labour market would affect the wage rate and employment level.

☐ Use a graph to explain why the equilib-rium wage rate and employment level is indeterminate when a labour market is a bilateral monopoly; and to predict the range within which the wage rate will be found.

☐ Present the case for and the case against a legally established minimum wage.

☐ State the two generalizations that emerge from an examination of the question whether unions have raised wages in Canada.

☐ List the three major factors that explain why wage differentials exist.

☐ Compare the economic status of female and male workers; explain the special kind of occupational discrimination to which women are subjected.

☐ State the crowding hypothesis and employ a simple model to explain why women receive lower wages and why the labour resources of society are more efficiently allocated when occupational discrimination is eliminated.

☐ Define investment in human capital; explain the cause-effect chain in the theory of human capital; and criticize this theory.

CHAPTER OUTLINE

1 A wage (or the wage rate) is the price paid per unit of time for any type of labour and can be measured either in money or in real terms. Earnings are equal to the wage multiplied by the amount of time worked.

2 The general level of wages in Canada is among the highest in the world because the demand for labour in Canada has been great relative to the supply of labour.

a. The demand for labour in Canada has been strong because labour has been highly productive; and it has been highly productive for several major reasons.

b. The real hourly wage rate and output per hour of labour are closely and directly related to each other; and real income per worker can increase only at the same rate as output per worker.

c. The increases in the demand for labour that have resulted from the increased productivity of labour over time have been greater than the increases in the supply of labour in Canada; and as a result the real wage rate in Canada has increased in the long run.

3 The wage rate received by a specific type of labour depends upon the demand for and the supply of that labour and upon the competitiveness of the market in which that type of labour is hired.

a. In a purely competitive and non-unionized labour market, the total demand for and the total supply of labour determine the wage rate; from the point of view of the individual firm, the supply of labour is perfectly elastic at this wage rate (that is, the marginal labour cost is equal to the wage rate) and the firm will hire the amount of labour at which the marginal revenue product of labour is equal to the marginal labour cost.

b. In a monopsonistic and non-unionized labour market, the firm's marginal labour costs are greater than the wage rates it must pay to obtain various amounts of labour; it hires the amount of labour at which marginal labour cost and the marginal revenue product of labour are equal. Both the wage rate and the level of employment are less than they would be under purely competitive conditions.

c. In labour markets in which unions represent workers, the unions attempt to raise wage rates by
(1) increasing the demand for labour by increasing the demands for the products produced by the union workers, by increasing the productivity of these workers, and by increasing the prices of resources that are substitutes for the labour provided by the members of the union;
(2) reducing the supply of labour; or
(3) imposing upon employers wage rates in excess of the equilibrium wage rate that would prevail in a purely competitive market.

d. Labour unions are aware that actions taken by them to increase wage rates also increase the unemployment of their members and may, therefore, limit their demands for higher wages; but the unemployment effect of higher wages is lessened by increases in and a relatively inelastic demand for labour.

e. In a labour market characterized by bilateral monopoly, the wage rate depends, within certain limits, on the relative bargaining power of the union and of the employer.

f. Whether minimum wage laws reduce poverty is a debatable question; but the evidence suggests that, while they increase the incomes of employed workers, they also reduce the number of workers employed.

g. The unionization of workers has increased the wages received by union members significantly above what they would have received in the absence of unionization; but these wage increases have been at the expense of unorganized workers, and unionization has not increased the average real wages of workers as a whole.

4 Not all labour receives the same wage.

a. Wage differentials exist because
(1) The labour force consists of non-competing groups;
(2) jobs vary in difficulty and attractiveness; and
(3) workers are not perfectly mobile.

b. The average income of women is substantially less than the average income of male workers.
(1) Women are subjected to occupational discrimination, and this discrimination has crowded them into a small number of occupations: in these occupations, the supply of workers is large relative to the demand for them and wage rates and incomes are, therefore, lower.
(2) A simple supply-and-demand model illustrates the effects of crowding women into a limited number of occupations.

5 Some economists have argued that differences in the earnings of workers are to a large extent the result of differences in the amounts invested in human capital.

a. An investment in human capital increases the productivity of workers, and is the amount spent to improve the education, health, and mobility of workers.

b. Like the investments a business firm makes in such real capital as a machine, a worker decides to invest in human capital if the discounted value of the additional lifetime earnings that result from the investment are greater than the cost of the investment.

c. The human capital theory explains not only wage diffentials and the rising level of real wages Canada has experienced historically, but other phenomena that would otherwise be mysteries.

d. But critics of the theory have questioned the effectiveness of investments in human capital in raising the productivity and incomes of the investors and in reducing poverty and income inequality.

IMPORTANT TERMS

Wage (rate)

Earnings

Money wage (rate)

Real wage (rate)

Marginal resource
  (labour) cost

Competitive labour
  market

Monopsony

Oligopsony

Exclusive unionism

Craft union

Occupational licensing

Inclusive unionism

Industrial union

Bilateral monopoly

Minimum wage

Wage differential

Non-competing groups

Equalizing differences

Immobility

Occupational
  discrimination

Female participation
  rate

Crowding hypothesis

Theory of human
  capital

Human capital
  investment

FILL-IN QUESTIONS

1 A wage rate is the price paid for labour

per unit of _____ ,

and the earnings of labour are equal to the

_____

multiplied by _____ ;

money wages are an amount of money, while

real wages are _____ .

2 The general level of wages is higher in Canada than in most foreign countries because

a. the demand for labour in Canada is

(great, small) _____ relative to the supply of labour;

b. Canadian labour tends to be highly productive, among other reasons, because it has

relatively large amounts of _____

and _____

with which to work, and employs a generally

superior _____ to produce

goods, and because of the high _____
of the Canadian labour force.

3 In a competitive labour market,

a. the supply curve slopes upward from left to right because it is necessary for employers

to pay higher _____

to attract workers from _____ ;

b. the demand is the sum of the _____

_____

of all firms hiring this type of labour;

c. the wage rate will equal the rate at which

the _____

and the _____
are equal.

4 Insofar as an individual firm hiring labour in a competitive market is concerned,

the supply of labour is _____
elastic because the individual firm is unable

to affect the _____ it must pay.

5 The individual employer who hires labour in a competitive market hires that quantity of labour at which the _____ of labour is equal to the _____ or the _____ .

6 A monopsonist employing labour in a market that is competitive on the supply side will hire that amount of labour at which _____ and _____ are equal. And because the marginal labour cost is (greater, less) _____ than the wage rate in such a market, the employer will pay a wage rate that is less than both the _____ of labour and the marginal _____ .

7 When compared with a competitive labour market, a market dominated by a monopsonist results in (higher, lower) _____ wage rates and in (more, less) _____ employment.

8 The basic objective of labour unions is to _____ ; they attempt to accomplish this goal either by increasing the _____ ; restricting the _____ of labour; or imposing _____ wage rates on employers.

9 Craft unions typically try to increase wages by _____ while industrial unions try to increase wages by _____ ;
a. if they are successful, employment in the craft or industry is (decreased, increased, not affected)_____ .
b. This effect on the employment of their members may lead unions to (increase, decrease) _____ their wage demands.

c. But unions will not worry too much about the effect on employment of higher wage rates if the economy is (growing, declining, stationary) _____ or if the demand for labour is relatively (elastic, inelastic) _____ .

10 Labour unions can increase the demand for the services of their members by increasing the demand for _____ , by increasing the _____ of their members, and by increasing the _____ of resources that are substitutes for the services supplied by their members.

11 In a bilateral monopoly labour market, the monopsonist will not pay a wage greater than_____ ;
the union will ask for some wage greater than the _____ ;
within these limits, the wage rate will depend on _____ .

12 The imposition of effective minimum wage rates, ignoring any shock effects, in
a. competitive labour markets is to (increase, decrease) _____ the wage rate and to _____ employment;
b. monopsonistic labour markets is to _____ the wage rate and to _____ employment;
c. the economy as a whole seems to have been to _____ the wage rate and to _____ employment.

13 The effect of the unionization of workers in the Canadian economy has been to (increase, decrease, have no effect on) _____

_____ wage rates in the organized industries, to _____ them in the unorganized industries, and to _____ the average level of wages of organized and unorganized workers.

14 Actual wage rates received by different workers tend to differ because workers are not _____ because jobs differ in _____ and because labour markets are _____ .

15 The total labour force is composed of a number of _____ groups of workers. Within each of these groups, some workers receive higher wages than others, and these wage differentials are called _____ .

16 Workers performing identical jobs often receive different wages; these differences are due to _____ of three basic types: _____ , _____ , and _____ .

17 The average earnings of a full-time female worker are only about ____% of the average earnings of a full-time male worker because of _____ discrimination.

18 The contention that occupational discrimination pushes women into a small number of occupations and results in the supply of labour being large relative to demand in these occupations is called the _____ hypothesis. Because supply is large relative to demand, wages and incomes in these occupations are (high, low)_____ .

19 Investment, according to the theory of human capital,
a. consists of expenditures for _____ , _____ , and _____ ;
b. increases the _____ and _____ of workers;
c. explains a good part of the increase in the level of _____ in Canada;
d. and accounts for the existence of _____ _____ groups and _____ in the wages and incomes among groups.

PROBLEMS AND PROJECTS

1 Suppose a single firm has, for a particular type of labour, the marginal revenue product schedule given in the following table.

Number of units of labour	MRP of labour
1	$15
2	14
3	13
4	12
5	11
6	10
7	9
8	8

a. Assume there are 100 firms with the same marginal revenue product schedules for this particular type of labour. Compute the total or market demand for this labour by completing column 1 in the table on the next page.
b. Using the supply schedule for labour given in columns 2 and 3,
(1) what will be the equilibrium wage rate?

$ _____
(2) what will be the total amount of labour hired in the market? _____

(1) Quantity of labour demanded	(2) Wage rate	(3) Quantity of labour supplied
_____	$15	850
_____	14	800
_____	13	750
_____	12	700
_____	11	650
_____	10	600
_____	9	550
_____	8	500

c. The individual firm will

(1) have a marginal labour cost of $ _____ ;

(2) employ _____ units of labour;

(3) pay a wage of $ _____ .

d. On the following graph , plot the market demand and supply curves for labour and indicate the equilibrium wage rate and the total quantity of labour employed.

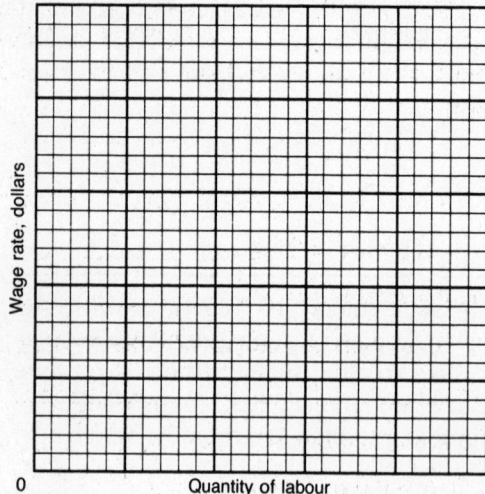

e. On the following graph, plot the individual firm's demand curve for labour, the supply curve for labour, and the marginal-labour-cost curve that confronts the individual firm; indicate the quantity of

labour the firm will hire and the wage it will pay.

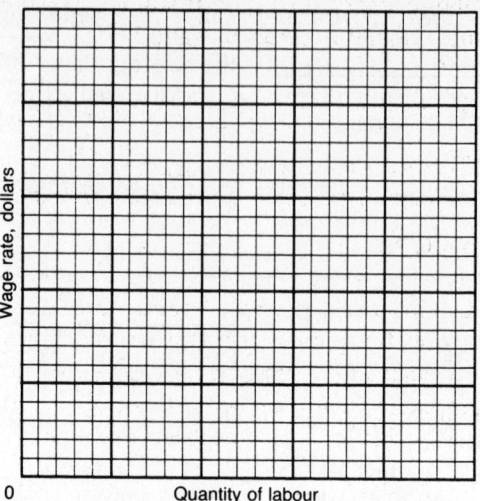

f. The imposition of a $12 minimum wage rate would change the total amount of labour hired in this market to _____ .

2 In the following table, assume that a monopsonist has the marginal revenue product schedule for a particular type of labour given in columns 1 and 2 and that the supply schedule for labour is that given in columns 1 and 3.

(1) Number of labour units	(2) MRP of labour	(3) Wage rate	(4) Total labour cost	(5) Marginal labour cost
0		$ 2	$_____	
1	$36	4	_____	$_____
2	32	6	_____	_____
3	28	8	_____	_____
4	24	10	_____	_____
5	20	12	_____	_____
6	16	14	_____	_____
7	12	16	_____	_____
8	8	18	_____	_____

a. Compute the firm's total labour costs at each level of employment and the marginal labour cost of each unit of labour, and enter these figures in columns 4 and 5.

b. The firm will

(1) hire _____ units of labour;

(2) pay a wage of $ _____ ;

(3) have a marginal revenue product for

labour of $ _____

for the last unit of labour employed.

c. Plot the marginal revenue product of labour, the supply curve for labour, and the marginal-labour-cost curve on the next graph; indicate the quantity of labour the firm will employ and the wage it will pay.

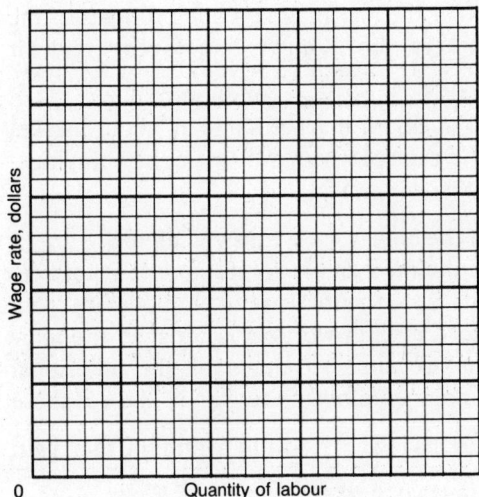

d. If this firm hired labour in a competitive labour market, it would hire at least _____ units and pay a wage of at least $_____ .

3 Assume that the employees of the monopsonist in problem 2 organize a strong industrial union. The union demands a wage rate of $16 for its members, and the mon-

opsonist decides to pay this wage because a strike would be too costly for it.

a. In the following table, compute the supply schedule for labour that now confronts the monopsonist by completing column 2.

(1) Number of labour units	(2) Wage rate	(3) Total labour cost	(4) Marginal labour cost
1	$____	$____	$____
2	____	____	____
3	____	____	____
4	____	____	____
5	____	____	____
6	____	____	____
7	____	____	____
8	____	____	____

b. Compute the total labour cost and the marginal labour cost at each level of employment, and enter these figures in columns 3 and 4.

c. The firm will

(1) hire _____ units of labour;

(2) pay a wage of $ _____ ;

(3) pay total wages of $ _____ .

d. As a result of unionization the wage rate has _____ , the level of employment has _____ , and the earnings of labour have _____ .

e. On the next graph, plot the firm's marginal-revenue-product-of-labour schedule, the labour supply schedule, and the marginal-labour-cost schedule. Indicate also the wage rate the firm will pay and the number of workers it will hire.

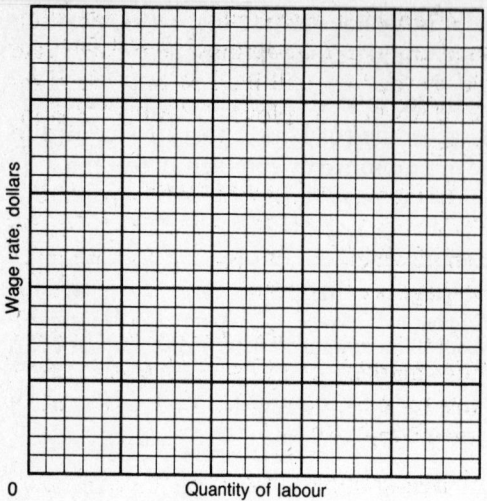

Wage rate, dollars

0   Quantity of labour

4 Suppose there are only three labour markets in the economy and that each of these markets is perfectly competitive. The table contains the demand (or marginal-revenue-product) schedule for labour in *each* of these three markets.

Wage rate (marginal revenue product of labour per hour)	Quantity of labour (millions per hour)
$11	4
10	5
9	6
8	7
7	8
6	9
5	10
4	11
3	12

a. Assume there are 24 million homogeneous workers in the economy and that one-half of these workers are male and one-half are female.

(1) If the 12 million female workers can be employed only in labour market Z, for all of them to find employment the hourly wage rate must be $ _____.

(2) If, of the 12 million male workers, 6 mil-

lion are employed in labour market X and 6 million are employed in labour market Y, the hourly wage rate in labour markets X and

Y will be $ _____.

b. Imagine now that the impediment to the employment of females in labour markets X and Y is removed and that, as a result (and because the demand and marginal revenue product of labour is the same in all three markets), 8 million workers find employment in each labour market.

(1) In labour market Z (in which only females had previously been employed)

(a) the hourly wage rate will rise to $ _____ ;
(b) the *decrease* in domestic output that results from the decrease in employment from 12 to 8 million workers is equal to the loss of the marginal revenue products of the workers no longer employed; and it

totals $ _____ million.

(2) In labour market X and in labour market Y (in each of which only males had previously been employed)

(a) the hourly wage rate will fall to $ _____ ;
(b) the *increase* in domestic output that results from the increase in employment from 6 to 8 million workers is equal to the marginal revenue products of the additional workers employed; the gain in *each* of these

markets is $ _____ million and the total gain

in the two markets is $ _____.

(c) The *net* gain to society from the reallocation of female workers is $ _____ million.

SELF-TEST

Circle T if the statement is true, F if it is false.

1 The general level of real wages is higher in Canada than in foreign countries because the supply of labour in Canada is great relative to the demand for it.   **T F**

2 The average real income per worker and

the average real output per worker in an economy are two names for the same thing.

T F

3 If an individual firm employs labour in a competitive market, it finds that its marginal labour cost is equal to the wage rate in that market.

T F

4 Given a competitive employer's demand for labour, the lower the wage it must pay the more workers it will hire.

T F

5 Both monopsonists and firms hiring labour in competitive markets hire labour up to the point where the marginal revenue product of labour and marginal labour cost are equal.

T F

6 Restricting the supply of labour is a means of increasing wage rates more commonly used by craft unions than by industrial unions.

T F

7 Occupational licensing has been one of the principal means employed by the federal government to increase the number of recent immigrants in certain skilled occupations and trades.

T F

8 The imposition of an above-equilibrium wage rate will cause employment to fall off more when the demand for labour is inelastic than it will when the demand is elastic. **T F**

9 Union members are paid wage rates that on the average are greater by 10% or more than the wage rates paid to non-union members.

T F

10 The actions of both exclusive and inclusive unions that raise the wage rates paid to them by competitive employers of labour also cause, other things remaining constant, an increase in the employment of their members.

T F

11 If a labour market is competitive, the imposition of an effective minimum wage will increase the wage rate paid and decrease employment in that market. **T F**

12 When an effective minimum wage is imposed upon a monopsonist, the wage rate paid by the firm will increase and the number of workers employed by it may also increase. **T F**

13 An increase in the minimum wage rate in the Canadian economy tends to increase the unemployment of teenagers and of others in low-wage occupations. **T F**

14 Actual wage rates received in different labour markets tend to differ because the demand for particular types of labour relative to their supply differ. **T F**

15 "Ben Robbins is a skilled artisan of a particular type, is unable to obtain membership in the union representing that group of artisans, and is, therefore, unable to practise his trade." This is an example of labour immobility. **T F**

Circle the letter that corresponds to the best answer.

1 Real wages would decline if the (*a*) prices of goods and services rose more rapidly than money wages rates; (*b*) prices of goods and services rose less rapidly than money wage rates; (*c*) prices of goods and services and wage rates both rose; (*d*) prices of goods and services and wage rates both fell.

2 Which of the following has *not* led to the generally high productivity of Canadian workers? (*a*) the high level of real wage rates in Canada; (*b*) the superior quality of the Canadian labour force; (*c*) the advanced technology utilized in Canadian industries; (*d*) the large quantity of capital available to assist the average worker in Canada.

3 Between 1926 and 1961 output per hour of labour and real hourly wage rates increased in Canada at an average annual rate of (*a*) 2.69%; (*b*) 2.09%; (*c*) 1.59%; (*d*) 1.29%.

4 The individual firm that hires labour under competitive conditions faces a supply curve for labour that (*a*) is perfectly inelastic; (*b*) is of unitary elasticity; (*c*) is perfectly elastic; (*d*) slopes upward from left to right.

5 A monopsonist pays a wage rate that is (*a*) greater than the marginal revenue product of labour; (*b*) equal to the marginal revenue product of labour; (*c*) equal to the firm's marginal labour cost; (*d*) less than the marginal revenue product of labour.

6 Compared with a competitive labour market, a monopsonistic market will result in (*a*) higher wage rates and higher level of employment; (*b*) higher wage rates and a lower level of employment; (*c*) lower wage rates and a higher level of employment; (*d*) lower wage rates and a lower level of employment.

7 Higher wage rates and a higher level of employment are the usual consequences of (*a*) inclusive unionism; (*b*) exclusive unionism; (*c*) an above-equilibrium wage rate; (*d*) an increase in the productivity of labour.

8 Which of the following would *not* increase the demand for a particular type of labour? (*a*) an increase in the productivity of that type of labour; (*b*) an increase in the prices of those resources that are substitutes for that type of labour; (*c*) an increase in the prices of those resources that are complements to that type of labour; (*d*) an increase in the demand for the products produced by that type of labour.

9 Industrial unions typically attempt to increase wage rates by (*a*) imposing an above-equilibrium wage rate upon employers; (*b*) increasing the demand for labour; (*c*) decreasing the supply of labour; (*d*) forming a bilateral monopoly.

Use the data in the following table to answer multiple-choice questions 10, 11, and 12.

Wage rate	Quantity of labour supplied	Marginal labour cost	Marginal revenue product of labour
$10	0	–	$18
11	100	$11	17
12	200	13	16
13	300	15	15
14	400	17	14
15	500	19	13
16	600	21	12

10 If the firm employing labour were a monopsonist, the wage rate and the quantity of labour employed would be, respectively, (*a*) $14 and 300; (*b*) $13 and 400; (*c*) $14 and 400; (*d*) $13 and 300.

11 But if the market for this labour were competitive, the wage rate and the quantity of labour employed would be, respectively, (*a*) $14 and 300; (*b*) $13 and 400; (*c*) $14 and 400; (*d*) $13 and 300.

12 If the firm employing labour were a monopsonist and the workers were represented by an industrial union, the wage rate would be (*a*) between $13 and $14; (*b*) between $13 and $15; (*c*) between $14 and $15; (*d*) below $13 or above $15.

13 Which of the following has been a consequence of unionization? (*a*) higher wage rates for unionized workers; (*b*) greater employment of unionized workers; (*c*) greater employment of the workers in the labour force; (*d*) a higher level of real wages in the economy.

14 The fact that a star hockey player receives a wage of $500,000 a year can best be explained in terms of (*a*) non-competing labour groups; (*b*) equalizing differences; (*c*) labour immobility; (*d*) imperfections in the labour market.

15 The fact that unskilled construction workers receive higher wages than gas station attendants is *best* explained in terms of (*a*) non-competing labour groups; (*b*) equalizing differences; (c) labour immobility; (d) imperfections in the labour market.

16 About what percentage of women aged 15 and older is in the labour force? (a) 36; (b) 44; (c) 55; (d) 56.

17 About what percentage of the total labour force is women? (a) 43; (b) 41; (c) 33; (d) 28.

18 The average annual earnings of full-time female workers is about what percentage of the average annual earnings of full-time male employees? (a) 60%; (b) 75%; (c) 90%; (d) 95%.

19 Those who have suggested the crowding hypothesis assert that the crowding of women into certain occupations (a) is the result of occupational discrimination; (b) results in the misallocation of resources; (c) explains the lower wage rates in the crowded occupations; (d) all of the above.

20 Which of the following is *not* true? (a) investment in human capital, according to the proponents of the human-capital theory, increases the productivity of workers; (b) expenditures for health, education, and mobility are investments in human capital; (c) whether to invest in real capital is a decision similar to the decision whether to invest in human capital; (d) differences in the amounts invested in human capital, human-capital theorists argue, explain the equalizing differences in wage rates.

DISCUSSION QUESTIONS

1 Why is the general level of real wages higher in Canada than in most foreign nations? Why has the level of real wages continued to increase even though the supply of labour has continually increased?

2 Explain why the productivity of the Canadian labour force increased in the past to its present high level.

3 In the competitive model, what determines the market demand for labour and the wage rate? What kind of supply situation do all firms as a group confront? Why? What kind of supply situation does the individual firm confront? Why?

4 In the monopsony model, what determines employment and the wage rate? What kind of supply situation does the monopsonist face? Why? How does the wage rate paid and the level of employment compare with what would result if the market were competitive?

5 In what sense is a worker who is hired by a monopsonist "exploited" while one who is employed in a competitive labour market "justly" rewarded? *Why* do monopsonists wish to restrict employment?

6 When supply is less than perfectly elastic, marginal labour cost is greater than the wage rate. Why?

7 What basic methods do labour unions employ to try to increase the wages received by their members? If these methods are successful in raising wages, what effect do they have on employment?

8 What three methods might labour employ to increase the demand for labour? If these methods are successful, what effects do they have upon wage rates and employment?

9 When labour unions attempt to restrict the supply of labour to increase wage rates, what devices do they employ to do this for the economy as a whole, and what means do they use to restrict the supply of a given type of worker?

10 How do industrial unions attempt to increase wage rates, and what effect does this method of increasing wages have upon employment in the industry affected?

11 Both exclusive and inclusive unions are able to raise the wage rates received by their members. Why might unions limit or temper their demands for higher wages? What two factors determine the extent to which they will or will not reduce their demands for higher wages?

12 What is bilateral monopoly? What determines wage rates in a labour market of this type?

13 What is the effect of minimum wage laws upon wage rates and employment in (*a*) competitive labour markets; (*b*) monopsony labour markets; (*c*) the economy as a whole?

14 How (*a*) do the wage rates paid to union members differ from those paid to non-union employees; (*b*) do minimum wage rates affect the employment of workers in high- and low-wage occupations?

15 Why are the wage rates received by workers in different occupations, by workers in the same occupations, and by workers in different localities different?

16 If labour markets were competitive, what would be the effect of reducing or eliminat-ing sexual discrimination in these labour markets upon the wage rates received by men and women and upon the domestic output?

17 Explain what is meant by investment in human capital and why the decision to invest in human capital is like the decision to invest in real capital. What, according to the proponents of the human-capital theory, is the effect of investment in human capital upon the productivity, the wage rate, and the income of workers?

18 Using the theory of human capital, explain (*a*) geographic differences in wage rates; (*b*) why younger people are more mobile; (*c*) why a society tends to educate younger rather than older people; and (*d*) the historic rise in real wages in the Canadian economy.

19 Outline the argument of the critics of the theory of human capital and the important public-policy issue that their criticism raises.

13

THE PRICING AND EMPLOYMENT OF RESOURCES: RENT, INTEREST, AND PROFITS

Chapter 13 concludes the study of the prices of resources by examining rent, interest, and profits. Compared with the study of wage rates in Chapter 12, each of the first three major sections in Chapter 13 is considerably briefer and a good deal simpler. You might do well to treat these sections as though they were actually three mini-chapters.

There is nothing especially difficult about Chapter 13. By now you should understand that the marginal revenue product of a resource determines the demand for that resource, and that this understanding can be applied to the demand for land and capital. It will be on the supply side of the land market that you will encounter whatever difficulties there are. The supply of land is unique because it is perfectly *inelastic*: changes in rent do not change the quantity of land supplied. Demand, given the quantity of land available, is thus the sole determinant of rent. Of course, land varies in productivity and can be used for different purposes, but these are merely the factors that explain why the rent on all land is not the same.

Capital, as the economist defines it, means capital goods. Is the rate of interest, then, the price paid for the use of capital goods? No, not quite. Capital is not one kind of good; it is many different kinds. In order to be able to talk about the price paid for the use of capital goods there must be a simple way of adding up different kinds of capital goods. The simple way is to measure the quantity of

capital goods in terms of money. The rate of interest is, then, the price paid for the use of money (or of financial capital). It is the demand for and the supply of money that determine the rate of interest in the economy. Business firms and households wish to hold — that is, demand — money for two principal reasons. Like the demand for any other good or service, the greater the price of money (the interest rate) the smaller is the amount of money firms and households will wish to hold. And, like other *normal* goods and services, the greater the economy's income (GDP), the greater will be the demand for money.

On the supply side, the Bank of Canada, the monetary authority in the Canadian economy, decides how much money will be available. At any time the supply of money is a fixed quantity. Since the determining of the supply of money is a problem of macroeconomics, the theory of interest rate determination is presented in Part 6 with footnote 4 in the text citing the relevant sections.

When it comes to profits, supply and demand analysis fails the economist. Profits are not merely a wage for a particular type of labour; rather, they are rewards for taking risks and the gains of the monopolist. Such things as "the quantity of risk taken" or "the quantity of effort required to establish a monopoly" simply can't be measured; consequently, it is impossible to talk about the demand for or the supply of them. Nevertheless, profits are important in the economy. They are largely rewards for doing things that have to be done if the economy is to allocate resources efficiently and to progress and develop; they are the lure or the bait that makes people willing to take the risks that result in efficiency and progress.

The final section of Chapter 13 answers two questions about the Canadian economy. What part of the national income goes to workers and what part goes to the capitalists—those who provide the economy with land, capital goods, and entrepreneurial ability? Have the shares going to workers and to capitalists changed in the past seventy-five or so years? You may be surprised to learn that the lion's share—about 80% — of the national income goes to workers today and went to workers in 1926; and that capitalists today and in 1926 got about 20%. There is, in short, no evidence to support the belief that workers get less and capitalists more, or the opposite belief that workers obtain a greater part and capitalists a smaller part of the national income today than they did over sixty years ago in Canada.

CHECK LIST

When you have studied this chapter you should be able to

☐ Define economic rent and explain what determines the amount of economic rent paid.

☐ Explain why economic rent is a surplus (or unearned income); state the means that Henry George and the socialists would use to recover this surplus.

☐ Explain why the owners of land do not all receive the same economic rent; explain why, if economic rent is a surplus, a firm must pay rent.

☐ Define the interest rate and explain why interest rates differ.

☐ Define economic profit and distinguish between economic profit, normal profit, and business profit.

☐ Explain why profits are received by some firms; explain the functions of profits in the Canadian economy.

☐ State the current relative size of labour's and of capital's share of the national income; describe what has happened to these shares in the Canadian economy since 1926.

CHAPTER OUTLINE

1 Economic rent is the price paid for the use of land or natural resources whose supply is perfectly inelastic.

a. Demand is the active determinant of economic rent because changes in the level of economic rent do not change the quantity of land supplied: economic rent is, therefore, a payment which, in the aggregate, need not be paid to ensure that the land will be available.

b. Some people have argued that land rents are unearned incomes and that either land should be nationalized or rents should be taxed away. The single tax advocated by Henry George would have no effect upon resource allocation.

(1) Critics have pointed out three disadvantages of such a tax.

(2) But there is a renewed interest in taxing land values to improve the equity and efficiency of local tax systems.

c. Economic rents on different types of land vary because land differs in its productivity.

d. Land has alternative uses; thus, rent is a cost to a firm because it must pay rent to lure land away from alternative employments.

2 The interest rate is the price paid for the use of money.

a. While it is convenient to speak as though there were but a single interest rate, there are actually a number of different rates of interest.

b. The interest rate plays two roles.

(1) Because of the inverse relationship between the interest rate and total investment, the level of the interest rate affects the total

output of capital goods and the equilibrium GDP of an economy.

(2) The interest rate rations (allocates) financial and real capital among competing firms and determines the composition of the total output of capital goods.

3 Economic profit is what remains of the firm's revenues after all its explicit and implicit opportunity costs have been deducted.

a. Profit is a payment for entrepreneurial ability, which involves combining and directing the use of resources in an uncertain and innovating world.

b. Profits are

(1) rewards for assuming the risks in an economy in which the future is uncertain and subject to change;

(2) rewards for assuming the risks and uncertainties inherent in innovation; and

(3) surpluses that business firms obtain from the exploitation of monopoly power.

c. The expectation of profits motivates business firms to innovate, and profits (and losses) guide business firms to produce products and to use resources in the way desired by society.

4 National income data for the Canadian economy indicate that

a. in the period 1971–85, wages and salaries were 72% of the national income; but using a broader definition of labour income (wages and salaries plus net income of farmers and unincorporated businesses—which is mostly a payment for labour), labour's share was 80% and capital's share (rent, interest, and corporation profits) was 20% of national income;

b. since 1926, wages and salaries have increased from 58 to 72%.

(1) But labour's share, employing the broader definition of labour income, has remained at about 80% and capital's share at about 20% of the national income because of the structural changes that occurred in the Canadian economy.

(2) The growth of labour unions in Canada

does not explain the increases in the wages and salaries received by workers.

(3) The pursuit-and-escape theory may explain the stability of labour's and capital's shares of the national income.

IMPORTANT TERMS

Economic rent

Incentive function

Single-tax movement

The (*or* pure) rate of interest

Normal profit

Economic (pure) profit

Static economy

Insurable risk

Uninsurable risk

Pursuit-and-escape theory

FILL-IN QUESTIONS

1 Rent is the price paid for the use of __

_____

and _____ ,

and their total supply is _____ .

2 The active determinant of rent is (demand, supply) _____ and the

passive determinant is _____ .

Because rent does *not* perform a(n) (rationing, incentive) _____ function, economists consider it to be a _____ .

3 Socialists argue that land rents are (earned, unearned) _____ incomes

and that land should be _____ so that these incomes can be used for the good of society as a whole. Proponents of the

_____ argue that economic rent could be completely taxed away without affecting the amount of land available for productive purposes.

4 Rents on different pieces of land are not

the same because _____

_____ .
And while rent, from the viewpoint of the economy as a whole, is a surplus, rent is a cost to _____ users of land, which must be paid because land has _____ .

5 Interest is the price paid for the use of _____ .

6 Interest rates on different loans tend to differ because of differences in _____ , _____ , and _____ , and because of _____ .

7 In the Canadian economy at any moment, the money supply is an amount determined by _____ .

8 As far as the individual business firm is concerned, the profit-maximizing amount of financial and real capital to employ in producing goods and services is the amount at which the _____ and the expected rate of _____ _____ are equal.

9 In the Canadian economy the interest rate is an "_____ price"; but it performs two important functions. It helps to determine how much ____ _____ will occur in the economy and then _____ it among various firms and industries.

10 Normal profits are a payment for the resource called (land, labour, capital, entrepreneurial ability) _____ , and this resource performs four functions: it combines the other _____ to produce goods and services; it makes

(routine, non-routine) _____ decisions for the firm; it (invents, innovates) _____ products and production processes; and it bears the economic (costs, risks, criticisms) _____ associated with the other three functions.

11 When the future is _____ , entrepreneurs necessarily assume risks, some of which are _____ and some of which are _____ . The risks entrepreneurs cannot avoid arise either because the _____ _____ is changing or because the firm itself deliberately engages in _____ .

12 Profits
a. are important in the Canadian ecomomy because the expectation of profits stimulates firms to innovate, and the more innovation there is, the higher will be the levels of _____ , _____ , and _____ in the economy;

b. and losses promote the efficient _____ _____ of resources in the economy unless the profits are the result of (competition, monopoly) _____ .

13 Defining labour income broadly to include both wages and salaries *and* net income of farmers and unincorporated business (proprietors),
a. labour's share of the national income is today about _____ %;
b. the capitalists' share is the sum of _____ , _____ , and _____ ; and is today about _____ % of the national income.

c. Since 1926

(1) labour's share has (increased, decreased, remained constant) _____ ;

(2) capital's share has _____ .

14 The pursuit-and-escape theory suggests that

a. when workers increase their money wages they are in pursuit of the ____ _____ of business firms;

b. businesses escape by raising _____

and _____ ;

c. and that as a result _____ remains constant.

Land rent, dollars

0   Number of hectares

PROBLEMS AND PROJECTS

1 Assume that the quantity of a certain type of land available is 300,000 hectares and that the demand for this land is that given in the table below.

Pure land rent, per hectare	Land demanded, hectares
$350	100,000
300	200,000
250	300,000
200	400,000
150	500,000
100	600,000
50	700,000

a. The pure rent on this land will be $ ____ .

b. The total quantity of land rented will be _____ hectares.

c. On the following graph , plot the supply and demand curves for this land, and indicate the pure rent for land and the quantity of land rented.

d. If landowners were taxed at a rate of $250 per hectare for their land, the pure rent on this land after taxes would be $_____ but the number of hectares rented would be _____ .

2 The table below shows estimated wages and salaries, proprietors' income, corporate profits, interest, rent, and the national income of Canada in 1985.

Wages and salaries	$256 billion
Proprietors' income, including rent	24 billion
Corporate profits	40 billion
Interest	35 billion
Farm income	4 billion
National income	359 billion

a. Wages and salaries were _____% of the national income.

b. Labour's share of the national income was _____% , and capital's share was _____% .

SELF-TEST

Circle T if the statement is true, F if it is false.

1 Rent is the price paid for the use of land and other property resources. **T F**

2 Rent is a surplus because it does not perform an incentive function. **T F**

3 Rent is unique because it is not determined by demand and supply. **T F**

4 The renewed interest in land taxation is the result of the federal government's search for additional revenue to balance its budget. **T F**

5 Money is an economic resource, and the interest rate is the price paid for this resource. **T F**

6 A normal profit is the minimum payment the entrepreneur must expect to receive to induce him or her to provide a firm with entrepreneurial ability. **T F**

7 If the economists' definition of profits were used, total profit in the economy would be greater than they would be if the business executive's definition were used. **T F**

8 The expectation of profits is the basic motive for innovation, while actual profits and losses aid in the efficient allocation of resources. **T F**

9 The increasing importance of the corporation in the Canadian economy is a part of the explanation of why wages and salaries have increased and proprietors' incomes have decreased as shares of the national income. **T F**

10 The growth of labour unions is the main cause of the expansion of wages and salaries as a share of the national income. **T F**

11 Over the past sixty years, there has been a shift from labour-intensive to capital- and land-intensive production. **T F**

Circle the letter that corresponds to the best answer.

1 The supply of land is (*a*) perfectly inelastic; (*b*) of unitary elasticity; (*c*) perfectly elastic; (*d*) elastic but not perfectly elastic.

2 Which of the following is *not* characteristic of the tax proposed by Henry George? (*a*) it would be equal to 100% of all land rent; (*b*) it would be the only tax levied by government; (*c*) it would not affect the supply of land; (*d*) it would reduce rents paid by the amount of the tax.

3 A single tax on land in Canada would (*a*) bring in tax revenues sufficient to finance all current government spending; (*b*) be impractical because it is difficult to distinguish between payments for the use of land and those for the use of capital; (*c*) tax all "unearned" incomes in the economy at a rate of 100%; (*d*) be or do all of the above.

4 Which of the following is *not* true? (*a*) the greater the demand for land, the greater will be the economic rent paid for the use of land; (*b*) a "windfall profits" tax on the increases in the profits of petroleum producers that have resulted from the rise in oil prices would be a good example of tax on economic rent; (*c*) individual users of land have to pay a rent to its owners because that land has alternative uses; (*d*) the less productive a particular piece of land is, the greater will be the rent its owner is able to earn from it.

5 The smaller the *rate* of interest on a loan (*a*) the greater the risk involved; (*b*) the shorter the length of the loan; (*c*) the smaller the amount of the loan; (*d*) the greater the imperfections in the money market.

6 Changes in the rate of interest do *not* (*a*) affect the total amount of investment in the economy; (*b*) affect the amount of investment occurring in particular industries; (*c*) guarantee that the demand for and the supply of money will be equal; (*d*) guarantee that there will be full employment in the economy.

7 The profit-maximizing amount of financial and real capital an individual firm would employ is the amount at which the interest rate is equal to be (a) expected rate of net profit; (b) marginal physical product of capital; (c) marginal cost of capital; (d) marginal resource cost of capital.

8 If the rate of interest were 12% and the rate of net profit a firm expects to earn by building a new plant were 14%, the firm would (a) not build the new plant; (b) build the new plant; (c) have to toss a coin to decide whether to build the new plant; (d) not be able to determine, from these figures, whether to build the plant.

9 Which of the following is an economic cost? (a) business profit; (b) normal profit; (c) economic profit; (d) windfall profit.

10 Which of the following would *not* be a function of the entrepreneur? (a) the introduction of a new product on the market; (b) the making of decisions in a static economy; (c) the incurring of unavoidable risks; (d) the combination and direction of resources in an uncertain environment.

11 Business firms obtain profits because (a) not all risks are insurable; (b) not all markets are competitive; (c) the economy is dynamic; (d) all of these.

12 The monopolist who earns an economic profit is able to do so because (a) he or she is an innovator; (b) all the risks are insurable; (c) uncertainty has been reduced to the minimum; (d) most of his or her decisions are non-routine.

13 Since 1926 (a) capital's share of national income has increased; (b) labour's share has increased; (c) labour's share has decreased; (d) capital's share has been almost constant.

14 In the pursuit-and-escape theory, (a) labour attempts by obtaining higher wages to reduce the profits of business firms; (b) business firms prevent decreases in their profits by increasing the productivity of labour; (c) business firms prevent decreases in their profits by increasing the prices they charge consumers; (d) all of the above occur.

DISCUSSION QUESTIONS

1 Explain what determines the economic rent paid for the use of land. What is unique about the supply of land?

2 Why is land rent a "surplus"? What economic difficulties would be encountered if the government adopted Henry George's single-tax proposal as a means of confiscating this surplus? What arguments are used to support the renewed interest in the heavy taxation of land values?

3 Even though land rent is an economic surplus, it is also an economic cost for the individual user of land. Why and how can it be both an economic surplus and an economic cost?

4 What is the interest rate?

5 Why are there actually many different rates in the economy at any given time?

6 What two important functions does the rate of interest perform in the economy?

7 What are profits? For what resource are they a payment? What tasks does this resource perform?

8 Why would there be no economic profits in a purely competitive static economy?

9 "The risks an entrepreneur assumes arise because of uncertainties that are external to the firm and because of uncertainties that are developed by the initiative of the firm itself." Explain.

10 What two important functions do profits or the expectations of profits perform in the economy? Why does monopoly impede the effective performance of these functions?

11 Monopoly results in profits and reduces uncertainty. Is it possible that monopolists may undertake more innovation as a result? Why?

12 What part of the Canadian national income is wages and salaries and what part is labour income? Why do your answers to these two questions differ? What part of the national income is the income of capitalists? What kinds of income are capitalist income?

13 What have been the historical trends in the shares of national income that are wages and salaries, labour income, and capitalist income? What changes in the Canadian economy can account for these trends?

14 Explain (a) why the growth of labour unions is not a good explanation of the expanding share of the national income going for wages and salaries; (b) the pursuit-and-escape theory.

14

RURAL ECONOMICS: THE FARM PROBLEM

Probably no economic problem has aroused public interest to the extent and for the number of years that the farm problem has. It has concerned not only those directly engaged in agriculture or living and working in rural areas, but every Canadian consumer and taxpayer. Other problems seem to come and go; the farm problem seems always to have been with us.

Chapter 14 is devoted exclusively to an examination of the farm problem — the first of the four specific trouble spots studied in this part of the book. The chapter opens with a brief history of the experiences of Canadian farmers. The *symptoms* of the farm problem are declining farm prices, declining farm incomes, farm incomes that are low relative to the incomes of non-farm families, and a highly unequal distribution of farm income among farm families.

The symptoms of the farm problem, however, are not the same thing as the *causes* of the farm problem. If the problem is to be solved, it is necessary to understand what has occasioned the straits in which agriculture finds itself. In fact, as we point out, the failure to solve the problem has been brought about by the failure to understand and treat its causes. Actually, there are two farm problems, a long-run problem and a short-run problem. Each problem has its own particular causes, and the chapter deals with each of the two problems in turn.

The long-run problem is that, measured in constant dollars, farm prices and incomes have tended to decline over the years; the short-run problem is that farm prices and incomes have fluctuated sharply from year to year. To understand the causes of each of these problems, you will have to make use of the concept of inelastic demand and to employ your knowledge of how demand and supply determine price in a competitive market. The effort you put into the study of these tools in previous chapters will now pay a handsome dividend: you will understand the causes of a real-world problem and the policies designed to solve the problem.

The policies of the federal and provincial governments are directed at raising farm incomes by supporting farm prices.

Consumers pay higher prices for and consume smaller quantities of the various farm products; and at the prices supported by the federal government, there tended to be surpluses of some products. The federal government bought these surpluses to keep the price above the competitive market price. The purchases of the surpluses were financed by Canadian taxpayers. To eliminate these surpluses, government looked for ways to increase the demand for or to decrease the supply of these commodities and switched from the offers-to-purchase to the deficiency payments method, often coupling this with crop restrictions. From 1973 to 1975, booming grain exports gave Canadians reason to hope that at least part of the farm problem was solved. However, by 1976, the average farm income was again below the national average and considerably below the average by 1982.

CHECK LIST

When you have studied this chapter you should be able to

☐ Outline briefly the economic history of Canadian agriculture during the twentieth century.

☐ Compare per capita farm and non-farm income and rural and non-rural poverty; and describe the three different groups within the farm sector and the diversity of income among these three groups.

☐ Identify both the long-run and the short-run farm problem; and explain the four causes of the former and the cause of the latter problem.

☐ Explain why the long-run farm problem is the result of a misallocation of resources in a growing economy.

☐ Enumerate the several arguments that are made in support of government assistance to agriculture.

☐ Explain how the farm policies of the federal and provincial governments try to increase farm prices and incomes; explain the effect and the costs to the consumer and the taxpayer of policies of price supports and supply restriction.

☐ Present two major criticisms of the farm policy.

☐ Present the arguments for and against the contention that the world will not be able to feed itself by the year 2000.

CHAPTER OUTLINE

1 A history of Canadian agriculture in the twentieth century makes it clear that agricultural prices and farm incomes have fluctuated with changes in foreign and domestic demand and with changes in supply resulting from improvements in agricultural technology.

2 The evidence also makes it clear that farmers are, on the average, poorer than people not engaged in agriculture (and that poverty among farm families is more common than among non-farm families); that there is a great diversity of incomes among farmers (who, based on their annual sales and incomes, can be divided into three groups); and that this diversity among farmers makes it difficult to devise farm policies to benefit farmers.

3 The farm problem is both a long-run and a short-run problem: the long-run problem is the tendency for farm prices and incomes to lag behind the upward trend of prices and incomes in the rest of the economy; and the short-run problem is the frequent sharp changes in the incomes of farmers from one year to the next.

a. The causes of the long-run (low farm-income) problem are the inelastic demand for farm products, the large increases in the supply of these products relative to the modest increases in the demand for them, and the relative immobility of agricultural resources.

b. The causes of the short-run (income-instability) problem are the inelastic demand for farm products, fluctuations in the output of agricultural products, fluctuations in the domestic demand, and the unstable foreign demand, which result in relatively large changes in agricultural prices and farm incomes.

c. The long-run problem is, therefore, the result of four factors; and the short-run problem is the result of inelastic demand and changes in the demand for and the supply of farm products.

d. Another explanation of the long-run problem is that as the Canadian economy grew and improved its agricultural technology, it reallocated too small an amount of its resources away from agriculture and into the non-agricultural sectors of the economy.

4 Those who represent farmers claim that they have a special right to assistance from government. In addition to several other arguments it is claimed that

a. farmers have made it possible for the

Canadian economy to have more food and fibre at relatively lower prices and that the cost of this progress has been borne (in the form of lower relative incomes) by farmers; and

b. farmers have no control over the prices they receive (because they sell their products in competitive markets) but the prices they pay are controlled (by oligopolists who sell in non-competitive markets).

5 Farmers have been successful in obtaining various forms of public aid, and the policy of both the federal and provincial governments towards agriculture has included programs designed to raise and stabilize farm prices and incomes.
a. Farm products marketing boards were first established, federally and provincially, in the 1930s, the best known one being the Canadian Wheat Board.
b. The Agricultural Stabilization Board, established under federal law in 1958, supports the prices of several commodities at 90% of their average price over the previous five years. The Board buys outright, grants deficiency payments, and makes direct payments to producers.
c. Other important federal farm agencies are the Agricultural Products Board, Canadian Dairy Commission, Canadian Livestock Feed Board, and the National Farm Products Marketing Council.

6 The different effects of the two types of price supports—offers to purchase and deficiency payments—are explained, as are the reasons for crop restriction.

7 Pessimists and optimists answer very differently the question as to whether the future will bring feast or famine to the world.

8 Canada's international competitiveness in agriculture lies overwhelmingly in grains. Without our grain exports, Canada would have a food import surplus.

IMPORTANT TERMS

Farm problem

Long-run farm problem

Short-run farm problem

Agricultural Products Marketing Act

Agricultural Stabilization Board

Agricultural Products Board

National Farm Products Marketing Council

Price support

Offers to purchase

Deficiency payments

Crop restriction

FILL-IN QUESTIONS

1 What was the economic condition—prosperity, mediocre, or depression—of Canadian agriculture in each of the following periods?

a. 1901 to 1913: _____

b. 1914 to 1919: _____

c. 1920 to 1929: _____

d. 1930 to 1940: _____

e. 1941 to 1952: _____

f. 1953 to 1972: _____

g. 1973 to 1975: _____

h. 1978 to 1986: _____

2 The per capita farm income tends to be (greater, less) _____ than per capita non-farm income; and the incomes of the three different groups within the farm sector of the economy are (similar, diverse, highly unequal) _____ .
a. The farms with annual receipts of $50,000 or more from farming are (12, 28, 71) _____% of all farms and receive (12, 19, 77)_____% of the total annual receipts from farming.
b. Farms with annual receipts of less than $25,000 are _____% of all

farms and receive _____% of the total annual receipts from farming.

c. And the farms with annual receipts between $25,000 and $50,000 are

_____% of all farms and

receive _____% of the total annual receipts from farming.

3 The long-run farm problem is farm prices and incomes that (run ahead of, lag

behind) _____ the trends of prices and incomes in the rest of the economy; and the short-run problem is the

(stability, instability) _____ of farm prices and incomes from one year to the next.

4 The basic causes of the long-run farm

problem are the (elastic, inelastic) _____ demand for agricultural products, increases

in supply that have been (greater, less) __

_____ than the increases in demand, and

the relative (mobility, immobility) _____ of agricultural resources.

5 The demand for farm products tends to be inelastic because farm products have few

good _____ .

6 The supply of farm commodities has increased rapidly since about the time of

World War I because of _____ progress.

7 The demand for agricultural products in Canada has not increased as rapidly as the supply of these products because the popula-

tion of Canada has not _____

_____

and because as the income of Canadians has increased their expenditures for farm pro-

ducts has increased (more, less) _____ than proportionally.

8 The price system has failed to reallocate farmers into occupations earning higher incomes because as resources, farmers, their

land, and their capital are highly_____ .

9 The basic cause of the short-run farm

problem is the _____ demand for agricultural commodities. This contributes to unstable farm prices and incomes in two ways. Relatively (large, small)

_____ changes in the output of farm

products result in relatively _____ changes in farm prices and incomes; and

relatively _____ changes in demand

result in relatively _____ changes in prices and incomes.

10 As the Canadian economy has grown and improved its agricultural technology, it has

failed to reallocate *enough* _____

from _____ to _____ sectors of the economy.

11 Two of the reasons advanced to support the farmers' claim to assistance from the federal government are the contentions that the farmer

a. has borne too large a share of the cost of

_____ in Canada;

b. sells the commodities produced in (competitive, non-competitive) _____

markets and is, therefore, (able, unable)__

_____ to control the prices of these commodities.

12 Farm policy is partly designed to restrict

farm (prices and incomes, output) _____

_____ in order to increase farm _____ .

13 If a farmer produces a commodity supported under the Agricultural Stabilization Act, he or she will receive not less than

_____% of its average price over the previous _____ years.

14 If the government supports farm prices at an above equilibrium level, the result will be (shortages, surpluses) _____ , which the government must _____ in order to maintain prices at their support level.
a. Farmers benefit from this price-support program because it increases their _____ .
b. But consumers are hurt by it because they must pay higher _____ and higher _____ .

15 To bring the equilibrium level of prices in the market up to their support level, government has attempted to (increase, decrease) _____ the demand for and to _____ the supply of farm products.

16 In their role as consumers, the public will prefer (an offers-to-purchase, a deficiency payments) _____ price support program. In their role as taxpayers, the public (will, will not) _____ prefer one program to another because total payments by the public to farmers are (identical, more, less) _____ with offers-to-purchase compared to deficiency payments.

17 A noteworthy program employed by the federal government to reduce wheat production was the _____ in (year) _____ .

18 The farm program has not been successful in solving the farm problem because it has not sufficiently _____ resources and it most benefits those farmers whose incomes are (high, low) _____ .

19 From 1973 to 1975, there was a sharp increase in the (domestic, foreign) _____ demand for Canadian farm products.

20 Canada runs an annual agricultural (export, import) _____surplus.

21 Canada's agricultural exports lie overwhelmingly in _____ and _____ .

PROBLEMS AND PROJECTS

1 In columns 1 and 2 in the following table is a demand schedule for agricultural product X.

(1) Price	(2) Bushels of X demanded	(3) Bushels of X demanded
$8.00	600	580
7.20	620	600
6.40	640	620
5.60	660	640
4.80	680	660
4.00	700	680
3.20	720	700
2.40	740	720

a. Is demand elastic or inelastic in the price range given? _____
b. If the amount of X produced should increase from 600 to 700 bushels, the income of producers of X would _____ from $ _____ to $_____ ; an increase of _____% in the amount of X produced would cause income to _____ _____ by _____ %.
c. If the amount of X produced were 700 bushels and the demand for X decreased from that shown in columns 1 and 2 to that shown in columns 1 and 3, the price of X would _____ from $ _____

to $ _____; the income of farmers would _____ from $ _____ to $ _____.

d. Assume that the government supports a price of $7.20, that the demand for X is that shown in columns 1 and 2, and that farmers grow 720 bushels of X.

(1) At the supported price, there will be a surplus of _____ bushels of X.

(2) If the government buys this surplus at the support price, the cost to the taxpayers of purchasing the surplus is $ _____ .

(3) The total income of the farmers producing product X when they receive the support price of $7.20 per bushel for their entire crop of 720 bushels is $ _____ .

(4) Had farmers to sell the crop of 720 bushels at the free-market price, the price of X would be only $_____ per bushel; and the total income of these farmers would be $ _____.

(5) The gain to farmers producing X from the price-support program is therefore, $ _____ .

(6) In addition to the cost to taxpayers of purchasing the surplus, consumers pay a price that is $_____ greater than the free-market price and receive a quantity of X that is _____ bushels less than they would have received in a free market.

2 The demand schedule for agricultural product Y is given in columns 1 and 2 of the following table.

a. If farmers were persuaded by the government to reduce the size of their crop from 41,000 to 40,000 bales, the income of farmers would _____ from $_____ to $ _____ .

(1) Price	(2) Bales of Y demanded	(3) Bales of Y demanded
$5.00	40,000	41,000
4.75	40,200	41,200
4.50	40,400	41,400
4.25	40,600	41,600
4.00	40,800	41,800
3.75	41,000	42,000
3.50	41,200	42,200

b. If the crop remained constant at 41,000 bales and the demand for Y increased to that shown in columns 1 and 3, the income of farmers would _____ from $_____ to $ _____ .

3 The demand and supply schedules for agricultural product Z are shown below.

Pounds of Z demanded	Price	Pounds of Z supplied
850	$2.60	1,150
900	2.40	1,100
950	2.20	1,050
1,000	2.00	1,000
1,050	1.80	950
1,100	1.60	900
1,150	1.40	850

a. The government considers supporting the price of Z at $2.60 a pound through offers-to-purchase. At this price

(1) the quantity demanded is _____ pounds, the quantity supplied is _____ pounds, and the surplus is _____ pounds.

(2) buyers spend $ _____ for Z, the government spends $ _____ to purchase the surplus of Z, and the total income of the farmers who produce Z is $ _____ .

b. As an alternative to the offers-to-purchase program the government considers a deficiency-payments program with the support price set at $2.60 a pound.

(1) Knowing that they are going to receive $2.60 a pound for Z, farmers will produce _____ pounds of Z and when they sell this quantity of Z to demanders the market price of Z is $ _____ a pound.

(2) At this market price the buyers of Z will spend $ _____ for Z. The difference between the support price and the market price is $ _____ a pound, and the government will make a total cash deficiency payment of $ _____ to the producers of Z. The total income of the producers of Z from both buyers and the government is $ _____ .

c. Regardless of whether government supports the price of Z at $2.60 through offers-to-purchase or deficiency payments, the total income of the farmers who produce Z is $ _____. But if the government selects the deficiency-payments program,

(1) the cost of the program to the government is (more, less)_____ than the cost of the offers-to-purchase program by $_____;

(2) the buyers of Z obtain _____ pounds more of Z, pay a price that is $ _____ lower, and spend $ _____ (more/less) _____ on Z.

4 The demand and supply schedules for butter are shown in the following table.

Pounds of butter demanded	Price	Pounds of butter supplied
550	$2.60	1,150
700	2.40	1,100
850	2.20	1,050
1,000	2.00	1,000
1,150	1.80	950
1,300	1.60	900
1,500	1.40	850

a. The government considers supporting the price of butter at $2.60 a pound through offers-to-purchase. At this price

(1) the quantity demanded is _____ pounds, the quantity supplied is _____ pounds, and the surplus is _____ pounds;

(2) buyers spend $ _____ for butter, the government spends $ _____ to purchase the surplus of butter, and the total income of the farmers who produce butter is $ _____ .

b. As an alternative to the offers-to-purchase program the government considers a deficiency-payments program with the support price set at $2.60.

(1) Knowing that they are going to receive $2.60 a pound for butter, farmers will produce _____ pounds of butter and when they sell this quantity of butter to demanders the market price of butter is $ _____ a pound.

(2) At this market price the buyers of butter will spend $ _____ for butter. The difference between the support price and the market price is $ _____ a pound; and the government will make a total cash deficiency payment of $ _____ to the producers of butter. The total income of the producers of butter from both buyers and the government is $ _____ .

c. Regardless of whether government supports the price of butter at $2.60 through offers-to-purchase or deficiency payments, the total income of the farmers who produce butter is $ _____ . But if the government selects the deficiency-payments program,

(1) the cost of the program to the government is (more, less) _____ than the cost of the offers-to-purchase program by $ _____ ;

(2) the buyers of butter obtain _____ pounds more of butter, pay a price that is $_____ lower, and spend $ _____ (more/less) _____ on butter.

5
a. In Problem 3 above, the price elasticity of demand for product Z over the whole range of the schedule is found by use of this formula:

$$E_d = \frac{\text{change in quantity}}{\text{sum of quantities/2}} \div \frac{\text{change in price}}{\text{sum of prices/2}}$$

$$= \frac{1150 - 850}{(1150 + 850)/2} \div \frac{\$2.60 - \$1.40}{(\$2.60 + \$1.40)/2}$$

$$= \frac{300}{2000/2} \div \frac{1.20}{4.00/2}$$

$$= \frac{3}{10} \div \frac{1.20}{2.00}$$

$$= \frac{3}{10} \times \frac{10}{6}$$

$$= \frac{1}{2}.$$

This demand curve, therefore, is (elastic/inelastic) _____ .

b. In Problem 4 above, the price elasticity of demand for butter over the whole range of the schedule is:

$$\underline{\hspace{2cm}} \div \underline{\hspace{2cm}} = \underline{\hspace{2cm}}.$$

This demand curve, therefore, is _____ .

c. (1) In Problem 3, the offer-to-purchase program cost the government (more/less) _____ ; and here the demand was (elastic/inelastic) _____ .

(2) In Problem 3, the deficiency payments program cost the government (more/less) _____ ; and here the demand was (elastic/inelastic) _____ .

(3) From this we conclude that if the aim is for the government's cost to be as low as possible while ensuring the same total income for farmers, the offer-to-purchase program should be used when demand is _____ and the deficiency payment program when demand is _____ .

(4) From the consumers' point of view, the _____ program is always preferable, since they get _____ and pay a _____ price.

d. On two of the four graphs following, draw the supply and demand curves of Problem 3 and on the other two those of Problem 4. On each set of two graphs draw on one the rectangle representing the cost to the government of the offer-to-purchase program of that problem and on the other the cost to the government of the deficiency payment program.

(1) On the Problem 3 set, the smaller rectangle is the one for the _____ program.

(2) On the Problem 4 set, the smaller rectangle is the one for the _____ program.

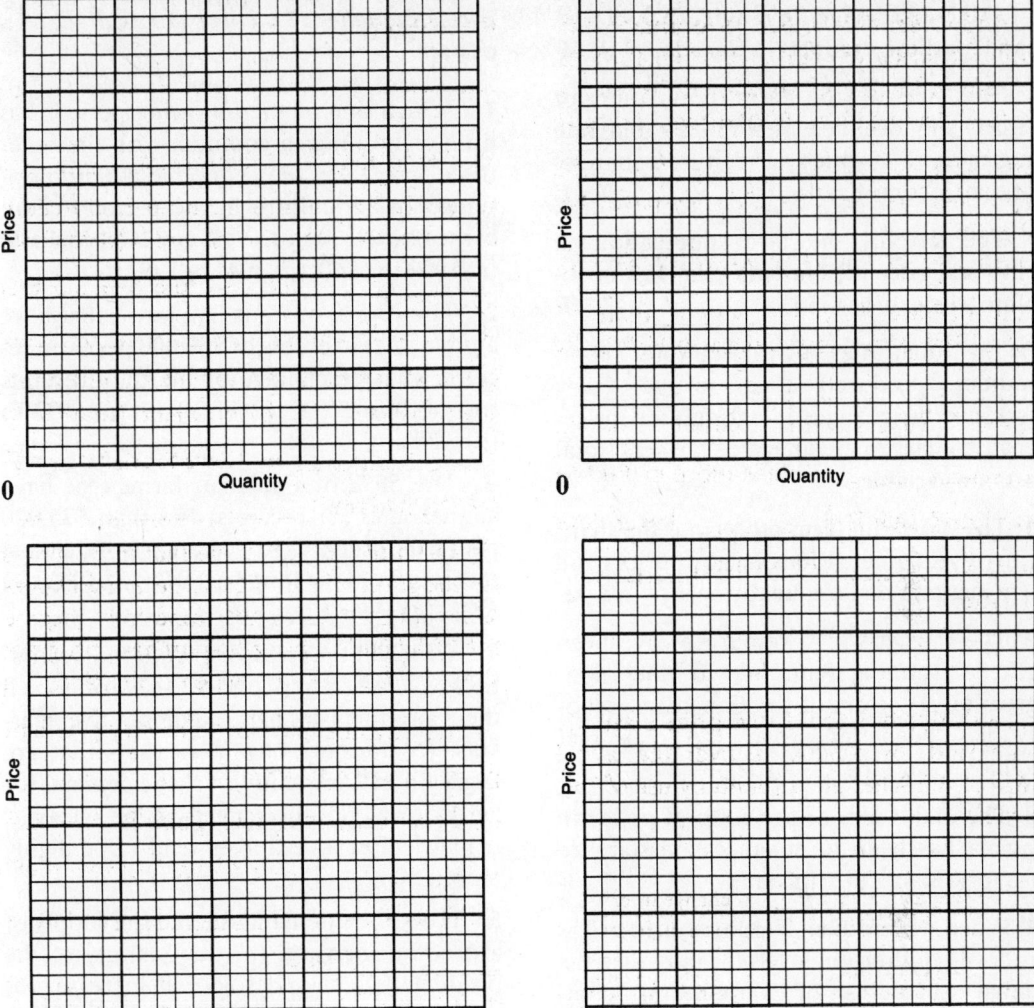

SELF-TEST

Circle T if the statement is true, F if it is false.

1 Per capita non-farm income is greater than per capita farm income. **T F**

2 A greater percentage of non-farm families live in poverty than farm families. **T F**

3 The diversity in farm incomes refers to the fact that a small percentage of the farms receives a large percentage of total farm income. **T F**

4 The diversity in the incomes of farm families simplifies the problem of formulating farm policies to enhance and stabilize farm prices and incomes. **T F**

5 The long-run farm problem is that the incomes of farmers have been low relative to incomes in the economy as a whole. **T F**

6 Most of the recent technological advances in agriculture have been initiated by farmers. **T F**

7 The supply of agricultural products has

tended to increase more rapidly than the demand for these products in Canada.   T F

8 The size of the farm population of Canada has declined at a more rapid rate than the rate at which agriculture's share of national income has declined.   T F

9 The size of the farm population in Canada has declined in both relative and absolute terms since 1950.   T F

10 The quantities of agricultural commodities produced tend to be fairly *insensitive* to changes in agricultural prices because a large percentage of farmers' total costs are variable.   T F

11 The short-run farm problem is the sharp year-to-year fluctuations in farm prices and farm incomes that frequently occur.   T F

12 The rate at which resources have been shifted from agricultural to the non-agricultural sectors of the Canadian economy has been less than the rate that technological progress made possible. T F

13 The major aim of agricultural policy in Canada has been to enhance and stabilize farm prices and farm incomes.   T F

14 When government supports farm prices at above-equilibrium levels it can reduce the annual surpluses of agricultural commodities either by increasing the supply or by decreasing the demand for them.   T F

15 Crop restriction is the only appropriate method for the government to use to boost farm incomes when supply is inelastic. T F

16 The deficiency payments method of price supports is appropriate when demand is elastic.   T F

17 As consumers, the public prefers the offers-to-purchase method of price support to deficiency payments.   T F

18 The offers-to-purchase method of price supports should be used when demand is elastic.   T F

Circle the letter that corresponds to the best answer.

1 Which one of the following periods has little or nothing in common with the other three insofar as the economic condition of Canadian agriculture in the period is concerned? (*a*) 1900 to 1913; (*b*) 1914 to 1919; (*c*) 1930 to 1940; (*d*) 1941 to 1952.

2 The 28.5% of Canadian farms that have annual sales in excess of $50,000 per farm receive what percentage of the total receipts from farming? (*a*) 12%; (*b*) 19%; (*c*) 33%; (*d*) 77%.

3 The 53% of Canadian farms that have annual sales (or receipts) less than $25,000 per farm receive what percentage of the total receipts from farming? (*a*) 9%; (*b*) 19%; (*c*) 33%; (*d*) 68%.

4 Which of the following is *not* characteristic of Canadian agriculture? (*a*) farmers sell their products in highly competitive markets; (*b*) farmers buy in markets that are largely non-competitive; (*c*) the demand for agricultural products tends to be inelastic; (*d*) agricultural resources tend to be highly mobile.

5 If both the demand for and the supply of a product increase, (*a*) the quantity of the product bought and sold will increase; (*b*) the quantity of the product bought and sold will decrease; (*c*) the price of the product will increase; (*d*) the price of the product will decrease.

6 Which one of the following is *not* a reason the increases in the demand for agricultural commodities have been relatively small? (*a*) the population of Canada has not increased as rapidly as the productivity of agriculture; (*b*) the increased per capita incomes of Canadian consumers have resulted in less than proportionate increases in their expenditures for farm products; (*c*) the demand for agricultural products is inelastic; (*d*) the standard of living in Canada is well above the level of bare subsistence.

7 The price system has failed to solve the problem of low farm incomes because (*a*) the demand for agricultural products is relatively inelastic; (*b*) the supply of agricultural products is relatively elastic; (*c*) agricultural products have relatively few good substitutes; (*d*) agricultural resources are relatively immobile.

8 If the demand for agricultural products is inelastic, a relatively small increase in supply will result in (*a*) a relatively small increase in farm prices and incomes; (*b*) a relatively small decrease in farm prices and a relatively large increase in farm incomes; (*c*) a relatively large decrease in farm prices and incomes; (*d*) a relatively large increase in farm prices and a relatively small decrease in farm incomes.

9 The year-to-year instability of farm prices and farm incomes is the result of fluctuations in (*a*) the outputs of farmers; (*b*) the domestic demand for farm products; (*c*) the foreign demand for agricultural commodities; (*d*) all of the above.

10 Which of the following is *not* one of the arguments used in support of public aid for agriculture in Canada? (*a*) farmers have had to bear a disproportionate part of the cost of economic progress; (*b*) farmers are subject to hazards to which other industries are not subject; (*c*) farmers sell their products in highly competitive markets; (*d*) farmers are more affected by competition from foreign producers than are other parts of the economy.

11 Deficiency payments mean that (*a*) the real income of the farmer remains constant; (*b*) through subsidies, the farmer enjoys a form of price support; (*c*) the purchasing power of the farmer's money income remains constant; (*d*) the money income of the farmer will buy a constant amount of goods and services.

12 Which statement is correct? (*a*) deficiency payments can lead to surpluses, which the government must then buy; (*b*) crop restriction is not appropriate if supply is elastic; (*c*) the offers-to-purchase method of price supports should not be used with an elastic demand; (*d*) consumers prefer the offers-to-purchase method of price supports.

Use the diagram below to answer multiple-choice questions 13 to 15. *D* is the demand for, and *S* is the supply of, a certain farm product.

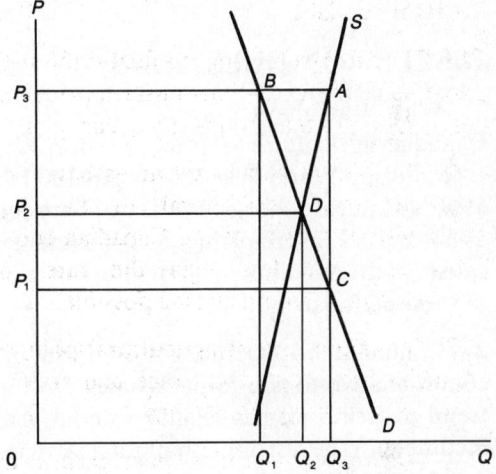

13 If the government supported the price of this product at P_3 through offers-to-purchase, the total amount it would have to spend to purchase the surplus of the product would be (*a*) $0Q_3AP_3$; (*b*) Q_1Q_3AB; (*c*) P_1CAP_3; (*d*) $0Q_1BP_3$.

14 If the government supported the price of this product at P_3, the total deficiency payments made by the government to producers of the product would be (*a*) $0Q_3AP_3$; (*b*) Q_1Q_3AB; (*c*) P_1CAP_3; (*d*) $0Q_1BP_3$.

15 Regardless of whether the government supports the price of the product at P_3 through offers-to-purchase or deficiency payments, the total income of producers of the product will be (a) $0Q_3AP_3$; (b) $0Q_1BP_3$; (c) $0Q_3CP_1$; (d) $0Q_2DP_2$.

16 Which one of the following is *not* a reason farm programs have been generally unsuccessful in accomplishing their aims? (a) the farm programs have not eliminated the basic cause of the problem; (b) restricting agricultural output increases farm prices but reduces farm income when demand is inelastic; (c) the human and non-human resources employed in agriculture have not been sufficiently reduced and reallocated; (d) the principal beneficiaries of government aid have been farmers with high, not low, incomes.

DISCUSSION QUESTIONS

1 What was the economic condition of Canadian agriculture (a) prior to World War I; (b) during World War I; (c) from 1930 to 1940; (d) during World War II; (e) between 1953 and 1972? Explain the fundamental causes of the condition of agriculture in each of these periods.

2 Comment on (a) the size of farm incomes relative to non-farm incomes; (b) the trend of farm incomes relative to non-farm incomes; (c) the distribution of total farm income among farmers.

3 What is the long-run farm problem; what are its specific causes? What is the short-run farm problem; what are its causes?

4 Why does the demand for agricultural products tend to be inelastic?

5 What have been the specific causes of the large increases in the supply of agricultural products since World War I?

6 Why has the demand for agricultural products failed to increase at the same rate as the supply of these products?

7 Explain why the farm population tends to be relatively immobile. If farmers were more mobile, how would the price system reallocate their labour away from agriculture and into more prosperous occupations?

8 Explain why the inelastic nature of the demand for and the supply of agricultural products results in prices and incomes that change by large amounts as a consequence of small changes in either demand or supply.

9 Why do agricultural interests claim that farmers have a special right to aid from government?

10 What devices does the government employ to support above-equilibrium agricultural prices? Why is the result of government-supported prices through offers-to-purchase invariably a surplus of farm commodities?

11 Explain why, as consumers, the public prefers price support through deficiency payments but, as taxpayers, the public does not prefer deficiency payments over offers-to-purchase.

12 Why has the farm program not been successful in preventing falling farm prices and incomes, surpluses, and an unequal distribution of farm income?

13 Give the arguments for and against the prediction that, by the turn of the century, the world will be unable to feed itself.

15

THE ECONOMICS OF INCOME DISTRIBUTION: INEQUALITY AND POVERTY

Chapter 15 examines the second of the so-called trouble spots in the Canadian economy—the unequal distribution of the total income of the economy among its families and the poverty of many of these families.

The things you should learn from this chapter are found in the "Check List" below. In addition to these things, the following ideas have an important bearing on the discussion of inequality and poverty. First, as you will see in Chapter 16, one of the functions of government in the Canadian economy is to modify the economic results that a *pure* price-market system would yield: it is the price-market system and the institutions of capitalism that bring about an unequal distribution of income, and government in Canada has worked to reduce—but by no means has eliminated—this unequal distribution.

Second, the critics of the price-market system (see Chapter 7) have attacked the system because it has unequally distributed income. But capitalism claims it has replied to its critics by repairing its faults. No group advocating a drastically different economic system has met with much success in Canada.

Third, the single most effective method of reducing the importance of income inequality and the extent of poverty in Canada has been the maintenance of full employment and an expanding average standard of living. Other programs have aided in the achievement of this goal, but the best cure has been the usually high and increasing output of the Canadian economy.

Fourth, very few people advocate an absolutely equal distribution of income; the question to be decided is not one of inequality or equality, but of how much or how little inequality there should be. The question can be looked at either ethically or economically, and economists have nothing to offer on the ethical question but their own personal value judgment. From the economic point of view, it is the task of economists to observe that less income inequality may result in a smaller domestic output and a lower employment rate. This is the big trade-off confronting the economy, and it requires that Canadians make a choice. The pros and cons of the income-inequality issue represent no more than different opinions on the degree to which we should reduce our economic efficiency (total output and employment) in order to reduce income inequality.

Finally, while poverty is caused by many forces, it is essentially an economic problem. Any attack on poverty will have to be basically an economic attack. There are reasons the problem of poverty may not be solved in Canada, but one of these reasons is not that the Canadian economy cannot afford to abolish poverty. The costs of poverty far outweigh the costs of eliminating it; and surely a rich nation can afford what it costs to provide the necessities of life for all of its citizens.

CHECK LIST

When you have studied this chapter you should be able to

☐ Present data from the textbook to support the conclusion that there is considerable income inequality in Canada.

☐ Report what has happened to the distribution of income in Canada since 1951.

☐ State what is measured on each axis when a Lorenz curve is used to describe the degree of income inequality; explain what area measures the extent of income inequality.

☐ Describe the effects of taxes and transfers on income distribution.

☐ Explain how much mobility between income classes there is in the short run (from one year to the next) and in the long run (from one generation to the next).

☐ Enumerate six causes of an unequal distribution of income.

☐ State the case *for* and the case *against* income equality; explain the trade-off between equality and efficiency that is at the heart of the debate over how much income inequality is desirable.

☐ Use current Statistics Canada standards to define poverty and to describe the extent of poverty in Canada; enumerate the groups in which poverty is concentrated; and explain why poverty tends to be invisible.

☐ List components of the Canadian social security system; list three criticisms levelled against this system.

☐ Explain how a negative income tax (NIT) might be employed to reduce poverty, and state the two crucial elements in any NIT plan.

☐ List the three goals of any NIT plan and explain why it is impossible to devise a program in which these three objectives do not conflict.

CHAPTER OUTLINE

1 There is considerable income inequality in the Canadian economy.

a. The extent of the inequality can be seen by examining a personal-distribution-of-income table.

b. Since 1951, the real incomes received by all income classes have increased but the relative distribution of personal income has barely changed at all; the income gap between the richest and the poorest families has widened.

c. The Lorenz curve is a geometric device for portraying the extent of inequality in any group at any time, for comparing the extent of inequality among different groups, and for contrasting the extent of inequality at different times.

d. The relative distribution of income after taxes is about the same as it was before taxes were collected; there is little movement in the short run and more than a little movement in the long run from one income class to another.

2 The impersonal price system does not necessarily result in a distribution of income that society deems just; at least six specific factors explain why income inequality exists.

3 The important question society must answer is not whether there will or will not be income inequality but what is the best amount of inequality.

a. Those who argue for equality contend that it leads to the maximum satisfaction of consumer wants (utility) in the economy.

b. But those who argue for inequality contend that equality would reduce the incentives to work, save, invest, and take risks; and that these incentives are needed if the economy is to be efficient: to produce as large an output (and income) as it is possible for it to produce from its available resources.

c. In the Canadian economy, there is a trade-off between economic equality and economic efficiency: a more nearly equal distribution of income results in less economic efficiency (a smaller real domestic output) and greater economic efficiency leads to a more unequal distribution of income. The debate over the right amount of inequality depends, therefore, upon how much output society is willing to sacrifice to reduce income inequality.

4 Aside from inequality in the distribution of income, there is great concern today with the problem of poverty in Canada.

a. Using Statistics Canada's definition of poverty, over 13% of the families and more than 36% of the individuals in the Canadian economy live in poverty; these poor tend to be concentrated among certain kinds of families.

b. Poverty in Canada tends to be invisible because it is obscured by the general affluence of the economy as a whole and hidden from the eyes of the remainder of society.

5 Canada's income-maintenance system consists of six principal programs.

a. The Old Age Security (OAS) Pension, for everyone on reaching the age of 65, and the Guaranteed Income Supplement (GIS), for those with no other income than the OAS.

b. The Canada and Quebec Pension Plans (CPP and QPP) at age 65; the amount of the pension depends on the size and number of the obligatory contributions previously made by the pensioner out of earnings.

c. Family Allowances, paid to mothers at so much a child.

d. Unemployment Insurance benefits, paid to the unemployed on the basis of previous contributions.

e. Health Insurance, which covers doctors' and hospital bills paid under provincial programs with federal assistance. Three provinces collect premiums from their citizens.

f. Welfare payments, covering assistance to disabled, handicapped, unemployed, and other needy persons not adequately provided for in the previous five programs.

g. The social insurance (or security) system has been criticized in recent years; and its critics argue that it impairs incentive to work, is abused by those who are not really in need and inequitably distributes benefits, and is costly to administer.

6 A new approach to income maintenance would employ a negative income tax (NIT) to subsidize families whose incomes are below a certain level.

a. In any NIT plan, a family would be guaranteed a minimum income and the subsidy to a family would decrease as its earned income increases. But a comparison of three alternative plans reveals that the guaranteed income, the (benefit-loss) rate at which the subsidy declines as earned income increases, and the (break-even) income at which the subsidy is no longer paid may differ.

b. The comparison of the plans also indicates there is a conflict among the goals of taking families out of poverty, maintaining incentives to work, and keeping the costs of the plan at a reasonable level; and that a trade-off among the three goals is necessary because none of the three plans can achieve all three goals.

c. A possible compromise plan would embody an increasing benefit-loss rate.

IMPORTANT TERMS

Income inequality	Guaranteed income supplement (GIS)
Lorenz curve	
Equality vs. efficiency (the big) trade-off	Family allowances
Poverty	Unemployment insurance benefits
Income-maintenance system	Health Insurance
Canada (Quebec) Pension Plan (CPP, QPP)	Negative income tax (NIT)
Old age security pension (OAS)	Guaranteed annual income
	Benefit-loss rate
	Break-even income

FILL-IN QUESTIONS

1 It can fairly be said that the extent of income inequality in Canada is _____ .

2 The percentage of total personal income received by the highest quintile since 1951 has (increased, decreased, barely changed) _____, and the percentage received by the lowest two quintiles has _____. These changes can fairly be said to have been (slight, significant) _____. Since 1951, the distribution of personal income in Canada (has, has not) _____ changed significantly.

3 Income inequality can be portrayed graphically by drawing a (Laffer, marginal utility, Lorenz) _____ curve.
a. When such a curve is plotted, the cumulative percentage of (income, families) _____ is measured along the horizontal and the cumulative percentage of _____ is measured along the vertical axis.
b. The curve that would show a completely (perfectly) equal distribution of income is a diagonal line, which would run from the (lower, upper) _____ left to the _____ right corner of the graph.
c. The extent or degree of income inequality is measured by the area that lies between the _____ and the _____ .

4 In Canada,
a. there is little noticeable difference in the before-_____ and the after-_____ distributions of income;
b. there is, in the short run, little _____ of income receivers between income classes;

c. a person's income status (is, is not)____ generally inherited.

5 The important factors that explain (or cause) income inequality are differences in _____; in _____ and _____; in job _____ and risk; in the ownership of _____; in market _____; and in luck, connections, misfortune, and discrimination.

6 Those who argue for the
a. equal distribution of income contend that it results in the maximization of total (income, utility) _____ in the economy;
b. unequal distribution of income believe it results in a greater total (income, utility) _____ .

7 The so-called "big trade-off" is between economic _____ and economic _____ . This means that
a. less income inequality leads to a (greater, smaller) _____ total output; and
b. a larger total output requires (more, less) _____ income inequality.

8 Using the Statistics Canada definition of poverty,
a. "the poor" includes any big-city family of four with less than $ _____ a year to spend;
b. approximately _____% of the families, and _____ % of the unattached individuals and about _____ million people are poor.

9 Poverty tends to be concentrated
a. among the (young, old) _____ ;
b. among (families, unattached individuals) _____ ;

c. in families headed by _____ ;

d. among those who are poorly _____ ;

e. in families in which the working members do not have _____ and _____ jobs;

f. in (large, small) _____ families.

10 What four reasons explain why, in the affluent Canadian economy, those living in poverty remain hidden or invisible?

a. _____

b. _____

c. _____

d. _____

11 The six parts of Canada's income maintenance system are: _____ pension, with the guaranteed _____ _____ ; the Canada and Quebec _____ ; family _____ ; unemployment _____ ; health _____ ; and _____ payments.

12 Critics of the income-maintenance system often refer to "the welfare mess" and point to its three *ins*: they contend that it is administratively *in*- _____ , is *in*-_____ , and impairs work *in*-_____ .

13 The two critical elements of any negative income tax plan are a _____ income below which family incomes would not be allowed to fall, and a _____ _____ rate that specifies the rate at which the subsidy would be reduced if earned income increases.

14 The three goals of any negative income tax plan

a. are to get families out of _____ , provide _____ to work, and assure the _____ of the program are reasonable;

b. are (complementary, conflicting) _____ _____ .

PROBLEMS AND PROJECTS

1 The distribution of personal income among families in a hypothetical economy is shown in the table below.

(1) Personal income class	(2) Percentage of all families in this class	(3) Percentage of total income received by this class	(4) Percentage of all families in this and all lower classes	(5) Percentage of total income received by this and all lower classes
Less than $5,000	18	4	_____	_____
5,000–9,999	12	6	_____	_____
10,000–14,999	14	12	_____	_____
15,000–19,999	17	14	_____	_____
20,000–24,999	19	15	_____	_____
25,000–49,999	11	20	_____	_____
50,000 or more	9	29	_____	_____

a. Complete the table by computing
(1) the percentage of all families in each income class and all lower classes; enter these figures in column 4;
(2) the percentage of total income received by each income class and all lower classes; enter these figures in column 5.
b. From the distribution of income data in columns 4 and 5, it can be seen that
(1) families with less than $10,000 a year income constitute the lowest _____% of all families and receive _____% of the total income;
(2) families with incomes of $25,000 a year or more constitute the highest _____% of all families and receive _____% of the total income.
c. Use the figures you entered in columns 4 and 5 to draw a Lorenz curve on the graph below. (Plot the seven points and the zero-zero point and connect them with a smooth curve.)

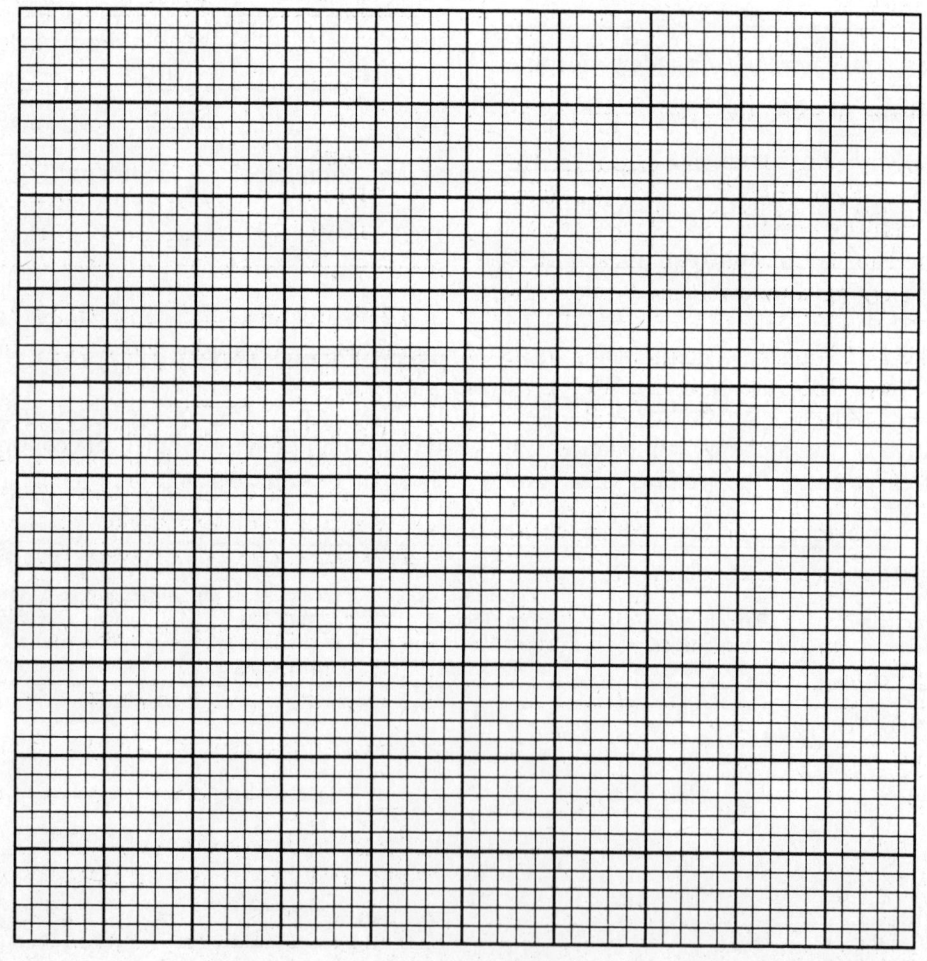

0

(1) On the same graph, draw the diagonal line that would indicate complete equality in the distribution of income.

(2) Shade the area of the graph that shows the degree of income inequality.

2 Following is a table containing different possible earned incomes for a family of a certain size.

Earned income	NIT subsidy	Total income
$ 0	$5,000	$5,000
5,000	_____	_____
10,000	_____	_____
15,000	_____	_____
20,000	_____	_____
25,000	_____	_____

a. Assume that $5,000 is the guaranteed annual income for a family of this size and that the benefit-loss rate is 20%. Enter the NIT subsidy and the total income at each of the five remaining earned-income levels. (*Hint*: 20% of $5,000 is $1,000.)

(1) This NIT program retains strong incentives to work because whenever the family earns an additional $5,000, its total income increases by $_____.

(2) But this program is costly because the family receives a subsidy until its earned income, the break-even income, is $ _____ .

b. To reduce the break-even income, the benefit-loss rate is raised to 50%. Complete the next table.

Earned income	NIT subsidy	Total income
$ 0	$5,000	$5,000
2,500	_____	_____
5,000	_____	_____
7,500	_____	_____
10,000	_____	_____

(1) This program is less costly than the previous one because the family only receives a subsidy until it earns the break-even income of $_____;

(2) but the incentives to work are less because whenever the family earns an additional $5,000, its total income increases by only $_____.

c. Both of the previous two NIT programs guaranteed an income of only $5,000. Assume the guaranteed income is raised to $7,500 and that the benefit-loss rate is kept at 50%. Complete the table below.

Earned income	NIT subsidy	Total income
$ 0	$7,500	$7,500
3,000	_____	_____
6,000	_____	_____
9,000	_____	_____
12,000	_____	_____
15,000	_____	_____

(1) This program is more costly than the previous one because the break-even income has risen to $_____.

(2) The incentives to earn additional income are no better in this program than in the previous one. But to improve these incentives by reducing the benefit-loss rate to 40% would raise the break-even income to $_____. (*Hint*: divide the guaranteed income by the benefit-loss rate.)

d. To summarize:

(1) given the guaranteed income, the lower the benefit-loss rate the (greater, less) ____ _____ are the incentives to earn additional income and the (greater, less) _____ is the break-even income and the cost of the NIT program;

(2) and given the benefit-loss rate, the greater the guaranteed income, the (greater,

less) _____ is the break-even income and the cost of the program;

(3) but to reduce the break-even income and the cost of the program requires either a(n)

(increase, decrease) _____ in the

benefit-loss rate or a(n) _____ in the guaranteed income.

SELF-TEST

Circle T if the statement is true, F if it is false.

1 According to the text, there is considerable income inequality in Canada. **T F**

2 Since 1951, the percentage of total personal income received by families and unattached individuals in the highest income quintile has decreased by several percentage points. **T F**

3 In drawing a Lorenz curve, the percentage of families in each income class is measured along the horizontal axis and the percentage of the total income received by those families is measured on the vertical axis. **T F**

4 In percentage or relative terms, the before-tax and after-tax distributions of income in Canada are approximately the same. **T F**

5 There appears to be little mobility between income classes from one generation to the next and considerable mobility between income classes from one year to the next. **T F**

6 Using Statistics Canada's definition of poverty, some 37% of the unattached individuals in Canada were poor in 1985. **T F**

7 Those who favour equality in the distribution of income contend that equality will lead to stronger incentives to work, save, invest, and take risks and to a greater domestic output and income. **T F**

8 In the trade-off between equality and economic efficiency, an increase in efficiency requires a decrease in inequality. **T F**

9 Using Statistics Canada's definition of poverty, over 13% of the families of Canada were poor in 1985. **T F**

10 Evidence suggests that the vast majority of the poor who obtain public assistance (welfare) are unable to support themselves. **T F**

11 Those who have been critical of the Canadian system of income maintenance contend that the welfare system impairs incentives to work. **T F**

12 In the NIT program, the benefit-loss rate is the rate at which subsidy benefits decrease as the earned income of a family increases. **T F**

13 The lower the benefit-loss rate, the smaller are the incentives to earn additional income. **T F**

Circle the letter that corresponds to the best answer.

1 Approximately what percentage of all Canadian families have personal incomes of $45,000 and over annually? (*a*) 5%; (*b*) 15%; (*c*) 25%; (*d*) 31%.

2 Approximately what percentage of all Canadian families have personal incomes of less than $10,000 a year? (*a*) 4%; (*b*) 6%; (*c*) 14%; (*d*) 20%.

3 Which of the following would be evidence of a decrease in income inequality in Canada? (*a*) a decrease in the percentage of total personal income received by the lowest quintile; (*b*) an increase in the percentage of total personal income received by the highest quintile; (*c*) an increase in the percentage of total personal income received by the four lowest quintiles; (*d*) a decrease in the percentage of total personal income received by the four lowest quintiles.

4 When a Lorenz curve has been drawn,

the degree of income inequality in an economy is measured by (*a*) the slope of the diagonal that runs from the southwest to the northeast corner of the diagram; (*b*) the slope of the Lorenz curve; (*c*) the area between the Lorenz curve and the axes of the graph; (*d*) the area between the Lorenz curve and the southwest-northeast diagonal.

5 In the post-World Ware II period, there has been (*a*) a significant decrease in the percentage of total personal income received by the highest quintile; (*b*) a significant increase in the percentage of total personal income received by the lowest quintile; (*c*) a significant increase in the percentage of total personal income received by the middle three quintiles; (*d*) no significant change in the percentage of total personal income received by any of the five quintiles.

6 Which of the following is *not* one of the causes of the unequal distribution of income in Canada? (*a*) the unequal distribution of property; (*b*) in-kind transfers; (*c*) the inability of the poor to invest in human capital; (*d*) luck and the unequal distribution of misfortune.

7 Suppose that Ms. Anne obtains 5 units of utility from the last dollar of income received by her and that Mr. Charles obtains 8 units of utility from the last dollar of his income. Those who favour an equal distribution of income would (*a*) advocate redistributing income from Charles to Anne; (*b*) advocate redistributing income from Anne to Charles; (*c*) be content with this distribution of income between Anne and Charles; (*d*) argue that any redistribution of income between them would increase total utility.

8 Poverty does not have a precise definition, but Statistics Canada's definition of "poor" is any family of four living in a big city and with less to spend annually than (approximately) (*a*) $20,800; (*b*) $10,200; (*c*) $13,100; (*d*) $8,900.

9 Which of the following is *not* a cause of the invisibility of the Canadian poor? (*a*) poverty in the cities is not easily seen from the more common means of transportation; (*b*) poverty in rural areas is not easily seen from the more common means of transportation; (*c*) poverty among the old and sick is not easily seen because these people seldom emerge from their dwelling places; (*d*) poverty among the unemployed is more than offset by unemployment insurance benefits.

10 Which of the following is one of the parts of the Canadian income-maintenance system? (*a*) public housing; (*b*) agricultural subsidies; (*c*) unemployment insurance; (*d*) minimum-wage laws.

11 Which of the following is designed to provide a nationwide income for all those aged 65 and over? (*a*) Canada Pension Plan; (*b*) Guaranteed Income Supplement; (*c*) Canada Assistance Plan; (*d*) Old Age Security Pension.

12 A negative income tax would (*a*) reduce incentives to work; (*b*) fail to eliminate poverty; (*c*) be too costly; (*a*) result in at least one but not necessarily all of the above.

DISCUSSION QUESTIONS

1 How much income inequality is there in the Canadian economy? Cite figures to support your conclusion. What causes income inequality in capitalism?

2 Has the distribution of income changed in Canada during the past 30 years? What does this imply about the efficiency of Canada's social insurance system?

3 What is measured along each of the two axes when a Lorenz curve is drawn? If the distribution of income were completely equal, what would the Lorenz curve look like? If one family received all of the income of the economy, what would the Lorenz curve look like? After the Lorenz curve for an economy has been drawn, how is the degree of income inequality in that economy measured?

4 How do taxes affect the relative distribution of income in Canada? Does the passage of time tend to change the income class in which a family is located?

5 State the case for an equal distribution of income and the case for an unequal distribution. What would be traded for what in the "big trade-off"?

6 What is the currently accepted and more or less official definition of poverty? How many people and what percentage of the Canadian population are poor if we use this definition of poverty?

7 What characteristics—other than the small amounts of money they have to spend—do the greatest concentrations of the poor families of the nation *tend* to have?

8 Why does poverty in Canada tend to be invisible or hidden?

9 What are the programs embodied in the social insurance or security system of Canada? Explain why this system has been called a "welfare mess" by its critics.

10 Explain how poverty and the unequal distribution of income would be reduced by a negative income tax. In your explanation, be sure to include definitions of guaranteed income, the benefit-loss rate, and break-even income.

11 What are the three goals or objectives of any NIT plan? Explain why there is a conflict among these objectives—why all three goals cannot be achieved simultaneously.

16

MIXED CAPITALISM AND THE ECONOMIC FUNCTIONS OF GOVERNMENT

Chapter 16 introduces you to the six basic functions performed by federal, provincial, and local governments in Canada's mixed capitalistic economy. This is an examination of the actual role of government (the public sector) in an economy that is neither a purely planned nor a purely market-type economy. The discussion points out the degree to and the ways in which government causes the Canadian economy to differ from pure capitalism. The chapter does not attempt to list all the *specific* ways in which government affects the behaviour of the economy. Instead, it provides a *general* classification of the tasks performed by government.

Following an explanation of each of the six functions of government in the Canadian economy, the chapter attempts to evaluate the economic role of government in Canada. Here it is pointed out that people generally agree that government should perform these functions. But they disagree on how far government should go in performing them and over whether specific government actions and programs are needed for government to perform these functions.

Governments today frequently employ benefit-cost analysis to determine whether they should or should not undertake some specific action—a particular act, project, or program. This kind of analysis forces government to estimate both the added costs and the additional benefits of the project or program; to expand its activities only where the additional benefits exceed the added costs; and to reduce or eliminate programs

and projects when the added costs exceed the additional benefits.

The latter part of Chapter 16 examines two important questions that are related to the economic role of government in the Canadian economy. The first question is whether government fails to solve social problems because the process it uses to make decisions is an inherently inefficient mechanism for allocating resources. The question is whether there has been a public sector failure; and you are given some of the reasons that the public sector's decision-making process may result in a misallocation of resources in the economy. The second question is whether an increase in the size of government's role in the economy reduces or expands the freedoms of the individual members of Canadian society. Two cases are presented: that of those who argue that expanded governmental activity reduces personal freedom and that of those who contend it may actually lead to greater individual freedom.

CHECK LIST

When you have studied this chapter you should be able to

☐ Explain in one or two sentences why the Canadian economy is *mixed* rather than *pure* capitalism.

☐ Enumerate the six economic functions of government in Canada and explain the difference between the purpose of the first two and the purpose of the last four functions.

☐ Define monopoly and explain why government wishes to prevent monopoly and to preserve competition in the economy.

☐ Explain why government believes it should redistribute income, and list the three principal policies it employs for this purpose.

☐ Define a spillover cost and a spillover benefit; explain why a competitive market fails to allocate resources efficiently when there are spillovers; and list the things government may do to reduce spillovers and improve the allocation of resources.

☐ Determine, when given the necessary data, the price (emission fee) a government agency should charge for pollution rights.

☐ Define a public good and a private good and explain how government goes about reallocating resources from the production of private to the production of public goods.

☐ Draw a circular flow diagram that includes businesses, households, and government; label all the flows in the diagram; and use the diagram to explain how government alters the distribution of income, the allocation of resources, and the level of activity in the economy.

☐ Use benefit-cost analysis to determine the extent to which government should apply resources to a project or activity when you are given the cost and benefit data.

☐ Explain what is meant by "public sector failure" and list several possible causes of this alleged failure.

☐ Present briefly the case for and the case against the proposition that an expanded public sector reduces personal freedom.

CHAPTER OUTLINE

1 The Canadian economy is neither a pure market economy nor a purely planned economy. It is an example of mixed capitalism, in which government affects the operation of the economy in important ways.

2 Government in the Canadian economy performs six economic functions. The first two of these functions are designed to enable the price system to operate more effectively; and the other four functions are designed to eliminate the major shortcomings of a purely market-type economy.

3 The first of these functions is to provide the legal and social framework that makes the effective operation of the price system possible.

4 The second function is the maintenance of competition and the regulation of monopoly.

5 Government performs its third function when it redistributes income to reduce income inequality.

6 When government reallocates resources it performs its fourth function.
a. It reallocates resources to take account of spillover costs and benefits.
b. To reduce pollution requires that the costs of pollution be made private instead of social costs (be transferred from society to the polluter); and this may be accomplished by legislated standards, by levying special taxes on polluters, or by creating a market for pollution rights.
c. It also reallocates resources to provide society with public (social) goods and services.
d. It levies taxes and uses the tax revenues to purchase or produce the public goods.

7 Its fifth function is stabilization of the price level and the maintenance of full employment.

8 Its sixth function is nation-building: encouraging, subsidizing, or carrying out itself large projects of general benefit to the country that private enterprise would not attempt alone, if at all.

9 A circular flow diagram that includes the public sector as well as business firms and households in the private sector of the economy reveals that government purchases public goods from private businesses, collects taxes from and makes transfer payments to these firms, purchases labour services from households, and collects taxes from and makes transfer payments to these households; and government can alter the distribution of income, reallocate resources, and change the level of economic activity by affecting the six flows in the diagram.

10 In evaluating government's role in the economy it should be noted that

a. it is generally agreed that it is desirable for government to perform these six functions; but there is a good deal of controversy about how far it should go in performing them.

b. Benefit-cost analysis may be employed by government to determine whether it should employ resources for a project and to decide upon the total quantity of resources it should devote to a project. Additional resources should be devoted to a project only so long as the marginal benefit to society from using the additional resources for the project exceeds the marginal cost to society of the additional resources.

c. In using benefit-cost analysis, however, government encounters the problem of measuring benefits and costs accurately.

11 Critics of the governmental or public sector of the economy argue that this sector has failed to find solutions for social problems; and the theory of public choice suggests that the public sector has failed because the process it uses to make decisions is inherently weak and results in an economically inefficient allocation of resources.

a. The weakness of the decision-making process in the public sector and the resulting inefficient allocation of resources is often the result of pressures exerted on government and the bureaucracy by special interests.

b. Those seeking election to public office frequently favour (oppose) programs whose benefits (costs) are clear and immediate and whose costs (benefits) are uncertain and deferred even when the benefits are less (greater) than the costs.

c. When the citizen must vote for candidates who represent different but complete programs, the voter is unable to select those parts of a program that he or she favours and to reject the other parts of the program.

d. It is argued that the public sector (unlike the private sector) is inefficient because those employed there are offered no incentive to be efficient; and because there is no way to measure efficiency in the public sector.

e. Just as the private or market sector of the economy does not allocate resources perfectly, the public sector does not perform its functions perfectly; and the imperfections of both sectors make it difficult to determine which sector will provide a particular good or service more efficiently.

12 The nature and amount of government activity and the extent of individual freedom may be related to each other.

IMPORTANT TERMS

Market economy	Benefit-cost analysis
Planned economy	Public sector
Mixed capitalism	Public-sector failure
Emission fees	Theory of public choice
Market for pollution rights	
Peak pricing	Special-interest effect
User charge	Fallacy of limited decisions

FILL-IN QUESTIONS

1 All actual economies are "mixed" because they combine elements of a _____ _____ economy and a _____ economy.

2 List the six economic functions of government:

a. _____

b. _____

c. _____

d. _____

e. _____

f. _____

3 To control monopoly in Canada, government has

a. created commissions to _____ the prices and the services of the _____ monopolies; and taken over at the provincial and local levels the _____ of electric and water companies;

b. enacted _____ laws to maintain competition.

4 The price system, because it is an impersonal mechanism, results in an (equal, unequal) _____ distribution of income. To redistribute income from the upper- to the lower-income groups, the federal government has

a. enacted _____ programs;

b. engaged in _____ intervention;

c. used the _____ tax to raise much of its revenues.

5 Government frequently reallocates resources when it finds instances of _____ failure; and the two major cases of such failure occur when the competitive price system either

a. _____ or

b. _____.

6 It has been suggested that to relieve highway congestion there be _____ on drivers and that _____ policies should be used on expressways and mass transit systems.

7 To reallocate resources from the production of private to the production of public goods government reduces the demand for private goods by _____ consumers and firms and then _____ public goods.

8 To stabilize the economy, government,

a. when there is less than full employment (increases, decreases) _____ aggregate spending by (increasing, decreasing) _____ _____ its expenditures for public goods and services and by (increasing, decreasing) _____ taxes;

b. when there are inflationary pressures _____ aggregate spending by _____ its expenditures for public goods and services by _____ taxes.

9 Throughout most of its history, government in Canada has performed in some degree each of the six functions except that of_____ .

10 In applying benefit-cost analysis, government should employ more resources in the public sector if the marginal (costs, benefits) _____ from the additional public goods exceed the marginal (costs, benefits) _____ that result from having fewer private goods.

11 When government employs benefit-cost analysis it often finds that

a. it is difficult to _____ the benefits and the costs of a program;

b. the program not only reallocates resources but also results in spillover _____ and _____ .

12 When governments use resources to attempt to solve social problems and the employment of these resources does not result in solutions to these problems, there has been _____

sector _____ .

13 Four possible reasons for public-sector failure are
a. that government, instead of promoting the general interests (or welfare) of its citizens, may promote the _____ interests of small groups in the economy;
b. that the benefits from a program or project are often (clear, hidden) _____ ;

and its costs are frequently _____ ;
c. that individual voters are unable to

_____ the particular quantities of each public good and service they wish the public sector to provide;

d. that there are weak _____ to be efficient in the public sector and no way

to _____ the efficiency of the public sector.

14 Those who allege that there are inherent deficiencies in the processes used to make decisions in the public sector and that these deficiencies produce economic inefficiency

are interested in the theory of public _____ .

15 Despite the recognition of inefficiency in the public sector,
a. it should be recognized that there is also

inefficiency in the _____ of the economy;
b. the institutions employed in both sectors

to allocate resources are _____ ;
c. it is, therefore, difficult to determine to

which sector the production of a particular good or service should be _____ .

16 To reason that increased governmental activity necessarily reduces private economic activity is an example of the fallacy of ____

_____ .

PROBLEMS AND PROJECTS

1 Below is a list of various government activities. Indicate in the space to the right of each into which of the six classes of government functions the activity falls. If the activity falls under more than one of the six functions, indicate this.

a. Maintaining an army. _____
b. Providing for a system of unemployment-insurance benefits. _____

c. Establishing the Bank of Canada.

_____
d. Insuring employees of business firms

against industrial accidents. _____
e. Establishing a Combines Investigation Branch in the Department of Consumer and

Corporate Affairs. _____
f. Making it a crime to sell stocks and bonds

under false pretences. _____

g. Providing Family Allowances. _____

_____

h. Taxing whisky and other spirits. _____

_____
i. Regulating organized stock, bond, and

commodity markets. _____
j. Setting tax *rates* higher for large incomes

than for smaller ones. _____

k. Building the St. Lawrence Seaway. ____

_____ .

2 Following is a table showing the average number of motor vehicles travelling each kilometre of expressway in a hypothetical metropolitan area, and the estimated cost to society of each vehicle-kilometre travelled during various periods of the day. Compute the total cost per kilometre of highway in each of the seven periods of the day.

a. In every twenty-four-hour period, the total number of vehicles travelling each kilometre of expressway is _____ and the total cost for each kilometre of highway travelled is $ _____.

b. The average cost to society for a vehicle to travel one kilometre is $_____.

c. Assuming that the number of vehicles per highway-kilometre is not affected by the imposition of a user charge and that the user charge is the same during all periods, the user charge that would enable society to recover the full cost of the highway system would be $ _____ per vehicle-kilometre.

Period of the day	Vehicles per highway-kilometre	Cost per vehicle-kilometre	Total cost
7 am–9 am	500	$ .60	$_____
9 am–12 noon	150	.10	_____
12 noon–2 pm	200	.15	_____
2 pm–4 pm	100	.10	_____
4 pm–6 pm	600	.85	_____
6 pm–10 pm	200	.15	_____
10 pm–7 am	50	.10	_____

d. Imagine now that the imposition of this user charge results in the following change in vehicular traffic during the various periods of the day. The cost per vehicle-kilometre remains the same in each period; the total cost in each period is shown in the table following.

Period of the day	Vehicles per highway-kilometre	Total cost	Total revenue
7 am–9 am	450	$270.00	$_____
9 am–12 noon	135	13.50	_____
12 noon–2 pm	180	27.00	_____
2 pm–4 pm	90	9.00	_____
4 pm–6 pm	540	459.00	_____
6 pm–10 pm	180	27.00	_____
10 pm–7 am	45	4.50	_____

(1) The total cost per day of each kilometre of highway is $ _____.

(2) Compute the total revenue in each period when a 50 cents-per-kilometre user charge is made. The total revenue per day on each kilometre of highway is $ _____.

(3) In what two periods are the revenues received less than the cost in that period?

_____ and _____ .

e. If it is desired to reduce the number of vehicles per kilometre of highway in these two periods to 400, and if each 1 cent increase in the user charge decreases the number of vehicles per kilometre by 10 vehicles, the user charge in the

(1) 7 am–9 am period should be increased to

_____ cents per kilometre;

(2) 4 pm–6 pm period should be increased

to _____ cents per kilometre.

3 Assume the atmosphere of Metropolitan Toronto is able to reabsorb 1,500 tonnes of pollutants per year. The following schedule shows the price polluters would be willing to pay for the right to dispose of 1 tonne of pollutants per year, and the total quantity of pollutants they would wish to dispose of at each price.

Price (per tonne of pollutant rights)	Total quantity of pollutant rights demanded (tonnes)
$ 0	4,000
1,000	3,500
2,000	3,000
3,000	2,500
4,000	2,000
5,000	1,500
6,000	1,000
7,000	500

a. If there were no emission fee, polluters would put _____ tonnes of pollutants in the air each year; this quantity of pollutants would exceed the ability of nature to reabsorb them by _____ tonnes.

b. To reduce pollution to the capacity of the atmosphere to recycle pollutants, an emission fee of $_____ per tonne should be set.

c. Were this emission fee set, the total emission fees collected would be $ _____ .

d. Were the quantity of pollution rights demanded at each price to increase by 500 tonnes, the emission fee could be increased by $_____ and total emission fees collected would increase by $ _____ .

4 The circular flow diagram below includes business firms, households, and government (the public sector).

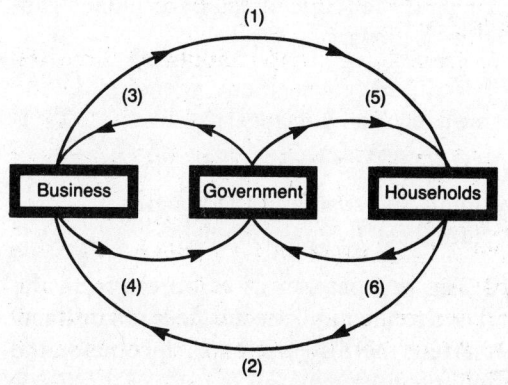

a. The flow labelled

(1) is the expenditures of (households, businesses, government) _____ for (products, resources) _____ obtained from _____ ;

(2) is the expenditures of _____ for _____ obtained from _____ ;

(3) is the expenditures of _____ for _____ obtained from _____ ;

(4) is the taxes minus the transfer payments collected by government from _____ ;

(5) is the expenditures of _____ for _____ obtained from _____ ; and

(6) is the taxes minus the transfer payments collected by government from _____ .

b. If government wished to

(1) expand output and employment in the economy, it would increase flows _____ or _____ , decrease flows _____ , or do both;

(2) increase the production of public (social) goods and decrease the production of private goods in the economy, it would increase flows _____ and _____ or _____ ;

(3) redistribute income from high-income to low-income households, it would (increase, decrease) _____ the taxes minus transfers paid by the former and _____ the taxes minus transfers paid by the latter in flow _____.

5 Imagine that a provincial government is considering the construction of a new highway to link its two largest cities. Its estimate

Project	Total cost	Marginal cost	Total benefit	Marginal benefit
No highway	$ 0		$ 0	
2-lane highway	500	$_____	650	$_____
4-lane highway	680	_____	750	_____
6-lane highway	760	_____	800	_____
8-lane highway	860	_____	825	_____

of the total costs and the total benefits of building two-, four-, six-, and eight-lane highways between the two cities is shown in the table above.(All figures are in millions of dollars).

a. Compute the marginal cost and the marginal benefit of the two-, four-, six-, and eight-lane highways.

b. Will it benefit the province to allocate resources to construct a highway? _____

c. If the province builds a highway,

(1) it should be a _____-lane highway;

(2) the total cost will be $_____ ;

(3) the total benefit will be $ _____ ;

(4) the *net* benefit to the province will be

$ _____ .

SELF-TEST

Circle T if the statement is true, F if it is false.

1 The Canadian economy cannot be called "capitalistic" because its operation involves some "planning." **T F**

2 When the federal government provides for a monetary system, it is functioning to provide the economy with public goods and services. **T F**

3 An economy in which strong and effective competition is maintained will find no need for programs designed to redistribute income. **T F**

4 Competitive product markets ensure an optimal allocation of an economy's resources. **T F**

5 An effective antipollution policy requires that the social costs of pollution be turned into private costs. **T F**

6 Because in any period of time and in any region the quantity of pollutants that can be absorbed by nature is fixed, the supply of pollution rights will be perfectly elastic. **T F**

7 When an urban bus company utilizes a peak-pricing system, the fares it charges riders are higher during rush hours than at other times of the day. **T F**

8 In performing its stabilization function when there is widespread unemployment and no inflation in the economy, government should decrease its spending for public goods and services and increase taxes. **T F**

9 If the economic role of government in Canada is evaluated objectively, it becomes clear that the scope of the government's activities is too large. **T F**

10 Reduced government spending is the same as economy in government. **T F**

11 In practice, it is usually quite simple to estimate the costs and the benefits of a project financed by government. **T F**

12 The reallocation of resources from the private to the public sector does not ordinarily affect the distribution of income or the stability of the economy. **T F**

13 There is a failure in the public sector whenever a governmental program or activity has been expanded to the level at which the marginal social cost exceeds the marginal social benefit. **T F**

14 The special-interest effect, it is argued by those concerned with the theory of public choice, tends to reduce public sector failures because the pressures exerted on government by one special-interest group are offset by the pressures brought to bear by other special-interest groups. **T F**

15 When the costs of programs are hidden and the benefits are clear, vote-seeking politicians tend to reject economically justifiable programs. **T F**

16 The non-selectivity of citizens refers to the inability of individual voters to select the precise bundle of public goods and services that best satisfies the citizen's wants when he or she must vote for a candidate or a party, and the candidate's or the party's entire program. **T F**

17 Both liberal and conservative economists agree that the expansion of government's role in the economy has reduced personal freedom in Canada. **T F**

Circle the letter that corresponds to the best answer.

1 Which of the following is *not* one of the methods utilized by government to control monopoly? (*a*) the imposition of special taxes on monopolists; (*b*) government ownership of monopolies; (*c*) government regulation of monopolies; *d*) anti-combines laws.

2 One of the following is *not* employed by government to redistribute income. Which one? (*a*) the negative income tax; (*b*) direct market intervention; (*c*) income taxes that take a larger part of the incomes of the rich than the poor; (*d*) public assistance programs.

3 Which of the following would do little or nothing to reduce pollution? (*a*) create a market for pollution rights; (*b*) charge polluters an emission fee; (*c*) enact legislation that prohibits pollution and fines polluters; (*d*) redesign and reconstruct the infrastructure.

4 An emission fee levied against polluters will (*a*) encourage the use of pollution-abatement equipment; (*b*) eliminate pollution; (*c*) reduce the revenues of governments that levy the fee; (*d*) externalize the internal costs of pollution.

5 An increase in the demand for pollution rights will (*a*) increase both the quantity of pollutants discharged and the market price of pollution rights; (*b*) increase the quantity discharged and have no effect on the market price; (*c*) have no effect on the quantity discharged and increase the market price; (*d*) have no effect on either the quantity discharged or the market price.

6 User charges imposed on those who drive on urban expressways would tend to (*a*) relieve congestion on the expressways; (*b*) discourage the use of public transportation facilities; (*c*) reduce the funds available for the expansion of the expressway system; (*d*) do all of the above.

7 In the Canadian economy the reallocation of resources needed to provide for the production of public goods is accomplished mainly by means of (*a*) government subsidies to the producers of public goods; (*b*) government purchases of public goods from producers; (*c*) direct control of producers of both private and public goods; (*d*) direct control of producers of public goods only.

8 In assessing the desirability of government performing the six basic economic functions in Canada, there seems to be rather general agreement that (*a*) the functions ought to be increased in number, and government's role in the economy expanded; (*b*) the functions ought to be decreased in number, and government's role in the economy reduced to a minimum; (c) the functions are those the government ought to perform, but there is no general agreement as to the extent to which government should go in performing them; (d) with the exception of stabilizing the economy, these are legitimate tasks for government to perform as long as government, in performing them, does not interfere with the operation of the economy.

9 Assume that a government is considering a new antipollution program and it may choose to include in this program any number of four different projects. The total cost and the total benefits of each of the four projects are given below. What total amount should this government spend on the antipollution program? (a) $2 million; (b) $7 million; (c) $17 million; (d) $37 million.

Project	Total cost	Total benefit
#1	$ 2 million	$ 5 million
#2	$ 5 million	$ 7 million
#3	$10 million	$ 9 million
#4	$20 million	$15 million

10 Which of the following is *not* one of the reasons for the alleged greater efficiency of the private sector? (a) the least efficient workers in the economy gravitate to the public sector; (b) strong incentives to be efficient are largely absent in the public sector; (c) there is no simple way to measure or test efficiency in the public sector; (d) there is a tendency, in the public sector, to increase the budgets of agencies that have failed to perform efficiently.

11 It is difficult to determine whether provision for a particular good or service should be assigned to the private or public sector of the economy because (a) the institutions in both sectors function efficiently; (b) markets function efficiently and the agencies of government perform imperfectly; (c) markets are faulty and government agencies function with much greater efficiency; (d) the institutions in both sectors are imperfect.

DISCUSSION QUESTIONS

1 Why is it proper to refer to the Canadian economy as "mixed capitalism"?

2 What are the six economic functions of government in Canada's mixed capitalistic economy? Explain what the performance of each of these functions requires government to do.

3 Would you like to live in an economy in which government undertook only the first two functions listed in the text? What would be the advantages and disadvantages of living in such an economy?

4 What is "market failure" and what are the two major kinds of such failures?

5 How, using the price system, might the urban transportation system be improved?

6 What basic method does government employ in Canada to reallocate resources away from the production of private goods and toward the production of public goods?

7 Is there agreement on whether government should perform its six economic functions? Why is there criticism of government activity?

8 Explain what benefit-cost analysis is and how it is used. What are the two major problems encountered when benefit-cost analysis is utilized by government?

9 Explain what is meant by "public sector failure."

10 The theory of public choice suggests that there are a number of possible causes of public sector failures. What are these causes? Explain how each would tend to result in the inefficient allocation of the economy's resources.

11 It is generally agreed that "national defence must lie in the public sector while wheat production can best be accomplished in the private sector." Why isn't there agreement on where many other goods or services should be produced?

12 Do you think government limits or expands personal freedom by performing its economic functions?

17

THE RADICAL CRITIQUE: THE ECONOMICS OF DISSENT

Chapter 17 is the last of the four chapters concerned with the "Current Economic Problems" of the Canadian economy. Unlike the first three chapters in this part of the text, Chapter 17 does not examine a particular trouble spot (such as agriculture or poverty). Instead, it asks if capitalism is one big trouble spot or problem.

Those who see capitalism as a giant sore spot are called radical economists, the New Left, or neo-Marxists. Their viewpoint is labelled the radical critique, radical economics, or the economics of dissent. It is their contention that modern capitalism, based on private property, the corporation, and the profit motive, is such a bad system that it ought to be abolished and replaced with a system of socialism. Their contention is essentially an updated or modern version of Marxian economics. Karl Marx argued that capitalism had brought about the tremendous rise in the standard of living in Western Europe, but that capitalism would eventually destroy itself. Its success, he believed, would lead to economic conditions that, in turn, would lead to the collapse of capitalism, revolution, and the coming of socialism. Chapter 17 begins, therefore, with a detailed examination of the radical economists' Marxian heritage and with an analysis of the New Left's historical predecessor, the Old Left.

From the Old Left we turn to an explanation of the two fundamental differences between orthodox economists—the kind of economics accepted by almost all econo-

mists, including the authors of the text—and radical economics. These two differences are differences in approach or methodology. Orthodox economists, the radical economists argue, don't see what is really going on in the world around them. They either have their eyes closed or are rather simpleminded, and see harmony where there is actually conflict. Moreover, orthodox economists, the New Left contends, have too narrow a viewpoint. They look only at economic matters and disregard the other aspects of modern society; and within economics they devote their efforts to nitpicking while ignoring real and important economic problems.

The most important section of Chapter 17 is a summary of the way in which the radical economists view capitalism. They see the economy dominated by a relatively few large monopoly corporations in league with the state (that is, all levels of government but especially the federal) and out to exploit workers and consumers. This exploitation leads to inequality in the distribution of income and wealth, alienation (which you should be sure to define), an economy that irrationally and wastefully uses its resources and imperialism, which exploits underdeveloped nations. The radical economists agree that they don't like what they see in capitalist economies, and that what is needed is socialism. They don't agree at all on just what socialism is—on what a better economic system would be like.

The chapter concludes with a rebuttal by

the orthodox economists. Their critique of radical economics has four parts. The first three parts add up to an attack on the objectivity of the radical economists. They are blinded by their preconceptions and ignore any facts that weaken their case. The fourth part is the most devastating, in the view of most of their critics. They don't present any of the details of the better economic system that is to replace the capitalism that they detest. Rejecting both the market system and a bureaucratic government, they don't tell us how they are going to allocate scarce resources to satisfy the unlimited wants of society. The histories of France and Russia suggest that revolution and the elimination of an old system do not always bring about the introduction of a better system. And many, like Hamlet, would

> . . . rather bear those ills we have
> Than fly to others we know not of . . .

CHECK LIST

When you have studied this chapter you should be able to

☐ Use the following six categories to explain, from the viewpoint of Marx and the Old Left, the development and eventual collapse of capitalism:
• the class struggle
• private property and the exploitation of labour
• capital accumulation and its consequences
• the increasing degradation of the working class
• monopoly capitalism and imperialism
• revolution and socialism

☐ Contrast the positions of the orthodox and the radical economists in the "harmony or conflict" controversy.

☐ Explain why the radical economists believe orthodox economics is plagued by "disciplinary narrowness."

☐ Outline the eight main features in the radical conception of capitalism.

☐ Enumerate the three characteristics found in every socialist (radical) vision of a new society.

☐ Present the four arguments offered by orthodox economists to rebut the contentions of the radical economists.

CHAPTER OUTLINE

1 Radical economists reject the orthodox explanation of the operation of capitalism and its analysis of the problems of a capitalistic society.

2 The radical explanation of capitalism builds upon the work of Karl Marx, who examined the development of capitalism and concluded that capitalism would eventually collapse.

a. Marx argued that as capitalist economies expanded the factory system, improved technology, and increased material well-being, one class of people (capitalists) struggled with another class (workers) to take some of the workers' output from them.

b. The capitalists, fortified by the institution of private property, control the machinery and equipment (the capital) needed to produce goods; and driven by their desire for profits (surplus value), they employ their superior bargaining power to exploit workers and pay them subsistence wages that are less than the value of their production.

c. Competition forces capitalists to reinvest their profits in more and better capital; and this capital accumulation not only expands the real domestic output but also results in technological unemployment, in a growing Industrial Reserve Army, and in a declining rate of profit.

d. These events operate to provide workers with a mere subsistence wage; to ever-increasing unemployment; and, in trying to prevent the profit rate from falling, to still further exploitation of workers.

e. Competition among capitalists in an atmosphere of falling profits and growing unemployment, Marx contended, would lead to the monopolization of industry by a few capitalists; and eventually, searching for cheap foreign labour and foreign markets for their products, to imperialism.

f. The ultimate result of the workings of capitalism is revolution by the workers, the overthrow of capitalism, and the establishment of a socialist state without classes.

3 There are, in the opinion of radical economists, two fundamental shortcomings in orthodox economics.

a. Orthodox economists see a harmony and the reconciliation of opposing interests in capitalism; but radical economists see an irreconcilable conflict between capitalists (and the government that they dominate) and the rest of society.

b. Orthodox economists, according to the radical economists, focus their attention only on the economic aspects of society, ignore the non-economic aspects of modern capitalism, and fail to understand the real problems of society.

4 The radical economists have a modern version of Marx and see capitalism in this light.

a. A small group of huge, multiproduct, multinational, monopolistic corporations dominates the capitalist economy.

b. These corporate giants also dominate government and

(1) prevent the control of monopoly,

(2) obtain subsidies from tax revenues, and

(3) have government create markets for them.

c. The expansion of capitalism and of the corporate giants requires the expansion of markets and output; and creates new problems while it fails to solve old problems.

d. The first of these problems is the exploitation of workers that is explained by three basic defects in the marginal productivity theory of income distribution of orthodox economists.

(1) The markets for products and labour are not competitive but are monopolies and monopsonies.

(2) Workers are unable to obtain wage rates equal to their potential marginal revenue products because they cannot develop their natural abilities and society discriminates among workers on the basis of race or sex.

(3) Owners of real capital obtain the income produced not by them but by their capital.

e. The second problem is the unequal distribution of income and wealth that the radical economists see to be the result of

(1) the unearned incomes received by owners of capital and the economic and political powers that accompany these incomes; and

(2) the existence of dual labour markets.

f. Alienation, or the absence of decision-making power and the inability of individuals to control their lives, is a third problem.

g. A fourth problem is the irrational and wasteful use of resources to produce goods that do not fulfil consumer needs.

h. The last problem is the exploitation of the less developed nations of the world and is the result of imperialism.

i. Radical economists, while agreeing that the socialism which should replace capitalism ought not to be based on private profits and ought to be decent, humane, and democratic, cannot agree on the exact nature of the new society.

5 In reply to the radical economists , orthodox economists contend

a. that the radical conception of capitalism is not consistent with reality;

b. that radical economics is non-objective because it ignores facts and interprets all events in terms of its conception of capitalism;

c. that the problems of capitalism cannot all be the result of ideology, because other economies with different ideological bases have the same problems;

d. that the radical economists have not explained the kind of system with which they would replace modern capitalism.

IMPORTANT TERMS

Radical economics

Marxian economics

Old Left

Class struggle

Bourgeois

Proletariat

Surplus value

Law of capitalist accumulation

Industrial Reserve Army

Monopoly capitalism

Imperialism

Dictatorship of the proletariat

New Left

Exploitation

Dual labour market

Alienation

Participatory socialism

FILL-IN QUESTIONS

1 Humanity, according to Marx, is engaged in a perpetual struggle with _____

_____ to obtain material wealth.
a. Simultaneously, some people attempt to improve their own material well-being by wresting output from _____ people.
b. And under the capitalistic system, this latter struggle is the struggle of capitalists (or the _____)
against workers (or the _____).

2 Because of the institution of private _____ , capitalists control the machinery and equipment necessary to produce goods and services; and workers are dependent upon the capitalists for _____ ; and the capitalists are driven by their desire for profits (or _____) to exploit workers by paying them a _____
that is less than the _____ of their output.

3 The accumulation of capital means that capitalists are forced by (government, workers, competition) _____ to invest their _____ in additional and superior machinery and equipment; and capital accumulation results in an expansion of the _____ output, the substitution of capital for _____ and a decline in the rate of _____ .

4 In an effort to offset the decline in the profit rate, capitalists will increase the (wages, exploitation) _____ of the working class.

5 As capitalism continues to develop,
a. Marx reasoned that unemployment and falling profits would lead to (the monopolization of, increasing competition in) _____ _____ industry.
b. Lenin reasoned that the final state of this development would be (socialism, democracy, imperialism)_____ .

6 Exploitation and unemployment would, Marx predicted, eventually result in a ____ _____ by the working class, the establishment of a dictatorship of the _____ , the socialization of _____ , the abolition of the _____ class, and finally in the formation of a _____ society.

7 The radical economists find two major methodological deficiencies in the orthodox approach to economics and believe
a. that the orthodox economists have an incorrect perception of reality and see (conflict, a harmony) _____ where there is actually _____ ;
b. that orthodox economics as a discipline is

too (narrow, broad) _____, is too re-mote from the real problems of society, and fails to recognize the importance of (economic, religious, political) _____ power in capitalistic societies.

8 In the radical conception of capitalism

a. the economy is dominated by _____ corporations, which also dominate the ____ _____, depend upon finding new _____ for their ever-increasing production, and exploit both _____ and _____ ;

b. capitalism brings about income (equal-ity, inequality) _____ , the alien-ation of individuals, the irrational use of society's resources, and _____ beyond the economy's national boundaries;

c. these evils can be eliminated only by replacing capitalism with_____ .

9 What are the three ways in which gov-ernment is alleged by the radical economists to cater to the large corporations?

a. _____

b. _____

c. _____

10 Orthodox economists argue that the wage rate of the workers will equal their _____ ; and that all resources will receive a reward (or income) in propor-tion to their contribution to the production of the _____ . But the radical economists challenge this theory by arguing

a. that these conclusions are true only when markets in the economy are_____ ;

b. capital goods were created in the past by _____;

c. and while capital goods are productive, the capitalist is not productive and his in-come from the ownership of capital is (earned, unearned) _____ .

11 Radical economists contend that the causes of inequality in the distribution of in-come and wealth in capitalist countries are

a. the capitalistic institutions, which in-clude (public, private) _____ prop-erty, and both economic and political (power, democracy, morality) _____ ;

b. \the existence of _____ labour markets and the payment of high wages in the (primary, secondary) labour market and the payment of low wages in the _____ labour market.

12 Alienation

a. means that individuals have little control over their own _____ and are remote from the _____ -making process;

b. is primarily the result, in the view of radi-cal economists, of the dominance and size of_____ .

13 It is the view of radical economists that capitalism uses its resources irrationally and engages in wasteful production.

a. The primary cause of this is the capital-ist's pursuit of _____ .

b. And some of the results are the deter-ioration of the _____ , the creation of wants, unnecessary (consumer, military, investment) _____ spending, and _____ activities throughout the world.

14 The radical economists advocate the re-placement of capitalism with some variety of _____; and agree that the new society should be _____, decent, and humane, and that there should be no private _____ .

15 The orthodox economists rebut the radical critique of capitalism by arguing that radical economics has an invalid perception of (ideology, reality) _____ and is not (objective, subjective)_____ , that not all of the problems of the capitalist economies are the result of capitalism's (ideology, ideals) _____ , and that the radical economists offer no viable or attainable _____ for the present economic system.

PROBLEMS AND PROJECTS

1 Suppose the subsistence wage for a worker is 4 units of output per day; and that the total daily output that can be produced by from 0 to 7 workers is as shown in the table in the next column.
a. Compute the daily marginal products of each worker and enter them in the table.
b. If a capitalist can employ as many workers as he or she wishes at the subsistence wage, to maximize profits he or she will employ _____ workers per day.
c. The total wages paid to workers each day will be _____ .
d. The daily output of the capitalist is _____ , and his or her daily surplus value is _____ .
e. Were the capitalist to employ this number of workers, in order to obtain no surplus

Number of workers	Output	Marginal product
0	0	_____
1	8	_____
2	15	_____
3	21	_____
4	26	_____
5	30	_____
6	33	_____
7	35	_____

value he or she would have to pay each worker a daily wage of _____ .
f. The daily exploitation of each worker is, therefore, _____ .

2 In the table below is a Marxian picture of what happens in a capitalistic economy as it develops.
a. In addition to the economy's gross national product, the table also shows its capital consumption allowances (CCA) in each of the three years. Compute and enter into the table the economy's net national product for each year.
b. Workers in this economy always receive a subsistence wage of 4 in each year. Find total employment in each year by dividing the wages paid in that year by the subsistence wage, and enter these employment figures into the table.
c. Marx defined surplus value as all of the NNP not paid to workers as wages. Compute the surplus value in the economy in each year, and enter these surplus values in the table.

Year	GNP	CCA	NNP	Wages	Employ-ment	Surplus value	CCA plus wages	Rate of profit
1	500	100	_____	280	_____	_____	_____	_____
2	504	110	_____	276	_____	_____	_____	_____
3	509	120.4	_____	272	_____	_____	_____	_____

d. Marx defined the rate of profit to be equal to surplus value divided by the sum of capital consumption allowances and wages.

(1) Compute capital consumption allowances plus wages in each year. Enter these into the table.

(2) Now compute the rate of profit in each year.

e. As the economy develops,

(1) employment (increases, decreases, remains constant) _____ ; and,

therefore, unemployment _____ ;

(2) the rate of profit _____ .

SELF-TEST

Circle T if the statement is true, F if it is false.

1 Among radical economists there is very little difference in their viewpoints. **T F**

2 Surplus value equals the value of the daily output of the workers less their daily wage. **T F**

3 Capitalists, according to Marx, are able to exploit workers because the capitalists have monopoly control of the machinery and equipment needed to produce goods in an industrial society. **T F**

4 Marx argued that in a capitalist society the demand for consumer goods would increase more rapidly than the economy's capacity to produce them and that unemployment would result. **T F**

5 In Marx's view the increasing degradation of the working class was the direct result of their tendency to have too many children. **T F**

6 Marx's *Capital* contained a clear and detailed picture of the society that would emerge after the overthrow of capitalism by a revolution of the working class. **T F**

7 Radical economists contend that the solution to the problems of capitalistic societies requires an end to the private ownership of capital goods and the abolition of the market system as the decision-making device for society. **T F**

8 Orthodox economists tend to emphasize the conflicts and the radical economists tend to stress the harmony found in modern capitalistic economies. **T F**

9 The modern, radical conception of capitalism is an extended and updated version of Marx's ideas. **T F**

10 Capitalism has reached a stage in modern industrial states in which, according to radical economists, monopoly corporations dominate the economy. **T F**

11 Radical economists argue that because labour markets are not competitive, workers receive a wage that is greater than their marginal revenue product. **T F**

12 Capitalistic institutions, in the opinion of radical economists, create and maintain most of the income inequality found in modern, capitalist states. **T F**

13 Orthodox and radical economists agree that the primary function of education in modern capitalistic economies is to increase the technical skills of workers. **T F**

14 Alienation refers to the increase in the proportion of the working class that is either foreign born or from a minority group. **T F**

15 The radical economists argue that capitalism uses its resources to produce little-needed goods and services and fails to produce goods and services that are more needed. **T F**

16 From the radical viewpoint, two basic causes of the irrational use of resources in capitalistic societies are the pursuit of profits and pollution. **T F**

17 The radical economists agree on almost all of the particulars of the socialism with which they would replace capitalism. **T F**

18 Most radical economists reject both the price-market system and government bureaucracy as a means of allocating scarce resources.   **T F**

19 The orthodox economists concede that only capitalistic societies are monopolistic, militaristic, and imperialistic; but argue that the abolition of private property and the profit motive will not solve these problems.   **T F**

20 In their rebuttal of the radical economists' critique of capitalism, orthodox economists argue that radical economists ignore any facts that do not support their conclusions.   **T F**

Circle the letter that corresponds to the best answer.

1 In the person-against-person struggle found in capitalistic societies, Marx envisioned the exploitation (*a*) of the bourgeois by capitalists; (*b*) of the proletariat by the bourgeois; (*c*) of workers by the proletariat; (*d*) of the bourgeois by the proletariat.

2 The institution that Marx believed made it possible for one class to exploit another in a capitalistic economy was (*a*) the use of money; (*b*) the use of capital goods; (*c*) the corporation; (*d*) private property.

3 Which of the following was *not* a consequence of capital accumulation in Marx's analysis of capitalism? (*a*) an increase in the profit rate; (*b*) an increase in unemployment; (*c*) an increase in domestic output; (*d*) an increase in the misery of the working class.

4 Marx argued that the development of capitalism would eventually result in (*a*) imperialism; (*b*) prolonged inflation: (*c*) a decline in the number of capitalists; (*d*) a rise in the real wages of workers.

5 Imperialism, according to Lenin, results from (*a*) the search of capitalists for cheap foreign labour; (*b*) the inability of capitalists to sell all of their output at home; (*c*) higher profit rates in less developed nations; (*d*) all of the above.

6 Which of the following is the process through which Marx predicted capitalism would be replaced by socialism? (*a*) revolution; (*b*) evolution; (*c*) unionization; (*d*) liberalization.

7 The socialism that would replace capitalism would have all but one of the following characteristics. Which one? (*a*) the dictatorship of the proletariat; (*b*) the abolition of the capitalist class; (*c*) the sale of the capitalists' machinery and equipment to the proletariat; (*d*) the establishment of a classless society.

8 The radical economists contend that orthodox economics (*a*) is too broad a discipline to come to grips with real-world problems; (*b*) is overly concerned with the power of large corporations; (*c*) devotes too much of its attention to the study of conflict; (*d*) fails to recognize the political character of the modern corporation.

9 Which of the following, in the view of the radical economists, is *not* a consequence of capitalism in the modern industrial state? (*a*) alienation; (*b*) anarchism; (*c*) inequality; (*d*) imperialism.

10 In the radical conception of capitalism, (*a*) the state dominates and controls the large corporations; (*b*) the presence in the economy of a large number of small businesses results in wasteful competition; (*c*) government employs progressive personal and corporation income taxes to subsidize greedy workers; (*d*) military spending by government provides markets for large corporations.

11 Capitalists, the radical economists contend, are able to exploit the working class because of (*a*) their monopsony position in labour markets; (*b*) their monopoly position in product markets; (*c*) the institution of private property; (d) all of the above.

12 The radical economists contend that (a) neither capital goods nor capitalists are productive; (b) capital goods are and capitalists are not productive; (c) capitalists are and capital goods are not productive; (d) both capital goods and capitalists are productive.

13 Which of the following, in the view of radical economists, is *not* a major factor in producing inequality in the distribution of income and in the ownership of wealth in the modern capitalist state? (a) weak inheritance taxes; (b) tax loopholes; (c) foreign competition; (d) the system of higher education.

14 In the primary labour market (a) wages are low and employment is unstable; (b) wages are low and employment is stable; (c) wages are high and employment is unstable; (d) wages are high and employment is stable.

15 Of the following, which is neither a cause nor a result of alienation? (a) the large size of corporate employers; (b) the unionization of workers; (c) the inability of individuals to influence business decisions; (d) assembly-line production.

16 Radical economists argue that the failure of the underdeveloped nations to grow (to expand their outputs of goods and services) is the result of their (a) overpopulation; (b) social systems; (c) shortages of natural resources; (d) inability to produce sufficient incomes to enable them to invest in capital goods.

17 The new society advocated by all radical economists is (a) socialism; (b) anarchy; (c) communism; (d) a reformed price-market system.

18 The radical critique of capitalism is, in the opinion of orthodox economists (a) scientific; (b) immoral; (c) valid; (d) ideological.

DISCUSSION QUESTIONS

1 Looking back into history, Marx saw people engaged in two kinds of struggle. What were these two struggles?

2 Who, according to Marx, were the protagonists of the person-against-person struggle in a capitalistic society?

3 Why, in Marx's explanation of capitalism, are capitalists able to exploit workers? What does "exploit" mean?

4 What does capital accumulation mean? What forced Marx's capitalist to accumulate, and what were the consequences of this accumulation?

5 Why did Marx believe that the working class would become increasingly more miserable?

6 What made Marx conclude that capitalistic development would lead to the monopolization of industry by a relatively few capitalists?

7 What is imperialism? Why did Lenin conclude that the development of capitalism would eventually lead to imperialism?

8 What did Marx envision as the causes and the results of the workers' revolution?

9 Explain the two methodological deficiencies that radical economists find in orthodox economics.

10 What evidence is there to suggest that a few large monopolistic corporations dominate the modern capitalist economy? In what ways does the state allegedly cater to these corporations?

11 What, according to the radical economists, are the major problems that result from corporate capitalism?

12 Explain (a) the orthodox economists' theory of income distribution; and (b) the faults the radical economists see in this theory.

13 In the view of the radical economists, how does the capitalistic system lead to inequality in the distribution of income and in the ownership of wealth? Why, in their view, are these causes "cumulative and self-reinforcing"?

14 Compare the economic conditions found in the primary labour market with those found in the secondary labour market. What historical reasons can be presented to explain the evolution of these dual labour markets?

15 What is alienation, and what do the radical economists see as the causes of alienation in the modern capitalist state?

16 Why do the radical economists argue that capitalistic production is irrational and its use of resources wasteful?

17 What are the three ways in which imperialism, if one accepts the view of radical economists, serves as an obstacle to the economic development of the poor nations of the world? According to John G. Gurley (quoted in the text), what forms has American imperialism taken in the last thirty years and what has been the aim of these imperialistic activities?

18 What kind of new society do the radicals envision or advocate? What are the different economic systems they recommend as replacements for capitalism?

19 How do the orthodox economists rebut the radical economists' critique of modern capitalism?

20 What evidence is there to suggest that radical economists (*a*) have invalid perceptions of reality; (*b*) are not objective; and (*c*) overemphasize the significance of ideology?

18

NATIONAL INCOME ACCOUNTING

The subject matter of Chapter 18 is national income (or social) accounting. This type of accounting measures or estimates the size of (1) the gross domestic product, (2) the gross national product, (3) the national income, (4) the personal income, and (5) the disposable income of the economy.

This is national income (or social) accounting because it involves estimating output or income for the nation or society as a whole, rather than for an individual business firm or family. Note that the terms "output" and "income" are interchangeable because the nation's output and its income are identical (except for "net investment income from non-residents"). The value of the nation's output equals the total expenditure for this output, and these expenditures become the income of those in the nation who have produced this output. Consequently, there are two equally acceptable methods, both discussed in the chapter, for obtaining each of the five income-output measures listed above. These two methods are the expenditures method and the income method.

Accounting is essentially an adding-up process. This chapter explains in detail, and lists the items that must be added, to obtain by both methods each of the five income-output measures. It is up to you to learn precisely *what* to add, that is, how to compute GDP, GNP, NI, PI, and DI by both methods. This is a fairly difficult chapter and the only way to learn the material is simply to sit down and learn it—memorize it if necessary! A careful reading of the chapter, however, will enable you to avoid the necessity of memorizing. You should first try to understand what each of the five income-output

measures measures and the two alternative approaches to these measurements. Remembering the items to be added will then be much simpler.

In addition to explaining the two methods of computing the five income-output measures and each of the items used in the computation process, the chapter discusses the purpose of social accounting; the means by which income-output measures for different years may be adjusted to take account of changes in the price level so that comparisons between years are possible; and the shortcomings and dangers inherent in using these income-output measures. It is especially dangerous to assume that the GDP is a good overall measure of the welfare of society as a whole. Chapter 18 is, however, the essential background for Parts Five and Six, which explain the history of and the factors that determine the level of total output and income in the economy. The chapter is important in itself because it presents one of the several means of measuring the well-being of the economy and the individuals comprising the economy in a given year and over the years.

CHECK LIST

When you have studied this chapter you should be able to
☐ State the purposes of national income accounting.
☐ Define GDP; and compute it using either the expenditures or the income approach when you are given the necessary data.

□ Explain: the difference between gross and net investment; why changes in inventories are investment; and the relation between net investment and economic growth.

□ Define each of the following; and, when you are given the needed data, compute each by two different methods: GNP, NI, PI, and DI.

□ Adjust the nominal GDP, when you are given the relevant price index, to find the real GDP.

□ Present seven reasons why GDP is not an index of social welfare.

CHAPTER OUTLINE

1 National income (or social) accounting consists of concepts that enable those who use them to measure the economy's output, to compare it with past outputs, to explain its size and the reasons for changes in its size, and to formulate policies designed to increase it.

2 The gross domestic product (GDP) is the market value of all final goods and services produced in the economy during a year.
a. GDP is measured in dollar terms rather than in terms of physical units of output.
b. To avoid double counting, GDP includes only *final* goods and services (goods and services that will not be processed further during the *current* year).
c. Non-productive transactions are not included in GDP; purely financial transactions and second-hand sales, are, therefore, excluded.
d. Measurement of GDP can be accomplished by either the expenditures or the income method, but the same result is obtained by the two methods.

3 Computation of the GDP by the expenditures method requires the addition of the total amounts of the four types of spending for final goods and services.
a. Personal consumption expenditures (C) are the expenditures of households for dura-

ble, semi-durable, and non-durable goods and for services.
b. Gross capital formation or gross investment (I_g) is the sum of the spending by governments and business firms for machinery, equipment, and tools; spending by firms and households for new buildings; and the changes in the inventories of business firms.
(1) A change in inventories is included in investment because it is the part of output of the economy that was not sold during the year.
(2) Investment does not include expenditures for stocks or bonds or for second-hand capital goods.
(3) Gross investment exceeds net investment by the value of the capital goods worn out during the year.
(4) An economy in which net investment is positive (zero, negative) is an expanding (a static, a declining) economy.
c. Government purchases of goods and services (G) are the *current* expenditures (that is, *excluding* investment) made by all governments in the economy for products produced by business firms and for resource services from households.
d. Net exports (X_n) in an economy equal the expenditures made by foreigners for goods and services produced in the economy *less* the expenditures made by the consumers, government, and investors of the economy for goods and services produced in foreign nations.
e. In symbols, $C + I_g + G + X_n = $ GDP

4 Computation of GDP by the income method requires the addition of the eight uses to which the income derived from the production and sale of final goods and services are put. These eight items are:
a. Wages, salaries, and supplementary labour income.
b. Corporation profits before taxes.
c. Interest, and miscellaneous investment income.
d. Accrued net income of farm operators from farm production.

e. Net income of non-farm unincorporated business, including rent.

f. Inventory valuation adjustment.

g. Indirect taxes less subsidies.

h. Capital consumption allowances (depreciation).

5 In addition to GDP, four other national income measures are important in evaluating the performance of the economy. Each has a distinct definition and can be computed by making additions to or deductions from another measure.

a. GNP is GDP less net investment income from non-residents ("less" because it is always negative in Canada).

b. NI is the total income *earned* by owners of land and capital and by the suppliers of labour and entrepreneurial ability during the year; and equals GNP less indirect taxes and depreciation (capital consumption allowances).

c. PI is the total income *received*—whether it is earned or unearned—by the households of the economy before the payment of personal taxes; and is found by *adding* transfer payments to and *subtracting* other earnings not paid out to persons, corporation income taxes, and undistributed corporation profits from the NI.

d. DI is the total income available to households after the payment of personal taxes; and is equal to PI less personal taxes and also equal to personal consumption expenditures plus personal saving and the interest paid by consumers.

e. The relations among the five income-output measures are summarized for you in Table 18-5.

f. Figure 18-2 is a more realistic and complex circular flow diagram that shows the flows of expenditures and incomes among the households, business firms, and governments in the economy.

6 Because price levels change from year to year, it is necessary to adjust the money or nominal GDP computed for any year to obtain the real GDP before year-to-year comparisons between the outputs of final goods and services can be made.

a. To adjust the nominal GDP figures, divide the nominal GDP in any year by the price index for that year; the result is the adjusted or real GDP.

b. When the price index in a year is below (above) the 100 it was in the base year, the nominal GDP figure for that year is inflated (deflated) by this adjustment.

7 GDP is not, for the following reasons, a measure of social welfare in the economy.

a. It excludes the value of final goods and services not bought and sold in the markets of the economy.

b. It excludes the amount of leisure the citizens of the economy are able to have.

c. It does not record the improvements in the quality of products that occur over the years.

d. It does not measure changes in the composition and the distribution of the domestic output.

e. It is not a measure of per capita output because it does not take into account changes in the size of the economy's population.

f. It does not record the pollution costs to the environment of producing final goods and services.

g. It does not measure the market value of the final goods and services produced in the hidden or underground sector of the economy.

IMPORTANT TERMS

National income
(social) accounting

Gross domestic
product

Final goods

Intermediate goods

Double counting

Value added

Non-productive
transaction

Non-market
transaction

Expenditure approach

Income approach

Personal consumption expenditures

Government current purchases of goods and services

Gross investment (gross capital formation)

Non-investment transaction

Net investment

Expanding economy

Static economy

Declining economy

Net exports

Capital consumption allowances (depreciation)

Non-income charges

Indirect taxes

Wages, salaries, and supplementary labour income

Gross national product

National income

Personal income

Disposable income

Personal saving

Real gross domestic product

Price index

Base year

Given year

Inflating

Deflating

GDP deflator

FILL-IN QUESTIONS

1 Social accounting is valuable because it provides a means of keeping track of the level of _____ in the economy and the course it has followed over the long run; it also provides the information required to devise and put into effect the public _____ that will improve the performance of the economy.

2 Gross domestic product is a monetary measure of all final goods and services produced during a year; to measure the value of these goods and services, the goods and services are valued at their _____ .

3 In measuring GDP, only final goods and services are included; if intermediate goods and services were included, the accountant would be_____ .

4 A firm buys materials for $200 from other firms in the economy and produces from them a product that sells for $315. The $115 is the _____ by the firm.

5 The total value added to a product at all stages of production equals the _____ value of the _____ product; and the total value added to all products produced in the economy during a year is the _____ product.

6 Personal consumption expenditures are the expenditures of households for _____, _____, and _____ goods and for _____ .

7 *a.* Gross investment basically includes _____ , _____ , and _____ .

b. Net investment is less than gross investment by an amount equal to _____ .

8 If gross investment is less than depreciation, net investment is (positive, zero, negative) _____ and the economy is (static, declining, expanding)_____ .

9 An economy's *net* exports equal its _____ less its_____ .

10 In symbols, the GDP by the expenditures approach = ___ + ___ + ___ + ___ .

11 The capital consumption allowances and indirect taxes, by the income approach, are referred to as _____ charges or allocations.

12 The compensation of employees in the

system of social accounting consists of actual wages and salaries *and* _____ labour income. The latter are the payments employers make to social _____ programs and to _____ pension funds.

13 Corporation profits are disposed of in three ways: _____ ,

_____ ,

and _____ .

14 Net investment income from non-residents is the difference between gross domestic product and _____ . This latter aggregate measures income received from production by (resident/non-resident) _____ factors of production. GNP in Canada is always (greater than/less than/equal to) _____ GDP because net investment income from non-residents is always (positive/negative/zero) _____ .

15 National income equals gross national product minus _____ and _____ .

16 Personal income

a. equals national income plus _____ and minus the sum of _____ ,

_____ ,

and _____ ;

b. also equals _____

plus _____

plus _____ .

17 Disposable income

a. equals personal income minus _____

_____ ;

b. also equals _____

_____ .

18 In order to compare the real gross domestic product in two different years, it is necessary to adjust the nominal GDP because _____ .

19 For several reasons the real GDP is not a measure of social welfare in an economy.

a. It does not include the _____ transactions that result in the production of goods and services or the amount of _____

_____ enjoyed by the citizens of the economy.

b. It fails to record improvements in the _____ of the products produced, changes in the composition and distribution of the economy's total _____ , the undesirable effects of producing the GDP upon the _____ of the economy, and the goods and services produced in the _____ economy.

c. And because it is a measure of the *total* output of the economy it does not measure the _____ output of the economy.

20 When the population of an economy grows at a more rapid rate than its GDP grows, the standard of living in that economy (rises, falls, remains constant) _____ .

PROBLEMS AND PROJECTS

1 On the next page are actual national accounts figures for Canada in 1985.
a. Compute each of the following.

(1) Dividends: $ _____

(2) Net exports: $ _____

(3) Net investment: $_____

b. Use any of these figures and any of your computations in (a) above to prepare in the table below an Income Statement for the Economy similar to the one found in Table 18-6 (on page 406 of the text).

c. In this economy:

(1) Net domestic income is $_____.

(2) National income is $_____.

(3) Personal income is $_____.

(4) Disposable income is $_____.

(5) Personal saving is $_____.

2   A farmer who owns a plot of ground sells the right to pump crude oil from his land to a crude-oil producer. The crude-oil producer agrees to pay the farmer $20 a barrel for every barrel pumped from the farmer's land.

a. During one year 10,000 barrels are pumped.

(1) The farmer receives a payment of $____ from the crude-oil producer.

(2) The value added by the farmer is $ ____ .

	Billions of dollars
Exports	$136
Corporations profits before taxes	47
Capital consumption allowances	54
Government current purchases of goods and services	94
Net investment income from non-residents	–15
Accrued net income of farm operators from farm production	4
Indirect taxes (less subsidies)	47
Wages, salaries, supplementary labour income	255
Gross investment	95
Personal saving	44
Corporation income taxes	16
Government transfer payments	99
Interest and miscellaneous investment income	40
Net income from non-farm unincorporated business, including rent	29
Personal consumption expenditures	274
Imports	123
Other earnings not paid out to persons	28
Undistributed corporation profits	18
Personal taxes	79

Receipts: Expenditure approach		Allocations: Income approach	
	$____		$____
	____		____
	____		____
	____		____
			____
			____
			____
Gross domestic product	$____	Gross domestic product	$____

b. The crude-oil producer sells the 10,000 barrels pumped to a petroleum refiner at a price of $25 a barrel.

(1) The crude-oil producer receives a payment of $_____ from the refiner.

(2) The value added by the crude-oil producer is $_____.

c. The refiner employs a pipeline company to transport the crude oil from the farmer's land to the refinery and pays the pipeline company a fee of $1 a barrel for the oil transported.

(1) The pipeline company receives a payment of $_____ from the refiner.

(2) The value added by the pipeline company is $_____.

d. From the 10,000 barrels of crude oil the refiner produces 1.8 million litres of gasoline and various by-products, which are sold to distributors and gasoline service stations at an average price of 25 cents a litre.

(1) The total payment received by the refiner from its customers is $_____.

(2) The value added by the refiner is $_____.

e. The distributors and service stations sell the 1.8 million litres of gasoline and by-products to consumers at an average price (tax *not* included) of 30 cents a litre.

(1) The total payment received by distributors and service stations is $_____.

(2) The value added by them is $_____.

f. The total value added by the farmer, crude-oil producer, pipeline company, refiner, and distributors and service stations is $_____, and the market value of the gasoline and by-products (the final good) is $_____.

3 Below is a list of items that may or may not be included in the five income-output measures. Indicate, in the space to the right of each, which of the income-output mea-

sures includes this item; it is possible for the item to be included in none, one, two, three, four, or all of the measures. If the item is included in none of the measures, indicate why it is not included.

a. Interest on the public debt. _____

b. The sale of a used computer. _____

c. The production of shoes that are not sold by the manufacturer. _____

d. The income of a bootlegger in a "dry" township. _____

e. The purchase of a share of common stock on the Vancouver Stock Exchange. _____

f. The interest paid on the bonds of Quebec Hydro. _____

g. The labour performed by a homemaker. _____

h. The labour performed by a paid baby-sitter. _____

i. The monthly cheque received by an idler from his rich aunt. _____

j. The purchase of a new tractor by a farmer. _____

k. The labour performed by an assembly-line worker in repapering his or her own kitchen. _____

l. The services of a lawyer. _____

m. The purchase of shoes from their manufacturer by a shoe retailer. _____

n. The cheque received from a provincial government by a student. _____

o. The rent a homeowner would receive if he or she did not live in his or her own home.

_____

4 In the following table are nominal (or unadjusted) GDP figures for three years and the price indices for each of the three years. (The GDP figures are in billions.)

Year	Nominal GDP	Price index	Adjusted (real) GDP
1929	$104	121	$_____
1933	56	91	_____
1939	91	100	_____

a. Which of the three years appears to be the base year? _____

b. Between
(1) 1929 and 1933 the economy experienced (inflation, deflation)_____ ;
(2) 1933 and 1939 it experienced _____ .

c. Use the price indices to compute the adjusted (real) GDP in each year. (You may round your answer to the nearest billion dollars.)

d. The nominal GDP figure
(1) for 1929 was (deflated, inflated, neither)

_____ ;

(2) for 1933 was _____ ;

(3) for 1939 was _____ .

SELF-TEST

Circle T if the statement is true, F if it is false.

1 Gross domestic product measures, at their market value, the total output of all goods and services produced in the economy during a year. **T F**

2 Both the nominal GDP and the real GDP of the Canadian economy are measured in dollars. **T F**

3 The total market value of the wine produced in Canada during a year is equal to the number of bottles of wine produced in that year multiplied by the average price at which a bottle sold during that year. **T F**

4 The total value added to a product and the value of the final product are equal. **T F**

5 The two approaches to the measurement of the gross domestic product yield identical results because one approach measures the total amount spent on the products produced by business firms during a year, while the second approach measures the total income of business firms during the year. **T F**

6 In computing gross domestic product, net domestic income and national income by the expenditure approach, transfer payments are excluded because they do not represent payments for currently produced goods and services. **T F**

7 The expenditure made by a household to have a new home built for it is a personal consumption expenditure. **T F**

8 In national income accounting any increase in the inventories of business firms is included in gross investment. **T F**

9 If gross investment is greater than capital consumption during a given year, the economy has declined during that year. **T F**

10 The net exports of an economy equal its exports of goods and services less its imports of goods and services. **T F**

The data in the following table should be used to answer true–false questions 11 to 14 and multiple-choice questions 8 to 14.

	Billions
Net investment	$32
Personal taxes	39
Government transfer payments	19
Indirect taxes	8
Corporation income taxes	11
Personal consumption expenditures	217
Capital consumption allowances	7
Exports	15
Dividends	15
Government current purchases of goods and services	51
Undistributed corporation profits	10
Other earnings not paid out to persons	4
Imports	12
Net investment income from non-residents	–5

11 The stock of capital goods in the economy has expanded. **T F**

12 Gross investment is equal to $25 billion. **T F**

13 National income equals the net domestic income minus $5 billion. **T F**

14 Disposable income is equal to $245 billion. **T F**

15 Comparison of a gross domestic product with the gross domestic product of an earlier year when the price level has risen between the two years necessitates the "inflation" of the GDP figure in the later year. **T F**

16 To adjust nominal gross domestic product for a given year so that a comparison between GDP in that year and in the base year can be made, it is necessary to divide nominal GDP in the given year by the price index—expressed as a decimal—for that year. **T F**

17 The price index used to adjust nominal GDP to measure the real GDP is the consumer price index (CPI). **T F**

18 The GDP is a measure of the social welfare of society. **T F**

Circle the letter that corresponds to the best answer.

1 Which of the following is *not* an important use to which national accounting is put? (*a*) provides a basis for the formulation and application of policies designed to improve the economy's performance; (*b*) permits measurement of the economic efficiency of the economy; (*c*) makes possible an estimate of the output of final goods and services in the economy; (*d*) enables the economist to chart the growth of the economy over a period of time.

2 To include the value of the parts used in producing the automobiles turned out during a year in gross domestic product for that year would be an example of (*a*) including a non-market transaction; (*b*) including a non-productive transaction; (*c*) including a non-investment transaction; (*d*) double counting.

3 Which of the following is *not* a purely financial transaction? (*a*) the sale of a used (second-hand) ironing board at a garage sale; (*b*) the sale of shares of stock in Stelco; (*c*) the payment of the Canada Pension to a retired worker; (*d*) the birthday gift of a cheque for $5 sent by a grandmother to her grandchild.

4 The sale in 1986 of an automobile produced in 1982 would not be included in the gross domestic product for 1986; doing so would involve (*a*) including a non-market transaction; (*b*) including a non-productive transaction; (*c*) including a non-investment transaction; (*d*) double counting.

5 The service a babysitter performs when she stays at home with her baby brother while her parents are out and for which she receives no payment is not included in the gross domestic product because (*a*) this is a non-market transaction; (*b*) this is a non-productive transaction; (*c*) this is a non-investment transaction; (*d*) double counting would be involved.

6 Which of the following does *not* represent investment? (*a*) an increase in the quantity of shoes on the shelves of a shoe store; (*b*) the construction of a house that will be occupied by its owner; (*c*) the purchase of newly issued shares of stock in Canadian Pacific Limited; (*d*) the construction of a factory building using money borrowed from a bank.

7 A refrigerator is produced by its manufacturer in 1986, sold during 1986 to a retailer, and sold by the retailer to a final consumer in 1987. The refrigerator is (*a*) counted as consumption in 1986; (*b*) counted as investment in 1987; (*c*) counted as investment in 1986 and consumption and disinvestment in 1987; (*d*) not included in the gross domestic product of 1986.

Questions 8 to 14 use the national income accounting data given in the table in the true-false section.

8 The non-income charges are equal to (*a*) $11 billion; (*b*) $15 billion; (*c*) $17 billion; (*d*) $19 billion.

9 Corporate profits are equal to (*a*) $15 billion; (*b*) $25 billion; (*c*) $26 billion; (*d*) $36 billion.

10 Net exports are equal to (*a*) -$3 billion; (*b*) $2 billion; (*c*) -$32 billion; (*d*) $32 billion.

11 The gross domestic product is equal to (*a*) $245 billion; (*b*) $284 billion; (*c*) $298 billion; (*d*) $310 billion.

12 The net domestic income is equal to (*a*) $295 billion; (*b*) $302 billion; (*c*) $317 billion; (*d*) $321 billion.

13 National income exceeds personal income by (*a*) $6 billion; (*b*) $15 billion; (*c*) $21 billion; (*d*) $44 billion.

14 Personal saving is equal to (*a*) -$28 billion; (*b*) -$8 billion; (*c*) $8 billion; (*d*) $28 billion.

15 If both nominal gross domestic product and the level of prices are rising, it is evident that (*a*) real GDP is constant; (*b*) real GDP is rising but not as rapidly as prices; (*c*) real GDP is declining; (*d*) no conclusion can be drawn concerning the real GDP of the economy on the basis of this information.

16 Suppose GDP rose from $500 billion to $600 billion while the GDP deflator increased from 125 to 150. The real GDP (*a*) remained constant; (*b*) increased; (*c*) decreased; (*d*) cannot be calculated from these figures.

17 The GDP includes (*a*) the goods and services produced in the underground economy; (*b*) expenditures for equipment to reduce the pollution of the environment; (*c*) the value of the leisure enjoyed by citizens; (*d*) the goods and services produced but not bought and sold in the markets of the economy.

18 Changes in the real GDP from one year to the next do *not* reflect (*a*) changes in the quality of the goods and services produced; (*b*) changes in the size of the population of the economy; (*c*) changes in the average length of the work week; (*d*) any of the above changes.

DISCUSSION QUESTIONS

1 Of what use is national income accounting to the economist and to the policy makers in the economy?

2 Why are GDP, GNP, and so on, monetary measures, and why is it necessary that they be monetary measures?

3 Why does GDP exclude non-productive transactions? What are the two principal types of non-productive transactions? List some examples of each.

4 Why are there two ways, both of which yield the same answers, of computing GDP, net domestic income, and so on?

5 Why are transfer payments excluded from GDP, GNP, and NI?

6 Is residential construction counted as investment or consumption? Why? Why is a change in inventories an investment?

7 How do you define a static, an expanding, and a declining economy? What is the relationship between gross investment and the capital consumption allowances in these three economies?

8 What is meant by a non-income charge or allocation? What are the two principal non-income charges included in GDP? Why are they excluded from NI?

9 Why do economists find it necessary to inflate and deflate GDP when comparing GDP in different years? How do they do this?

10 Why is GDP not a measure of the social welfare of society?

19

MACROECONOMIC INSTABILITY: UNEMPLOYMENT AND INFLATION

In the last chapter you learned how to define and how to compute the gross domestic product and gross national product and national, personal, and disposable income in any year. This chapter begins the explanation of what determines how large each of these five income-output measures will tend to be. In the chapters that follow our study of money and banking, you will learn what causes the income and output of the economy to be what they are, what causes them to change, and how they might be controlled for the welfare of society.

Chapter 19 is concerned with the instability of the Canadian economy, or with what is commonly called the business cycle: the ups and downs in employment of labour and the real output of the economy that occur over the years. That there have been expansions and contractions in economic (or business) activity since before Confederation is evident from even a casual look at Canadian economic history. What is not immediately evident, however, is that these alternating and relatively short periods of prosperity and "hard times" have taken place over a very long period in which the trends in output, employment, and the standard of living have been upward. During this long history, booms and busts have occurred quite irregulary; and their duration and intensity have been so varied that it is better to think of economic instability than of business cycles.

There are two principal problems that result from the instability of the economy—from the business cycle. After a brief

look, in the first major section of the chapter, at the business cycle, its phases, and its impact on the production of different kinds of goods, we turn to the first of these two problems in the second major section. Here you will find an examination of the unemployment that accompanies a downturn in the level of economic activitiy in the economy. You will discover that there are different kinds of unemployment, that full employment means about 6% of the labour force is unemployed, and that there are at least three problems encountered in measuring what percentage of the labour force is actually unemployed at any time. That unemployment has an economic cost, and that this cost is unequally distributed among different sectors of our society, you will also learn; and you probably won't be too surprised to discover that widespread unemployment can be the cause of other social problems.

The second of the two problems that result from economic instability is inflation, and it is examined in the remainder of the chapter. Inflation is an increase in the general (or average) level of prices in an economy. It does not have a unique cause: it may result from increases in demand; increases in costs; or from both. But regardless of its cause, it works a real hardship on certain sectors within the economy. If it occurs at too rapid a rate, it may bring about a severe breakdown in the economy.

One last word. The thing to keep your eye on when you consider economic fluctuations and unemployment and inflation in the

Canadian economy are the changes in total or aggregate spending that can occur because consumers, business firms, the public sector or non-residents decide to spend more or less for goods and services.

CHECK LIST

When you have studied this chapter you should be able to

☐ Explain what is meant by the business cycle; describe the four phases of an idealized cycle; and identify the two types of non-cyclical fluctuations.

☐ Identify the "immediate determinant" or cause of the levels of output and employment.

☐ Distinguish between the impact of cyclical fluctuations on industries producing capital and consumer durable goods and on those producing consumer semi- and non-durable goods; and on high- and low-concentration industries.

☐ Distinguish between frictional, structural, and cyclical unemployment; and explain the causes of these three kinds of unemployment.

☐ Define full employment.

☐ Describe the process employed (by Statistics Canada) to measure the rate of unemployment; and list the three criticisms of Statscan data.

☐ Define the GDP gap, and state Okun's law.

☐ Identify the economic cost of unemployment and two groups that bear the unequal burdens of unemployment.

☐ Define inflation and describe the two kinds of inflation.

☐ Explain the effects of an increase in total spending on output and employment *and* on the rate of increase in the price level of ranges 1, 2, and 3.

☐ List three groups that are hurt by and two groups that benefit from inflation.

☐ Present three scenarios that describe the possible effects of inflation on output and employment.

CHAPTER OUTLINE

1 The history of the Canadian economy is a record of exceptional economic growth.
a. But this growth has been accompanied by periods of inflation, of depression, or of both.
b. The business cycle means alternating periods of prosperity and depression. These recurrent periods of ups and downs in employment, output, and prices are irregular in their duration and intensity; but the typical pattern is: peak, recession, trough, and recovery to another peak.
c. Changes in the levels of output and employment are largely the result of changes in the level of total spending or demand in the economy.
d. Not all changes in employment and output that occur in the economy are cyclical; some are due to seasonal and secular influences.
e. The business cycle affects the entire economy, but it does not affect all parts in the same way and to the same degree. In particular, the production of capital and durable consumer goods fluctuates more than the production of consumer non-durable and semi-durable goods during a cycle because
(1) the purchase of capital and durable consumer goods can be postponed, and
(2) the industries producing these goods are largely dominated by a few large firms that hold prices constant and let output decline when demand falls.

2 Full employment does not mean that all workers in the labour force are employed and that there is no unemployment; some unemployment is normal.
a. There are at least three kinds of unemployment.
(1) There is always some frictional unemployment, and this kind of unemployment is

generally desirable.

(2) And in addition there is the structural unemployment that is the result of changes in technology and in the types of goods and services consumers wish to buy.

(3) Cyclical unemployment is the result of insufficient aggregate spending in the economy.

b. Because some frictional and structural unemployment is unavoidable, the full-employment unemployment rate (the natural rate of unemployment) is the sum of frictional and structural unemployment; is achieved when cyclical unemployment is zero (real output of the economy is equal to its potential output) and is about 6% of the labour force.

c. Surveying 55,000 households each month, Statistics Canada finds the unemployment rate by dividing the number of persons in the civilian labour force who are unemployed by the number of people in the civilian labour force; but the figures collected in the survey have been criticized for at least three reasons.

d. Unemployment has an economic cost.

(1) The economic cost is the unproduced output (or the GDP gap), and Okun's law is that for every 1% the actual unemployment rate exceeds the natural rate of unemployment there is 2.5% GDP gap.

e. Unemployment also leads to serious social problems.

3 Over its history the Canadian economy has experienced not only periods of unemployment but periods of inflation.

a. Inflation is an increase in the general level of prices in the economy; and a decline in the level of prices is deflation.

b. The rate of inflation in any year is equal to the percentage change in the price index between that year and the preceding year; and the rule of 70 can be used to calculate the number of years it will take for the price level to double at any given rate of inflation.

c. There are at least two causes of inflation; and these two causes may operate separately

or simultaneously to raise the price level.

(1) Demand-pull inflation is the result of excess aggregate demand in the economy. While increases in aggregate demand do not increase the price level when the unemployment rate is high (in a depression), they do bring about inflation as the economy moves toward and reaches full employment.

(2) Cost-push inflation is the result of the ability of strong labour unions and large business firms with market power to raise wage rates and prices; and it may occur when aggregate demand is not excessive and output and employment are declining.

4 Even if the total output of the economy did not change, inflation would arbitrarily redistribute real income and wealth; and would benefit some groups and hurt other groups in the economy.

a. Inflation injures those whose nominal incomes rise less rapidly and benefits those whose nominal incomes rise more rapidly than the price level.

b. It also injures savers because it decreases the real value of any savings the nominal value of which is fixed.

c. And it benefits debtors and hurts creditors because it lowers the real value of debts.

d. But when the inflation is anticipated and people can adjust their nominal incomes to reflect the expected rise in the price level, the redistribution of income and wealth is lessened.

e. Since World War II, inflation in Canada has redistributed wealth from the household to the public sector of the economy.

f. In short, inflation acts to tax some groups and to subsidize other groups.

5 Inflation may also affect the total output of the economy, but economists disagree over whether it is likely to expand or contract total output.

a. Mild demand-pull inflation seems likely to expand output and employment in the economy.

b. Cost-push inflation is apt to contract

output and employment.

c. And hyperinflation may well lead to the breakdown of the economy.

IMPORTANT TERMS

Business cycle	GDP gap
Seasonal variation	Okun's law
Secular trend	Inflation
Frictional unemployment	Deflation
	Rule of 70
Structural unemployment	Demand-pull inflation
Cyclical unemployment	Cost-push inflation
	Nominal income
Full employment	Real income
Full-employment— unemployment rate	Cost-of-living adjustment (COLA)
Natural rate of unemployment	Anticipated inflation
Potential output	Unanticipated inflation
Unemployment rate	Hyperinflation
Civilian labour force	Wage-price inflationary spiral
Discouraged workers	

FILL-IN QUESTIONS

1 The history of the Canadian economy is one of (steady, unsteady) _____ economic growth; at times, its growth has been accompanied by _____ , and at other times its expansion has been interrupted by low levels of _____ and _____ .

2 The business cycle is a term that means the recurrent _____ and _____ in the level of business activity in the economy; the four phases of a typical business cycle are peak, _____ , _____ , and _____ .

3 The basic determinant of the levels of employment and output in an economy is the level of total _____ or aggregate _____ in the economy.

4 In addition to the changes brought about by the operation of the business cycle, changes in output and employment may be due to _____ variations and to a _____ trend.

5 Production and employment in the (durable, non-durable) _____ and (capital, consumer) _____ goods industries are affected to a greater extent by the expansion and contraction of the economy than they are in the _____ goods industries; and prices vary to a greater extent in the (low-, high-) _____ concentration industries.

6 The three types of unemployment are:

a. _____ ;

b. _____ ;

c. _____ .

7 The full-employment unemployment rate is

a. sometimes called the _____ rate of unemployment;

b. equal to the total of the _____ and the _____ unemployment in the economy;

c. realized when the _____ unemployment in the economy is equal to zero and when the _____ output of the economy is equal to its _____ output; and

d. assumed in this chapter to be about _____%.

8 When the economy achieves its natural rate of unemployment, the number of job seekers is (greater than, less than, equal to) _____ the number of job vacancies; and the price level is (rising, falling, constant) _____.

9 The unemployment *rate* is found by dividing _____ by the _____ .

10 The GDP gap is equal to _____ GDP *minus* _____ GDP.

11 The burdens of unemployment are borne more heavily by _____ , (adult, teenage) _____ , and (educated, uneducated) _____ workers.

12 Inflation means a _____ in the general level of _____ in the economy; and the rate of inflation in year 1987 is equal to the price index for year _____ less the price index for year _____ all divided by the price index for year _____ .

13 The basic cause of
a. demand-pull inflation is (an increase, a decrease) _____ in aggregate demand;
b. cost-push inflation is the result of the _____ power of strong _____ and large _____ .

14 Inflation
a. hurts those whose money incomes are relatively (fixed, flexible) _____ ;
b. penalizes savers when the inflation is

(expected, unexpected) _____ ;
c. hurts (creditors, debtors) _____ and benefits _____ ;
d. has since World War II shifted wealth from (the public sector, households) _____ _____ to _____ .

15 Despite considerable disagreement and uncertainty among economists, it seeems that
a. demand-pull inflation, unless there is full employment in the economy, will (increase, decrease) _____ total output and employment;
b. cost-push inflation will _____ output and employment in the economy;
c. hyperinflation may bring about an economic _____ .

PROBLEMS AND PROJECTS

1 In the following table are statistics* showing the civilian labour force and total employment in Canada in June 1982 and July 1982. Make the computations necessary to complete the statistics. (Numbers of persons are in thousands.)

	June 1982	July 1982
Civilian labour force	12,192	12,388
Employed	10,888	11,002
Unemployed	_____	_____
Employment Rate	____%	____%
Unemployment Rate	____%	____%

Source: Statistics Canada, *Canadian Statistical Review*, January 1983 (Ottawa, 1983), p. 38.

a. How is it possible that *both* employment and unemployment increased? _____ _____

b. In relative terms, if unemployment

increases, employment will decrease. Why?

_____

c. Would you say that the summer of 1982 was a period of full employment? _____

d. Why is the task of maintaining full employment over the years more than just a problem of finding jobs for those who happen to be unemployed at any given time?

_____

2 In the space below, indicate for each of the following situations the effects of an increase in total spending on *real GDP*, *nominal GDP*, the *unemployment rate*, and the *price level*, respectively, using the following symbols: A: little or no effect; B: increase; C: decrease; and D: sharp increase.

a. Depression and widespread unemployment

_____ _____ _____ _____

b. Prosperity, but moderate unemployment

_____ _____ _____ _____

c. Prosperity and full employment

_____ _____ _____ _____

3 Indicate in the space to the right of each of the following, the effect [beneficial (B), detrimental (D), or indeterminate (I)] of inflation on these persons:

a. A retired, self-employed business executive who now lives by spending, each month, a part of the amount saved and deposited in a savings and loan association. _____

b. A retired private-school teacher who lives on the dividends she receives from the shares of stocks she owns. _____

c. A farmer who (by mortgaging his farm) borrowed at the local bank $500,000 that must be repaid during the next ten years.

_____

d. A retired couple whose sole source of income is the pension they receive from her former employer. _____

e. A widow whose income consists entirely of interest received from the corporate bonds she owns. _____

f. A public-school teacher. _____

g. A member of a union who works for a firm that produces computers. _____

h. The Canadian government. _____

4 Suppose that in 1987 the economy is at full employment, and has a potential and actual real GDP of $700 billion, and an unemployment rate of 6%.

a. Compute the GDP gap in 1987 and enter it in the table below.

Year	Potential GDP	Actual GDP	GDP gap
1987	$700	700	$_____
1988	760	741	_____
1989	825	742.5	_____

b. The potential and actual real GDPs in 1988 and 1989 are also shown in the table. Compute and enter into the table the GDP gaps in these two years.

c. In 1988 the actual real GDP is _____ % of the potential real GDP. (*Hint*: divide the actual real GDP by the potential real GDP.)

(1) The actual real GDP is _____ % less than the potential real GDP.

(2) Using Okun's law, the unemployment rate will rise from 6% in 1987 and be _____ % in 1988.

d. In 1989 the actual real GDP is _____ % of the potential real GDP.

(1) The actual real GDP is _____ % *less* than the potential real GDP.

(2) The unemployment rate, according to Okun's law, will be _____ %.

5 The following table shows the price index in the economy at the end of four different years.

Year	Price index	Rate of inflation
1	100.00	
2	112.00	_____ %
3	123.20	_____
4	129.36	_____

a. Compute and enter in the table the rates of inflation in years 2, 3, and 4.
b. Employing the "rule of 70," how many years would it take for the price level to double at each of these three inflation rates?

_____

_____

6   On the two following graphs, the price *level* is measured along the vertical axis and *real* domestic output is measured along the horizontal axis. The demand for and the supply of domestic output are shown by the curves labelled *D* and *S*.
a. Applying the principles of demand and supply that you learned in Chapter 3, the equilibrium price level is the price level at which the domestic output demanded and

the domestic output supplied are _____

and the equilibrium domestic output is ____

_____ .

b. Draw, on the first graph, a new demand curve that represents an *increase* in the demand for domestic output.

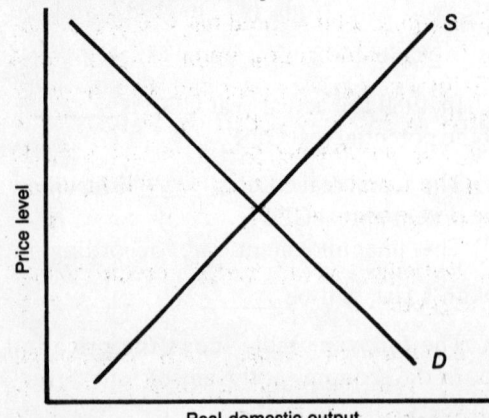

Real domestic output

(1) The effect of this increase in demand is a rise in the equilibrium price level and a(n)

_____ in the equilibrium domestic output.
(2) This rise in the price level is an example

of _____ inflation.
c. On the second graph, draw a new supply curve that represents a *decrease* in the supply of domestic output.

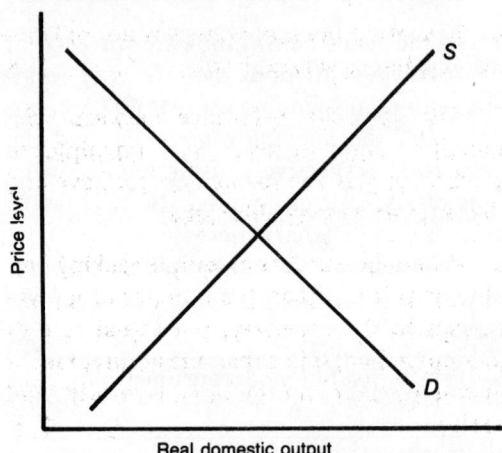

Real domestic output

(1) The effect of this decrease in supply is a

_____ in the equilibrium

price level and a _____ in the equilibrium domestic output.

(2) These effects are an example of _____

_____ .

SELF-TEST

Circle T if the statement is true, F if it is false.

1   The Canadian economy has experienced a long period of substantial economic growth and shorter periods of inflation and of high unemployment.   **T F**

2   The business cycle is best defined as alternating periods of increases and decreases in the rate of inflation in the economy. **T F**

3 Individual business cycles tend to be of roughly equal duration and intensity. **T F**

4 Not all changes that occur in output and employment in the economy are due to the business cycle. **T F**

5 Industries that are highly concentrated show small relative decreases in output and large relative decreases in prices during a downswing of the business cycle. **T F**

6 Frictional unemployment is not only inevitable but largely desirable. **T F**

7 The essential difference between frictionally and structurally unemployed workers is that the former *do not* have and the latter *do* have salable skills.

8 When the number of people seeking employment is less than the number of job vacancies in the economy, the actual rate of unemployment is less than the natural rate of unemployment and the price level will tend to rise. **T F**

9 If unemployment in the economy is at its natural rate, the actual and potential outputs of the economy are equal. **T F**

10 The natural rate of unemployment in the Canadian economy is a constant 6% of the labour force. **T F**

11 An economy cannot produce indefinitely an actual real GDP that exceeds its potential real GDP. **T F**

12 The unemployment rate is equal to the number of persons in the civilian labour force divided by the number of people who are unemployed. **T F**

13 The percentage of the labour force unemployed for fourteen or more weeks is always less than the unemployment rate and tends to rise during a recession. **T F**

14 The economy's GDP gap is measured by deducting its actual GDP from its potential GDP. **T F**

15 The economic costs of cyclical unemployment are the goods and services that are not produced. **T F**

16 Inflation is defined as an increase in the total output of an economy. **T F**

17 Between 1984 and 1985 the consumer price index rose from 122.3 to 127.2. The rate of inflation was, therefore, 4.9%. **T F**

18 If the price level increases by 10% each year, the price level will double every ten years. **T F**

19 With a moderate amount of unemployment in the economy, an increase in total spending will generally increase both the price level and the output of the economy. **T F**

20 If the economy is operating at full employment, a decrease in total spending can be expected to reduce both the price level and employment in the economy. **T F**

21 A person's real income is the amount of goods and services that the person's money (or nominal) income will enable him or her to purchase. **T F**

22 Whether the inflation is anticipated or unanticipated, the effects of inflation on the distribution of income are much the same. **T F**

23 Suppose a household has $10,000 on deposit in a credit union upon which it earns 7% interest during a year and the rate of inflation is 9% in that year. By the end of the year the purchasing power of the $10,000 and the interest it has earned will have decreased to about $9,817. **T F**

24 Deflation would benefit creditors and hurt debtors. **T F**

25 Inflation in Canada has transferred wealth from the public sector of the economy to the households. **T F**

Circle the letter that corresponds to the best answer.

1 Which one of the following is *not* one of the four phases of an idealized business cycle? (*a*) inflation; (*b*) recession; (*c*) recovery; (*d*) trough.

2 Most economists believe that the immediate determinant of the levels of domestic output and employment is (*a*) the price level; (*b*) the size of the civilian labour force; (*c*) the nation's stock of capital goods; (*d*) the level of aggregate spending.

3 Total employment in December of this year was greater than total employment in December 1928. This is no doubt due to the effect of (*a*) seasonal variations; (*b*) secular trend; (*c*) the business cycle; (*d*) business fluctuations.

4 If employment in the forest products sector of the Canadian economy during last August and September was 112% of what it normally is in those months, this is probably a consequence of (*a*) seasonal variations; (*b*) secular trend; (*c*) the business cycle; (*d*) both seasonal variations and the business cycle.

5 Production and employment in which of the following industries would be least affected by a depression? (*a*) non-durable consumer goods; (*b*) durable consumer goods; (*c*) capital goods; (*d*) iron and steel.

6 A worker who loses his job at a petroleum refinery because consumers and business firms switch from the use of oil to the burning of coal is an example of (*a*) frictional unemployment; (*b*) structural unemployment; (*c*) cyclical unemployment; (*d*) disguised unemployment.

7 A worker who has quit one job and is taking two weeks off before reporting to a new job is an example of (*a*) frictional unemployment; (*b*) structural unemployment; (*c*) cyclical unemployment; (*d*) disguised unemployment.

8 Insufficient aggregate demand results in (*a*) frictional unemployment; (*b*) structural unemployment; (*c*) cyclical unemployment; (*d*) disguised unemployment.

9 The full-employment unemployment rate in the economy has been achieved when (*a*) frictional unemployment is zero; (*b*) structural unemployment is zero; (*c*) cyclical unemployment is zero; (*d*) the natural rate of unemployment is zero.

10 Which of the following has increased the natural rate of unemployment in Canada? (*a*) the increased participation of women and teenagers in the Canadian labour force; (*b*) the expansion of unemployment insurance benefits in Canada; (*c*) the increases in the legal minimum wage; (*d*) all of the above.

11 The civilian labour force includes those who are (*a*) less than fifteen years of age; (*b*) in mental institutions; (*c*) not seeking work; (*d*) employed.

12 The data collected by Statistics Canada have been criticized because (*a*) part-time workers are not counted in the number of workers employed; (*b*) discouraged workers are treated as a part of the civilian labour force; (*c*) some workers who are not looking for work are included in the civilian labour force; (*d*) all of the above.

13 Okun's law predicts that when the actual unemployment rate exceeds the natural rate of unemployment by two percentage points the GDP gap will equal (*a*) 2% of the potential GDP; (*b*) 3% of the potential GDP; (*c*) 4% of the potential GDP; (*d*) 5% of the potential GDP.

14 If the GDP gap were equal to 7.5% of the potential GDP, the actual unemployment rate would exceed the natural rate of unemployment by (*a*) two percentage points; (*b*) three percentage points; (*c*) four percentage points; (*d*) five percentage points.

15 The burden of unemployment is *least* felt by (*a*) the uneducated; (*b*) teenagers; (*c*) workers 15—24 years of age; (d) workers 25 years of age and older.

16 If the resources of the economy are fully employed, an increase in aggregate spending will cause (a) output and employment to increase; (b) output and prices to increase; (c) nominal incomes and prices to increase; (d) employment and nominal incomes to increase.

17 If the economy is experiencing a depression with substantial unemployment, an increase in total spending will cause (a) a decrease in the *real* income of the economy; (b) little or no increase in the level of prices; (c) an increase in the *real* income and a decrease in the *nominal* income of the economy; (d) proportionate increases in the price level, output, and income in the economy.

18 If a person's nominal income increases by 8% while the price level increases by 10%, the person's real income will have (a) increased by 2%; (b) increased by 18%; (c) decreased by 18% (d) decreased by 2%.

19 If no inflation were anticipated, a bank would be willing to lend a business firm $10 million at an annual interest of 8%. If the rate of inflation were expected to be 6%, the bank would charge the firm an annual interest rate of (a) 2%; (b) 6%; (c) 8%; (d) 14%.

20 Of the following, who would *not* be hurt by inflation? (a) those living on fixed money incomes; (b) those who find prices rising more rapidly than their money incomes; (c) those who have money savings; (d) those who became debtors when prices were lower.

21 Mild demand-pull inflation, many economists argue, results in (a) rising output; (b) rising real income; (c) falling unemployment; (d) all of the above.

22 Which of the following is *not* related to the cost-push theory of inflation? (a) an increase in employment and output; (b) the market power of aggressive labour unions; (c) the ability of large corporations to administer prices; (d) a decrease in supply.

23 Which of the following is *not* associated with hyperinflation? (a) war or its aftermath; (b) rising output in the economy; (c) the hoarding of goods and speculation; (d) a halt to the use of money as both a medium of exchange and a standard of value.

24 Inflation in the Canadian economy has been caused by (a) increases in aggregate demand; (b) decreases in aggregate supply; (c) either a or b; (d) both a and b.

25 Since 1983 (a) both the rate of inflation and the unemployment rate have increased; (b) the rate of inflation has increased and the unemployment rate has decreased; (c) the rate of inflation has increased and the unemployment rate has decreased; (d) both the rate of inflation and the unemployment rate have decreased.

DISCUSSION QUESTIONS

1 What is the historical record of the Canadian economy with respect to economic growth, full employment, and price-level stability?

2 Define the business cycle. Why do some economists prefer the term "business fluctuation" to "business cycle"? Describe the four phases of an idealized cycle.

3 What, in the opinion of most economists, is the immediate determinant or cause of the levels of output and employment in the economy?

4 The business cycle is only one of three general causes of changes in output and employment in the economy. What are the other influences that affect these variables?

5 Compare the manner in which the business cycle affects output and employment in the industries producing capital and durable goods with industries producing non-durable goods and services. What causes these differences?

6 Distinguish between frictional, structural, and cyclical unemployment.

7 When is there full employment in the Canadian economy? (Answer in terms of the unemployment rate, the actual and potential output of the economy, and the markets for labour.)

8 How is the unemployment rate measured in Canada? What criticisms have been made of Statistics Canada's method of determining the unemployment rate?

9 What is the economic cost of unemployment, and how is this cost measured? What is the quantitative relationship (called Okun's law) between the unemployment rate and the cost of unemployment?

10 What groups in the economy tend to bear the burdens of unemployment? How are blue-collar workers affected by unemployment and how is the percentage of the labour force unemployed fourteen or more weeks related to the unemployment rate in the economy?

11 What is inflation and how is the rate of inflation measured?

12 Compare and contrast demand-pull and cost-push inflation.

13 What groups benefit from and what groups are hurt by inflation, and how has the public sector of the economy been affected by it?

14 What is the difference between the effects of unanticipated and the effects of anticipated inflation on the redistribution of real incomes in the economy?

15 Explain what will tend to happen to employment, output, money income, and the price level if total spending increases and the resources of the economy are: (*a*) widely unemployed, (*b*) moderately unemployed, (*c*) fully employed. If total spending *decreased*, would the effects on employment, output, income, and the price level be just the opposite?

16 Write three scenarios that describe the effects of inflation on the real domestic output.

20

MONEY AND BANKING IN CANADA

By and large, Chapter 20 is descriptive and factual. It contains only a brief explanation of how the financial system affects the operation of the economy. The purpose of this chapter is, however, to prepare you for a more detailed explanation (in Chapters 21 and 22).

Of special importance in this chapter are the many terms and definitions that will be new to you. These must be learned if the following two chapters and their analysis of how the financial system affects the performance of the economy are to be understood. Chapter 20 also contains a factual description of the institutions that comprise the Canadian banking system—the Bank of Canada and the chartered banks—and the functions of these institutions.

You will do well to pay particular attention to the following: (1) what money is and the functions it performs, what types of money exist in the Canadian economy and their relative importance, and how four measures of the money supply (M1, M1A, M2, and M3) are defined; (2) what gives value to, or "backs," Canadian money; (3) why people want to have money in their possession, and what determines how much money they want to have on hand at any time; (4) how the total demand for money and the money supply together determine the equilibrium rate of interest; and (5) the two basic institutions of the Canadian banking system, their functions, and their relationships.

Several points are worth repeating here because so much depends upon their being fully understood. First, money is whatever performs the three functions of money, and in Canada money consists of Bank of Canada notes and the debts (promises to pay) of chartered banks. In Canada, this money is "backed" by the goods and services for which its owners can exchange it and not by gold or any other precious metal.

Second, because money is used as a medium of exchange, consumers and business firms wish to have money on hand to use for transactions purposes; and the quantity of money they demand for this purpose is directly related to the size of the economy's money (or nominal) gross domestic product. This means that when either the price level or the real gross domestic product increases, they will want to have more money on hand to use for transactions. But money is also used as a store of value: consumers and firms who own assets may choose to have some of their assets in the form of money (rather than in stocks, bonds, goods, or property). There is, therefore, also an asset demand for money. Holding money, however, imposes a cost on those who hold it. This cost is the interest they lose when they own money rather than, say, bonds. This means that people will demand less money for asset purposes when the rate of interest (the cost of holding money) is high and more money when the rate of interest is low: the quantity of money demanded for this purpose is inversely related to the interest rate. The total demand for money is the sum of the transactions demand and the asset demand and, therefore, depends upon the nominal GDP and the rate of interest. This total demand and the money supply determine interest rates in the economy.

Third, the central bank is the Bank of Canada, which operates as an agency of the federal government—not for profit, but primarily to regulate the nation's money supply in the best interests of the economy as a whole, and secondarily to perform other services for the banks, the government, and the economy. It is able to perform its primary function because it is a banker's bank, where chartered banks can deposit and borrow money. The Bank of Canada does not deal directly with the public.

Fourth, chartered banks, like many other financial institutions, accept deposits and make loans, but they also—and this distinguishes them from financial intermediaries—are literally able to create money by lending deposits. However, trust companies, credit unions, and other such non-bank financial intermediaries, in effect, also create money when they lend chequable deposits—except that the Bank of Canada does not count these non-bank deposits in its official definition of the money supply. Because banks are able to create money, they have a strong influence on the size of the money supply and the value of money. The Bank of Canada exists primarily to regulate the money supply and its value by influencing and controlling the amount of money the chartered banks create.

CHECK LIST

When you have studied this chapter you should be able to

☐ List the three functions of money, and explain the meaning of each function.

☐ Define the money supply, M1.

☐ Explain the meaning of near-money and identify the principal near-monies; and then define M2 and M3.

☐ Present three reasons why near-monies are important.

☐ Explain why money in the Canadian economy is debt, and whose debts paper money and deposits are.

☐ Present three reasons why currency and demand deposits are money and have

value.

☐ Indicate the precise relationship between the value of money and the price level.

☐ Explain what is meant by stabilizing the value of money and enumerate the two devices government utilizes to try to stabilize its value.

☐ Identify the two demands for money and the determinant of each of these demands; and explain the relationship between each demand and its determinant.

☐ Explain what determines the equilibrium rate of interest; and how changes in the nominal GDP and the money supply will affect this interest rate.

☐ Describe the structure of the Canadian banking system.

☐ List several kinds of financial intermediaries; explain the role played by these intermediaries; and state the distinction between a financial intermediary and a chartered bank.

☐ Explain why the Bank of Canada is a central, public, bankers' bank.

☐ Enumerate the five functions of the Bank of Canada; explain the meaning of each of these functions; indicate which is the most important.

CHAPTER OUTLINE

1 Money is whatever performs the three basic functions of money: a medium of exchange, a standard of value, and a store of value.

2 In the Canadian economy, money is whatever is generally used as a medium of exchange; and consists of the debts of the federal government, of chartered banks, and, in effect, of other financial intermediaries that have set up chequing accounts.

a. The narrowly defined money supply is called M1 and consists of

(1) coins, which are token money and the smallest part of the total money supply;

(2) paper money, which is Bank of Canada

notes; and

(3) demand deposits, which are bank-created money and the largest component of the money supply.

(4) Currency and deposits owned by the federal government and the chartered banks are *not* included in M1 or in any of the more broadly defined money supplies.

b.   A more broadly defined money supply is called M1A, and is equal to M1 plus *chequable* personal savings and non-personal notice deposits in chartered banks. M2 and M3 are yet broader definitions.

c.   The amount of these near-monies held by the public is important for at least three reasons.

d.   Credit cards are not money but are a device by which the cardholders obtain a loan (credit) from the issuer of the card.

3   In Canada,

a.   money is largely the promise of either a chartered bank or the Bank of Canada to pay; but the central bank's "debts" cannot be redeemed for anything tangible: all the Bank of Canada will give you in exchange for a dollar bill is another one;

b.   money has value only because people can exchange it for desirable goods and services;

c.   the value of money is inversely related to the price level;

d.   money is "backed" by the confidence the public has that the value of money will remain stable; the federal government can use monetary and fiscal policy to keep the value of money relatively stable.

4   Business firms and households wish to hold and, therefore, demand money for two reasons.

a.   Because they use money as a medium of exchange, they have a transactions demand, which is directly related to the nominal gross domestic product of the economy.

b.   Because they also use money as a store of value, they have an asset demand, which is inversely related to the rate of interest.

c.   Their total demand for money is the sum of the transactions and asset demands.

d.   This total demand for money along with the supply of money determine the equilibrium interest rate in the money market of the economy.

5   The centralized Canadian banking system consists of 63 privately owned and operated chartered banks (8 Canadian-owned, 55 foreign-owned) and the Bank of Canada, which is owned by the federal government. The foreign-owned banks will always remain a small part of the whole, because of legal restrictions on their growth.

a.   The banking system is centralized because the requirement in the Bank Act that each commercial bank must be separately chartered by Parliament has resulted in few banks—each of the Canadian-owned banks has many branches. The five largest banks have more than a thousand branches each. The banks perform the two essential functions of holding deposits and making loans.

b.   The Bank of Canada, established as the central bank in 1935, is owned by the government. It exercises control over the supply of money and the banking system.

c.   Both the chartered banks and the non-bank financial intermediaries act as intermediaries between savers and investors; both create and destroy chequable deposit money but the Bank of Canada counts only deposits in the chartered banks in its official definitions of the money supply.

d.   The Bank of Canada performs five functions aimed at providing certain essential services, assisting the Department of Finance in the supervision of the chartered banks, and regulating the supply of money.

IMPORTANT TERMS

Medium of exchange	Token money
Standard of value	Intrinsic value
Store of value	Face value
Money supply	Paper money
M1	Bank of Canada Note

Chequable deposit

Demand deposit

Currency

Near-money

Savings, term, and
notice deposits

M1A

M2

M3

Near-bank

Legal tender

Fiat money

Value of money

Canada Deposit
Insurance
Corporation

Transactions
demand
for money

Asset demand for
money

Total demand for
money

Money market

Prime rate

Central bank

Bankers' bank

Chartered bank

Financial
intermediary

Cheque clearing

FILL-IN QUESTIONS

1 Three functions of money are

a. _____ ;

b. _____ ;

c. _____ .

2 The supply of money, M1, in Canada
consists of _____ ,

_____ ,

and _____

not owned by _____

or_____ .

3 The *other* financial intermediaries

a. include such institutions as _____

companies, _____

companies, _____ unions, and

_____ companies;

b. channel funds from _____

to_____ ;

c. like banks, can set up chequable deposits
and thus can, like banks, _____

and _____ money; however,

their deposits (are, are not) _____
counted in the money supply by the

_____ unless it is majority-

owned by a _____ .

4 The most important near-monies in the

Canadian economy are _____, _____,

and _____ deposits in chartered banks

and _____ institutions. Another important near-money is Government of

Canada _____ .

5 The money supply, M1A, is equal to

chequable near-monies plus _____ .

6 List three reasons why the discussion of
near-monies is important.

a. _____

b. _____

c. _____

7 Money in Canada consists largely of

_____ banknotes

and the debts of _____ .

8 In Canada currency and chequable deposits

a. (are, are not) _____
"backed" by gold and silver;

b. are money because they are used as a

medium of _____ , they are in

the case of currency _____

tender, and they are relatively (abundant,

scarce) _____ .

9 Money has value because it can be

exchanged for _____

and its value varies (directly, inversely) _____ with changes in the _____ level.

10 The total demand for money is the sum of

a. the transactions demand, which depends (directly, inversely) _____ upon the_____ ;

b. and the asset demand, which depends _____ upon the _____ .

11 The total demand for money and the _____ of money determine the equilibrium _____ rate in the _____ market.

12 If a bank is a bankers' bank, it means that it accepts the _____ of and stands ready to _____ to (households, business firms, chartered banks, the public sector) _____ .

13 Chartered banks are banks that accept _____ make loans, and in doing so _____ .

14 The five major functions of the Bank of Canada are

a. _____

b. _____

c. _____

d. _____

e. _____

The most important of the functions that the Bank of Canada performs is that of _____ .

15 When it is said that the Bank of Canada acts as a fiscal agent for the federal government, it is meant that the central bank holds part of the federal government's _____ , helps the government to collect _____ , and administers the sale and redemption of government _____ .

PROBLEMS AND PROJECTS

1 From the data in the table below, it can be concluded that on the date to which the figures pertain:

	Billions
Total currency outstanding	$13
Total chequable personal savings and chequable non-personal notice deposits of the public at chartered banks	8
Deposits of the federal government at the Bank of Canada	0.1
Currency owned by chartered banks	2
Demand deposits of the public at chartered banks	18
Government bonds owned by the public	40
Deposits of the federal government at chartered banks	3

a. The amount of currency in the money supply, M1, is $ _____ billion.

b. The money supply, M1, is $ _____ billion.

c. M1A is equal to $ _____ billion.

2 If the price level

a. fell by 20%, the value of money would _____ by _____ %;

b. rose by 10%, the value of money would _____ by _____ %.

3 The total demand for money is equal to the transactions plus the asset demand for money.

a. Assume each dollar held for transaction purposes is spent (on the average) four times per year to buy final goods and services.
(1) This means that transactions demand for money will be equal to (what fraction or percent) _____ of the nominal GDP and
(2) if the nominal GDP is $500 billion, the transactions demand will be $ _____ billion.
b. The schedule below shows the number of dollars demanded for asset purposes at each rate of interest.

Rate of Interest	Amount of Money Demanded (billions)	
	For Asset Purposes	Total
16%	$10	$_____
14	20	_____
12	30	_____
10	40	_____
8	50	_____
6	60	_____
4	70	_____

(1) Given the transactions demand for money in (*a*) above, complete the table above.
(2) On the following graph, plot the total demand for money (D_m) at each rate of interest.
c. Assume the money supply (S_m)is $165 billion.
(1) Plot this money supply on the same graph.
(2) Using either the graph or the table, the equilibrium rate of interest is _____%.
d. Should the money supply
(1) increase to $175 billion the equilibrium interest rate would (rise, fall) _____ to _____%.
(2) decrease to $145 billion the equilibrium interest rate would _____ to _____%.

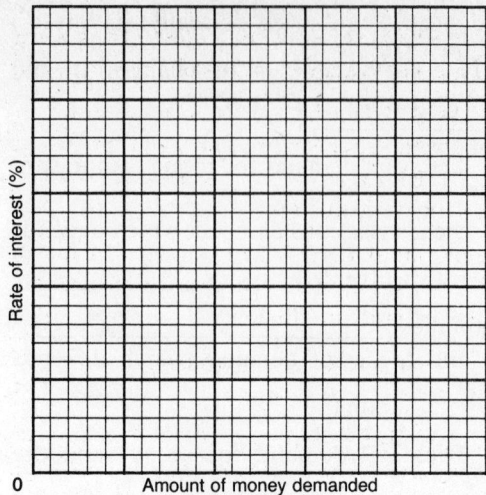

Rate of interest (%)

0   Amount of money demanded
              (billions of dollars)

e. If the nominal GDP
(1) increased by $40 billion, the total demand for money would (increase, decrease) _____ by $_____ billion at each rate of interest and the equilibrium rate of interest would (rise, fall) _____ by _____ percentage points;
(2) decreased by $60 billion, the total demand for money would _____ by $ _____ billion at each rate of interest and the equilibrium interest rate would _____ by _____ percentage points.

SELF-TEST

Circle T if the statement is true, F if it is false.

1 The money supply designated M1 is the sum of currency and non-chequable deposits. **T F**

2 The currency component of M1 includes both coins and paper money. **T F**

3 If a coin is "token money," its face value is less than its intrinsic value. **T F**

4 The demand deposits of the federal government in the chartered banks are a component of M1. **T F**

5 Both chartered banks and savings institutions accept chequable deposits. **T F**

6 M1A exceeds M1 by the amount of chequable savings and notice deposits in chartered banks but excludes those in various thrift institutions. **T F**

7 Economists and public officials are in general agreement on how to define the money supply in Canada. **T F**

8 A near-money is a medium of exchange. **T F**

9 The larger the volume of near-monies owned by consumers, the larger will be their average propensity to save. **T F**

10 Currency and chequable deposits are money because they are acceptable to sellers in exchange for goods and services. **T F**

11 If money is to have a fairly stable value, its supply must be limited relative to the demand for it. **T F**

12 There is a transactions demand for money because households and businesss firms use money as a store of value. **T F**

13 An increase in the price level would, *ceteris paribus*, increase the transactions demand for money. **T F**

14 An increase in the nominal GDP, other things remaining the same, will increase both the total demand for money and the equilibrium rate of interest in the economy. **T F**

15 The governor and deputy governor of the Bank of Canada are appointed for seven-year terms by the Bank's board of directors with the approval of the government. **T F**

16 The Bank of Canada is owned by the federal government. **T F**

17 The Bank of Canada is a bankers' bank because it stands ready to make loans to and because it accepts deposits from chartered banks. **T F**

18 The most important function of the Bank of Canada is the control of the size of the economy's money supply. **T F**

Circle the letter that corresponds to the best answer.

1 Which of the following is *not* one of the functions of money? (*a*) a factor of production; (*b*) a medium of exchange; (*c*) a store of value (*d*) a standard of value.

2 Chequable deposits are (*a*) all deposits in chartered banks; (*b*) demand deposits in chartered banks; (*c*) deposits in thrift institutions on which cheques may be written; (*d*) the sum of *b* and *c* above.

3 Which of the following constitutes the largest element in the nation's money supply, M1? (*a*) currency; (*b*) Bank of Canada notes; (*c*) term and notice deposits; (*d*) demand deposits.

4 Demand deposits are money because they are (*a*) legal tender; (*b*) fiat money; (*c*) a medium of exchange; (*d*) token money.

5 The supply of money, M1, consists almost entirely of the debts of (*a*) the federal government; (*b*) the Bank of Canada; (*c*) chartered banks; (*d*) the Bank of Canada and chartered banks.

6 Which of the following *best* describes the "backing" of money in Canada? (*a*) the gold bullion stored in the Bank of Canada's vaults; (*b*) the belief of holders of money that it can be exchanged for desirable goods and services; (*c*) the willingness of banks and the government to surrender something of value in exchange for money; (*d*) the faith and confidence of the public in the ability of government to pay its debts.

7 If the price level increases 20%, the value of money decreases (*a*) 14 $^1/_7$%; (*b*) 16 $^2/_3$%; (*c*) 20%; (*d*) 25%.

8 To keep the value of money fairly constant, the federal government (*a*) utilizes price and wage controls; (*b*) employs fiscal policy; (*c*) controls the money supply; (*d*) does both *b* and *c* above.

9 The total quantity of money demanded is

(a) directly related to nominal GDP and the rate of interest; (b) directly related to nominal GDP and inversely related to the rate of interest; (c) inversely related to nominal GDP and directly related to the rate of interest; (d) inversely related to GDP and the rate of interest.

10 There is an asset demand for money because money is (a) a medium of exchange; (b) a standard of value; (c) a store of value; (d) a standard of deferred payment.

11 If the dollars held for transactions purposes are, on the average, spent five times a year for final goods and services, then the quantity of money people will wish to hold for transactions is equal to (a) five times the nominal GDP; (b) 20% of the nominal GDP; (c) five divided by the nominal GDP; (d) 20% divided by the nominal GDP.

12 An increase in the rate of interest would increase (a) the opportunity cost of holding money; (b) the transactions demand for money; (c) the asset demand for money; (d) the prices of bonds.

13 Suppose the transactions demand for money is equal to 10% of the nominal GDP, the supply of money is $45 billion, and the asset demand for money is that shown in the table below. If the nominal GDP is $300 billion, the equilibrium interest rate is (a) 14%; (b) 13%; (c) 12%; (d) 11%.

Interest rate (%)	Asset demand (billions)
14	$10
13	15
12	20
11	25

14 Using the information in multiple-choice question 13, if the nominal GDP remains constant, an increase in the money supply from $45 billion to $50 billion would cause the equilibrium interest rate to (a) rise to 14%; (b) fall to 11%; (c) remain unchanged; (d) fall to 12%.

15 Which of the following functions distinguishes a commercial bank from other financial intermediaries? (a) accepts deposits; (b) creates and destroys money as defined by the Bank of Canada; (c) makes loans; (d) deals in debts.

DISCUSSION QUESTIONS

1 How would you define money? What constitutes the supply of money, M1, in Canada? Which of these components is the largest?

2 What is a near-money? What are the most important near-monies in the Canadian economy? Define M2 and explain why the existence of near-monies is important.

3 For what reasons are chequable deposits included in the money supply?

4 What "backs" the money used in Canada? What determines the value of money? Explain the relationship between the value of money and the price level.

5 What must government do if it is to stabilize the value of money?

6 What are the two reasons people wish to hold money? How are these two reasons related to the "functions" of money?

7 Explain the determinant of each of the two demands for money; explain how a change in the size of these determinants will affect the amount of money people wish to hold.

8 The rate of interest is a price. Of what good or service is it the price? Explain how demand and supply determine this price.

9 Why is it necessary to have a central bank in Canada?

10 What are the chief functions the Bank of Canada performs? Explain briefly the meaning of each of these functions. Which function is the most important?

21

HOW BANKS CREATE MONEY

Chapter 20 explained the institutional structure of banking in Canada today, the functions that banks and money perform, and the composition of the money supply in Canada. Chapter 21 explains how banks literally create money—deposit account money—and the factors that determine and limit the money-creating ability of chartered banks. Even though the other depository institutions also create chequable deposits, this chapter focuses its attention on the chartered banks because they have and will continue to create a very large part of the total amount of money created by all the depository institutions in Canada—quite apart from the fact that the Bank of Canada counts only chartered bank deposits in its official money supply totals. But where the term *chartered bank* (or *bank*) appears, it is legitimate to substitute *depository institution*; and it is permissible to substitute *chequable deposit* for *demand deposit* (or chequing account).

The device (and a most convenient and simple device it is) employed to explain chartered banking operations and money creation is the balance sheet. All banking transactions affect this balance sheet, and the first step to understanding how money is created is to understand how various simple and typical transactions affect the chartered bank balance sheet.

In reading this chapter, you must analyse for yourself the effect upon the balance sheet of each and every banking transaction discussed. The important terms in the balance sheet are deposits and reserves, because deposits *are* money, and the ability of a bank to create new deposits is determined by the amount of reserves the bank has. Expansion of the money supply depends upon the possession by the chartered banks of excess cash reserves. Excess reserves do not appear explicitly in the balance sheet but do appear there implicitly because excess reserves are the difference between the actual reserves and the required reserves of chartered banks.

Two cases—the single chartered bank and the banking system—are presented in order to help you build an understanding of banking and money creation. It is important here to understand that the money-creating potential of a single chartered bank differs in an important way from the money-creating potential of the entire banking system; it is equally important to understand how the money-creating ability of many single chartered banks is *multiplied* and results in the money-creating ability of the banking system as a whole.

Certain assumptions are used throughout most of the chapter to analyse money-creating ability; in certain instances, these assumptions may not be completely realistic and may need to be modified. The chapter concludes with a discussion of how the earlier analysis must be modified—but not changed in its essentials—to take account of these slightly unrealistic assumptions.

CHECK LIST

When you have studied this chapter you should be able to

☐ Recount the story of how goldsmiths came to issue paper money and became bankers who created money and held fractional reserves.

☐ Explain the effects of the deposit of currency in a bank account on the composition and size of the money supply.

☐ Compute a bank's required and excess reserves when you are given the needed balance-sheet figures.

☐ Explain why a chartered bank is required to maintain a reserve; and why this reserve is not sufficient to protect the depositors from losses.

☐ Indicate how the deposit of a cheque drawn on one chartered bank in a second chartered bank will affect the reserves and excess reserves of the two banks.

☐ Show what happens to the money supply when a chartered bank makes a loan (or buys securities); and what happens to the money supply when a loan is repaid (or a bank sells securities).

☐ Explain what happens to a chartered bank's reserves and deposits after it has made a loan, a cheque has been written on the newly created deposit, deposited in another chartered bank, and cleared; and what happens to the reserves and deposits of the chartered bank in which the cheque was deposited.

☐ Describe what would happen to a chartered bank's reserves if it made loans (or bought securities) in an amount that exceeded its excess reserves.

☐ State the money-creating potential of a chartered bank (the amount of money a chartered bank can safely create by lending or buying securities).

☐ State the money-creating potential of the banking system; and explain how it is possible for the banking system to create an amount of money that is a multiple of its excess reserves, when no individual chartered bank ever creates money in an amount greater than its excess reserve.

☐ Compute the size of the monetary multiplier and the money-creating potential of the banking system when you are provided with the necessary data.

☐ List the two leakages that reduce the money-creating potential of the banking system.

☐ Explain why the size of the money supply needs to be controlled.

CHAPTER OUTLINE

1 The balance sheet of the chartered bank is a statement of the assets, liabilities, and net worth of the bank at a specific time; and in the balance sheet the bank's assets equal its liabilities plus its net worth.

2 The history of the goldsmiths illustrates how paper money came into being, how they became bankers when they began to make loans and issue money in excess of their gold holdings; and how the currently-used fractional reserve system, with its two significant characteristics, was developed.

3 By examining the ways in which the balance sheet of the chartered bank is affected by various transactions, it is possible to understand how a single chartered bank in a multibank system can create money.

a. Once a chartered bank has been founded

(1) by selling shares of stock and obtaining cash in return;

(2) and acquired the property and equipment needed to carry on the banking business;

(3) the deposit of cash in the bank does not affect the total money supply; it only changes its composition by substituting deposits for currency in circulation.

(4) Three reserve concepts are essential to an understanding of the money-creating potential of a chartered bank:

(*a*) the *primary or cash reserve deposit* (required reserve) that a chartered bank *must* maintain at the Bank of Canada (or as vault cash) equals

(i) 10% of Canadian currency *demand* deposits;

(ii) 3% of Canadian currency *notice* deposits (2% on the first $500 million of such deposits);

(iii) 3% of foreign currency deposit liabilities used to finance domestic transactions;

(iv) (The actual average required cash reserve ratio in November 1986 was 3.86%.)

(*b*) the *actual reserves* of a chartered bank are its deposits at the Bank of Canada (plus the vault cash);

(*c*) the *excess reserves* equal the actual reserves less the required reserves.

(5) The writing of a cheque upon the bank and its deposit in a second bank results in a loss of reserves and deposits for the first and a gain in reserves and deposits for the second bank.

b. When a single chartered bank lends or buys securities, it increases its own deposit liabilities and, therefore, the supply of money by the amount of the loan or security purchase. But the bank only lends or buys in securities an amount equal to its excess reserves because it fears the loss of reserves to other chartered banks in the economy.

c. An individual chartered bank balances its desire for profits (which result from the making of loans and the purchase of securities) with its desire for safety (which it achieves by having excess reserves).

4 The ability of a banking system composed of many individual chartered banks to lend and to create money is a multiple (greater than one) of its excess reserves; and is equal to the excess reserves of the banking system multiplied by the monetary (or deposit) multiplier.

a. The banking system as a whole can do this even though no single chartered bank ever lends an amount greater than its excess reserve because the banking system, unlike a single chartered bank, does not lose reserves.

b. The monetary multiplier is equal to the reciprocal of the required reserve ratio; the maximum expansion of demand deposits is equal to the excess reserves in the banking system times the monetary multiplier.

c. The potential lending ability of the banking system may be not fully achieved if there are leakages because borrowers choose to have additional currency or if bankers choose to have excess reserves.

d. If bankers lend as much as they are able during periods of prosperity and less than they are able during recessions, they add to the instability of the economy; and to reduce the instability the Bank of Canada must control the size of the money supply.

IMPORTANT TERMS

Balance sheet

Fractional reserve
  system of banking

Vault cash
  (till money)

Primary reserve
  assets

Primary or cash
  reserve ratio

Fractional reserve

Actual reserve

Excess reserve

The lending potential
  of an individual
  chartered bank

Chartered banking
  system

Monetary (deposit)
  multiplier

The lending
  potential of the
  banking system

Leakage

FILL-IN QUESTIONS

1 The balance sheet of a chartered bank is a statement of the bank's _____ , _____ , and _____ at some specific point in time.

2 The coins and paper money that a bank has in its possession are called _____ cash or _____ money.

3 Deposit liabilities of a bank are of two main types: _____ deposits and _____ , _____ and _____ deposits.

4 When a person deposits cash in a chartered bank and receives a deposit account in return, the size of the money supply has (increased, decreased, not changed) _____ _____ .

5 The primary or cash reserves of a chartered bank (ignoring vault cash) must be kept in the _____ and must equal (at least) its _____ multiplied by the _____ .

6 The excess reserves of a chartered bank equal its _____ less its _____ .

7 If chartered banks are allowed to accept (or create) deposits in excess of their reserves, the banking system is operating under a system of _____ reserves.

8 When a cheque is drawn upon bank X, deposited in bank Y, and cleared, the reserves of bank X are (increased, decreased, not changed) _____ and the reserves of bank Y are _____ ; deposits in bank X are _____ , and deposits in bank Y are _____ .

9 A single chartered bank in a multibank system can safely make loans or buy securities equal in amount to the _____ of that chartered bank.

10 When a chartered bank makes a new loan of $10,000, it (increases, decreases) _____ the supply of money by $_____ .

11 When a chartered bank sells a $2,000 government bond to a securities dealer, the supply of money (increases, decreases) _____ by $_____ .

12 A bank ordinarily pursues two conflict-

ing goals; they are _____ and _____ .

13 The banking system can make loans (or buy securities) and create money in an amount equal to its excess reserves multiplied by the _____
_____ .
Its lending potential per dollar of excess reserves is greater than the lending potential of single chartered bank because it does not lose _____ to other banks.

14 The greater the reserve ratio is, the (larger, smaller) _____ is the monetary multiplier.

15 If the required cash reserve ratio is 5%, the banking system is $6 million short of reserves and the banking system is unable to increase its reserves, the banking system must _____ the money supply by $_____ .

16 The money-creating potential of the chartered banking system is lessened by the withdrawal of _____ from banks and by the decision of bankers to keep _____ reserves.

17 Chartered banks, in the past
a. have kept considerable excess reserves during periods of (prosperity, recession) _____ and have kept few or no excess reserves during periods of _____ ;
b. and by behaving in this way have made the economy (more, less)_____ unstable.

PROBLEMS AND PROJECTS

1 Following is the simplified balance sheet of a chartered bank. Assume that the figures given show the bank's assets and the demand-deposit liabilities *prior to each of the following four transactions*. Draw up the balance sheet as it would appear after each of these transactions is completed, and place the balance-sheet figures in the appropriate column. *Do not* use the figures you place in columns *a*, *b*, or *c* when you work the next part of the problem: start all parts of the problem with the printed figures.

	(a)	(b)	(c)	(d)
Assets:				
Reserves	$100 $___	$___	$___	$___
Loans	700 ___	___	___	___
Securities	200 ___	___	___	___
Liabilities and net worth:				
Deposits	900 ___	___	___	___
Capital Stock	100 100	100	100	100

a. A cheque for $50 is drawn by one of the depositors of the bank, given to a person who deposits it in another bank, and cleared (column *a*).

b. A depositor withdraws $50 in cash from the bank, and the bank restores its vault cash by obtaining $50 in additional cash from the Bank of Canada (column *b*).

c. A cheque for $60 drawn on another bank is deposited in this bank and cleared (column *c*).

d. The bank sells $100 of government bonds to the Bank of Canada (column *d*).

2 At the bottom of this page are five balance sheets for a single chartered bank (columns 1*a*-5*a*). The required reserve ratio is 10%.

a. Compute the required reserves (A), the excess reserves* (B), and the amount of new loans it can extend (C).

*If the bank is short of reserves and must reduce its loans or obtain additional reserves, show this by placing a minus sign in front of the amounts by which it is short of reserves.

b. For the individual bank, draw up the five balance sheets below as they appear after the bank has made the new *loans* that it is capable of making (columns 1*b*-5*b*).

	(1b)	(2b)	(3b)	(4b)	(5b)
Assets:					
Reserves	$___	$___	$___	$___	$___
Loans	___	___	___	___	___
Securities	___	___	___	___	___
Liabilities and net worth:					
Deposits	___	___	___	___	___
Capital Stock	___	___	___	___	___

	(1a)	(2a)	(3a)	(4a)	(5a)
Assets:					
Reserves	$22.50	$ 20	$ 10	$ 22	$ 23
Loans	127.50	140	135	138	187
Securities	50	60	30	70	60
Liabilities and net worth:					
Deposits	175	200	150	180	220
Capital Stock	25	20	25	50	50
A. Required reserve	$___	$___	$___	$___	$___
B. Excess reserve	___	___	___	___	___
C. New Loans	___	___	___	___	___

3 Following are several reserve ratios. Compute the monetary multiplier for each of the reserve ratios and enter the figures in column 2. In column 3, show the maximum amount by which a single chartered bank can increase its loans for each dollar's worth of excess reserves it possesses. In column 4, indicate the maximum amount by which the banking system can increase its loans for each dollar's worth of excess reserves in the system.

(1)	(2)	(3)	(4)
5%	___	$___	$___
6%	___	___	___
6¼%	___	___	___
8%	___	___	___
10%	___	___	___
12%	___	___	___

4 Below is the simplified consolidated balance sheet for *all* chartered banks in the economy. Assume that the figures given show the bank's assets and liabilities *prior to each of the following three transactions*, and that the reserve ratio is 5%. *Do not* use the figures you placed in columns 2 and 4 when you begin parts *b* and *c* of the problem: start parts *a*, *b*, and *c* of the problem with the printed figures.

a. The public deposits $5 in cash in the banks, and the banks send the $5 to the Bank of Canada, where it is added to their reserves. Fill in column 1. If the banking system extends the new loans it is capable of extending, show in column 2 the balance sheet as it would then appear.

b. The banking system sells $8 worth of securities to the Bank of Canada. Complete column 3. Assuming the system extends the maximum amount of credit of which it is capable, fill in column 4.

c. The Bank of Canada sells $1 worth of securities to the chartered banks; complete column 5. Complete column 6 showing the condition of the banks after they have contracted their loans by the amount necessary to meet the reserve requirement.

		(1)	(2)	(3)	(4)	(5)	(6)
Assets:							
Reserves	$ 25	$___	$___	$___	$___	$___	$___
Loans	425	___	___	___	___	___	___
Securities	100	___	___	___	___	___	___
Liabilities and net worth:							
Deposits	500	___	___	___	___	___	___
Capital Stock	50	50	50	50	50	50	50
Advances (loans) from Bank of Canada	0	___	___	___	___	___	___
Excess Reserves		___	___	___	___	___	___
Maximum possible expansion of the money supply		___	___	___	___	___	___

SELF-TEST

Circle T if the statement is true, F if it is false.

1 The balance sheet of a chartered bank shows the transactions in which the bank has engaged during a given period of time. **T F**

2 A chartered bank's assets plus its net worth equal the bank's liabilities. **T F**

3 Goldsmiths increased the money supply when they accepted deposits of gold and issued paper receipts to the depositors. **T F**

4 Roberta Lynn, the dancing star, deposits a $30,000 cheque from the Royal Alex in a chartered bank and receives a deposit account in return; an hour later, the Manfred Iron and Coal Company borrows $30,000 from the same bank. The money supply has increased $30,000 as a result of the two transactions. **T F**

5 A chartered bank may maintain its required cash reserve either as a deposit in the Bank of Canada or as government bonds in its own vault. **T F**

6 The required cash reserve that a chartered bank maintains must equal its own deposit liabilities multiplied by the required reserve ratio. **T F**

7 The actual reserves of a chartered bank equal excess reserves plus required reserves. **T F**

8 The reserve of a chartered bank in the Bank of Canada is an asset of the Bank of Canada. **T F**

9 A cheque for $1,000 drawn on bank X by a depositor and deposited in bank Y will increase the excess reserves of bank Y by $1,000. **T F**

10 A single chartered bank can safely loan an amount equal to its excess reserves multiplied by the required reserve ratio. **T F**

11 When a borrower repays a loan of $500, either in cash or by cheque, the supply of money is reduced by $500. **T F**

12 The granting of a $5,000 loan and the purchase of a $5,000 government bond from a securities dealer by a chartered bank have the same effect on the money supply. **T F**

13 A chartered bank seeks both profits and liquidity, but these are conflicting goals. **T F**

14 If the banking system has $10 million in excess reserves and if the reserve ratio is 5%, it can increase its loans by $200 million. **T F**

15 While a single chartered bank can only increase its loans by an amount equal to its excess reserves, the entire banking system can increase its loans by an amount equal to its excess reserves multiplied by the reciprocal of the reserve ratio. **T F**

16 When borrowers from a chartered bank wish to have cash rather than demand deposits, the money-creating potential of the banking system is increased. **T F**

Circle the letter that corresponds to the best answer.

1 The goldsmiths became bankers when (*a*) they accepted deposits of gold for safe storage; (*b*) they issued receipts for the gold stored with them; (*c*) their receipts for deposited gold were used as paper money; (*d*) they issued paper money in excess of the amount of gold stored with them.

2 When cash is deposited in a deposit account in a chartered bank, there is (*a*) a decrease in the money supply; (*b*) an increase in the money supply; (*c*) no change in the composition of the money supply; (*d*) a change in the composition of the money supply.

3 A chartered bank has actual reserves of $2,000 and deposit liabilities of $30,000; the required reserve ratio is 5%. The excess reserves of the bank are (a) $500; (b) $0; (c) minus $1,000; (d) $1,500.

4 A chartered bank is required to maintain a cash reserve either on deposit in the Bank of Canada or as vault cash in order (a) to protect the deposits in the chartered bank against losses; (b) to provide the means by which cheques drawn on the chartered bank and deposited in other chartered banks can be collected; (c) to add to the liquidity of the chartered bank and protect it against a "run" on the bank; (d) to provide the Bank of Canada with a means of controlling the lending ability of the chartered bank.

5 A depositor places $1,000 in cash in a chartered bank, and the reserve ratio is 5%; the bank sends the $1,000 to the Bank of Canada. As a result, the *reserves* and the *excess reserves* of the bank have been increased, respectively, by (a) $1,000 and $50; (b) $1,000 and $950; (c) $1,000 and $1,000; (d) $500 and $500.

6 A chartered bank has no excess reserves, but then a depositor places $600 in cash in the bank, and the bank adds the $600 to its reserves by sending it to the Bank of Canada. The bank then loans $300 to a borrower. As a consequence of these transactions, the size of the money supply has (a) not been affected; (b) increased by $300; (c) increased by $600; (d) increased by $900.

7 A chartered bank has excess reserves of $500 and a required cash reserve ratio of 10%; it grants a loan of $1,000 to a borrower. If the borrower writes a cheque for $1,000, which is deposited in another chartered bank, the first bank will be short of reserves, after the cheque has been cleared, in the amount of (a) $100; (b) $500; (c) $700; (d) $1,000.

8 A chartered bank sells a $1,000 government security to a securities dealer. The dealer pays for the bond in cash, which the bank adds to its vault cash. The money supply has

(a) not been affected; (b) decreased by $1,000; (c) increased by $1,000; (d) increased by $1,000 multiplied by the reciprocal of the cash reserve ratio.

9 A chartered bank has deposit liabilities of $100,000, reserves of $17,000, and a required cash reserve ratio of 10%. The amount by which a *single* chartered bank and the amount by which the banking *system* can increase loans are, respectively, (a) $7,000 and $70,000; (b) $10,000 and $100,000; (c) $7,000 and $100,000; (d) $10,000 and $60,000.

10 If the required cash reserve ratio were 4%, the value of the monetary multiplier would be (a) 16; (b)20; (c)24; (d)25.

11 The banking system has excess reserves of $700 and makes new loans of $7,000 and is just meeting its reserve requirements. The required cash reserve ratio is (a) 5%; (b) $6^1/_4$%; (c) 8%; (d) 10%.

12 The chartered banking system, because of a recent switch in deposits from notice to demand, finds that the required cash reserve ratio has changed from 5% to $6^1/_4$% with the result that it is $100 million short of reserves. If it is unable to obtain any additional reserves, it must decrease its money supply by (a) $100 million; (b) $125 million; (c) $1,600 million; (d) $2,000 million.

13 Only one chartered bank in the banking system has excess reserves, and its excess reserves are $100,000. This bank makes a new loan of $80,000 and keeps excess reserves of $20,000. If the required reserve ratio for all banks is 5%, the potential expansion of the money supply because of the loan (but not counting the loan) is (a) $80,000; (b) $100,000; (c) $1,520,000; (d) $2,000,000.

14 The money-creating potential of the banking system is reduced when (a) bankers choose to have excess reserves; (b) borrowers choose to hold none of the funds they have borrowed in currency; (c) the Bank of

Canada lowers the required secondary reserve ratio; (d) bankers borrow from the Bank of Canada.

15 The excess reserves held by banks tend to (a) rise during periods of prosperity; (b) fall during periods of recession; (c) rise during periods of recession; (d) fall when interest rates in the economy fall.

16 Unless controlled, the money supply will (a) fall during periods of prosperity; (b) rise during periods of recession; (c) change in a pro-cyclical fashion; (d) change in an anti-cyclical fashion.

DISCUSSION QUESTIONS

1 How did the early goldsmiths come to issue paper money and then become bankers? Explain the difference between 100% and a fractional reserve system of banking, and why the latter system is subject to "runs" and requires public regulation.

2 Chartered banks seek both profits and safety. Explain how the balance sheet of the chartered banks reflects the desires of bankers for income and for liquidity.

3 Do the reserves held by chartered banks satisfactorily protect the bank's depositors? Are the reserves of banks needed? Explain your answers.

4 Explain why the granting of a loan by a chartered bank increases the supply of money. Why does the repayment of a loan decrease the supply of money?

5 The owner of a sporting goods store writes a cheque on his account in a Calgary, Alberta, bank and sends it to one of his suppliers, who deposits it in a different bank in Edmonton, Alberta. How does the Edmonton bank obtain payment from the Calgary bank? If the two banks were in Calgary and Halifax, Nova Scotia, is payment any more complicated? How are the reserves of the two banks affected?

6 Why is a single bank only able to loan safely an amount equal to its excess reserves?

7 No one chartered bank ever lends an amount greater than its excess reserve, but the banking system as a whole is able to extend loans and expand the money supply by an amount equal to the system's excess reserves multiplied by the reciprocal of the reserve ratio. Explain why this is possible and how the multiple expansion of deposits (that is, money) takes place.

8 On the basis of a given amount of excess reserves and a given reserve ratio, a certain expansion of the money supply may be possible. What are two reasons the potential expansion of the money supply may not be fully achieved?

9 Why is there a "need for monetary control" in the Canadian economy?

22

THE BANK OF CANADA AND MONETARY POLICY

Chapter 22 is the third chapter dealing with money and banking. It explains how the Bank of Canada affects output, income, employment, and the price level in the economy. Central-bank policies designed to affect these variables are called monetary policies, the goal of which is full employment without inflation.

You should have little difficulty with this chapter if you have understood the material in Chapter 21. In Chapter 22 attention should be concentrated on the following: (1) the cause-effect chain, as Keynesians see it, between monetary policy; chartered bank reserves and excess reserves; the supply of money; the rate of interest; investment spending, aggregate expenditures, output, employment, and the price level; (2) the principal item on the balance sheet of the Bank of Canada; (3) the three major controls available to the Bank of Canada, and how employment of these controls can affect the reserves, excess reserves, the actual money supply, and the money-creating potential of the banking system; (4) the actions the Bank of Canada would take if it were pursuing a tight money policy to curb inflation, and the actions it would take if it were pursuing an easy money policy to prevent or eliminate depression; (5) the relative importance of the three major controls; and (6) the two minor selective controls that the Bank of Canada uses to influence the economy.

In order to acquire a thorough knowledge of the manner in which each of the Bank of Canada transactions affects reserves, excess reserves, the actual money supply, and the potential money supply, you must study very carefully each of the sets of balance sheets that are used to explain these transactions. On these balance sheets the items to watch are again reserves and deposits! Be sure that you know why each of the balance-sheet changes is made and are able, *on your own*, to make the appropriate balance-sheet entries to trace through the effects of any transaction.

CHECK LIST

When you have studied this chapter you should be able to

☐ Explain, using the Keynesian cause-effect chain, the links between a change in the money supply and a change in the equilibrium GDP.

☐ List the principal assets and liabilities of the Bank of Canada.

☐ Identify the three tools of monetary policy; explain how each may be employed by the central bank to expand and to contract the money supply.

☐ Prescribe the three specific monetary policies the Bank of Canada utilizes to reduce unemployment, and the three specific policies it employs to reduce inflationary pressures in the economy.

☐ State which of the three monetary-policy tools is the most effective.

☐ Identify the two minor selective controls; explain how each is used to promote economic stability.

CHAPTER OUTLINE

1 The objective of monetary policy is full employment without inflation.

a. The Bank of Canada, according to Keynesians, can accomplish this objective by exercising control over the amount of excess reserves held by the chartered banks and thereby influencing the size of the money supply, the rate of interest, and the level of aggregate expenditures.

b. Decreases (increases) in the rate of interest tend to increase (decrease) planned investment and, therefore, aggregate expenditures.

2 By examining the statement of assets and liabilities of the Bank of Canada, an understanding of the ways in which the central bank can control and influence the reserves of chartered banks and the money supply can be obtained.

a. The principal assets of the Bank of Canada (in order of size) are securities issued or guaranteed by the Government of Canada, other securities, other assets, and— a very minor item—advances (*normally* very short-term loans) to the chartered banks.

b. Its principal liabilities are its bank notes in circulation, the reserve deposits of the chartered banks, and Government of Canada deposits.

3 The Bank of Canada employs three principal tools (techniques or instruments) to control the reserves of banks and the size of the money supply.

a. It can can buy and sell government bonds in the open market.

(1) Buying securities in the open market from either banks or the public increases the reserves of banks.

(2) Selling securities in the open market to either banks or the public decreases the reserves of banks.

b. It can change the Bank Rate. Changes in the Bank Rate directly affect the cost, and hence, the volume of credit.

c. It can switch Government of Canada deposits between itself and the chartered banks; and thus affect the amount of chartered bank reserves.

d. A tight (easy) money policy involves selling (buying) bonds in the open market, increasing (decreasing) the Bank Rate, switching government reserves out of (into) the chartered banks.

e. Open-market operations are the most effective device for controlling the money supply.

f. The Bank of Canada also employs two selective controls to affect the volume of credit available for and the amount of spending on certain types of goods and securities. The first such control consists in changing the *secondary* reserve ratio, secondary reserves being bank cash in excess of cash reserve requirements, Government of Canada Treasury bills of one year or less, and day-to-day loans to a select group of investment dealers. In addition, moral suasion is used to influence chartered bank lending.

IMPORTANT TERMS

Monetary policy

Monetary control

Open-market operations

Bank Rate

Switching Government of Canada deposits

Easy money policy

Tight money policy

Selective control

Secondary reserve ratio

Moral suasion

FILL-IN QUESTIONS

1 The objective of monetary policy in Canada is a _____ level of total output. Responsibility for these monetary policies rests with the _____ .

2 To eliminate inflationary pressures in the economy, Keynesians contend the monetary authority should seek to (increase, decrease) _____ the reserves of chartered banks; this would tend to _____ the money supply and to _____ the rate of interest; and this, in turn, would cause investment spending, aggregate expenditures, and output to _____ .

3 The largest asset of the Bank of Canada is Government of Canada _____ . Its two largest liabilities are _____ and _____ _____ .

4 The three tools (or instruments) employed by the monetary authority to control the money supply are _____ _____ , changing _____ , and switching _____ .

5 The Bank of Canada buys and sells government securities in the open market in order to change the amount of new _____ that chartered banks are able to create, and the rate of _____ in the economy.

6 If the Bank of Canada were to sell $10 million in government bonds to the *public*, who paid for them by cheque, and the reserve ratio were 5%, the supply of money would immediately be reduced by $ _____ , the reserves of the chartered banks would immediately be reduced by $ _____ , and the excess reserves of the banks would immediately be reduced by $ _____ . But if these bonds were sold to the chartered banks, the supply of money would immediately be reduced by $ the reserves of the banks would immediately be reduced by $ _____ ,

and the excess reserves of the banks would immediately be reduced by $ _____ .

7 To increase the supply of money, the Bank of Canada should _____ government securities in the open market; to decrease the supply of money, it should _____ securities in the open market.

8 The most effective major monetary control is _____ .

9 The two selective (or minor) controls are changes in _____ and _____ .

PROBLEMS AND PROJECTS

1 Below are various items that belong in the balance statement of the Bank of Canada. Place them in their proper place in the blank balance sheet by listing them either on the asset or on the liability side in the order of their dollar importance.

Chartered bank reserves (deposits)
Government of Canada deposits
Securities
Advances (loans) to banks
Bank of Canada notes

Assets	Liabilities
_____	_____
_____	_____
_____	_____
_____	_____

2 Assume that the consolidated balance sheet on the next page is for all chartered banks. Assume, also, that the required reserve ratio is 5%.

Assets		Liabilities	
Reserves	$ 20	Deposits	$400
Loans	280	Net Worth	100
Securities	200		
	$500		$500

a. To *increase* the supply of money by $100, the Bank of Canada could _____ securities worth $_____ in the open market.

b. To *reduce* the supply of money by $50, the Bank of Canada could _____ securities worth $_____ in the open market.

3 Below are the initial balance sheet of the Bank of Canada and the consolidated balance sheets of the chartered banks. Assume that the cash reserve ratio is 5%. The figures in column (1) show the balance sheets of the Bank of Canada and the chartered banks *prior to each of the following three transactions.* Place the new balance-sheet figures in the appropriate columns and complete A, B, C, D, and E in the columns. *Do not* use the figures you place in columns (2) and (3) when you work the next part of the problem: start all parts of the problem with the printed figures in column (1).

a. The Bank of Canada sells $1 in securities to the public (security dealer), which pays by cheque (column 2).

	(1)	(2)	(3)	(4)
Bank of Canada				
Assets:				
Securities	$ 21	$_____	$_____	$_____
Advances (loans) to chartered banks	0	_____	_____	_____
Liabilities:				
Reserves of chartered banks	10	_____	_____	_____
Government of Canada deposits	2	_____	_____	_____
Bank of Canada notes	9	_____	_____	_____
Chartered Banks				
Assets:				
Reserves	$ 10	$_____	$_____	$_____
Securities	20	_____	_____	_____
Loans	170	_____	_____	_____
Liabilities:				
Deposits	200	_____	_____	_____
Advances (loans) from Bank of Canada	0	_____	_____	_____
A. Required Reserves		_____	_____	_____
B. Excess Reserves		_____	_____	_____
C. How much has the money supply changed?		_____	_____	_____
D. How much *more* can the money supply change?		_____	_____	_____
E. What is the total of C and D?		_____	_____	_____

b. The Bank of Canada buys $1 in securities from the chartered banks (column 3).

c. The Government of Canada buys $1 worth of goods from the Canadian manufacturers and pays the manufacturers by cheques drawn on its accounts at the Bank of Canada (column 4).

SELF-TEST

Circle T if the statement is true, F if it is false.

1 Consumer spending is more sensitive to changes in the rate of interest than is investment demand. **T F**

2 The securities owned by the Bank of Canada are practically entirely Canadian government bonds. **T F**

3 If the Bank of Canada buys $15 in government securities from the public in the open market, the effect will be to increase the excess reserves of chartered banks by $15. **T F**

4 When the Bank of Canada sells bonds in the open market, the price of these bonds falls. **T F**

5 A change in the secondary reserve ratio will not affect the multiple by which the banking system can create money, but it will affect the actual or excess cash reserves of chartered banks. **T F**

6 If the secondary reserve ratio is lowered, some required secondary reserves are turned into excess secondary reserves. **T F**

7 When chartered banks get an advance (borrow) from the Bank of Canada, they increase their reserves. **T F**

8 If the monetary authority wished to follow a tight money policy, it would seek to reduce the reserves of the chartered banks. **T F**

9 An increase in the secondary reserve ratio tends to reduce the profits of banks. **T F**

Circle the letter that corresponds to the best answer.

1 The agency directly responsible for monetary policy in Canada is (*a*) Canadian Bankers' Association; (*b*) the Bank of Canada; (*c*) the Parliament of Canada; (*d*) Department of Finance.

2 In the Keynesian chain of cause and effect between changes in the excess reserves of chartered banks and the resulting changes in output and employment in the economy, (*a*) an increase in excess reserves will decrease the money supply; (*b*) a decrease in the money supply will increase the rate of interest; (*c*) an increase in the rate of interest will increase aggregate expenditures; (*d*) an increase in aggregate expenditures will decrease output and employment.

3 Which of the followings is most likely to be affected by changes in the rate of interest? (*a*) consumer spending; (*b*) investment spending; (*c*) the spending of the federal government; (*d*) the exports of the economy.

4 The largest single asset in the Bank of Canada's consolidated balance sheet is (*a*) securities; (*b*) gold; (*c*) cash; (*d*) the reserves of the chartered banks.

5 The largest single liability of the Bank of Canada is (*a*) the reserves of the chartered banks; (*b*) the deposits of the Government of Canada; (*c*) Bank of Canada Notes; (*d*) loans to chartered banks.

6 Assuming that the Bank of Canada sells $20 million in government securities to the chartered banks and the reserve ratio is 10%, then the effect will be (*a*) to reduce the actual supply of money by $20 million; (*b*) to reduce the actual supply of money by $2 million; (*c*) to reduce the potential money supply by $20 million; (*d*) to reduce the potential money supply by $200 million.

7 Which of the following acts would *not* have the same general effect upon the economy as the other three? (*a*) the Bank of

Canada sells bonds in the open market; (b) the Bank of Canada increases the Bank Rate; (c) the Bank of Canada lowers the secondary reserve ratio; (d) the Bank of Canada switches Government of Canada deposits out of chartered banks.

8 Which of the following is the most important control used by the Bank of Canada to regulate the money supply? (a) changing the secondary reserve ratio; (b) open-market operations; (c) changing the Bank Rate; (d) moral suasion.

9 Which of the followings is *not* one of the controls that has been employed by the Bank of Canada? (a) setting tariff rates; (b) moral suasion; (c) setting the secondary reserve ratio; (d) setting the Bank Rate.

DISCUSSION QUESTIONS

1 Explain, from a Keynesian viewpoint, how the Bank of Canada can influence income, output, employment, and the price level. In your explanation, employ the following concepts: reserves, excess reserves, the supply of money, the availability of bank credit, and the rate of interest.

2 Why are changes in the rate of interest more likely to affect investment spending than consumption and saving?

3 What are the principal assets and liabilities of the Bank of Canada? Which of these items seems most crucial in its effect on the levels of income, output, employment, and prices in the economy?

4 Explain how the open-market operations of the Bank of Canada would be used to contract the supply of money. How would they be used to expand the supply of money?

5 What is the difference between the effects of the central bank's buying (selling) government securities in the open market from (to) chartered banks and from (to) investment dealers?

6 Which of the monetary-policy tools available to the Bank of Canada is more effective? Why is it more effective than other tools?

7 How do the selective controls differ from general or quantitative controls? What are the principal selective controls? Explain how the central bank would use these controls in following a tight and easy money policy.

23

MACROECONOMICS: AN OVERVIEW

You learned in Chapter 18 how the GDP is measured and how to adjust it when the price level changes to find the real GDP. Then in Chapter 19 you found that over the years the Canadian economy has at times suffered from unemployment, has at other times experienced inflation, and has at still other times had both unemployment and inflation.

In Chapter 23 you will begin learning what determines how large the real domestic output (the real GDP) and the price level at any time will be; what causes them to change; and what policies the federal government can use to prevent unemployment and inflation.

The tools employed to explain what determines the economy's real output and price level are demand and supply. You first encountered these tools in Chapter 3, where they were used to explain what determines the output and the price of a particular product. These same tools are now employed in a slightly different way. To use these tools of aggregate demand and aggregate supply you will have to think not of the price of a particular good or service but of the price level in the economy. And instead of thinking about the quantity of a particular good or service demanded or supplied it is necesary to think about the total (the aggregate) quantity of all final goods and services demanded (purchased) and supplied (produced) in the economy. You will have no difficulty with the way demand and supply are used in this chapter once you adjust the way you think about them from a particular good or service and its price to all final goods and services

and their average price.

Having made this adjustment in your way of thinking about demand and supply, the rest is not too difficult. The aggregate-demand curve is downsloping because of the interest-rate, real-balances, and foreign-trade effects of changes in the price level. The aggregate-supply curve is, however, somewhat peculiar. It is horizontal at low levels, vertical at high levels, and upsloping at intermediate levels of real domestic output.

Like the ordinary demand and supply curves of Chapter 3, the intersection of the aggregate-demand and the aggregate-supply curves determines equilibrium quantity and price: the equilibrium quantity is the equilibrium real domestic output and the equilibrium price is the equilibrium price level. With the knowledge of how aggregate demand and supply determine the real domestic output and the price level, you have acquired the ability to explain the basic causes of inflation (an increase in demand or a decrease in supply), of a decrease in domestic output and employment (a decrease in demand or in supply), and of stagflation (a decrease in supply). You have also acquired the economic principles that will enable you to know what the federal government might do to increase output and employment, prevent inflation, and eliminate stagflation in the economy.

Aggregate demand and aggregate supply are the skeleton upon which macroeconomic theory and policies are based. The next five chapters "flesh-out" this skeleton. As you study these chapters you may forget the aggregate-demand–aggregate-supply framework. Don't!

CHECK LIST

When you have studied this chapter you should be able to

☐ Define aggregate demand and aggregate supply.

☐ Explain why the aggregate-demand curve slopes downward.

☐ Describe and name the three ranges on the aggregate-supply curve.

☐ Explain what the equilibrium real domestic output and the equilibrium price level will be; and why the economy will tend to produce this output (rather than a larger or smaller one).

☐ State the effects on the real domestic output and on the price level of an increase in aggregate demand when the economy is in the Keynesian, classical, and intermediate ranges.

☐ Explain why a decrease in aggregate demand will not reduce the price level so much as an equal increase in aggregate demand would have raised it.

☐ Explain the basic cause of changes in aggregate supply; and the effects of increases and decreases in aggregate supply upon the real domestic output and the price level.

CHAPTER OUTLINE

1 Aggregate demand and aggregate supply determine the real domestic output and the price level of the economy; and are used in this chapter to explain both why output and the price level fluctuate.

2 Aggregate demand is a curve that shows the total quantity of goods and services that will be purchased (demanded) at different price levels; and the curve slopes downward for three reasons.

a. With the supply of money fixed, an increase in the price level increases the demand for money, increases interest rates, and as a result reduces those expenditures (by consumers and business firms) that are sensitive to increased interest rates; and a de-

crease in the price level has the opposite effects.

b. An increase in the price level also decreases the real value (purchasing power) of financial assets with a fixed money value, and because those who own such assets are now poorer they spend less for goods and services; and a decrease in the price level has the opposite effects.

c. In addition, an increase in the price level (relative to foreign price levels) will reduce Canadian exports, expand Canadian imports, and decrease the quantity of goods and services demanded in the Canadian economy; and a decrease in the price level (relative to foreign price levels) will have opposite effects.

3 Aggregate supply is a curve that shows the total quantity of goods and services that will be produced (supplied) at different price levels; and the curve has three ranges.

a. In the Keynesian range (when the economy is in a severe recession or depression) the aggregate-supply curve is horizontal: the price level need not rise to induce producers to supply larger quantities of goods and services.

b. In the classical range (when the economy is at full employment) the aggregate-supply curve is vertical: a rise in the price level cannot result in an increase in the quantity of goods and services supplied.

c. Between these two ranges is the intermediate range in which the supply curve slopes upward: the price level must rise to induce producers to supply larger quantities of goods and services.

4 The equilibrium real domestic output and the equilibrium price level are the intersection of the aggregate-demand and the aggregate-supply curves. Were the actual output greater (less) than the equilibrium output, producers would find that their inventories were increasing (decreasing) and they would contract (expand) their output to the equilibrium output.

a. An increase in aggregate demand in

(1) the Keynesian range would result in an increase in real output but the price level would remain unchanged;

(2) the classical range would result in an increase in the price level but the real domestic output would remain unchanged;

(3) the intermediate range would result in an increase in both real domestic output and the price level.

b. But a decrease in aggregate demand would not have the opposite effect on the price level because prices (for several reasons) tend to be inflexible (sticky) downward.

c. An increase (a decrease) in the costs of producing goods and services will decrease (increase) aggregate supply—move the aggregate supply curve to the left (right)—and reduce (expand) the real domestic output and push the price level upward (downward).

d. To recap, both aggregate demand and aggregate supply affect real domestic output and the price level; both demand-management and supply-side policies may be used to combat recession and inflation. These are analysed in Chapters 26 and 27.

IMPORTANT TERMS

Stagflation	**Aggregate-supply curve**
Aggregate-demand curve	
Interest-rate effect	**Keynesian range**
Real-balances effect	**Classical range**
Foreign-trade effect	**Intermediate range**
	Ratchet effect

FILL-IN QUESTIONS

1 Aggregate demand and aggregate supply together determine the equilibrium real domestic _____

and the equilibrium price _____ .

2 The aggregate-demand curve shows the quantity of goods and services that will be

_____ at various price _____ .

a. It slopes (upward, downward) _____

b. because of the _____ ,

the _____ ,

and the _____ effects.

3 The aggregate-supply curve shows the quantity of goods and services that will be

_____ at various price _____ ;
and in the

a. Keynesian range is (vertical, horizontal, upsloping) _____ ;

b. the intermediate range is _____ ;

c. the classical range is _____ .

4 The equilibrium real domestic output and price level are found at the _____ of the aggregate-demand and aggregate-supply curves.

a. At this price level, the aggregate quantity of goods and services _____ is equal to the aggregate quantity of goods

and services _____ .

b. And at this real domestic output, the prices producers are willing to (pay, accept)

_____ are equal to the prices buyers

are willing to _____ .

5 Were the actual real domestic output

a. greater than the equilibrium domestic output, producers would find that their

inventories are (increasing, decreasing) ____

_____ , and they would (expand, reduce) _____ their production;

b. less than the equilibrium domestic output, producers would find that their inven-

tories are _____ , and they would

_____ their production.

6 When the economy is producing in

a. the Keynesian range, an increase in aggregate demand will (increase, decrease,

have no effect on) _____
real domestic output and will _____ the price level;

b. the intermediate range an increase in aggregate demand will _____

real domestic output and will _____ the price level;

c. the classical range an increase in aggregate demand will _____

real domestic output and will _____ the price level.

7 Were the economy operating in the intermediate or classical ranges and aggregate demand were to decrease, the price level would decline by (a larger, a smaller, the same) _____

amount as an equal increase in aggregate demand would have raised the price level; this is called the (interest-rate, real-balances, ratchet) _____ effect.

8 The basic cause of a decrease in aggregate supply is a(n) (increase, decrease) _____ in the costs of producing goods and services; and the basic cause of an increase in aggregate supply is _____ .

a. An increase in aggregate supply will not only (raise, lower) _____ real domestic output and (lead to, prevent) _____ inflation but will also (increase, decrease) _____ the full-employment level of domestic output.

b. A decrease in aggregate supply will _____ real output and _____ the price level.

9 Demand-pull inflation is the result of a(n) (increase, decrease) _____ in aggregate demand and is accompanied by a (rise, fall) _____ in real output; but cost-push inflation is the result of a(n)

_____ in aggregate supply and is accompanied by a _____ .

PROBLEMS AND PROJECTS

1 In the table below is an aggregate-supply schedule. _____

Price level	Real domestic output produced
$7.00	2,000
6.00	2,000
5.00	1,900
4.00	1,700
3.00	1,400
2.00	1,000
2.00	500
2.00	0

a. The economy is in the
(1) Keynesian range when the real domestic output is between _____ and _____ ;
(2) the classical range when the real domestic output is _____ and the price level is $ _____ or more;
(3) intermediate range when the real domestic output is between _____ and _____ .

b. Plot this aggregate-supply schedule on the graph below.

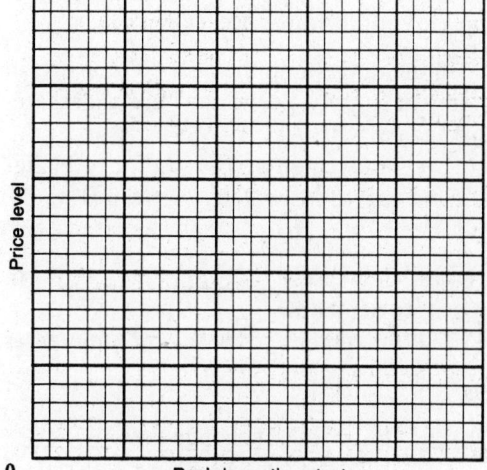

Price level

0   Real domestic output

c. In the table below are three aggregate-demand schedules.

REAL DOMESTIC OUTPUT PURCHASED

Price level (1)	(2)	(3)	(4)
$7.00	1,400	1,900	400
6.00	1,500	2,000	500
5.00	1,600	2,100	600
4.00	1,700	2,200	700
3.00	1,800	2,300	800
2.00	1,900	2,400	900
1.00	2,000	2,500	1,000

(1) Plot the aggregate-demand curve shown in columns (1) and (2) on the graph above; and label this curve D_1. At this level of aggregate demand the equilibrium real domestic output is _____

mestic output is _____

and the equilibrium price level is $_____ .
(2) On the same graph plot the aggregate-demand curve shown in columns (1) and (3); and label this curve D_2. The equilibrium real

domestic output is _____

and the equilibrium price level is $_____ .
(3) Now plot the aggregate-demand curve in columns (1) and (4) and label it D_3. The

equilibrium real domestic output is _____

and the equilibrium price level is $_____ .

2 In the diagram in the next column are an aggregate-supply curve and six aggregate-demand curves.
a. The movements of the aggregate-demand curves from D_1 to D_2, from D_3 to D_4, and from D_5 to D_6 all portray (in-

creases, decreases) _____ in aggregate demand.
(1) The movement from D_1 to D_2 increases

the (real domestic output, price level) ____

_____ but does not change the _____ .

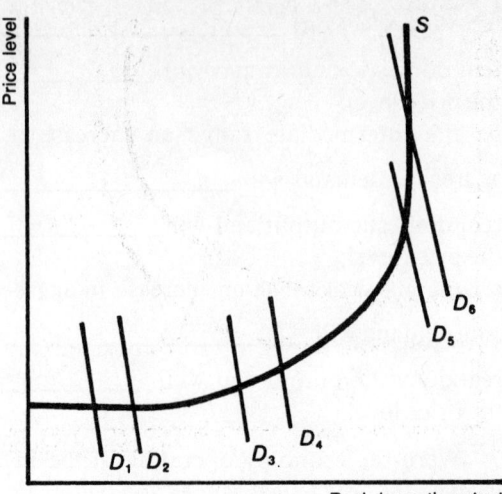

Real domestic output

(2) The movement from D_3 to D_4 will (raise,

lower) _____ the price level and will

(expand, contract) _____ the real domestic output.

(3) The movement from D_5 to D_6 will ____

_____ .

b. The movements the aggregate-demand curves to the left all portray (increases,

decreases) _____ in aggregate demand.
(1) If prices are flexible in a downward direction, what effects will these changes in aggregate demand have upon the real do-

mestic output and the price level? _____

_____

(2) If prices are *not* flexible in a downward direction, what effects will these changes in

aggregate demand have? _____

_____

3 Following is a diagram in which there are two aggregate-supply curves and three aggregate-demand curves.

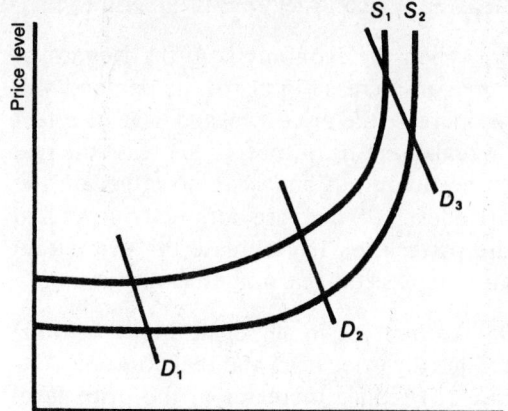

Price level

Real domestic output

a. The movement of the aggregate-supply curve from S_1 to S_2 represents a(n) (increase, decrease) _____ in aggregate supply.
(1) If the price level is flexible downward and upward, this change in aggregate supply in each of the three ranges along the aggregate supply curve will (raise, lower) _____ the price level and (expand, contract) ____ the real domestic output.
(2) But if prices are inflexible in a downward direction, this change in aggregate supply will (increase, decrease) _____ real domestic output but (will, will not) _____ affect the price level.
b. The movement of aggregate supply from S_2 to S_1 portrays a(n) _____ in aggregate supply and in each of the three ranges will _____ the price level and _____ the real domestic output.

SELF-TEST

Circle T if the statement is true, F if it is false.

1 The aggregate-demand curve slopes downward. **T F**

2 A fall in the price level increases the real value of financial assets with fixed money values and, as a result, increases spending by the holders of these assets. **T F**

3 A fall in the price level reduces the demand for money in the economy and drives interest rates upward. **T F**

4 A rise in the price level of an economy (relative to foreign price levels) tends to increase that economy's exports and to reduce its imports of goods and services. **T F**

5 The aggregate-supply curve is horizontal in the classical range. **T F**

6 At the equilibrium price level the real domestic output purchased is equal to the real domestic output produced. **T F**

7 In the intermediate range on the aggregate-supply curve an increase in aggregate demand will increase both the price level and the real domestic output. **T F**

8 A decrease in aggregate demand will lower the price level by the same amount as an equal increase in aggregate demand would have raised it. **T F**

9 An increase in aggregate supply increases both the equilibrium real domestic output and the full-employment output of the economy. **T F**

10 The basic cause of a decrease in aggregate supply is an increase in the costs of producing goods and services. **T F**

11 Stagflation is a rise in the price level accompanied by declining or stable levels of real domestic output and employment in the economy. **T F**

12 A decrease in aggregate supply is "doubly good" because it increases the real domestic output and prevents inflation. **T F**

Circle the letter that corresponds to the best answer.

1 The slope of the aggregate-demand curve is the result of (*a*) the real-balances effect; (*b*) the interest-rate effect; (*c*) the foreign-trade effect; (*d*) all of the above effects.

2 The aggregate-demand curve is the relationship between the (*a*) price level and the real domestic output purchased; (*b*) price level and the real domestic output produced; (*c*) price level producers are willing to accept and the price level purchasers are willing to pay; (*d*) real domestic output purchased and the real domestic output produced.

3 The aggregate-supply curve is the relationship between the (*a*) price level and the real domestic output purchased; (*b*) price level and real domestic output produced; (*c*) price level producers are willing to accept and the price level purchasers are willing to pay; (*d*) real domestic output purchased and the real domestic output produced.

4 In the Keynesian range the aggregate-supply curve is (*a*) upsloping; (*b*) downsloping; (*c*) vertical; (*d*) horizontal.

5 In the intermediate range the aggregate-supply curve is (*a*) upsloping; (*b*) downsloping; (*c*) vertical; (*d*) horizontal.

6 When the price level rises (*a*) holders of financial assets with fixed money values increase their spending; (*b*) the demand for money and interest rates rise; (*c*) spending that is sensitive to interest-rate changes increases; (*d*) holders of financial assets with fixed money values have more purchasing power.

7 If the real domestic output is less than the equilibrium real domestic output, producers find (*a*) their inventories decreasing and expand their production; (*b*) their inventories increasing and expand their production; (*c*) their inventories decreasing and contract their production; (*d*) their inventories increasing and contract their production.

8 When the economy is in the Keynesian range an increase in aggregate demand will (*a*) increase the price level and have no effect on real domestic output; (*b*) increase the real domestic output and have no effect on the price level; (*c*) increase both real output and the price level; (*d*) increase the price level and decrease the real domestic output.

9 An increase in aggregate supply will (*a*) reduce the price level and real domestic output; (*b*) reduce increases in the price level and increase the real domestic output; (*c*) increase the price level and real domestic output; (*d*) reduce increases in the price level and decrease the real domestic output.

10 If there were stagflation in the economy and aggregate supply were to increase (*a*) both the real domestic output and the price level would decrease; (*b*) the real domestic output would increase and rises in the price level would become smaller; (*c*) the real domestic output would decrease and the price level would rise; (*d*) both the real domestic output and rises in the price level would become greater.

11 Which of the following seems to be the most effective way of eliminating stagflation? (*a*) an increase in aggregate demand; (*b*) a decrease in aggregate demand; (*c*) an increase in aggregate supply; (*d*) a decrease in aggregate supply.

12 A decrease in aggregate supply generally results in (*a*) inflation and prosperity; (*b*) stagflation; (*c*) deflation and unemployment; (*d*) deflation and prosperity.

DISCUSSION QUESTIONS

1 What is an aggregate-demand and an aggregate-supply curve?

2 Explain (*a*) the interest-rate effect, (*b*) the real-balances effect, and (*c*) the foreign-trade effect of change in the price level on the quantity of goods and services demanded in an economy.

3 The aggregate-supply curve is divided into three distinct ranges. Describe the slope of this curve in each of the three ranges. What conditions prevail in the economy in each of the ranges? Why is one range called the Keynesian and another called the classical range?

4 Why does the aggregate-supply curve slope upward in the intermediate range?

5 What real domestic output is the equilibrium real domestic output? Why will business firms that produce the domestic output reduce or expand their production when they find themselves producing more or less than the equilibrium output?

6 What are the effects on the real domestic output and the price level when aggregate demand increases in each of the three ranges along the aggregate-supply curve?

7 If prices were as flexible downward as they are upward, what would be the effects on real domestic output and the price level of a decrease in aggregate demand in each of the three ranges along the aggregate-supply curve?

8 Prices in the economy tend to be "sticky" or inflexible in a downward direction. Why? How does this downward inflexibility alter your answers to question 7 above?

9 What have been some of the causes of decreases in aggregate supply in the Canadian economy during recent years? What might cause aggregate supply to increase?

10 What are the effects on the real domestic output and the price level of a decrease in aggregate supply? What are the effects of an increase in aggregate supply on the real domestic output, the price level, and the maximum real output the economy is able to produce?

11 Why is a decrease in aggregate supply "doubly bad" and an increase in aggregate supply "doubly good"?

12 Using the aggregate-demand and aggregate-supply concepts, explain the difference between demand-pull and cost-push inflation.

24

NEOCLASSICAL AND KEYNESIAN THEORIES OF EMPLOYMENT

Most of the material contained in this chapter deals with the mainstream Keynesian theory or explanation of what determines the demand for the real domestic output (the real GDP) and how the equilibrium level of output (and of employment) is determined. The Keynesian explanation is not the only possible explanation, however. It is with the alternative neoclassical theory that the first part of Chapter 24 deals. The neoclassical theory is described there for several reasons: to impress upon you the fact that an alternative theory does exist; to examine its assumptions and its "cures" for depression; and to prepare you for both Keynesian and "monetarist" macroeconomic theory.

The outstanding thing about the neoclassical theory is its conclusion that the economy will *automatically* function to produce the maximum output it is capable of producing and to provide employment for all those who are willing and able to work. Compare this with the conclusion drawn by the exponents of the Keynesian theory that the economy functions in no such way, that both depression and inflation can prevail with no automatic tendency to be corrected, and that full employment and maximum output, when achieved, are accidental. Compare also the political philosophies of the proponents of the two theories. Those accepting the neoclassical theory have advocated as little government interference with the economy as possible in the belief that such interference prevents the achievement of full employment and maximum output. Adherents of

the Keynesian theory argue that government action is necessary to eliminate the periods of depression that occur. The basic proposition contained in the Keynesian theory is that the level of total or aggregate expenditures in the economy determine the location of the economy's aggregate-demand curve and, as a result, determine real output and employment and, as you learned in the last chapter, therefore determine the price level.

The last section in the chapter outlines the criticism of mainstream Keynesianism by the post-Keynesians—those who claim that mainstream Keynesianism is in fact a synthesis of Keynes and the neoclassical theory.

CHECK LIST

When you have studied this chapter you should be able to

☐ State Say's Law and explain how neoclassical economists were able to reason that all saving would be borrowed and spent for capital goods.

☐ Explain how neoclassical economists were able to reason that price-wage flexibility would eliminate a recession and unemployment.

☐ Present three reasons why the rate of interest may not guarantee the equality of saving and investment; and two reasons why price-wage flexibility may not guarantee full employment; and state the neoclassical response to the latter Keynesian contention.

☐ Compare the neoclassical and Keynesian aggregate-supply curves and the effects of a decrease in aggregate demand in the two theories; and explain why neoclassical (and monetarist) economists argue that the price level and the real domestic output are inversely related if the money supply is constant.

☐ State why the post-Keynesians call mainstream Keynesianism the "neoclassical synthesis."

☐ List the five ways in which the post-Keynesians state mainstream Keynesianism is different from Keynes.

☐ State three reasons why the neoclassical synthesis is not of mere historic or academic interest.

CHAPTER OUTLINE

1 Neoclassical economists contend that full employment is the norm in a market (or capitalistic) economy and *laissez-faire* is the best policy for government to pursue; but Keynesian economists argue that unemployment is typical of such economies and activist policies are required to eliminate it.

2 The neoclassical theory of employment reached the conclusion that the economy would automatically tend to employ its resources fully and produce a full-employment level of output; this conclusion was based on Say's Law and the assumption that prices and wages were flexible.

a. Say's Law stated that the production of goods produced an equal demand for these goods because changes in the rate of interest would ensure that all income not spent (that is, income saved) by consumers would be loaned to investors, who would spend these borrowed funds for capital goods.

b. If there were an excess supply of goods or an excess supply of labour (unemployment), prices and/or wages would fall until the excesses were eliminated and full employment and maximum output again prevailed in the economy.

c. Believing that capitalism would automatically ensure a full-employment level of output, the neoclassical economists saw no need for government interference with the operation of the economy.

3 J.M. Keynes, in *The General Theory of Employment, Interest, and Money,* denied that flexible interest rates, prices, and wages would automatically promote full employment; he set forth the theory that there was nothing automatic about full employment and that both depression and inflation might prevail without any tendency existing for them to be self-correcting.

a. According to Keynes, flexible interest rates do not guarantee that all income saved by consumers will be spent by investors for capital goods because savers and investors are different groups and are differently motivated and because saving is neither the only source of the funds to finance investment nor the only use to which consumers can put these funds.

b. Keynes also argued that prices and wages

(1) are not, in fact, flexible downward; and

(2) that even if they were, a reduction in prices and wages would not reduce unemployment in the economy; but

(3) the defenders of neoclassical theory responded that they would be flexible downward if it were not for government policies that prevented them from falling.

4 Neoclassical and Keynesian economics can be compared by examining their aggregate-demand–aggregate-supply models of the economy.

a. In the neoclassical model the aggregate-supply curve is vertical at the economy's full-employment output; and a decrease in aggregate demand will lower the equilibrium price level and have no effect on the real output of (or employment in) the economy.

b. In the Keynesian model the aggregate-supply curve is horizontal at the current price level; and a decrease in aggregate demand will lower the real output of (and employment in) the economy and have no effect on the equilibrium price level.

c. In both the neoclassical and Keynesian models the aggregate-demand curve slopes downward; but in the neoclassical model it slopes downward because (with a fixed money supply in the economy) a fall in the price level increases the purchasing power of money and enables consumers and business firms to purchase a larger real output.

5 Post-Keynesians claim that mainstream Keynesianism should be called the neoclassical synthesis, which, the post-Keynesians claim, is distinguished from Keynes in five important ways:
a. Acceptance of Say's Law as "really" correct if frictions in the economy could be overcome.
b. Acceptance of creation of unemployment by government to control inflation.
c. Acceptance of high interest rates at any time.
d. Neglect of Keynes' analysis of financial instability.
e. Neglect of Keynes' analysis of aggregate supply.

6 The neoclassical synthesis—mainstream Keynesianism—is not of mere academic interest, for three reasons:
a. The *initial* analysis is greatly simplified by keeping as many things as possible constant, including price.
b. A constant-price model is useful for analysing that which is desirable: a non-inflationary economy.
c. The neoclassical synthesis is the model learned by today's policy-makers.

IMPORTANT TERMS

Classical theory of
  employment
Say's Law
Rate of interest
Money market
Saving
Investment

Price-wage flexibility
Keynesian economics
Post-Keynesians
Neoclassical synthesis
Incomes policy
Constant-cost supply
  curve

FILL-IN QUESTIONS

1 Neoclassical economists believe a market (or capitalistic) economy will tend to produce an output at which its labour force is (fully, less than fully) _____ employed, but Keynesian economists argue it will tend to produce an output at which its labour force is _____ employed; and for this reason the neoclassical economists favour a(n) (activist, *laissez-faire*) _____ government policy and the Keynesian economists favour a(n) _____ policy.

2 Full employment, in the neoclassical theory, was assured by the operation of _____ Law and price-wage _____ .

3 According to Say's Law, the production of goods and services creates an equal ____ _____ .

4 Changes in _____ , according to the neoclassical economists, ensure that what is not spent on consumer goods is spent on capital goods.

5 In the neoclassical theory, if saving is greater than investment the rate of interest will (rise, fall) _____ ; and if investment is greater than saving it will _____ ; and the rate of interest will move to the level at which _____ and _____ are equal.

6 According to the neoclassical way of thinking, if the investment rate did not equate saving and investment, and if total output exceeded the level of spending, prices in the output markets would tend to (rise, fall) _____ because of competition among business firms; this would make some production unprofitable and temporarily

cause _____ in labour markets; but competition among workers would tend to drive resource prices (upward, downward) _____ and (increase, decrease) _____ their employment. This process would continue until _____

_____ .

7 According to the Keynesian theory of employment
a. saving and investment are done by different _____
and for different _____ ;
b. the funds to finance investment come not only from current saving but from the _____ of households and from _____ ;
c. current saving may not be lent to investors in the money market but added to the money _____ of consumers or used to retire outstanding bank _____ .

8 Keynes, in attacking the neoclassical theory of employment, contended that in the modern economy prices and wages (do, do not) _____ fall when there is unemployment; and that wage reductions would lead to (smaller, larger) _____ money incomes, a (fall, rise) _____ in total spending, a(n) (increase, decrease) _____ in prices, and little or no change in total _____ in the economy.

9 Reasoning that if a price and wage-rate reduction would increase the output and employment of an individual firm, then a general reduction in prices and wages will increase output and employment in the economy as a whole is an example of the (*post hoc, ergo propter hoc* fallacy, fallacy of

composition, fallacy of limited decisions)

_____ .

10 The aggregate-supply curve of the neoclassical economists is (horizontal, vertical) _____ , and the aggregate-supply curve of the Keynesian economists is _____ . For this reason, a decrease in aggregate demand will have no effect on the price level and will decrease output and employment in the (classical, Keynesian) _____ and will decrease in the price level and have no effect on output and employment in the _____ model.

11 In the neoclassical and present-day monetarist way of thinking, if the price level falls and the money supply is constant the purchasing power of money will (fall, rise) _____ and consumers and business firms will (expand, contract) _____ their expenditures for goods and services.

12 The post-Keynesians claim mainstream Keynesianism is really the neoclassical

_____ .

13 Post-Keynesians claim mainstream Keynesianism should be distinguished from Keynes in five ways because it:
a. Accepts Say's Law as "really" correct if only it were not for such _____ as money _____ and administered _____ .
b. Accepts that government should create _____ to control inflation.
c. Ignores Keynes' insistence that interest rates should be kept permanently _____ .
d. Neglects Keynes' analysis of financial _____ .
e. Ignores Keynes' analysis of aggregate _____ .

PROBLEMS AND PROJECTS

1 Indicate, in the space to the right of each of the following statements, whether it is made by a neoclassical economist (NC), a Keynesian (K), or a post-Keynesian (PK).

a. Supply creates its own demand.

_____

b. The neoclassical synthesis accepts Say's Law as "really" correct if it were not for frictions. _____

c. The changing interest rate equates saving and investment. _____

d. Capitalism does not contain any mechanism capable of guaranteeing full employment. _____

e. Saving and investment plans can be at odds. _____

f. Prices and wages are not flexible downward. _____

g. Neoclassical economists were guilty of the fallacy of composition. _____

h. To the extent that downward wage-price flexibility does not exist, it is the government's fault. _____

i. Interest rates should be kept permanently very low. _____

j. Financial instability is characteristic of capitalist finance. _____

SELF-TEST

Circle T if the statement is true, F if it is false.

1 According to the neoclassical economists, full employment is normal in market economies. **T F**

2 The neoclassical economists believed that government assistance was *not* required to bring about full employment and full production in the economy. **T F**

3 Say's Law states that demand for goods and services creates an equal supply of goods and services. **T F**

4 In both the neoclassical and Keynesian theories of employment, saving is income not expended for consumer goods and services. **T F**

5 In the neoclassical theory, if saving exceeds investment the rate of interest will rise until saving and investment are equal. **T F**

6 Keynesians contend that most saving is done by business firms and most investment is done by households in the economy. **T F**

7 Neoclassical economists contend that prices and wages would be sufficiently flexible to assure full employment in the economy if it were not for the government policies that reduce their downward flexibility. **T F**

8 The neoclassical economists' view of aggregate demand is that if the money supply is constant, a decrease in the price level will decrease the purchasing power of money and increase the quantities of goods and services demanded by consumers and business firms. **T F**

9 The "neoclassical synthesis" is the post-Keynesian term for mainstream Keynesianism. **T F**

10 Post-Keynesians call for a monetary policy of rising interest rates to stem inflation. **T F**

Circle the letter that corresponds to the best answer.

1 Keynesian economists believe that (*a*) unemployment is characteristic of capitalistic economies and in activist government policies; (*b*) unemployment is characteristic of capitalistic economies and in a government policy of *laissez-faire*; (*c*) full employment is characteristic of capitalistic economies and in activist government policies; (*d*) full employment is characteristic of capitalistic economies and in a government policy of *laissez-faire*.

2 In the neoclassical theory of employment, a decline in the rate of interest will (*a*) decrease saving and investment; (*b*) decrease saving and increase investment; (*c*) increase saving and decrease investment; (*d*) increase saving and investment.

3 The neoclassical theory predicts that an increase in the supply of saving will (*a*) lower interest rates and reduce investment; (*b*) raise interest rates and reduce investment; (*c*) lower interest rates and expand investment; (*d*) raise interest rates and expand investment.

4 If the rate of interest did not equate saving and investment and total output was greater than total spending, the neoclassical economists argued, competition would tend to force (*a*) product and resource prices down; (*b*) product prices up and resource prices down; (*c*) product prices up and resource prices up; (*d*) product prices down and resources prices up.

5 Which of the following is *not* involved in Keynes' criticism of the neoclassical theory of employment? (*a*) a reduction in wage rates will lead only to a reduction in total spending, not to an increase in employment; (*b*) investment spending is not influenced by the rate of interest; (*c*) prices and wages are simply not flexible downward in modern capitalistic economies; (*d*) saving in modern economies depends largely upon the level of disposable income and is little influenced by the rate of interest.

6 Keynesian economists argue the source of the funds that finance investment are (*a*) current saving; (*b*) the accumulated money balances of households; (*c*) commercial banks; (*d*) all of the above.

7 The Keynesian economists also argue that saving is (*a*) used to finance investment expenditures; (*b*) added to the money balances of savers; (*c*) used to retire the loans made previously by banks; (*d*) utilized for all of the above.

8 The Keynesian aggregate-supply curve (*a*) is horizontal; (*b*) slopes upward; (*c*) is vertical; (*d*) slopes downward.

9 The aggregate-supply curve of neoclassical economists (*a*) is horizontal; (*b*) slopes upward; (*c*) is vertical; (*d*) slopes downward.

10 In the neoclassical theory of employment a decrease in aggregate demand results in (*a*) a decrease in both the price level and domestic output; (*b*) a decrease in the price level and no change in domestic output; (*c*) no change in the price level and a decrease in the domestic output; (*d*) no change in either the price level or domestic output.

11 A decrease in aggregate demand, in the Keynesian theory of employment, results in (*a*) a decrease in both the price level and domestic output; (*b*) a decrease in the price level and no change in domestic output; (*c*) no change in the price level and a decrease in domestic output; (*d*) no change in either the price level or domestic output.

DISCUSSION QUESTIONS

1 How do the neoclassical and Keynesian economists differ on (*a*) the normal amount of unemployment that will prevail in a capitalistic (or market) economy; and (*b*) the role they would assign to government in such an economy?

2 According to the neoclassical economists, what level of employment would tend to prevail in the economy? On what two basic assumptions did their analysis of the level of employment rest?

3 What is Say's Law? How were the neoclassical economists able to reason that whatever is saved is spent?

4 In the neoclassical analysis, Say's Law made it certain that whatever was produced would be sold. How did flexible prices, flexible wages, and competition drive the economy to full employment and maximum output?

5 On what grounds did J.M. Keynes argue that flexible interest rates would not assure the operation of Say's Law? What were his reasons for asserting that flexible prices and wages would not assure full employment, and what was the neoclassical response to his assertion?

6 "Savers and investors are largely different groups and are motivated by different factors." Explain in detail who these groups are and what motivates them. Does the rate of interest play any role in determining saving and investment?

7 What is (*a*) the difference between the neoclassical and the Keynesian aggregate-supply curve; and (*b*) the difference between the effects a decrease in aggregate demand would have on the price level and on the real domestic output in the two models? Why does the neoclassical aggregate-demand curve have a negative (downward) slope?

8 *If* the criticisms by the post-Keynesians of mainstream Keynesianism are valid, why study it?

25

EQUILIBRIUM DOMESTIC OUTPUT IN THE KEYNESIAN MODEL

Chapter 25 develops the Keynesian explanation of what determines the equilibrium level of GDP—the actual size of the GDP that will tend to be produced in the economy. You *must* understand this chapter if you are to acquire an understanding of what causes GDP to rise and fall; of what causes unemployment, depression, inflation, and prosperity; and of what can be done to prevent recession and inflation and to foster price stability, full employment, and economic growth.

In the Keynesian model of the economy, the equilibrium level of real GDP is determined *only* by the level of *aggregate expenditures* because it is assumed in this model that the economy is operating in the Keynesian (or depression) range of the aggregate-supply curve (and that the price level does not rise or fall). It is through examining the components of aggregate expenditures that we can determine the location of the aggregate-demand curve discused in Chapter 23.

The first part of the chapter analyses the economic factors that determine two principal components of aggregate expenditures—consumption expenditures and investment expenditures. You should pay particular attention to the relationships called the consumption schedule, the saving schedule, and their characteristics; to the four propensity concepts; and to the "non-income" determinants of consumption and saving.

Investment expenditures—that is, the purchase of capital goods—depend upon the rate of net profits that business firms *expect* to earn from an investment and upon the real rate of interest they have to pay for the use of money. Because firms are anxious to make profitable investments and to avoid unprofitable ones, they undertake all investments that have an expected rate of net profit greater than (or equal to) the real rate of interest and do not undertake an investment when the expected rate of net profit is less than the interest rate. You should see that because business firms behave this way, the lower the real rate of interest the larger will be the dollar amount invested; and that this relationship between the real interest rate and the level of investment spending, called the investment-demand schedule, is an inverse one. But you should not confuse the investment-demand schedule (or curve) with the investment schedule (or curve), which relates investment spending to the GDP and which may show investment is either unrelated to or directly related to the GDP. Five non-interest determinants of investment spending influence the profit expectations of business firms; these are analysed. You should learn how changes in these determinants affect investment; and why investment spending is unstable.

The total amount a nation exports and the total amount it imports also have important macroeconomic effects upon the nation's output and income and upon its level of employment. *Net* exports are the third component of aggregate expenditures. The more a nation exports (or the less it imports), the greater will be the levels of income, output, and employment in that nation; and the less it exports (or the more it imports), the smaller these levels will be.

Government purchases of goods and services add to aggregate expenditures, while taxation subtracts from aggregate expenditures. But while government purchases do so directly, (personal) taxation does so indirectly, since it reduces the disposable income of consumers and thereby reduces both the amount of consumption and the amount of saving that will take place at any level of GDP.

With the four elements of aggregate expenditures (C, I_g, G, and X_n) now before us, the equilibrium level of GDP is explained with both tables and graphs, first by using the expenditures-output approach and then by employing the leakages-injections approach. These two approaches are complementary and are simply two different ways of analysing the same process and of reaching the same conclusions. For each approach it is important for you to know, given the consumption (or saving) schedule, the level of investment expenditures, the net export schedule, and the level of government purchases and taxation, *what* GDP will tend to be produced and *why* this will be the GDP that will be produced.

It is essential that you understand *why* the only sustainable GDP is the one where the *sum* of the leakages of saving, imports, and taxation are exactly offset by the *sum* of the injections of investment, exports and government purchases.

All the schedules are subject to change, and when they change, equilibrium GDP will also change. The relationship between a change in any schedule and a change in equilibrium GDP is called the multiplier. Three things to note here are: *how* the multiplier is defined, *why* there is a multiplier effect, and upon *what* the size of the multiplier depends. Special attention should be directed to the exact effect taxes have upon the consumption and saving schedules and to the multiplier effects of changes in government purchases and taxes. Because of the multiplier, the paradoxical consequence of an attempt by the economy to save more, that is, to consume less—in the absence of a simultaneous increase in investment, net exports, and/or government purchases—is, at best, less of an increase in saving than desired.

It is important to be aware that the equilibrium real GDP is not necessarily the real GDP at which full employment without inflationary pressures is achieved. Aggregate expenditures may be greater or less than the full-employment non-inflationary real GDP; if they are greater there is an inflationary gap and if they are less there exists a recessionary gap. Be sure that you know how to measure the size of each of these gaps: the amount by which the aggregate-expenditures schedule (or curve) must change to bring the economy to its full-employment real GDP without there being inflation in the economy.

The price level in the Keynesian model, as noted above, is assumed to be constant; but in the aggregate-demand–aggregate-supply model (examined in Chapter 23) the price level can rise or fall. These two models do not, however, contradict each other; and the last section of the chapter reconciles them. The important thing to understand is that prices can be constant at different levels. The price index in the economy, for example, might be constant at 100, at 75, or at 120. The AD curve is derived from the Keynesian model by letting prices be *constant at different levels*. Once you realize this it is no great problem to see that the lower (the higher) the level at which prices are constant in the Keynesian model the larger (the smaller) will be the equilibrium real GDP in that model of the economy; and that the AD curve slopes downward.

The AD curve derived in this way from the Keynesian model and the AS curve together determine the price level and the equilibrium real GDP in the aggregate-demand–aggregate-supply model. But aggregate demand can increase (or decrease); and when it does both the price level and the equilibrium real GDP may be changed. How the price level and real GDP are affected depends upon the range on the aggregate-supply curve in which the economy is initially operating. Here the important thing to see is that because the change in AD may also affect the price level in the economy, the change in AD may not have its *full* multiplier effect on the real GDP of the economy.

The next chapter deals with the fiscal policies that can be employed by government to eliminate recessionary and inflationary gaps in the economy.

CHECK LIST

When you have studied this chapter you should be able to

☐ State the range along the aggregate-supply curve in which the economy is assumed to operate and the assumption made about the price level in the Keynesian model.

☐ State the other simplifying assumption and its implication.

☐ State what determines the amount of goods and services produced and the level of employment in the Keynesian theory.

☐ Explain how consumption and saving are related to disposable income.

☐ Compute, when you are given the necessary data, the four propensities.

☐ Explain what happens to the size of the two average propensities as income increases.

☐ List the five non-income determinants of consumption and saving; and explain how a change in each of these determinants will affect the consumption and saving schedules.

☐ Explain the difference between a change in the amount consumed (or saved) and a change in the consumption (or saving) schedule.

☐ List the two basic determinants of investment; explain when a firm will and will not invest.

☐ Compute, when given the appropriate data, the investment-demand schedule; and explain why the relationship between investment spending and the real rate of interest is inverse.

☐ List the five non-interest determinants of investment demand; explain how a change in each of these determinants will affect the investment-demand curve.

☐ Explain the two variables found in an investment schedule; explain the two kinds of relationships that might be found to exist between these two variables.

☐ List the four factors that explain why investment spending tends to be unstable.

☐ Identify the major determinant of a nation's exports and the major determinant of its imports.

☐ Compute, when you are given the necessary data, the marginal propensity to import and the net export schedule.

☐ Outline the linkage between the real GDP and the level of employment in one nation with the real GDP and employment in other nations.

☐ State the two simplifying assumptions made concerning government tax collection.

☐ Explain the effect on consumption and saving of an increase and of a decrease in net tax revenues and the consequent effect on aggregate expenditures.

☐ Find the equilibrium GDP when you are given the necessary tabular or graphical data, by employing either the aggregate-expenditures–domestic-output or the leakages-injections approach.

☐ Explain why the economy will tend to produce its equilibrium GDP rather than some smaller or larger GDP.

☐ Determine the economy's new equilibrium GDP when there is a change in any of the schedules.

☐ Find the value of the multiplier when you are given the needed information; and cite the two facts upon which the multiplier affect (a multiplier greater than one) is based.

☐ Explain the balanced-budget multiplier.

☐ Draw a graph to explain the paradox of thrift.

☐ Distinguish between the equilibrium GDP and the full-employment, noninflationary level of GDP.

☐ Find the recessionary and the inflationary gaps when you are provided with the relevant data.

☐ Contrast the Keynesian expenditures-output and the aggregate-demand–aggregate-supply models by comparing the variability of the price level and real GDP in the two models in the three ranges along the aggregate-supply curve.

☐ Derive the aggregate-demand curve (or schedule) from the Keynesian model; and explain the effect of a change in aggregate expenditures (in the Keynesian model) on the aggregate-demand curve (or schedule).

☐ Predict the effects of a change in aggregate demand on the price level and the equilibrium real GDP in the three ranges along the aggregate-supply curve; and explain what determines how large the multiplier effect on the equilibrium real GDP will be in the aggregate-demand–aggregate-supply model.

CHAPTER OUTLINE

1 In this chapter it is assumed (unless otherwise explicitly specified) that the economy is operating within the Keynesian range of the aggregate-supply curve and the price level is, therefore, constant; two approaches are used to explain what *real* domestic output (or GDP) the economy will tend to produce; but both approaches yield the same conclusion.

2 A second simplifying assumption is that all saving is personal saving.

3 Aggregate output and employment in the Keynesian theory are directly related to the level of total or aggregate expenditures in the economy; and to understand what determines the level of total expenditures at any time it is necessary to explain the factors that determine the levels of consumption, investment, net exports, and government purchases.

4 Consumption is the largest component of aggregate expenditures; and saving is disposable income not spent for consumer goods.
a. Disposable income is the most important determinant of both consumption and saving; the relationships between income and consumption and between income and saving are both direct (positive) ones.
b. The consumption schedule shows the amounts that households plan to spend for consumer goods at various levels of income.
c. The saving schedule indicates the amounts households plan to save at different income levels.
d. The average propensities to consume and to save and the marginal propensities to consume and to save can be computed from the consumption and saving schedules.
(1) The APC and the APS are, respectively, the percentages of income spent for consumption and saved; and their sum is equal to 1.
(2) The MPC and the MPS are, respectively, the percentages of *additional* income spent for consumption and saved; and their sum is equal to 1.
e. In addition to income, there are several other important determinants of consumption and saving; changes in these non-income determinants will cause the consumption and saving *schedules* to change.
f. A change in the amount consumed (or saved) is not the same thing as a change in the consumption (or saving) schedule. If

these schedules change they change in opposite directions; but the schedules are very stable.

5 The two important determinants of the level of net investment spending in the economy are the expected rate of net profit from the purchase of additional capital goods and the real rate of interest.

a. The expected rate of net profit is directly related to the net profit (revenues less operating costs) that is expected to result from an investment and inversely related to the cost of making the investment (purchasing capital goods).

b. The rate of interest is the price paid for the use of money. When the expected real rate of net profit is greater (less) than the real rate of interest, a business will (will not) invest because the investment will be profitable (unprofitable).

c. For this reason, the lower (higher) the real rate of interest, the greater (smaller) will be the level of investment spending in the economy; and the investment-demand curve (schedule) indicates this inverse relationship between the real rate of interest and the level of spending for capital goods.

d. There are at least five non-interest determinants of investment demand; and a change in any of these determinants will shift the investment-demand curve (schedule).

e. Investment spending in the economy may also be either independent or directly related to the real GDP; and the investment schedule may show that investment either remains constant or increases as real GDP increases.

f. Because the five non-interest determinants of investment are subject to sudden changes, investment spending tends to be unstable.

6 International trade and specialization have macroeconomic effects upon aggregate expenditures and, as a result, upon the total income, output, and employment of a nation.

a. Net exports equal exports minus imports; and a nation's exports depend directly upon the GDPs of foreign nations, while its imports depend directly upon its own GDP.

b. The net export schedule shows the amounts of net exports at various levels of GDP.

(1) The MPM is the percentage of *additional* income spent for imports.

c. The economies of nations that engage in international trade are linked by the effect a change in one nation's real GDP has on the real GDPs of other nations: an increase (a decrease) in real GDP in one nation will expand (contract) its M, expand (contract) the X of other nations, and increase (decrease) their real GDPs and employment.

7 Discretionary fiscal policy involves deliberate changes in tax rates and government spending to offset cyclical fluctuations and to increase economic growth.

a. Two assumptions are made in order to simplify the explanation of the effects of government spending and taxes on aggregate expenditures.

b. Government purchases of goods and services add to the aggregate-expenditures schedule.

c. Taxes decrease consumption and the aggregate-expenditures schedule by the amount of the tax times the MPC (and decrease saving by the amount of the tax times the MPS).

8 Employing the aggregate-expenditures–domestic-output approach, the equilibrium real GDP is the real GDP at which:

a. aggregate expenditures $(C_a + I_g + X_n + G)$ equal the real GDP; or

b. in graphical terms, the aggregate-expenditures curve crosses the 45° line.

9 Using the leakages-injections approach, the equilibrium real GDP is the real GDP at which:

a. $S_a + M + T = I_g + X + G$; or

b. in graphical terms, the leakages curve crosses the injections curve.

10 When leakages and injections are not equal, either unplanned investment or unplanned disinvestment in inventories has occurred; and the real GDP will change until leakages and injections are equal and there is no unplanned investment or disinvestment.

11 Changes in any of the spending schedules will cause the equilibrium level of real GDP to change in the same direction by an amount greater than the change in spending.
a. This is called the multiplier effect; and the multiplier is equal to the ratio of the change in the real GDP to the initial change in spending.
(1) The multiplier effect occurs because a change in the dollars spent by one person alters the income of another person in the same direction and because any change in the income of one person will change the person's consumption and saving in the same direction by a fraction of the change in income.
(2) The value of the open-economy multiplier is equal to the reciprocal of the marginal propensity to save plus the marginal propensity to import.
(3) The significance of the multiplier is that relatively small changes in the spending plans of business firms or households bring about larger changes in the equilibrium real GDP.
b. An increase in taxes has a negative multiplier effect on the equilibrium real GDP. Equal increases (decreases) in taxes and in government purchases increase (decrease) equilibrium real GDP by an amount determined by the balanced-budget multiplier.
c. The paradox of thrift is that an increase in the saving schedule may result in a smaller increase than that intended, or in no increase, and may even result in a decrease, in saving; the increase in the saving schedule causes a multiple contraction in real GDP; and at the lower real GDP, saving is less than that desired at the original GDP.

12 The equilibrium level of real GDP may turn out to be an equilibrium at less than full employment, at full employment, or at full employment with inflation.
a. If the equilibrium real GDP is *less* than the real GDP consistent with full employment, there exists a recessionary gap; the size of the recessionary gap equals the amount by which the aggregate-expenditures schedule must increase (shift upward) to increase the real GDP to its full-employment non-inflationary level.
b. If equilibrium real GDP is *greater* than the real GDP consistent with stable prices, there is an inflationary gap. The size of the inflationary gap equals the amount by which the aggregate-expenditures schedule must decrease (shift downward) if the economy is to achieve full employment without inflation.
c. It is, however, likely that a full-employment non-inflationary real GDP is unattainable in the real world; and this likelihood complicates the elimination of an inflationary gap.

13 The Keynesian expenditures-output model and the aggregate-demand–aggregate-supply model are reconciled by recalling that the price level is assumed to be constant in the former and is a variable (can rise or fall) in the latter model.
a. The AD curve is derived from the intersections of the aggregate-expenditures curves and the 45° curve: as the price level falls (rises) the consumption and the aggregate-expenditure curves shift upward (downward) because of the real balances effect and the equilibrium real GDP increases (decreases); and this inverse relationship between the price level and the equilibrium real GDP is the AD schedule (or curve).
b. If the price level is constant, any change in the non-price level determinants of consumption, investment, net exports, and government purchases that shifts the aggregate-expenditures curve upward (downward) will increase (decrease) the equilibrium real GDP and shift the AD curve

to the right (left) by an amount equal to the increase (decrease) in aggregate expenditures times the multiplier.

c. If the economy is operating along the

(1) Keynesian range of the AS curve, an increase in AD will have no effect on the price level and the increase in the equilibrium real GDP will equal the full multiplier effect of the increase in aggregate expenditures;

(2) intermediate range, the increase in AD will increase the price level and the increase in the equilibrium real GDP will be less than the full multiplier effect of the increase in aggregate expenditures;

(3) classical range, the increase in AD will increase the price level and have no effect on the equilibrium real GDP.

IMPORTANT TERMS

Total (aggregate) expenditures

Dissaving

Consumption schedule

Saving schedule

Break-even income

Average propensity to consume

Average propensity to save

Marginal propensity to consume

Marginal propensity to save

Non-income determinants of consumption and saving

Change in amount consumed (saved)

Change in the consumption (saving) schedule

Expected rate of net profit

Real rate of interest

Investment-demand schedule (curve)

Non-interest determinants of investment

Investment schedule (curve)

Open economy

Net exports

Net export schedule

Marginal propensity to import

Discretionary fiscal policy

Net taxes

Lump-sum tax

Real domestic output (GDP)

Aggregate-expenditures—domestic-output approach

Leakages-injections approach

Aggregate-expenditures schedule

Equilibrium real GDP

45° line

Leakage

Injection

Multiplier effect

Multiplier

Open-economy multiplier

Complex multiplier

Paradox of thrift

Supermultiplier

Balanced-budget multiplier

Recessionary gap

Inflationary gap

FILL-IN QUESTIONS

1 In this chapter (unless explicitly indicated to the contrary)

a. it is assumed that the economy is operating within the (Keynesian, classical) _____ range of the aggregate-supply and the price level is (variable, constant) _____ ;

b. the explanation is in terms of the (real, nominal) _____ domestic output or (GNP, GDP) _____ .

2 It is also assumed, initially, that government does not collect _____ , make _____ payments, or _____ for goods and services; and that all saving is (personal, business, government) _____ saving.

a. The implications of these assumptions are

GDP = _____ = _____ = _____ = _____ .

3 The largest single component of total expenditures is _____ expenditures.

4 Keynes argued that

a. domestic output and employment depend (directly, inversely) _____

upon the level of total or aggregate _____
in the economy;

b. the most important determinant of consumption and of saving in the economy is the

economy's _____ ;

c. and that both consumption and saving

are (directly, inversely) _____
related to this determinant.

5 As disposable income falls, the average propensity to consume will (rise, fall)

_____ and the average propensity to

save will _____ .

6 The most important determinants of consumption spending, other than the level of income, are

a. the wealth or the sum of the

_____ and the _____ assets
households have accumulated;

b. _____ ;

c. _____ ;

d. _____ ;

e. _____ .

7 A change in the consumption (or saving)

schedule means that _____

_____ ;
but a change in the amount consumed (or

saved) means that _____

_____ .

8 Investment is defined as spending for

additional _____ ;
and the total amount of investment spending in the economy depends upon

a. the _____ rate of net _____ ;

b. the real rate of_____ .

9 A business firm will invest in more capital if the expected rate of net profit on

this investment is (greater, less) _____
than the real rate of interest it must pay for the use of money.

10 The relation between the real rate of interest and the total amount of investment in

the economy is (direct, inverse) _____ .
This means that if the real rate of interest

a. rises, investment will _____ ;

b. falls, investment will _____ .

11 Five non-interest determinants of investment-demand are

a. _____

b. _____

c. _____

d. _____

e. _____ .

12 The consumption schedule and the saving schedule tend to be (stable or unstable)

_____, while investment

demand tends to be _____ .

13 The demand for new capital goods tends

to be unstable because of the _____

of capital goods, the _____ of

innovation, and the _____ of actual
and expected profits.

14 When a nation is able to export and import goods and services,

a. its net exports equal its _____

minus its_____ ;

b. the volume of its total exports depends

(directly, indirectly) _____

upon the level of _____ in foreign countries;

c. the volume of its total imports depends (directly, indirectly) _____ upon the level of _____ .

15 Suppose an economy experienced a recession in which its real GDP and employment fell.
a. Its imports from other nations would (rise, fall) _____, and the exports of the other nations would _____.
b. Real GDP and employment in the other nations would (rise, fall) _____.

16 An open economy's marginal propensity to import is equal to the fraction (or percentage) of an increase in its _____ that is spent on _____ .

17 Taxes tend to reduce consumption at each level of GDP by an amount equal to the taxes multiplied by the _____ ; saving will decrease by an amount equal to the taxes multiplied by the _____ .

18 Two complementary approaches that are employed to explain the equilibrium levels of real domestic output are the _____ _____ approach and the _____ approach.

19 The equilibrium level of GDP is the GDP at which
a. aggregate _____ equal real domestic_____ ;
b. GDP equals _____ plus _____ plus _____ plus _____ ;

c. the aggregate-expenditures schedule or curve intersects the _____ line.
d. When the leakages-injection approach is used:
(1) leakages considered are _____ , _____ , and _____ ;
(2) injections considered are _____ , _____, and _____ .

20 If
a. aggregate expenditures are greater than the real domestic output, leakages are (greater, less) _____ than injections, there is unplanned (investment, disinvestment) _____ in inventories, and the real GDP will (rise, fall) _____ ;
b. aggregate expenditures are less than the real domestic output, leakages are _____ _____ than injections, there is unplanned _____ in inventories, and the real GDP will _____ ;
c. aggregate expenditures are equal to the real domestic output, leakages are _____ _____ injections, unplanned investment in inventories is _____, and the real GDP will _____ .

21 Only where leakages equal injections will aggregate expenditures equal_____ .
a. But if injections are greater than leakages by $10,
(1) there is $10 of unplanned (investment, disinvestment) _____ in inventories;
(2) the real GDP will (rise, fall) _____ by an amount equal to $10 times_____ .
b. And if injections are less than leakages by $5,

(1) there is $5 of unplanned _____ in inventories;

(2) the real GDP will _____

by _____ .

22 The multiplier effect is based on two facts:

a. an initial increase in spending by business firms, government, foreigners, or consumers will increase the _____ of the households in the economy; and

b. the latter increase will expand the (consumption, investment) _____ spending of the households by an amount equal to the increase in income times the

_____ .

23 The open-economy multiplier

a. is the ratio of the change in _____

to the change in _____ ;

b. has a value equal to one divided by the

_____ plus the _____ .

24 What would be the effect—increase (+) or decrease (−)—of each of the following upon an open economy's equilibrium real GDP?

a. An increase in its imports. _____

b. An increase in its exports. _____

c. A decrease in its imports. _____

d. A decrease in its exports. _____

25 When any of the spending schedules increases, the equilibrium real GDP (increases, decreases) _____ ; and when spending decreases, the equilibrium real GDP _____ .

a. The changes in the equilibrium real GDP are (greater, less) _____ than the changes in spending on domestic production.

b. The size of the multiplier varies (directly, inversely) _____ with the size of the marginal propensity to consume.

26 Equal reductions in taxes and government purchases will (increase, decrease) _____ real GDP by an amount (less than, equal to, greater than) _____ the reductions.

27 If the economy decides to save more (consume less) at every level of real GDP, equilibrium real GDP will (increase, decrease) _____ and the equilibrium level of saving in the economy (will, will not) _____ increase as much as desired. This consequence of an increased desire to save is called the _____

_____ .

28 A recessionary gap exists when equilibrium real GDP is (greater, less) _____ than the full-employment real GDP; to bring real GDP to the full-employment level, the aggregate-expenditures schedule must (increase, decrease) _____ by an amount equal to the difference between the equilibrium and the full-employment noninflationary real GDP divided by the _____ .

29 When equilibrium *money* or *nominal* GDP is greater than the full-employment real GDP at which prices are stable, there is a(n) _____ gap; to eliminate this gap _____ must decrease by

_____

_____

divided by the multiplier.

30 In the aggregate-demand–aggregate-supply model the price level is a (constant, variable) _____ and in the Keynesian expenditures-output model it is a _____ .

a. But if the price level were lower in the Keynesian model the _____ effect would (raise, lower) _____ the consumption and aggregate-expenditures curves; and the equilibrium real GDP would (rise, fall) _____ .

b. And if the price level were higher in the Keynesian model, this effect would _____ the consumption and aggregate-expenditures curves; and the equilibrium real GDP would_____ .

c. This (direct, inverse) _____ relationship between the price level and the equilibrium real GDP in the Keynesian model is the aggregate- (demand, supply) _____ curve (or schedule).

31 If the price level were a constant, a(n)
a. increase in the aggregate-expenditures curve would shift the aggregate-demand curve to the (right, left) _____ by an amount equal to the upward shift in aggregate expenditures times the _____ ;
b. decrease in the aggregate-expenditures curve would shift the aggregate-demand curve to the _____ by an amount equal to the _____ _____ .

32 Were aggregate demand to increase,
a. the flatter the aggregate-supply curve, the (greater, smaller) _____ is the multiplier effect on the equilibrium real GDP and the _____ is the effect on the equilibrium price level; and

b. the steeper the aggregate-supply curve, the _____ is the multiplier effect on the equilibrium real GDP and the _____ is the effect on the equilibrium price level.

PROBLEMS AND PROJECTS

1 Below is a consumption schedule. Assume taxes and transfer payments are zero and that all saving is personal saving.

GDP	C	S	APC,%	APS,%
$1,500	$1,540	$_____	1.027	−.027
1,600	1,620	_____	1.025	−.025
1,700	1,700	_____	_____	_____
1,800	1,780	_____	.989	.011
1,900	1,860	_____	.979	.021
2,000	1,940	_____	_____	_____
2,100	2,020	_____	.962	.038
2,200	2,100	_____	_____	_____

a. Compute saving at each of the eight levels of GDP and the missing average propensities to consume and to save.
b. The break-even level of income (GDP) is $_____ .
c. As GDP rises, the marginal propensity to consume remains constant. Between each two GDPs, the MPC can be found by dividing $_____ by $_____, and is equal to _____% .
d. The marginal propensity to save also remains constant when the GDP rises. Between each two GDPs, the MPS is equal to $_____ divided by $_____, or to _____% .
e. Plot the consumption schedule, the saving schedule, and the 45° line on the graph on the next page.

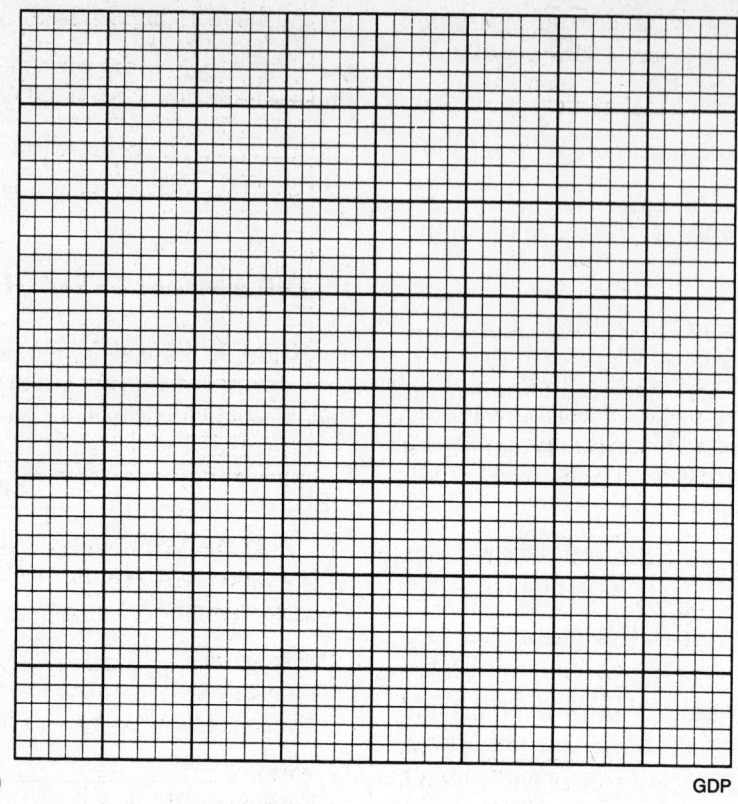

0   GDP

2 Indicate, in the space to the right of each of the following events, whether the event will tend to increase (+) or decrease (−) the *saving* schedule.

a. Development of consumer expectations that prices will be higher in the future.

_____

b. Gradual shrinkage in the stock of durable goods owned by consumers. _____

c. Increase in the volume of consumer indebtedness.   _____

d. Growing belief that disposable income will be lower in the future.   _____

e. Rumours that a current shortage of consumer goods will soon disappear.

_____

f. Rise in the actual level of disposable income.   _____

g. A build-up in the dollar size of liquid assets owned by consumers.   _____

h. Development of a belief by consumers that the federal government can and will prevent depressions in the future.

_____

3 The following schedule has eight different expected rates of net profit and the dollar amounts of investment expected to have each of these net-profit rates.

a. If the real rate of interest in the economy were 18%, business firms would plan to spend $ _____ billion for investment; but if the real interest rate were 16%, they would plan to spend $ _____ billion for investment.

Expected rate of net profit	Amount of investment (billions)
18%	$ 0
16	10
14	20
12	30
10	40
8	50
6	60
4	70

b. Should the real interest rate be 14%, they would still wish to make the investments they were willing to make at real interest rates of 18% and 16%; they would also plan to spend

an additional $ _____ billion for investment; and their total investment would

be $ _____ billion.

c. Were the real rate of investment 12%, they would make all the investments they had planned to make at higher real interest

rates plus an additional _____ billion; and their total investment spending would

be $ _____ billion.

d. Complete the next table by computing the amount of planned investment at the four remaining real interest rates.

Real rate of interest	Amount of investment (billions)
18%	$ 0
16	10
14	30
12	60
10	____
8	____
6	____
4	____

e. Graph the schedule you completed above on the graph in the next column. Plot the rate of interest on the vertical axis and the amount of investment planned at each rate of interest on the horizontal axis.

0

f. Both the graph and the table show that the relation between the real rate of interest and the amount of investment spending in

the economy is _____ .
This means that when the real rate of interest
(1) increases, investment will (increase, decrease) _____ ;
(2) decreases, investment will (increase, decrease) _____ .
g. It also means that should we wish to
(1) increase investment, we would need to

_____
the real rate of interest;
(2) decrease investment, we would have to

_____
the real rate of interest.

h. This graph (or table) is the _____ curve (or schedule).

4 Indicate in the space to the right of each of the following events whether the event would tend to increase (+) or decrease (−) investment expenditures.

a. Rising stock market prices. _____
b. Development of expectations by entrepreneurs that business taxes will be higher in

the future. _____

c. Step-up in the rates at which new products and new production processes are being introduced. _____

d. Business belief that wage rates may be lower in the future. _____

e. A mild recession. _____

f. A belief that business is "too good" and the economy is due for a period of "slow" consumer demand. _____

g. Rising costs in the construction industry. _____

h. A rapid increase in the size of the economy's population. _____

i. A period of a high level of investment spending that has resulted in productive capacity in excess of the current demand for goods and services. _____

5 Below are two schedules showing several GDPs and the level of investment spending (I) at each GDP. (All figures are in billions of dollars.)

Schedule Number 1		Schedule Number 2	
GDP	I	GDP	I
$ 850	$90	$ 850	$ 75
900	90	900	80
950	90	950	85
1,000	90	1,000	90
1,050	90	1,050	95
1,100	90	1,100	100
1,150	90	1,150	105

a. Each of these schedules is a(n) _____ schedule.

b. When such a schedule is drawn up, it is assumed that the real rate of interest is

_____ .

c. In schedule
(1) number 1, GDP and I are (unrelated, directly related)_____ ;

(2) number 2, GDP and I are _____ .

d. Should the real rate of interest rise, investment spending at each GDP would (increase, decrease) _____ and the curve relating GDP and investment spending would shift (upward, downward)_____ .

6 In the table on the following page are a consumption function, a saving function, and an import function.

a. Assume the government levies a lump-sum tax of $10 at all levels of real GDP, and the marginal propensities to consume and to import remain constant.
(1) Because the marginal propensity to consume in this problem is _____, the imposition of this tax will reduce consumption at all levels of real GDP by $ _____ .
Complete the C_a column to show consumption at each real GDP after the levying of this tax.
(2) Because the marginal propensity to save in this problem is ____, this tax will reduce saving at all levels of real GDP by
Complete the S_a column to show saving at each real GDP after this tax has been levied.

b. Compute the (after-tax) saving-plus-taxes-plus-imports at each real GDP and put them in the $S_a + T + M$ column.

c. Suppose that investment is $15, government purchases of goods and services are $20, and exports are $20. Complete the investment-plus-government spending plus net-exports column, $(I_g + G + X_n)$, and the after-tax consumption-plus-investment-plus-government spending-plus-net-exports column $(C_a + I_g + G + X_n)$.

d. On the following two graphs plot
(1) $C_a + I_g + G + X_n$, and the 45° line. Show the equilibrium real GDP.
(2) $S_a + T + M$ and $I_g + G + X$. Show the equilibrium real GDP.

e. The equilibrium real GDP is $ _____ .

Real GDP	C	S	M	X	X_n	C_a	S_a	$S_a + T + M$	$I_g + G + X_n$	$C_a + I_g + G + X_n$
$350	$325	$25	$17	$20	___	___	___	___	___	___
360	334	26	20	20	___	___	___	___	___	___
370	343	27	23	20	___	___	___	___	___	___
380	352	28	26	20	___	___	___	___	___	___
390	361	29	29	20	___	___	___	___	___	___
400	370	30	32	20	___	___	___	___	___	___
410	379	31	35	20	___	___	___	___	___	___
420	388	32	38	20	___	___	___	___	___	___
430	397	33	41	20	___	___	___	___	___	___
440	406	34	44	20	___	___	___	___	___	___
450	415	35	47	20	___	___	___	___	___	___
460	424	36	50	20	___	___	___	___	___	___
470	433	37	53	20	___	___	___	___	___	___

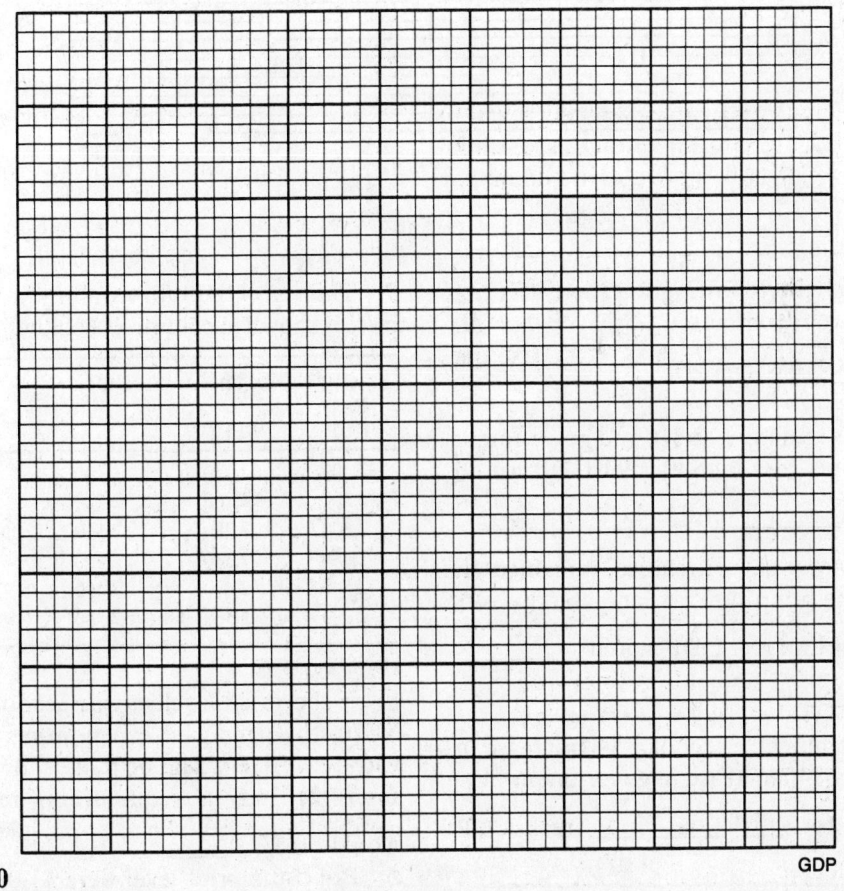

0

GDP

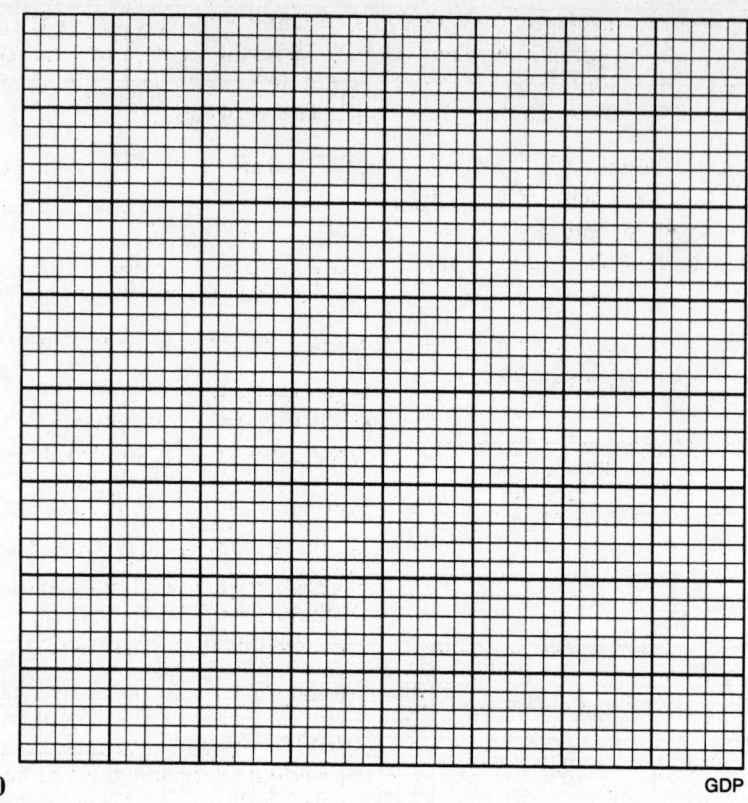

0   GDP

(To answer the following question it is not necessary to recompute C_a, S_a, $S_a + T + M$, $I_g + G + X$, or $C_a + I_g + G + X_n$. Use the multipliers.)

f. If taxes remained at $10 and government expenditures rose by $40, real GDP would (rise, fall) _____ by $ _____ .

g. If government purchases remained at $20 and the lump-sum tax increased by $40, the equilibrium real GDP would _____ by $_____ .

h. The combined effect of a $40 increase in taxes *and* a $40 increase in government purchases is to _____ real GDP by $_____ .

7 The real GDP an economy might produce is shown in column (1) below.

(1) Real GDP	(2) $AE_{1.20}$	(3) $AE_{1.00}$	(4) $AE_{0.80}$
$2,100	$2,110	$2,130	$2,150
2,200	2,200	2,220	2,240
2,300	2,290	2,310	2,330
2,400	2,380	2,400	2,420
2,500	2,470	2,490	2,510
2,600	2,560	2,580	2,600

a. If the price level in this economy were $1.20, the aggregate expenditures (AE) at each real GDP would be those shown in column (2) and the equilibrium real GDP would be $_____ .

b. But if the price level were $1.00, the aggregate expenditures at each real GDP would be those shown in column (3) and the equilibrium real GDP would be $ _____ .

c. And if the price level were $0.80, the aggregate expenditures at each real GDP would be those shown in column (4) and the equilibrium real GDP would be $ _____ .

d. show in the schedule below the equilibrium real GDP at each of the three price levels.

Price level	Equilibrium real GDP
$1.20	$_____
1.00	_____
.80	_____

(1) This schedule is the _____ schedule; and
(2) in it the equilibrium real GDP is _____ related to the price level.

8 Columns (1) and (2) in the table below are the aggregate-supply schedule of an economy.
a. The economy is in the
(1) classical range when its real GDP is $ _____ and the price level is $ _____ or higher;
(2) Keynesian range when its real GDP is $ _____ or less and its price level is $ _____ .
b. If the aggregate demand in the economy were columns (1) and (3), the equilibrium real GDP would be $ _____ and the equilibrium price level would be $ _____ ; and if aggregate demand should increase by $100 to that shown in columns (1) and (4), the equilibrium real GDP would increase by $ _____ and the price level would _____ .
c. Should aggregate demand be that shown in columns (1) and (5), the equilibrium real

(1) Price level	(2) Real GDP	(3) AD$_1$	(4) AD$_2$	(5) AD$_3$	(6) AD$_4$	(7) AD$_5$	(8) AD$_6$
$2.60	$2,390	$ 840	$ 940	$1,900	$2,000	$2,190	$2,290
2.40	2,390	940	1,040	2,000	2,100	2,290	2,390
2.20	2,390	1,040	1,140	2,100	2,200	2,390	2,490
2.00	2,390	1,140	1,240	2,200	2,300	2,490	2,590
1.90	2,350	1,190	1,290	2,250	2,350	2,540	2,640
1.80	2,300	1,240	1,340	2,300	2,400	2,590	2,690
1.60	2,200	1,340	1,440	2,400	2,500	2,690	2,790
1.40	2,090	1,440	1,540	2,500	2,600	2,790	2,890
1.20	1,970	1,540	1,640	2,600	2,700	2,890	2,990
1.00	1,840	1,640	1,740	2,700	2,800	2,990	3,090
1.00	1,740	1,640	1,740	2,700	2,800	2,990	3,090
1.00	1,640	1,640	1,740	2,700	2,800	2,990	3,090

GDP would be $ _____ and the equilib-
rium price would be $ _____ ; and if ag-
gregate demand should increase by $100 to
that shown in columns (1) and (6), the equilibrium real GDP would increase by
$ _____ and the price level would rise
to $ _____ .
d. And if aggregate demand were that
shown in columns (1) and (7), the equilibrium real GDP would be $ _____ and
the equilibrium price level would be
$ _____ ; but if aggregate demand in-
creased by $100 to that shown in columns (1)
and (8), the price level would rise to
$ _____ and the equilibrium real GDP
would _____ .

SELF-TEST

Circle T if the statement is true, F if it is false.

1 The level of saving in the economy, according to the Keynesians, depends primarily upon the level of its disposable income.
                                          T   F

2 The consumption schedule that is
employed as an analytical tool is also a historical record of the relationship of consumption to disposable income.   **T   F**

3 Statistics show and economists tend to
agree that the marginal propensity to consume rises and the marginal propensity to
save falls as disposable income rises.   **T   F**

4 An increase in the price level will increase the consumption schedule (shift the
consumption curve upward).   **T   F**

5 An increase in the taxes paid by consumers will decrease both the amount they spend
for consumption and the amount they save.
                                          T   F

6 Both the consumption schedule and the
saving schedule tend to be relatively stable
over time.   **T   F**

7 The *real* interest rate is the nominal interest rate minus the rate of inflation.   **T   F**

8 A business firm will purchase additional
capital goods if the real rate of interest it
must pay exceeds the expected rate of net
profit from the investment.   **T   F**

9 An increase in an economy's income may
induce an increase in investment spending.
                                          T   F

10 The relationship between the real rate of
interest and the level of investment spending
is called the investment schedule.   **T   F**

11 The investment-demand schedule (or
curve) tends to be relatively stable over time.
                                          T   F

12 The irregularity of innovations and the
variability of business profits contribute to
the instability of investment expenditures.
                                          T   F

13 If GDP were to decline by $40, consum-
ers would probably reduce their consumption expenditures by an amount less than
$40.   **T   F**

14 A decrease in the real rate of interest will,
other things remaining the same, result in a
decrease in the equilibrium real GDP.   **T   F**

15 Net exports increase as real GDP decreases.   **T   F**

16 The purposes of discretionary fiscal policy are reduced inflation, the elimination of
unemployment, and the stimulation of economic growth.   **T   F**

17 If the MPS were 0.3 and the MPM 0.2,
and taxes were levied by the government so
that consumers paid $20 in taxes at each level
of real GDP, consumption expenditures at
each level of real GDP would be $14 less and
imports would not change.   **T   F**

18 If taxes only are reduced by $10 at all levels of real GDP, and the combined marginal propensities to save and import are 0.4, equilibrium real GDP will rise by $25.   **T   F**

19 The larger the marginal propensity to consume, the larger the size of the multiplier.   **T   F**

20 If investment increases when the real GDP rises, the size of the multiplier is less than 1/MPS + MPM.   **T   F**

21 The equilibrium real GDP is the real GDP at which there is full employment in the economy.   **T   F**

22 The existence of a recessionary gap in the economy is characterized by the full employment of labour.   **T   F**

23 The evidence suggests that the Canadian economy is capable of achieving both full employment and stable prices.   **T   F**

24 The higher the level at which the price level is constant in the Keynesian model of the economy, the smaller are the real balances of consumers and the lower is the consumption schedule (curve).   **T   F**

25 An increase in the price level will shift the aggregate-demand curve to the right.   **T   F**

26 In the Keynesian range on the aggregate-supply curve, an increase in aggregate demand will have no effect on the equilibrium real GDP of the economy and will raise its price level.   **T   F**

27 The greater the increase in the price level that results from an increase in aggregate demand, the greater will be the increase in the equilibrium real GDP.   **T   F**

28 The Keynesian model of the economy does not adequately predict the effects of changes in aggregate expenditures on the equilibrium real GDP if the price level is not constant.   **T   F**

Circle the letter that corresponds to the best answer.

1 If the government neither taxes nor spends, and all saving done in the economy is personal saving, (*a*) gross domestic product equals gross national product; (*b*) gross domestic product equals national income; (*c*) gross domestic product equals disposable income; (*d*) all the above are true.

2 In the Keynesian theory, output and employment in the economy depend (*a*) directly on the level of total expenditures; (*b*) inversely on the quantity of resources available to it; (*c*) directly on the level of disposable income; (*d*) directly on the rate of interest.

3 As disposable income decreases, *ceteris paribus*, (*a*) both consumption and saving increase; (*b*) consumption increases and saving decreases; (*c*) consumption decreases and saving increases; (*d*) both consumption and saving decrease.

4 If consumption spending increases from $358 to $367 billion when disposable income increases from $412 to $427 billion, it can be concluded that marginal propensity to consume is (*a*) 0.4; (*b*) 0.6; (*c*) 0.8; (*d*) 0.9.

5 If when disposable income is $375 billion the average propensity to consume is 0.8, it can be concluded that (*a*) the marginal propensity to consume is also 0.8; (*b*) consumption is $325 billion; (*c*) saving is $75 billion; (*d*) the marginal propensity to save is 0.2.

6 As the disposable income of the economy increases, (*a*) both the APC and the APS rise; (*b*) the APC rises and the APS falls; (*c*) the APC falls and the APS rises; (*d*) both the APC and the APS fall.

7 Which of the following would *not* cause the consumption schedule to increase (that is, cause the consumption curve to rise)? (*a*) decrease in consumers' stocks of durable goods; (*b*) an increase in consumers' ownership of liquid assets; (*c*) a decrease in the amount of consumers' indebtedness; (d) an increase in the income received by consumers.

8 A decrease in the price level tends to (a) increase the amount consumed; (b) decrease the amount consumed; (c) shift the consumption schedule upward; (d) shift the consumption schedule downward.

9 A decrease in the level of investment spending would be a consequence of (a) a decline in the rate of interest; (b) a decline in the level of wages paid; (c) a decline in business taxes; (d) a decline in stock market prices.

10 Which of the following relationships is an inverse one? (a) the relationship between consumption spending and disposable income; (b) the relationship between investment spending and the rate of interest; (c) the relationship between saving and the rate of interest; (d) the relationship between investment spending and gross domestic product.

Use the data in the table below to answer questions 11 to 13.

Real GDP	C + I + G	Net exports
$ 900	$ 913	$7
920	929	6
940	945	5
960	961	4
980	977	3
1,000	993	2
1,020	1,009	1

11 If exports in this economy are constant, its marginal propensity to import must be (a) .04; (b) .05; (c) .06; (d) .07.

12 The equilibrium real GDP is (a) $960; (b) $980; (c) $1,000; (d) $1,020.

13 If the marginal propensity to save in this economy is 0.2, a $10 increase in its net exports would increase its equilibrium real GDP by (a) $40; (b) $50; (c) $100; (d) $200.

14 An increase in the real GDP of an economy will, other things remaining constant, (a) increase its imports and the real GDPs in other economies; (b) increase its imports and decrease the real GDPs in other economies; (c) decrease its imports and increase the real GDPs in other economies; (d) decrease its imports and the real GDPs in other economies.

15 Which of the following is an injection? (a) investment; (b) saving; (c) taxes; (d) imports.

16 If leakages are greater than injections, (a) businesses will be motivated to increase their investments; (b) aggregate expenditures will be greater than the real domestic output; (c) real GDP will be greater than aggregate expenditures; (d) saving will tend to increase.

17 On a graph the equilibrium real GDP is found at the intersection of the 45° line and (a) the consumption schedule; (b) the investment-demand schedule; (c) the saving schedule; (d) the aggregate-expenditures schedule.

The next four questions are based on the consumption and import schedules below.

Real GDP	C	M
$300	$287	27
310	296	28
320	305	29
330	314	30
340	323	31
350	332	32
360	341	33

18 If taxes were zero, government purchases of goods and services $10, investment $6, and exports $30, equilibrium real GDP would be (a) $310; (b) $320; (c) $330; (d) $340.

19 If taxes were $10, government purchases of goods and services $10, investment $11, and exports $30, equilibrium real GDP would be (a) \$300; (b) \$310; (c) \$320; (d) \$330.

20 Assume investment is \$42, taxes \$40, government purchases of goods and services zero, and exports \$33. If the full-employment level of real GDP is \$340, the deflationary gap can be eliminated by reducing taxes by (a) \$8; (b) \$10; (c) \$13; (d) \$40.

21 Assume that investment is zero, that taxes are zero, that government purchases of goods and services is \$20, and exports \$30. If the full-employment-without-inflation level of real GDP is \$330, the inflationary gap can be eliminated by decreasing government expenditures by (a) \$4; (b) \$5; (c) \$10; (d) \$20.

22 If the marginal propensity to consume is $^2/_3$ and the marginal propensity to import is $^1/_6$, and both taxes and government expenditures on goods and services increase by \$24, real GDP will (a) fall by \$24; (b) rise by \$16; (c) fall by \$16; (d) rise by \$24.

23 Which of the following policies would do the *most* to reduce inflation? (a) increase taxes by \$5 billion; (b) reduce government expenditures for goods and services by \$5 billion; (c) increase taxes and government expenditures by \$5 billion; (d) reduce both taxes and government expenditures by \$5 billion.

24 The paradox of thrift means that (a) an increase in saving lowers the level of real GDP; (b) an increase in the average propensity to save lowers or leaves unchanged the level of savings; (c) an increase in the marginal propensity to save lowers the value of the multiplier; (d) an increase in real GDP increases investment demand.

25 If the economy's full-employment, non-inflationary real GDP is \$1,200 and its equilibrium real GDP is \$1,100, there is a recessionary gap of (a) \$100; (b) \$100 divided by the multiplier; (c) \$100 multiplied by the multiplier; (d) \$100 times the reciprocal of the marginal propensity to consume.

26 To eliminate the inflationary gap of \$50 in an economy in which the sum of the marginal propensities to save and import are 0.1, it will be necessary to (a) decrease the aggregate-expenditures schedule by \$50; (b) decrease the aggregate-expenditures schedule by \$5; (c) increase the aggregate-expenditures schedule by \$50; (d) increase the aggregate-expenditures schedule by \$5.

27 If the price level in the Keynesian model were lower, the consumption and aggregate-expenditures curves would be (a) lower and the equilibrium real GDP would be smaller; (b) lower and the equilibrium real GDP would be larger; (c) higher and the equilibrium real GDP would be larger; (d) higher and the equilibrium real GDP would be smaller.

28 An increase in aggregate expenditures in the Keynesian model shifts the aggregate-demand curve to the (a) right by the amount of the increase in aggregate expenditures; (b) right by the amount of the increase in aggregate expenditures times the multiplier; (c) left by the amount of the increase in aggregate expenditures; (d) left by the amount of the increase in aggregate expenditures times the multiplier.

29 An increase in aggregate demand will increase the equilibrium real GDP if the economy is operating in the (a) Keynesian range; (b) intermediate range; (c) Keynesian or intermediate ranges; (d) classical range.

30 An increase in aggregate demand will increase both the equilibrium real GDP and the price level if the economy is operating in the (a) Keynesian range; (b) intermediate range; (c) intermediate or classical ranges; (d) classical range.

DISCUSSION QUESTIONS

1 Describe the relation between consumption and disposable income called the consumption schedule and the one between saving and disposable income known as the saving schedule; and then define the two average propensities and the two marginal propensities.

2 Explain briefly how the average propensity to consume and the average propensity to save vary as disposable income varies. Why do APC and APS behave this way? What happens to consumption and saving as disposable income varies?

3 Why do the sum of the APC and the APS and the sum of the MPC and the MPS always equal exactly one?

4 Explain briefly and explicitly *how* changes in the five non-income determinants will affect the consumption schedule and the saving schedule and *why* such changes will affect consumption and saving in the way you have indicated.

5 Explain: (*a*) when a business firm will or will not purchase additional capital goods; (*b*) how changes in the five non-interest determinants of the investment spending will affect the investment-demand curve; (*c*) why investment spending tends to rise when the rate of interest falls; and (*d*) how changes in GDP might affect investment spending.

6 Why does the level of investment spending tend to be highly unstable?

7 Explain why the amount consumers spend and the amount investors spend matter all that much to the performance of the economy.

8 What are the primary determinants of the volume of a nation's exports and imports? How do exports and how do imports affect aggregate expenditures within a nation?

9 To what is the equilibrium real GDP equal in an open economy (in the Keynesian model)? How does a change in the volume of exports and in the volume of imports affect real GDP and employment in a nation?

10 What determines the size or value of the multiplier in an open economy? Why is the multiplier larger in a closed than in an open economy?

11 How are real output and employment in one nation linked to real output and employment in other nations?

12 What is meant by fiscal policy?

13 What is the exact effect that taxes will have on the consumption schedule? On the saving schedule? On the import schedule?

14 Explain why, with government taxing and purchases, the equilibrium real GDP is the real GDP at which real GDP equals consumption plus planned investment plus government purchases of goods and services plus net exports; and saving plus taxes plus imports equals planned investment plus government purchases plus exports. What will cause real GDP to move to its equilibrium level?

15 If both taxes and government purchases increase by equal amounts, real GDP will increase. Why?

16 Explain what is meant by a leakage and by an injection. What are the three major leakages and the three major injections in the flow of income in the Candian economy? Which leakages and which injections are considered in this chapter? Why is the equilibrium real GDP the real GDP at which the leakages equal the injections?

17 What is the multiplier effect? *Why* does there tend to be a multiplier effect (that is, on what basic economic facts does the multiplier effect depend)? What determines how large the open-economy multiplier will be?

18 What is meant by the paradox of thrift? When would an increase in the saving schedule cause saving (at equilibrium) to decrease?

19 What relationship is there between the equilibrium level of real GDP and the level of real GDP at which full employment without inflation is achieved?

20 Explain what is meant by a recessionary gap and an inflationary gap. What economic conditions are present in the economy when each of these gaps exists? How is the size of each of these gaps measured?

21 How is the aggregate-demand curve used in the aggregate-demand–aggregate-supply model of the economy derived from the Keynesian model?

22 What is the effect of an increase in aggregate expenditures in the Keynesian model on (*a*) the aggregate-demand curve; (*b*) on the equilibrum real GDP and price level in the Keynesian, intermediate, and classical ranges of the aggregate-supply curve; and (*c*) on the size of the multiplier effect on real GDP in each of these three ranges? What is the relationship between the effect of an increase in aggregate expenditures on real GDP and the rise in the price level that accompanies it?

26

FISCAL POLICY, THE PUBLIC DEBT, AND MONETARY POLICY RESTATED

Chapter 26 is really a continuation of the preceding chapter and is concerned with the chief practical application of the principles discussed in it.

It is worth recalling that principles of economics are generalizations about the way the economy works, and that these principles are studied in order that policies may be devised to solve real problems. Over the past one hundred or so years, the most serious problems encountered by the Canadian economy have been those problems that resulted from the business cycle. Learning what determines the output, employment, and price levels of an economy and what causes them to fluctuate will make it possible to discover ways to bring about full employment, maximum output, and stable prices. Economic principles, in short, suggest the policies that will eliminate both recessionary and inflationary gaps.

Government spending and taxing have a strong influence on the economy's output and employment and its price level. Federal expenditure and taxation policies designed to affect total production and employment and the level of prices are called fiscal policies. The Bank of Canada is also able to affect these variables by applying monetary policy, as you will recall from Chapter 22. Monetary policy is analysed in more detail in conjunction with fiscal policy at the end of the present chapter.

The brief first section of the chapter makes it clear that the federal government now considers itself committed merely to "fuller" employment.

Since you learned in the previous chapter how government purchases and taxing affect the equilibrium real GDP, it is fairly easy to understand what fiscal policies will be expansionary and reduce a recessionary gap and what fiscal policies will be contractionary and lessen an inflationary gap. In addition to this, you should be aware (1) that if the government has a budget deficit or surplus there are several ways of financing the deficit or disposing of the surplus, and the way the deficit or surplus is handled can affect the economy's operation as much as the size of the deficit or surplus; and (2) that the federal government has the option of changing its expenditures or altering the taxes it collects when it applies fiscal policy to reduce unemployment or lessen inflation in the economy. *Discretionary* fiscal policy requires that Parliament take action to change tax rates, transfer payment programs, or purchases of goods and services. *Non*-discretionary fiscal policy does not require Parliament to take any action, and is a built-in stabilizer of the economy. You should be sure that you understand *why* net taxes increase when the GDP rises and decrease when the GDP falls, and *how* this tends to stabilize the economy.

Unfortunately, non-discretionary fiscal policy by itself is not able to eliminate any recessionary or inflationary gap that might develop; discretionary fiscal policy will be necessary if the economy is to produce its full-employment GDP and avoid inflation. And the built-in stabilizers make it more difficult to use discretionary fiscal policy to achieve this goal, because they produce fiscal drag, and create the illusion that the federal government's policy is expansionary or contractionary when, in fact, its policy is just the opposite. Because of the illusions created by the built-in stabilizers, economists developed the cyclically adjusted budget to enable them to discover whether federal fiscal policy was actually expansionary or contractionary and to determine what policy should have been followed to move the economy toward full employment or slow the rate of inflation.

In addition to the problems of timing and the political problems encountered in using fiscal policies in the real world, you will discover in the last major section of the chapter that many economists and other people are concerned by two other important complications. They fear, first of all, that all expansionary fiscal policy that requires the federal government to borrow in the money market will raise the level of interest rates in the economy and reduce (or crowd out) investment spending; this is called the crowding-out effect and if it is large it will reduce the effect of the expansionary fiscal policy on real GDP and unemployment. The second fear is that an expansionary fiscal policy, if the economy is operating in the intermediate range along the aggregate-supply curve, will drive up the price level and have only a small effect on real output and employment. But all is not gloom. The supply-side economists argue that a reduction in tax rates will not only increase aggregate demand but will also (for number of reasons explained in the text) expand aggregate supply. In this way, they contend, the real equilibrium GDP of the economy can be increased with little or no rise in the price level. This is, however, the problem of stagflation, which will be dealt with in more detail in the next chapter.

When the federal government applies fiscal policies to lessen inflation in the economy, it *could* have a budget surplus; and when it uses fiscal policies to reduce unemployment, it is likely to have a budget deficit. Over the past quarter of a century the federal government has had very few budget surpluses: it has had budget deficits in all but one year.

Any budget surplus or deficit affects the size of the public (sometimes called the national) debt; surpluses decrease it and deficits increase it. As a consequence of its persistent deficits during World War II and since the late 1950s, the public debt has increased; and since 1980 the deficits have grown larger and the public debt has increased by increasing amounts from one year to the next. The federal government finances public debt by selling securities (bonds). To those who have purchased these securities the government pays interest each year; and as the size of the debt has increased (and interest rates in the economy have risen) the annual interest payments on the debt have also increased.

These facts are the background. After defining a budget deficit and the public debt, the chapter examines three budget philosophies. You should be aware that the philosophy adopted by the federal government has a significant impact on the output of and employment in the economy *and* on the public debt. A brief explanation of the reasons for the increases in the public debt (wars and recessions) and of the absolute and relative sizes of the debt and the interest payments on the debt is next. Then comes an examination of the economic implications or consequences of the debt. Here you will learn that the debt creates problems for the economy (but these problems do not include bankrupting the federal government or shifting the cost of a war—or other government programs—to future generations).

The problems created by the public debt and the payment of interest of the debt are four in number. They appear to make the distribution of income in the economy more unequal, to reduce the incentives that induce people and business firms to produce and expand their outputs, to decrease the Canadian standard of living if a part of the debt is owed to foreigners, and to have a crowding-out effect on investment in plant and equipment in Canada.

Crowding-out is probably the most serious of these four problems; and you should be sure that you understand how crowding-out works and how it imposes a burden on future generations by reducing the growth of the nation's capital stock. To understand why it reduces the growth of the capital stock, borrowing to finance an increase in government expenditures is compared with increasing taxes to finance these expenditures.

Finally the chapter shows that government borrowing not only crowds-out investment in the economy but results in a chain of events that lead to the contraction of output and employment in Canada. Be sure you follow each of the steps in this cause-and-effect chain.

The chapter concludes with a restatement of monetary policy and its contrasting with fiscal policy. We explain again how the demand for and the supply of money determine the interest rate (in the "money market"); how the interest rate determined there and the investment-demand schedule determine the level of investment in the economy; and how the investment and the saving schedule together determine the equilibrium real GDP. This restatement makes it clear that the effectiveness of a change in the money supply depends upon just how steep or flat the downsloping demand-for-money and investment-demand curves are. We also use the aggregate-supply and the aggregate-demand curves to show how changes in the money supply affect domestic output and the price level in the three stages along the aggregate-supply curve.

The strengths and shortcomings of monetary policy in reducing unemployment (and expanding domestic output) and in reducing inflation are examined in the next-to-last major section of the chapter. Here you will also encounter the dilemma faced by the Bank of Canada: it cannot simultaneously control both the money supply and the level of interest rates in the economy. The reason it can't will be explained for you.

The last section of Chapter 26 is a summary of Chapters 18 to 26. It will recall for you the main outline of the Keynesian theory of employment and the principal public policies that may be used to promote full employment without creating inflation. They will help you to see that the various principles discussed in the previous chapters are *not* separate theories but are, in fact, connected parts of the one Keynesian theory; and that the public policies discussed in earlier chapters are *not* really separate policies but are alternative means of achieving the goal of economic stabilization.

This one theory of employment and the alternative means of achieving this one goal are summarized for you in Figure 26-2. This is probably the single most important figure in the textbook. A few of the "Complications and Problems" that are hidden by Figure 26-2 are examined at the end of the chapter.

CHECK LIST

When you have studied this chapter you should be able to

☐ State the nature of the federal government's commitment to "fuller" employment.

☐ Explain when government should pursue an expansionary and a contractionary fiscal policy; what each of these policies might entail; and the effect of each upon the federal budget.

☐ Describe the best way to finance a government deficit and to dispose of a surplus.

☐ Distinguish between discretionary and non-discretionary fiscal policy.

☐ Indicate how the built-in stabilizers help to eliminate recession and inflationary pressures.

☐ Outline the timing and political problems encountered in applying fiscal policy in the real world.

☐ Describe the crowding-out effect of an expansionary fiscal policy and how it may lessen the impact of an expansionary fiscal policy on real output and employment.

☐ Distinguish between the effects of an expansionary fiscal policy in the Keynesian and intermediate ranges of the aggregate-supply curve; and explain how the impact of such a policy is reduced when the economy is in the latter range.

☐ State the effects supply-side economists argue a reduction in tax rates would have on aggregate supply, real GDP, and the price level; and explain why they believe it would have these effects.

☐ Define a budget deficit (and surplus) and the public debt; and explain how the latter is related to the former.

☐ Explain each of the three budget philosophies.

☐ State the absolute and relative size of the public debt and of the annual interest charges on this debt; the principal cause of the debt; and why it is also, for the most part, a public credit.

☐ Compare the effects of an internal debt with the effects of an external debt on the economy.

☐ Explain how adjusting the size of the nominal public debt for inflation affects the real size of the debt and the real size of a budget deficit; and why the accounting procedures employed by the federal government do not accurately reflect its financial condition.

☐ Settle the two false issues related to the public debt.

☐ Enumerate the four real issues related to the public debt.

☐ Describe the crowding-out effect of borrowing to finance an increase in government expenditures and the burden this method of financing expenditures places on future generations; compare the burden imposed on future generations by this method of finance with the burden placed on them if the increased expenditures are financed by increased taxation; and qualify in two ways this comparison.

☐ Explain why increasing debt is necessary in a growing economy if the economy is to remain at full employment and when it is necessary for the public debt to expand.

☐ Draw the demand-for-money and the supply-of-money curves and use them to show how a change in the supply of money will affect the interest rate; draw an investment-demand curve to explain the effects of changes in the interest rate on investment spending; and construct a leakages-injections graph to show the effects of a change in planned investment on the equilibrium GDP.

☐ State precisely how the steepness of the demand-for-money and of the investment-demand curves affects the impact of a change in the money supply on the equilibrium GDP.

☐ List three strengths and four shortcomings of monetary policy.

☐ State the target (or policy) dilemma confronted by the Bank of Canada; and explain why it faces this dilemma.

☐ Summarize the Keynesian theory of employment and the policies that may be utilized to promote a full-employment, non-inflationary GDP.

☐ Enumerate the four "complexities and problems" found in the Keynesian theory and its application.

CHAPTER OUTLINE

1 Fiscal policy is the manipulation by the federal government of its expenditures and tax receipts in order to expand or contract aggregate expenditures in the economy; and by doing so either increase its real output (and employment) or decrease its rate of inflation.

2 Since World War II, the federal government has committed itself to full employment, though the commitment becomes less well-defined as the unemployment rate climbs.

3 Discretionary fiscal policy involves deliberate changes in tax rates and government spending to offset cyclical fluctuations and to increase economic growth.

a. The elimination of the inflationary (recessionary) gap is accomplished by contractionary (expansionary) fiscal policy and by increasing (decreasing) taxes, decreasing (increasing) purchases, and incurring budget surpluses (deficits).

b. In addition to the size of the deficit or surplus, the manner in which the government finances its deficit or disposes of its surplus affects the level of total spending in the economy.

c. Whether government purchases or taxes should be altered to reduce recessionary and inflationary gaps depends to a large extent upon whether an expansion or a contraction of the public sector is desired.

4 In the Canadian economy, net-tax revenues (tax receipts minus government transfer payments) are not a fixed amount or lump sum; they increase as the GDP rises and decrease as the GDP falls.

a. This net-tax system serves as a built-in stabilizer of the economy because it reduces purchasing power during periods of inflation and expands purchasing power during periods of recession.

b. But built-in stability

(1) can only reduce and cannot eliminate economic fluctuations;

(2) creates fiscal drag and makes it difficult to reduce unemployment during a recession and to maintain full employment in a growing economy;

(3) and requires that the cyclically adjusted budget be used to determine whether the federal budget is actually expansionary or contractionary.

5 Certain problems and complications arise in enacting and applying fiscal policy.

a. There will be problems of timing because it requires time to recognize the need for fiscal policy; to bring a budget or even a mini-budget before Parliament; and for the action taken there to affect output and employment, and the rate of inflation in the economy.

b. There will also be political problems because

(1) the economy has goals other than full employment and stable prices;

(2) there is an expansionary bias (for budget deficits and against surpluses);

(3) there may be a political business cycle (if politicians lower taxes and increase expenditures before and then do the opposite after elections).

c. An expansionary fiscal policy may, by raising the level of interest rates in the economy, reduce (or crowd out) investment spending and weaken the effect of the policy on real GDP; but this crowding-out effect may be small and can be offset by an expansion in the nation's money supply.

d. The effect of an expansionary fiscal policy on the real GDP will also be weakened to the extent that it results in a rise in the price level (inflation).

e. Aggregate-demand and aggregate-supply curves can be used to show how crowding-out and inflation weaken the effects of an expansionary fiscal policy on real GDP.

f. But an expansionary fiscal policy that includes a reduction in taxes (tax rates) may, by increasing aggregate supply in the economy, expand real GDP (and employment), and reduce inflation.

6 The budget deficit of the federal government is the amount by which its expenditures exceed its revenues in any year; and the public debt at any time is the sum of the federal government's previous annual deficits (less any annual supluses).

7 If the federal government utilizes fiscal

policy to combat recession and inflation, its budget is not likely to be balanced in any paricular year. Three budgetary philosophies may be adopted by government; and the adoption of any of these philosophies will affect employment, real output, and the price level of the economy.

a. Proponents of an annually balanced budget would have government expenditures and tax revenues equal in every year; such a budget is pro- rather than counter-cyclical; but conservative economists favour it to prevent the expansion of the public sector (and the contraction of the private sector) of the economy without the increased payment of taxes by the public.

b. Those who advocate a cyclically balanced budget propose matching surpluses (in years of prosperity) with deficits (in depression years) to stabilize the economy; but there is no assurance that the surpluses will equal the deficits over the years.

c. Advocates of functional finance contend that deficits, surpluses, and the size of the debt are of minor importance; that the goal of full employment without inflation should be achieved regardless of the effects of the necessary fiscal policies upon the budget and the size of the public debt.

8 Any government surplus or deficit automatically affects the size of the public debt.

a. The Government of Canada's public debt has grown substantially since 1926. This debt is *not* primarily the result of federal borrowing during wartime; it *is* primarily the consequence of fiscal policies — government deficits of the past decade.

b. The public debt currently exceeds $220 billion.

(1) The size of the debt as a percentage of GNP did not grow so rapidly as the absolute size of the debt between 1954 and 1986; but relative to GNP it has increased significantly since the late 1970s.

(2) Since the late 1970s the interest payments on the debt (because of increases in the size of the debt and higher interest rates

in the economy) have also increased significantly; and the interest payments as a percentage of the economy's GNP have grown dramatically.

(3) About 7% of the public debt is owed to the Bank of Canada and 93% to others; but more importantly, about 12% of it is owed to foreign citizens, firms, and governments.

(4) Because the accounting system used by the federal government records its debts but not its assets, the public debt is not a true picture of its financial position; and when adjusted for inflation, the decrease in the real value of its debt can exceed its nominal deficit and result in a real budget surplus.

9 The contentions that a large debt will eventually bankrupt the government and that borrowing to finance expenditures passes the cost onto future generations are false.

a. The debt cannot bankrupt the government

(1) because the government need not retire (reduce) the debt and can refund (or refinance) it; and

(2) because the government can always print (or create) money to pay both the principal and the interest on it.

b. The debt cannot shift the burdens of the debt to future generations because the debt is largely internally held, and repayment of any portion of the principal and the payment of interest on it does not reduce the wealth or purchasing power of Canadians.

10 But the debt does create real and potential problems in the economy.

a. The payment of interest on the debt probably increases the extent of income inequality.

b. The payment of taxes to finance these interest payments may also reduce the incentives to bear risks, to innovate, to invest, and to save, and so slow economic growth in the economy.

c. The portion of the debt that is externally held requires the repayment of principal and the payment of interest to foreign citizens and institutions and transfers a part of the real output of the Canadian economy to them.

d. An increase in government spending may or may not impose a burden on future generations.

(1) If the increase in government spending is financed by increased personal taxes, the burden of the increased spending is on the present generation whose consumption is reduced; but if it is financed by an increased public debt, the increased borrowing of the federal government will raise interest rates, crowd out investment spending, and future generations will inherit a smaller stock of capital goods.

(2) The burden imposed on future generations is lessened if the increase in government expenditures is for real or human capital or if the economy were initially operating at less than full employment (and it stimulates an increase in investment demand).

11 Since the mid-1970s the federal government has incurred increasingly large deficits and the public debt has risen.

a. This has caused concern because the deficits and the increases in the public debt have grown larger, because interest costs of the debt have risen, and because the deficits have taken place in a peace-time economy operating close to full employment.

b. These large deficits have produced a cause-and-effect chain of events: they have increased interest rates, and higher interest rates have crowded out real private investment.

c. Despite the problems associated with deficits and the public debt, private and public debt has an important role to play: it absorbs the saving done in a growing economy at full employment and sustains the aggregate expenditures of consumers, businesses, and governments at the full-employment level; and if consumers and firms do not borrow sufficient amounts, the public debt must

be increased to maintain full employment and economic growth in the economy.

12 To restate the effects of monetary policy on the equilibrium GDP

a. In the money market the demand-for and the supply-of-money curves determine the real interest rate; the investment-demand curve and this rate of interest determine planned investment; and total injections (including planned investment) along with the leakages curve determine the equilibrium GDP.

b. And:

(1) The steeper the demand-for-money curve and the flatter the investment-demand curve, the greater will be the effect on the equilibrium GDP of a change in the money supply.

(2) Changes in the equilibrium GDP that result from a change in the money supply will alter the demand for money and dampen the effect of the change in the money supply on the GDP.

c. Or, restated in terms of the aggregate-demand–aggregate-supply model: the flatter (steeper) the aggregate-supply curve is, the greater (smaller) is the effect of a change in the money supply on real domestic output and employment and the smaller (greater) is the effect on the price level.

13 Whether monetary policy is effective in promoting full employment without inflation is a debatable question because monetary policy has both strengths and shortcomings in fighting recession and inflation.

a. Its strengths are that it can be more quickly changed than fiscal policy; it is more politically acceptable than fiscal policy; and (some economists believe) it is the key determinant of economic activity and, therefore, more effective than fiscal policy.

b. Its weaknesses are that it is more effective in fighting inflation than it is in curbing recession; it can be offset by changes in the velocity of money; it is relatively ineffective in controlling cost-push inflation, and it may not have a significant impact on investment spending in the economy.

c. A most difficult problem for the Bank of Canada is its inability to control both the money supply and the level of interest rates at the same time.

(1) If the central bank's policy target is the stabilization of interest rates, an increase in the nominal GDP (and the resulting increase in the demand for money) will require it to increase the money supply; and if its policy target is the stabilization of the money supply, an increase in the nominal GDP (and the demand for money) will force interest rates upward.

(2) Controversy surrounds the issue of which of these two policy targets is preferable; and the Bank of Canada switched from controlling interest rates to controlling (unsuccessfully) the money supply in 1975. In late 1982 the Bank abandoned monetary targeting.

14 The income, employment, output, and prices of an economy are in Keynesian theory positively related to the level of aggregate expenditures, which has three principal components (assuming net exports are zero).

a. These three components are consumption spending, which depends upon the stable consumption schedule and the income of the economy; investment spending, which is more unstable; and government spending, which depends partly on the level of spending needed to achieve full employment and price stability.

b. To achieve economic stability, government employs both fiscal and monetary policy; but to be effective these two types of policy must be co-ordinated.

IMPORTANT TERMS

Fiscal policy

Discretionary fiscal policy

Expansionary fiscal policy

Contractionary fiscal policy

Non-discretionary fiscal policy

Built-in stability

Fiscal drag

Actual budget

Cyclically-adjusted budget balance

Political business cycle

Crowding-out effect

Budget deficit

Public debt

Annually balanced budget

Cyclically balanced budget

Functional finance

External debt

Money market

Velocity of money

Feedback effects

FILL-IN QUESTIONS

1 The use of monetary and fiscal policy to reduce inflationary and recessionary gaps became national economic policy at the end

of _____ .

2 In order to increase real GDP during a recession, taxes should be (increased, decreased) _____ and government purchases should be _____ ; to decrease the rise in the price level during a period of inflation (according to the Keynesians), taxes should be _____ and government purchases should be

_____ .

3 If fiscal policy is to have a counter-cyclical effect, it will probably be necessary for the federal government to incur a budget (surplus, deficit) _____ during a recession and a budget _____ during inflation.

4 The two principal means available to the federal government for financing budget deficits are _____ and _____ ; and the (former, latter) _____ is more expansionary.

5 Those who wish to expand the public sector of the economy would, during a period of *inflation*, advocate a(n) (increase, decrease) _____ in (government purchases, taxes) _____ ; and those who wish to contract the public sector during a *recession* would advocate a(n) _____ in _____ .

6 Net taxes

a. equal _____ minus _____ ;

b. in Canada will (increase, decrease) _____ as the GDP rises and will _____ as the GDP falls.

7 When net tax receipts are directly related to the GDP the economy has some _____ stability because
a. when the GDP rises, leakages (increase, decrease) _____ and the budget surplus will (increase, decrease) _____ (or the budget deficit will _____);

b. when the GDP falls, leakages _____ and the budget deficit will _____ (or the budget surplus will _____).

8 Fiscal drag means that when net tax receipts vary directly with the GDP and are not a lump sum, it is more difficult for discretionary fiscal policy to raise the level of _____ in the short run and to maintain _____ in the long run.

9 The cyclically-adjusted budget balance

a. indicates what the federal _____ _____ would have been if the economy had operated at _____ during the year;

b. tells us whether the federal budget was in fact _____ or_____ .

10 There is a problem of timing in the use of discretionary fiscal policy because of the _____, _____, and _____ lags.

11 Political problems arise in the application of discretionary fiscal policy to stabilize the economy because government has _____ goals; because voters have a bias in favour of budget (surpluses, deficits) _____ ; and because politicians use fiscal policies in a way that creates a _____ business cycle.

12 When the federal government employs an expansionary fiscal policy to increase real GDP and employment in the economy, it usually has a budget (surplus, deficit) _____ and (lends, borrows) _____ in the money market.

a. This will (raise, lower) _____ interest rates in the economy and (contract, expand) _____ investment spending.
b. This change in investment spending is the _____ effect of the expansionary fiscal policy, and it tends to (weaken, strengthen) _____ the impact of the expansionary fiscal policy on real GDP and employment.

13 An expansionary fiscal policy when the economy is operating in the intermediate range of the aggregate-supply curve will increase the real GDP and employment in the economy and (raise, lower) _____ the price level.

a. This change in the price level will (weaken, strengthen) _____ the impact of the expansionary fiscal policy on output and employment in the economy.
b. But if the expansionary fiscal policy is

the result of reduction in taxes, the supply-side effects of the policy may be to (increase, decrease) _____ aggregate supply, to _____ the productive capacity of the economy, to _____ _____ real GDP and employ-ment, to _____ the rate of inflation, and to (weaken, strengthen) _____ the impact of the fiscal policy on output and employment.

14 The budget deficit of the federal govern-ment in any year is equal to its (expenditures, revenues) _____ less its _____ in that year; and the public debt is equal to the sum of the federal government's past budget _____ _____ less its budget _____ .

15 An annually balanced budget is (pro-, counter-) _____ cyclical because gov-ernments tend to (raise, lower) _____ taxes and to _____ their pur-chases of goods and services during a reces-sion (and to do just the opposite during an inflation).

16 A cyclically balanced budget suggests that to ensure full employment without in-flation, the government incur deficits dur-ing periods of _____ and surpluses during periods of _____ _____ , with the deficits and surpluses equalling each other over the business cycle.

17 Functional finance has as its main goal the achievement of _____ _____ ,

and would regard budget _____ and increases in the _____ as being of secondary importance.

18 The principal causes of the public debt are past _____ and _____ and high _____ .

19 The public debt is
a. equal to about $ _____ billion and about _____ % of the GNP, and the an-nual interest changes on this debt are about $ _____ billion and equal about _____ % of the GNP;
b. for the most part an (internal, external) _____ debt.

20 About
a. 87% of the public debt is owed to _____ and to the Bank of _____ ; and
b. _____ % of this debt is owed to for-eigners.

21 The accounting procedures used by the federal government reflect its (assets, debts) _____ but do not reflect its _____ .
a. William Krehm demonstrated that in 1985 the value of the government's assets were (greater, less) _____ than the public debt.
b. He also showed that because inflation (increases, decreases) _____ the real value of the public debt, when the (surplus, deficit) _____ of the federal government in 1983–84 was adjusted for the change in the real value of the debt it ended up with a $9 billion _____ .

22 The possibility that the federal govern-ment will go bankrupt is a false issue. It need not (reduce, refinance) _____ its debt; and it can retire maturing securities by _____ them or by creating _____ .

23 As long as the government expenditures that lead to the increase in the public debt are not financed by borrowing from foreigners, the public debt of Canada is also an _____ of the Canadian people who own government securities; and the cost of a government program financed by borrowing from the Canadian public is equal to their decreased _____ of goods and services and is a burden on (the present, a future) _____ generation.

24 The public debt is a burden on an economy if it is (internally, externally) _____ held. It and the payment of interest on it, may, however, (increase, decrease) _____ income inequality in the economy, dampen the _____ to work, take risks, save, and invest in the economy, and have a _____ effect on investment.

25 A public debt that is internally held imposes a burden on future generations if the borrowing done to finance an increase in government expenditures (increases, decreases) _____ interest rates, _____ investment spending, and leaves future generations with a smaller stock of _____ goods.
a. But if the increased government expenditures are financed by an increase in the taxes on personal income, the present generation will have fewer _____ goods and the burden of the increased government expenditures will be on the _____ generation.
b. These generalizations are subject to two qualifications: The size of the burden of in-

creased government expenditures financed by borrowing on future generations is weakened if the government expenditures finance increases in physical or human _____ or if the economy had been operating at (full, less than full) _____ employment.

26 The increased concern of the public with federal deficits and the expanding public debt in the 1980s is the result the large _____ of these deficits, the increased interest _____ of the debt, and the fact that the economy was at (peace, war) _____ .

27 Graphically, in an economy in which government neither purchases goods and services nor collects net taxes, and which neither exports nor imports goods and services,
a. the equilibrium interest rate is determined by the demand for and the supply of _____ curves;
b. this equilibrium real interest rate, and the _____ curve determine the level of investment;
c. and the level of investment, using the leakages-injections approach, and the _____ curve determine the equilibrium GDP;
d. but when the supply-of-money curve increases (shifts to the right), the real interest rate will (increase, decrease) _____ , investment will _____ , and the equilibrium GDP will_____ .

28 The effect of a $1 billion increase or decrease in the money supply upon the equilibrium GDP is greater the (flatter, steeper) _____ the demand-for-money curve and the _____ the investment-demand curve.

29 An increase in the money supply will shift the aggregate (supply, demand) _____ curve to the (right, left) _____ .

a. In the Keynesian (or depression) range, along the aggregate-supply curve this increase in the money supply will have a (small, large) _____ effect on real domestic output and a _____ effect on the price level.

b. In the classical range, along the aggregate-supply curve this increase in the money supply will have a _____ effect on real domestic output and a _____ effect on the price level.

c. In the intermediate range along the aggregate-supply curve the effect of an increase in the money supply on the real domestic output is greater the (steeper, flatter) _____ the aggregate-supply curve, and the effect on the price level is greater the _____ the aggregate-supply curve.

30 The

a. strengths of monetary policy are that it is more _____ , more politically _____ , and (in the view of the monetarists) more _____ than fiscal policy;

b. weaknesses of monetary policy are that it is more effective in curbing (recession, inflation) _____ than _____ , can be ineffective if the _____ of money changes in the (same, opposite) _____ direction as the money supply, cannot be used to fight (demand-pull, cost-push) _____ inflation, and will not be effective if changes in the interest rate have little or no effect on _____

spending in the economy.

31 The target dilemma faced by the Bank of Canada is that it is (able, unable) _____ to control both the money supply and the level of interest rates simultaneously.

a. If it is to stabilize the interest rate it must (increase, decrease) _____ the money supply when the nominal GDP rises.

b. And if it stabilizes the money supply it must allow the interest rate to _____ when the nominal GDP rises.

32 In the Keynesian theory the levels of output, employment, income, and prices depend on the level of aggregate _____ , which in turn depend (in a closed economy) upon the amounts of _____ , _____ , and _____ spending in the economy.

33 Government seeks to bring about a full-employment, non-inflationary GDP by employing both _____ and _____ policies.

PROBLEMS AND PROJECTS

1 In the following table are seven GDPs and the net tax receipts of government at each GDP.

GDP	Net tax receipts	Government purchases	Government surplus
$ 850	$170	$_____	$_____
900	180	_____	_____
950	190	_____	_____
1,000	200	_____	_____
1,050	210	_____	_____
1,100	220	_____	_____
1,150	230	_____	_____

a. Looking at the two columns on the left of the table, it can be seen that

(1) when real GDP increases by $50, net tax receipts (increase, decrease) _____ by $ _____;

(2) when real GDP decreases by $100, net tax receipts _____ by $ _____;

(3) the relation between real GDP and net tax receipts is (direct, inverse)_____ .

b. Assume the investment multiplier has a value of 10 and that investment spending in the economy decreases by $10.

(1) *If* net tax receipts remained constant, the equilibrium real GDP would decrease by $ _____.

(2) But when real GDP decreases, net tax receipts also decrease; and this decrease in net tax receipts will tend to (increase, decrease) _____ the equilibrium real GDP.

(3) And, therefore, the decrease in real GDP brought about by the $10 decrease in investment spending will be (more, less) _____ than $100.

(4) The direct relationship between net tax receipts and real GDP has (lessened, expanded) _____ the impact of the $10 decrease in investment spending on real GDP.

c. Suppose the government-purchases multiplier is also 10 and government wishes to increase the equilibrium real GDP by $50.

(1) *If* net tax receipts remained constant, government would have to increase its expenditures on goods and services by $ _____ .

(2) But when real GDP rises, net tax receipts also rise; and this rise in net tax receipts will tend to (increase, decrease) _____ the equilibrium real GDP.

(3) The effect therefore, of the $5 increase in government expenditures will be to increase the equilibrium real GDP by (more, less) _____ than $50.

(4) The direct relation between net tax receipts and real GDP has (lessened, expanded) _____ the effect of the $5 increase in government purchases; and to raise the equilibrium real GDP by $50, government will have to increase its purchases by (more, less) _____ than $5.

d. Imagine that the full-employment real GDP of the economy is $1,150 and that government current purchases of goods and services are $200.

(1) Complete the table at the beginning of the question by entering the government purchases and by computing the budget surplus at each of the real GDPs. (Show a government deficit by placing a minus sign in front of the amount by which expenditures exceed net tax receipts.)

(2) The full-employment surplus equals $ _____ .

(3) Were the economy in a recession and producing a real GDP of $900, the budget would show a (surplus, deficit) _____ of $ _____ .

(4) This budget deficit or surplus makes it appear that government is pursuing a(n) (expansionary, contractionary) _____ fiscal policy; but this deficit or surplus is not the result of counter-cyclical fiscal policy, but the result of the _____ .

(5) If the government did not change its net tax *rates*, it could increase the equilibrium real GDP from $900 to the full-employment real GDP of $1,150 by increasing its purchases by $75. At the full-employment real GDP the budget would show a (sur-

plus, deficit) _____

of $_____ .

(6) If the government did not change its purchases it could increase the equilibrium real GDP from $900 to the full-employment real GDP of $1,150 by decreasing net tax receipts at all real GDPs by a lump sum of (approximately) $107. The full-employment budget would have a (surplus, deficit)

_____ of $_____ .

2 Columns (1) and (2) in the table below are the aggregate-supply schedule, and columns (1) and (3) are the aggregate-demand schedule.

(1) Price level	(2) Real GDP₁	(3) AD₁	(4) AD₂	(5) Real GDP₂
$2.20	$2,390	$2,100	$2,200	$2,490
2.00	2,390	2,200	2,340	2,490
1.90	2,350	2,250	2,350	2,450
1.80	2,300	2,300	2,400	2,400
1.60	2,200	2,400	2,500	2,300

a. The equilibrium real GDP is

$ _____ , and the price level is

$ _____ .

b. Suppose that an expansionary fiscal policy increases aggregate demand from that shown in columns (1) and (3) to that shown in columns (1) and (4).

(1) If the price level remained constant, the equilibrium real GDP would increase to

$ _____ .

(2) But the increase in aggregate demand does raise the price level to _____ ; and this rise in the price level results in real

GDP increasing to only $ _____ .

c. If the expansionary fiscal policy that increased aggregate demand also has supply-side effects and increased aggregate supply from that shown in columns (1) and (2) to that shown in columns (1) and (5),

(1) the equilibrium real GDP would increase

to $ _____ ; and

(2) the price level would _____ .

3 Columns (1) and (2) in the table below are the investment-demand schedule and show planned investment (*I*) at different rates of interest (*i*). Assume the marginal propensity to consume in the economy is 0.8 and the MAM is 0.

(1) i	(2) I	(3) I'
.08	$115	$125
.07	140	150
.06	165	175
.05	190	200
.04	215	225

a. If the federal government were to spend an additional $20 for goods and services, the equilibrium real GDP would (increase, de-

crease) _____ by $ _____ .

b. If the federal government had obtained the additional $20 by

(1) increasing taxes by $20, the equilibrium real GDP would have (increased, decreased)

_____ a total of $ _____ ;

(2) borrowing $20 in the money market and this borrowing had increased the interest rate from 5% to 6%,

(a) planned investment spending would

have (increased, decreased) _____ by

$ _____ ,

(b) the equilibrium real GDP would have

_____ by $ _____ , and

(c) the net effect of the increased government spending of the $20 borrowed in the money market would have been to

_____ the equilibrium real GDP by

$ _____ .

c. But if the government deficit-spending had improved business profit expectations and shifted the investment-demand schedule to the one shown in columns (1) and (3) in the table on page 291, the total effect of the increased government spending of the $20 borrowed in the money market would have been to _____ the equilibrium real GDP by $ _____ .

4 On the following graph is the demand-for-money curve, which shows the amounts of money that consumers and firms wish to hold at various rates of interest (when the nominal GDP in the economy is given).

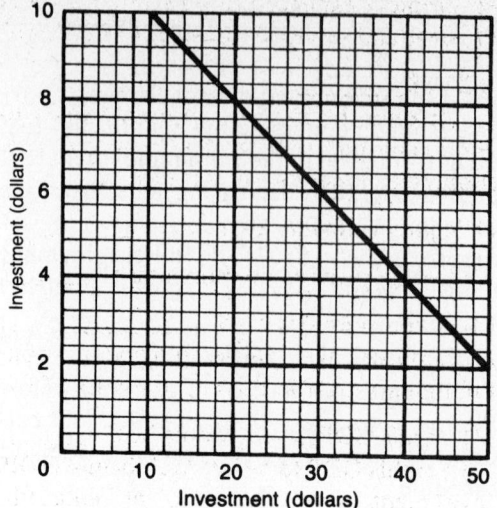

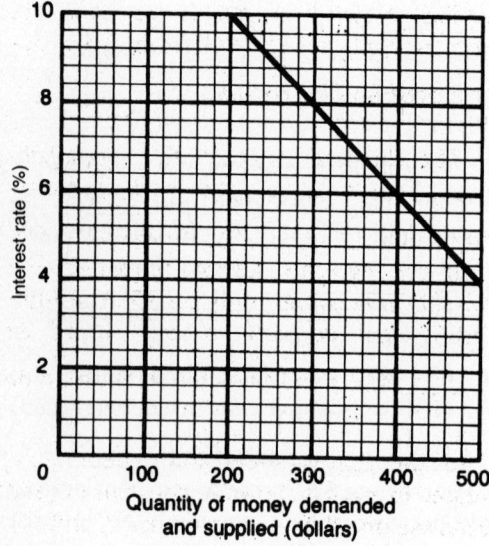

a. Suppose the supply of money is equal to $300.

(1) Draw on this graph the supply-of-money curve.

(2) The equilibrium rate of interest in the economy is _____ %.

b. On the next graph is an investment-demand curve, which shows the amounts of planned investment at various rates of interest. Given your answer to (2) above, how much will investors plan to spend for capital goods? $ _____

c. On the last graph is the saving curve in an economy in which the only leakage from the GDP is saving. (There are no taxes collected and no imports of goods and services).

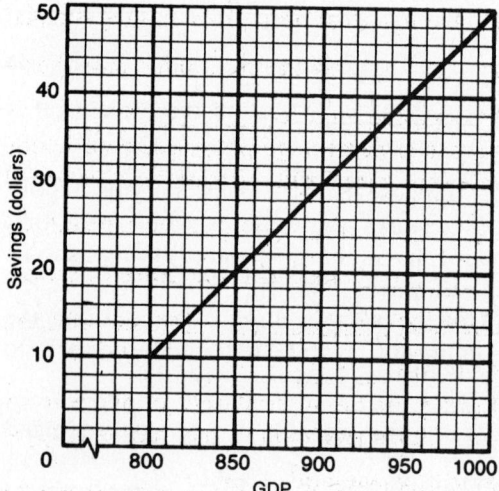

(1) On this graph, plot the investment curve when planned investment is the amount given by you in your answer to (b) above.

(2) If the only injection into this economy is investment spending (that is, if there is no

government expenditure on and no exports of goods and services), the equilibrium GDP

will be $_____ .

d. Assume the money supply increases to $400. On the first graph, plot the new supply-of-money curve. The new

(1) equilibrium interest rate is _____ %;

(2) level of planned investment is $ _____ ;

(3) equilibrium GDP is $_____ .

e. Suppose the full-employment, non-inflationary GDP in this economy is $875.

(1) At this GDP, saving would be $ _____ .
(2) For this GDP to be the equilibrium GDP, investment would have to be equal to

$_____ .

(3) For investment to be at this level, the

rate of interest would have to be _____ %.
(4) And for the interest rate to be at this level, the supply of money would have to be

equal to $_____ .

f. In this economy
(1) the marginal propensity to save is equal

to _____ and the multiplier has, there-

fore, a value equal to _____ ;
(2) a one-percentage-point decrease in the interest rate will (increase, decrease)

_____ planned investment by

$_____ and, will, therefore (increase,

decrease) _____ the equilibrium

GDP by $_____ ;
(3) but for the interest rate to decrease by one percentage point, the money supply

must (increase, decrease) _____

by $_____ .

5 Columns (1) and (2) of the table following are the aggregate-supply schedule. (The price level is a price index and real domestic output is measured in billions of dollars.)

(1) Price level	(2) Domestic output	(3) AE$_1$	(4) AE$_2$	(5) AE$_3$	(6) AE$_4$	(7) AE$_5$	(8) AE$_6$
.30	$1,500	$1,600	$1,700	$2,070	$2,400	$2,920	$3,020
.30	1,600	1,600	1,700	2,070	2,400	2,920	3,020
.30	1,700	1,600	1,700	2,070	2,400	2,920	3,020
.40	1,790	1,500	1,600	1,970	2,300	2,820	2,920
.50	1,870	1,400	1,500	1,870	2,200	2,720	2,820
.60	1,940	1,300	1,400	1,770	2,100	2,620	2,720
.70	2,000	1,200	1,300	1,670	2,000	2,520	2,620
.80	2,050	1,100	1,200	1,570	1,900	2,420	2,520
.90	2,090	1,000	1,100	1,470	1,800	2,320	2,420
1.00	2,120	900	1,000	1,370	1,700	2,220	2,320
1.10	2,120	800	900	1,270	1,600	2,120	2,220
1.20	2,120	700	800	1,170	1,500	2,020	2,120

a. The Keynesian range on this aggregate-supply schedule is from a real domestic output of zero to $_____ billion.

b. The classical range on this aggregate-supply curve is at the real domestic

output of $_____ billion.

c. If the aggregate-demand schedule were that shown in columns (1) and (3), the equilibrium real domestic output would be

$_____ billion and the price level would be

_____ .

d. If the aggregate-demand schedule increased from that shown in columns (1) and (3) to the one shown in columns (1) and (4), the equilibrium real domestic output would

_____ and the price level would

_____ .

e. If the aggregate-demand schedule increased from that shown in columns (1) and (5) to the one shown in columns (1) to (6), the equilibrium real domestic output would

_____ and the price level

would _____ .

f. And if the aggregate-demand schedule increased from that shown in columns (1) and (7) to the one shown in columns (1) to (8), the equilibrium real domestic output would _____ and the price

level would _____ .

6 Columns (1) and (2) in the following table show the money supply, and columns (2) and (3) show the demand for money. (Dollar figures are in billions and the interest rate is a percentage.)

(1) Supply of money	(2) Interest rate	(3) Demand for money	(4) Demand for money
$400	.08	$100	$200
400	.07	200	300
400	.06	300	400
400	.05	400	500
400	.04	500	600
400	.03	600	700
400	.02	700	800

a. The equilibrium interest rate is _____%.

b. Suppose the Bank of Canada wishes to stabilize the interest rate at this level; but the nominal GDP produced by the economy increases, and as a result the demand for money in the economy increases to that shown in columns (2) and (4). The Bank will have to (increase, decrease) _____ the supply of money to $ _____ billion.

c. But if the Bank stabilizes the supply of money at $400 billion and the nominal GDP increases to increase the demand for money to that shown in columns (2) and (4), the interest rate will (rise, fall) _____ to _____ %.

d. If the Bank stabilizes the interest rate it must (increase, decrease) _____ the supply of money when the nominal GDP rises and _____ it when the nominal GDP falls; and if it holds the supply of money constant the interest rate will (rise, fall) _____ when the nominal GDP increases and _____ when the nominal GDP decreases.

SELF-TEST

Circle T if the statement is true, F if it is false.

1 The federal government is committed, by Act of Parliament, to using monetary and fiscal policy to achieve economic stability. **T F**

2 Even a balanced budget can be a weapon in fighting depression and inflation. **T F**

3 A governmental deficit is contractionary. **T F**

4 A reduction in taxes during a recession would tend to contract the public sector of the economy. **T F**

5 Built-in stabilizers are not sufficiently strong to prevent recession or inflation, but they can reduce the severity of a recession or of inflation. **T F**

6 The automatic (or built-in) stabilizers also increase the sizes of the government expenditures and investment multipliers. **T F**

7 The cyclically-adjusted budget balance indicates how much government must spend and tax if there is to be full employment in the economy. **T F**

8 Recognition, administrative, and operational lags in the timing of federal fiscal policy make fiscal policies more effective in reducing the rate of inflation and decreasing unemployment in the economy. **T F**

9 The fiscal policies of provincial and local governments have tended to assist and reinforce the efforts of the federal government to mitigate depression and inflation. **T F**

10 The spending and taxing policies of the federal government are designed solely to reduce unemployment and limit inflation in the economy. **T F**

11 It comes more naturally to the federal government to bring in budgets providing for decreases in tax rates and for increases in government purchases than for increased taxes and decreased purchases. **T F**

12 Economists who see evidence of a political business cycle argue that the government tends to increase taxes and reduce expenditures before and to reduce taxes and increase expenditures after elections. **T F**

13 Supply-side economists maintain that reductions in tax rates decrease aggregate supply and are, therefore, inflationary. **T F**

14 The budget deficit of the federal government in any year is equal to its revenues less its expenditures. **T F**

15 There is no assurance that a nation can use fiscal policy both to promote full employment and balance its budget cyclically. **T F**

16 Proponents of functional finance argue that a balanced budget, whether it is balanced annually or over the business cycle, is of minor importance when compared with the objective of full employment without inflation. **T F**

17 The primary reason for the large increase in the public debt since 1930 is the deficit spending during the years of the Great Depression. **T F**

18 The public debt was about $220 billion at the beginning of 1987. **T F**

19 Between 1940 and the present, both the public debt and the interest charges on this debt as percentages of the GNP have decreased. **T F**

20 About one-tenth of the public debt is currently held by foreigners and about three-fourths of it is held by agencies of the federal government and the Bank of Canada. **T F**

21 Inflation increases the *real* value of the *nominal* public debt. **T F**

22 William Krehm found that, when the budget was adjusted for inflation, the federal government had a budget surplus rather than a budget deficit in 1983–84. **T F**

23 Selling government securities to foreigners to finance increased expenditures by the federal government imposes a burden on future generations. **T F**

24 The crowding-out effect of borrowing in the money market to finance an increase in government expenditures is the result of the rise in interest rates in these markets. **T F**

25 Financing increased government expenditures by increasing personal taxes imposes a burden on future generations. **T F**

26 Crowding-out shifts the investment-demand curve to the left. **T F**

27 The amount of saving done at full employment increases in a growing economy. **T F**

28 To maintain full employment in a growing economy, it is necessary for the total of public and private debt to increase. **T F**

29 The equilibrium rate of interest is found at the intersection of the demand-for-money and the supply-of-money curves. **T F**

30 An increase in the equilibrium GDP will shift the demand-for-money curve to the left and increase the equilibrium interest rate. **T F**

31 Monetary policy is more effective in fighting recession than it is in curbing inflation. **T F**

32 Unlike fiscal policy, monetary policy is an effective means of controlling cost-push inflation. **T F**

33 In an economy in which the GDP is either rising or falling, the Bank of Canada must choose between controlling either the money supply or interest rates. **T F**

34 When the economy is at or near full employment, an increase in the money supply tends to be inflationary. **T F**

35 It is generally agreed that fiscal policy is more effective than monetary policy in controlling the business cycle because fiscal policy is more flexible.　　　　**T F**

Circle the letter that corresponds to the best answer.

1 If the government wishes to increase the level of GDP, it might (*a*) reduce taxes; (*b*) reduce its purchases of goods and services; (*c*) reduce transfer payments; (*d*) reduce the size of the budget deficit.

2 Which of the following, by itself, is the most expansionary (least contractionary)? (*a*) redemption of government bonds held by the public; (*b*) borrowing from the public to finance a budget deficit; (*c*) a build-up in the size of the government's account in the central bank; (*d*) issuing new money to finance a budget deficit.

3 Which of the following, by itself, is the most contractionary (least expansionary)? (*a*) redemption of government bonds held by the public; (*b*) borrowing from the public to finance a budget deficit; (*c*) a build-up in the size of the government's account in the central bank; (*d*) issuing new money to finance a budget deficit.

4 If the economy is to have built-in stability, when real GDP falls (*a*) tax receipts and government transfer payments should fall; (*b*) tax receipts and government transfer payments should rise; (*c*) tax receipts should fall and government transfer payments should rise; (*d*) tax receipts should rise and government transfer payments should fall.

5 A direct relation between net tax receipts and real GDP (*a*) automatically produces budget surpluses during a recession; (*b*) makes it easier for discretionary fiscal policy to move the economy out of a recession and toward full employment; (*c*) makes it easier to maintain full employment in a growing economy; (*d*) reduces the effect of a change in planned investment spending upon the domestic output and employment.

6 The length of time it takes for the fiscal action taken by Parliament to affect output, employment, or the price level is referred to as the (*a*) administrative lag; (*b*) operational lag; (*c*) recognition lag; (*d*) fiscal lag.

7 The crowding-out effect of an expansionary (deficit) fiscal policy is the result of government borrowing in the money market, which (*a*) increases interest rates and investment spending in the economy; (*b*) increases interest rates and decreases investment spending; (*c*) decreases interest rates and increases investment spending; (*d*) decreases interest rates and investment spending.

8 The effect of an expansionary (deficit) fiscal policy on the real GDP of an economy operating in the Keynesian range on the aggregate-supply curve is lessened by (*a*) increases in aggregate supply; (*b*) the crowding-out effect; (*c*) increases in the price level; (*d*) by both *b* and *c*.

9 The effect of an expansionary (deficit) fiscal policy on the real GDP of an economy operating in the intermediate range on the aggregate-supply curve is lessened by (*a*) increases in aggregate supply; (*b*) the crowding-out effect; (*c*) increases in the price level; (*d*) by both *b* and *c*.

10 The public debt is the sum of all previous (*a*) expenditures of the federal government; (*b*) budget deficits of the federal government; (*c*) budget deficits less the budget surpluses of the federal government; (*d*) budget surpluses less the budget deficits of the federal government.

11 Which of the following would involve reducing government expenditures and increasing tax rates during a depression? (*a*) an annually balanced budget policy; (*b*) functional finance; (*c*) a cyclically balanced budget policy; (*d*) a policy employing built-in stability.

12 As a percentage of the gross national product, the public debt and interest on the debt are respectively about (a) 47% and 1%; (b) 45% and 5.4%; (c) 105% and 5%; (d) 125% and 6%.

13 The annual interest payments on the public debt today are about (a) $26 billion; (b) $37 billion; (c) $17 billion; (d) $21 billion.

14 Since 1980 (a) both the public debt and the interest charges on the debt relative to the GNP have increased; (b) the public debt relative to the GNP has decreased, and the interest charges on the debt relative to the GNP have increased; (c) the public debt relative to the GNP has increased, and the interest charges on the debt relative to the GNP have decreased; (d) both the public debt and the interest charges on the debt relative to the GNP have decreased.

15 The accounting procedures used by the federal government record (a) only its assets; (b) only its debts; (c) both its assets and debts; (d) its net worth.

16 Inflation is a tax on (a) the holders of the public debt and reduces the real size of a budget deficit; (b) the holders of the public debt and expands the real size of a budget deficit; (c) the federal government and reduces the real size of a budget deficit; (d) the federal government and expands the real size of a budget deficit.

17 The public debt cannot bankrupt the federal government because the federal government (a) need not reduce the size of the debt; (b) is able to refinance the debt; (c) can create money to repay the debt and pay the interest on it; (d) all of the above.

18 Incurring internal debts to finance a war does not pass the cost of war on to future generations because (a) the opportunity cost of the war is borne by the generation that fights it; (b) the government need not pay interest on internally held debts; (c) there is never a need for government to refinance the debt; (d) wartime inflation reduces the relative size of the debt.

19 Which of the following would be a consequence of the retirement of the internally held portion of public debt? (a) a reduction in the nation's productive capacity; (b) a reduction in the nation's standard of living; (c) a redistribution of the nation's wealth among its citizens; (d) an increase in aggregate expenditures in the economy.

20 Which of the following is a consequence of the public debt of Canada? (a) it increases incentives to work and invest; (b) it transfers a portion of the Canadian output of goods and services to foreign nations; (c) it reduces income inequality in Canada; (d) it leads to greater saving at every level of disposable income.

21 The crowding-out effect of borrowing in the money market to finance an increase in government expenditures (a) reduces current private investment expenditures; (b) decreases the rate at which the privately owned stock of real capital increases; (c) imposes a burden on future generations; (d) does all of the above.

22 The crowding-out effect of government borrowing to finance its increased expenditures is reduced (a) when the economy is operating at less than full employment; (b) when the expenditures expand human capital in the economy; (c) when the government's deficit financing improves the profit expectations of business firms; (d) when any one or more of the above are true.

23 Which one of the following is *not* one of the sources of the recent concern with the deficits of the federal government and the growth of the public debt? (a) the large increases in the size of the deficits and in the public debt; (b) the operation of the economy at full employment; (c) the mounting interest costs of the debt; (d) the fact that the nation was not at war.

24 Suppose the multiplier is 3. Were the amount of saving done at full employment to increase by \$20, and were private borrowing to increase by \$5, to maintain full employment the public debt would have to increase by (a) \$5; (b) \$15; (c) \$45; (d) \$60.

25 A change in the money supply has the *least* effect on the equilibrium GDP when (a) both the demand-for-money and investment-demand curves are steep; (b) both the demand-for-money and investment-demand curves are flat; (c) the demand-for-money curve is flat and the investment-demand curve is steep; (d) the demand-for-money curve is steep and the investment-demand curve is flat.

26 An increase in the money supply will have little or no effect on the real domestic output and employment in (a) the Keynesian range on the aggregate-supply curve; (b) the intermediate range along the aggregate-supply curve; (c) the classical range on the aggregate-supply curve; (d) any of the three ranges on the aggregate-supply curve.

27 An increase in the money supply will have little or no effect on the price level in (a) the Keynesian range; (b) the intermediate range; (c) the classical range; (d) any of the three ranges.

28 An increase in the money supply is *least* effective in stimulating aggregate expenditures when the velocity of money (a) falls as the money supply increases; (b) remains constant; (c) rises as the money supply increases; (d) is equal to 5.

29 The Bank of Canada (a) can stabilize both the interest rate and the money supply; (b) cannot stabilize the interest rate; (c) cannot stabilize the money supply; (d) cannot stabilize both the interest rate and the money supply.

30 Between 1975 and late 1982 the Bank of Canada attempted to (a) stabilize interest rates and allowed the money supply to fluc-

tuate; (b) stabilize the money supply and allowed interest rates to fluctuate; (c) stabilize neither the money supply nor interest rates; (d) stabilize both the money supply and interest rates.

31 Which of the following are co-ordinated policies? (a) an increase in government expenditures and in the money supply; (b) a decrease in income tax rates and in the money supply; (c) an increase in transfer payments and a decrease in the money supply; (d) an increase in corporation tax rates and in the money supply.

DISCUSSION QUESTIONS

1 What three things might the federal government do if its fiscal policy were to be (a) expansionary and (b) contractionary? When would it invoke each of these two kinds of policy and what would be their effects on the federal budget?

2 What are the alternative means of financing deficits and disposing of surpluses available to the federal government? What is the difference between these methods insofar as their expansionary and contractionary effect is concerned?

3 Explain the fiscal policy that would be advocated during a recession and during a period of inflation (a) by those whose wish to expand the public sector and (b) by those who wish to contract the public sector.

4 What is the difference between discretionary and non-discretionary fiscal policy? How do the built-in stabilizers work to reduce rises and falls in the level of nominal GDP?

5 Explain why a tax system in which net tax receipts vary directly with the level of nominal GDP makes it difficult to achieve and to sustain full employment.

6 What is the cyclically-adjusted budget balance? What was the problem that its use was designed to solve?

7 Explain the three kinds of time lags that make it difficult to use fiscal policy to stabilize the economy.

8 What are the three political problems that complicate the use of fiscal policy to stabilize the economy?

9 How do (*a*) crowding-out and (*b*) inflation reduce the effect of an expansionary (deficit) fiscal policy on real GDP and employment?

10 What might be the supply-side effects of a reduction in tax rates on the capacity output of the economy, the equilibrium levels of real GDP and employment, and the price level?

11 What is the difference between the (federal) budget deficit and the public debt?

12 Explain why an annually balanced budget is not "neutral" and how it can intensify, rather than reduce, the tendencies for GDP to rise and fall.

13 How does a cyclically balanced budget philosophy differ from the philosophy of functional finance? Why do advocates of functional finance argue that budget deficits and a mounting public debt are of secondary importance?

14 How big is the public debt of Canada, absolutely and relatively? How large are the interest charges on the debt absolutely and relatively? What has happened to the size of the debt and interest charges since 1926 and since 1975? Why have these changes occurred?

15 In what way do the accounting procedures of the federal government misstate its actual financial position (its net worth)? How does inflation affect the *real* size of the public debt and the real size of the federal government's budget deficits?

16 Why can't the public debt result in the bankruptcy of the federal government?

17 Explain the difference between an internally held and an externally held public debt. If the debt is internally held, government borrowing to finance a war does not pass the cost of the war on to future generations. Why?

18 How does the public debt and the payment of interest of this debt affect (*a*) the distribution of income and (*b*) incentives? Why does the portion of the public debt externally held impose a burden on the economy?

19 How can deficit financing impose a burden on future generations? Why don't increases in government expenditures financed by increased personal taxes impose the same burden on future generations? What will lessen the burden on future generations of deficit financing?

20 What tends to happen to the amount of saving done at full employment as the full-employment GDP grows? Why, in a growing economy, must debt increase in order to maintain full employment and economic growth?

21 Using the Keynesian theory and three graphs, explain what determines (*a*) the equilibrium real rate of interest; (*b*) investment; and (*c*) the equilibrium GDP. Now employ these three graphs to show the effects of a decrease in the money supply upon the equilibrium GDP.

22 Utilizing your answers to the question above, (*a*) what determines how large the effect of the decrease in the money supply on the equilibrium GDP will be; and (*b*) how would the change in the equilibrium GDP affect the demand-for-money curve, the interest rate, investment, and the GDP itself?

23 How does a change in the money supply affect the aggregate-demand curve? How will a change in the money supply and the resulting shift in the aggregate-demand curve affect the real domestic output and the price level in (*a*) the Keynesian range, (*b*) the classical range, and (*c*) the intermediate range along the aggregate-supply curve?

24 What are the strengths and shortcomings of monetary policy?

25 Why is monetary policy more effective in controlling inflation than in reducing unemployment?

26 What is the target (or policy) dilemma of the Bank of Canada? What target did the Bank set (*a*) before 1975; (*b*) between 1975 and late 1982; and (*c*) after late 1982?

27 Suppose the nominal GDP in the Canadian economy is increasing or decreasing. Why is the Bank of Canada unable to keep *both* interest rates and the size of the money supply from changing?

28 Explain, as briefly as possible, what Keynesians believe determines the level of domestic output in the Canadian economy.

29 Distinguish between fiscal and monetary policy, and explain how we may use each of them to achieve reasonably full employment and relatively stable prices.

27

INFLATION, UNEMPLOYMENT, AND AGGREGATE SUPPLY

Not too many years ago most economists believed that it was possible for the Canadian economy to have both full employment and stable prices. This belief was based on the assumption that the price level would not rise until the labour force was fully employed. All that was necessary for there to be full employment without inflation was just the right level of total expenditures. Fiscal and monetary policy, thought economists, could be used to assure that aggregate spending was adequate but not excessive.

But the assumption that was the basis of the economists' belief that monetary and fiscal policy could guarantee a stable price level and the full employment of the labour force was not at all realistic. The price level rises before full employment is achieved; and the closer the economy moves to full employment, the more rapid appears to be the rate at which prices rise. This premature inflation (that is, inflation *before* full employment is reached) seems to be the result of the ability of big unions—especially public service unions—to raise wage rates, of the power of big business firms to raise prices, and of the fact that some types of labour become fully employed while other kinds of workers have not yet all found jobs. But no matter what the causes of this premature inflation, the economy finds itself on the spot. It can have full employment with inflation or it can have stable prices with unemployment; *but* it can't have both full employment and stable prices.

Is there any way for the economy to avoid this problem? It may be possible for the economy to avoid both horns of this dilemma. But whether the market policies and the wage-price policies (discussed in this chapter) will enable us to escape from both inflation and unemployment is doubtful.

While this problem, and the policy dilemma it created, were bad enough, an even worse problem emerged in Canada during the 1970s. This was the problem of stagflation. Rising prices were accompanied not by falling but by rising unemployment rates. This inflation was not the result of excessively high levels of total expenditures and the failure to utilize fiscal and monetary policies to control these expenditures. It was the consequence of decreases in aggregate supply rather than increases in aggregate demand.

When the aggregate-supply curve moves upward (that is, when aggregate supply decreases), the equilibrium price level in the economy will increase and the equilibrium real output will decrease. As a direct result the employment of workers declines: the unemployment rate rises. Rising prices and rising unemployment rates were the experience of the Canadian economy in the 1970s and early 1980s, and this *is* stagflation.

The group of economists who explain stagflation by emphasizing the decreases in aggregate supply are labelled supply-side economists; their brand of economics is called supply-side economics. This breed of economists points to the role of government—especially the federal government—in increasing costs and in decreasing aggregate supply; their remedies for stagflation are less government regulation and a massive reduction in both personal and corporation taxes.

In sympathy with the contention of the supply-side economists that the federal government is the chief cause of stagflation are the economists who are called accelerationists (because they accept the accelerationist hypothesis) and rational-expectations theorists. Both contend that the downsloping Phillips Curve is a figment of Keynesian imagination; that it is actually a vertical line; and that government attempts to reduce the unemployment rate below the rate at which the vertical Phillips Curve meets the horizontal axis produce a higher rate of inflation. The only difference between the accelerationists and the rational-expectations theorists is that the former believe that expansionary monetary or fiscal policies can bring about a temporary decline in the unemployment rate and the latter argue that such policies do not even reduce the unemployment rate temporarily.

Whether the supply-side economists and "Reaganomics"—the policies of the Reagan administration in the United States—or their Keynesian critics are right is more than a theoretical detail. It is a matter of great practical importance. The selection of the correct policies for controlling inflation and reducing unemployment depends upon it. But regardless of which view and set of policies are correct, the macroeconomic events of the past twenty years in Canada have taught Canadians a lot about the problems of unemployment and inflation and of controlling them.

CHECK LIST

When you have studied this chapter you should be able to

☐ Explain how Keynesian analysis was able to conclude that the economy could achieve both full employment and stable prices; and what was needed to reach these two goals simultaneously.

☐ Use the aggregate-demand–aggregate-supply model to explain and distinguish demand-pull and cost-push inflation.

☐ Draw a traditional Phillips Curve (after properly labelling the two axes); and explain how to derive this curve by using the aggregate-demand–aggregate-supply model.

☐ Explain what is meant by premature inflation; and state the two basic causes of the premature inflation shown on the Phillips Curve.

☐ Explain and use the Phillips Curve to illustrate the stabilization policy dilemma.

☐ Define stagflation; and contrast stagflation with the relationship shown by a Phillips Curve.

☐ Enumerate the five supply-side shocks experienced by the Canadian economy in the 1970s and early 1980s; and use the aggregate-demand–aggregate-supply model to explain why these shocks led to stagflation.

☐ State what demand-management (fiscal and monetary) policies government might employ to increase the real domestic output or to prevent a rise in the price level.

☐ Describe the dilemma government faces if it uses demand-management policies to deal with stagflation; and how the use of supply-side policies would enable it to avoid this dilemma.

☐ State the accelerationist hypothesis and the rational-expectations theory; and explain how the economists who employ this hypothesis and this theory come to the conclusion that the Phillips Curve is vertical.

☐ State the two kinds of market policies that might be used to combat stagflation.

☐ Distinguish between wage-price guideposts and wage-price controls; and explain why they are called incomes policies.

☐ Explain what the advocates of supply-side economics see as the three basic causes of stagflation in the Canadian economy.

☐ List the four policies advocated by the Reagan Administration in the United States to deal with stagflation.

☐ Criticize the program of the Reagan Administration (Reaganomics) and evaluate the effectiveness of that program.

☐ List the four macroeconomic lessons of the 1970s.

CHAPTER OUTLINE

1 In the Keynesian expenditures-output model it is possible for the economy to experience either a recession or inflation and to achieve both full employment and a stable price level simultaneously; but to understand stagflation it is necessary to use the aggregate-demand–aggregate-supply model.

2 Aggregate demand and aggregate supply determine the real domestic output (and employment) and the price level of the economy.
a. In the intermediate range along the aggregate-supply curve, an increase in aggregate demand results in a higher level of output (and employment) and demand-pull inflation; but a decrease in aggregate supply results in a lower level of output (and employment) and cost-push inflation.
b. In the real world it is difficult to distinguish between the two kinds of inflation and to control inflation; and while cost-push inflation tends to be self-limiting, demand-pull inflation continues as long as aggregate demand continues to increase.

3 If aggregate supply is constant and the economy is operating in the intermediate range on the aggregate-supply curve, the greater the rate of increase in aggregate demand the greater the rate of increase in the price level and in real output, and the lower is the rate of unemployment (and *vice versa*); and there is , therefore, an inverse relationship (or trade-off) called the Phillips Curve between the inflation rate and the unemployment rate.
a. There are at least two reasons inflation occurs before the economy reaches full employment.

(1) Scarcities of some kinds of labour develop before the economy's entire labour force is fully employed; and these scarcities increase wage rates, production costs, and prices.

(2) Labour unions and business firms have market power, and they raise wage rates and prices as the economy approaches full employment.

b. While fiscal and monetary policy can be employed to manage aggregate demand and to affect unemployment and the rate of inflation, the nation faces a serious policy dilemma: if fiscal and monetary policy alone are used, full employment without inflation and price stability without unemployment are impossible and the nation must choose one of the combinations of inflation and unemployment that lie on the Phillips Curve.

c. Events in the 1960s seemed to confirm the inverse relationship between the unemployment and inflation rates; but the relationship is complicated by the downward inflexibility of prices (the reversibility problem) and by shifts in aggregate supply.

4 In the 1970s and early 1980s, however, the Canadian economy experienced both higher rates of inflation and greater unemployment rates; and this stagflation suggests either that there is no dependable relationship between the inflation and unemployment rates or that the Phillips Curve had shifted to the right.
a. During these years five cost- or supply-side shocks decreased aggregate supply (moved the aggregate-supply curve upward) to increase prices and unemployment and the experiences of the Canadian economy suggest that the Phillips Curve is not a stable relationship and cannot be used as the basis for economic policy.
b. The federal government is able to manage aggregate demand.
(1) To increase aggregate demand, it uses an expansionary fiscal policy (increases its expenditures or reduces taxes) or an easy

money policy (increases the money supply).
(2) To decrease aggregate demand, it employs a contractionary fiscal policy (decreases its expenditures or increases taxes) or a tight money policy (decreases the money supply).

c. But demand-management policies are not an effective means of treating stagflation: restricting aggregate demand will increase unemployment without lowering the price level (because of the reversibility problem) and stimulating aggregate demand will increase the price level without reducing unemployment (because it induces offsetting effects on the supply side).

5 The accelerationist hypothesis is that an increase in aggregate demand sponsored by government which reduces unemployment and increases the price level also reduces the real wages of workers who demand and obtain higher nominal wages; this expands unemployment to its original level; the process is repeated when government again tries to reduce unemployment; and the rise in the price level accelerates. The downsloping Phillips Curve does not, in short, exist; and the real Phillips Curve is a vertical line.

6 In the rational expectations theory, workers anticipate that government policies to reduce unemployment will also be inflationary, and they increase their nominal wage demands to offset the anticipated inflation; and not even temporary increases in employment will occur.

7 Because of the ineffectiveness of demand-management policies in coping with stagflation, the Canadian economy has sought other kinds of policies to prevent decreases in or to increase aggregate supply (to shift the Phillips Curve to the left).

a. Market policies try to eliminate the causes of premature inflation and include:
(1) manpower policies to reduce the scarcities of particular kinds of labour that occur before the labour force is fully employed;
(2) pro-competition policies to reduce the power of labour unions and business firms to raise wage rates and prices.

b. Wage-price (or incomes) policies restrict increases in wages and prices by utilizing either guideposts or controls.
(1) Wage-price guideposts are voluntary restraints. The Kennedy-Johnson guideposts in the United States restricted money wage increases in all industries to the rate at which the productivity of labour in the economy had increased; and allowed an industry to increase the price of its product by an amount equal to the increase in its unit labour cost.
(2) Wage-price controls are mandatory (or legal) restraints; and were introduced in Canada in October 1975, in an effort to stem the inflation then running at a rate of more than 10% a year.
(3) Whether to employ wage-price policies has been a vigorously debated issue; and the proponents and opponents have based their arguments on the questions of workability and compliance, allocative efficiency, and economic freedom of choice.
(4) To improve the effectiveness of incomes policies it has been suggested that special tax rebates be given to (tax penalties imposed on) those who comply with (ignore) the guideposts.

c. Supply-side economists argue that the Keynesians have overemphasized the aggregate-demand side and neglected the aggregate-supply side in their explanation of the price level and unemployment.
(1) Taxes, they argue, are business costs and increased taxes result in an upward shift—that is, a decrease—in aggregate-supply.
(2) They also argue that taxes and transfer payments reduce the incentives to work, to save, and to invest and lead to a misallocation of resources, which reduces aggregate supply.
(3) And the increased regulation of industry has adversely affected costs and productivity.

d. Reaganomics is based on supply-side economics and is the policies of the Reagan

Administration in the United States to reduce almost all government spending (except defence expenditures), reduce government regulation of private business firms, prevent the growth in the money supply from being inflationary, and reduce personal and corporation income tax rates.

(1) Sizable reductions in personal and business tax rates were contained in the Economic Recovery and Tax Act of 1981 and were aimed at increasing aggregate supply to bring about a reduction in the rates of inflation and unemployment (and an expansion in real output); and Professor Laffer contended that this would increase tax revenues and prevent inflationary government deficits.

(2) But critics replied that these tax-rate reductions would have little effect on incentives (and would be slow to expand domestic output), would so increase aggregate demand (relative to supply) that large budget deficits and more rapid inflation would result, would actually decrease tax revenues, and would increase income inequality.

e. While the programs of the Reagan Administration reduced the inflation rate sharply, they appear to have brought on a sharp recession between 1980 and 1982, increased the budget deficits of the American government, failed to increase tax revenues, may have crowded-out private investment, and have not increased saving and investment or incentives to work; and the recovery of the economy since 1982 can be attributed to the expansionary effects of the budget deficit.

8 From the Canadian economic experiences of the last two decades have emerged three lessons.

a. Macroeconomic instability in the Canadian economy is more and more related to events outside Canada.

b. Expectations of inflation lead to inflation and make inflation difficult to control.

c. Both aggregate demand and aggregate supply affect output, employment, and the price level of an economy; and both demand-side and supply-side policies have limitations and effects on the other side of a market economy.

IMPORTANT TERMS

Demand-pull inflation	Market policies
Cost-push inflation	Wage-price (incomes) policy
Premature inflation	
Phillips Curve	Wage-price guideposts
Stagflation	Wage guidepost
Demand management	Price guidepost
Stabilization policy dilemma	Tax-based income policy (TIP)
Reversibility problem	Supply-side economics
Supply-side shock	Tax "wedge"
Accelerationist hypothesis	Reaganomics
Rational-expectations theory	Economic Recovery Tax Act (ERTA) (USA)
Wage-price controls	Tax-transfer disincentives
Inflationary expectations	Laffer Curve

FILL-IN QUESTIONS

1 In the Keynesian view, the price level of the economy would not increase until the economy reached _____ and inflation was the result of (excess, insufficient) _____ aggregate demand; and the economy can have (either, both) _____ unemployment or/and inflation.

2 In the aggregate-demand–aggregate-supply model, when the economy is producing in the intermediate range along the aggregate-supply curve,

a. an increase in aggregate demand will (increase, decrease) _____ real output and employment and result in _____ inflation;

b. a decrease in aggregate supply will
_____ real output and employment and
result in _____ inflation.

3 If aggregate supply remains constant,
along the intermediate range of aggregate
supply,
a. the greater the increase in aggregate
demand, the (greater, smaller) _____
will be the increase in the price level, the
_____ will be the increase in real output,
and the _____ will be the unemployment
rate;
b. there will be a(n) (direct, inverse)
_____ relationship between the rate of
inflation and the unemployment rate.

4 Premature inflation
a. means that prices rise before _____
_____ ;
b. is the result of the market power of
_____ and _____
and of imbalances or bottlenecks in _____
markets.

5 The Phillips Curve
a. is the relation between the annual rate of
increase in the _____ and the
_____rate;
b. has a (positive, negative) _____
slope.

6 The policy dilemma faced by the Canadian economy is that
a. to have full employment it must also
have _____, and to have stable prices it
must tolerate _____ ;
b. to reduce the unemployment rate the
rate of inflation must (increase, decrease)
_____ ; and to reduce the rate of inflation

the unemployment rate must _____ .

7 Demand-management policies can be
used to (shift the Phillips Curve, select a
point on the Phillips Curve) _____ .

8 List the five factors (supply-side shocks)
that shifted the Phillips Curve to the right
after 1972.

a. _____

b. _____

c. _____

d. _____

e. _____

9 In the equation that relates unit labour
costs to money-wage rates and the productivity of labour,
a. if the rate at which money wages increases is greater than the rate at which
productivity increases, unit labour costs will
(increase, decrease) _____ ;
b. if the productivity of labour decreases
and money-wage rates are constant, unit labour costs will_____ .

10 The expectation of inflation by workers
and employers leads to (higher, lower)
_____ wage rates and in turn to a
(rise, fall) _____ in production costs, to a(n)
(increase, decrease) _____ in
aggregate supply, to a (higher, lower)
_____ prices level, and to a _____
rate of unemployment in the economy.

11 The rising unemployment rates and the
sharp inflation following the supply-side
shocks can be understood by using the
aggregate-demand–aggregate-supply model.

a. The shocks (increased, decreased) ____
_____ aggregate supply;
b. which in turn increased both the _____

level and the _____ rate;

c. and these two events when they occur simultaneously are called_____ .

12 The stagflation of the 1970s and early 1980s led

a. some economists to believe that the Phillips Curve had shifted to the (right, left) _____;

b. and other economists to conclude that the conventional downsloping Phillips Curve did not _____.

13 Should the federal government use demand-management policies

a. to increase the real domestic output, it might employ either

(1) a(n) (expansionary, contractionary) ____ _____ fiscal policy by (increasing, decreasing) ____ _____ its expenditures or by ____ _____ taxes,

(2) or a(n) (tight, easy) _____ money policy by (increasing, decreasing) _____ the money supply;

b. to prevent a rise in the price level it might employ either

(1) a(n) _____ fiscal policy by _____ its expenditures or by _____ taxes,

(2) or a(n) _____ money policy by _____ the money supply.

14 If the federal government uses demand-management policies to deal with stagflation,

a. an increase in aggregate demand will increase real domestic output but will _____ the price level;

b. a decrease in aggregate demand will

prevent further inflation but will _____ real domestic output.

15 It is the contention of those who accept

a. the accelerationist hypothesis that

(1) the Phillips Curve is actually a (vertical, horizontal) _____ line at an unemployment rate that is (greater, less) _____ than the unemployment rate government would like to achieve; and

(2) attempts by government to reduce the unemployment rate bring about a rate of inflation that (increases, decreases) _____ ;

b. the rational expectations theory that

(1) attempts by government to reduce the unemployment rate lead workers to anticipate perfectly the amount of _____ this will cause and to keep their (real, nominal) _____ wages constant they obtain a(n) (increase, decrease) _____ in their _____ wages; and

(2) this brings about (a rise, a fall, no change) _____ in the price level and _____ in the unemployment rate.

16 Supply-side policies to deal with stagflation try to (increase, decrease) _____ aggregate supply. This will both increase the (price level, real output) _____ and reduce (inflation, real output)_____ .

17 Three kinds of economic policies might be used to deal with stagflation.

a. These three policies are _____ policies, _____ - _____ policies, and the policies identified with _____ economics.

b. If effective, these policies would move

the Phillips Curve to the (right, left) _____ .

18 Market policies to reduce unemployment include

a. those designed to reduce bottlenecks in labour markets and are called _____ policies; and

b. those aimed at reducing the market power of business firms and labour unions and are called pro- _____ policies.

19 Wage-price policies

a. are sometimes called _____ policies;

b. involve either

(1) wage-price (controls, guideposts) _____, which rely upon the voluntary co-operation of labour unions and business firms,

(2) or wage-price _____ , which have the force of law to make them effective.

20 The wage-price guideposts for curbing inflation during the United States Kennedy-Johnson administrations limited *wage* increases in an industry to the overall rate of increase in the _____ of labour and limited *price* increases to an amount equal to the increase in _____ costs in that industry.

21 It is the view of supply-side economists that

a. business costs and product prices have increased because

(1) government has raised taxes, and these taxes are a business _____ and a "_____" between the price of a product and the cost of resources;

(2) high marginal tax rates reduce _____ to work, save, invest, and take risks; and

(3) increased government _____ of industry has decreased its productivity;

b. the remedy for stagflation is a substantial

(increase, decrease) _____ in taxes.

22 The program of the United States Reagan Administration ("Reaganomics") to reduce inflation and unemployment in the economy had four principal elements. These were

a. _____

b. _____

c. _____

d. _____

23 What three lessons have emerged from Canadian macroeconomic experiences during the last twenty years?

a. _____

b. _____

c. _____

PROBLEMS AND PROJECTS

1 Following is a traditional Phillips Curve.

a. At full employment (a 4% unemployment rate), the price level would rise by _____% each year.

b. If the price level were stable (increasing

by 0% a year), the unemployment rate would be _____%.

c. Which of the combinations along the Phillips Curve would you choose for the economy? _____ Why would you select this combination? _____

_____

2 In columns (1) and (2) of the table below is a portion of an aggregate-supply schedule. Column (3) shows the number of full-time workers (in millions) that would have to be employed to produce each of the seven real domestic outputs (in billions) in the aggregate-supply schedule. The labour force is 80 million workers, and the full-employment output of the economy is $ _____ .

a. If the aggregate-demand schedule were that shown by columns (1) and (4),

(1) the price level would be $_____ and the real output would be _____ ;

(2) the number of workers employed would be _____, the number of workers unemployed would be _____, and the unemployment *rate* would be _____%.

b. If aggregate demand were to increase to that shown in columns (1) and (5) and aggregate supply remained constant,

(1) the price level would rise to $_____ and the real output would rise to $ _____ ;

(2) employment would increase by _____ workers and the unemployment rate would fall to _____%;

(3) the price level has increased by_____ %.

c. If aggregate demand were to decrease to that shown in columns (1) and (6) and aggregate supply remained constant,

(1) the price level would fall to $_____ and the real output would fall to $ _____ ;

(2) employment would decrease by _____ workers and the unemployment rate would rise to _____%;

(3) the price level has decreased and the rate of inflation has been (positive, negative) _____ .

3 On the graph on the next page are two aggregate-demand and two aggregate-supply curves. If aggregate demand is AD_1 and aggregate supply is AS_1, the equilibrium price level is _____ and the equilibrium real output is _____ .

(1) Price level	(2) Real output produced	(3) Employment	(4) Real output purchased	(5) Real output purchased	(6) Real output purchased
$3	$ 800	69	$2,300	$2,600	$1,900
4	1,300	70	2,200	2,500	1,800
5	1,700	72	2,100	2,400	1,700
6	2,000	75	2,000	2,300	1,600
7	2,200	78	1,900	2,200	1,500
8	2,300	80	1,800	2,100	1,400
9	2,300	80	1,700	2,000	1,300

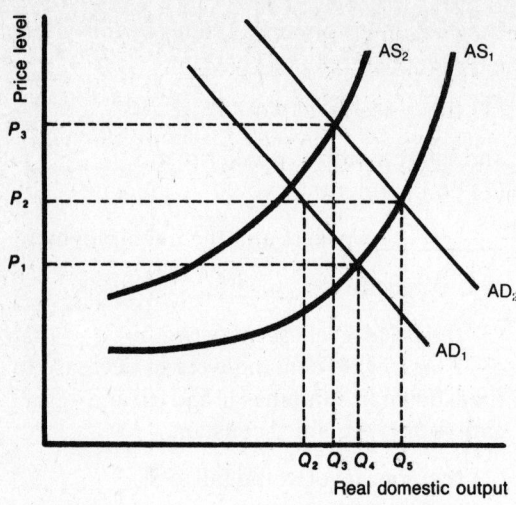

Price level

P_3

P_2

P_1

AS_2 AS_1

AD_2

AD_1

Q_2 Q_3 Q_4 Q_5

Real domestic output

a. Suppose that to increase the real output of the economy and to reduce the unemployment rate the federal government uses fiscal and monetary policies to increase aggregate demand from AD_1 to AD_2.

(1) If aggregate supply remains fixed at AS_1,

(*a*) the price level will (rise, fall) _____ to _____;

(*b*) the output of the economy will _____ to _____; and

(*c*) the unemployment rate will _____ .

(2) But, if aggregate supply were to decrease from AS_1 to AS_2 when aggregate demand increases from AD_1 to AD_2,

(*a*) the price level will (rise, fall) _____ to _____;

(*b*) the output of the economy will _____ to _____; and

(*c*) the unemployment rate will _____ .

b. Suppose that aggregate demand had increased from AD_1 to AD_2 while aggregate supply remained at AS_1 and the price level had risen to P_2; and that to reduce inflation in the economy the federal govenment had used fiscal and monetary policies to decrease

aggregate demand from AD_2 to AD_1.

(1) If prices were *flexible* downward,

(*a*) the price level would fall from P_2 to

_____;

(*b*) the output of the economy would

_____ to _____; and

(*c*) the unemployment rate would _____ .

(2) But if prices were *inflexible* downward,

(*a*) the price level would remain at P_2;

(*b*) the output of the economy would

_____ to _____; and

(*c*) the unemployment rate would _____ .

(3) When prices are inflexible rather than flexible downward, the effects of a decrease in aggregate demand on

(*a*) the price level is (smaller, larger)

_____; and

(*b*) output and unemployment is _____ .

4 Assume that the overall rate of increase in the productivity of labour in the economy is 4% per year.

a. The general level of wages in the economy can increase by _____ % a year without increasing unit labour costs and inducing cost-push inflation.

b. If the wage rate were increased by this percentage,

(1) in an industry in which the productivity of labour had increased 3%, labour costs per

unit would (increase, decrease) _____

by _____%, and the application of the United States Kennedy-Johnson price guidepost would permit the price of the product produced by this industry to (rise, fall)

_____ by _____%;

(2) in an industry in which the productivity of labour had increased by 6%, labour costs per unit would _____ by _____%, and the price guidepost would permit the price of

the product to _____ by _____%;

(3) in an industry in which the productivity of labour had *decreased* by 2%, labour costs per unit would have _____ by _____%, and the price guidepost would permit the price of the product to _____ by _____%.

SELF-TEST

Circle T if the statement is true, F if it is false.

1 In the Keynesian expenditures-output model the aggregate-supply curve has no intermediate range.   **T F**

2 The Keynesian model is a reasonably satisfactory explanation of the macrocomomic behaviour of the Canadian economy between 1930 and 1970, but does not explain the stagflation of the 1970s and early 1980s.
                                          T F

3 Cost-push inflation is accompanied by increases in real output and employment.
                                          T F

4 It is usually not too difficult to determine whether the inflation experienced by an economy is demand-pull or cost-push inflation.   **T F**

5 Cost-push inflation tends to be self-limiting.   **T F**

6 When aggregate supply is constant, higher rates of inflation are accompanied by higher rates of unemployment.   **T F**

7 According to the conventional Phillips Curve, the rate of inflation increases as the level of unemployment decreases.   **T F**

8 As the economy approaches full employment, some types of labour become fully employed before all of the labour force is fully employed.   **T F**

9 Prices in the Canadian economy tend to be flexible upward and inflexible downward.
                                          T F

10 Stagflation refers to a situation in which both the price level and the unemployment rate are rising.   **T F**

11 The Phillips Curve seems to have shifted to the right during the 1970s and early 1980s.
                                          T F

12 Expectations of inflation induce workers to demand and their employers to pay them higher money wages.   **T F**

13 When the nominal-wage rate increases at a rate greater than the rate at which the productivity of labour increases, the unit labour cost will rise.   **T F**

14 If the money-wage rate increases by 8% and the productivity of labour remains constant, unit labour costs will rise by 8%. **T F**

15 Because of the negative slope of the Phillips Curve, fiscal and monetary policies cannot be used to increase employment or to reduce the rate of inflation in the economy.
                                          T F

16 Demand-management policies are an effective method of eliminating stagflation.
                                          T F

17 When government uses demand-management policies in the intermediate range along the aggregate-supply curve, it is able to increase the real domestic output or reduce the rise in the price level but it is unable to do both.   **T F**

18 Accelerationists contend that when the price level rises, the conventional downsloping Phillips Curve moves to the left.   **T F**

19 Rational-expectations theorists maintain that workers believe expansionary monetary and fiscal policies will be inflationary and lower their real wages and that the reaction of workers to these expectations results in higher nominal wages, higher labour costs, and no change in employment in the economy.   **T F**

20 Of the policies that might be employed

to deal with stagflation, the market, wage-price, and the supply-side policies are designed to move the Phillips Curve to the left.
T F

21 Application of the competition (anti-combines) law has proved effective in the past in curbing the market power of big business, so it is a promising technique for fighting stagflation. **T F**

22 Voluntary restraint by business and labour leaders is not apt to be effective in preventing price and wage increases, because such restraint requires them to abandon their major goals. **T F**

23 The wage-price guideposts of the United States Kennedy-Johnson administrations for preventing cost-push inflation were to limit wage increases to the overall rate of increase in labour productivity in the economy. **T F**

24 The tax-based incomes policy discussed in the text would impose a 3% surtax on the personal incomes of workers who receive wage increases in excess of those granted to them by the wage guidepost. **T F**

25 Supply-side economists contend that Keynesian economics is unable to explain stagflation because costs and aggregate supply play an "active" role in the Keynesian model. **T F**

26 To reduce both the rate of inflation and the unemployment rate, supply-siders advocate an increase in aggregate supply. **T F**

27 Supply-siders recommend that tax rates be increased to lower the rate of inflation in the economy. **T F**

28 The use of supply-side policies requires the economy to trade higher levels of real output and employment for a more rapid rise in the price level. **T F**

29 Supply-siders advocate the use of economic policies that stimulate the incentives to work, save, invest, and undertake risks.
T F

30 The tax "wedge" to which supply-side economists refer is the difference between the price of a product and the cost of the economic resources required to produce it. **T F**

31 If the economy were at Point A on the Laffer Curve shown, a decrease in tax rates would increase tax revenue. **T F**

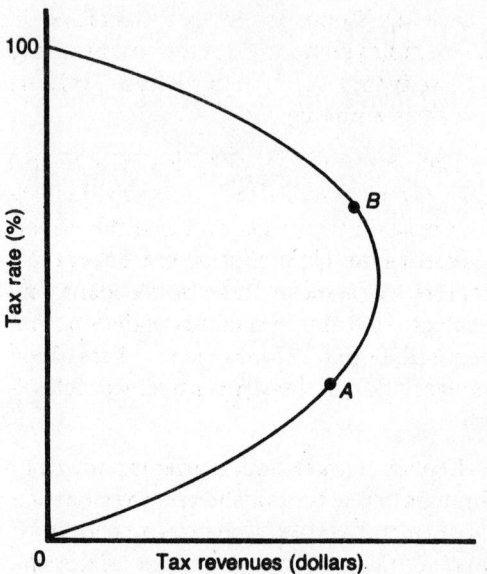

32 The supply-side economists believe that the economy is at a point such as Point B on the Laffer Curve in question 31 (above), and that a substantial reduction in tax rates would both increase tax revenues and increase incentives to work, invest, innovate, and take risks. **T F**

Circle the letter that corresponds to the best answer.

1 In the Keynesian expenditures-output model it is impossible for the economy to experience (a) full employment; (b) inflation; (c) unemployment and inflation; (d) full employment and stable prices.

2 Demand-pull inflation (a) is the result of a decrease in aggregate demand; (b) is accompanied by a decrease in real output and employment; (c) is the result of the increased cost of producing goods and services; (d) may be accompanied by a decrease in the unemployment rate.

3 As long as aggregate supply remains constant and the economy operates along the intermediate range of the aggregate-supply curve, the greater the increase in aggregate demand (a) the greater is the increase in the price level; (b) the greater is the increase in the unemployment rate; (c) the smaller is the increase in real output; (d) the smaller is the increase in employment.

4 The conventional Phillips Curve (a) shows the inverse relation between the rate of increase in the price level and the unemployment rate; (b) makes it possible for the economy to achieve full employment and stable prices; (c) indicates that prices do not rise until full employment has been achieved; (d) slopes upward from left to right.

5 Labour-market adjustments do not eliminate bottleneck problems when there is less than full employment in the economy. Which of the following is *not* one of the reasons for these labour-market imbalances? (a) unemployed workers often lack the skills or training needed for a new occupation; (b) the demand for workers in the markets in which there are labour shortages is inadequate; (c) there are artificial restrictions that prevent unemployed workers from filling the job openings; (d) unemployed workers do not know of the shortages of workers in other labour markets in the economy.

6 If inflation during periods of less than full employment is to be explained by market power, it must be assumed that (a) only unions possess considerable market power; (b) only employers possess considerable market power; (c) both unions and employers possess considerable market power; (d) neither unions nor employers possess considerable market power.

7 The public policy dilemma illustrated by a Phillips Curve is the mutual inconsistency of (a) more employment and price stability; (b) a higher unemployment rate and price stability; (c) inflation and more employment; (d) inflation and a lower unemployment rate.

8 Demand-management (monetary and fiscal) policies can be employed to (a) shift the Phillips Curve to the right; (b) shift the Phillips Curve to the left; (c) achieve full employment without inflation; (d) reduce the unemployment rate.

9 A demand-management policy for increasing the real domestic output is (a) an increase in government expenditures; (b) an increase in taxes; (c) a decrease in the money supply; (d) a decrease in government expenditures and an increase in taxes.

10 A contractionary fiscal policy requires (a) an increase in government expenditures; (b) an increase in taxes; (c) a decrease in the money supply; (d) an increase in the money supply.

11 When government increases aggregate demand to deal with stagflation, (a) both real domestic output and the price level increase; (b) the real domestic output increases and the price level falls; (c) the real domestic output decreases and the price level rises; (d) the real domestic output decreases and the price level falls.

12 An increase in aggregate demand will increase the price level and decrease the unemployment rate; but if the increase in aggregate demand is accompanied by a decrease in aggregate supply, (a) the increase in the price level will be smaller; (b) the decrease in the unemployment rate will be smaller; (c) the decrease in the unemployment rate will be larger; (d) the rate of inflation will be negative.

13 Which of the following was *not* one of the supply-side shocks to the Canadian economy during the 1970s and early 1980s? (a) the imposition of wage and price controls; (b) the devaluation of the dollar; (c) the rise in the price charged by OPEC nations for oil; (d) worldwide agricultural shortfalls.

14 If the percentage change in the productivity of labour is 2% and the percentage change in money-wage rates is 5%, the percentage change in unit labour costs is (a) 1%; (b) 3%; (c) 7%; (d) 10%.

15 Suppose the overall rate of increase in the productivity of labour in the economy is 4%. If the productivity of labour in a particular industry has increased at a rate of only 3%, the Kennedy-Johnson wage-price guideposts would have allowed this industry (a) to increase both the wage rate and the price of its product by 3%; (b) to increase the wage rate by 3% and would have allowed no increase in price; (c) to increase the wage rate by 4% and would have allowed no increase in price; (d) to increase the wage rate by 4% and to increase price by about 1%.

16 A leftward shift in the aggregate-supply curve, aggregate demand remaining constant, will (a) decrease the price level; (b) decrease the unemployment rate; (c) increase real output; (d) increase both the price level and the unemployment rate.

17 A likely result of treating stagflation by stimulating aggregate demand with monetary and fiscal policies is (a) more inflation and less unemployment; (b) less inflation and more unemployment; (c) more inflation and more unemployment; (d) less inflation and unemployment.

18 A likely result of treating stagflation by restricting aggregate demand with monetary and fiscal policies is (a) a fall in the price level and the unemployment rate; (b) a rise in the price level and the unemployment rate; (c) no change in the price level and a fall in the unemployment rate; (d) no change in the price level and a rise in the unemployment rate.

19 In the view of the accelerationists, the long-run Phillips Curve is (a) horizontal; (b) vertical; (c) downsloping; (d) upsloping.

20 Accelerationists argue that if increases in money-wage rates lag behind increases in the price level, when government attempts to reduce unemployment by using fiscal and monetary policies (a) employment and the price level rise in the long run; (b) employment remains constant and the price level rises in the short run; (c) employment rises and the price level remains constant in the short run; (d) employment remains constant and the price level rises in the long run.

21 The rational-expectations theorists contend that when government attempts to reduce unemployment by using fiscal and monetary policies (a) unemployment decreases temporarily and the price level rises; (b) unemployment decreases permanently and the price level rises; (c) unemployment decreases neither temporarily nor permanently and the price level rises; (d) unemployment decreases both temporarily and permanently and the price level falls.

22 Which of the following is *not* one of the *manpower* policies that might reduce premature inflation? (a) application of anti-monopoly laws to labour unions; (b) removal of discrimination as an obstacle to employment; (c) improvement of the flow of job information between workers without jobs and employers with unfilled positions; (d) expansion of job training programs.

23 Which one of the following proposals for fighting inflation is aimed more at demand-pull inflation than at premature inflation? (a) restriction of total spending; (b) restriction of the market power of labour unions; (c) restriction of the market power of business firms; (d) restriction by government of price and wage increases.

24 From the viewpoint of supply-side economists, stagflation is the result of excessive (a) taxes; (b) government regulation; (c) transfer payments; (*d*) all of the above.

25 Supply-side economists contend that the system of taxes and transfer payments reduce incentives to (*a*) work; (*b*) save; (*c*) invest; (*d*) all of the above.

26 Which was *not* an element in the Reaganomics program for reducing stagflation in the American economy? (*a*) a reduction in defence expenditures; (*b*) a reduction in personal and corporation income tax rates; (*c*) a reduction in the regulation of private business firms; (*d*) a reduction in the rate of growth in the money supply.

27 Critics of the proposal of supply-side economists to reduce tax rates by a substantial percentage contend that decreased tax rates would (*a*) reduce aggregate demand and increase unemployment; (*b*) increase tax revenues; (*c*) have little effect on incentives; (*d*) all of the above.

28 During the 1980–82 period the program of the United States Reagan Administration reduced (*a*) unemployment; (*b*) the rate of inflation; (*c*) the federal budget deficit; (*d*) all of the above.

29 Which of the following is *not* one of the economic lessons of the 1970s and early 1980s? (*a*) both aggregate demand and aggregate supply affect the state of the macroeconomy; (*b*) expectations of inflation contribute to and make the control of inflation difficult; (*c*) Canadian macroeconomic instability can often be traced to events outside of Canada; (*d*) central economic planning is the only means by which the economy's resources can be efficiently allocated and full employment without inflation achieved.

DISCUSSION QUESTIONS

1 Why does the Keynesian expenditures-output model imply that the economy may have either unemployment and infla-
tion but will not experience unemployment and inflation simultaneously? What do Keynesians believe must be done if the economy is to realize full employment and stable prices simultaneously?

2 Use the aggregate-demand–aggregate-supply model to explain demand-pull and cost-push inflation and the differences between these two types of inflation.

3 What is a Phillips Curve? Explain how a Phillips Curve with a negative slope may be derived by holding aggregate supply constant and mentally increasing aggregate demand.

4 Explain what is meant by premature inflation and the two major causes of it.

5 What is the public policy dilemma illustrated by the Phillips Curve? Do demand-management (monetary and fiscal) policies enable the federal government to move the curve or to move from one point to another point on the curve?

6 How do the "reversibility problem" and shifts in the aggregate-supply curve complicate the public policy dilemma imposed on the economy by the Phillips Curve?

7 Were the rates of inflation and of unemployment consistent with the Phillips Curve in the 1950s and 1960s? What do these two rates suggest about the curve in the 1970s and 1980s?

8 What were the supply-side shocks to the Canadian economy during the 1970s and early 1980s? How did these shocks affect aggregate supply and the Phillips Curve in Canada?

9 How do expectations of inflation and declines in the productivity of labour affect aggregate supply and the Phillips Curve?

10 When do increases in money-wage rates increase unit labour costs, decrease aggregate supply, and increase the price level in the economy?

11 What is stagflation? Why is it difficult to treat stagflation with demand-management policies?

12 What are the appropriate demand-management policies for dealing with recession and unemployment? (Be sure to include both fiscal and monetary policies.) What are the appropriate demand-management policies for slowing inflation in the economy? Cite two real-world examples of each type of policy.

13 Explain the dilemma faced by the federal government if it were to employ demand-management policies to deal with stagflation. How can it avoid this dilemma?

14 What are the views of accelerationists on (*a*) the effects of expansionary monetary and fiscal policy on employment in the short run and the short-run Phillips Curve; and (*b*) the long-run Phillips Curve? How do they reach these conclusions?

15 How do rational-expectations theorists believe expansionary monetary and fiscal policy affects the price level and employment in the short run and in the long run? By what logic do they reach these conclusions, and in what way do their conclusions differ from those of the accelerationists?

16 What are the two kinds of market policies that might be employed to shift the Phillips Curve to the left? Within each of these two categories, what specific things might be done to reduce the causes of premature inflation?

17 Explain (*a*) what is meant by wage-price policy; (*b*) why wage-price policy is often called incomes policy; and (*c*) the difference between wage-price guideposts and wage-price controls.

18 What (*a*) was the wage guidepost and (*b*) the price guidepost of the United States

Kennedy-Johnson administration? Why would adherence to these guideposts by labour and management have limited the rate of inflation?

19 What wages and prices were controlled during the Nixon Administration? Why did it seem necessary to control them?

20 State the cases *for* and *against* the use of wage-price (or incomes) policy to limit inflation. Build each case upon the three points on which the wage-price policy debate has centred.

21 How might a tax-based incomes policy be used to control increases in money wage rates?

22 Why do supply-side economists believe Keynesian economics "does not come to grips with stagflation"? In the view of the supply-siders, what have been the three principal causes of stagflation in Canada?

23 What were the four major steps the Reagan administration proposed to increase employment and reduce inflation in the American economy?

24 Explain (*a*) the provisions of the United States Economic Recovery Tax Act of 1981 and (*b*) the Laffer Curve. Contrast the positions of the supply-side economists and Keynesians with respect to the Act and the Curve.

25 Criticize and defend the contention that Reaganomics has worked well to reduce stagflation in the United States.

26 What are the three economic lessons to be found in the macroeconomic events of the past twenty years?

27 What policies do supply-side economists advocate to reduce unemployment and inflation in the economy?

28

ALTERNATIVE VIEWS: MONETARISM AND RATIONAL EXPECTATIONS

Economics has always been an arena in which conflicting theories and policies opposed each other. This field of intellectual combat, in major engagements, has seen Adam Smith do battle with the defenders of a regulated economy. It witnessed the opposition of Karl Marx to the orthodox economics of his day. In more recent times it saw Keynes in conflict with the neoclassical economists. Around these major engagements have been countless minor skirmishes between opposing viewpoints. Out of these major and minor confrontations have emerged, not winners and losers, but the advancement of economic theory and the improvement of economic policy.

Monetarism and (more recently) rational-expectations theory are the latest challengers to enter this intellectual arena. The opponent is the reigning champion, Keynesianism, which bested neoclassical economics in the same arena during the 1940s. Monetarists and rational-expectation theorists wish to free the economy from what they see as the destabilizing effects of discretionary fiscal and monetary policies. They view the Keynesians as the proponents of government intervention and see themselves as the defenders of *laissez-faire*.

Chapter 28 examines both monetarism and rational-expectations theory; but it directs most of its attention toward monetarism. But this chapter is more than a comparison of the attitudes of Keynesians and monetarists toward the role of government in the economy. And it is more than a comparison of the basic equations of the two

schools of thought. The basic equation of the Keynesians and the equation of exchange of the monetarists say pretty much the same thing. The equation of exchange ($MV = PQ$) is another way of saying that the economy will produce the GDP that is equal to the aggregate quantity of goods and services demanded.

The issue is whether the income velocity of money—the V in the equation of exchange—is stable or unstable. If it is stable, as the monetarists contend, then the only kind of policy that can be used to control (to increase or decease) nominal GDP is monetary policy; fiscal policy cannot expand or contract nominal GDP. But if V is unstable, as the Keynesians argue, then the fiscal policy is the only effective means and monetary policy is an ineffective means of controlling nominal GDP. The issue of whether V is stable or unstable becomes an issue of whether the size of the money supply matters very much or very little. Monetarists argue that the M in the equation of exchange is the only thing that matters, and their Keynesian rivals contend that it doesn't matter very much.

The emphasis in Chapter 28 is on monetarism because earlier chapters have emphasized Keynesianism. You are not expected, however, to determine which of the two groups is correct. But you should see that monetarism is an alternative to Keynesianism; that the economic issue is the stability of V; and that the political issue is, therefore, whether monetary or fiscal policy is more effective.

Rational-expectations theorists take a

more extreme position in the debate over the relative effectiveness of monetary and fiscal policies. Their position is that the economy tends to produce its full-employment output and that neither of the two types of policy can expand real output and employment in either the short run and the long run: the only effect on the economy of an expansionary monetary or fiscal policy is inflation. They are modern-day (or the new) classical economists who argue that neither the size of the money supply nor the fiscal policies of government has any effect on real output and employment. While this extreme position will be strange to those who have come to believe government can bring about full employment without inflation in the economy, advocates of the rational-expectations theory are careful to explain how they reach these conclusions; and you should be sure you understand the assumptions they make in order to reach their unusual conclusions before you dismiss their extreme position.

Out of the debate among Keynesians, monetarists, and rational-expectationists, as out of the confrontations of the past, will eventually come better economic theory and the policies that solve economic problems. In the meantime, you can adopt an eclectic position: neither the Keynesians, monetarists, nor rational-expectation theorists are entirely correct and neither of them is wholly wrong.

CHECK LIST

When you have studied this chapter you should be able to

☐ Compare the positions of Keynesian and monetarist economists on the competitiveness of a capitalistic economy and its inherent stability and on the role government should play in stabilizing it.

☐ Write the equation of exchange, and define each of the four terms in the equation.

☐ Show how the basic Keynesian equation is "translated" into the equation of exchange.

☐ Compare the monetarist and Keynesian views on the functions of money; on why households and firms demand money; and on what determines the quantity of money demanded.

☐ Explain why the monetarists believe nominal GDP is directly and predictably linked to M.

☐ Write a brief scenario that explains what monetarists believe will happen to change the nominal GDP and what will happen to V when M is increased.

☐ Construct a scenario that explains what Keynesians believe will happen to the interest rate and to V and nominal GDP if M is increased.

☐ Explain why Keynesians favour and monetarists reject the use of fiscal policy to stabilize the economy.

☐ State the monetary rule of the monetarists, and the two reasons they propose a rule instead of discretionary monetary policy.

☐ Use the aggregate-demand–aggregate-supply models of the Keynesians and the monetarists to compare and contrast the effects of an expansionary monetary or fiscal policy on the real domestic output and the price level.

☐ State the two basic assumptions of the rational-expectations theory; and explain how the advocates of this theory believe firms, workers, and consumers react to the announcement of an expansionary monetary or fiscal policy to frustrate the achievement of the goal of the policy.

☐ Use aggregate demand and aggregate supply to show the effects of an expansionary monetary or fiscal policy on real output and the price level in the RET.

☐ Write a brief scenario to explain why rational-expectations theorists believe discretionary monetary and fiscal policies are pro-cyclical; and state what type of government policy is advocated by these theorists.

☐ Present three criticisms of the RET.

CHAPTER OUTLINE

1 Monetarism and rational-expectations theory (RET) are alternatives to the Keynesian macroeconomic theory and policy recommendations; and while this chapter examines both of these alternatives, it stresses monetarism.

2 Keynesians and monetarists differ over the inherent stability of capitalistic economies and ideologically over the role government should play in the economy.

a. Keynesians believe that because many markets in a capitalistic economy are non-competitive it is unstable, that government should intervene to stabilize the economy, and that fiscal policy is a more effective stabilizer than monetary policy.

b. Monetarists believe that because markets in a capitalistic economy are competitive the economy would be stable if it were not for government interference, that government intervention destabilizes the economy, and that government should not use either discretionary fiscal or monetary policy to try to stabilize it.

3 In the Keynesian model, the equilibrium output of the economy is the output at which

$$C_a + I_g + G + X_n = \text{GDP}$$

a. In the monetarist model the basic equation is the equation of exchange,

$$MV = PQ$$

but because MV (total spending) $= C_a + I_g + G + X_n$, and $PQ = \text{GDP}$, the two equations are different ways of stating the same relationship.

b. Keynesians assign a secondary role to money because they believe the links in the cause-effect chain of Chapter 26 are loose ones; monetarists believing that V, in the equation of exchange, is constant, find that

while a change in M may affect Q in the short run, it will in the long run affect only P.

4 Whether V in the equation of exchange is stable or unstable is a critical question, because if it is stable, PQ is closely linked to M, and if it is unstable, the link between PQ and M is loose and uncertain.

a. Reasoning that money is a medium of exchange and that the only demand for money is the transactions demand, monetarists conclude that the quantity of money demanded is a stable percentage of GDP (that GDP/M is constant); that an increase (a decrease) in M will leave firms and households with more (less) money than they wish to have; that they will, therefore, increase (decrease) spending for consumer and capital goods; and that this will cause the GDP and the amount of money they wish to hold for transactions purposes to rise (fall) until their demand for money is equal to M and GDP/M = V.

b. But Keynesians argue that consumers and business firms also have an asset demand for money; that this asset demand for money is inversely related to the rate of interest; and that an increase (decrease) in M will decrease (increase) the interest rate, increase (decrease) the amount of money people wish to hold as an asset, lower (raise) V, and leave the effect on GDP uncertain.

c. Empirical evidence confirms neither the contention of the monetarist that V is stable nor the contention of the Keynesians that it is variable (or unstable).

5 Because their theories (their views on the stability of V) differ, Keynesians and monetarists disagree over the effectiveness of fiscal and monetary policies in stabilizing the economy.

a. Keynesians favour the use of fiscal policy to stabilize the economy because they believe it is a more powerful stabilizer; but the monetarists argue that the use of fiscal policy is both harmful and ineffective because of the crowding-out effect it has on investment expenditures in the economy.

b. Arguing that discretionary changes in M have produced monetary mismanagement and macroeconomic instability, the monetarists have proposed the monetary rule that M be increased at the same annual rate as the potential annual rate of increase in the real GDP.

c. In the aggregate-demand–aggregate-supply model the monetarists see an aggregate-supply curve that is very steep (or vertical) and in which an increase in aggregate demand has little (or no) effect on real domestic output and increases the price level by a relatively large amount; but the Keynesians see an aggregate-supply curve that is nearly flat (or horizontal) and in which an increase in aggregate demand has little (or no) effect on the price.

6 The RET, developed since the mid-1970s and called the new classical economics, is an alternative to Keynesian economics and to monetarism.

a. Economists who advocate the RET make two basic assumptions:

(1) business firms, consumers, and workers understand how the economy works so that they can anticipate the effect on the economy of an economic event or a change in economic policy, and use all available information to make decisions in a way to further their own self-interests; and

(2) all markets in the economy are so competitive that equilibrium prices and quantities quickly adjust to these events and changes in public policy.

b. From these assumptions the proponents of the RET conclude that the response of the public to the expected inflationary effect of an expansionary monetary (or fiscal) policy will cancel the intended effect on output and employment in the economy.

c. In an aggregate-demand–aggregate-supply model of the RET the aggregate supply curve is vertical; and any monetary or fiscal policy that increases or decreases aggregate

demand affects only the price level, and has no effect on real output or employment, real wages, or real interest rates in either the short or the long run.

d. Rational-expectations theorists argue that discretionary monetary and fiscal policies are pro- (rather than counter-) cyclical; and would (like the monetarists) replace discretionary policies with rules.

e. The appeal of the RET comes from the inability of Keynesian economics to explain and to develop policies to correct stagflation, and from the long-sought connection between micro- and macroeconomics; but RET has been subjected to three basic criticisms.

(1) One criticism is that people are not so well informed on the workings of the economy and the effect of economic policy on it as the rational-expectations theorists assume.

(2) A second criticism is that many markets in the economy are not so competitive as assumed in the RET, and do not, therefore, adjust their prices as rapidly as asssumed.

(3) And the third criticism is that monetary and fiscal policies have worked in the past to expand real output and employment in the economy.

f. The debate among Keynesians, monetarists, and rational-expectationists will continue into the future; and three concluding comments put this debate into perspective.

IMPORTANT TERMS

Keynesianism	Crowding-out effect
Monetarism	Monetary rule
Equation of exchange	Rational-expectations theory
Income (circuit) velocity of money	

FILL-IN QUESTIONS

1 Keynesians believe that capitalism is inherently (stable, unstable) _____ because many of its markets are (com-

petitive, non-competitive) _____ , advocate (government intervention, *laissez-faire*) _____ , and favour (monetary, fiscal) _____ over _____ policy.

2 Monetarists argue that capitalism is inherently _____ because most of its markets are _____ , advocate _____ , and favour the use of (discretionary, non-discretionary) _____ (monetary, fiscal) _____ policy.

3 The basic equation of the monetarists is _____ = _____ .

a. This equation is called the _____ _____ .

b. Indicate below what each of the four letters in this equation represents.

(1) M: _____

(2) V: _____

(3) P: _____

(4) Q: _____

4 The basic equation of the Keynesians is

$$C_a + I_g + G + X_n = \text{GDP}.$$

a. $C_a + I_g + G + X_n$ is _____ and in the equation of exchange is equal to _____ .

b. Nominal GDP is equal to _____ in the equation of exchange.

5 Monetarists argue that

a. any increase in M will (increase, decrease) _____ PQ;

b. in the *short run* any increase in M may (increase, decrease) _____ both P and Q; but

c. in the *long run* any increase in M will (increase, decrease) _____ only (P,Q) _____ .

6 In the debate on the stability of V,

a. monetarists argue that money is used only as a _____ , that the only demand for money is the _____ demand, that this demand is a fixed percentage of _____ and that V is, therefore, _____ ;

b. Keynesians contend that money is also used as a _____ and that there is also an _____ demand for money, that this demand is inversely related to the _____ and that V is, therefore, _____ .

7 An increase in M,

a. to the monetarists' way of thinking, will

(1) leave the public with (more, less) _____ money than it wishes to have,

(2) induce the public to (increase, decrease) _____ its spending for consumer and capital goods,

(3) which will result in a(n) _____ in nominal GDP,

(4) until the nominal GDP (or MV) is equal to _____ times _____ ;

b. to the Keynesians' way of thinking, it will

(1) result in a(n) _____ in the rate of interest,

(2) which will _____ the demand for money

(3) and _____ V,

(4) and the effect on nominal GDP will be _____ .

8 It is, in short, the view of the

a. monetarists that V (in the equation of exchange) is stable and that there is a direct relationship between _____ and _____;

b. Keynesians that V is (directly, inversely) _____ related to the interest rate; that the interest rate (increases, decreases) _____ when M increases; and that, therefore, M and V are (directly, inversely) _____ related to each other.

9 In the debate on the use of fiscal policy
a. the Keynesians contend that for the purpose of stabilization of the economy, the more effective tool is _____ policy; but
b. the monetarists reply that government borrowing to finance a budget deficit will (raise, lower) _____ the rate of interest and have a _____ effect on investment spending.

10 Monetarists would have the supply of money increase at the same annual rate as the potential rate of growth of _____ and this is a rate of from _____ to _____%.

11 Monetarists proposed the adoption of the "Monetary Rule" because they believe that discretionary monetary policy tends to (stabilize, destabilize) _____ the economy.

12 In the
a. Keynesian model of the economy, the aggregate supply curve is relatively (steep, flat) _____, and an increase in aggregate demand will have a relatively (large, small) _____ effect on the price level and a relatively _____ effect on the real domestic output;
b. monetarist model, the aggregate supply curve is relatively _____, and an increase in aggregate demand will have a relatively _____ effect on price price and a relatively _____ effect on real domestic output.

13 In the rational-expectations theory
a. individuals correctly anticipate the effects of any economic event or a change in public policy on the economy and make decisions based on their anticipations to maximize their own _____;
b. the markets in the economy are (non-competitive, purely competitive) _____, and prices in these markets are perfectly (inflexible, flexible) _____; and that as a result,
c. an expansionary monetary or fiscal policy will lead the public to expect (inflation, a recession) _____, and they will react in a way that results in (an increase, a decrease, no change) in _____ the real output of the economy and in _____ in the price level.

14 The aggregate-supply curve in the RET is (vertical, horizontal) _____, and a change in aggregate demand brings about a change in (the price level, the real output) _____ and no change in _____ of the economy.

15 Proponents of the RET
a. contend that discretionary monetary and fiscal policies are (pro-, counter-) _____ cyclical; and
b. like the monetarists, favour (policy rules, discretionary policy) _____ .

16 The critics of the RET maintain that people are (less well, better) _____ informed than assumed in the theory; markets are (more, less) _____ competitive than assumed in the theory and prices are, therefore, (sticky, flexible) _____; and monetary and fiscal policies have been employed in the past to (stabilize, destabilize) _____ the economy and to expand its (real, nominal) _____ output.

PROBLEMS AND PROJECTS

1   You must imagine that you are a monetarist in this problem and assume that V is constant and equal to 4. In the table below is the aggregate-supply schedule: the real output Q that producers will offer for sale at seven different price levels P.

P	Q	PQ	MV
$1.00	100	$_____	$_____
2.00	110	_____	_____
3.00	120	_____	_____
4.00	130	_____	_____
5.00	140	_____	_____
6.00	150	_____	_____
7.00	160	_____	_____

a.   Compute and enter in the table above the seven values of PQ.
b.   Assume M is $90. Enter the values of MV on each of the seven lines in the table. The equilibrium
(1) nominal domestic output (PQ or MV) is

$ _____ ;

(2) price level is $ _____ ;

(3) real domestic output Q is $ _____ .
c.   When M increases to $175, MV at each price level is $_____; and the equilibrium
(1) nominal   domestic   output   is

$_____ ;

(2) price level is $ _____ ;

(3) real domestic output is $ _____ .

2   In this problem, you are a Keynesian. The table below, at the left, shows the amounts of money firms and households wish to have for transactions at different levels of nominal GDP. On the right, the table shows the amounts of money they want to have as assets at different rates of interest.

Nominal GDP	Transactions Demand	Interest Rate	Asset Demand
$ 500	$ 50	7.0%	$ 75
600	60	6.8	80
700	70	6.6	85
800	80	6.4	90
900	90	6.2	95
1,000	100	6.0	100

a.   Suppose the nominal GDP is $500, the interest rate is 7%, and the supply of money is $125.
(1) The amount of money demanded for transactions is $ _____ .
(2) The amount of money demanded as an asset is $ _____ .
(3) The total amount of money demanded for both purposes is $ _____ .
(4) The amount of money firms and households wish to have is (greater than, less than, equal to) _____ the amount of money they actually have.
(5) The velocity of money (equal to nominal GDP divided by the supply of money) is

_____ .

b.   Assume the Bank of Canada expands the supply of money to $160 by purchasing securities in the open market; and that as a result the rate of interest falls to 6% and the nominal GDP rises to $600.
(1) The amount of money demanded for transactions is now $ _____ , and the amount demanded as an asset is now

$ _____ .

(2) The total amount of money demanded is

$_____, and the amount of money

the public wishes to have is _____ the
amount of money they actually have.

(3) The velocity of money is _____ .

c. Suppose the federal government pursues
an expansionary fiscal policy that raises the
nominal GDP from $600 to $800 and the interest rate from 6% to 6.8%; and the money
supply remains at $160.

(1) The transactions demand for money is

$_____, the asset demand is

$_____, and the total demand is

$_____ .

(2) The velocity of money is _____ .

d. The effect of the easy money policy was

to (increase, decrease) _____ the
velocity of money, and the effect of the

expansionary fiscal policy was to _____
it.

3 On the following graph are three
aggregate-supply curves: AS_1, AS_2, and AS_3.

a. AS_1 is the (Keynesian, classical, rational-

expectations) _____ supply

curve, AS_2 is the _____ supply

curve, and AS_3 is the _____
supply curve.

b. Regardless of which is the economy's
supply curve, if the aggregate-demand curve
is AD_1, the equilibrium real domestic output

is _____ and the equilibrium

price level is _____ .

c. Should aggregate demand increase from
AD_1 to AD_2 in the

(1) classical model, the equilibrium real domestic output would (increase, decrease, re-

main constant) _____ to (at)

_____ , and the equilibrium

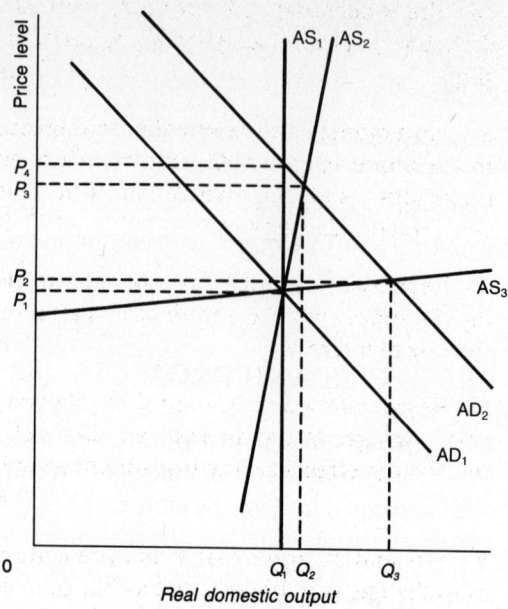

Real domestic output

price level would (increase, decrease, remain

constant) _____ to (at)

_____ ;

(2) Keynesian model, the equilibrium real

domestic output would _____ to

(at) _____, and the equilibrium

price level would _____ to (at)

_____ ;

(3) rational-expectations model, the equilib-

rium real domestic output would _____

to (at) _____, and the equilibri-

um price level would _____ to (at)

_____ .

SELF-TEST

Circle T if the statement is true, F if it is false.

1 The chief exponent of the monetarist position is Milton Friedman.   **T   F**

2 The basic equations of the Keynesians

and the monetarists are no more than two different ways of stating the same relationship. **T F**

3 Most monetarists believe that an increase in the money supply will have no effect on real output and employment in either the short run or the long run. **T .F**

4 Keynesians contend that changes in the money supply will have little or no effect on the rate of interest. **T F**

5 Keynesians also maintain that relatively small changes in the interest rate have relatively large effects on the investment spending. **T F**

6 Monetarists argue that V, in the equation of exchange, is stable and that a change in M will bring about a direct and proportional change in P. **T F**

7 In the monetarists' analysis, the demand for money is directly related to nominal GDP. **T F**

8 From the monetarist viewpoint, the economy is in equilibrium when the amount of money firms and households want to hold is equal to the money supply. **T F**

9 Keynesians contend that the velocity of money is unstable. **T F**

10 In the Keynesians' analysis, the demand for money is directly related to the rate of interest. **T F**

11 Keynesians argue that a decrease in the rate of interest will decrease the velocity of money. **T F**

12 Statistical evidence reveals that the velocity of money has remained almost constant from one year to the next. **T F**

13 An expansionary fiscal policy will, the Keynesians contend, decrease the velocity of money. **T F**

14 Monetarists conclude that discretionary monetary policy has resulted in macroeconomic instability. **T F**

15 Economists who have advanced the rational-expectations theory argue that discretionary fiscal and monetary policy have helped to stabilize the economy. **T F**

16 Most economists are proponents of the rational-expectations theory (the new classical economics). **T F**

Circle the letter that corresponds to the best answer.

1 Keynesians (*a*) believe capitalism is inherently stable; (*b*) believe the markets in a capitalistic economy are highly competitive; (*c*) argue against the use of discretionary monetary policy; (*d*) contend that government intervention in the economy is desirable.

2 Monetarists (*a*) argue for the use of discretionary monetary policy; (*b*) contend that government policies have reduced the stability of the economy; (*c*) believe a capitalistic economy is inherently unstable; (*d*) believe the markets in a capitalistic economy are largely non-competitive.

3 Which of the following is *not* true? (*a*) MV is total spending; (*b*) PQ is the real GDP; (*c*) MV is nominal GDP; (*d*) $MV = C_a + I_g + G + X_n$.

4 If V, in the equation of exchange, is constant, an increase in M will necessarily increase (*a*) P; (*b*) Q; (*c*) both P and Q; (*d*) P times Q.

5 Monetarists contend that (*a*) the only demand for money is the transactions demand; (*b*) the only demand for money is the asset demand; (*c*) there is no transactions demand; (*d*) there is both a transactions and an asset demand for money.

6 From the monetarist viewpoint, an increase in the supply of money will (a) raise the rate of interest; (b) increase spending for consumer and capital goods; (c) increase the asset demand for money; (d) increase the demand for government securities.

7 Keynesians argue that (a) the only demand for money is the asset demand; (b) the only demand for money is the transactions demand; (c) there is no transactions demand; (d) there is both a transactions and an asset demand for money.

8 From the Keynesian viewpoint, an increase in supply of money will (a) raise the rate of interest; (b) increase spending for consumer and capital goods; (c) increase the asset demand for money; (d) decrease the demand for government securities.

9 The crowding-out effect is the effect of borrowing funds to finance a government deficit on (a) imports into the economy; (b) the money supply; (c) investment spending; (d) consumer expenditures.

10 Keynesians contend that borrowing to finance a government deficit incurred in order to increase employment and output in the economy will (a) have little or no effect on the rate of interest; (b) have little or no effect on investment spending; (c) have a significant effect on Q in the equation of exchange; (d) have all of the above effects.

11 The rule suggested by the monetarists is that the money supply increase at the same rate as (a) the price level; (b) the real output of the economy; (c) the velocity of money; (d) none of the above.

12 In the classical model, (a) the aggregate-supply curve is very steep and an increase in aggregate demand will have little or no effect on the price level; (b) the aggregate-supply curve is nearly flat and an increase in aggregate demand will have little or no effect on the price level; (c) the aggregate-supply curve is very steep and an increase in aggregate demand will have a large effect on the price level; (d) the aggregate-supply curve is nearly flat and an increase in aggregate demand will have a large effect on the price level.

13 In the Keynesian model, (a) the aggregate-supply curve is very steep and an increase in aggregate demand will have a large effect on real domestic output; (b) the aggregate-supply curve is nearly flat and an increase in aggregate demand will have a large effect on real domestic output; (c) the aggregate-supply curve is very steep and an increase in aggregate demand will have little or no effect on real domestic output; (d) the aggregate-supply curve is nearly flat and an increase in aggregate demand will have little or no effect on real domestic output.

14 In the rational-expectations theory, (a) individuals understand how the economy works and can correctly anticipate the effects of an event or a change in public policy on the economy; (b) the markets in the economy are purely competitive; (c) to maximize their own self-interests, individuals respond to any expansionary fiscal or monetary policy in a way that prevents an increase in real output and fosters an increase in the price level; (d) all of the above are true.

15 In the model of the rational-expectations theorists, an increase in aggregate demand will (a) increase the price level and have no effect on real domestic output; (b) increase real domestic output and have no effect on the price level; (c) increase both the price level and the real domestic output; (d) have none of the above effects.

16 To stabilize the economy, rational-expectation theorists favour the use of (a) price controls; (b) discretionary fiscal policy; (c) discretionary monetary policy; (d) policy rules.

DISCUSSION QUESTIONS

1 How do the views of Keynesians and monetarists on the competitiveness of capitalistic economies, its stability, and the need for government intervention in the economy differ?

2 What is the basic equation of the Keynesians and the basic equation of the monetarists? Define all terms in both equations and explain how the Keynesian equation can be converted to the monetarist equation.

3 Why do Keynesians believe that monetary policy is an "uncertain, unreliable, and weak stabilization tool as compared to fiscal policy"?

4 Explain how a change in M in the equation of exchange will, to the monetarist way of thinking, affect (a) P times Q, (b) P and Q in the short run, and (c) P and Q in the long run.

5 Explain the differences between the monetarist and Keynesian views on why firms and households demand money (or liquid balances); on what determines the demand for money; and the stability, therefore, of the velocity of money.

6 Suppose firms and households, because of an increase in the money supply, find themselves with more money than they wish to have. What do the monetarists believe they will do with this excess money? What effect will this have on the velocity of money and nominal GDP?

7 Suppose the supply of money increases. What do Keynesians believe will happen to the rate of interest, the amount of money firms and households will wish to hold, planned investment spending, and to the nominal GDP?

8 What empirical evidence is there to support the Keynesian contention that V is unstable or the monetarist contention that it is relatively stable?

9 Why do the Keynesians advocate and the monetarists reject the use of fiscal policy to stabilize the economy?

10 What is the monetary rule? Why do monetarists suggest this rule to replace discretionary monetary policy?

11 How do the aggregate-demand–aggregate-supply models of the Keynesians and monetarists differ? What effect will an expansionary monetary or fiscal policy have upon real domestic output and price level in each of these models?

12 In as few words as possible, explain how and why rational-expectations theorists believe firms, workers, and consumers will respond to an expansionary monetary or fiscal policy; and how these responses make the policy ineffective and promote economic instability.

13 How will an expansionary monetary or fiscal policy affect real domestic output and the price level in the rational-expectations theorists' aggregate-demand–aggregate-supply model? Why does it have these effects?

14 What criticisms have been made of the RET by its opponents?

15 Why has the debate among Keynesians, monetarists, and rational-expectationists been "healthy"?

29

INTERNATIONAL TRADE: COMPARATIVE ADVANTAGE AND PROTECTIONISM

This is the first of three chapters dealing with international trade and finance. International trade is a subject with which most people have little firsthand experience. For this reason many of the terms, concepts, and ideas encountered in these chapters will be unfamiliar and may not be readily grasped. However, most of this material is fairly simple if you will take some pains to examine it. The ideas and concepts employed are new, but they are not especially complex or difficult.

At the beginning, it is essential to recognize that international trade is important to Canada. Canada's merchandise exports and imports were, respectively, $116 and $113 billion in 1986. In relative terms, some other nations have merchandise exports and imports that are larger percentages of their GDPs. They may export and import more than 40% of GDP, but the Canadian percentage of 23% is not trivial, and when services are included the proportion of GDP devoted to exports increases to almost 30%. It is equally important for you to understand from the beginning that international trade differs from the trade that goes on within nations. Different nations use different monies, not just one money; resources are less mobile internationally than they are *intra*nationally; and governments interfere even more with foreign than they do with domestic trade.

But while foreign trade differs from domestic trade in these three ways, nations trade for the same basic reason that people within a nation trade: to take advantage of the benefits of specialization. Nations specialize in and export those goods and services in the production of which they have comparative advantage. A comparative advantage means that the opportunity cost of producing a particular good or service is lower in that nation than in another nation. These nations will avoid the production of and import the goods and services in the production of which other nations have a comparative advantage. In this way, all nations are able to obtain products that are produced as inexpensively as possible. Put another way, when nations specialize in those products in which they have a comparative advantage, the world as a whole can obtain more goods and services from its resources; and each of the nations of the world can enjoy a standard of living higher than it would have if it did not specialize and export and import.

But regardless of the advantages of specialization and trade among nations, people in Canada and throughout the world have for well over 200 years debated whether free trade or protection was the better policy for their nation. Economists took part in this debate and, with few exceptions, argued for free trade and against protection. Those who favour free trade contend that free trade benefits both the nation and the world as a whole. "Free traders" argue that tariffs, import quotas, and other barriers to international trade prevent or reduce specialization and decrease both a nation's and the world's production and standard of living.

But nations have erected and continue to erect barriers to trade with other nations. The questions upon which the latter part of this chapter focuses attention are (1) what motivates nations to impose tariffs and to limit the quantities of goods imported from abroad; (2) what effects do protection have upon a nation's own prosperity and upon the prosperity of the world; and (3) what kinds of arguments do those who favour protection employ to support their position — on what grounds do they base their contention that their nation will benefit from the erection of barriers that reduce imports from foreign nations?

The chapter's final major section is a review of Canadian trade policy over the past century. In 1934 began a series of gradual but substantial tariff-rate reductions, which have continued almost up to the present year. Despite this progress in decreasing the barriers to trade with other nations, protectionism is not dead. Advocates of protection are alive — though not quite well — and living in Canada. And, more importantly for Canada, in the United States — which is the reason Canada opened free-trade talks with the United States in 1986.

Whether free trade or protection will be the policy of Canada in the years to come may well depend upon whether you understand that free trade helps everyone and that protection helps no one but the selfish. It is for this reason that Chapter 29 is important.

CHECK LIST

When you have studied this chapter you should be able to

☐ Explain the importance of international trade to the Canadian economy as a whole and to particular industries in the economy; and list the major exports and imports of Canada.

☐ Enumerate the three features of international trade that distinguish it from the trade that takes place within a nation.

☐ State the two economic circumstances that make it desirable for nations to specialize and trade.

☐ Compute, when you are given the necessary figures, the cost of producing two commodities in two countries; determine which nation has the comparative advantage in the production of each commodity; calculate the range in which the terms of trade will be found; and explain the gains to each nation and to the world from specialization and trade.

☐ Restate the case for free trade.

☐ Identify the four principal types of artificial barriers to international trade and the four motives for erecting these barriers.

☐ Explain the economic effects of a protective tariff on resource allocation, the price of the commodity, the total production of the commodity, and the outputs of foreign and domestic producers of the commodity.

☐ Enumerate the arguments used to support the case for protection and find the weakness in each of these arguments.

☐ Describe the National Policy and its effects on the structure of Canadian industry; and explain how free trade could be especially beneficial for Canada.

☐ List the major provisions of the General Agreement on Tariffs and Trade of 1947.

☐ Identify the four major goals of the European Economic Community (the Common Market).

☐ Contrast Canada's desire for access *for* her *upgraded* raw materials with the other developed nations' desires for access *to* Canada's raw materials; and contrast the resulting divergent policies.

☐ Identify the interrelated factors that explain the rebirth of protectionism in Canada and especially in the United States; and present examples of this rebirth.

☐ Give arguments for and against free trade between Canada and the United States.

CHAPTER OUTLINE

1 Trade between nations is large enough and unique enough to warrant special attention.

a. While the relative importance of international trade to Canada is less than it is to some other nations,

(1) this country's merchandise imports and exports are both about 23% of its GDP and both close to $115 billion a year in 1986;

(2) this trade provides both important capital goods and markets for raw materials;

(3) over 73% of Canada's trade, both exports and imports, is with the United States; about 15% is with Japan and the Common Market (including the United Kingdom); and the balance, about 12%, is with the rest of the world.

b. International trade has three characteristics that distinguish it from domestic trade: resources are less mobile, the nations use different currencies (or money), and the trade is subjected to more government interference.

2 Specialization and trade between nations are advantageous because the world's resources are not evenly distributed and the efficient production of different commodities necessitates different methods and combinations of resources.

3 A simple hypothetical example explains comparative advantage and the gains from trade.

a. Suppose the world is composed of only two nations, each of which is capable of producing two different commodities and in which the production possibilities curves are different straight lines (whose cost ratios are constant but different).

b. With different cost ratios, each nation will have a comparative (cost) advantage in the production of one of the two commodities; and if the world is to use its re-

sources economically, each nation must specialize in the commodity in the production of which it has a comparative advantage.

c. The ratio at which one product is traded for another—the terms of trade—lies between the cost ratios of the two nations.

d. Each nation gains from this trade because specialization permits a greater total output from the same resources and a better allocation of the world's resources.

e. If costs ratios in the two nations are not constant, specialization may not be complete.

f. The basic argument for free trade among nations is that it leads to a better allocation of resources and a higher standard of living in the world; but it also increases competition and deters monopoly in these nations.

4 Nations, however, retard international trade by erecting artificial barriers; and tariffs, import quotas, a variety of non-tariff barriers, and voluntary export restrictions are the principal barriers to trade.

a. Special-interest groups within nations benefit from protection and persuade their governments to erect trade barriers; but the costs to consumers of this protection exceed the benefits to the economy.

b. The imposition of a tariff on a good imported from abroad has both direct and indirect effects on an economy.

(1) The tariff increases the domestic price of the good, reduces its domestic consumption, expands its domestic production, decreases foreign production, and transfers income from domestic consumers to government.

(2) It also reduces the income of foreign producers and the ability of foreign nations to purchase goods and services in the nation imposing the tariff, causes the contraction of relatively efficient industries in that nation, decreases world trade, and lowers the real output of goods and services.

5 The arguments for protection are military self-sufficiency, increasing the domestic employment of labour, diversification to stabilize the economy, the support of infant industries, and shielding the economy from the competition of cheap foreign labour; while most of these arguments are fallacious or based on half-truths, at least two of them warrant the protection of certain industries under certain conditions; and historical evidence suggests free trade promotes and protectionism deters prosperity and economic growth in the world.

6 Since Sir John A. Macdonald's National Policy of 1879, Canada has been a high-tariff country, with harmful effects to its industrial structure.

a. Since 1934, tariff rates have been substantially reduced; many nations, including Canada, have signed the 1947 General Agreement on Tariffs and Trade in an attempt to eliminate trade barriers.

b. The European Common Market has sought the economic integration of Western Europe, and the Common Market nations have achieved considerable integration and have increased their growth rates; but their success has created problems for non-member nations.

c. Canada has been disappointed by her lack of success in gaining access for her *upgraded* raw materials and should consider imposing export taxes on her non-upgraded raw materials.

d. In recent years pressures for protection from goods produced abroad have re-emerged in Canada.

(1) There are several interrelated causes of these pressures for protection.

(2) And both Canada and the United States, among many others, have in a number of ways restricted imports into their economies.

e. The need to have assured access to its main market prompted Canada in 1986 to start free-trade talks with the United States.

IMPORTANT TERMS

Open economy	Voluntary export restrictions (VERs)
Labour- (land-, capital-) intensive commodity	National Policy
	Miniature replica
Cost ratio	Most favoured nation clause
Comparative advantage	General Agreement on Tariffs and Trade (GATT)
Specialization	
Terms of trade	
Trading possibilities line	Economic integration
	European Common Market (European Economic Community)
Tariff	
Revenue tariff	
Protective tariff	Export tax
Import quota	Free trade
Non-tariff barriers (NTBs)	

FILL-IN QUESTIONS

1 The merchandise imports and exports of Canada in 1986 each amount to about ____% of the economy's GDP or about $ _____ billion.

2 Ranked in order of their importance, the four principal exports of Canada are _____

_____ ,

_____ ,

_____ ,

and _____ ;

the four most important imports are _____

_____ ,

_____ ,

_____ ,

and _____ .

3 Special attention is devoted to international trade because resources are (more, less) _____ mobile between nations than within a nation; because each nation employs a different _____ ; and because international trade is subject to (more, fewer) _____ political interferences and controls than domestic trade.

4 Nations tend to trade among themselves because the distribution of economic resources among them is (even, uneven) _____ and because the efficient production of various goods and services necessitates the (same, different) _____ technologies or combinations of resources.

5 The nations of the world tend to specialize in those goods in the production of which they have a _____ , to export those goods, and to import those goods in the production of which they do not have a _____ .

6 If the cost ratio in country X is 4 Panama hats equal 1 kilogram of bananas, while in country Y, 3 Panama hats equal 1 kilogram of bananas,
a. hats are relatively (expensive, inexpensive) _____ in country X and bananas relatively _____ ;
b. hats are relatively _____ in country Y and bananas relatively _____ ;
c. X has a comparative advantage and should specialize in the production of _____ and Y has a comparative advantage and should specialize in the production of _____ ;
d. when X and Y specialize and trade, the terms of trade will be somewhere between _____ and _____ hats for each kilogram of bananas; and will depend upon _____

_____ ;
e. when the actual terms of trade turn out to be 3 $\frac{1}{2}$ hats for 1 kilogram of bananas, the cost of obtaining
(1) 1 Panama hat has been decreased from _____ to _____ kilograms of bananas in Y;
(2) 1 kilogram of bananas has been decreased from _____ to _____ Panama hats in X.
f. This international specialization will not be complete if the cost of producing either good (increases, decreases, remains constant) _____ as a nation produces more of it.

7 The basic argument for free trade is that it results in a better _____ of resources and a higher _____ of living.

8 The barriers to international trade include _____, _____ quotas, the non-_____ barriers, and _____ restrictions.

9 Nations erect barriers to international trade to benefit the economic positions of _____ groups even though these barriers (increase, decrease) _____ economic efficiency and trade among nations, and the benefits to a nation are (greater, less) _____ than the costs to it.

10 When Canada imposes a tariff on a good that is imported from abroad,
a. the price of that good in Canada will (increase, decrease) _____ ;
b. the total purchases of the good in Canada will _____ ;
c. the output of
(1) Canadian producers of the good will

_____ ;
(2) foreign producers of the good will

_____ ;

d. the ability of foreigners to buy goods and

services in Canada will _____ ,
and, as a result, output and employment in
Canadian industries that sell goods and

services abroad will _____ .

11 List the five arguments that protection-
ists employ to justify trade barriers.

a. _____

b. _____

c. _____

d. _____

e. _____

The only two arguments containing any reasonable justification for protection are the

_____ and the

_____ arguments.

12 Canada became a high tariff country in

1879 as a result of the _____ ,

but since the signing of a treaty with ____

_____ that took effect in

_____ , the trend has been

_____ .

This and subsequent trade agreements in-

corporated the _____ clause.

13 The three main principles set down in the
General Agreement on Tariffs and Trade are

a. _____

b. _____

c. _____

14 The specific aims of the European Com-

mon Market were the abolition of _____

_____
among member nations, the establishment
of common tariffs on goods imported from

_____ nations, the free movement of

_____ and _____ among
member nations, and common policies with
respect to other matters.

15 The National Policy has created an (ef-

ficient, inefficient) _____ industrial structure, which is characterized

by _____ , _____ ,

and _____ .

16 What are the five interrelated factors
that have resulted in the recent resurgence of
pressures for the protection of Canadian industries?

a. _____

b. _____

c. _____

d. _____

e. _____

17 Those who advocate that Canada seek assured access to the United States market

a. stress the threat from the _____ ;
b. state Canada—U.S. free trade

(1) would stimulate _____ initiative,

(2) force industrial _____ that would

(3) lead to a more _____ economy with

(4) (higher, lower) _____ real wages.

PROBLEMS AND PROJECTS

1 Following are the production possibilities curves for two nations: Canada and
Chile. Suppose these two nations do not currently engage in international trade or spe-

cialization, and suppose that points *A* and *a* show the combinations of wheat and copper they now produce and consume.

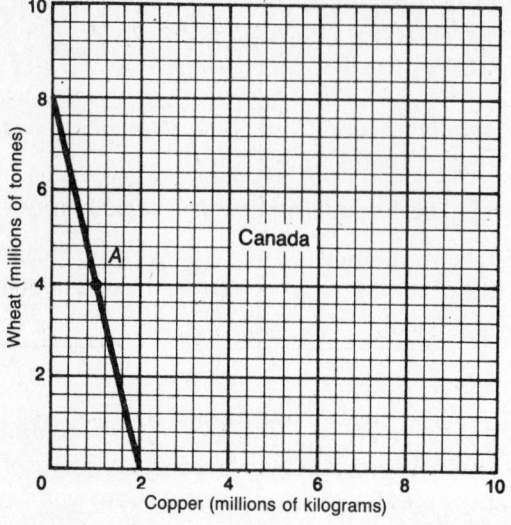

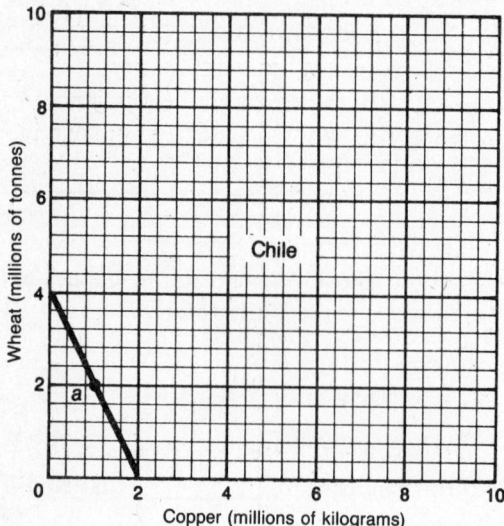

a. The straightness of the two curves indicates that the cost ratios in the two nations are (changing, constant) _____ .

b. Examination of the two curves reveals that the cost ratio in

(1) Canada is _____ million tonnes of wheat

for _____ million kilograms of copper.

(2) Chile is _____ million tonnes of wheat

for _____ million kilograms of copper.

c. If these two nations were to specialize and trade wheat for copper

(1) Canada would specialize in the production of wheat because _____

_____ ;

(2) Chile would specialize in the production of copper because _____ .

d. The terms of trade, if specialization and trade occur, will be greater than 2 and less than 4 million tonnes of wheat for 1 million

kilograms of copper because _____

_____ .

e. Assume the terms of trade turn out to be 3 million tonnes of wheat for 1 million kilograms of copper. Draw in the trading possibilities curve for Canada and Chile.

f. With these trading possibilities curves, suppose Canada decides to consume 5 million tonnes of wheat and 1 million kilograms of copper while Chile decides to consume 3 million tonnes of wheat and 1 million kilograms of copper. The gains from trade to

(1) Canada are _____ million tonnes of

wheat and _____ million kilograms of copper.

(2) Chile are _____ million tonnes of

wheat and _____ million kilograms of copper.

2 The table following shows the quantities of woollen gloves demanded (*D*) in Canada at several different prices (*P*). Also shown in the table are the quantities of woollen gloves that would be supplied by Canadian producers (S_c) and the quantities that would be supplied by foreign producers (S_f) at the nine different prices.

a. Compute and enter in the table the total quantities that would be supplied (S_t) by Canadian and foreign producers at each of the prices.

P	D	S_c	S_f	S_t	S'_f	S'_t
$2.60	450	275	475	___	___	___
2.40	500	250	450	___	___	___
2.20	550	225	425	___	___	___
2.00	600	200	400	___	___	___
1.80	650	175	375	___	___	___
1.60	700	150	350	___	___	___
1.40	750	125	325	___	___	___
1.20	800	0	300	___	___	___
1.00	850	0	0	___	___	___

b. If the market for woollen gloves in Canada is a competitive one, the equilibrium prices for woollen gloves is $_____

and the equilibrium quantity is _____ .

c. Suppose now that the Canadian government imposes an 80 cents ($0.80) per pair of gloves tariff on all gloves imported into Canada from abroad. Compute and enter into the table the quantities that would be supplied (S'_f) by foreign producers at the nine different prices. (*Hint*: if foreign producers were willing to supply 300 pairs at a price of $1.20 when there was no tariff, they are now willing to supply 300 pairs at $2.00, the $0.80 per pair tariff plus the $1.20 they will receive for themselves. The quantities supplied at each of the other prices may be found in a similar fashion).

d. Compute and enter into the table the total quantities that would now be supplied (S'_t) by Canadian and foreign producers at each of the nine prices.

e. As a result of the imposition of the tariff, the equilibrium price has risen to $ _____ and the equilibrium quantity has fallen to

_____ .

f. The number of pairs sold by
(1) Canadian producers has (increased, decreased) _____ by _____ ;

(2) foreign producers has (increased, decreased) _____ by _____ .

g. The total revenues (after the payment of the tariff) of
(1) Canadian producers—who do *not* pay the tariff—have (increased, decreased) _____ by $ _____ ;

(2) foreign producers — on whose products the tariff *is* paid by Canadian consumers — have (increased, decreased) _____ by $ _____ .

h. The total amount spent by Canadian buyers of woollen gloves has _____

by $ _____ .

i. The tariff revenue of the Canadian government has _____

by $ _____ .

j. The total number of dollars earned by foreigners has _____ by

$ _____ ; and, as a result, the total foreign demand for goods and services produced in

Canada will _____ by $ _____ .

SELF-TEST

Circle T if the statement is true, F if it is false.

1 The principal import of Canada is non-ferrous metals.　　　　　　　　　**T F**

2 Canada's exports are heavily weighted toward staples, her imports toward end products.　　　　　　　　　　　　　**T F**

3 Canada's trade with non-industrialized countries is more than 15% of its total trade.
　　　　　　　　　　　　　　　T F

Use the following production possibilities to answer questions 4, 5, and 6 below and to answer multiple-choice questions 8 and 9.

Nepal Production Possibilities Table

Product	Production Alternatives					
	A	B	C	D	E	F
Yak fat	0	4	8	12	16	20
Camel hides	40	32	24	16	8	0

Kashmir Production Possibilities Table

Product	Production Alternatives					
	A	B	C	D	E	F
Yak fat	0	3	6	9	12	15
Camel hides	60	48	36	24	12	0

4 In Kashmir, the cost of 1 camel hide is 3 units of yak fat. **T F**

5 Nepal has a comparative advantage in producing camel hides. **T F**

6 With specialization and trade, the trading possibilities curve of both nations would move to the right of their production possibilities curves. **T F**

7 Increasing production costs tend to prevent specialization among trading nations from being complete. **T F**

8 Trade among nations tends to bring about a more efficient use of the world's resources and a greater world output of goods and services. **T F**

9 Free trade among nations tends to increase monopoly and lessen competition in these nations. **T F**

10 A tariff on coffee in Canada is an example of a protective tariff. **T F**

11 The imposition of a tariff on a good imported from abroad will raise the price of the good and lower the quantity of it bought and sold. **T F**

12 To advocate tariffs that would protect domestic producers of goods and materials essential to national defence is to substitute a political-military objective for the economic objective of efficiently allocating resources. **T F**

13 An increase in a nation's imports will, other things remaining constant, expand aggregate expenditures, real output, and employment in that nation. **T F**

14 One-crop economies may be able to make themselves more stable and diversified by imposing tariffs on goods imported from abroad; but these tariffs are apt also to lower the standard of living in these economies. **T F**

15 The only argument for tariffs that has, in the appropriate circumstances, any economic justification is the increase-domestic-employment argument. **T F**

16 If Canada concludes a trade agreement with and lowers the tariff rates on goods imported from another nation, the lower tariff rates are then charged on those goods when they are imported from other nations in the world with which Canada has trade agreements containing a most-favoured-nation clause. **T F**

17 The members of the European Economic Community have had rapid economic growth since they formed the Common Market in 1958. **T F**

18 The economic integration of nations creates larger markets for firms within the nations that integrate, and makes it possible for these firms and their customers to benefit from the economies of large-scale (mass) production. **T F**

19 The formation of the European Economic Community (Common Market) has made it more difficult for Canadian firms to compete for customers there with firms located within the Community. **T F**

20 According to the Macdonald Royal Commission Report, Canada–United States free trade would reduce the birth of new businesses in areas where Canada is competitive.

T F

Circle the letter that corresponds to the best answer.

1 In 1986, the merchandise imports of Canada amounted to approximately what percentage of Canada's GDP? (*a*) 15%; (*b*) 23%; (*c*) 10%; (*d*) 30%.

2 To which of the following does the largest percentage of the Canadian exports of merchandise go? (*a*) Western Europe; (*b*) U.S.A; (*c*) Japan; (*d*) United Kingdom.

3 From which does the largest percentage of the Canadian imports of merchandise come? (*a*) Western Europe; (*b*) U.S.A.; (*c*) Japan; (*d*) United Kingdom.

4 The *second* most important Canadian export market is (*a*) European Economic Community (*less* U.K.); (*b*) Japan; (*c*) Latin America; (*d*) United Kingdom.

5 The *second* most important supplier of Canadian imports is (*a*) European Economic Community (*less* U.K.); (*b*) Japan; (*c*) Latin America; (*d*) United Kingdom.

6 International trade is a special and separate area of economic study because (*a*) international trade involves the movement of goods over greater distances than trade within a nation; (*b*) resources are more mobile internationally than domestically; (*c*) countries engaged in international trade use different monies; (*d*) international trade is based on comparative advantage.

7 Nations would not need to engage in trade if (*a*) all products were produced from the same combinations of resources; (*b*) world resources were evenly distributed among nations; (*c*) world resources were perfectly mobile; (*d*) all of the above.

Use the tables preceding true–false question 4 to answer the following two questions.

8 If Nepal and Kashmir engage in trade, the terms of trade will be (*a*) between 2 and 4 camel hides for 1 unit of yak fat; (*b*) between $\frac{1}{3}$ and $\frac{1}{2}$ units of yak fat for 1 camel hide; (*c*) between 3 and 4 units of yak fat for 1 camel hide; (*d*) between 2 and 4 units of yak fat for 1 camel hide.

9 If Nepal and Kashmir, in the absence of trade between them, both produced combination *C*, the gains from trade would be (*a*) 6 units of yak fat; (*b*) 8 units of yak fat; (*c*) 6 units of yak fat and 8 camel hides; (*d*) 8 units of yak fat and 6 camel hides.

10 Which one of the following is characteristic of tariffs? (*a*) they prevent the importation of goods from abroad; (*b*) they specify the maximum amounts of specific commodities that may be imported during a given period of time; (*c*) they often protect domestic producers from foreign competition; (*d*) they enable nations to reduce their exports and increase their imports during periods of depression.

11 The motive for the erection by a nation of barriers to the importation of goods and services from abroad is to (*a*) improve economic efficiency in that nation; (*b*) protect and benefit special interest-groups in that nation; (*c*) reduce the prices of the goods and services produced in that nation; (*d*) expand the export of goods and services to foreign nations.

12 When the tariff is imposed on a good imported from abroad, (*a*) the demand for the good increases; (*b*) the demand for the good decreases; (*c*) the supply of the good increases; (*d*) the supply of the good decreases.

13 Tariffs lead to (*a*) the contraction of relatively efficient industries; (*b*) an overallocation of resources to relatively efficient industries; (*c*) an increase in the foreign demand for domestically produced goods; (*d*) an underallocation of resources to relatively inefficient industries.

14 Which one of the following arguments for protection is the least fallacious and most pertinent in modern industrial countries today? (*a*) the military self-sufficiency argument; (*b*) the increase-domestic-employment argument; (*c*) the cheap foreign labour argument; (*d*) the infant-industry argument.

15 Which of the following is the likely result of Canada employing tariffs to protect its high wages and standard of living from cheap foreign labour? (*a*) an increase in Canadian exports; (*b*) a rise in the Canadian real GDP; (*c*) a decrease in the average productivity of Canadian workers; (*d*) a decrease in the quantities of resources employed by industries producing the goods on which tariffs have been levied.

16 Which of the following is a likely result of imposing tariffs to increase domestic employment? (*a*) a short-run increase in domestic employment; (*b*) retaliatory increases in the tariff rates of foreign nations; (*c*) a long-run decline in exports; (*d*) all of the above.

17 The infant-industry argument for tariffs (*a*) is especially pertinent to the advanced industrial nations; (*b*) generally results in tariffs that are removed after the infant industry has matured; (*c*) makes it rather easy to determine which infant industries will become mature industries with comparative advantages in producing their goods; (*d*) might better be replaced by an argument for outright subsidies for infant industries.

18 Under the National Policy (*a*) infant industries have grown to world-scale; (*b*) domestic oligopolies have declined; (*c*) Canadian secondary industry is composed of miniature replicas; (*d*) Canadian secondary industry has become competitive.

19 Which of the following is *not* characteristic of the General Agreement on Tariffs and Trade? Nations signing the agreement were committed to (*a*) the elimination of import quotas; (*b*) the reciprocal reduction of tariffs by negotiation; (*c*) the non-discriminatory treatment of all trading nations; (*d*) the establishment of a world customs union.

20 The European Common Market (*a*) is designed to eliminate tariffs and import quotas among its members; (*b*) aims to allow the eventual free movement of capital and labour within the member nations; (*c*) imposes common tariffs on goods imported into the member nations from outside the Common Market area; (*d*) does all of the above.

21 Pressures for the protection of Canadian industries have increased in recent years because of (*a*) previous decreases in the barriers to trade; (*b*) recession and unemployment in Canada; (*c*) increased competition from imported products; (*d*) all of the above.

DISCUSSION QUESTIONS

1 In relative and absolute terms, how important is international trade to Canada? What are the principal exports and imports of the Canadian economy? What commodities used in the economy come almost entirely from abroad, and what Canadian industries sell large percentages of their output abroad?

2 Which nations are the principal "trading partners" of Canada? How much of this trade is with the developed, and how much of it is with the underdeveloped nations of the world?

3 Are the Canadian economy's exports of merchandise to the following greater or less than its imports of merchandise from them? (*a*) Japan; (*b*) the United Kingdom; (*c*) European Economic Community (*less* U.K.); and (*d*) the rest of the world.

4 In what ways is international trade different from the trade that takes place within a nation?

5 Why do nations specialize in certain products and export their surplus production of these goods at the same time that they are importing other goods? Why do they not use the resources employed to produce the surpluses they export to produce the goods they import?

6 What two facts—one dealing with the distribution of the world's resources and the other related to the technology of producing different products—are the basis for trade among nations?

7 Explain (*a*) the theory or principle of comparative advantage; (*b*) what is meant by and what determines the terms of trade; and (*c*) the gains from trade.

8 What is the "case for free trade"?

9 What motivates nations to erect barriers to the importation of goods from abroad, and what types of barriers do they erect?

10 Suppose Canada were to increase the tariff on radios imported from West Germany (and other foreign countries). What would be the effect of this tariff-rate increase in (*a*) the price of radios in Canada; (*b*) the total number of radios sold in Canada during a year; (*c*) the number of radios produced by and employment in the West German radio industry; (*d*) production by and employment in the Canadian radio industry; (*e*) West German income obtained by selling radios in Canada; (*f*) the West German demand for goods produced in Canada; (*g*) the production of and employment in those Canadian industries that now export goods to West Germany; (*h*) the standards of living in Canada and in West Germany; (*i*) the allocation of resources in the Canadian economy; and (*j*) the allocation of the world's resources?

11 What is the "case for protection"? How valid and pertinent to Canada is each of the basic arguments for protection?

12 What were the three cardinal principles contained in the General Agreement on Tariffs and Trade?

13 What were the four main goals of the European Economic Community? How does the achievement of these goals bring about an increased standard of living within the Community? What problems and what benefits does the success of the EEC create for Canada?

14 Since import taxes (tariffs) are harmful both to the country imposing them and to the countries against whose products they are imposed, how can export taxes be any good?

15 Why is free trade more necessary for Canada than for most other industrialized countries, and why must tariff barriers *not* be removed gradually?

16 Explain why the pressures for the protection of Canadian firms and workers have increased in the last few years.

30

EXCHANGE RATES AND THE BALANCE OF PAYMENTS

In the last chapter you learned *why* nations engage in international trade and *why* they erect barriers to trade with other nations. In Chapter 30 you will learn *how* nations using different monies (or currencies) are able to trade with each other. The means they employ to overcome the difficulties that result from the use of different monies is fairly simple. When the residents of a nation (its consumers, business firms, or governments) wish to buy goods or services or real or financial assets from, make loans or gifts to, or pay interest and dividends to the residents of other nations, they *buy* some of the money used in that nation. They pay for the foreign money with some of their own money. In other words, they *exchange* their own money for foreign money. And when the residents of a nation sell goods or services or real or financial assets to, receive loans or gifts from, or are paid dividends or interest by the residents of foreign nations and obtain foreign money they *sell* this foreign money—often called foreign exchange—in return for some of their own money. That is, they *exchange* foreign money for their own money. The markets in which one money is sold and is paid for with another money are called foreign-exchange markets. The price that is paid (in one money) for a unit of another money is called the foreign-exchange rate (or the rate of exchange). And like most prices, the foreign-exchange rate for any foreign currrency is determined by the demand for and the supply of that foreign currency.

As you know from Chapter 29, nations buy and sell large quantities of goods and ser-

vices across national boundaries. But the residents of these nations also buy and sell such financial assets as stocks and bonds and such real assets as land and capital goods in other nations; and the governments and individuals in one nation make gifts (remittances) in other nations. At the end of a year, nations summarize their foreign transactions with the rest of the world. This summary is called the nation's balance of international payments: a record of how it obtained foreign money during the year and what it did with this foreign money. Of course, all foreign money obtained was used for some purpose—it did not evaporate—and consequently the balance of payments *always* balances. The balance of international payments is an extremely important and useful device for understanding the amounts and kinds of international transactions in which the residents of a nation engage. But it also enables us to understand the meaning of a balance of payments imbalance (a deficit or a surplus), the causes of these imbalances, and how to deal with them.

Probably the most difficult section of this chapter is concerned with balance of payments deficits and surpluses. A balance of payments deficit (surplus) is found when the receipts of foreign money are less (greater) than the payments of foreign money and the nation's official international reserves are reduced (expanded). You should pay particular attention to the way in which a system of *flexible* exchange rates and the way in which a system of *fixed* exchange rates will correct balance of payments deficits and surpluses; and the advantages and disadvantages of these two alternative methods of eliminating imbalances.

As examples of these two types of exchange-rate systems you will find in the final section of the chapter an examination of the gold standard, of the Bretton Woods system, and of the managed floating exchange rate system. In the first two systems exchange rates are fixed; and in the third system exchange rates are fixed in the short run (to obtain the advantages of fixed exchange rates) and flexible in the long run (to enable nations to correct balance of payments deficits and surpluses).

One last word for you. This chapter is filled with new terms. Some of these are just special words used in international economics to mean things with which you are already familiar. Be very sure to learn what all of the new terms mean. It will simplify your comprehension of this chapter and enable you to understand more readily the foreign investment problem considered in Chapter 3l.

CHECK LIST

When you have studied this chapter you should be able to

☐ Explain how Canadian exports create a demand for dollars and generate a supply of foreign exchange; and how Canadian imports create a demand for foreign exchange and generate a supply of dollars.

☐ Put unarranged data into an organized balance of international payments statement for a nation; and find the amount due to (or from) that nation, that is, its balance of payments surplus or deficit, as a result of its exports and imports of goods and services and its capital account transactions.

☐ Explain how a nation finances a payments deficit and what it does with a payments surplus.

☐ Show how a nation can export more goods and services than it imports and still have a balance of payments deficit; and how it can have a trade deficit and still have a balance of payments surplus.

☐ Explain the relationship between the current and capital account balances; and between the balance of payments and changes in the official international reserves of a nation.

☐ Provide an explanation of how flexible (floating) exchange rates function to eliminate payments deficits and surpluses; and enumerate the three disadvantages of this method of correcting imbalances.

☐ Identify the five principal determinants of the demand for and supply of a particular foreign money; and explain how a change in each of these determinants would affect the rate of exchange for that foreign money.

☐ Enumerate the four means by which a nation may fix (or "peg") foreign-exchange rates.

☐ Explain how a nation with a payments deficit might employ its international reserves to prevent a fall in the international value of its currency.

☐ Describe how a nation with a payments deficit might use fiscal and monetary policies, trade policies, and exchange controls to eliminate the deficit.

☐ List the three conditions a nation had to fulfil if it was to be on the gold standard; explain how gold flows operated to reduce payments deficits and surpluses; and identify its two advantages and its two basic drawbacks.

☐ Explain how the Bretton Woods system stabilized exchange rates and attempted to provide for orderly changes in exchange rates to eliminate payments imbalances.

☐ Define the international monetary reserves of nations in the Bretton Woods system; explain why the United States had to incur balance of payments deficits to expand these reserves; and describe the dilemma this created for the United States.

☐ Describe how the United States severed the link between gold and the international value of the dollar in 1971 that led to the floating of the dollar and brought to an end the old Bretton Woods system.

☐ Explain what is meant by a system of managed floating exchange rates; and enumerate its two alleged virtues and its three alleged shortcomings.

☐ Contrast the adjustments necessary to correct payments deficits and surpluses when exchange rates are flexible and when they are fixed.

☐ Identify the assumed domestic (or internal) and international (or external) goals of the Canadian economy; and state which goal is assumed to have the higher priority.

☐ State when a nation's policies to reduce unemployment (or to reduce inflationary pressures) are compatible with and when they are in conflict with the policies it might utilize to eliminate trade surpluses or deficits.

☐ List three things a nation might do to reduce the conflicts between the domestic and international goals of the economy.

CHAPTER OUTLINE

1 Trade between two nations differs from domestic trade because the nations use different monies; but this problem is resolved by the existence of foreign-exchange markets in which the money used by one nation can be purchased and paid for with the money of the other nation.

a. Canadian exports create a demand for dollars and generate a supply of foreign money in the foreign-exchange markets; increase the money supply in Canada and decrease foreign money supplies; and earn monies that can be used to pay for Canadian imports.

b. Canadian imports create a supply of dollars and generate a demand for foreign money in foreign-exchange markets; decrease the money supply in Canada and increase for-

eign money supplies; and use monies obtained by exporting.

2 The balance of international payments for a nation is an annual record of all its transactions with the other nations in the world; and it records all the payments received from and made to the rest of the world. It contains twelve major sections.

a. The first three sections record a nation's exports of goods and services, its imports of these things, and the difference between exports and imports—its balance of trade.

b. The fourth section lists the two-way flow of investment income resulting from foreign investment.

c. The next section records the transfers (private and governmental gifts, inheritances, and immigrants' funds). The balance of transfers added to the balance of trade gives the current account balance, the sixth section.

d. The seventh and eighth sections reveal the balance on direct and portfolio investment flows.

e. The ninth section gives the balance on the Goverment of Canada's transactions.

f. Sections 10 and 11 reveal the allocation of Special Drawing Rights and other capital movements.

g. The addition of sections 7 to 11 gives the capital account balance, the twelfth section.

h. The ninth section records the statistical discrepancy and is the difference between the *known* inpayments and the outpayments and the *actual* change in the official international reserves recorded on line 9(*a*).

i. Line 9 (*a*) gives the balance of payments; a positive sign indicates a balance of payments *deficit*, a negative sign a *surplus*.

j. The merchandise deficit of a nation implies its producers are losing their competitiveness in foreign markets, but is beneficial to consumers in that nation who receive more goods (imports) from abroad than they must pay for (export); and a balance of payments deficit is undesirable to the extent that the nation's official international reserves are limited and require the nation to take painful macroeconomic adjustments to correct it.

3 A capital account surplus causes a current account deficit through the net inflow of foreign investment capital pushing up the Canadian dollar's international value, thus simultaneously reducing Canada's international competitiveness and increasing the net outflows of investment income.

4 The kinds of adjustments a nation with a balance of payments deficit or surplus must make to correct the imbalance depends upon whether exchange rates are flexible (floating) or fixed.

a. If foreign-exchange rates float freely the demand for and the supply of foreign-exchange determine foreign-exchange rates; and the exchange rate for any foreign money is the rate at which the quantity of that money demanded is equal to the quantity of it supplied.

(1) A change in the demand for or supply of a foreign money will cause the exchange rate for that money to rise or fall; and when there is a rise (fall) in the price paid in dollars for a foreign money, it is said that the dollar has depreciated (appreciated) and that the foreign money has appreciated (depreciated).

(2) Changes in the demand for or supply of a foreign currency are largely the result of changes in tastes, relative income changes, relative price changes, changes in relative real interest rates, and speculation.

(3) When a nation has payments deficit (surplus), foreign-exchange rates will rise (fall); this will make foreign goods and services more (less) expensive, decrease (increase) imports, make a nation's goods and services less (more) expensive for foreigners to buy, increase (decrease) its exports; and these adjustments in foreign-exchange rates and in imports and exports correct the nation's payments deficit (surplus).

(4) But flexible exchange rates increase the

A Helpful Hint

The application of the terms *depreciate* and *appreciate* to foreign exchange confuses many students. Here are some hints that will help reduce the confusion.
First:
- depreciate means decrease; and appreciate means increase.

Second: what decreases when Country A's currency depreciates and increases when its currency appreciates is
- the quantity of Country B's currency that can be purchased for *one unit* of Country A's currency.

Third: when the exchange rate for B's currency
- *rises*, the quantity of B's currency that can be purchased for one unit of A's currency *decreases* (just as a rise in the price of cigars decreases the number of cigars that can be bought for a dollar) and A's currency has *depreciated*;
- *falls*, the quantity of B's currency that can be purchased for one unit of A's currency *increases* (just as a fall in the price of cigars increases the number of cigars that can be bought for a dollar) and A's currency has *appreciated*.

uncertainties faced by exporters, importers, and investors (and reduce international trade); change the terms of trade; and destabilize economies (by creating inflation or unemployment).

b. When nations fix (or "peg") foreign-exchange rates, the governments of these nations must intervene in the foreign-exchange markets to prevent shortages and surpluses of foreign monies.

(1) One way for a nation to stabilize foreign-exchange rates is for its government to sell (buy) a foreign money in exchange for its own money (or gold) when there is a shortage (surplus) of the foreign money.

(2) A nation with a payments deficit might

also discourage imports by imposing tariffs, import quotas, and special taxes; and encourage exports by subsidizing them.

(3) To eliminate a payments deficit, a nation might require exporters who earn foreign exchange to sell it to the government; and the government would then ration the available foreign exchange among importers and make the value of imports equal to the value of exports.

(4) Another way for a nation to stabilize foreign-exchange rates is to employ fiscal and monetary policies to reduce its national income and price level and to raise interest rates relative to those in other nations; and, thereby, reduce the demand for and increase the supply of the different foreign monies.

5 The nations of the world in their recent history have employed three different exchange-rate systems.

a. Between 1879 and 1934 (with the exception of the World War 1 years) the operation of the gold standard kept foreign-exchange rates relatively stable.

(1) A nation was on the gold standard when it:

(*a*) defined its monetary unit in terms of a certain quantity of gold;

(*b*) maintained a fixed relationship between its stock of gold and its money supply; and

(*c*) allowed gold to be exported and imported without restrictions.

(2) Foreign-exchange rates between nations on the gold standard would fluctuate only within a narrow range (determined by the cost of packing, insuring, and shipping gold from country to country); and if a foreign-exchange rate rose (fell) to the upper (lower) limit of the range, gold would flow out of (into) a nation.

(3) But if a nation has a balance of payments deficit (surplus) and gold flowed out of (into) the country, its money supply would decrease (increase); this would raise (lower) interest rates and reduce (expand) aggregate demand, domestic output, employment, and prices in that country; and the balance of

payments deficit (surplus) would be eliminated.

(4) The gold standard resulted in nearly stable foreign-exchange rates (which by reducing uncertainty stimulated international trade), and automatically corrected balance of payments deficits and surpluses; but it required that nations accept such unpleasant adjustments as recession and inflation to eliminate their balance of payments deficits and surpluses, and it could operate only so long as nations with deficits did not run out of gold.

(5) During the worldwide Great Depression of the 1930s, nations decided that remaining on the gold standard threatened their recoveries from the depression, and the devaluations of their currencies (to expand exports and reduce imports) led to the breakdown and abandonment of the gold standard.

b. From the end of World War II until 1971, the Bretton Woods System, committed to the adjustable-peg system of exchange rates and managed by the International Monetary Fund (IMF), kept foreign-exchange rates relatively stable.

(1) The adjustable-peg system required the United States to sell gold to other member nations at a fixed price and the other members of the IMF to define their monetary units in terms of either gold or U.S. dollars (which established fixed exchange rates among the currencies of all member nations); and for the other member nations to keep the exchange rates for their currencies from rising by selling foreign currencies, selling gold, or borrowing on a short-term basis from the IMF.

(2) The system also provided for orderly changes in exchange rates to correct a fundamental imbalance (persistent and sizable balance of payments deficits) by allowing a nation to devalue its currency (increase its defined gold or dollar equivalent).

(3) The other nations of the world used gold and U.S. dollars as their international monetary reserves in the Bretton Woods System;

for these reserves to grow, the United States had to continue to have balance of payments deficits, but to continue the convertibility of dollars into gold it had to reduce the deficits; and, faced with this dilemma, the United States in 1971 suspended the convertibility of the dollar, brought an end to the Bretton Woods System of fixed exchange rates, and allowed the exchange rates for the U.S. dollar and the other currencies to float.

c. Exchange rates today are managed by individual nations to avoid short-term fluctuations and allowed to float in the long term to correct balance of payments deficits and surpluses; and this new system of managed floating exchange rates is favoured by some and critized by others.

(1) Its proponents contend that this system has not led to any decrease in world trade and has enabled the world to adjust to severe economic shocks.

(2) Its critics argue that it has resulted in volatile exchange rates and has not reduced balance of payments deficits and surpluses; that it reinforces inflationary pressures in a nation; and that it is a "non-system" that a nation may employ to achieve its own domestic economic goals.

6 The international goals of a nation complicate and may conflict with its use of monetary and fiscal policy to achieve domestic goals.

a. It is assumed that foreign-exchange rates are fixed; and that

(1) the goal of the economy domestically (or internally) is full employment without inflation, and this is its primary goal; and

(2) the goal of the economy internationally (or externally) is a current account balance of zero.

b. The policies designed to achieve full employment without inflation affect the current account balance (because the imports of a nation are directly related to its national income); and policies designed to reach a zero current account balance affect employment and the price level in the nation.

(1) The use of restrictive monetary and fiscal policies to retard inflation are *compatible* with a reduction in a current account deficit.

(2) But the use of expansionary monetary and fiscal policies to reduce unemployment *conflict* with a reduction in a current account deficit.

(3) And the use of restrictive policies to retard inflation *conflict* with a reduction in a current account surplus.

(4) While expansionary policies to reduce unemployment are *compatible* with a reduction in a current account surplus.

c. The conflicts between the domestic and international goals of a nation in (2) and (3) above may lead to the use of other policies.

(1) The imposition of tariffs and the devaluation of its currency may reduce a nation's current account deficit and expand its output and employment; but these policies are apt to induce retaliation and to be ineffective.

(2) If foreign-exchange rates are flexible, the depreciation of a nation's currency may also reduce its current account deficit by increasing its exports and decreasing its imports, and expanding its output and employment.

(3) And when exchange rates are flexible, an expansionary (easy) monetary policy will be more effective than fiscal policy in reducing unemployment *and* a current account deficit because it lowers interest rates and the international value of its currency, expands its exports, and reduces its imports.

IMPORTANT TERMS

Financing exports and imports	Balance of international payments
Foreign-exchange market	Current account
Export transaction	"Invisibles"
Import transaction	Balance of trade
Rate of exchange (foreign-exchange rate)	(Balance of) trade surplus
	(Balance of) trade deficit

Net investment
  income

Transfers

Remittances

Withholding tax

Net transfers

Non-merchandise
  balance

Balance on current
  account

Current account
  deficit

Current account
  surplus

Capital account

Official international
  reserves

Special Drawing
  Rights

Balance on the
  capital account

Capital account
  surplus

Capital account deficit

(Balance of) payments
  surplus

(Balance of) payments
  deficit

Exchange Fund
  Account (EFA)

Flexible (floating)
  exchange rate

Fixed exchange rate

Exchange rate
  (currency)
  depreciation

Exchange rate
  (currency)
  appreciation

Foreign-exchange
  control

Gold standard

Gold flow

Gold export point

Gold import point

Devaluation

Bretton Woods system

Adjustable pegs

International
  Monetary Fund

International
  monetary reserves

Managed floating
  exchange rate

Domestic (internal)
  economic goal

International
  (external) economic
  goal

FILL-IN QUESTIONS

1 The rate of exchange for the French
franc is the number of (francs, dollars)

_____ that a Canadian must pay to

obtain one (franc, dollar) _____ .

2 When the rate of exchange for the Saudi
Arabian riyal is 30 Canadian cents, the rate
of exchange for the Canadian dollar

is _____ riyals.

3 Canadian
a. exports create a (demand for, supply of)

_____ foreign money, generate a

_____ dollars, (increase, decrease)

_____ the money supply in

Canada, and _____ mon-
ey supplies abroad;
b. imports create a _____ foreign

money, generate a _____ dollars,

_____ the money supply in Canada,

and _____ money supplies abroad.

4 In addition to the demand for foreign exchange by Canadian firms that wish to
import goods from foreign countries, Canadians also demand foreign money to pur-

chase _____ and _____

and _____ services abroad and to pay

_____ and _____ on foreign investments in Canada.

5 The balance of payments of a nation
records all payments its residents make to

and receive from residents in _____

_____ .
a. Any transaction that *earns* foreign exchange for that nation is a (debit, credit)

_____ and is shown with a (+ , −)

_____ sign.
b. A transaction that *uses up* foreign ex-

change is a _____ and is shown with

_____ sign.

6 When a nation has a
a. balance of trade deficit, its exports are

(greater, less) _____ than its imports

of _____ ;
b. balance of trade surplus, its exports are

_____ than its imports of goods

and services;

c. current account deficit, its balance on goods and services plus its net _____ _____ income and net _____ is (positive, negative) _____ .

7 The capital account records the capital inflows and capital outflows of a nation.

a. The capital inflows are the expenditures made (in that nation, abroad) _____ by residents of (that nation, other nations) _____ ; and the capital outflows are the expenditures made _____ by residents of _____ for _____ and _____ assets.

b. A nation has a capital account surplus when its capital account inflows are (greater, less) _____ than its outflows.

8 A nation

a. may finance a current account deficit by (buying, selling) _____ assets or by (borrowing, lending) _____ abroad; and

b. may use a current account surplus to (buy, sell) _____ assets or to (borrow, lend) _____ abroad.

9 a. When Canada has a (current, capital) _____ account deficit, _____ it is caused by the (current, capital) _____ account (surplus, deficit) _____ .

b. The mechanism through which this occurs is that a capital account surplus (increases, decreases) _____ the international value of the Canadian dollar, leading to (increased, decreased) _____ Canadian exports and _____ im-

ports, creating a current account (surplus, deficit) _____ .

10 a. The official international reserves of a nation are the quantities of (foreign monies, its own money) _____ owned by its _____ bank.

b. In Canada these reserves are held in the _____ Account.

c. When the entry on line 9(a) in text Table 30-1 has a + (plus) sign, this means the Bank of Canada, on behalf of the government, has put (up, down) _____ -ward pressure on the Canadian by (buying, selling) _____ U.S. dollars (for, out of) _____ the Exchange Fund Account.

d. Thus a + (plus) sign on line 9(a) in text Table 30-1 means Canada has had a balance of payments (surplus, deficit) _____ ; and a − (minus) sign means Canada has had a payments _____ .

11 If foreign exchange rates float freely (that is, the central bank is *not* supporting the value of the currency: line 9(a) in text Table 30-1 has value of 0) and a nation is tending towards a balance of payments *deficit*,

a. that nation's money in the foreign exchange markets will (appreciate, depreciate) _____ and foreign monies will _____ ;

b. as a result of these changes in foreign exchange rates, the nation's imports will (increase, decrease) _____ its exports will _____ , and the size of its deficit will _____ .

12 What effect (depreciation or appreciation) would each of the following have upon the value of the Canadian dollar in U.S. dollar terms (other things equal)?

a. A rise in real interest rates in Canada:

_____

b. A rise in the national income of Canada:

_____

c. An increase in the price level in the United States:

_____

d. The expectation in the United States that inflation will be more rapid in Canada than in the United States:

_____

e. The belief of speculators that the Canadian dollar will appreciate against the U.S. dollar:

_____

13 There are three disadvantages of freely floating foreign-exchange rates: the risks and uncertainties associated with flexible rates tend to (expand, diminish) _____ trade between nations; when a nation's currency depreciates, its terms of trade with other nations are (worsened, bettered) _____; and fluctuating exports and imports can destabilize an economy and result in _____ or in _____ in that economy.

14 To fix or "peg" the rate of exchange for the West German mark when
a. the exchange rate for the mark is rising, Canada would (buy, sell) _____ marks in exchange for dollars;
b. the exchange rate for the mark is falling, Canada would _____ marks in exchange for dollars.

15 A nation with a balance of payments deficit
a. might attempt to eliminate the deficit by (taxing, subsidizing) _____

imports or by _____ exports;
b. might employ exchange controls and ration foreign exchange among those who wish to (export, import) _____ goods and services and require all those who _____ goods and services to sell the foreign exchange they earn to the _____ .

16 If Canada has a payments deficit and the international value of the Canadian dollar is falling, Canada might employ (expansionary, contractionary) _____ fiscal and monetary policies to reduce the demand for foreign currency; but this would tend to bring about (inflation, recession) _____ in Canada.

17 A nation is on the gold standard when it defines its money in terms of _____ , maintains a fixed relationship between its _____ supply and gold _____ , and allows gold to be freely _____ from and _____ into the nation.

18 When the nations of the world were on the gold standard,
a. exchange rates were relatively (stable, unstable) _____ ;
b. but when a nation had a payments deficit
(1) gold flowed (into, out of) _____ the nation;
(2) its money supply and price level (increased, decreased) _____ , and its interest rates _____ ;
(3) its payments deficit (rose, fell) _____ , and it experienced (inflation, recession) _____ .

19 The Bretton Woods system was established to bring about (flexible, fixed)

_____ exchange rates; and, to accomplish this, it employed the _____ system of exchange rates. Under the Bretton Woods system

a. a member nation defined its monetary unit in terms of _____ or_____ ;

b. each member nation stabilized the exchange rate for its currency and prevented it from rising by (buying, selling) _____ foreign currency, which it obtained from its _____ fund, by (buying, selling) _____ gold, or by (borrowing from, lending to) _____ from the International Monetary Fund;

c. a nation with a deeply rooted payments deficit could (devalue, revalue) _____ its currency;

d. official international reserves included both _____ and _____ ;

e. it was hoped that exchange rates in the short run would be (stable, flexible) _____ enough to promote international trade and in the long run would be _____ enough to correct balance of payments imbalances.

20 The role of the U.S. dollar as a component of official international reserves produced a dilemma:

a. For these reserves to grow, the United States had to incur balance of payments (surpluses, deficits) _____.

b. This resulted in an increase in the foreign holding of American dollars and in a decrease in the American reserves (stock) of _____.

c. The ability of the United States to convert dollars into gold and the willingness of foreigners to hold dollars (because they were

"as good as gold"), therefore (increased, decreased) _____ .

d. For the U.S. dollar to remain an acceptable official international reserve, the U.S. payments deficits had to be (eliminated, continued) _____; but for official international reserves to grow, the U.S. payments deficits had to be _____ .

21 The United States completed the destruction of the Bretton Woods system in 1971 when it suspended the convertibility of dollars into _____ and allowed the value of the dollar to be determined by _____ .

Since then the international monetary system has moved from exchange rates that (for all practical purposes) were (fixed, floating) _____ to exchange rates that are _____ .

22 The system of exchange rates that has developed since 1971 has been labelled a system of _____ exchange rates. This means that individuals nations will

a. in the short term, buy and sell foreign exchange to keep exchange rates _____ ;

b. in the long term, allow exchange rates to rise or fall to correct payments_____ .

23 It is assumed that

a. the domestic (or internal) goal of Canada is _____ ;

b. the international (or external) goal of Canada is _____ ;

c. its primary goal is its (domestic, international) _____ goal.

24 The domestic policy that would

a. reduce inflation (conflicts, is compatible) _____ with the policies needed to eliminate a trade *surplus*;

b. reduce unemployment _____ with the policies required to eliminate a trade *deficit*.

25 The conflicts between the domestic and international goals of Canada can be reduced by

a. changing its _____ on imported goods and the international value of its _____ ;

b. allowing the exchange rates for its currency to _____ ;

c. employing expansionary (monetary, fiscal) _____ policy to reduce unemployment and a current account deficit.

PROBLEMS AND PROJECTS

1 Assume a Canadian exporter sells $3 million worth of wheat to an import firm in Colombia. If the rate of exchange for the Colombian peso is $0.02 (two cents), the wheat has a total value of 150 million pesos.

a. There are two ways the import firm in Colombia may pay for the wheat. It might write a cheque for 150 million pesos drawn on its bank in Bogota and send it to the Canadian exporter.

(1) The Canadian exporter would then sell the cheque to its bank branch in Vancouver and its demand deposit there would increase by $_____ million.

(2) This Vancouver bank branch sells the cheque for 150 million pesos to its main branch, that is, the head office branch of the bank that keeps an account in the Bogota bank.

(*a*) The Vancouver bank branch's account in the main branch increases by _____ million (dollars, pesos) _____ ; and

(*b*) the main branch's account in the Bogota bank increases by _____ million (pesos, dollars) _____ .

b. The second way for the importer to pay for the wheat is to buy from its bank in Bogota a draft on a Canadian bank for $3 million, pay for this draft by writing a cheque for 150 million pesos drawn on the Bogota bank, and send the cheque to the Canadian exporter.

(1) The Canadian exporter would then deposit the draft in its account in the Vancouver bank branch and its demand deposit account there would increase by $_____ million.

(2) The Vancouver bank branch collects the amount of the draft from the Canadian bank on which it is drawn through the Vancouver clearing house.

(*a*) The account at the Bank of Canada of the bank of which the Vancouver branch forms a part increases by $_____ million; and

(*b*) the account of the bank on which the draft was drawn decreases by $_____ million.

c. Regardless of the way employed by the Colombian importer to pay for the wheat,

(1) the export of the wheat created a (demand for, supply of) _____ dollars and a _____ pesos;

(2) the number of dollars owned by the Canadian exporter has (increased, decreased _____ and the number of pesos owned by the Colombian importer has

_____ .

2 Use the hypothetical balance of international payments data for Canada given in the following table.

a. Using the data in the table and your computations, complete Canada's balance of international payments on the next page. (Use Table 30-1 in the text as a model and assume that there is no statistical discrepancy.)

	Dollars (in billions)
Balance on personal and institutional remittances	−0.1
Investment income — receipts	+7.4
Balance on direct investment	−8.0
Balance on official international reserves	+0.1
Balance on portfolio securities (a) bonds	+5.5
Investment income — payments	−22.0
Allocation of SDRs	0
Balance on travel (tourism)	−2.1
Balance on portfolio securities (b) stocks	+1.2
Balance on business services	−2.1
Balance on withholding tax	+0.9
Balance on merchandise	+17.5
Balance on government transactions	−0.7
Balances on inheritances and immigrants' funds	+1.4
Balance on other services	+0.1
Balance on freight and shipping	+0.5
Balance on official contributions	−1.4
Balance on Government of Canada loans and subscriptions	−0.9
Balance on other capital movements	+2.7

b. Compute with the appropriate sign (+ or −).

(1) Balance of trade $ _____

(2) Non-merchandise balance $ _____

(3) Current account balance $ _____

(4) Total capital account balance, net flow $ _____

c. Canada had a balance of payments (surplus, deficit) _____ of $ _____ , which is found by referring to line _____ .

The (plus, minus) _____ $ _____ billion means that Canadian dollar worth of foreign exchange was (bought for, sold out of) _____ the EFA to exert (up, down) _____ -ward pressure on the Canadian dollar.

Balance

(1) _____

(2a) _____

(2b) _____

(2c) _____

(2d) _____

(2e) _____

(2f) _____

(3) _____

(4) _____

(5a) _____

(5b) _____

(5c) _____

(5d) _____

(5e) _____

(6) _____

(7) _____

(8a) _____

(8b) _____

(9a) _____

(9b) _____

(10) _____

(11) _____

(12) _____

(13) _____

3 Below are the supply and demand schedules for the British pound.

Quantity of pounds supplied	Price $	Quantity of pounds demanded
400	5.00	100
360	4.50	200
300	4.00	300
286	3.50	400
267	3.00	500
240	2.50	620
200	2.00	788

a. If the exchange rates are flexible,
(1) what will be the rate of exchange for the pound? $ _____
(2) what will be the rate of exchange for the dollar? £ _____
(3) how many pounds will be purchased in the market? _____
(4) how many dollars will be purchased in the market? _____
b. If the Government of Canada wished to fix or "peg" the price of the pound at $5.00, it would have to (buy, sell) _____ (how many) _____ pounds for $ _____ .
c. And if the British government wished to fix the price of the dollar at £ 2/5, it would have to (buy, sell) _____ (how many) _____ pounds for $_____ .

4 Assume
a. the Canadian economy has fully employed its labour force, is experiencing inflation, and has a current account *deficit*.
(1) To reduce the inflationary pressures in the economy requires a(n) (expansionary, contractionary) _____ fiscal policy or a(n) (tight, easy) _____ monetary policy.

(2) If these measures are successful in curbing inflation without reducing employment, the economy's
(*a*) exports will tend to (increase, decrease) _____,
(*b*) imports will tend to _____ ,
(*c*) the trade deficit of the Canadian economy will tend to (increase, decrease)_____ .
(3) The measures undertaken to reduce inflation in Canada worked to (reduce, widen) _____ the trade deficits.
(4) But if the economy had begun with a trade *surplus*, the fiscal and monetary measures taken to fight inflation would have (widened, narrowed) _____ the trade surplus.

b. the Canadian economy has a relatively large portion (say 10%) of its labour force unemployed, is experiencing a recession, and has a current account *deficit*.
(1) To reduce unemployment and increase the economy's real output requires a(n) _____ fiscal policy or a(n) _____ monetary policy.
(2) If these measures are successful in expanding employment and output in the economy,
(*a*) exports will tend to_____ ,
(*b*) imports will tend to _____ ,
(*c*) the trade deficit of the Canadian economy will tend to_____ .
(3) The measures undertaken to reduce unemployment in Canada worked to (reduce, widen) _____ the trade deficit.
(4) But if the economy had begun with a payments *surplus*, the fiscal and monetary policies employed to fight recession would have (widened, narrowed) _____ the surplus.

SELF-TEST

Circle T if the statement is true, F if it is false.

1 The importation of goods by Canadians from abroad creates a supply of dollars in the foreign-exchange market. **T F**

2 Canadian exports expand foreign money supplies and reduce the supply of money in Canada. **T F**

3 The balance of international payments of Canada records all the payments its residents receive from and make to the residents of foreign nations. **T F**

4 Exports are a debit item and are shown with a plus sign (+), and imports are a credit item and are shown with a minus sign (−), in the balance of international payments of a nation. **T F**

5 If a nation's exports of goods, services, and transfers are less than its imports of goods, services, and transfers, the nation's balance of international payments will show a balance is due from other nations in the current account. **T F**

6 The sum of Canada's current and capital account balances and the statistical discrepancy always equals zero. **T F**

7 Canada normally has a merchandise trade surplus. **T F**

8 Any nation with a balance of payments deficit will lose official international reserves. **T F**

9 When the Bank of Canada buys U.S. dollars for the Exchange Fund Account, it is putting upward pressure on the international value of the Canadian dollar. **T F**

10 Canada's capital account surplus is caused by the current account deficit. **T F**

11 If a nation has a balance of payments deficit and exchange rates are flexible, the price of that nation's money in the foreign exchange markets will fall, and this will reduce its imports and increase its exports. **T F**

12 An increase in the number of dollars earned as dividends by Japanese investors in Canadian corporations will increase the demand for dollars and the supply of the yen, and the price of the dollar will appreciate in Japan. **T F**

13 Were Canada's terms of trade with Venezuela to worsen, Venezuela would obtain a greater quantity of Canadian goods and services for every barrel of oil it exported to Canada. **T F**

14 To increase its official international reserves (foreign exchange reserves), a nation must have a balance of payments surplus. **T F**

15 If Canada wishes to fix (or "peg") the value of the Canadian dollar in terms of the U.S. dollar, the Bank of Canada must sell U.S. dollars (in exchange for Canadian dollars) when the Canadian dollar is tending to depreciate. **T F**

16 The expectations of speculators in Canada that the exchange rate for the Japanese yen will fall in the future will increase the supply of yen in the foreign-exchange market and decrease the exchange rate for the yen. **T F**

17 If exchange rates are stable and a nation has a payments surplus, prices and money incomes in that nation will tend to rise. **T F**

18 A nation using exchange controls to eliminate a payments surplus might devalue its currency. **T F**

19 If country A defined its money as worth 100 grains of gold and country B defined its money as worth 20 grains of gold, then, ignoring packing, insuring, and shipping charges, 5 units of country A's money would be worth 1 unit of country B's money. **T F**

20 When nations were on the gold standard,

foreign-exchange rates fluctuated only within limits determined by the cost of moving gold from one nation to another.   **T   F**

21 If a nation maintains an exchange stabilization fund, it would purchase its own money with gold or foreign monies when the value of its money falls in foreign-exchange markets.   **T   F**

22 In the Bretton Woods system, a nation could not devalue its currency by more than 10% without the permission of the International Monetary Fund.   **T   F**

23 In the Bretton Woods system, a nation with persistent balance of payments surpluses had an undervalued currency and should have increased the pegged value of its currency.   **T   F**

24 Because the world's stock of gold did not grow very rapidly it became necessary for the United States to have payments deficits for official international reserves to increase.   **T   F**

25 One of the basic shortcomings of the Bretton Woods system was its inability to bring about the changes in exchange rates needed to correct persistent payments deficits and surpluses.   **T   F**

26 Another basic shortcoming of the Bretton Wood system was its failure to maintain stable foreign exchanges.   **T   F**

27 The United States shattered the Bretton Woods system in August 1971 by raising tariff rates on nearly all the goods it imported by an average of 40%.   **T   F**

28 Using the managed floating system of exchange rates, a nation with a persistent balance of payments surplus should allow the value of its currency in foreign exchange markets to decrease.   **T   F**

29 The external (or international) goal of Canada can be reasonably assumed to have a higher priority than its internal (or domestic) goal.   **T   F**

30 As the incomes of Canadians rise, they buy more goods and services produced in Canada and more goods and services produced abroad.   **T   F**

31 The policies used by a country to eliminate unemployment are compatible with the elimination of that country's current account deficit.   **T   F**

32 The policies used by a country to reduce inflation conflict with the elimination of a current account surplus.   **T   F**

33 Tariff reductions and the revaluation of its currency would (if there were no retaliation) enable a nation to reduce both its rate of inflation and a current account surplus.
     T   F

34 A fall in the exchange rate for a nation's currency tends to increase its exports and to decrease its imports.   **T   F**

35 A rise in the exchange rate for its currency will help to lessen a nation's unemployment and reduce its current account deficit.
     T   F

36 An expansionary fiscal policy tends to increase interest rates in the economy. **T   F**

37 An easy monetary policy is more effective in reducing unemployment and a current account deficit than an expansionary fiscal policy.   **T   F**

Circle the letter that corresponds to the best answer.

1 If a Canadian could buy £ 25,000 for $100,000, the rate of exchange for the pound would be (*a*) $40; (*b*) $25; (*c*) $4; (*d*) $.25.

2 There is an increased demand for foreign currency (increased supply of Canadian dollars) when Canadians (*a*) pay for goods and services imported from foreign countries; (*b*) make payments of interest and dividends to foreign countries on their investments in Canada; (*c*) make real and financial investments in foreign countries; (*d*) do all of the above.

3 A nation's balance of trade is equal to its (*a*) exports less its imports of merchandise (goods); (*b*) exports less its imports of goods and services; (*c*) exports less its imports of goods and services plus its net investment income and transfers; (*d*) exports less its imports of goods, services, and capital.

4 A nation's balance on the current account is equal to its (*a*) exports less its imports of merchandise (goods); (*b*) exports less its imports of goods and services; (*c*) exports less its imports of goods and services plus its net investment income and net transfers; (*d*) exports less its imports of goods, services, and capital.

5 Investment income in Canada's balance of payments is (*a*) highly positive and includes interest and dividends; (*b*) highly negative and includes interest and dividends; (*c*) positive and includes interest only; (*d*) negative and includes interest only; (*e*) positive and includes dividends only.

6 Capital flows into Canada include the purchase by foreign residents of (*a*) a factory building owned by Canadians; (*b*) shares of stock owned by Canadians; (*c*) bonds owned by Canadians; (*d*) an apartment building owned by Canadians; (*e*) all of the above.

7 A Canadian current account deficit may be caused by (*a*) borrowing abroad; (*b*) selling real assets to foreigners; (*c*) selling financial assets to foreigners; (*d*) any of the above.

8 Assuming the Bank of Canada is neither buying nor selling foreign exchange, if Canada has a capital account surplus, she *must* also have a (*a*) current account surplus; (*b*) current account deficit; (*c*) balance of payments surplus; (*d*) balance of payments deficit.

9 A nation may be able to correct or eliminate a persistent (long-term) balance of payments deficit by (*a*) lowering the barriers on imported goods; (*b*) reducing the international value of its currency; (*c*) expanding its national income; (*d*) reducing its official international reserves.

10 If exchange rates float freely, the exchange rate for any currency is determined by (*a*) the demand for it; (*b*) the supply of it; (*c*) the demand for and the supply of it; (*d*) the official reserves that "back" it.

11 If a nation had a balance of payments surplus and exchange rates floated freely, (*a*) the foreign-exchange rate for its currency would rise, its exports would increase, and its imports would decrease; (*b*) the foreign-exchange rate for its currency would rise, its exports would decrease, and its imports would increase; (*c*) the foreign-exchange rate for its currency would fall, its exports would increase, and its imports would decrease; (*d*) the foreign-exchange rate for its currency would fall, its exports would decrease, and its imports would increase.

12 Assuming exchange rates are flexible, which of the following would increase the Canadian dollar price of the Swedish krona? (*a*) a rate of inflation greater in Sweden than in Canada; (*b*) real interest-rate increases greater in Sweden than in Canada; (*c*) national income increases greater in Sweden than in Canada; (*d*) expectations that the price of the krona will be lower in the future.

13 Which of the following would be one of the results associated with the use of freely floating foreign-exchange rates to correct a nation's balance of payments surplus? (*a*) the nation's terms of trade with other nations would be worsened; (*b*) importers in the nation who had made contracts for the future delivery of goods would find that they had to pay a higher price than expected for the goods; (*c*) if the nation were at full employment, the decrease in exports and the increase in imports would be inflationary; (*d*) exporters in the nation would find their sales abroad had decreased.

14 When exchange rates are stable and a nation at full employment has a payments surplus, the result in that nation will be (a) a declining price level; (b) falling nominal income; (c) inflation; (d) rising real income.

15 The use of exchange controls to eliminate a nation's balance of payments deficit results in (a) decreasing the nation's imports; (b) decreasing the nation's exports; (c) decreasing the nation's price level; (d) decreasing the nation's income.

16 A nation with a balance of payments surplus might attempt to eliminate this surplus by employing (a) imports quotas; (b) higher tariffs; (c) subsidies on items the nation exports; (d) none of the above.

17 Which one of the following conditions did a nation *not* have to fulfil if it was to be one under the gold standard? (a) use only gold as a medium of exchange; (b) maintain a fixed relationship between its gold stock and its money supply; (c) allow gold to be freely exported from and imported into the nation; (d) define its monetary unit in terms of a fixed quantity of gold.

18 If the nations of the world were on the gold standard and one nation had a balance of payments surplus, (a) foreign-exchange rates in that nation would rise toward the gold import point; (b) gold would tend to be imported into that country; (c) the level of prices in that country would tend to fall; (d) employment and output in that country would tend to fall.

19 Under the gold standard, a nation with a balance of payments deficit would experience all but one of the following. Which one? (a) gold would flow out of the nation; (b) the nation's money supply would contract; (c) interest rates in the nation would fall; (d) real domestic output, employment, and prices in the nation would decline.

20 Which of the following was the principal disadvantage of the gold standard? (a) unstable foreign-exchange rates; (b) persistent payments imbalances; (c) the uncertainties and decreased trade that resulted from the depreciation of gold; (d) the domestic macroeconomic adjustments experienced by a nation with a payments deficit or surplus.

21 All but one of the following were elements in the adjustable-peg system of foreign-exchange rates. Which one? (a) each nation defined its monetary unit in terms of gold or dollars; (b) nations bought and sold their own currencies to stabilize exchange rates; (c) nations were allowed to devalue their currencies when faced with persistent payments deficits; (d) the deposit by all nations of their international reserves with the IMF.

22 Which one of the following was *not* characteristic of the International Monetary Fund in the Bretton Woods system? (a) made short-term loans to member nations with balance of payments deficits; (b) tried to maintain relatively stable exchange rates; (c) required member nations to maintain exchange stabilization funds; (d) extended long-term loans to underdeveloped nations for the purpose of increasing their productive capacities.

23 The objective of the adjustable-peg system was exchange rates that were (a) adjustable in the short run and fixed in the long run; (b) adjustable in both the short and long run; (c) fixed in both the short and long run; (d) fixed in the short run; adjustable in the long run.

24 Which of the following is the best definition of international monetary reserves in the Bretton Woods system? (a) gold; (b) dollars; (c) gold and dollars; (d) gold, dollars and British pounds.

25 The dilemma created by the U.S. payments deficits was that (a) to maintain the status of the dollar as an acceptable international monetary reserve the deficit had to be reduced and to increase these reserves the deficits had to be continued; (b) to maintain the status of the dollar the deficit had to be continued and to increase reserves the deficit had to be eliminated; (c) to maintain the status of the dollar the deficit had to be increased and to expand reserves the deficit had to be reduced; (d) to maintain the status of the dollar the deficit had to be reduced and to expand reserves the deficit had to be reduced.

26 "Floating" the U.S. dollar means (a) the value of the dollar is determined by the demand for and the supply of the dollar; (b) the dollar price of gold has been increased; (c) the price of the dollar has been allowed to crawl upward at the rate of one-fourth of 1% a month; (d) the IMF decreased the value of the dollar by 10%.

27 A system of managed floating exchange rates (a) allows nations to stabilize exchange rates in the short term; (b) requires nations to stabilize exchange rates in the long term; (c) entails stable exchange rates in both the short and long term; (d) none of the above.

28 Floating exchange rates (a) tend to correct payments imbalances; (b) reduce the uncertainties and risks associated with international trade; (c) increase the world's need for official international reserves; (d) tend to expand the volume of world trade.

29 The domestic (or internal) goal of the Canadian economy is (a) full employment; (b) a relatively stable price level; (c) full employment with little or no inflation; (d) a zero current account balance.

30 The international (or external) goal of Canada is (a) full employment with little or no inflation; (b) a current account surplus; (c) a current account deficit; (d) a zero current account balance.

31 Which of the following policies are compatible? (a) those designed to eliminate inflation and a current account deficit; (b) those utilized to eliminate unemployment and a trade surplus; (c) both of the above; (d) neither of the above.

32 Which of the following policies conflict? (a) those designed to reduce unemployment and a trade deficit; (b) those designed to reduce inflation and a trade surplus; (c) both of the above; (d) neither of the above.

33 Which of the following would (if there were no retaliation) enable a nation to reduce both unemployment and a current-account deficit? (a) a reduction in its tariffs and the devaluation of its currency; (b) a reduction in its tariffs and the revaluation of its currency; (c) an increase in its tariffs and the devaluation of its currency; (d) an increase in its tariffs and the revaluation of its currency.

34 An easy money policy will (a) expand output and employment and increase interest rates in the economy; (b) expand output and employment and decrease interest rates in the economy; (c) contract output and employment and increase interest rates in the economy; (d) contract output and employment and decrease interest rates in the economy.

DISCUSSION QUESTIONS

1 What is foreign exchange and the foreign-exchange rate? Who are the demanders and suppliers of a particular foreign exchange, say, the French franc? Why is a buyer (demander) in the foreign-exchange markets always a seller (supplier) also?

2 What is meant when it is said that "a nation's exports pay for its imports"? Do nations pay for all their imports with exports?

3 What is a balance of international payments? What are the principal sections of a nation's balance of payments? What are the three kinds of exports and imports listed in it?

4 How does a capital account surplus cause a current account deficit? How does a nation finance a balance of payments deficit and what does it do with a balance of payments surplus?

5 Is it good or bad for a nation to have a balance of payments deficit or surplus?

6 What types of events cause the exchange rate for a foreign currency to appreciate or depreciate? How will each of these events affect the exchange rate for a foreign money and for a nation's own money?

7 How can freely floating foreign-exchange rates eliminate balance of payments deficits and surpluses? What are the problems associated with this method of correcting payments imbalances?

8 How may a nation employ its foreign-exchange reserves to fix or "peg" foreign-exchange rates? Be precise. How does a nation obtain or acquire these official international reserves?

9 What kinds of trade controls may nations with payments deficits employ to eliminate their deficits?

10 How can foreign-exchange controls be used to overcome a payments deficit? Why do such exchange controls necessarily involve the rationing of foreign exchange? What effect do these controls have upon prices, output, and employment in nations that use them?

11 If foreign-exchange rates are fixed, what kind of domestic macroeconomic adjustments are required to eliminate a payments deficit? To eliminate a payments surplus?

12 When was a nation on the gold standard? How did the international gold standard correct payments imbalances? What were the disadvantages of this method of eliminating payments deficits and surpluses?

13 Why does the operation of the international gold standard ensure relatively stable

foreign-exchange rates, that is, rates that fluctuate only within very narrow limits? What are the limits, and what are the advantages of stable exchange rates?

14 What is the "critical difference" between the adjustment necessary to correct payments deficits and surpluses under the gold standard and those necessary when exchange rates are flexible? How did this difference lead to the demise of the gold standard during the 1930s?

15 Explain (a) why the International Monetary Fund was established, and what the objectives of the adjustable-pegs (or Bretton Woods) system were; (b) what the adjustable-peg system was, and the basic means it employed to stabilize exchange rates in the short run; and (c) when and how the system was to adjust exchange rates in the long run.

16 What did nations use as official international reserves under the Bretton Woods system? Why was the dollar used by nations as an international money, and how could they acquire additional dollars?

17 Explain the dilemma created by the need for expanding official international reserves and for maintaining the status of the U.S. dollar.

18 Why and how did the United Stated shatter the Bretton Woods system in 1971? If the international value of the U.S. dollar is no longer determined by the amount of gold for which it can be changed, what does determine its value?

19 Explain what is meant by a managed floating system of foreign exchange rates. When are exchange rates managed, and when are they allowed to float?

20 Explain the arguments of the proponents and the critics of the managed floating system.

21 What domestic and international goals is

the economy assumed to have? Which of these goals is assumed to have the higher priority?

22 Explain when (and why) the policies employed by a nation to reduce unemployment or inflation conflict, and when (and why) they are compatible with the elimination of trade deficits or surpluses.

23 What might a nation do to lessen the incompatibility of its domestic and international economic goals?

31

FOREIGN INVESTMENT IN CANADA

As the preceding two chapters have surely made clear, international trade is of prime importance to Canada. Keeping foreign investment to the last of these three chapters is *not* meant to suggest it is a subsidiary or lesser aspect of Canada's foreign dealings. Quite the contrary: the effects of foreign investment on Canada are all-pervasive, overwhelming. Having a well-thought-out policy on foreign investment, firmly based on the analysis of its economic effects, *should* be a matter of the highest priority for every Canadian government. It is the object of this chapter to analyse foreign investment in the light of the economic principles studied in the previous 30 chapters.

Chapter 30, on the balance of payments, is an essential prerequisite to this one. Ignoring the effect of foreign investment on the balance of payments and consequently on the international value of the Canadian dollar is at the root of most misconceptions concerning the *total* effect of foreign investment.

The two types of foreign investment, direct and portfolio, are first defined. The analysis that follows concerning the balance-of-payments effect of foreign investment is important: it should serve to dispel the notion that foreign investment is costless and always implies a net addition to Canada's supply of foreign exchange. On the contrary, not only can foreign direct investment occur without Canada gaining *any* foreign exchange, but a successful direct investment will be a potential or actual *continuously increasing* charge on Canada's foreign exchange. It is true that the direct investment

may, in a sense, pay for itself through increased exports, but the more successful the foreign-owned business is, either in exporting or in supplying the Canadian domestic market, the greater will become the foreign stake in Canada, and the more Canada will have to export in the future should Canadians ever decide to buy back their economy. This section ends with a discussion of the employment effect of foreign investment and notes that it is by no means always favourable.

The next section analyses the circumstance that justifies a country seeking foreign investment. It is easily stated: a country that cannot earn through its exports enough foreign capital equipment imports to develop at the rate it desires must encourage foreign investment. Canada, however, has been a successful exporter for centuries. Thus Canada has not needed to encourage foreign investment for centuries! Yet Canada is *the* major international debtor per capita among industrialized nations.

The present percentage of foreign ownership of Canadian industries is briefly surveyed before a longer section explains how it came about that a country that never needed to be a debtor has so evidently become one. It is fundamentally important to understand that a government's time horizon is bounded by the next election. If it appears that encouraging foreign investment will create new jobs, then foreign investment will be encouraged, for jobs mean votes. The relevance here of the fallacy of composition and of how foreign investment can displace domestic investment should both be noted.

Though Canada's present international indebtedness is huge—and growing more rapidly than ever in absolute terms—you should note carefully that, relative to GNP, Canada's indebtedness has been much greater in the past. The percentages of Table 31-4 bear careful study. You should also note, however, that the continually growing direct investment is, in total, occurring entirely through reinvestment: decade by decade, billions more flow out of Canada as dividends than flow in as new direct investment.

It is important to note why Canada has grown faster in the past while *exporting* capital (investing net abroad). The case against direct investment, because of its employment- and growth-reducing effects, is made briefly, but is none the less important.

The chapter concludes with an analysis of Canada's capacity for getting out of debt and the means of doing so. The last section is controversial, not because of the analysis—after all, the *only* way for Canada to repay its foreign debts is to earn foreign exchange by attaining sizable current account surpluses—but because it remains the policy of every government in Canada, federal, provincial, and municipal, to continue to increase Canada's indebtedness.

CHECK LIST

When you have studied this chapter you should be able to

☐ Define and distinguish between direct and portfolio investment.

☐ Explain the balance-of-payments effect of a foreign investment, with regard both to the usual initial inflow of foreign funds and to the eventual transfer effect or burden.

☐ Explain how, working through the foreign-exchange rate, all inflows of funds for foreign investment in Canada always decrease Canada's net exports by an equal amount.

☐ Explain when a country needs foreign investment and how a successful exporting country can always earn enough foreign exchange not to need foreign investment.

☐ State the present extent of foreign ownership in Canada's major industrial sectors.

☐ List Canada's eight staple exports.

☐ Explain why New England's economic elite developed differently, and more successfully, than Canada's.

☐ State the major provisions of the Regional Development Incentives Act.

☐ State the basic reason all governments in Canada encourage direct investment.

☐ Explain how foreign direct investment can displace domestic investment.

☐ State Canada's net international indebtedness as a percent of GNP in 1930 and in 1986.

☐ Explain how Canada's real GNP grew so rapidly from 1942 to 1944 while Canada was investing net abroad or giving away a total of $3,372 million and while almost a million men and women were in uniform and thus out of the civilian labour force.

☐ Explain the fallacy of composition as applied to foreign investment.

☐ List the possible harmful effects of direct investment.

☐ Explain why the international value of the Canadian dollar must not be held up by central bank action if Canada is to begin reducing its net international indebtedness.

☐ Explain, with reference to the elasticity of demand, when export taxes are appropriate.

☐ Explain how Canada could earn a strong dollar.

CHAPTER OUTLINE

1 There are two fundamental types of foreign investment, direct and portfolio.

a. Direct investment always implies non-

resident control and sufficient ownership to ensure that control; it is accomplished
(1) by non-residents establishing a new firm or
(2) by non-residents taking over an already existing Canadian-owned firm, or
(3) through growth of a non-resident-owned firm.
b. Portfolio investment is the non-resident buying of shares (but not enough for control) and of bonds, for the sake of dividends, interest and capital gains.

2 *The transfer effect* or *transfer burden* has nothing to do with government transfer payments but is the cost of foreign investment in terms of the outflow or transfer abroad of interest and dividends. *The balance-of-payments effect* is a broader term: it is both the inflow of foreign funds that usually—but not necessarily—accompanies a takeover or the establishment of a new foreign-controlled firm, and the resulting transfer effect outflow of interest and dividends abroad.

3 An inflow of funds for foreign investment in Canada pushes up the international value of the Canadian dollar and, other things equal, *necessarily* causes a decline in net exports equal to the capital inflow.

4 A country needs foreign investment when it cannot earn enough foreign exchange to buy the foreign capital equipment or services it needs to develop. However, a country, such as Canada, that has many goods in high international demand, need not be an international debtor. It has but to use its foreign-exchange reserves to buy the foreign capital equipment it requires. If it lets its currency float, this loss of reserves will lead to speculation against its currency until its international value has decreased sufficiently to bring foreign trade back into balance: imports of non-essentials will decrease while exports will increase.

5 In 1984 the percentage of assets in corporations controlled by non-residents was 51% for manufacturing, 50% for petroleum and natural gas, and 41% for mining and smelting. No other industrialized nation has so encouraged foreign investment as has Canada; no other has so large a proportion of its industry foreign-owned.

6 Canada has remained a staple (raw material) exporter because of the colonial mentality of her economic elite of merchants and financiers, who preferred assured markets first in France, later in England, and now in the United States, to taking the risks of industrial development. The northeastern United States, on the other hand, is supreme in international economic affairs because, having no staples desired by the mother country, the Yankee entrepreneurs were forced from the very first generation 340 years ago to roam the North Atlantic selling their produce where they could and establishing commercial ties wherever they went.

7 More than a hundred years ago, the Bank of Montreal was lending vast amounts of Canadian savings in New York rather than backing Canadian entrepreneurs. This Canadian banking pattern has not changed to this day. It is still often considered more profitable to lend to foreign corporations, including the large number of foreign-owned ones now established in Canada, than to Canadian-owned businesses. The governments of Canada and the provinces also encourage foreign investment in Canada with grants, low-cost loans, lower taxes, and other incentives.

8 Ottawa and the provinces behave thus because of their belief that foreign investment results in more jobs in Canada. No account is taken of the fact that Canadian savings diverted to foreign investors cannot then be used for investment by Canadians.

9 The only time foreign direct investment does not *directly* displace Canadian investment is when the foreign investment is entirely financed from abroad. However, overwhelmingly, foreign direct investment is now financed *within* Canada. In the twenty-seven year period 1960–1986, the excess of the outflow of dividends (*net* of withholding tax) over the inflow of foreign capital for new direct investment was more than $36 billion. The *book* value of Canada's *net* international indebtedness rose from $35.4 billion at the end of 1974 to $185 billion just twelve years later. Moreover, in this time of inflation, the *market* value of Canada's net indebtedness has probably reached $350 billion. However, the book value of net indebtedness as a percentage of current dollar GNP was only 37% in 1986, compared to 1930's 114%. Thus, it is still possible for Canadians to buy back control of their economy, should they desire to do so.

10 Canada grew rapidly during World War II while her net indebtedness was decreasing in absolute terms (and even more so relative to GNP). Thus Canada did not need foreign investment to grow far more rapidly than it has ever done since and, indeed, during this period, was a net investor abroad. Investing abroad stimulates Canada's exports and, therefore, its economic growth.

11 The fallacy of composition is relevant to a consideration of the effects of foreign investment. Provided one ignores, as governments do, the offsetting decrease in net exports caused by an inflow of foreign investment funds, practically any proposed foreign investment can be justified on job-creating grounds *in isolation*. Yet the *total* effects of foreign investment can be harmful. Canadian savings lent to foreign investors in Canada subtract from the savings available to domestic investors. And foreign money invested in Canada must be repaid through constantly increased exports—or such investment will compound forever through re-

investment. Moreover, foreign subsidiaries are far more import-prone than Canadian-owned firms.

12 If Canada had a zero balance of international indebtedness, the import-inducing nature of direct investment in Canada would be balanced by the export-inducing nature of Canadian investment abroad. To achieve this zero balance, Canada need only stop encouraging foreign investment and start discouraging it by lowering interest rates to the United States, levels and by gradually raising the withholding tax on interest and dividends paid to non-residents. This would depress the Canadian dollar, possibly as low as U.S. $.65, greatly increasing Canadian net exports until a current account surplus was achieved —provided Canadian business *knew* that it was now government policy no longer to force the Canadian dollar to an artificially high level against the U.S. dollar by encouraging net inflows on capital account. Thus Canada would gain the foreign exchange necessary to achieve a *deficit* on the capital account—indicating Canada was repatriating Canadian bonds and shares held abroad. As the Canadian dollar dropped in international value, export taxes would have to be placed on Canadian exports in inelastic foreign demand to ensure Canada's foreign-exchange earnings did not drop as the dollar dropped.

13 Once Canada had reduced its net international indebtedness to zero, there would no longer be a net outflow of interest and dividends on current account and no further requirement for a net outflow on capital account. Then the Canadian dollar could rise again in international value, which would allow Canada to buy cheap and sell dear abroad. But this strong dollar has to be *earned* through successful exporting and import-replacement. It is not earned through the massive foreign borrowings of 1975–1981 that have returned after 1983 as the recession receded and imports increased.

IMPORTANT TERMS

Direct investment

Portfolio investment

Balance-of-payments effect

Transfer burden or effect

Net international debtor

Forced "savings"

Staple exports

Staple trap

Colonial mentality

Regional Development Incentives Act

Export taxes

FILL-IN QUESTIONS

1 The two fundamental types of foreign investment are _____ and _____ .

2 Direct investment always implies foreign _____ and sufficient _____ to ensure this _____ .
Portfolio investment, on the other hand, is the buying of _____ and _____ for the sake of _____, _____, and _____. To the extent that partial ownership is gained through the buying of _____, the quantity bought is insufficient for _____ .

3 The three types of direct investment are non-residents

_____ ,

_____ ,

_____ .

4 Which type of direct investment is *not* considered "investment" as economists define the term? _____

5 The balance-of-payments effect refers to the usual inflow of _____ when a foreign investment is initiated and to the

subsequent continuous outflow of _____ so long as the investment exists in the case of a loan or as long as the investment is profitable in the case of shares or _____ .

6 The transfer effect is also called the transfer _____. It refers to the (in, out) _____-flow of _____ _____ as a result of a foreign investment.

7 An inflow of funds for foreign investment in Canada drives (up, down) _____ the international value of the Canadian dollar so that, other things equal, Canadian net _____ are (increased, decreased) _____ by an amount equal to the foreign investment inflow. Thus, if the foreign investment is a portfolio investment, a takeover, or an especially capital intensive direct investment in a new or growing foreign-owned plant, the net result of the foreign investment inflow will be to increase, decrease, not change) _____ Canadian employment.

8 It (is, is not) _____ possible for a foreign investment to occur in Canada without the use of foreign funds. The federal and provincial governments (do, do not) _____ make grants and loans to foreign investors in Canada. Canadian banks (do, do not) _____ make loans to foreign investors and (do, do not) _____ assist in the taking over of Canadian businesses and the setting up of new foreign-owned companies.

9 A country needs foreign investment when it wishes to develop and cannot earn the _____ needed to buy foreign _____ .

Thus a country that can achieve an export _____ in goods and services never needs to be a net international _____.

10 If a normally successful exporting country cannot achieve sufficient exports at the present foreign exchange rate for its currency, it can, despite this, increase its imports of capital equipment, thus running down its _____ and causing an eventual (decrease, increase) _____ in the international value of its _____ , leading to an increase in its net _____ .

11 The percentage of the assets of Canadian industry in foreign-controlled corporations is _____ %; for petroleum and natural gas the percentage is _____ %; for manufacturing it is _____ %; and for mining and smelting it is _____ %.

12 Canada's concentration on the export of raw materials is related to the _____ mentality of Canada's _____ and _____ economic elite.

13 Canada has (always, never) _____ been short of savings. Canada's problem is that its governments and banks often prefer to lend to _____ corporations.

14 Canada's governments at all levels encourage foreign investment in the belief that it will create _____. No account is taken of the fact that foreign investment may displace _____ or that the inflow of foreign funds will force (up, down) _____ the exchange rate, creating a current account (deficit, surplus) _____.

15 From 1960 to 1986, the excess of the outflow of dividends (net of withholding tax) over the net inflow for new investment was more than $ _____ .

16 Canada's net international indebtedness at the end of 1986 came to $_____ at _____ value. The market value was probably close to $_____. As a percentage of GNP, it was _____ and this is several times (higher, lower) _____ than it has been in the past. However, this is relevant only if all our GNP is readily (exportable, importable) _____ .

17 During the 1940s, while Canada was a net (exporter, importer) _____ of capital, its rate of economic growth was higher than in any subsequent decade while Canada has been a net (exporter, importer) _____ of capital.

18 Placing an export tax on goods in inelastic foreign demand would (increase, decrease) _____ the foreign exchange Canada derives from such exports.

19 To get out of debt, Canada must achieve sizable current account _____. Repayment of international debt implies having a capital account _____ .

PROBLEMS AND PROJECTS

1 In column 1 in the table on the next page is given in modified form the balance (exports less imports of goods and services, inflows less outflows of capital) of Canada's 1985 balance of payments—a year in which the current account deficit was, because of the lingering recession, still abnormally low

| | | Balances (in billions of dollars) | | |
	(1) Debtor	(2) Repayer	(3) Zero balance	(4) Creditor
Current Account				
Merchandise	$ + 17.5	$_____	$_____	$_____
Services				
— travel	$ −2.1	$_____	$_____	$_____
— freight & shipping	$ +0.5	$_____	$_____	$_____
— business services	$ −2.1	$_____	$_____	$_____
— government transactions	$ −0.7	$_____	$_____	$_____
— other services	$ +0.1	$_____	$_____	$_____
Services balance	$ −4.3	$_____	$_____	$_____
Investment income (interest & dividends)	$ −14.6	$_____	$_____	$_____
Transfers	$ +0.8	$_____	$_____	$_____
Current Account balance	$ −0.6	$_____	$_____	$_____
Capital Account balance	$ +0.6	$_____	$_____	$_____

(compared to the "normal" massive deficit of 1986). The statistical discrepancy of $5.5 billion has been subtracted from the capital account surplus.

(a) In column 2 (Repayer), insert figures showing what would have been Canada's 1985 balance of payments had Canada adopted a policy of reducing its net international indebtedness. Make the following assumptions:

(i) Because of a lower international value of the Canadian dollar, the travel (tourist) balance is zero;

(ii) All other Services balances are unchanged;

(iii) The Current Account surplus is $8.0 billion;

(iv) The Capital Account outflow is $8.0 billion.

(b) In column 3 (Zero balance), insert figures showing what would be Canada's balance of payments, say, 25 years after adopting a policy of debt repayment by which time Canada has achieved, let us suppose, a zero balance of net international in-

debtedness. Make the following assumptions:

(i) The Current Account and the Capital Account are individually in balance and there is no change in Canada's foreign exchange reserves.

(ii) All the services ("invisibles") are individually in balance.

(c) In column 4 (Creditor), insert figures showing Canada's position one year after the column 3 position, assuming there are no changes except that Canada achieves a merchandise trade surplus of $15 billion and decides to invest the entire proceeds abroad.

SELF-TEST

Circle T if the statement is true, F if it is false.

1   Direct investment always implies more than 50% ownership.   T   F

2   A takeover by non-residents of a previously Canadian-owned firm is an example of portfolio investment.   T   F

3 All three forms of direct investment meet the economist's definition of investment. **T F**

4 Portfolio investment is not investment as an economist defines investment. **T F**

5 Portfolio investment is accomplished by non-residents buying shares and bonds. **T F**

6 The transfer burden or transfer effect of foreign investment is its cost in terms of the outflow abroad of interest and dividends. **T F**

7 Working through the foreign-exchange rate, an inflow of funds for investment in Canada increases Canada's net exports. **T F**

8 A country with a current account surplus does not need a net inflow of foreign investment. **T F**

9 Seventy percent of Canada's manufacturing assets are in foreign-controlled corporations. **T F**

10 Canada is a successful staple exporter. **T F**

11 Canada's indigenous economic elite are merchants and financiers, not captains of industry. **T F**

12 In Canada, as in the United States, Germany, and Japan, the major economic governmental policies favouring their economic elites have also favoured the countries themselves. **T F**

13 In mid-nineteenth century, the Bank of Montreal was acting as the channel for large Canadian direct investments in New York. **T F**

14 Non-residents can make direct investments in Canada without putting up a cent of their own money, the entire investment being Canadian savings and grants. **T F**

15 Under the Federal Regional Development Incentives Act, grants may only be made to Canadian residents. **T F**

16 The inflow of foreign currency during the past 20 years for new direct investment was greater than the outflow of dividends. **T F**

17 At the end of 1986, the book value of Canada's net international indebtedness as a percentage of GNP was approximately one-third as high as it had been 60 years earlier. **T F**

18 During the 1940s, Canada was a net exporter of capital. **T F**

19 During World War II, Canada showed herself capable of full employment and very fast economic growth while reducing her net international indebtedness. **T F**

20 Foreign subsidiaries in Canada are more import-prone than their Canadian-owned domestic competitors. **T F**

21 If the Canadian dollar's value sank to U.S. $0.65, Canada would derive nothing but benefits. **T F**

22 As the Canadian dollar's international value drops, export taxes should be placed on all goods in elastic foreign demand. **T F**

23 A strong dollar can only be earned through capital account surpluses. **T F**

Circle the letter that corresponds to the best answer.

1 Which of the following is a portfolio investment? (*a*) establishment of a new firm in Canada by non-residents; (*b*) buying of bonds by non-residents; (*c*) takeover of an existing Canada firm by non-residents; (*d*) reinvestment of a firm's profits in new capital equipment by its non-resident owners.

2 To Canada, foreign exchange (*a*) is Canadian dollars held by non-residents; (*b*) entirely in the form of gold; (*c*) represents real wealth; (*d*) represents command over foreign goods and services; (*e*) both *c* and *d*.

3 The balance of payments effect is (a) both the inflow of funds usually accompanying a foreign investment as well as the subsequent transfer effect; (b) equivalent to the transfer effect; (c) equivalent to the transfer burden; (d) both b and c.

4 An inflow of foreign funds for investment in Canada, other things equal, creates both a capital account (a) surplus and a current account surplus; (b) surplus and a current account deficit; (c) deficit and a current account deficit; (d) deficit and a current account surplus.

5 A "staple trap" occurs when (a) a country's diversification is limited to developing new staple exports; (b) the demand for a country's exported staple is inelastic and it tries to earn more foreign exchange by increasing exports of this staple; (c) the demand for a country's exported staple is elastic and it tries to earn more foreign exchange by increasing exports of this staple; (d) the supply of a staple export is inelastic; (e) the supply of a staple export is elastic.

6 Which of the following statements is *not* correct? Under the Regional Development Incentives Act, the federal government will (a) make capital grants amounting to 25% of approved capital costs; (b) make grants only to Canadian-owned businesses; (c) make grants of $30,000 for each job created; (d) allow the non-resident investor to receive a government grant even if the rest of the capital is also raised in Canada.

7 During the 27 years, 1960–1986, the sum of net capital inflow for new direct investment in Canada less payment of dividends (net of withholding tax) to non-residents was (a) minus $35 billion; (b) minus $1 billion; (c) zero; (d) plus $1 billion; (e) plus $35 billion.

8 In 1986, as a percentage of GNP, which of the following had grown by more than 100% since 1975? (a) current account investment income negative balance; (b) current account non-merchandise transactions negative balance; (c) current account negative balance; (d) net international indebtedness; (e) both a and b.

9 In which of the following years was Canada's net international indebtedness, at book value, at its lowest level as a percentage of GNP? (a) 1926; (b) 1930; (c) 1950; (d) 1975; (e) 1978.

10 When did Canada's net international indebtedness, at book value, decrease? (a) from 1926 to 1930; (b) from 1930 to 1945; (c) from 1945 to 1956; (d) from 1956 to 1976; (e) none of the above.

DISCUSSION QUESTIONS

1 Why is it that a country that has many goods in high international demand need never be a net international debtor?

2 Contrast the transfer burden of direct and of portfolio investments in prosperous times and, alternatively, during a depression.

3 How can foreign investment in Canada grow each year by *more* than the capital account surplus?

4 How could an inflow of foreign funds for direct investment that in itself creates jobs have the total effect of decreasing jobs in Canada?

5 In comparing the development of the economic elites of Canada and the northeastern United States, what is meant by "New England's fortunate lack of staples"?

6 Explain the staple trap and how it is that though Canada can be described as a permanent staple exporter, she avoids the trap.

7 What is meant by "a persistent colonial mentality" in Canada, and how has this affected Canada's development?

8 Contrast the economic effects of the channelling of Canadian savings to the New

York money market by the Bank of Montreal in the 1860s to the Canadian banks' assistance to foreign investors in Canada today.

9 Explain how Michelin's "foreign investment" in Nova Scotia, carried out entirely with Canadian savings, may in the long run be of greater benefit to Canada than a foreign investment in a Canadian mine carried out entirely with foreign currency.

10 How is it that, despite the conventional view of foreign investment as being essential for her growth, Canada achieved a very high rate of growth of real GNP during World War II while her net international indebtedness was dropping?

11 Explain how the fallacy of composition relates to government encouragement of foreign investment in Canada.

12 Since practically any investment creates jobs and is therefore better than no investment, how can foreign investment ever be decribed as harmful?

13 Why must the international value of the Canadian dollar be at U.S. $0.70, or lower, for Canada to be able to start decreasing her net international indebtedness?

14 If it is true that, viewed in isolation, a policy of discouraging foreign investment might also discourage domestic investment, how can such a policy work without massive unemployment?

15 With the Canadian dollar dropping in international value, what is the economic rationale for placing export taxes on goods in inelastic foreign demand? When should export taxes be placed on goods in *elastic* foreign demand?

16 How might Canada earn a strong dollar (that is, one worth more than U.S. $1.00)? Why was it incorrect to talk of a strong Canadian dollar in mid-1976 when its value was U.S. $1.03?

17 Why might Canadians prefer to have a strong dollar, assuming they can earn it?

18 What effect does the drop in the international value of the Canadian dollar have on Canada's inflation rate?

19 How might a policy of reducing Canada's net international indebtedness help achieve Canada's goals of fast economic growth and full employment?

32

THE ECONOMICS OF GROWTH

This is the first of three chapters dealing with the important and controversial topic of economic growth. Chapter 32 presents the theory of growth; Chapter 33 examines the Canadian economic growth record and the debate surrounding further growth in Canada; Chapter 36 explains the special problems that underdeveloped nations encounter in their attempts to grow.

The purpose of Chapter 32 is to explain what makes economic growth possible. After briefly defining and pointing out the significance of growth, the text analyses the six factors that make growth possible. The four *supply* factors increase the output potential of the economy. Whether the economy actually produces its full potential—that is, whether the economy has both full employment and full production—depends upon the two other factors: the level of aggregate expenditures (the *demand* factor) and the efficiency with which the economy reallocates resources (the *allocative* factor).

The crucial thing to note about the supply factors is that when labour increases more rapidly than natural resources, or capital, or both of these, the economy is subject to diminishing returns and eventually to decreasing output per worker and to a declining standard of living. This will breed the misery and poverty forecast by Malthus more than 185 years ago. Diminishing returns can, however, be offset—and more than offset—by increasing the productivity of labour. The productivity of labour is improved by expanding the stock of capital, by technological progress, and by improvements in the *quality* of the labour force and of management. Diminishing returns have been *more*

than offset by those nations that have experienced economic growth. The nations that have not experienced growth have found the force of diminishing returns too great for them: their improvements in technology, capital, and labour just barely offset the effect of diminishing returns.

Probably the most important principle or generalization developed in the chapter employs the theory of employment presented in Chapter 25. Here we discover that the maintenance of full employment in an economy whose productive capacity is increasing annually requires that investment increase annually to ensure sufficient aggregate expenditures for the expanding full employment output. And because investment increases an economy's productive capacity, not only must investment increase from year to year, but it must also increase by increasing amounts to assure the production of the full employment output. You must be sure you understand the "why" of this principle, because it is fundamental to an understanding of full-employment without inflation in a growing economy.

Actually, Chapter 32 contains very little that is really new. It uses a few of the ideas, terms, and theories found in earlier chapters to explain what makes an economy capable of growing (that is, what increases the size of its full-employment or capacity output) and what is necessary if it is actually to grow (that is, if it is to produce all its expanding capacity allows). With careful reading, you should have little or no trouble with Chapter 32, providing you have done a good job on the earlier chapters and providing you keep in mind the fundamental distinction between the supply factors and the demand and allocative factors.

CHECK LIST

When you have studied this chapter you should be able to
☐ Distinguish between employment theory and growth economics.
☐ Define economic growth in two different ways.
☐ Explain why economic growth is important to any economy.
☐ Identify the four supply factors in economic growth.
☐ State the law of diminishing returns.
☐ State the Malthusian thesis and explain why Malthus reached this conclusion.
☐ Explain how the effects of diminishing returns on the standard of living can be offset or forestalled.
☐ Contrast the income-creating and capacity-creating effects of net investment.
☐ Calculate the full-employment rate of growth when you are supplied with the needed data; explain why GDP must grow at this rate to maintain full employment.
☐ Outline the three types of economic policies that might be utilized to stimulate economic growth in Canada.

CHAPTER OUTLINE

1 While employment theory is concerned with the short run and an economy with a fixed productive capacity, growth economics deals with the long run and changes in productive capacity over time.
a. Economic growth means an increase in either the total or the per capita real output of an economy; and is measured in terms of the annual percentage rate of growth of either total or per capita real output.
b. Economic growth is important because it lessens the burden of scarcity: it provides the means of satisfying existing wants more fully and of fulfilling new wants.

c. One or two percentage point differences in the rate of growth result in substantial differences in annual increases in the economy's output.

2 Whether economic growth *can* occur depends upon four supply factors (or, said another way, upon the quantity of labour employed and the productivity of labour); and whether it will occur depends upon the demand factor and the allocative factor.

3 The classical model of economic growth analysed the effects of population growth and diminishing returns upon total and per capita real output.
a. In an economy where the quantities of land and capital are relatively fixed, the law of diminishing returns operates so that increases in the quantity of labour employed eventually result in a decline in output per worker (the productivity of labour).
b. The optimum population is the population at which the output per worker (per capita output and income) is a maximum.
c. Because of diminishing returns and the tendency for population to increase, Malthus predicted widespread poverty as time passed.

4 But growth can occur and poverty can be avoided if diminishing returns are offset by the increases in the productivity of workers that are brought about by more capital, technological progress, and improvements in the quality of the labour force and management.

5 The amounts the actual output of the economy increases depends not only upon the supply factors but also upon the demand factor.
a. To maintain full employment without inflation, aggregate expenditures must grow at the same rate as the economy's productive capacity.
b. In the simple macroeconomic growth model, the full-employment rate of growth equals the average propensity to save divided by the capital-output ratio; achievement of

the full-employment rate of growth requires that net investment grow at the same rate.

6 For economic growth to be possible, the economy must also be capable of reallocating its resources with reasonable speed and completeness.

7 To stimulate economic growth in the Canadian economy, Keynesians stress policies that would expand aggregate expenditures and constrain government spending and consumption; supply-side economists stress policies that would expand the economy's capacity output by increasing saving, investment, work effort, and risk-taking; and others advocate the use of an industrial policy that would shape the structure and the composition of industry in the economy.

IMPORTANT TERMS

Economic growth

Supply factor

Demand factor

Allocative factor

Law of diminishing returns

Average product

Increasing returns

Optimum population

Labour productivity

Income-creating aspect of investment

Capacity-creating aspect of investment

Capital-output ratio

Full-employment rate of growth

Industrial policy

FILL-IN QUESTIONS

1 Employment theory assumes that the productive capacity of the economy is (fixed, variable) _____, while growth economics is concerned with an economy whose productive capacity (increases, remains constant) _____ over time.

2 Economic growth can mean an increase in either the _____ or the _____ of an economy.

3 A rise in output per capita (increases, decreases) _____ the standard of living and _____ the burden of scarcity in the economy.

4 Assume that an economy has a GDP of $400 billion. If the growth rate is 6%, GDP will increase by $ _____ billion a year; but if the rate of growth is only 4%, the annual increase in GDP will be $_____ billion. A two-percentage-point difference in the growth rate results in a $ _____ billion difference in the annual increase in GDP.

5 The four supply factors in economic growth are _____ , _____ , _____ , and _____ . The other two factors are the _____ _____ factor and the _____ factor.

6 The law of diminishing returns states that when additional equal quantities of labour are used with fixed quantities of other resources, (beyond some point) the _____ per worker or the (total, average) _____ product of labour will diminish.

7 The population size that results in the maximum output per worker (or the maximum average product of labour) is the _____.

8 Malthus predicted that because of diminishing returns and the tendency for the _____ of an economy to increase, the standard of living would _____.

9 The tendency for the standard of living to fall as the population increases can be lessened or even overcome by increasing the _____ of workers. The three principal means of doing this are to increase the stock of _____ , to improve _____ , and to improve the quality of _____ .

10 In an economy increasing its productive capacity each year, it is necessary that _____ increase by the right amount each year if full employment is to be maintained.

11 Expenditures for new capital goods both increase _____ and add to the _____ of the economy; the amount by which investment expenditures expand the latter depend upon the volume of investment expenditures and the _____ _____ .

12 To have the economic growth that the supply and demand factors make possible, an economy must also be able to _____ its resources from one use to another.

13 To stimulate economic growth in Canada,
a. Keynesians stress the (supply, demand) _____-side of growth, favour (high, low) _____ interest rates to expand _____ spending, and would use fiscal policies to (expand, contract) _____ government spending and consumption;
b. supply-side economists stress policies that would stimulate _____ , _____ , _____ , and entrepreneurial _____ to expand (aggregate expenditures, capacity output) _____ .

c. Others stress policies that would shape the _____ and _____ of Canadian industry and are called _____ policy.

PROBLEMS AND PROJECTS

1 If, between 1984 and 1985,
a. the real GDP increased from $375 billion to $390 billion, it increased at a rate of _____ %;
b. the real GDP per capita increased from $15,000 to $15,450, it increased at a rate of _____ %.

2 The table below shows the total production of an economy as the quantity of labour employed increases. The quantities of all other resources employed are constant.

Units of labour	Total production	Average product of labour
0	0	0
1	80	_____
2	200	_____
3	330	_____
4	400	_____
5	450	_____
6	480	_____
7	490	_____
8	480	_____

a. Compute the average products of labour and enter them in the table.
b. There are increasing returns from the first to the _____ unit of labour, and decreasing returns from the _____ to the eighth unit.
c. The optimum population in this economy would be _____ units of labour, because with this many units of labour, the

(total, average) _____ output of labour is a maximum.

3 Column 1 of the table below lists the various quantities of labour an economy might employ. Columns 2 and 3 show total production and the average product of labour for each quantity of labour, respectively.

(1)	(2)	(3)	(4) New	(5) New
Quantity of labour	Total production	Average product of labour	total production	average product of labour
0	0	0	0	0
1	80	80	100	_____
2	200	100	220	_____
3	330	110	360	_____
4	400	100	500	_____
5	450	90	600	_____
6	480	80	660	_____
7	490	70	700	_____
8	480	60	720	_____

a. Assume the economy has and employs 4 units of labour. The average product of labour is _____ .

b. Now suppose that a rise in the productivity of workers increases the figures shown in column 2 to those in column 4. Compute the new average products of labour and enter them in column 5.

c. If the economy continued to employ 4 units of labour, the average productivity of labour would have increased by _____ %.

d. As a result of this increase in productivity, the optimum population for this economy has (increased, decreased) _____ from 3 to _____ units of labour.

e. If, while the productivity of workers increased, the number of units of labour this economy had, and employed, increased from 4 to

(1) 5, the average product of labour would have (increased, decreased) _____ from 100 to _____ ;

(2) 7, the average product of labour would have _____ ;

(3) 8, the average product of labour would have _____ .

4 Assume that, in an economy in which aggregate expenditures contain only consumption and net investment components, the average propensity to consume is 0.80; that in year 1, the economy's equilibrium output (GDP) is its full-employment of $1,000; and that the supply factors make it possible for the full-employment output to increase at a rate of 10% per year.

a. Complete the table below by computing
(1) the full-employment output in year 2 and in year 3;
(2) the amounts that would be spent for consumption and saved if the economy produced its full-employment output in year 2 and year 3;
(3) the amounts that would have to be invested and aggregate expenditures in years 2 and 3 if the equilibrium output of the econo-

		Full employment			
Year	Output (GDP)	Consumption	Saving	Investment	Aggregate expenditures $(C + I)$
1	$1,000	$800	$200	$200	$1,000
2	_____	_____	_____	_____	_____
3	_____	_____	_____	_____	_____

my is to equal its full-employment output. (Investment will have to be equal to the saving done when the economy produces a full-employment output; $C + I$ must equal the full-employment output.)

b. Examination of the table completed in a reveals that, to maintain full employment in an economy in which the average propensity to save is a constant and in which the full-employment output is growing at the rate of 10% annually,

(1) aggregate expenditures must grow at a rate of _____% per year; and
(2) net investment must grow at an annual rate of _____%.

c. Further examination of the completed table in a shows that when the
(1) average propensity to consume is constant and equal to 0.8, the *marginal* propensity to consume is equal to _____.
(2) average propensity to save is constant and equal to 0.2, the *marginal* propensity to save is equal to _____.

d. Employing your knowledge of the multiplier, had net investment increased by 5% from $200 to $210 between year 1 and year 2, the equilibrium output of the economy would have increased from $1,000 to $_____.

(1) This is a _____% increase in GDP.
(2) The equilibrium GDP is (greater than, less than, equal to) _____ the full-employment output of the economy.
(3) In year 2, there will be (recession, inflation) _____ in the economy.

e. Still employing the multiplier, if net investment increased by 15% from $200 to $230 between year 1 and year 2, the equilibrium output of the economy would have tried to increase from $1,000 to $_____.
(1) This equilibrium output is (greater than, less than, equal to) _____ the full-employment output and (can, cannot) _____ actually be produced.

(2) In year 2, there will be _____ in the economy.
f. Still further examination of the table completed above reveals that for the economy to grow at any given rate—such as 10%—the *amount* that net investment must increase (increases, decreases, remains constant) _____ .

5 This problem is much like problem 4 above; but it is a little more difficult because it does not ignore the capacity-creating aspect of investment as problem 4 did.

Assume, in an economy in which the only two components of aggregate spending are consumption and net investment, that the average propensity to consume is 0.7, the capital-output ratio is 3, and, in year 1, the economy is producing a full-employment output of $900.

a. In the following table, compute the amount of saving that would be done in year 1 if the economy produced its full-employment output, and the amount of investment that would be needed if the economy were to produce an equilibrium output equal to its full-employment output; and enter these two figures in the table.

b. Now compute the increase in full-employment output between year 1 and year 2 that results from the investment undertaken in year 1 (*Hint*: Divide the investment in year 1 by the capital-output ratio.)

c. Add the increase in full-employment output that results from the investment in year 1 to the full-employment output of year 1 to find the full-employment output of year 2; calculate the amount of saving that would be done at full employment in year 2, the amount of investment needed to bring about full employment, and the increase in the full-employment output between year 2 and year 3.

				Full employment		
Year	Output (GDP)	Saving	Investment	Increase in full-employment output
1	$900	$_____	$_____	$_____
2	_____	_____	_____	_____
3	_____	_____	_____	_____

d. Find the full-employment output and saving in year 3, the necessary amount of investment in year 3, and the increase in full-employment output between year 3 and year 4.

e. This economy's full-employment rate of growth is 10% and

(1) will be achieved if _____ grows at a rate of 10%;

(2) can be computed by dividing the economy's _____ by

_____ .

f. Were the economy's average propensity to save 0.1 and its capital-output ratio 4, its full-employment rate of growth would be

_____%.

SELF-TEST

Circle T if the statement is true, F if it is false.

1 Growth economics is concerned with an economy in which productive capacity is not fixed.   **T   F**

2 The better of the two definitions of economic growth is an increase in the per capita real output of the economy.   **T   F**

3 Suppose two economies each have GDPs of $500 billion. If the GDPs grow at annual rates of 3% in the first and 5% in the second economy, the difference in their amounts of growth in one year is $10 billion.   **T   F**

4 The demand factor in economic growth refers to the ability of the economy to expand its production as the demand for products grows.   **T   F**

5 The allocative factor in economic growth refers to the ability of the economy to move resources from one use to another as the productive capacity of the economy grows.   **T   F**

6 Diminishing returns for labour are the eventual result of increasing the employment of labour by larger percentages than the employment of other resources is increased.   **T   F**

7 The effect of diminishing returns to labour upon the standard of living is overcome whenever the average productivity of labour is increased.   **T   F**

8 Malthus predicted that diminishing returns and increases in the size of the population would cause the standard of living to fall to the subsistence level.   **T   F**

9 If the volume of investment expands more rapidly than is necessary to keep the full-employment output of the economy expanding at the rate the supply factors allow, the result will be unemployment.   **T   F**

10 Other things being constant, the productive capacity of an economy will increase by an amount equal to net investment multiplied by the capital-output ratio.   **T   F**

11 One of the requirements for allocative efficiency is the reasonably rapid and complete employment of the new workers in the labour force. **T F**

12 Supply-side economists favour increasing taxes to stimulate saving, investment, and economic growth in the economy. **T F**

Circle the letter that corresponds to the best answer.

1 Which of the following is *not* one of the benefits of economic growth to a society? (*a*) everyone enjoys a greater real income; (*b*) the standard of living in that society increases; (*c*) the burden of scarcity decreases; (*d*) the society is better able to satisfy new wants.

2 If the real output of an economy were to increase from $2,000 billion to $2,100 billion in one year, the rate of growth of real output during that year would be (*a*) 0.5%; (*b*) 5%; (*c*) 10%; (*d*) 50%.

3 Suppose an economy has a GDP of $700 billion and an annual growth rate of 5%. Over a *two*-year period, GDP will increase by (*a*) $14 billion; (*b*) $35 billion; (*c*) $70 billion; (*d*) $71.75 billion.

4 If the production possibilities curve of an economy moves from *AB* to *CD* on the graph in the next column, and the economy changes the combination of goods it produces from *X* to *Y*, there has been (*a*) an improvement in both the supply and the other growth factors; (*b*) an improvement in only the supply factor; (*c*) an improvement in only the demand and allocative growth factors; (*d*) an improvement in the level of total employment in the economy.

5 Which of the following is *not* a supply factor in economic growth? (*a*) an expansion in purchasing power; (*b*) an increase in the economy's stock of capital goods; (*c*) more natural resources; (*d*) technological improvements.

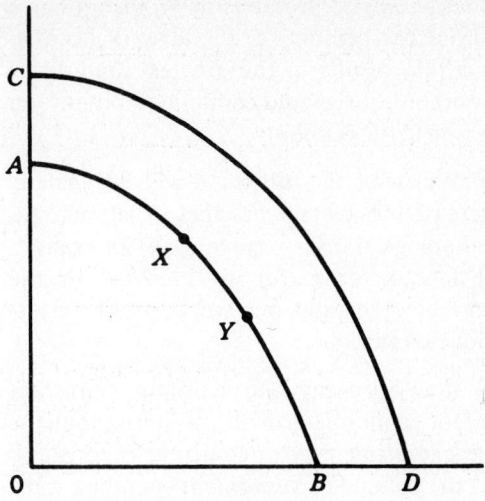

6 Using the data given in the table below, the average product of 4 units of labour is (*a*) 70; (*b*) 60; (*c*) 50; (*d*) 40.

Units of labour	Total production
0	0
1	50
2	110
3	160
4	200
5	230
6	250
7	260
8	265

7 The law of diminishing returns states that, as increased quantities of one resource are added to fixed quantities of other resources, there will eventually be a decrease in (*a*) total production; (*b*) the average product of the resource that is increased; (*c*) the average product of the resources that are fixed; (*d*) the optimum population.

8 The "optimum population" of an economy is (*a*) the largest population the resources of that economy are capable of supporting; (*b*) the level of population that enables the economy to produce the largest possible output; (*c*) the level of population that enables the economy to produce the largest possible output per person; (d) the level of population that results in the greatest amount of natural resources and capital equipment per person in the economy.

9 Which of the following will *not* usually increase the average product of labour? (a) technological improvements; (b) an expanded labour force; (c) an increase in the amount of capital per worker; (d) better-educated workers.

10 If an economy is to maintain a constant *rate* of economic growth, assuming that the average propensity to consume is constant, (a) the volume of investment spending must increase at a more rapid rate; (b) the volume of investment spending must increase at the same rate; (c) the volume of investment spending need only remain constant; (d) the volume of investment spending must increase by the same amount that the output of the economy increases.

11 The rate at which the full-employment output of an economy grows is greater (a) the greater are its APS and capital-output ratio; (b) the greater is its APS and the smaller is its capital-output ratio; (c) the smaller is its APS and the greater is its capital-output ratio; (d) the smaller are its APS and capital-output ratio.

12 To stimulate economic growth, Keynesians favour (a) an easy-money policy; (b) constraints on government spending; (c) constraints on consumption spending; (d) all of the above.

DISCUSSION QUESTIONS

1 How does growth economics differ from the theory of employment (or the theory of national income determination)?

2 What is meant by economic growth? Why should Canadians be concerned with economic growth?

3 What are the six basic ingredients of economic growth? What is the essential difference between the supply factors and the other two factors? Is there any relationship between the strength of the supply factors and the strength of the demand factor?

4 State the law of diminishing returns. What is the cause of diminishing returns?

5 What is an optimum population? Why is this concept important?

6 What predictions did Malthus make for the economic future of mankind? On what bases did he make this prediction?

7 What can be done to offset or overcome the tendency for the productivity of labour and the standard of living to decline as the employment of labour and the population increase?

8 Explain why an increasing level of aggregate expenditures is necessary in an economy whose productive capacity is increasing if full employment is to be maintained. Why does the maintenance of full employment in a growing economy in which the average propensity to save is constant require that investment increase at the same rate as the full-employment output?

9 What determines (a) how much the investment of one year will increase the full-employment output of the economy; (b) the full-employment rate of growth in an economy? What two events would bring about an increase in the full-employment rate of growth?

10 What is meant by allocative efficiency? Why is this kind of efficiency important if there is to be economic growth?

11 What (a) policies do Keynesians advocate to stimulate economic growth; (b) policies do supply-side economists favour to stimulate economic growth; (c) is meant by "industrial policy"?

33

GROWTH: FACTS AND ISSUES

Chapter 33 is the second of the three chapters concerned with economic growth. It is concerned primarily with economic growth in Canada.

Using the two definitions of growth found in Chapter 32, Chapter 33 begins by describing how much and how fast the Canadian economy has grown. That it has grown rapidly is fairly obvious. The net result of this rapid growth is that Canadians now enjoy one of the highest standards of living in the world.

Why has Canada grown economically? First, because Canada's population and the size of its labour force have grown. Second, and more important, the productivity of the labour force in Canada has increased. The increase in the productivity of labour is the result of technological advances; the expansion of the stock of capital goods in the Canadian economy; the improved education and training of its labour force; economies of scale; the reallocation of resources; the generous quantities of natural resources with which the Canadian economy was endowed; and its social, cultural, and political environment. (Note, however, that the regulations of government tend to slow the rates at which the productivity of labour and the output of the economy grow.) But in addition to the increases in the ability of the economy to produce goods and services made possible by the supply and allocative factors, aggregate expenditures expanded sufficiently (though unsteadily) to bring about most of the actual growth made possible by the increases in the quantity and the productivity of labour.

In the last ten or fifteen years, however, the rate at which the productivity of labour in Canada increased was dramatically less than it had been in earlier years. This slowdown has a number of causes and a number of consequences for the Canadian economy. None of the consequences is good, however; and the consequences add to the problems that we face. You should be sure you understand the causes, because the solutions to problems require elimination of the causes.

The latter part of Chapter 33 asks two important questions. Whether further economic growth is *desirable* in the already affluent Canadian economy is the first of these questions. The controversy over whether growth should be a social goal with a high priority in Canada has, of course, two sides to it. The case in defence of and the case against growth are both considered. You will have to decide for yourself which case is the stronger and whether the social benefits from growth are worth the costs.

The second question is whether further economic growth in the world is *possible*. Here we look at the dismal predictions of the Club of Rome. The Club of Rome is an informal group of all kinds of people from all over the world, who first met in that city in 1968 and later commissioned a team of professors from the Massachusetts Institute of Technology to prepare a report on the "Predicament of Mankind." Their report, a book entitled *The Limits To Growth*, aroused a storm of controversy throughout the world. Their prediction was that, the way things were going throughout the world, not only would world growth end within the next 100 years, but population and the standard of living would also suddenly decline or collapse.

More optimistically, the critics of the Doomsday model, in the last section of the chapter, point out that there are good reasons to be suspicious of these dismal predictions. The end of the world may not be at hand.

CHECK LIST

When you have studied this chapter you should be able to

☐ Describe the growth record of the Canadian economy in the twentieth century, and its two long-term rates of economic growth.

☐ State the two fundamental means by which an economy can increase its real GDP, and the relative importance of these two means of increasing the real GDP in Canada since 1958.

☐ Enumerate the several sources of the growth of the productivity of labour in Canada since World War II; and state their relative importance in the growth of its real national income.

☐ Identify the chief detriment to the increase in labour productivity.

☐ Explain why the actual rate of growth in Canada has been less than its potential rate of growth and why it has been unstable.

☐ Enumerate the three principal causes and the three principal implications of the slowdown in the rate at which labour productivity has increased in Canada since the early 1970s.

☐ Present the case against further economic growth in Canada.

☐ Defend further economic growth.

☐ Outline the assumptions and conclusions of the Doomsday models.

☐ Critizice the assumptions of the Doomsday models and explain how the feedback mechanisms might work to prevent the collapse of the economy.

CHAPTER OUTLINE

1 Since the beginning of the century, the growth record of the Canadian economy has been impressive, but Canadian growth in recent years has been slower than in many of the developed nations.

2 An economy can increase its real output by increasing the quantity of labour employed, by increasing the productivity of labour, or by doing both of these things.
a. The population of Canada and the size of its labour force have grown historically.
b. In addition, the productivity of labour has increased because
(1) the quality of labour has improved as a consequence of its improved education and training;
(2) the availability of the two property resources has been conducive to growth, inasmuch as
(a) natural resources have been generally abundant in Canada and
(b) investment has expanded the Canadian economy's stock of capital goods and provided the Canadian worker with more tools, equipment, and machinery with which to work than any other worker in the world;
(3) technological progress has increased the efficiency with which the human and property resources are employed.
c. However,
(1) Canadian investment has been less successful in increasing labour productivity than has been the case in other developed nations;
(2) only 20% of Canadian plants are at or above the minimum efficient size;
(3) new technologies spread more slowly in Canada than elsewhere;
(4) R & D spending in Canada is the lowest among our main trading partners;
(5) Canadian managerial entrepreneurship is below par;
(6) because of the previous five points, the reallocation of resources in Canada has been less than optimum.

d. Moreover, such detriments (or deterrents) to the growth of productivity as the government regulation of industry, of pollution, and of worker health and safety, and many taxes and transfers, divert investment away from productivity-increasing additions to capital.

e. Thus, labour productivity increases have been less than they could have been.

f. From 1958 to 1973, increases in the quantity of labour and capital accounted for about 54% and increases in the productivity of labour and capital accounted for roughly 46% of the increases in the total output of the Canadian economy.

3 Since the early 1970s, the annual rates of increase in the productivity of labour have slowed down substantially.

a. This slowdown is the result of smaller

(1) increases in investment, a decline in capacity utilization;

(2) a slowing of technological progress; and

(3) unfavourable intersectoral shifts;

(4) but the main cause of the productivity slowdown was the depressed demand induced by the federal government in an effort to control the inflation started by the oil-price shocks.

b. The significance of this slowdown is that

(1) it decreases the rates at which real wage rates and the standard of living can rise;

(2) it contributes to rising unit labour costs and to inflation in the Canadian economy; and

(3) it leads to higher prices for Canadian goods in world markets and the loss of these markets to Canadian producers.

4 Canadians today debate whether economic growth is or is not desirable.

a. Those opposed to rapid economic growth contend that

(1) it pollutes the environment;

(2) it is not needed to resolve domestic problems;

(3) it makes people more anxious and insecure; and

(4) while providing more goods and services, it does not result in a better life.

b. Those in favour of growth argue that

(1) it results in a higher standard of living and lessens the burden of scarcity;

(2) it is not the cause of pollution;

(3) it is the easiest way to bring about a more equitable distribution of income; and

(4) ending or slowing growth will not improve the quality of life.

5 The Doomsday models not only forecast an end to economic growth, but also predict sudden collapses in the world's population and its capacity to produce goods and services.

6 Critics of the Doomsday models argue that the forecasters have

a. made unrealistic assumptions;

b. underestimated future technological progress;

c. made inadequate allowances for such feedback mechanisms as the price system and changes in human behavioural patterns; and

d. underestimated future technological progress.

IMPORTANT TERMS

Labour productivity	Productivity
Minimum efficient size	slowdown
	Club of Rome
R & D	Doomsday model
Creative destruction	Feedback mechanism
Total factor productivity	

FILL-IN QUESTIONS

1 In Canada,

a. since 1900, real GDP has increased about

_____-fold, and since 1956 real

per capita GDP has _____ .

2 Since 1870, the rates of growth in real GNP and per capita GNP have, on the average, been _____% and _____%, respectively.

3 The real GDP of any economy in any year is equal to the _____ of labour employed *multiplied* by the _____ of labour.
a. The former is measured by the (number of workers, hours of labour) _____ employed.
b. The latter is equal to the real GDP per _____ per _____ .

4 The quantity of labour employed in the economy in any year depends upon the size of the employed _____ force and the _____ of the average work week. The size element depends upon the size of the working-age _____ and the labour-force _____ rate.

5 The productivity of labour will increase when the (quantity, quality) _____ of labour increases; this particular increase in labour productivity can be achieved by improving the _____ of the labour force.

6 One of the factors explaining the high productivity of Canadian workers is the relatively fixed but generous quantity and quality of _____ with which the economy is endowed.

7 The average Canadian worker in 1987 had about $_____ worth of capital equipment with which to work; about _____ times as much real capital as the average worker in 1946.

8 Technological progress means that we learn how to employ given quantities of resources to obtain greater _____ ; and, more often than not, this progress requires _____ in new machinery and equipment.

9 If there is to be economic growth in a society the social environment must encourage changes in _____ , in productive _____ , and capital facilities.

10 Increases in Canadian labour productivity have been (optimum, less than optimum) _____ because
a. only about _____% of Canadian plants are at or above minimum efficient size;
b. spread of new technologies has been _____ ;
c. R & D spending has been _____ ;
d. entrepreneurship has been (adequate, inadequate) _____ , especially in (big, small) _____ companies, and especially if they are (Canadian-owned, branch plants) _____ ;
e. reallocation of resources has been (adequate, inadequate) _____ .

11 Other detriments to growth have been increased government _____ and taxes and _____ that
a. distort _____ decisions;
b. discourage and distort _____ decisions;
c. penalize _____ .

12 Between 1958 and 1973, about _____% of Canadian economic growth has been due to increases in the quantities of capital and labour; the remainder has been due to _____ .

13 The annual rates of increase in the productivity of labour since the early 1970s have (risen, fallen, remained constant) _____.

a. This has resulted in a (rise, fall) _____ in the rates at which the standard of _____ and the (money, real) _____ wages of labour have increased, in a (rise, fall) _____ in unit labour costs and (inflation, deflation) _____ in Canada, and the loss of international markets to (Canadian, foreign) _____ producers of goods and services.

b. Its causes have been the (rise, fall) _____ in investment spending as a percentage of GDP and a _____ in capacity utilization and _____ in technological progress; but the main cause was the depressed _____ induced by the _____ .

14 Influential economists arguing against the need for growth in Canada believe that growth _____ the environment, does not lead to the solution of _____ , breeds _____ and _____ , and does not result in the _____ .

15 Those who favour growth for the Canadian economy argue that it is the basic way to raise the standard of _____ and lessen the _____ dilemma, that economic growth does not necessarily result in _____ , that growth is the only practical way of obtaining a more _____ distribution of _____ and that limiting growth will not bring about _____ .

16 The Doomsday models
a. are based on current and projected trends in world _____ , _____ , _____ , _____ , and _____ ;

b. predict that within the next _____ years there will be a sudden collapse in the world's _____ and _____ .

17 The criticisms of the Doomsday models are that the models employ _____ assumptions, underestimate future _____ _____ progress, and make inadequate allowance for _____ mechanisms.

PROBLEMS AND PROJECTS

1 Suppose the real GDP and the population of an economy in six different years were those shown in the table below.

Year	Population, millions	Real GDP, billions of dollars	Per capita real GDP
1	30	$ 9	$300
2	60	24	$_____
3	90	45	$_____
4	120	66	$_____
5	150	90	$_____
6	180	99	$_____

a. How large would the real per capita GDP of the economy be in each of the other five years? Put your figures in the above table.

b. What would have been the size of the optimum population of this economy? ____

c. What was the *amount* of growth in real GDP between year 1 and year 2? $ _____

d. What was the *rate* of growth in real GDP between year 3 and year 4? _____ %

2 The table below shows the quantity of labour (measured in hours) and the productivity of labour (measured in real GDP per hour) in a hypothetical economy in three different years.

Year	Quantity of labour	Productivity of labour	Real GDP
1	1,000	$100	$_____
2	1,000	105	$_____
3	1,100	105	$_____

a. Compute the economy's real GDP in each of the three years and enter them in the table.

b. Between years 1 and 2, the quantity of labour remained constant; but

(1) the productivity of labour increased by _____ %; and

(2) as a consequence, real GDP increased by _____ %.

c. Between years 2 and 3, the productivity of labour remained constant; but

(1) the quantity of labour increased by _____ %; and

(2) as a consequence, real GDP increased by _____ %.

d. Between years 1 and 3,

(1) real GDP increased by _____ %; and

(2) this rate of increase is approximately equal to the sum of the rates of increase in the _____ and the _____ of labour.

SELF-TEST

Circle T if the statement is true, F if it is false.

1 Real GDP has tended to increase more rapidly than per capita GDP in Canada.
T F

2 Growth and rates-of-growth estimates generally attempt to take account of changes in the quality of goods produced and in the amount of leisure that members of the economy enjoy.
T F

3 The real GDP of an economy in any year is equal to its input of labour divided by the productivity of labour.
T F

4 The population of Canada is almost five times what it was in 1900.
T F

5 Investment in capital has been a smaller percent of real GDP in Canada during recent years than in West Germany and Japan, and this helps to account for the slower rates of economic growth in Canada.
T F

6 More often than not, technological progress requires the economy to invest in new machinery and equipment.
T F

7 The Canadian social, cultural, and political environment has, in general, worked to slow Canadian economic growth.
T F

8 Increased labour productivity was more important than increased labour inputs in the growth of the Canadian economy between 1958 and 1973.
T F

9 Since the early 1970s, the productivity of labour in Canada has fallen.
T F

10 Changes in the supply factors do not cause changes in the demand factor, and vice versa.
T F

11 Increases in labour productivity can, at least in the Canadian economy, be taken pretty much for granted, because the rate of increase has been nearly constant for much more than half a century.
T F

12 Since 1958, increased inputs of labour and capital have together accounted for the major part of real GDP growth in Canada.

T   F

13 Poor work attitudes and disruptive industrial relations are part of the reason for the Canadian labour productivity slowdown, 1974–1982.

T   F

14 Depressed demand had little to do with the Canadian labour productivity slowdown, 1974–1984.

T   F

15 The Club of Rome model predicts that if present trends continue the world's population and its per capita outputs of industrial products and food will decline before the year 2100.

T   F

Circle the letter that corresponds to the best answer.

1 Since 1900, real GDP in Canada has increased about (*a*) fivefold; (*b*) tenfold; (*c*) twenty-seven fold; (*d*) fortyfold.

2 Since about 1870, the total output of the Canadian economy has increased at an average *annual* rate of about (*a*) 0.5 to 1%; (*b*) 2%; (*c*) 3.6%; (*d*) 5%.

3 Total output per capita in Canada since about 1870 has increased at an average annual rate of about (*a*) 0.8%; (*b*) 1.8%; (*c*) 2.8%; (*d*) 3.8%.

4 There are, in the Canadian labour force, approximately how many million workers? (*a*) 9; (*b*) 11; (*c*) 13; (*d*) 15.

5 The supply of which of the following is the most nearly fixed? (*a*) natural resources; (*b*) labour; (*c*) capital; (*d*) money.

6 By 1983–84, the percentage of grade 2 students who reached the last year of high school was (*a*) 42; (*b*) 57; (*c*) 80; (*d*) 90.

7 In which of the following factors is the Canadian economy at a disadvantage relative to other industrialized countries? (*a*) per-

centage of plants of minimum efficient size; (*b*) speed of diffusion of new technology; (*c*) percentage of GDP spend on R & D; (*d*) entrepreneurial spirit in branch plants and large companies; (*e*) all of the above.

8 About what percentage of the increase in the total output of the Canadian ecomomy between 1958 and 1973 was due to increases in the quantities of capital and labour employed? (*a*) 20%; (*b*) 23%; (*c*) 54%; (*d*) 43%.

9 During the 1974–1982 period the productivity of labour in Canada increased at an average annual rate of about (*a*) 0.8%; (*b*) 2.0%; (*c*) 3.5%; (*d*) 4.0%.

10 The decline in the rate at which the productivity of labour increased between 1974 and 1982 in Canada can be attributed to a number of factors. Which of the following is *not* one of these factors? (*a*) an increase in the relative prices of Canadian goods in world markets; (*b*) stagflation in Canada; (*c*) the decrease in industrial capacity utilization; (*d*) the decline in research and development expenditures as a percentage of GDP in Canada.

11 The decline in the rate at which the productivity of labour has increased since 1973 in Canada has tended to cause (*a*) a decline in the international value of the Canadian dollar; (*b*) a decline in the standard of living in Canada; (*c*) deterioration in the quality of the Canadian labour force; (*d*) increased pollution in Canada.

12 Which of the following is *not* one of the consequences when aggregate expenditures increase by less than the productive capacity of the economy? (*a*) inflation; (*b*) a GDP gap; (*c*) a slower rate of economic growth; (*d*) unemployed labour.

13 Which of the following is *not* a part of the case against economic growth? (*a*) growth produces pollution; (*b*) growth impedes the increased production of consumer goods; (*c*) growth prevents the attainment of a better life; (*d*) growth is not needed to provide us with the means of solving domestic social problems.

14 Which of the following is *not* a part of the case in defence of economic growth? (*a*) growth lessens the unlimited wants–scarce resources problem; (*b*) growth lessens the extent of anxiety and insecurity; (*c*) growth need not to be accompanied by the pollution of the environment; (*d*) growth is the only practical way to reduce poverty.

15 Which is *not* one of the criticisms levelled against the Doomsday models? (*a*) the assumptions are less plausible than other assumptions that might have been made; (*b*) future technological progress has been underestimated; (*c*) feedback mechanisms have been neglected; (*d*) the extent of world poverty has been overstated.

DISCUSSION QUESTIONS

1 What has been the growth record of the Canadian economy since 1900 and since 1870? Compare recent Canadian growth rates with those in other nations.

2 What is the relationship between the real GDP produced in any year and the quantity of labour employed and the labour productivity?

3 In what units are the quantity of labour and the productivity of labour measured? What (*a*) are the two principal determinants of the quantity of the labour input; (*b*) determines the size of the labour force; (*c*) are the four factors that affect the productivity of labour?

4 What long-run changes have occurred in the size of the Canadian population and labour force?

5 What is meant by the "quality" of labour? What tends to increase the quality of labour? How can this quality be measured?

What are the difficulties encountered in measuring it in this way?

6 What is the relationship between investment and the stock of capital? By how much has real capital per worker increased since 1946? What is the connection between increases in the capital stock and the rate of economic growth?

7 What is technological advance, and why are technological advance and capital formation closely related processes?

8 What is meant by and, therefore, tends to increase the "quality" of labour? How is this quality usually measured?

9 What is the most widely accepted indicator of a nation's effort to advance technologically? What does this indicator tell us about Canadian technological progress and growth in labour productivity in recent years?

10 What have been the sources of the economic growth that Canada has experienced since 1958?

11 By how much have the annual increases in the productivity of labour declined in Canada during recent years? What have been (*a*) the causes and (*b*) the consequences of this decline?

12 What are the economic consequences if aggregate expenditures increase more than the productive capacity of the economy increases? If aggregate expenditures increase less than productive capacity increases?

13 What arguments can be presented on both sides of the question of whether growth in Canada is desirable?

14 What are the assumptions and conclusions of the Club of Rome models?

15 What have the critics had to say about the Doomsday models and the predictions made by the forecasters who use these models?

34

GROWTH AND THE UNDERDEVELOPED NATIONS

Chapter 34 is the third of the three chapters concerned with economic growth. Chapter 32 dealt with the theory of growth; Chapter 33 examined the record and problems of economic growth in Canada.

This chapter looks at the problem of raising the standard of living faced by the underdeveloped nations of the world. Economic growth both in these underdeveloped nations and in the developed or the advanced nations requires that the nations' resources and technological knowledge be expanded. Application of this principle in the underdeveloped nations, however, faces a set of obstacles quite different from those that limit economic growth in Canada. The emphasis in this chapter is on the obstacles to economic growth in the poor and underdeveloped nations of the world. You should concentrate your attention on these obstacles. You will then understand why increasing the quantity and quality of resources and improving technology is especially difficult in the world's underdeveloped nations.

The existence of these special obstacles does not mean that increases in the living standards of the underdeveloped nations are impossible. What it does mean is that the underdeveloped nations are going to have to do things that did not need to be done in Canada (or in the other developed nations) in order to grow. Governments of the poor countries will have to take an active role in promoting growth. Population increases are going to have to be limited. And dramatic changes in social practices and institutions will be required. If these things are not done, it will

not be possible to eliminate or reduce the obstacles to growth.

No matter how successful the underdeveloped nations are in eliminating these obstacles they probably will still not be able to grow very rapidly without the help of the developed nations. There seem to be at least two reasons the developed nations will offer the less-developed ones some amount of assistance. The citizens of the more advanced nations feel some moral obligation to aid the less-fortunate peoples of the world; and they may feel it is in their own self-interest to aid the poor of the world.

Underdeveloped nations have (on the whole) grown during the past thirty years; but the rate at which they have grown has been about the same as that at which the developed nations have grown. This has meant (because the GDPs per capita in the former nations were initially so much smaller) that the gap between the two groups has widened over this period of time. For this and other reasons, nations in the Third World have become increasingly dissatisfied with their relationships with the more advanced nations; and they have argued for the establishment of a New International Economic Order. Here you should look at these relationships from the viewpoint of the Third World nations that are not oil exporters. To understand the proposals they have made you must understand why they feel their relationships with the developed nations benefit mostly the developed and largely hurt the underdeveloped nations.

The question that remains to be answered

is the one posed in the final section of this chapter. Will the poor nations increase their standard of living by substantial amounts in the future? What appears to be the best available answer—no one can really see into the future—is well expressed by the term "cautious optimism." Many of the underdeveloped nations will raise their living standards substantially *if* they do the many things that have to be done. The terrible *if*! Can these things be done?

On this note of uncertainty we conclude the topic of economic growth and end our study of macroeconomics.

CHECK LIST

When you have studied this chapter you should be able to

☐ Distinguish between developed, semideveloped, and underdeveloped nations; and locate the former and latter nations geographically.

☐ Identify the Third World nations; describe the population and output of the Third World nations; and explain why the gap between the standards of living of the Third World and the developed nations has widened over the past thirty years.

☐ Enumerate the human implications of the poverty in the underdeveloped nations.

☐ Identify the four factors that make growth in real GDP possible.

☐ Identify the three specific problems related to human resources that plague the underdeveloped nations; and the five problems population growth creates in these nations.

☐ Contrast the traditional and the more recent views of unemployment in the underdeveloped countries.

☐ Present three reasons for the emphasis on capital formation in the underdeveloped nations; and explain the obstacles to saving and the obstacles to investment in these nations.

☐ Explain why transferring the technologies used in the advanced nations to the underdeveloped ones may not be a realistic method of improving the technology of the latter nations.

☐ Provide an explanation of the relationship between investment, the capital-output ratio, the rate of growth in real GDP, in population, and in the standard of living.

☐ Enumerate several of the sociocultural and institutional factors that inhibit growth in the underdeveloped nations.

☐ Explain why poverty in the poor nations is a vicious circle.

☐ List five reasons why governments in the underdeveloped nations will have to play a crucial role if the vicious circle is to be broken.

☐ Identify the three ways in which the developed nations may help the underdeveloped nations to grow economically.

☐ Identify the six proposals made by Third World nations that would, if implemented, result in a New International Economic Order; and the arguments made by them in support of these proposals.

☐ Write three scenarios describing the future of the Third World.

CHAPTER OUTLINE

1 The underdeveloped nations of the world comprise two-thirds of the world's population.

a. Most of the countries of Asia, Africa, and South America are underdeveloped, and all of them have one common characteristic—poverty (that is, a low per capita income or standard of living).

b. The world's nations can be divided into the industrially advanced market economies, the centrally planned economies, and the Third World Countries; and it is the last that are underdeveloped (or semideveloped), contain one-half the world's population, and produce only one-seventh of the world's output. Despite equal rates of growth in per capita output over the past thirty years, the gap between the per capita outputs of rich and poor nations has widened.

c. While all Third World nations have low standards of living, they are different in many ways and have experienced different rates of growth.

d. Compared with the developed nations, the underdeveloped or Third World nations have lower life expectancies, more disease, less food per person and more malnutrition, less schooling and literacy, and fewer non-human sources of energy.

e. Because of an increasing disparity between the standards of living in the developed and the underdeveloped nations, and because many of the underdeveloped nations became politically independent only after World War II, these nations are discontented and determined to raise their standards of living.

f. The economic and social environment of the underdeveloped nations is vastly different from that in which Canada found itself when it began its development; consequently, the underdeveloped nations cannot develop merely by following the examples of Canada and other advanced nations.

2 Economic development requires that the quantity and quality of economic resources be increased and that technological knowledge be expanded; but there are many special obstacles to such a program in the underdeveloped nations.

a. Many (but not all) underdeveloped nations possess inadequate natural resources, and this limits their ability to develop.

b. Many underdeveloped nations are overpopulated, are plagued by unemployment, and have poor quality labour forces.

c. Usually very short of capital goods, underdeveloped nations find it difficult to accumulate capital because of their low saving potentials and the absence of investors and incentives to invest.

d. Technological knowledge is primitive in underdeveloped nations, and they might adopt the technologies employed in the advanced nations; but the technologies of the advanced nations are not appropriate to the resource endowments of the underdeveloped nations, and they will have to develop their own technologies.

e. In addition, a nation must have a strong will to develop and alter its own social, cultural, and institutional environment to grow economically.

3 In summary, underdeveloped nations save little and, therefore, invest little in real and human capital because they are poor; and because they do not invest, their output per capita remains low and they remain poor. Even if this vicious circle were to be broken, a rapid increase in population would leave the standard of living unchanged.

4 It is probable that the governments of these nations will have to play a major role by sponsoring and directing many of the early development plans if the obstacles to growth are to be overcome.

5 The advanced nations of the world can help the poor nations to develop in a number of ways.

a. They can lower the barriers that prevent the underdeveloped nations from selling their products in the developed nations.

b. The flow of private capital from the advanced nations helps the underdeveloped nations increase their productive capacities and per capita outputs.

c. Loans and grants from governments and international organizations also enable the underdeveloped nations to accumulate capital.

6 Because they have not grown as rapidly as they had hoped and are dissatisfied with their relationships with industrially advanced nations, Third World countries during the past decade or so have urged the creation of a New International Economic Order that would involve six basic changes.

7 No one can now predict whether the Third World nations will in the future grow or stagnate; but at least three scenarios can be written to forecast the courses of events during the next thirty or so years.

IMPORTANT TERMS

Underdeveloped nation

Third World

Investment in human capital

Domestic capital formation

Non-financial (in-kind) investment

Basic social capital

Capital-saving technological advance

Capital-using technological advance

The will to develop

World Bank

Neo-colonialism

Green revolution

New International Economic Order (NIEO)

Preferential tariff treatment

Stabilization fund

Terms of trade

FILL-IN QUESTIONS

1   The common characteristic of underdeveloped nations is _____ .

2   The underdeveloped nations are found chiefly in the following areas of the world:

_____ ,

_____ ,

and _____ ;
and they account for approximately (one-third, one-half, two-thirds) _____ of the world's population.

3   The nations of the world can be divided into the industrially advanced countries with either market or centrally planned economies and the _____ countries. In these latter countries are found _____ % of the world's population but only _____ % of the world output of goods and services; and the annual rate of growth of output per capita is _____%.

4   To grow, every economy must increase its supplies of _____ ,

_____ ,

and _____

or improve its _____ .

5   Which resource is *least* easily increased in most underdeveloped nations? _____

_____ .

6   Three characteristics of the human resources in most underdeveloped nations are

a. _____

b. _____

c. _____

7   The per capita standard of living = _____ divided by

_____ ;

and social unrest = _____ · _____

minus _____ .

8   If the process of capital accumulation is "cumulative," investment increases the (population, output, natural resources) _____ of the economy, and this in turn makes it possible for the economy to save more and to _____ more in capital goods.

9   Domestic capital accumulation requires that a nation save and invest. The former is difficult in underdeveloped nations because of a low _____, and the latter is difficult because of a lack of _____ and of _____ to invest.

10 Non-financial (or in-kind) investment involves the transfer of surplus labour from

(agriculture, industry) _____ to the improvement of agricultural facilities or the construction of basic (private, social) _____ capital.

11 The technologies used in the advanced industrial nations might be borrowed by and used in the underdeveloped nations; but
a. the technologies used in the advanced nations are based upon a labour force that is (skilled, unskilled) _____, labour that is relatively (abundant, scarce) _____, and a capital that is relatively _____, and their technologies tend to be (labour, capital) _____-using; while
b. the technologies required in the underdeveloped countries must be based on a labour force that is _____, labour that is relatively _____, and capital that is relatively _____, and their technologies need to be _____-using.

12 If technological advances make it possible to replace a worn-out plow, costing $10 when new, with a new $5 plow, the technological advance is capital- (saving, using) _____ .

13 The "will to develop" in underdeveloped nations involves a willingness to change the _____ and _____ arrangements of the nation.

14 In most underdeveloped nations, saving is small because the _____ per capita is small. Because saving is small, _____ in real and human capital is also small. And for this reason the _____ _____ of labour and _____

per capita remain small.

15 List five reasons why the role of government in fostering economic development will need to be large in the underdeveloped nations, especially during the early stages of development.

a. _____
b. _____
c. _____
d. _____
e. _____

16 The three major ways in which Canada can assist economic development in the underdeveloped nations are _____ _____ , _____ , and _____ .

17 In pressing for the establishment of an New International Economic Order, the Third World nations have argued (among other things) that
a. because Third World nations had no part in their formation and because they are "stacked" against them, there should be a change in the _____ by which international trade, finance, and investment are conducted;
b. the advanced nations, to deprive Third World nations of their export markets, have erected barriers to _____ and the Third World nations should be accorded preferential _____ ;
c. the dealings of the Third World nations with corporations in the advanced nations have led to the greater part of the benefits from the _____ of their natural resources going to others and to the increased _____ of Third World nations on world markets;

d. there has been, as a result of the higher prices charged for manufactured goods by corporations in the advanced nations, a shift against them in the _____ of _____ and that these might be improved by the establishment of _____ funds and by _____ ;

e. except for the oil-exporting countries of the Third World, the size of their _____ abroad have increased, and these should either be _____ or _____ ;

f. the foreign aid that they have received has been _____ and should be increased to _____ % of the GDP of the advanced nations, have no _____ attached to it, and should be provided on a long-term and _____ basis.

18 No one can forecast the future course of events in the Third World nations; but at least three scenarios can be written.

a. In the most optimistic scenario, real GDP grows at a rate of 5% to 6% a year; and there is little or no growth in the _____ and an improved _____ .

b. In a second scenario, groups of underdeveloped nations form (common markets, cartels) _____ to raise the prices of the (manufactured goods, raw materials) _____ they export.

c. And in the third scenario, the poor nations acquire nuclear capabilities and engage in wars of (redistribution, national liberation) _____ with the rich nations.

PROBLEMS AND PROJECTS

1 Suppose that the real GDP per capita in the average advanced industrialized nation is $8,000 per year and in the average underdeveloped nation is $500 per year.

a. The gap between their standards of living is $_____ per year.

b. If GDP per capita were to grow at a rate of 5% during a year in both the advanced and the underdeveloped nations,

(1) the standard of living in the advanced nations would rise to $_____ a year;

(2) the standard of living in the underdeveloped nations would rise to $_____ a year; and

(3) the gap between their standards of living would (narrow, widen) _____ to $_____ a year.

2 While economic conditions are not identical in all underdeveloped nations, there are certain conditions common to or typical of most of them. In the spaces after each of the following characteristics, indicate briefly the nature of this characteristic in most underdeveloped nations.

a. Standard of living (per capita income).

_____

b. Average life expectancy. _____

c. Extent of employment. _____

d. Literacy. _____

e. Technology. _____

f. Percentage of the population engaged in agriculture. _____

g. Size of the population relative to the land and capital available. _____

h. The birth and death rates. _____

i. Quality of the labour force. _____

j. Amount of capital equipment relative to

the labour force. _____

k. Level of saving. _____

l. Incentive to invest. _____

m. Amount of basic social capital. _____

n. Extent of industrialization. _____

o. Size and quality of the entrepreneurial class and the supervisory class. _____

_____

p. Per capita public expenditures for education and per capita energy consumption.

_____

q. Per capita consumption of food. _____

r. Disease and malnutrition. _____

3 Suppose it takes a minimum of 5 units of food to keep a person alive for a year, and the population can double itself every 10 years, and that the food supply can increase every 10 years by an amount equal to what it was in the beginning (Year 0).

a. Assume that both the population and the food supply grow at these rates. Complete the table by computing the size of the population and the food supply in years 10 to 60.

Year	Food supply	Population
0	200	20
10	_____	_____
20	_____	_____
30	_____	_____
40	_____	_____
50	_____	_____
60	_____	_____

b. What happens to the relationship between the food supply and the population in the 30th year? _____

c. What would actually prevent the population from growing at this rate following the 30th year? _____

d. Assuming that the actual population growth in the years following the 30th does not outrun the food supply, what would be the size of the population in

(1) Year 40: _____

(2) Year 50: _____

(3) Year 60: _____

e. Explain why the standard of living failed to increase in the years following the 30th even though the food supply increased by 75% between years 30 and 60. _____

_____

SELF-TEST

Circle T if the statement is true, F if it is false.

1 Among the nations of the world with populations greater than one million persons, Canada had the seventh-highest per capita income in 1983. **T F**

2 The difference between the per capita incomes in the underdeveloped nations and the per capita incomes in the developed nations has been decreasing over the past years. **T F**

3 The rates of growth in GDP per capita in Third World nations are all approximately 3% a year. **T F**

4 Economic growth in the underdeveloped nations can be accelerated by adopting the policies that history shows led to the rapid growth of the Canadian economy. **T F**

5 Economic growth in both advanced and underdeveloped nations requires using resources more efficiently or increasing the supplies of these resources. **T F**

6 It is impossible to achieve a high standard of living with a small supply of natural resources. **T F**

7 Nations with large populations are overpopulated. **T F**

8 The chief factor preventing the elimination of underemployment in the agricultural sector of underdeveloped nations is the small number of job openings available in industry.   **T   F**

9 Saving in the underdeveloped nations is a smaller percentage of national income than in the more advanced industrial nations, and this is the chief reason total saving in the underdeveloped nations is small.   **T   F**

10 Before private investment can be increased in underdeveloped nations, it is necessary to reduce the amount of investment in basic social capital.   **T   F**

11 Technological advances in the underdeveloped nations will be made rapidly because they do not require pushing forward the frontiers of technological knowledge and the technologies used in the advanced nations can be easily transferred to the underdeveloped ones.   **T   F**

12 When technological advances are capital-saving, it is possible for an economy to increase its productivity without any *net* investment in capital goods.   **T   F**

13 The policies of the governments of underdeveloped nations have often tended to reduce the incentives of foreigners to invest in the underdeveloped nations.   **T   F**

14 Underdeveloped nations would not need foreign aid if the advanced nations would reduce tariffs and import quotas on the goods that the underdeveloped nations export.
T   F

15 An increase in the output and employment of the developed nations works to the advantage of the underdeveloped nations because it provides the underdeveloped nations with larger markets for their exports.
T   F

16 Foreign aid from Canada to the underdeveloped nations has consistently exceeded 1% of its GDP.   **T   F**

17 Many in the Third World nations believe that the public and private aid extended by the developed to the underdeveloped nations is designed to increase profits in the former and to exploit the latter nations. **T   F**

18 Were a fund to be established to stabilize the price of a commodity such as copper, the fund would be used to purchase the commodity when its price fell.   **T   F**

19 Preferential tariff treatment for Third World nations means that the developed nations would set their tariffs on commodities imported from underdeveloped nations below those established for the same commodities imported from developed nations.
T   F

20 One of the proposals associated with the establishment of a New International Economic Order is that the aid from the developed to the Third World nations be automatic, have no "strings" attached to it, and equal at least 1% of the GDP of the advanced nations.   **T   F**

Circle the letter that corresponds to the best answer.

1 Which of the following is the most underdeveloped nation? (*a*) U.S.S.R.; (*b*) Israel; (*c*) Canada; (*d*) India.

2 Which of the following is a Third World nation? (*a*) U.S.S.R.; (*b*) Canada; (*c*) Belgium; (*d*) Egypt.

3 When the rate of growth in per capita GDP is greater in the underdeveloped than in the developed nations, the gap between their standards of living (*a*) will decrease; (*b*) will increase; (*c*) will remain unchanged; (*d*) may do any of the above.

4 Which of the following is high in the underdeveloped nations? (*a*) life expectancy; (*b*) infant mortality; (*c*) literacy; (*d*) per capita energy consumption.

5 In the "equation" for social unrest, (*a*)

social unrest = the standard of living – aspirations; (*b*) social unrest = real GDP ÷ population; (*c*) social unrest = real GDP per capita – the standard of living; (*d*) social unrest = aspirations – the standard of living.

6 Which of the following is the most serious obstacle to economic growth in underdeveloped nations? (*a*) the supply of natural resources; (*b*) the size and quality of the labour force; (*c*) the supply of capital equipment; (*d*) technological knowledge.

7 An increase in the total output of consumer goods in an underdeveloped nation may not increase the average standard of living because (*a*) of diminishing returns; (*b*) it may provoke an increase in the population; (*c*) of disguised unemployment; (*d*) the quality of the labour force is so poor.

8 Which of the following best describes the unemployment found in the underdeveloped nations? (*a*) the result of cyclical fluctuations in aggregate spending; (*b*) the agricultural workers who have migrated from rural to urban areas and failed to find employment in the cities; (*c*) the workers in excess of the optimum population; (*d*) workers whose productivity is subject to diminishing returns.

9 Which of the following is *not* a reason for placing special emphasis on capital accumulation in underdeveloped nations? (*a*) the inflexible supply of arable land; (*b*) the low productivity of workers; (*c*) the low marginal contribution of capital equipment; (*d*) the possibility that capital accumulation will be "cumulative."

10 Which of the following is *not* a factor limiting saving in underdeveloped nations? (*a*) the output of the economy is too low to permit a large volume of saving; (*b*) those who do save do not make their saving available to their own economies; (*c*) the highly unequal distribution of income; (*d*) the low marginal contribution of capital equipment to production.

11 Which of the following is *not* an obstacle to capital formation (investment) in underdeveloped nations? (*a*) the absence of strong incentives to invest; (*b*) the lack of basic social capital; (*c*) the absence of a large entrepreneurial class; (*d*) the lack of capital-saving changes in technology.

12 Which of the following is an example of basic social capital? (*a*) a steel plant; (*b*) an electric power plant; (*c*) a farm; (*d*) a demand deposit in a commercial bank.

13 Which of the following seems to be the *most* needed and widespread institutional change required of underdeveloped nations? (*a*) adoption of birth control; (*b*) development of strong labour unions; (*c*) increase in the nation's basic social capital; (*d*) land reform.

14 Suppose the average propensity to save in an underdeveloped nation is .09 and that the capital-output ratio is 3. At what rate can total real output increase? (*a*) 2.7%; (*b*) 3.0%; (*c*) 3.3%; (*d*) 3.9%.

15 Assume the total real output of an underdeveloped economy increases from $100 billion to $115.5 billion while its population expands from 200 million to 210 million people. Real income per capita has, as a result, increased by (*a*) $50; (*b*) $100; (*c*) $150; (*d*) $200.

16 The role of government in the early stages of economic development will probably be a major one for several reasons. Which one of the following is *not* one of these reasons? (*a*) only government can provide a large amount of the needed basic social capital; (*b*) the absence of private entrepreneurs to accumulate capital and take risks; (*c*) the necessity of creating *new* money to finance capital accumulation; (*d*) the slowness and uncertainty of the price system in fostering development.

17 The terms of trade for a nation exporting tin worsen whenever (*a*) the price of tin rises;

(b) the price of tin falls; (c) the price of tin rises and the prices of imported goods decline; (d) the price of tin falls and the prices of imported goods rise.

18 Which one of the following is *not* one the proposals included in the New International Economic Order for which Third World nations have argued? (a) a change in the rules by which international financial institutions are governed; (b) the elimination of OPEC; (c) the renegotiation and cancellation of the debts of Third World nations to the developed nations; (d) abandonment of the neo-colonial policies of the developed nations.

19 The long-term external debt of the Third World nations that do not export oil is currently about (a) $300 billion; (b) $450 billion; (c) $625 billion; (d) $970 billion.

20 During the remainder of this and in the next century, the underdeveloped nations will (a) increase their standards of living; (b) form cartels to control the supplies of raw materials and bring about a redistribution of wealth and income in the world; (c) obtain nuclear capabilities and (threaten to) wage war to force the developed nations to share their wealth and income with them; (d) do one or more or none of the above.

DISCUSSION QUESTIONS

1 What nations of the world can be called "developed"? Which can be classified as "semideveloped"? Where are the "underdeveloped" nations of the world found?

2 Compare the incomes (per capita) and rates of growth in the developed and the Third World nations. What are the "human implications" of the poverty found in the latter nations? (Use the socioeconomic indicators found in Table 34-2 of the text to contrast the quality of life in the developed and underdeveloped nations.)

3 What recent events have increased the desire of the underdeveloped nations to improve their standard of living? Why should social unrest increase in the underdeveloped nations even though their standards of living have been increasing?

4 Why is advice to the underdeveloped nations to follow the example of the developed nations inappropriate and unrealistic?

5 What must any nation, developed or underdeveloped, do if it is to increase its standard of living? Answer in terms of the production possibilities curve concept.

6 What obstacles do the human resources of underdeveloped nations place in the path of economic development? What is the difference between the traditional view and the more recent view of the unemployment problem in the underdeveloped nations?

7 What reasons exist for placing special emphasis on capital accumulation as a means of promoting economic growth in underdeveloped nations?

8 Why is domestic capital accumulation difficult in underdeveloped nations? Answer in terms of both the saving side and the investment side of capital accumulation. How does a lack of basic social capital inhibit investment in underdeveloped nations?

9 In addition to the obstacles that limit domestic investment, what other obstacles tend to limit the flow of foreign capital into underdeveloped nations?

10 How might the underdeveloped nations improve their technology without engaging in slow and expensive research? Why might this be an inappropriate method of improving the technology used in the underdeveloped nations?

11 What is meant by "will to develop"? How is it related to social and institutional change in underdeveloped nations?

12 Explain the "vicious circle" of poverty found in the underdeveloped nations. How does population growth make an escape from this vicious circle difficult?

13 Why is the role of government expected to be a major one in the early phases of development in underdeveloped nations?

14 How can Canada help underdeveloped nations? What types of aid can be offered?

15 How is it possible for Canada to assist underdeveloped nations without spending a penny on "foreign aid"? Is this type of aid sufficient to ensure rapid and substantial development in the underdeveloped nations?

16 Discuss the World Bank in terms of its purposes, characteristics, sources of funds, promotion of private capital flows, and success. What are its affiliates and their purposes?

17 Explain the principal proposals that constitute the program of the Third World nations for the establisment of a New International Economic Order. Explain the arguments made by the Third World to support each of these proposals.

18 Write the three scenarios that might plausibly forecast the future of the Third World nations.

ANSWERS

1

THE NATURE AND METHOD OF ECONOMICS

Fill-in questions

1. *a.* production, distribution, consumption; *b.* limited (scarce), maximum

2. citizens, vocational

3. descriptive

4. generalizations, abstraction

5. "other things equal" (*ceteris paribus*)

6. *a.* failure to distinguish between relevant and irrelevant facts; *b.* failure to recognize economic models for what they are—useful first approximations; *c.* tendency to impute ethical or moral qualities to economic models

7. control, prepare

8. *a.* full employment; *b.* economic growth; *c.* reasonable price stability; *d.* viable balance of payments; *e.* equitable distribution of rising incomes

9. *a.* a clear statement of the objectives and goals of the policy; *b.* a statement and analysis of all possible alternative solutions to the problem; *c.* an evaluation of the results of the policy selected after it has been put into operation

10. total, general, individual industry, particular product

Problems and projects

1. An increase in the demand for an economic good will cause the price of that good to rise.

2. *a.* The validity of the statement depends upon the phase of business cycle; *b.* the fallacy of composition; *c.* loaded terminology; *d.* the *post hoc, ergo propter hoc* fallacy.

3. *a.* direct, up; *b.* inverse, down; *c.* (1) are, is not, (2) coincidental, incomes (standard of living, or some other such answer).

Self-test

1. T; 2. F; 3. F; 4. T; 5. T; 6. F; 7. T; 8. F; 9. T; 10. F; 11. F; 12. F

1. *b*; 2. *b*; 3. *c*; 4. *a*; 5. *d*; 6. *a*; 7. *b*; 8. *a*; 9. *d*; 10. *d*; 11. *b*; 12. *a*

2

AN INTRODUCTION TO THE ECONOMIZING PROBLEM

Fill-in questions

1. *a.* society's material wants are unlimited; *b.* economic resources, which are the ultimate means of satisfying these wants, are scarce in relation to these wants

2. *a.* property resources; (1) land or raw materials, (2) capital; *b.* human resources; (1) labour, (2) entrepreneurial ability

3. directly, indirectly

4. rental income, interest income, wages, profits

5. the social science concerned with the problem of using or administering scarce resources to attain maximum fulfilment of unlimited wants

6. employment, production

7. *a.* the economy is operating at full employment and full production; *b.* the available supplies of the factors of production are fixed; *c.* technology does not change during the course of the analysis; *d.* the economy produces only two products

8. *a.* fewer, more; *b.* unemployed, underemployed; *c.* more, more; *d.* increase resource supplies, improve its technology

9. values, non-scientific

10. opportunity cost

11. economic resources are not completely adaptable among alternate uses

12. less

13. *a.* at what level to utilize resources in the productive process; *b.* what collection of goods and services best satisfies its wants; *c.* how to produce this total output; *d.* how to divide this output among the various economic units of the economy; *e.* how to make the responses required to remain efficient over time

14. *a.* consumer tastes; *b.* the supplies of resources; *c.* technology

15. *a.* privately, market; *b.* publicly, planning

16. the extensive use of capital, specialization, the use of money

17. efficient

18. interdependent, exchange (trade)

19. inefficient

20. medium of exchange

21. coincidence of wants

22. generally acceptable by sellers in exchange

23. *a.* product, resource; *b.* real, money (either order); *c.* cost, income

Problems and projects

1. *a.* L_d; *b.* K; *c.* L_d; *d.* K; *e.* EA; *f.* L_d; *g.* K;

h. K; *i.* L; *j.* EA

2. *b.* 1, 2, 3, 4, 5, 6, 7 wheat

4. *a.* D; *b.* K; *c.* K; *d.* K; *e.* K; *f.* K; *g.* D; *h.* D; *i.* D; *j.* D; *k.* K; *l.* D

5. *a.* goods and services; *b.* expenditures for goods and services; *c.* money income payments (wages, rent, interest and profit); *d.* services of resources (labour, land, capital, and entrepreneurial ability)

Self-test

1. T; **2.** F; **3.** F; **4.** T; **5.** T; **6.** T; **7.** T; **8.** F; **9.** T; **10.** T; **11.** F; **12.** F; **13.** F; **14.** T; **15.** T; **16.** T; **17.** F; **18.** T; **19.** F

1. *d*; **2.** *d*; **3.** *b*; **4.** *c*; **5.** *d*; **6.** *a*; **7.** *b*; **8.** *b*; **9.** *b*; **10.** *d*; **11.** *a*; **12.** *c*; **13.** *c*; **14.** *b*; **15.** *a*; **16.** *d*; **17.** *c*; **18.** *d*; **19.** *d*; **20.** *a*

3

DEMAND, SUPPLY, AND ELASTICITY

Fill-in questions

1. buyers (demanders), sellers (suppliers) (either order); *a.* business firms, households; *b.* demand decisions of households, supply decisions of business firms

2. vertical, horizontal

3. inverse, direct

4. diminishing marginal utility

5. *a.* income; *b.* substitution

6. *a.* the tastes or preferences of consumers; *b.* the number of consumers in the market; *c.* the money income of consumers; *d.* the prices of related goods; *e.* consumer expectations with respect to future prices and incomes

7. smaller, less

8. demand for, a change in the quantity demanded of the product

9. *a.* the technique of production; *b.* resource prices; *c.* taxes and subsidies; *d.* prices of other goods; *e.* price expectations; *f.* the number of sellers in the market

10. quantity demanded and quantity supplied are equal

11. below, shortage, rise

12. *a.* +, +; *b.* −, +; *c.* −, −; *d.* +, −; *e.* ?, +; *f.* +, ?; *g.* ?, −; *h.* −, ?

13. rationing

14. other things being equal

15. inelastic, elastic

16. inversely, directly

17. elastic: greater than 1, decrease, increase; inelastic: less than 1, increase, decrease; of unitary elasticity: equal to 1, remain constant, remain constant

18. inelastic, vertical, perfectly elastic, horizontal

19. *a.* greater than; *b.* less than; *c.* equal to

20. *a.* the number of good substitute products available; *b.* the relative importance of the product in the total budget of the buyer; *c.* whether the good is a necessity or a luxury; *d.* the period of time in which demand is being considered

21. the amount of time that a seller has to respond to a price change

22. *a.* 7.00, 15,000; *b.* shortage, 4,000; *c.* surplus, 2,000

23. war, shortages, rationing

24. surplus, attempt to reduce supply or increase demand, purchase the surplus and store or dispose of it

25. minimum wages, agricultural price supports

26. rationing

27. the amount the price of the commodity rises as a result of the tax; *a.* less, more; *b.* more, less

Problems and projects

1. *b.* $6.60; *c.* 25; *e.* surplus, 20

2. Total: 5, 9, 17, 27, 39

3. Each quantity in column 3 is greater than in column 2, and each quantity in column 4 is less than in column 2.

4. *a.* 30, 4. *b.* (1) 20, 7; (2) inferior; (3) normal (superior)

5. *a.* complementary; *b.* substitute

6. *a.* 45,000, 33,000; 22,500; 13,500; 6,000; 0 *b.* shortage, 28,500

7. *a.* decrease demand, decrease price; *b.* decrease supply, increase price *c.* decrease supply, increase price; *d.* increase demand, increase price; *e.* decrease supply, increase price; *f.* increase demand, increase price; *g.* increase supply, decrease price; *h.* decrease demand, decrease price; *i.* increase demand, increase price; *j.* decrease supply, increase price

8. total revenue: $300, 360, 400, 420, 420, 400, 360; elasticity coefficient: $2^5/_7$ (2.71), $1^8/_9$ (1.89), $1^4/_{11}$ (1.36), 1, $^{11}/_{15}$ (0.73), $^9/_{17}$ (0.53); character of demand: elastic, elastic, elastic, unitary elasticity, inelastic, inelastic

9. elasticity coefficient: $1^4/_{15}$ (1.27), $1^4/_{13}$ (1.31), $1^4/_{11}$ (1.36), $1^4/_9$ (1.44), $1^4/_7$ (1.57), $1^4/_5$ (1.8); character of supply: elastic, elastic, elastic, elastic, elastic, elastic

10. *a.* (1) S_3; (2) S_2; (3) S_1; *b.* p_1, q_1; *c.* (1) p_4, remain at q_1; (2) p_3, q_2; (3) p_2, q_3; *d.* more; *e.* less, greater

11. *a.* $3.60; *b.* (reading down) 600, 500, 400, 300, 200, 100; *c.* $4.00; *d.* (1) $.40, $66^2/_3$; (2) $.20, $33^1/_3$

12. *a.* (2) has not changed; (3) none, all; (4)

smaller, larger; (5) larger, smaller; *b.* (2) increased by the amount of the tax; (3) all, none; (4) larger, smaller; (5) smaller, larger

Self-test

1. T; **2.** F; **3.** F; **4.** F; **5.** F; **6.** T; **7.** F; **8.** F; **9.** F; **10.** F; **11.** T; **12.** F; **13.** T; **14.** F; **15.** T; **16.** T; **17.** F; **18.** F; **19.** F; **20.** T; **21.** T

1. *d*; **2.** *a*; **3.** *b*; **4.** *b*; **5.** *a*; **6.** *c*; **7.** *d*; **8.** *a*; **9.** *c*; **10.** *d*; **11.** *c*; **12.** *b*; **13.** *a*; **14.** *a*; **15.** *c*; **16.** *b*; **17.** *b*; **18.** *c*; **19.** *a*; **20.** *b*; **21.** *b*

4

FURTHER TOPICS IN THE THEORY OF CONSUMER DEMAND

Fill-in questions

1. increase, decrease, income

2. more, lower, less, more, substitution

3. decrease

4. rational, preferences

5. limited, prices, budget restraint

6. ratio of the marginal utility of the last unit purchased of a product to its price

7. increase, decrease

8. *a.* MU of product X; *b.* price of X; *c.* MU of product Y; *d.* price of Y

9. *a.* the income of the consumer; *b.* the prices of other products

10. time: *a.* scarce; *b.* the income that can be earned by using the time for work; *c.* market price, value of the consumption time

Problems and projects

1. *a.* (1) increase, $1\frac{1}{2}$; (2) inelastic; *b.* (1) decrease, 1; (2) elastic

2. marginal utility of good A: 21, 20, 18, 15,

11, 6, 0; marginal utility of good B: 7, 6, 5, 4, 3, 2, 1.2; marginal utility of good C: 23, 17, 12, 8, 5, 3, 2

3. *a.* marginal utility per dollar of good A: $4\frac{1}{5}$, 4, $3\frac{3}{5}$, 3, $2\frac{1}{5}$, $1\frac{1}{5}$, 0; marginal utility per dollar of good B: 7, 6, 5, 4, 3, 2, $1\frac{1}{5}$; marginal utility per dollar of good C: $5\frac{3}{4}$, $4\frac{1}{4}$, 3, 2, $1\frac{1}{4}$, $\frac{3}{4}$, $\frac{1}{2}$; *b.* the marginal utility per dollar spent on good B (7) is greater than the marginal utility per dollar spent on good A (3), and the latter is greater than the marginal utility per dollar spent on good C (2); *c.* he would be spending more than his $37 income; *d.* (1) 4; (2) 5; (3) 3; 151; 3. *e.* A, he would obtain the greatest marginal utility for his dollar ($2\frac{1}{5}$)

4. *a.* 2, 3, 4, 6, 8; *b.* the demand schedule (for good D)

5. *a.* Yes; *b.* (1) 10, (2) 3; *c.* no, the marginal utility to price ratios is not the same for the two goods; *d.* of M, because its MU/P ratio is greater; *e.* less

Self-test

1. F; **2.** T; **3.** T; **4.** F; **5.** F; **6.** T; **7.** F

1. *c*; **2.** *b*; **3.** *a*; **4.** *b*; **5.** *c*; **6.** *c*; **7.** *b*

APPENDIX TO CHAPTER 4

INDIFFERENCE CURVE ANALYSIS

Fill-in questions

1. money income, the price of X, the price of Y

2. *a.* right; *b.* inward, F

3. total satisfaction (utility); *a.* downward, rate, substitution; *b.* convex

4. smaller, decreases

5. greater

6. tangent to an indifference curve, the ra-

tio of the price of the product the quantity of which is measured on the horizontal axis to the price of the product the quantity of which is measured on the vertical axis

7. up

8. is, does not

9. *a.* outward, right; *b.* higher; *c.* more

10. demand

Problems and projects

1. *b.* (1) 30, 25, 20, 15, 10, 5, 0; (3) 5; *c.* (1) 3, 15; (2) 36, 36

2. *a.* (1) 5, 10; (2) 50, 50; *b.* (1) 12, 4; (2) 80, 20; *c.* (1) 19, 1; (2) 95, 5; *e.* elastic, substitutes

Self-test

1. F; **2.** T; **3.** T; **4.** T; **5.** F; **6.** F; **7.** F; **8.** T; **9.** T; **10.** T

1. *d*; **2.** *b*; **3.** *b*; **4.** *b*; **5.** *c*; **6.** *b*; **7.** *b*; **8.** *d*; **9.** *b*; **10.** *b*

5

CAPITALISM, ITS MARKET STRUCTURES, AND CANADIAN BUSINESS

Fill-in questions

1. private property

2. enterprise, choice

3. do what is best for itself, competition

4. *a.* large numbers of independently acting buyers and sellers operating in the markets; *b.* freedom of those buyers and sellers to enter or leave these markets.

5. communicating, synchronizing (co-ordinating)

6. markets, prices

7. a limited

8. *a.* a large number of independent sellers in a highly organized market; *b.* the firms produce a standardized or virtually standardized product; *c.* individual firms exert no significant control over product price; *d.* new firms are free to enter and existing firms are free to leave the industry; *e.* there is virtually no room for non-price competition

9. sellers', buyers'

10. standardized, differentiated; close substitutes

11. barriers

12. public relations, goodwill

13. large, easy, some

14. *a.* there is only one firm in the industry; *b.* the firm produces a product for which there are no close substitutes; *c.* the firm exercises considerable control over the price of its product; *d.* there are barriers to entry into the industry; *e.* advertising is limited and of a goodwill or public relations nature

15. small

16. *a.* a large number of independent sellers; *b.* the product is differentiated; *c.* the firm has a limited amount of control over the price of its product; *d.* entry into the industry is relatively easy; *e.* there is extensive and vigorous non-price competition

17. the product is standardized in pure competition and differentiated in monopolistic competition

18. standardized, differentiated

19. raw, semi-finished, finished, consumer

20. few, significant

21. interdependence

22. *a.* the legislation and policies of government; *b.* business policies and practices; *c.* technology; *d.* capitalistic institutions; *e.* foreign direct investment

23. (1) pure competition, monopsony, monopsonistic competition, oligopsony; (2) large number of buyers, one buyer, fairly large number of buyers, a few buyers

24. one, sole proprietorship, corporation

25. unlimited, limited

26. *a.* CORP; *b.* PRO and PART; *c.* PRO; *d.* CORP; *e.* CORP; *f.* CORP; *g.* PART; *h.* PART; *i.* CORP

27. 32, 68

28. manufacturing; community, business, and personal service

29. 2.5

30. few, large

Problems and projects

1. number of firms: d, a, c, b; type of product: e, e, f, e or f; control over price: m, h, g, g; entry: i, j, k, l; non-price competition: m, g, h, g or h

2. *a.* oligopoly or monopolistic competition, standardized product, number of firms is fairly large, easy entry; *b.* oligopoly or monopolistic competition; differentiated product, number of firms is fairly large, entry is moderately difficult; *c.* pure competition; large number of firms, standardized product, easy entry; *d.* oligopoly; small number of firms, difficult entry; *e.* oligopoly or monopolistic competition; differentiated product, number of firms is fairly large, easy entry; *f.* oligopoly; small number of firms, entry is fairly difficult

3. *a.* yes, railroads, buses, automobiles; *b.* yes; synthetic fibres (nylon, rayon); *c.* yes, aluminum, steel, wood, copper, glass; *d.* yes; radios, movies, books, records, all forms of entertainment; *e.* yes; aluminum, steel, wood, glass, plastics

4. *a.* Firms a, b, c, d, and f are in wholesale and retail trade; firms b, g, h, and j are in manufacturing; firms h and i are in mining; firm e is in public utilities; Alcan Aluminium is engaged in aluminium rolling and casting and Inco is engaged in smelting and refining.

Self-test

1. F; **2.** T; **3.** T; **4.** T; **5.** F; **6.** T; **7.** T; **8.** F; **9.** T; **10.** F; **11.** T; **12.** F; **13.** T; **14.** T; **15.** F; **16.** F; **17.** F; **18.** T; **19.** F; **20.** T; **21.** T; **22.** F; **23.** T

1. *b*; **2.** *a*; **3.** *c*; **4.** *d*; **5.** *c*; **6.** *b*; **7.** *b*; **8.** *a*; **9.** *a*; **10.** *b*; **11.** *b*; **12.** *d*; **13.** *a*; **14.** *d*; **15.** *a*; **16.** *b*; **17.** *a*; **18.** *c*; **19.** *b*; **20.** *d*; **21.** *a*; **22.** *b*; **23.** *b*; **24.** *b*

6

THE COSTS OF PRODUCTION

Fill-in questions

1. other, opportunity

2. attract, explicit, implicit

3. entrepreneur(s); *a.* revenues, costs; *b.* explicit

4. variable, fixed, short-, long-

5. variable, fixed, marginal

6. *a.* rising; *b.* falling; *c.* maximum

8. fixed, variable, variable

10. average variable, average total, marginal

11. total variable, total cost

12. falling, rising

13. *a.* falling; *b.* rising; *c.* maximum; *d.* minimum; *e.* (1) marginal, equal, (2) marginal, equal

14. plant

16. *a.* increased specialization in the use of labour; *b.* better utilization of and increased specialization in management; *c.* more efficient productive equipment; *d*. greater utilization of by-products

17. managerial complexities (problems)

18. structure, competitiveness

Problems and projects

1. *a*. 80, 120, 130, 70, 50, 30, 10, −10; *b*. third, fourth; *c*. positive, negative; *d*. 80, 100, 110, 100, 90, 80, 70, 60

2. *a*. $0, 10, 20, 30, 40, 50, 60, 70, 80, 90, 100; *b*. $2.00, 1.67, 1.43, 1.67, 2.00, 2.50, 3.33, 5.00, 10.00; *c*. (1) decreases; (2) increases; *d*. 2.00, 1.82; 1.67, 1.67, 1.72, 1.82, 1.94, 2.11, 2.31, 2.56; *e*. (1) decreases, (2) increases

3. *a*.

Total cost	Average fixed cost	Average total cost	Marginal cost
$ 200	–	–	–
250	$200.00	$250.00	$ 50
290	100.00	145.00	40
320	66.67	106.67	30
360	50.00	90.00	40
420	40.00	84.00	60
500	33.33	83.33	80
600	28.57	85.71	100
720	25.00	90.00	120
870	22.22	96.67	150
1,100	20.00	111.00	230

4. *a*. $7.00, 6.00, 5.00, 4.00, 4.00, 3.00, 4.00, 5.00, 6.00, 5.00, 7.00, 10.00; *b*. (1) 10, 40; (2) 50, 80; (3) 90, 120

Self-test

1. T; **2.** F; **3.** T; **4.** F; **5.** F; **6.** F; **7.** T; **8.** F; **9.** T; **10.** T; **11.** T; **12.** F; **13.** F; **14.** F; **15.** T

1. *b*; **2.** *b*; **3.** *d*; **4.** *a*; **5.** *b*; **6.** *a*; **7.** *d*; **8.** *a*; **9.** *c*; **10.** *d*; **11.** *c*; **12.** *b*; **13.** *b*; **14.** *a*; **15.** *d*

7

PRICE AND OUTPUT DETERMINATION: PURE COMPETITION

Fill-in questions

1. *a*. a large number of independent sellers; *b*. a standardized product; *c*. no single firm supplies enough to influence market price; *d*. no obstacles to the entry of new firms or the exodus of old firms.

2. elastic, equal to

3. total revenue minus total cost

4. total-receipts–total-cost, marginal-revenue–marginal-cost

5. profit, fixed costs; *a*. maximum, minimum; *b*. cost, revenue (either order)

6. variable

7. that portion of the firm's marginal-cost curve which lies above the average-variable-cost curve, the sum of the short-run supply curves of all firms in the industry

8. total quantity demanded, total quantity supplied (either order), the quantity demanded and supplied at the equilibrium price

9. fixed, variable

10. average, marginal (either order), minimum

11. the firms in the industry are realizing profits in the short run, the firms in the industry are realizing losses in the short run

12. increasing-, upsloping

13. productive, allocative (either order)

14. *a*. normal; *b*. economic

15. enter, fall, more, larger, decrease, zero

16. cost

17. *a*. dollars; *b*. sovereign; *c*. restrict

18. average, minimum

19. marginal

20. *a.* income, *b.* prices

21. *a.* preferences (tastes), technology, resources; *b.* guiding

22. *a.* profit; *b.* losses (bankruptcy)

23. private, public (social), invisible hand

24. it efficiently allocates resources, it emphasizes personal freedom

25. market; *a.* produces the "wrong" amounts of certain goods and services; *b.* fails to allocate any resources to the production of certain goods and services whose production is economically justified

26. spillover

27. people other than the buyers and sellers (third parties)

28. *a.* over; *b.* under

29. *a.* (1) enact legislation, (2) impose specific taxes; *b.* (1) subsidize production, (2) finance or take over the production of the product

30. exclusion, indivisible, benefits

31. taxing, spends the revenue to buy

Problems and projects

1. *a.* average revenues: all are $10.00; total revenue: $0, 10.00, 20.00, 30.00, 40.00, 50.00, 60.00; marginal revenue: all are 10.00; *b.* yes, because price (average revenue) is constant and equal to marginal revenue; *d.* infinity; *e.* they are equal

2. *a.* see table at the bottom of this page

b. (1) 0, −$300; (2) 5, −$100; (3) 7, $380;

c.

Price	Quantity supplied	Profit
$360	10	$1,700
290	9	1,070
230	8	590
180	7	240
140	6	0
110	5	−150
80	4	−270
60	0	−300

d. (1) quantity supplied: 1,000, 900, 800, 700, 600, 500, 400; (2) (*a*) 180; (*b*) 7; (*c*) 240; (*d*) enter, profits in the industry will attract them into the industry

2. a.

Market price = $55		Market price = $120		Market price = $200	
Revenue	Profit	Revenue	Profit	Revenue	Profit
$ 0	$ −300	$ 0	$−300	$ 0	$−300
55	−345	120	−280	200	−200
110	−340	240	−210	400	−50
165	−345	360	−150	600	90
220	−370	480	−110	800	210
275	−425	600	−100	1,000	300
330	−510	720	−120	1,200	360
385	−635	840	−180	1,400	380
440	−810	960	−290	1,600	350
495	−1,045	1,080	−460	1,800	260
550	−1,350	1,200	−700	2,000	100

3. *a.* 140; *b.* 6; *c.* 133 = 800 (the total quantity demanded at $140) ÷ 6 (the output of each firm); *d.* 150 = 900 ÷ 6; *e.* (1) the curve is a horizontal line, (2) the curve slopes upward

4. $6, −$5; $10; *a.* C; *b.* produce A and have an economic profit of $14; *c.* it would increase

5. *a.* method 2; *b.* 15; *c.* (1) 13, 8; 3, 4, 2, 4; (2) 15, 4

6. *a.* under; *b.* over; *c.* Q_2, optimum

7. *a.* (1) supply, taxing, (2) decreases, increases; *b.* (2) subsidize, lower, (4) greater than, below

Self-test

1. F; **2.** T; **3.** T; **4.** T; **5.** T; **6.** T; **7.** T; **8.** T; **9.** T; **10.** T; **11.** T; **12.** T; **13.** F; **14.** T; **15.** T; **16.** T; **17.** T; **18.** T; **19.** T; **20.** T; **21.** T; **22.** T; **23.** T; **24.** T; **25.** T; **26.** T; **27.** T; **28.** T; **29.** F; **30.** T; **31.** T; **32.** T; **33.** F

1. *c;* **2.** *c*; **3.** *a*; **4.** *b*; **5.** *b*; **6.** *b*; **7.** *c*; **8.** *c*; **9.** *b*; **10.** *a*; **11.** *b*; **12.** *c*; **13.** *d*; **14.** *d*; **15.** *a*; **16.** *a*; **17.** *c*; **18.** *b*; **19.** *a*; **20.** *d*; **21.** *b*; **22.** *d*; **23.** *c*; **24.** *b*; **25.** *a*; **26.** *b*

8

PRICE AND OUTPUT DETERMINATION: PURE MONOPOLY

Fill-in questions

1. close substitutes, blocked

2. *a.* the economies of scale; *b.* natural monopolies; *c.* ownership of essential raw materials; *d.* patents and research; *e.* unfair competition; *f.* the economies of being established

3. greater, money capital

4. natural, regulated

5. less than, less, decrease

6. marginal revenue, marginal cost, greater

7. *a.* highest possible; *b.* a maximum; *c.* profit

8. a minimum, price (or average revenue), marginal cost

9. costs (or cost schedules); *a.* scale; *b.* X-inefficiency

10. techniques (technology), costs (or cost schedules), products

11. upper

12. prices, cost

13. *a.* the seller has some monopoly power; *b.* the seller is able to separate buyers into groups that have different elasticities of demand for the product; *c.* the original buyers cannot resell the product

14. increase, increase

15. marginal cost, average (total) cost

16. average (total) cost, misallocation

Problems and projects

1. *a.* total revenue: $0, 650, 1,200, 1,650, 2,000, 2,250, 2,400, 2,450, 2,400, 2,250, 2,000; marginal revenue: $650, 550, 450, 350, 250, 150, 50, −50, −150, −250; *b.* inelastic; *c.* (1)6; (2) 400; (3) 1,560; *d.* (1) total revenue: $0, 650, 1,250, 1,800, 2,300, 2,750, 3,150, 3,500, 3,800, 4,050, 4,250; marginal revenue: $650, 600, 550, 500, 450, 400, 350, 300, 250, 200; (2) price; (3) 8,300, 2,550; (4) larger, larger

2. *a.* 4, 11.50, 4.00; *b.* 6, 850, −7.50, bankrupt, subsidize; *c.* 73.50, 58.50, 15.00; *d.* 5, 10.00, zero; *e.* b, a, d

Self-test

1. F; **2.** T; **3.** F; **4.** T; **5.** F; **6.** T; **7.** T; **8.** F; **9.** F;

10. T; 11. T; 12. F; 13. F; 14. T; 15. F; 16. F; 17. T

1. *b*; 2. *c*; 3. *d*; 4. *a*; 5. *c*; 6. *d*; 7. *b*; 8. *c*; 9. *a*; 10. *d*; 11. *b*; 12. *d*; 13. *b*; 14. *a*; 15. *b*; 16. *a*

9

PRICE AND OUTPUT DETERMINATION: MONOPOLISTIC COMPETITION

Fill-in questions

1. relatively large number of, differentiated, do not, price, non-price, fairly easy

2. limited, rivalry

3. *a.* more, less; *b.* number of rivals the firm has, the degree of product differentiation; *c.* marginal cost, marginal revenue

4. reduce, increase

5. average cost, zero, greater

6. average cost is greater than minimum average cost, price is greater than marginal cost

7. product differentiation, product promotion

8. variety, quality

9. both

10. product, promotion

Problems and projects

2. *a.* marginal cost: $30, 10, 20, 30, 40, 50, 60, 70, 80, 90; marginal revenue: $110, 90, 70, 50, 30, 10, −10, −30, −50, −70; *b.* (1) 4; (2) $80; (3) $180; *c.* (1) decrease; (2) average cost; (3) equal to zero

Self-test

1. F; 2. T; 3. F; 4. T; 5. F; 6. T; 7. F; 8. T; 9. F; 10. F

1. *c*; 2. *b*; 3. *c*; 4. *d*; 5. *d*; 6. *b*; 7. *d*; 8. *b*; 9. *b*; 10. *a*

10

PRICE AND OUTPUT DETERMINATION: OLIGOPOLY

Fill-in questions

1. few, standardized, differentiated, difficult

2. the economies of scale, other barriers to entry, the advantages of merger

3. mutually interdependent, the reactions of rivals, no, so many

4. many, uncertain

5. inflexible, simultaneously

6. elastic, elastic, inelastic

7. not raise their prices, lower their prices

8. gap, price the oligopolist will charge

9. by a pure monopolist

10. price, output, share

11. informal, prices, the ingenuity of each seller (*i.e.,* non-price competition)

12. *a.* demand and cost differences; *b.* a large number of firms; *c.* cheating (secret price cutting); *d.* a recession; *e.* legal obstacles (anti-combines laws)

13. tacit, price leadership

14. markup, average

15. price, non-price, share of the market, *a.* price cuts can be quickly matched by rival firms; *b.* oligopolists tend to have the greater financial resources required to engage in non-price competition

16. higher, smaller, slower

17. *a.* means, incentives; *b.* product improvement, costs, prices, output, employment

18. have not

19. a few firms, both absolutely and relatively

20. competition, monopoly

21. the public

22. *a.* internal growth or superior efficiency; *b.* economic efficiency; *c.* services

23. anti-combines; *a.* labour unions, co-operatives, *caisses populaires,*credit unions; agriculture; *b.* patents, protective tariffs

24. natural, agencies, commissions

25. *a.* cost, capital, labour; *b.* the industry (firms) they are supposed to regulate; *c.* natural, competitive

26. monopoly, cartel

27. quality; *a.* conditions, society, character; *b.* industrial, economic (either order)

28. *a.* greater; *b.* inflation, slower, less

Problems and projects

1. *a.* total revenue: 290, 560, 810, 1,040, 1,250, 1,260, 1,265, 1,265, 1,260; *b.* marginal revenue: 2.70, 2.50, 2.30, 2.10, 0.40, 0.20, 0, −0.20; *c.* 2.50, 500; *e.* (1) 2.50, 500; (2) 2.50, 500, they have decreased; (3) 2.50, 500, they have increased

2. *a.* marginal cost: $30, 20, 30, 40, 50, 60, 70, 80; marginal revenue: $130, 110, 90, 70, 50, 30, 10, −10; *b.* $90; *c.* (1) 5; (2) $280; *d.* (1) 15; (2) $840; *e.* no; *f.* $90

3. *a.* 400; *b.* 800; *c.* (1) 533.33, (2) 7033.33, (3) 8.2

4. *a.* B; *b.* C; *c.* H; *d.* F; *e.* A; *f.* D; *g.* E

Self-test

1. T; **2.** F; **3.** T; **4.** F; **5.** T; **6.** F; **7.** F; **8.** F; **9.** T; **10.** T; **11.** F; **12.** T; **13.** F; **14.** F; **15.** T; **16.** F; **17.** T; **18.** F; **19.** F; **20.** F; **21.** T; **22.** F; **23.** F; **24.** T; **25.** T; **26.** T

1. *b*; **2.** *d*; **3.** *d*; **4.** *d*; **5.** *c*; **6.** *c*; **7.** *d*; **8.** *c*; **9.** *c*; **10.** *b*; **11.** *d*; **12.** *d*; **13.** *a*; **14.** *d*; **15.** *d*; **16.** *b*; **17.** *b*; **18.** *b*; **19.** *a*; **20.** *d*; **21.** *d*; **22.** *c*; **23.** *d*; **24.** *d*; **25.** *a*; **26.** *b*

11

PRODUCTION AND THE DEMAND FOR ECONOMIC RESOURCES

Fill-in questions

1. resources, incomes, costs

2. derived, productivity, value (price)

3. marginal revenue product, marginal resource cost; price, marginal resource cost (either order)

4. marginal revenue product, prices

5. lower, less

6. adding up the demand curves for the resource of all the firms hiring the resource

7. product, productivity, prices

8. *a.* +; *b.* −; *c.* +; *d.* −; *e.* +

9. more, less, substitution, more, output

10. marginal physical product, substituted, price-elasticity, proportion of total production costs accounted for by the resource

11. marginal physical product, price

12. marginal revenue product, price

13. one

14. *a.* marginal physical product, marginal resource cost; *b.* marginal revenue product, marginal resource cost, marginal revenue product, marginal revenue cost, one

15. marginal revenue product (marginal contribution to the firm's revenue)

Problems and projects

1. *a.* marginal physical product of A: 12, 10,

8, 6, 4, 2, 1; *b.* total revenue: 0, 18.00, 33.00, 45.00, 54.00, 60.00, 63.00, 64.50; marginal revenue product of A: 18.00, 15.00, 12.00, 9.00, 6.00, 3.00, 1.50; *c.* 0, 1, 2, 3, 4, 5, 6, 7

2. *a.* total product: 0, 22, 43, 62, 78, 90, 97, 98; *b.* (1) total revenue: 0, 22.00, 38.70, 49.60, 54.60, 54.00, 48.50, 39.20; (2) marginal revenue product of B: 22.00, 16.70, 10.90, 5.00, -0.60, -5.50, -9.30; *c.* 0, 1, 2, 3, 4, 4

3. *a.* (1) 1, 3; (2) 3, 5; *b.* 5, 6; *c.* the marginal physical product of C divided by its price, the marginal physical product of D divided by its price; *d.* purely, $.50; *e.* (1) 114; (2) $57; (3) $28; (4) $29

Self-test

1. T; 2. T; 3. F; 4. T; 5. T; 6. T; 7. F; 8. F; 9. T; 10. F; 11. F; 12. T; 13. F; 14. F; 15. T

1. *d*; 2. *c*; 3. *a*; 4. *d*; 5. *c*; 6. *a*; 7. *c*; 8. *c*; 9. *a*; 10. *b*; 11. *c*; 12. *d*; 13. *a*; 14. *b*; 15. *b*

12

THE PRICING AND EMPLOYMENT OF RESOURCES: WAGE DETERMINATION

Fill-in questions

1. time, wage rate, the amount of time worked, the goods and services money wages will purchase

2. *a.* great; *b.* capital equipment, natural resources, technology, quality

3. *a.* wages, alternative employment; *b.* marginal-revenue-product (demand) schedules; *c.* total quantity of labour demanded, total quantity of labour supplied (either order)

4. perfectly, wage rate

5. marginal revenue product, wage rate, marginal labour cost

6. marginal revenue product, marginal labour cost, greater, marginal revenue product, labour cost

7. lower, less

8. increase wages, demand, supply, above-equilibrium

9. restricting the supply of labour, imposing above-equilibrium wage rates; *a.* decreased; *b.* decrease; *c.* growing, inelastic

10. products they produce, productivity, prices

11. the marginal revenue product of labour, competitive and monopsonistic equilibrium wage, the relative bargaining strength of the union and monopsonist

12. *a.* increase, decrease; *b.* increase, increase; *c.* increase, decrease

13. increase, decrease, have no effect on

14. homogeneous, attractiveness, imperfect

15. non-competing, equalizing differences

16. immobilities, geographical, sociological, institutional

17. 60, occupational

18. crowding, low

19. *a.* education, health, mobility; *b.* productivity, wage rates (income); *c.* real wages; *d.* non-competing, differences

Problems and projects

1. *a.* quantity of labour demanded: 100, 200, 300, 400, 500, 600, 700, 800; *b.* (1) 10.00; (2) 600; *c.* (1) 10.00; (2) 6; (3) 10.00; *f.* 400.

2. *a.* total labour cost: 0, 4.00, 12.00, 24.00, 40.00, 60.00, 84.00 112.00, 144.00; marginal labour cost: 4.00, 8.00, 12.00, 16.00, 20.00, 24.00, 28.00, 32.00; *b.* (1) 5; (2) 12.00; (3) 20.00; *d.* 6, 14.00

3. *a.* wage rate: 16.00, 16.00, 16.00, 16.00, 16.00, 16.00, 16.00, 18.00; *b.* total labour cost: 16.00, 32.00, 48.00, 64.00, 80.00, 96.00, 112.00, 144.00; marginal labour cost: 16.00, 16.00, 16.00, 16.00, 16.00, 16.00, 16.00, 32.00; *c.* (1) 6; (2) 16.00; (3) 96.00; *d.* increased, increased, increased

4. *a.* (1) 3, (2) 9; *b.* (1) (a) 7, (b) 18, (2) (a) 7, (b) 15,30, (c) 12

Self-test

1. F; **2.** T; **3.** T; **4.** T; **5.** T; **6.** T; **7.** F; **8.** F; **9.** T; **10.** F; **11.** T; **12.** T; **13.** T; **14.** T; **15.** T

1. *a*; **2.** *a*; **3.** *a*; **4.** *c*; **5.** *d*; **6.** *d*; **7.** *d*; **8.** *c*; **9.** *a*; **10.** *d*; **11.** *c*; **12.** *b*; **13.** *a*; **14.** *a*; **15.** *b*; **16.** *c*; **17.** *a*; **18.** *a*; **19.** *d*; **20.** *d*

13

THE PRICING AND EMPLOYMENT OF RESOURCES: RENT, INTEREST, AND PROFITS

Fill-in questions

1. land, natural resources, fixed (perfectly inelastic)

2. demand, supply, incentive, surplus

3. unearned, nationalized, single tax

4. land differs in productivity (quality), individual, alternative uses

5. money

6. risk, the length of loan, the amount of the loan, market imperfections

7. the monetary authority (the Bank of Canada)

8. the rate of interest, net profits

9. administered, investment, rations

10. entrepreneurial ability, resources, non-routine, innovates, risks

11. uncertain, insurable, uninsurable, economy as a whole, innovation

12. *a.* investment, employment, output; *b.* allocation, monopoly

13. *a.* 80; *b.* rent, interest, corporation profit, 20; *c.* (1) remained constant, (2) remained constant

14. *a.* profits; *b.* productivity, the prices of the products they produce; *c.* labour's share of the national income

Problems and projects

1. *a.* 250; *b.* 300,000; *d.* 0, 300,000

2. *a.* 71.3; *b.* 79.1, 20.9

Self-test

1. F; **2.** T; **3.** F; **4.** F; **5.** F; **6.** T; **7.** F; **8.** T; **9.** T; **10.** F; **11.** F.

1. *a*; **2.** *d*; **3.** *b*; **4.** *d*; **5.** *b*; **6.** *d*; **7.** *a*; **8.** *b*; **9.** *b*; **10.** *b*; **11.** *d*; **12.** *c*; **13.** *d*; **14.** *d*

14

RURAL ECONOMICS: THE FARM PROBLEM

Fill-in questions

1. *a.* prosperity; *b.* prosperity; *c.* mediocre; *d.* depression; *e.* prosperity; *f.* depression; *g.* prosperity; *h.* mediocre

2. less, highly unequal; *a.* 28, 77; *b.* 53, 9; *c.* 19, 14

3. lag behind, instability

4. inelastic, greater, immobility

5. substitutes

6. technological

7. increased rapidly enough, less

8. immobile

9. inelastic, small, large, small, large

10. resources, the agricultural, non-agricultural

11. *a.* progress (economic growth); *b.* competitive, unable

12. output, prices and incomes

13. 90, five

14. surpluses, purchase; *a.* incomes; *b.* prices, taxes to finance the government purchases

15. increase, decrease

16. deficiency payments, will not, identical

17. Lower Inventory for Tomorrow (LIFT), 1970-1971

18. reallocated, high

19. foreign

20. export

21. grains, cereal preparations

Problems and projects

1. *a.* inelastic; *b.* decrease, 4,800, 2,800, 16 $^2/_3$, decrease, 41 $^2/_3$; *c.* fall 4.00, 3.20, fall, 2,800, 2,240; *d.* (1) 100, (2) 720, (3) 5,184; (4) 3.20, 2,304 (5) 2,880, (6) 4.00, 100

2. *a.* increase, 153,750.00, 200,000.00; *b.* increase, 153,750.00, 205,000.00

3. *a.* (1) 850, 1,150, 300, (2) 2,210, 780, 2,990; *b.* (1) 1,150, 1.40; (2) 1,610, 1.20, 1,380, 2,990; *c.* 2,990; (1) more, 600, (2) 300, 1.20, 600, less

4. *a.* (1) 550, 1,150, 600, (2) 1,430, 1,560, 2,990; *b.* (1) 1,150, 1.80; (2) 2,070, 0.80, 920, 2,990; *c.* 2,990, (1) less, 640, (2) 600, 0.80, 640, more

5. *a.* inelastic;

b. $\dfrac{1,500 - 550}{(1,500 + 550)/2} \div \dfrac{\$2.60 - \$1.80}{(\$2.60 + \$1.80)/2}$

2.55, elastic; *c.* (1) less, inelastic, (2) less, elastic, (3) inelastic, elastic, (4) deficiency payment, more, lower; *d.* (1) offer-to-purchase,

(2) deficiency payment

Self-test

1. T; **2.** F; **3.** T; **4.** F; **5.** T; **6.** F; **7.** T; **8.** F; **9.** T; **10.** F; **11.** T; **12.** T; **13.** T; **14.** F; **15.** F; **16.** T; **17.** F; **18.** F

1. *c*; **2.** *d*; **3.** *a*; **4.** *d*; **5.** *a*; **6.** *c*; **7.** *d*; **8.** *c*; **9.** *d*; **10.** *d*; **11.** *b*; **12.** *c*; **13.** *b*; **14.** *c*; **15.** *a*; **16.** *b*

15

INCOME DISTRIBUTION: INEQUALITY AND POVERTY

Fill-in questions

1. considerable

2. barely changed, barely changed, slight, has not

3. Lorenz; *a.* families, income; *b.* lower, upper; *c.* Lorenz curve, the line of complete equality (either order)

4. *a.* tax, tax; *b.* mobility; *c.* is not

5. ability, education, training, tastes, property, power

6. *a.* utility; *b.* income

7. equality, efficiency (either order); *a.* smaller; *b.* more

8. *a.* $20,812; *b.* 13.1, 36.6, 3.9

9. *a.* old; *b.* unattached individuals; *c.* females; *d.* educated; *e.* full-time, year-round; *f.* large

10. *a.* much of it is isolated and unseen in the hearts of large cities; *b.* the sick and old seldom venture onto the streets; *c.* rural poverty is away from the main highways; *d.* the poor have no political voice

11. old age security, income supplement; pension plans; allowances; insurance benefits; insurance; welfare

12. efficient, equitable, incentives

13. guaranteed annual, benefit-loss

14. *a.* poverty, incentives, costs; *b.* conflicting

Problems and projects

1. *a.* (1) column 4: 18, 30, 44, 61, 80, 91, 100; (2) column 5: 4, 10, 22, 36, 51, 71, 100; *b.* (1) 30, 10; (2) 20, 49

2. *a.* NIT subsidy: 4,000, 3,000, 2,000, 1,000, 0; Total income: 9,000, 13,000, 17,000, 21,000, 25,000; (1) 4,000, (2) 25,000; *b.* NIT subsidy: 3,750, 2,500, 1250, 0; Total income: 6,250, 7,500, 8,750, 10,000; (1) 10,000, (2) 2,500; *c.* NIT subsidy: 6,000, 4,500, 3,000, 1,500, 0; Total income: 9,000, 10,500, 12,000, 13,500, 15,000; (1) 15,000, (2) 18,750; *d.* (1) greater, greater, (2) greater, (3) increase, decrease

Self-test

1. T; **2.** F; **3.** F; **4.** T; **5.** F; **6.** T; **7.** F; **8.** F; **9.** T; **10.** T; **11.** T; **12.** T; **13.** F

1. *d*; **2.** *b*; **3.** *c*; **4.** *d*; **5.** *d*; **6.** *b*; **7.** *b*; **8.** *a*; **9.** *d*; **10.** *c*; **11.** *d*; **12.** *d*

16

MIXED CAPITALISM AND THE ECONOMIC FUNCTIONS OF GOVERNMENT

Fill-in questions

1. market, centrally planned (either order)

2. *a.* provide legal foundation and social environment; *b.* maintain competition; *c.* redistribute income and wealth; *d.* reallocate resources; *e.* stabilize the economy; *f.* nation-building

3. *a.* regulate, natural, ownership of; *b.* anti-combines (anti-monopoly)

4. unequal; *a.* social insurance; *b.* market; *c.* income

5. market; *a.* produces the "wrong" amounts of certain goods and services; *b.* fails to allocate any resources to the production of certain goods and services whose production is economically justified

6. user charges, peak-pricing

7. taxing, spends the revenue to buy

8. *a.* increases, increasing, decreasing; *b.* decreases, decreasing, increasing

9. stabilizing the economy

10. benefits, costs

11. *a.* estimate (measure); *b.* costs, benefits

12. public, failure

13. *a.* special; *b.* clear, hidden; *c.* select; *d.* incentives, test (measure)

14 choice

15 *a.* private sector; *b.* imperfect; *c.* assigned

16 limited decisions

Problems and projects

1. *a.* reallocates resources; *b.* redistributes income; *c.* provides a legal foundation and social environment *and* stabilizes the economy; *d.* reallocates resources; *e.* maintains competition; *f.* provides a legal foundation and a social environment *and* maintains competition; *g.* reallocates income; *h.* reallocates resources; *i.* provides a legal foundation and social environment; *j.* reallocates income; *k.* nation-building

2. 300, 15, 30, 10, 510, 30, 5; *a.* 1,800, 900; *b.* $.50; *c.* $.50; *d.* (1) 810, (2) Total revenue: 225, 67.50, 90, 45, 270, 90, 22.50; 810, (3) 7am-9am, 4pm-6pm; *e.* (1) 55, (2) 64

3. *a.* 4,000, 2,500; *b.* 5,000; *c.* 7,500,000; *d.* 1,000, 1,500,000

4. *a.* (1) businesses, resources, households,

(2) households, products, businesses, (3) government, products, businesses, (4) businesses, (5) government, resources, households, (6) households; *b.* (1) 3, 5 (either order), 4, 6 (either order), (2) 3, 4, 6 (any order), (3) increase, decrease, 6

5. *a.* marginal cost: $500, $180, $80, $100; marginal benefit: $650, $100, $50, $25; *b.* yes; *c.* (1) 2, (2) $500, (3) $650, (4) $150.

Self-test

1. F; **2.** F; **3.** F; **4.** F; **5.** T; **6.** F; **7.** T; **8.** F; **9.** F; **10.** F; **11.** F; **12.** F; **13.** T; **14.** F; **15.** F; **16.** T; **17.** F

1. *a*; **2.** *a*; **3.** *d*; **4.** *a*; **5.** *c*; **6.** *a*; **7.** *b*; **8.** *c*; **9.** *a*; **10.** *a*; **11.** *d*

17

THE RADICAL CRITIQUE: THE ECONOMICS OF DISSENT

Fill-in questions

1. nature; *a.* other; *b.* bourgeois, the proletariat

2. property, employment (a livelihood), surplus value, wage, value

3. competition, profits (surplus value), real domestic, labour, profit

4. exploitation

5. *a.* the monopolization of; *b.* imperialism

6. revolution, proletariat, capital, capitalistic, socialistic (classless)

7. *a.* harmony, conflict; *b.* narrow, political

8. *a.* large (monopolistic), state (government), markets, workers, consumers; *b.* inequality, imperialism; *c.* socialism

9. *a.* It fails to control monopolies; *b.* It uses revenues from regressive taxes to subsidize them; *c.* It provides markets for them

10. marginal product, national income; *a.* competitive; *b.* labour; *c.* unearned

11. *a.* private, power; *b.* dual, primary, secondary

12. *a.* lives, decision; *b.* large corporations

13. *a.* profit; *b.* environment, military, imperialistic

14. socialism, democratic, profits

15. reality, objective, ideology, option

Problems and projects

1 *a.* 8, 7, 6, 5, 4, 3, 2; *b.* 5; *c.* 20; *d.* 30, 10; *e.* 6; *f.* 2

2 *a.* 400; 394, 388.6; *b.* 70, 69, 68; *c.* 120, 118, 116.6; *d.* (1) 380, 386, 392.4, (2) .316, .306, .297; *e.* (1) decreases, increases, (2) decreases

Self-test

1. F; **2.** T; **3.** T; **4.** F; **5.** F; **6.** F; **7.** T; **8.** F; **9.** T; **10.** T; **11.** F; **12.** T; **13.** F; **14.** F; **15.** T; **16.** F; **17.** F; **18.** T; **19.** F; **20.** T;

1. *b*; **2.** *d*; **3.** *a*; **4.** *c*; **5.** *d*; **6.** *a*; **7.** *c*; **8.** *d*; **9.** *b*; **10.** *d*; **11.** *d*; **12.** *b*; **13.** *c*; **14.** *d*; **15.** *b*; **16.** *b*; **17.** *a*; **18.** *d*

18

NATIONAL INCOME ACCOUNTING

Fill-in questions

1. production, policies

2. market prices

3. double counting

4. value added

5. market, final, gross domestic

6. durable, semi-durable, non-durable, services

7. *a.* all final purchases of machinery, tools, and equipment by business firms and government; all construction; changes in inventories; *b.* capital consumption allowances

8. negative, declining

9. exports, imports

10. C, I_g, G, X_n

11. non-income

12. supplementary, insurance, private (or company)

13. corporation income taxes, dividends, undistributed corporation profits

14. gross national product, resident, less than, negative

15. indirect taxes, capital consumption allowances

16. *a.* transfer payments; corporation income taxes, undistributed corporation profits, other earnings not paid out to persons; *b.* personal taxes, personal consumption expenditures (including interest paid by consumers), personal saving

17. *a.* personal taxes; *b.* personal consumption expenditures (including interest paid by consumers) plus personal saving

18. the price level changes

19. *a.* non-market, leisure; *b.* quality, output, environment, hidden; *c.* per capita

20. falls

Problems and projects

1. *a.* (1) 13, (2) 13, (3) 41; *b.* see table at bottom of page; *c.* (1) 375, (2) 360, (3) 397, (4) 318, (5) 44

2 *a.* (1) 200,000, (2) 200,000; *b.* (1) 250,000, (2) 50,000; *c.* (1) 10,000, (2) 10,000; *d.* (1) 450,000, (2) 190,000; *e.* (1) 540,000, (2) 90,000; *f.* 540,000, 540,000

3. *a.* personal income and disposable income, a public transfer payment; *b.* none; a second-hand sale; *c.* all, represents investment (additions to inventories); *d.* all; *e.* none, a purely financial transaction; *f.* all; *g.* none, a non-market transaction; *h.* all; *i.* none, a private transfer payment; *j.* all; *k.* none, a non-market transaction; *l.* all; *m.* all, represents additions to the inventory of the retailer; *n.* personal income and disposable income, a public transfer payment; *o.* all; estimate of rental value of owner-occupied homes is included in rents

4. *a.* 1939; *b.* (1) deflation, (2) inflation, *c.* 86, 62, 91; *d.* (1)deflated, (2) inflated, (3) neither

Receipts: expenditures approach		Allocations: income approach	
C	$274	Wages, salaries & supp. L income	$255
G	94	Corp profits before taxes	47
I_g	95	Interest & misc. investment income	40
X_n	13	Accrued net income of farmers	4
		Net income of non-farm unincorp. business	29
		Net domestic income	375
		Indirect taxes (less subsidies)	47
		Capital consumption allowances	54
GDP	$476	GDP	$476

1. F; 2. T; 3. T; 4. T; 5. F; 6. T; 7. F; 8. T; 9. F; 10. T; 11. T; 12. F; 13. T; 14. T; 15. F; 16. T; 17. F; 18. F

1. *b*; 2. *d*; 3. *a*; 4. *b*; 5. *a*; 6. *c*; 7. *c*; 8. *b*; 9. *d*; 10. *a*; 11. *d*; 12. *a*; 13. *a*; 14. *d*; 15. *d*; 16. *a*; 17. *b*; 18. *d*

19

MACROECONOMIC INSTABILITY: UNEMPLOYMENT AND INFLATION

Fill-in questions

1. unsteady, inflation, output, employment

2. ups (increases), downs (decreases), recession, trough, recovery

3. expenditures, demand

4. seasonal, secular

5. durable, capital, non-durable, low-

6. *a*. frictional unemployment; *b*. structural unemployment; *c*. cyclical unemployment (any order)

7. *a*. natural; *b*. frictional, structural (either order); *c*. cyclical, actual, potential (either order); *d*. 6

8. equal to, constant

9. the number of persons unemployed, civilian labour force

10. potential, actual

11. teenage, uneducated

12. rise (increase), prices, 1987, 1986, 1986

13. *a*. an increase; *b*. market, labour unions, business firms (corporations);

14. *a*. fixed; *b*. unexpected; *c*. creditors, debtors; *d*. households, the public sector

15. *a*. increase; *b*. decrease; *c*. breakdown (collapse)

Problems and projects

1. The following figures complete the table. June: 1,304, 89.3, 10.7; July: 1,386, 88.8, 11.2; *a*. the labour force increased more than employment increased; *b*. because unemployment and employment in relative terms are percentages of the civilian labour force and *always* add up to 100%, and if one increases the other must decrease; *c*. no economist would argue that the full-employment unemployment rate is as high as 11% and the summer of 1982 was not a time of full employment; *d*. the number of people looking for work expands

2. *a*. B, B, C, A; *b*. B, B, C, B; *c*. A, D, A, D

3. *a*. D; *b*. I; *c*. B; *d*. D; *e*. D; *f*. I; *g*. B; *h*. B

4. *a*. 0; *b*. 19, 82.5; *c*. 97.5, (1) 2.5, (2) 7; *d*. 90, (1) 10, (2) 10

5. *a*. 12, 10, 5; *b*. 5.83, 7, 14

6. *a*. equal, the domestic output demanded and supplied at the equilibrium price level; *b*. (1) increase, (2) demand-pull; *c*. (1) rise, fall, (2) cost-push inflation

Self-test

1. T; 2. F; 3. F; 4. T; 5. F; 6. T; 7. F; 8. T; 9. T; 10. F; 11. T; 12. F; 13. T; 14. T; 15. T; 16. F; 17. F; 18. F; 19. T; 20. F; 21. T; 22. F; 23. T; 24. T; 25. F

1. *a*; 2. *d*; 3. *b*; 4. *c*; 5. *a*; 6. *b*; 7. *a*; 8. *c*; 9. *c*; 10. *d*; 11. *d*; 12. *c*; 13. *d*; 14. *b*; 15. *d*; 16. *c*; 17. *b*; 18. *d*; 19. *d*; 20. *d*; 21. *d*; 22. *a*; 23. *b*; 24. *d*; 25. *d*

20

MONEY AND BANKING IN CANADA

Fill-in questions

1. *a.* medium of exchange; *b.* standard of value; *c.* store of value

2. coins, paper money, demand deposits, banks, the federal government

3. *a.* trust, mortage loan, credit, insurance; *b.* savers, investors; *c.* create, destroy, are not, Bank of Canada, chartered bank

4. savings, term, notice, savings, Canada Savings Bonds

5. M1

6. *a.* their existence influences consuming-saving habits; *b.* conversion from near-money to money or from money to near-money may affect the stability of the economy; *c.* important when monetary policy is to be employed

7. Bank of Canada, chartered banks

8. *a.* are not; *b.* exchange, legal, scarce

9. desirable goods and services, inversely, price

10. *a.* directly, nominal GDP; *b.* inversely, rate of interest

11. supply, interest, money

12. deposits, make loans, chartered banks

13. deposits, create money

14. *a.* holding the deposits of the chartered banks; *b.* supplying the economy with paper currency; *c.* acting as fiscal agents for the government; *d.* supervising the chartered banks; *e.* regulating the money supply; regulating the money supply

15. deposits, taxes, bonds

Problems and projects

1. *a.* 11 (= 13 − 2); *b.* 29 (= 11 + 18); *c.* 37 (= 29 + 8)

2. *a.* rise, 25; *b.* fall, 9.1

3. *a.* (1) $\frac{1}{4}$ (25%), (2) 125; *b.* (1) 135, 145, 155, 165, 175, 185, 195; *c.* (2) 10; *d.* (1) fall, 8, (2) rise, 14; *e.* (1) increase, 10, rise, 2, (2) decrease, 15, fall, 3

Self-test

1. F; **2.** T; **3.** F; **4.** F; **5.** T; **6.** T; **7.** F; **8.** F; **9.** F; **10.** T; **11.** T; **12.** F; **13.** T; **14.** T; **15.** T; **16.** T; **17.** T; **18.** T

1. *a*; **2.** *d*; **3.** *d*; **4.** *c*; **5.** *d*; **6.** *b*; **7.** *b*; **8.** *d*; **9.** *b*; **10.** *c*; **11.** *b*; **12.** *a*; **13.** *b*; **14.** *d*; **15.** *b*

21

HOW BANKS CREATE MONEY

Fill-in questions

1. assets, liabilities, net worth

2. vault, till

3. demand, savings, term, notice

4. not changed

5. Bank of Canada, deposit liabilities, cash reserve ratio

6. actual reserves, required reserves

7. fractional

8. decreased, increased; decreased, increased

9. excess reserves

10. increases, 10,000

11. decreases, 2,000

12. profits, liquidity (safety)

13. monetary multiplier (reciprocal of the reserve ratio), reserves

14. smaller

15. decrease, 120 million

16. currency, excess

17. *a.* recession, prosperity; *b.* more

Problems and projects

1.

	(a)	*(b)*	*(c)*	*(d)*
Assets:				
Reserves	50	50	160	200
Loans	700	700	700	700
Securities	200	200	200	100
Liabilities and net worth:				
Deposits	850	850	960	900
Capital stock	100	100	100	100

2.

a.	*(1a)*	*(2a)*	*(3a)*	*(4a)*	*(5a)*
A. Required reserve	$17.50	$20	$15	$18	$22
B. Excess reserve	5	0	–5	4	1
C. New loans — single bank	5	0	*	4	1

b.	*(1b)*	*(2b)*	*(3b)*	*(4b)*	*(5b)*
Assets:					
Reserves	$ 22.50	$ 20	$10	$ 22	$23
Loans	132.50	140	*	142	188
Securities	50	60	30	70	60
Liabilities and net worth:					
Deposits	180	200	*	184	221
Capital stock	25	20	25	50	50

* If an individual bank is $5 short of reserves, it must either obtain additional reserves of $5 by selling $5 worth of securities, or by getting a $5 advance (very short-term loan) from the Bank of Canada, or by contracting its loans by $50 (for contracting loans by $50 will simultaneously contract deposits by $50, thus, in this case, bringing them to $100 — precisely right for reserves of $10)

3. column 2: 20, $16^2/_3$, 16, $12^1/_2$, 10, $8^1/_3$; column 3: 1, 1, 1, 1, 1, 1; column 4: 20, $16^2/_3$, 16, $12^1/_2$, 10, $8^1/_3$

4.

	(1)	(2)	(3)	(4)	(5)	(6)
Assets:						
Reserves	$ 30	$ 30	$ 33	$ 33	$ 24	$ 24
Loans	425	520	425	585	425	405
Securities	100	100	92	92	101	101
Liabilities and net worth:						
Deposits	505	600	500	660	500	480
Capital stock	50	50	50	50	50	50
Advances (loans) from Bank of Canada	0	0	0	0	0	0
Excess reserves	4.75	0	8	0	–1	0
Maximum possible expansion of the money supply	95	0	160	0	–20	0

Self-test

1. F; **2.** F; **3.** F; **4.** T; **5.** F; **6.** T; **7.** T; **8.** F; **9.** F; **10.** F; **11.** T; **12.** T; **13.** T; **14.** T; **15** T; **16.** F

1. *d*; **2.** *d*; **3.** *a*; **4.** *d*; **5.** *b*; **6.** *b*; **7.** *b*; **8.** *b*; **9.** *a*; **10.** *d*; **11.** *d*; **12.** *c*; **13.** *c*; **14.** *a*; **15.** *c*; **16.** *c*

22

THE BANK OF CANADA AND MONETARY POLICY

Fill-in questions

1. full-employment non-inflationary, Bank of Canada

2. decrease, decrease, increase, decrease

3. securities, bank notes in circulation, reserves of the chartered banks

4. open-market operations, the Bank Rate, Government of Canada deposits

5. money, interest

6. 10 million, 10 million, 9.5 million; 0,10

million, 10 million

7. buy; sell

8. open-market operations

9. the secondary reserve ratio, moral suasion

Problems and projects

1. Assets: securities, advances (loans) to banks; liabilities: Bank of Canada Notes, bank reserves (deposits), Government of Canada deposits

2. *a.* buy, 5; *b.* sell, 2 $^{1}/_{2}$

3.

	(2)	(3)	(4)
	Bank of Canada		
Assets:			
Securities	$20	$22	$21
Advances (loans) to chartered banks	0	0	0
Liabilities:			
Reserves of chartered banks	9	11	11
Government of Canada deposits	2	2	1
Bank of Canada Notes	9	9	9
	Chartered Banks		
Assets:			
Reserves	$ 9	$ 11	$ 11
Securities	20	19	20
Loans	170	170	170
Liabilities:			
Deposits	199	200	201
Advances (loans) from Bank of Canada	0	0	0
A. Required reserves	9.95	10	10.5
B. Excess reserves	−0.95	1	0.95
C. How much has the money supply changed?	−1	0	1
D. How much more can the money supply change?	−19	+20	+19
E. What is the total of C and D?	−20	+20	+20

Self-test

1. F 2. T; 3. F; 4. T; 5. F; 6. T; 7. T; 8. T; 9. T

1. *b*; 2. *b*; 3. *b*; 4. *a*; 5. *c*; 6. *d*; 7. *c*; 8. *b*; 9. *a*

23

MACROECONOMICS: AN OVERVIEW

Fill-in questions

1. output, level

2. purchased (demanded), levels; *a.* downward; *b.* real-balances, interest-rate, foreign-trade (any order)

3. produced (supplied), levels; *a.* horizontal; *b.* upsloping; *c.* vertical

4. intersection; *a.* purchased (demanded), produced (supplied) (either order); *b.* accept, pay

5. *a.* increasing, reduce; *b.* decreasing, expand

6. *a.* increase, have no effect; *b.* increase, increase; *c.* have no effect on, increase

7. smaller, ratchet

8. increase, a decrease in the costs of producing goods and services; *a.* raise, prevent, increase; *b.* lower, raise

9. increase, rise, decrease, fall in real output

Problems and projects

1. *a.* (1) 0, 1,000, (2) 2,000, 6.00, (3) 1,000, 2,000; *c.* (1) 1,700, 4.00, (2) 2,000, 6.00, (3) 900, 2.00

2. *a.* increases, (1) real domestic output, price level, (2) raise, expand, (3) increase the price level but will not affect domestic output; *b.* decreases, (1) Decrease the price level in the classical and intermediate ranges and decrease domestic output in the intermediate and Keynesian ranges, (2) Decrease only output in the intermediate and Keynesian ranges

3. *a.* increase, (1) lower, expand, (2) increase, will not; *b.* decrease, increase, decrease

Self-test

1. T; **2.** T; **3.** F; **4.** F; **5.** F; **6.** T; **7.** T; **8.** F; **9.** T; **10.** T; **11.** T; **12.** F

1. *d*; **2.** *a*; **3.** *b*; **4.** *d*; **5.** *a*; **6.** *b*; **7.** *a*; **8.** *b*; **9.** *b*; **10.** *b*; **11.** *c*; **12.** *b*

24

NEOCLASSICAL AND KEYNESIAN THEORIES OF EMPLOYMENT

Fill-in questions

1. fully, less than fully, *laissez-faire*, activist

2. Say's, flexibility

3. demand for these goods and services

4. the rate of interest

5. fall, rise, saving, investment

6. fall, unemployment, downward, increase, all who are willing to work at the going wage rate are employed and total output equals total spending

7. *a.* groups, reasons (motives); *b.* accumulated money balances, commercial banks; *c.* balances, loans (debts)

8. do not, smaller, fall, decrease, employment (output)

9. fallacy of composition

10. vertical, horizontal, Keynesian, neoclassical

11. rise, expand

12. synthesis

13. *a.* frictions, illusion, prices; *b.* unemployment; *c.* very low; *d.* instability; *e.* supply

Problems and projects

1. *a.* NC; *b.* PK; *c.* NC *d.* K, PK; *e.* K, PK;

f. K, PK; *g.* K, PK; *h.* NC; *i.* PK; *j.* PK

Self-test

1. T; **2.** T; **3.** F; **4.** T; **5.** F; **6.** F; **7.** T; **8.** F; **9.** T; **10.** F

1. *b*; **2.** *b*; **3.** *c*; **4.** *a*; **5.** *b*; **6.** *d*; **7.** *d*; **8.** *a*; **9.** *c*; **10.** *b*; **11.** *c*

25

EQUILIBRIUM DOMESTIC OUTPUT IN THE KEYNESIAN MODEL

Fill-in questions

1. *a.* Keynesian, constant; *b.* real, GDP

2. taxes, transfer, spend, personal; *a.* gross national product, national income, personal income, disposable income

3. consumption

4. *a.* directly, expenditures; *b.* disposable income; *c.* directly

5. rise, fall

6. *a.* real, financial; *b.* the price level; *c.* expectations; *d.* the current amount of consumer credit outstanding; *e.* taxation of consumer income

7. the amount consumers plan to consume (save) will be different at every level of income; the level of income has changed and that consumers will change their planned consumption (saving) as a result

8. capital goods; *a.* expected, profit; *b.* interest

9. greater

10. inverse; *a.* decrease; *b.* increase

11. *a.* the cost of acquiring, maintaining, and operating the capital goods; *b.* business taxes; *c.* technological change; *d.* the stock of

capital goods on hand; *e.* expectations

12. stable, unstable

13. durability, irregularity, variability

14. *a.* exports, imports; *b.* directly, total income; *c.* directly, its own total income (or gross domestic product)

15. *a.* fall, fall; *b.* fall

16. national income (or gross domestic product), imports

17. marginal propensity to consume, marginal propensity to save

18. (aggregate) expenditures-(real domestic) output, leakages-injections

19. *a.* expenditures, output; *b.* consumption, investment, net exports, government purchases; *c.* 45°; *d.* (1) saving, imports, taxes; (2) investment, exports, government purchases

20. *a.* less, disinvestment, rise; *b.* greater, investment, fall; *c.* equal to, zero, neither rise nor fall

21. real GDP; *a.* (1) disinvestment, (2) rise, the multiplier; *b.* (1) investment, (2) fall, $5 times the multiplier

22. *a.* income; *b.* consumption, marginal propensity to consume

23. *a.* equilibrium real GDP, spending; *b.* marginal propensity to save, marginal propensity to import

24. *a.* −; *b.* +; *c.* +; *d.* −

25. increases, decreases; *a.* greater; *b.* directly

26. decrease, less than

27. decrease, will not, paradox of thrift

28. less, increase, multiplier

29. inflationary, the aggregate-expenditures schedule, the amount by which equilibrium nominal GDP exceeds the full-employment non-inflationary real GDP

30. variable, constant; *a.* real-balances, raise, rise; *b.* lower, fall; *c.* inverse, demand

31. *a.* right, multiplier; *b.* left, downward shift in aggregate expenditures times the multiplier

32. *a.* greater, smaller; *b.* smaller, greater

Problems and projects

1. *a.* S: −40, −20, 0, 20, 40, 60, 80, 100; APC: 1.000, 0.970, 0.955; APS: 0.000, 0.030, 0.045; *b.* 1700; *c.* 80, 100, 80; *d.* 20, 100, 20

2. *a.* −; *b.* −; *c.* +; *d.* +; *e.* +; *f.* *none*; *g.* −; *h.* −

3. *a.* 0,10, *b.* 20, 30; *c.* 30, 60; *d.* 100, 150, 210, 280; *f.* inverse, (1) decrease, (2) increase; *g.* (1) lower, (2) raise; *h.* investment-demand

4. *a.* +; *b.* −; *c.* +; *d.* +; *e.* −; *f.* −; *g.* −; *h.* +; *i.* −

5. *a.* investment; *b.* constant (given); *c.* (1) unrelated, (2) directly related; *d.* decrease, downward

6. *a.* (1) 0.9, 9, C_a: 316, 325, 334, 343, 352, 361, 370, 379, 388, 397, 406, 415, 424, (2) 0.1, 1, S_a: 24, 25, 26, 27, 28, 29, 30, 31, 32, 33, 34, 35, 36; *b.* $S_a + T$: 34, 35, 36, 37, 38, 39, 40, 41, 42, 43, 44, 45, 46; *c.* $I_g + G + X_n$: 38, 35, 32, 29, 26, 23, 20, 17, 14, 11, 8, 5, 2; $C_a + I_g + G + X_n$: 354, 360, 366, 372, 378, 384, 390, 396, 402, 408, 414, 420, 426; *e.* 360; *f.* 100; *g.* fall, 90; *g.* increase, 10

7. *a.* 2,200; *b.* 2,400; *c.* 2,600; *d.* 2,200, 2,400, 2,600, (1) aggregate-demand, (2) inversely

8. *a.* (1) 2,390, 2.00, (2) 1,840, 1.00; *b.* 1,640, 1.00, 100, remain constant; *c.* 2,300, 1.80, 2,350, 1.90; *d.* 2,390, 2.20, 2.40, remain constant

Self-test

1. T; **2.** F; **3.** F; **4.** F; **5.** T; **6.** T; **7.** T; **8.** F; **9.** T; **10.** F; **11.** F; **12.** T; **13.** T; **14.** F; **15.** T; **16.** T; **17.** T; **18.** F; **19.** T; **20.** F; **21.** F; **22.** F; **23.** F; **24.** T; **25.** F; **26.** F; **27.** F; **28.** T

1. *d*; **2.** *a*; **3.** *d*; **4.** *b*; **5.** *c*; **6.** *c*; **7.** *d*; **8.** *c*; **9.** *d*; **10.** *b*; **11.** *b*; **12.** *b*; **13.** *a*; **14.** *a*; **15.** *a*; **16.** *c*; **17.** *d*; **18.** *c*; **19.** *b*; **20.** *b*; **21.** *a*; **22.** *b*; **23.** *b*; **24.** *b*; **25.** *b*; **26.** *a*; **27.** *c*; **28.** *b*; **29.** c; **30.** *b*

26

FISCAL POLICY, THE PUBLIC DEBT, AND MONETARY POLICY RESTATED

Fill-in questions

1. World War II

2. decreased, increased, increased, decreased

3. deficit, surplus

4. borrowing from the public, creating new money, latter

5. increase, taxes, decrease, taxes

6. *a.* taxes, transfer payments; *b.* increase, decrease

7. built-in; *a.* increase, increase, decrease; *b.* decrease, increase, decrease

8. employment, full employment

9. *a.* budget surplus or deficit, an average level; *b.* expansionary, contractionary

10. recognition, administrative, operational

11. other, deficits, political

12. deficit, borrows; *a.* raise, contract; *b.* crowding-out, weaken

13. raise; *a.* weaken; *b.* increase, increase, increase, decrease, strengthen

14. expenditures, revenues, deficits, surpluses

15. pro-, raise, lower

16. recession, inflation

17. full employment without inflation, deficits, public debt

18. wars, recessions, interest rates

19. *a.* 220, 45, 26, 5.4; *b.* internal

20. *a.* Canadian public, Canada; *b.* 13

21. debts, assets; *a.* greater; *b.* decreases, deficit, surplus

22. reduce, refinancing, money

23. asset, consumption, the present

24. externally, increase, incentives, crowding-out

25. increases, decreases, capital; *a.* consumer, present; *b.* capital, less than full

26. size, costs, peace

27. *a.* money; *b.* investment-demand; *c.* saving; *d.* decrease, increase, increase

28. steeper, flatter

29. demand, right; *a.* large, small; *b.* small, large; *c.* flatter, steeper

30. *a.* flexible, acceptable, effective; *b.* inflation, recession, velocity, opposite, cost-push, investment

31. unable; *a.* increase; *b.* increase

32. expenditures, consumption, investment, government

33. fiscal, monetary

Problems and projects

1. *a.* (1) increase, $10, (2) decrease, $20, (3) direct; *b.* (1) $100, (2) increase, (3) less, (4) lessened; *c.* (1) $5, (2) decrease, (3) less, (4) lessened, more; *d.* (1) government expenditures are $200 at all GDPs, government surplus: −30, −20, −10, 0, 10, 20, 30, (2) $30, (3) deficit, $20, (4) expansionary, recession, (5) deficit, $45, (6) deficit, 53⅓

2. *a.* 2,300, 1.80; *b.* (1) 2,400, (2) 1.90, 2,350; *c.* (1) 2,400, (2) remain constant

3. *a.* increase, 100; *b.* (1) increased, 20, (2) (*a*) decreased, 25, (*b*) decreased, 125, (*c*) decrease, 25; *c.* increase, 25

4. *a.* (2) 8; *b.* 20; *c.* (2) 850; *d.* (1) 6, (2) 30, (3) 900; *e.* (1) 25, (2) 25, (3) 7, (4) 350; *f.* (1) 0.20, 5, (2) increase, 5, increase, 25, (3) increase, 50

5. *a.* 1,700; *b.* 2,120; *c.* 1,600, .30; *d.* rise to $1,700 billion, remain constant; *e.* rise from $1,870 billion to $2,000 billion, rise from .50 to .70; *f.* remain constant at $2,120 billion, rise from 1.10 to 1.20

6. *a.* 5; *b.* increase, 500; *c.* rise, 6; *d.* increase, decrease, rise, fall

Self-test

1. T; 2. T; 3. F; 4. T; 5. T; 6. F; 7. F; 8. F; 9. F; 10. F; 11. T; 12. F; 13. F; 14. F; 15. T; 16. T; 17. F; 18. T; 19. F; 20. F; 21. F; 22. T; 23. T; 24. T; 25. F; 26. F; 27. T; 28. T; 29. T; 30. F; 31. F; 32. F; 33. T; 34. T; 35. F

1. *a*; 2. *d*; 3. *c*; 4. *c*; 5. *d*; 6. *b*; 7. *b*; 8. *b*; 9. *d*; 10. *c*; 11. *a*; 12. *b*; 13. *a*; 14. *a*; 15. *b*; 16. *a*; 17. *d*; 18. *a*; 19. *c*; 20. *b*; 21. *d*; 22. *d*; 23. *b*; 24. *b*; 25. *c*; 26. *c*; 27. *a*; 28. *a*; 29. *d*; 30. *b*; 31. *a*

27

INFLATION, UNEMPLOYMENT, AND AGGREGATE SUPPLY

Fill-in questions

1. full employment, excess, either

2. *a.* increase, demand-pull; *b.* decrease, cost-push

3. *a.* greater, greater, smaller; *b.* inverse

4. *a.* full employment is reached; *b.* business firms, labour unions, labour

5. *a.* price level, unemployment; *b.* negative

6. *a.* inflation, unemployment; *b.* increase, increase

7. select a point on the Phillips Curve

8. *a.* the dramatic rise in the oil prices of OPEC; *b.* agricultural shortfalls throughout the world (higher agricultural prices) *c.* the devaluation of the dollar; *d.* the fall in the rate of growth of labour productivity; *e.* inflationary expectations

9. *a.* increase; *b.* increase

10. higher, rise, decrease, higher, higher

11. *a.* decreased; *b.* price, unemployment; *c.* stagflation

12. *a.* right; *b.* exist

13. *a.* (1) expansionary, increasing, decreasing, (2) easy, increasing; *b.* contractionary, decreasing, increasing (2) tight, decreasing

14. *a.* increase; *b.* decrease

15. *a.* (1) vertical, greater, (2) increases; *b.* (1) inflation, real, increase, nominal, (2) a rise, no change

16. increase, real output, inflation

17. *a.* market, wage price, supply-side; *b.* left

18. *a.* manpower, *b.* competition

19. *a.* incomes; *b.* (1) guideposts, (2) controls

20. productivity, unit labour

21. *a.* (1) cost, wedge, (2) incentives, (3) regulation; *b.* decrease

22. *a.* substantial reduction in federal expenditures except for those for defence; *b.* reduction in government regulation of private business; *c.* limitation of the rate of growth in the money supply; *d.* sharp reduction in personal and corporation income tax rates

23. *a.* Canada is increasingly linked to the world economy and this growing international interdependence is an added source of macroeconomic instability; *b.* expectations of inflation play a causal role in inflation and make it difficult for policy to control it; *c.* both aggregate demand and aggregate supply affect the state of the macroeconomy and the kinds of policy that may be used to control it

Problems and projects

1. *a.* 20; *b.* 9; *c.* (it's your choice)

2. 2300; *a.* (1) 6, 2000, (2) 75, 5, 6.25; *b.* (1) 7, 2200, (2) 3, 2.5, (3) 16.67; *c.* (1) 5, 1700, (2) 3, 10, (3) negative

3. P_1, Q_4; *a.* (1) (a) rise, P_2, (b) rise Q_5, (c) fall, (2) (a) rise, P_3, (b) fall, Q_3, (c) rise; *b.* (1) (a) P_1, (b) fall, Q_4, (c) rise, (2) (b) fall, Q_2, (c) rise, (3) (a) smaller, (b) larger

4. *a.* 4; *b.* (1) increase, 1, rise, 1; (2) decrease, 2, fall, 2; (3) increased, 6, rise, 6

Self-test

1. T; **2.** T; **3.** F; **4.** F; **5.** T; **6.** F; **7.** T; **8.** T; **9.** T; **10.** T; **11.** T; **12.** T; **13.** T; **14.** T; **15.** F; **16.** F; **17.** T; **18.** F; **19.** T; **20.** T; **21.** F; **22.** T; **23.** T; **24.** F; **25.** F; **26.** T; **27.** F; **28.** F; **29.** T; **30.** T; **31.** F; **32.** T

1. *c*; **2.** *d*; **3.** *a*; **4.** *a*; **5.** *b*; **6.** *c*; **7.** *a*; **8.** *d*; **9.** *a*; **10.** *b*; **11.** *a*; **12.** *b*; **13.** *a*; **14.** *b*; **15.** *d*; **16.** *d*; **17.** *a*; **18.** *d*; **19.** *b*; **20.** *d*; **21.** *c*; **22.** *a*; **23.** *a*; **24.** *d*; **25.** *d*; **26.** *a*; **27.** *c*; **28.** *b*; **29.** *d*

28

ALTERNATIVE VIEWS: MONETARISM AND RATIONAL EXPECTATIONS

Fill-in questions

1. unstable, non-competitive, government intervention, fiscal, monetary

2. stable, competitive, *laissez-faire*, non-discretionary, monetary

3. $MV = PQ$; *a.* equation of exchange; *b.* (1) the money supply, (2) the (income or circuit) velocity of money, (3) the average price of each unit of physical output, (4) the physical volume of goods and services produced

4. *a.* total spending, MV; *b.* PQ

5. *a.* increase; *b.* increase, increase, P

6. *a.* medium of exchange, transactions, nominal GDP, stable; *b.* store of value, asset, interest rate, unstable

7. *a.* (1) more, (2) increase, (3) increase, (4) P, Q; *b.* (1) decrease, (2) increase, (3) decrease, (4) uncertain

8. *a.* M, PQ; *b.* directly, decreases, inversely

9. *a.* fiscal; *b.* raise, crowding-out

10. real GDP, 3, 5

11. destabilize

12. *a.* flat, small, large; *b.* steep, large, small

13. *a.* self-interests; *b.* purely competitive, flexible; *c.* inflation, no change, an increase

14. vertical, the price level, the real output

15. *a.* pro-; *b.* policy rules

16. less, less, sticky, stabilize, real

Problems and projects

1. *a.* 100, 220, 360, 520, 700, 900, 1120; *b.* 360, 360, 360, 360, 360, 360, 360, (1) 360, (2) 3.00, (3) 120; *c.* 700, (1) 700, (2) 5.00 (3) 140

2. *a.* (1) 50, (2) 75, (3) 125, (4) equal to, (5) 4; *b.*(1) 60, 100. (2) 160, equal to, (3) 3.75; *c.* (1) 80, 80, 160, (2) 5; *d.* decrease, increase

3. *a.* rational-expectations, classical, Keynesian; *b.* Q_1, P_1; *c.* (1) increase, Q_2, increase, P_3, (2) increase, Q_3, increase, P_2, (3) remain constant, Q_1, increase, P_4

Self-test

1. T; **2.** T; **3.** F; **4.** T; **5.** F; **6.** T; **7.** T; **8.** T; **9.** T; **10.** F; **11.** T; **12.** F; **13.** F; **14.** T; **15.** F; **16.** F

1. *d*; **2.** *b*; **3.** *b*; **4.** *d*; **5.** *a*; **6.** *b*; **7.** *d*; **8.** *c*; **9.** *c*; **10.** *d*; **11.** *d*; **12.** *c*; **13.** *b*; **14.** *d*; **15.** *a*; **16.** *d*

29

INTERNATIONAL TRADE, COMPARATIVE ADVANTAGE, AND PROTECTIONISM

Fill-in questions

1. 23, 115

2. transportation equipment, wood and paper, non-ferrous metals, chemicals; transportation equipment, industrial machinery, chemicals, non-ferrous metals

3. less, money (currency), more

4. uneven, different

5. comparative advantage, comparative advantage

6. *a.* inexpensive, expensive; *b.* expensive, inexpensive; *c.* hats, bananas; *d.* 3, 4, world demand and supply for hats and bananas; *e.* (1) $\frac{1}{3}$, $\frac{2}{7}$, (2) 4, $3\frac{1}{2}$; *f.* increases

7. allocation, standard

8. tariffs, import, tariff, voluntary export

9. special-interest, decrease, less

10. *a.* increase; *b.* decrease; *c.* (1) increase, (2) decrease; *d.* decrease, decrease

11. *a.* military self-sufficiency; *b.* infant industry; *c.* increase domestic employment; *d.* diversification for stability; *e.* cheap foreign labour; military-self-sufficiency, infant-industry

12. National Policy, the United States, 1936, downward; most-favoured nation

13. *a.* equal non-discriminatory treatment of all trading nations; *b.* reduction of tariffs by negotiation; *c.* elimination of import quotas

14. tariffs and import quotas, non-member, capital, labour

15. inefficient, oligopoly, high cost, international uncompetitiveness

16. *a.* the freer trade that resulted from past reductions in trade barriers; *b.* the increased competition from abroad that resulted from a more open economy; *c.* the increased competitiveness of foreign products that resulted from lower labour costs and prices abroad; *d.* the increased international value of the Canadian dollar against all currencies except the U.S. dollar; *e.* worldwide recession

17. *a.* newly industrializing countries (NICs); *b.* (1) entrepreneurial, (2) restructuring, (3) competitive, (4) higher

Problems and projects

1. *a.* constant; *b.*(1) 8, 2, (2) 4, 2; *c.*(1) it has a comparative advantage in producing wheat (its cost of producing wheat is less than Chile's), (2) it has a comparative advantage in producing copper (its cost of producing copper is less than Canada's); *d.* one of the two nations would be unwilling to trade if the terms of trade were outside this range; *f.*(1) 1, 0, (2) 1, 0

2. 750, 700, 650, 600, 550, 500, 450, 300, 0; *b.* $2.00, 600; *c.* 375, 350, 325, 300, 0, 0, 0, 0,

0; *d.* 650, 600, 550, 500, 175, 150, 125, 0, 0; *e.* $2.20, 550; *f.* (1) increased, 25, (2) decreased, 75; *g.* (1) increased, $95, (2) decreased, $345; *h.* increased, $10; *i.* increased, $260; *j.* decreased, $345, decrease, $345

Self-test

1. F; **2.** T; **3.** F; **4.** F; **5.** F; **6.** T; **7.** T; **8.** T; **9.** F; **10.** F; **11.** T; **12.** T; **13.** F; **14.** T; **15.** F; **16.** T; **17.** T; **18.** T; **19.** T; **20.** F

1. *b*; **2.** *b*; **3.** *b*; **4.** *b*; **5.** *a*; **6.** *c*; **7.** *d*; **8.** *a*; **9.** *a*; **10.** *c*; **11.** *b*; **12.** *d*; **13.** *a*; **14.** *a*; **15.** *c*; **16.** *d*; **17.** *d*; **18.** *c*; **19.** *d*; **20.** *d*; **21.** *d*

30

EXCHANGE RATES AND THE BALANCE OF PAYMENTS

Fill-in questions

1. dollars, franc

2. $3^1/_3$

3. *a.* supply of, demand for, increase, decrease; *b.* demand for, supply of, decrease, increase

4. tourism, freight, shipping (either order), interest, dividends (either order)

5. the other nations of the world; *a.* credit, +; *b.* debit, −

6. *a.* less, merchandise and services; *b.* greater; *c.* investment, transfers, negative

7. *a.* in that nation, other nations, in other nations, that nation, real, financial (either order); *b.* greater

8. *a.* selling, borrowing; *b.* buy, lend

9. *a.* current, capital, surplus; *b.* increases, decreased, increased, deficit

10. *a.* foreign monies, central; *b.* Exchange Fund; *c.* up, selling, out of; *d.* deficit, surplus

11. *a.* depreciate, appreciate; *b.* decrease, increase, decrease

12. *a.* appreciation; *b.* depreciation; *c.* appreciation; *d.* depreciation; *e.* appreciation

13. diminish, worsened; recession, inflation (either order)

14. *a.* sell, *b.* buy

15. *a.* taxing, subsidizing; *b.* import, export, government

16. contractionary, recession

17. gold, money, stock, exported, imported

18. *a.* stable; *b.* (1) out of, (2) decreased, rose, (3) fell, recession

19. fixed, adjustable-peg; *a.* gold, U.S. dollars (either order); *b.* selling, exchange-stabilization, selling, borrowing from; *c.* devalue; *d.* gold, U.S. dollars (either order); *e.* stable, flexible

20. *a.* deficits; *b.* gold; *c.* decreased; *d.* eliminated, continued

21. gold, market forces (demand and supply), fixed, floating

22. managed floating; *a.* stable; *b.* imbalances

23. *a.* full employment without inflation; *b.* a zero current-account balance; *c.* domestic

24. *a.* conflicts; *b.* conflicts

25. *a.* tariffs, currency; *b.* fluctuate; *c.* monetary

Problems and projects

1. *a.* (1) 3, (2) (a) 3, dollars, (b) 150, pesos; *b.* (1) 3, (2) (a) 3, (b) 3; *c.* (1) demand for, supply of, (2) increased, decreased

2. *a.* (reading down) + 17.5, −2.1, + 0.5, −2.1, −0.7, + 0.1, −4.3, + 13.2, −14.6, + 1.4, −0.1, −1.4, + 0.9, + 0.8, −0.6, −8.0, + 5.5, + 1.2, + 0.1, −0.9, 0, + 2.7, + 0.6, 0; *b.* (1) + 13.2, (2) −18.1, (3) −0.6, (4) + 0.6; *c.* deficit, 0.1, 9*a*, plus, 0.1, sold out of, up

3. *a.* (1) 4.00, (2) $^1/_4$, (3) 300, (4) 1200; *b.* buy, 300, 1500; *c.* sell, 380, 950

4. *a.* (1) contractionary, tight, (2) (*a*) increase, (*b*) decrease, (*c*) decrease, (3) reduce, (4) widened; *b.* (1) expansionary, easy, (2) (*a*) decrease, (*b*) increase, (*c*) increase, (3) widen, (4) narrowed

Self-test

1. T; 2. F; 3. T; 4. F; 5. F; 6. T; 7. T; 8. T; 9. F; 10. F; 11. T; 12. F; 13. T; 14. T; 15. T; 16. T; 17. T; 18. F; 19. F; 20. T; 21. T; 22. T; 23. T; 24. T; 25. T; 26. F; 27. F; 28. F; 29. F; 30. T; 31. F; 32. T; 33. T; 34. T; 35. F; 36. T; 37. T

1. *c*; 2. *d*; 3. *b*; 4. *c*; 5. *b*; 6. *e*; 7. *d*; 8. *b*; 9. *b*; 10. *c*; 11. *b*; 12. *b*; 13. *d*; 14. *c*; 15. *a*; 16. *d*; 17. *a*; 18. *b*; 19. *c*; 20. *d*; 21. *d*; 22. *d*; 23. *d*; 24. *c*; 25. *a*; 26. *a*; 27. *a*; 28. *a*; 29. *c*; 30. *d*; 31. *c*; 32. *c*; 33. *c*; 34. *b*

31

FOREIGN INVESTMENT IN CANADA

Fill-in questions

1. direct, portfolio

2. control, ownership, control; bonds, shares, interest, dividends, capital gains; shares, control

3. establishing a new firm, taking over a Canadian-owned firm, increasing their investment in a firm they already own (growth)

4. taking over a Canadian-owned firm

5. foreign exchange, foreign exchange, direct investment

6. burden; out, foreign exchange

7. up, exports, decreased; decrease

8. is; do; do, do

9. foreign exchange, capital equipment; surplus, debtor

10. foreign-exchange reserves, decrease, currency, exports

11. 26, 50, 51, 41

12. colonial, merchant, financial

13. never; foreign

14. jobs; domestic investment, up, deficit

15. 37 billion

16. 185 billion, book; 350 billion; 37, lower; exportable

17. exporter, importer

18. increase

19. surpluses; deficit

Problems and projects

1.

	a. (1) Debtor	*b.* (2) Re-payer	(3) Zero balance	*c.* (4) Cred-itor
	Balances (in billions of dollars)			
Current Account				
Merchandise	+ 17.5	+ 24.0	0	+ 15.0
Services				
— travel	–2.1	0	0	0
— freight & shipping	+ 0.5	+ 0.5	0	0
— business services	–2.1	–2.1	0	0
— government transactions	–0.7	–0.7	0	0
— other services	+ 0.1	+ 0.1	0	0
Services balance	–4.3	–2.2	0	0
Investment income (interest & dividends)	–14.6	–14.6	0	0
Transfers	+ 0.8	+ 0.8	0	0
Current Account balance	–0.6	+ 8.0	0	+ 15.0
Capital Account balance	+ 0.6	–8.0	0	–15.0

Self-test

1. F; 2. F; 3. F; 4. T; 5. T; 6. T; 7. F; 8. T; 9. F;
10. T; 11. T; 12. F; 13. F; 14. T; 15. F; 16. F;
17. T; 18. T; 19. T; 20. T; 21. F; 22. F; 23. F

1. b; 2. e; 3. a; 4. b; 5. b; 6. b; 7. a; 8. a; 9. c;
10. b

32

THE ECONOMICS OF GROWTH

Fill-in questions

1. fixed, increases

2. total real output (GDP), real output (GDP) per capita

3. increases, reduces

4. 24, 16, 8

5. quantity and quality of natural resources, quantity and quality of human resources, the supply or stock of capital goods, technology, demand, allocative

6. output, average

7. optimum population

8. population, decrease

9. productivity, capital, technology, labour

10. aggregate expenditures (or investment)

11. aggregate expenditures, productive capacity, capital-output ratio

12. reallocate

13. *a.* demand, low, investment, contract; *b.* saving, investment, work effort, risk-taking, capacity output; *c.* structure, composition, industrial

Problems and projects

1. *a.* 4; *b.* 3

2. *a.* 0, 80, 100, 110, 100, 90, 80, 70, 60; *b.*

third, fourth; *c.* 3, average

3. *a.* 100; *b.* 100, 110, 120, 125, 120, 110, 100, 90; *c.* 25; *d.* increased, 4; *e.* (1) increased, 120, (2) remained constant, (3) decreased to 90

4. *a.* (1) 1,100, 1,210; (2) consumption: 880, 968; saving: 220, 242; (3) investment: 220, 242; aggregate expenditures: 1,100, 1,210; *b.* (1) 10; (2) 10; *c.* (1) 0.8, (2) 0.2; *d.* 1,050; (1) 5; (2) less than; (3) recession; *e.* 1150; (1) greater than, cannot; (2) inflation; *f.* increases

5. *a.* 270, 270; *b.* 90; *c.* 990, 297, 297, 99; *d.* 1,089, 326.7, 326.7, 108.9; *e.* (1) investment; (2) average propensity to save, capital-output ratio; *f.* 2.5

Self-test

1. T; 2. F; 3. T; 4. F; 5. T; 6. T; 7. T; 8. T; 9. F;
10. F; 11. T; 12. F

1. a; 2. b; 3. d; 4. b; 5. a; 6. c; 7. b; 8. c; 9. b;
10. b; 11. b; 12. d

33

GROWTH: FACTS AND ISSUES

Fill-in questions

1. 27, doubled

2. 3.6, 1.8

3. quantity, productivity; *a.* hours of labour; *b.* worker, hour (either order)

4. labour, length, population, participation

5. quality, education and training

6. natural resources

7. 70,000, 2.7

8. output (production), investment

9. products, techniques

10. less than optimum; *a.* 20; *b.* slow; *c.* low; *d.* inadequate, big, branch plants; *e.* inadequate

11. regulations, transfers; *a.* investment; *b.* saving; *c.* work

12. 54, rising productivity

13. fallen, *a.* fall, living, real, rise, inflation, foreign; *b.* fall, decline, slow down, demand, federal government

14. pollutes, domestic problems, anxiety, insecurity, good life

15. living, unlimited wants–scarce resources, pollution, equitable, income, a better life

16. *a.* population, natural resources, pollution, food output per capita, industrial output per capita; *b.* 100, population, industrial output (or capacity)

17. unrealistic, technological, feedback

Problems and projects

1. *a.* 400, 500, 550, 600, 550; *b.* 150 million; *c.* \$15 billion; *d.* $46^2/_3\%$

2. *a.* 100,000, 105,000, 115,500; *b.* (1) 5, (2) 5; *c.* (1) 10, (2) 10; *d.* (1) 15.5, (2) quantity, productivity

Self-test

1. T; **2.** F; **3.** F; **4.** T; **5.** T; **6.** T; **7.** F; **8.** T; **9.** F; **10.** F; **11.** F; **12.** T; **13.** F; **14.** F; **15.** T

1. *c*; **2.** *c*; **3.** *b*; **4.** *c*; **5.** *a*; **6.** *c*; **7.** *e*; **8.** *c*; **9.** *a*; **10.** *a*; **11.** *a*; **12.** *a*; **13.** *b*; **14.** *b*; **15.** *d*

34

GROWTH AND THE UNDERDEVELOPED NATIONS

Fill-in questions

1. poverty (*i.e.,* a low standard of living)

2. Asia, South America, Africa, $^2/_3$

3. Third World, 50, 15, 3

4. natural resources, human resources, capital goods; technology

5. natural resources

6. *a.* overpopulation; *b.* widespread unemployment; *c.* the poor quality of the labour force

7. consumer goods (food) production, population, aspirations, standard of living

8. output, invest

9. saving potential, investors, incentives

10. agriculture, social

11. *a.* skilled, scarce, abundant, capital; *b.* unskilled, abundant, scarce, labour

12. saving

13. institutions, social

14. income; investment; productivity, output (income)

15. *a.* the existence of widespread banditry and intertribal warfare in many underdeveloped nations; *b.* the absence of a sizable and vigorous entrepreneurial class; *c.* the great need for public goods and services; *d.* government action may be the only means of promoting saving and investment; *e.* government can more effectively deal with the social-institutional obstacles to growth

16. by expanding trade with the underdeveloped nations (lowering the barriers to trade), private flows of capital, foreign aid (public loans and grants)

17. *a.* rules; *b.* trade, tariff treatments; *c.* exploitation, dependence; *d.* terms, trade, stabilization, indexing; *e.* debts, cancelled, rescheduled; *f.* insufficient; 0.7, strings, automatic

18. *a.* population, standard of living; *b.* cartels, raw materials; *c.* redistribution

Problems and projects

1. *a.* 7,500; *b.*(1) 8,400, (2) 525, (3) widen, 7,875

2. *a.* low; *b.* short; *c.* widespread; *d.* low; *e.* primitive; *f.* large; *g.* large; *h.* high; *i.* poor; *j.* small; *k.* low; *l.* absent; *m.* small; *n.* small; *o.* small and poor; *p.* small; *q.* low; *r.* common

3. *a.* food supply; 400, 600, 800, 1,000, 1,200, 1,400; population: 40, 80, 160, 320, 640, 1,280; *b.* the food supply is just able to support the population; *c.* the inability of the food supply to support a population growing at this rate; *d.* (1) 200, (2) 240, (3) 280; *e.* the population increased as rapidly as the food supply

Self-test

1. T; **2.** F; **3.** F; **4.** F; **5.** T; **6.** F; **7.** F; **8.** T; **9.** F; **10.** F; **11.** F; **12.** T; **13.** T; **14.** F; **15.** T; **16.** F; **17.** T; **18.** T; **19.** T; **20.** F

1. *d*; **2.** *d*; **3.** *d*; **4.** *b*; **5.** *d*; **6.** *a*; **7.** *b*; **8.** *b*; **9.** *c*; **10.** *d*; **11.** *d*; **12.** *b*; **13.** *d*; **14.** *b*; **15.** *a*; **16.** *c*; **17.** *d*; **18.** *b*; **19.** *d*; **20.** *d*

Ability-to-pay principle The belief that those who have the greater income (or wealth) should be taxed absolutely and relatively more than those who have less.

Abstraction Elimination of irrelevant and non-economic facts to obtain an economic principle.

Accelerationist hypothesis The contention that the negatively sloped Phillips curve (*see*) does not exist in the long run and that attempts to reduce the Unemployment rate bring about an accelerating rate of Inflation.

Actual budget The amount spent by the federal government (to purchase goods and services and for transfer payments) less the amount of tax revenue collected by it in any (fiscal) year; and which is *not* to be used to determine whether it is pursuing an expansionary or contractionary fiscal policy. Compare with the Cyclically-adjusted budget (*see*).

Actual investment The amount that business Firms do invest; equal to Planned investment plus unplanned investment.

Actual reserve The amount a bank has on deposit at the Bank of Canada (plus its Vault cash).

Adjustable pegs The device utilized in the Bretton Woods system (*see*) to change Exchange rates in an orderly way to eliminate persistent Payments deficits and surpluses: each nation defined its monetary unit in terms of (pegged it to) gold or the U.S. dollar, kept the Rate of exchange for its money stable in the short run, and changed (adjusted) it in the long run when faced with International disequilibrium.

Adult Occupational Training Act The federal Act of 1967, which replaced the Technical and Vocational Training Act and which changed the emphasis from the training of students to the training of those already in the labour force.

Aggregate demand A schedule or curve that shows the total quantity of goods and services demanded (purchased) at different price levels.

Aggregate-demand–aggregate-supply model The macroeconomic model that uses Aggregate demand and Aggregate supply (*see both*) to determine and explain the Price level and the real domestic output.

Aggregate expenditures The total amount spent for final goods and services in the economy.

Aggregate expenditures–domestic output approach Determination of the Equilibrium gross domestic product (*see*) by finding the real GDP at which Aggregate expenditures are equal to the real domestic output.

Aggregate-expenditures schedule A schedule or curve that shows the total amount spent for final goods and services at different levels of real GDP.

Aggregate supply A schedule or curve that shows the total quantity of goods and services supplied (produced) at different price levels.

Agricultural Stabilization Board The federal agency established in 1958 to support the following commodities at not less than 90% of their average price over the previous five years, with adjustments according to production costs: cattle, hogs, and sheep; industrial milk and cream; and oats and barley not produced on the Prairies [where the Canadian Wheat Board (*see*) has jurisdiction].

Alienation The inability of individuals to take part in the process by which the decisions that affect them are made and to control their own lives and activities.

Allocative efficiency The apportionment of resources among firms and industries to obtain the production of the products most wanted by society (consumers): the output of each product at which its Marginal cost and Price are equal.

Allocative factor The ability of an economy to reallocate resources to achieve the Economic growth that the Supply factors (*see*) make possible.

American Federation of Labor (AFL) The organization of affiliated Craft unions formed in the United States in 1886.

Annually balanced budget The equality of government expenditures and tax collections during a year.

Anticipated inflation Inflation (*see*) at a rate that was equal to the rate expected in that period of time.

Anti-combines (*See* Combines Investigation Act.)

Anti-Inflation Board The federal agency established in 1975 (and disbanded in 1979) to administer the government's inflation control program.

Applied economics (*See* Policy economics.)

Appreciation An increase in the international price of a currency caused by market forces; not caused by the central bank; the opposite of Depreciation.

Arbitration The designation of a neutral third party to render a decision in a dispute by which both parties (the employer and the labour union) agree in advance to abide.

Asset Anything with a monetary value owned by a firm or an individual.

Asset demand for money The amount of money people want to hold as a Store of value (the amount of their financial assets they wish to have in the form of Money); and which varies inversely with the Rate of interest.

Authoritarian capitalism An economic system (method of organization) in which property resources are privately owned and government extensively directs and controls the economy.

Authoritarian socialism (*See* Command economy.)

Average fixed cost The total Fixed cost (*see*) of a Firm divided by its output (the quantity of product produced).

Average product Average physical product; the total output produced per unit of a resource employed (total product divided by the quantity of a resource employed).

Average propensity to consume Fraction of Disposable income that households spend for consumer goods and services; consumption divided by Disposable income.

Average propensity to save Fraction of Disposable income that households save; Saving divided by Disposable income.

Average revenue Total revenue from the sale of a product divided by the quantity of the product sold (demanded); equal to the price at which the product is sold so long as all units of the product are sold at the same price.

Average tax rate Total tax paid divided by total (taxable) income; the tax rate on total (taxable) income.

Average (total) cost The Total cost of a Firm divided by its output (the quantity of product produced); equal to Average fixed cost (*see*) plus Average variable cost (*see*).

Average variable cost The total Variable cost (*see*) of a Firm divided by its output (the quantity of product produced).

Balanced budget multiplier The effect of equal increases (decreases) in government spending for goods and services and in taxes is to increase (decrease) the Equilibrium gross domestic product.

Balance of (international) payments The annual statement of a nation's international economic dealings showing the Current account (*see*) balance and the Capital account (*see*) balance, the latter including the balance in Official international reserves (*see*).

Balance of payments deficit When the balance in Official international reserves (*see*) is *positive*.

Balance of payments effect The inflow of foreign funds that usually accompanies a takeover or the establishment of a new foreign-controlled firm, and the resulting Transfer effect (*see*) outflow of interest and dividends abroad.

Balance of payments surplus When the balance in Official international reserves (*see*) is *negative*.

Balance of trade The addition of the balances on goods (merchandise) and services in the Current account (*see*) of the Balance of payments (*see*).

Balance on the capital account The Capital inflows (*see*) of a nation less its Capital outflows (*see*), both of which include Official international reserves (*see*).

Balance on current account The exports of goods (merchandise) and services of a nation less its imports of goods (merchandise) and services plus its Net investment income from non-residents (*see*) and its Net transfers.

Balance on goods and services The Balance of trade (*see*).

Balance sheet A statement of the Assets (*see*), Liabilities (*see*), and Net worth (*see*) of a Firm or individual at some given time.

Bank Rate The interest rate that the Bank of Canada charges on advances (*normally* very short-term loans) made to the chartered banks and other members of the Canadian Payments Association (*see*), equivalent to Discount rate in the United States.

Bankers' bank The bank that accepts the deposits of and makes loans to chartered banks: the Bank of Canada.

Barrier to entry Anything that artificially prevents the entry of Firms into an industry.

Barter The exchange of one good or service for another good or service.

Base year The year with which prices in other years are compared when a Price index (*see*) is constructed.

Basic social capital Public utilities, roads, communication systems, railways, housing, and educational and public health facilities; the Capital goods that must exist before there can be profitable (productive) investments in manufacturing, agriculture, and commerce.

Beggar-my-neighbour policy A government policy that expands a nation's exports or reduces its imports and thereby lessens its Balance-of-payments deficit and increases its rates of employment and economic growth by reducing the exports or expanding imports and worsening the Balance-of-payments position, employment, and economic growth in other nations.

Benefit-cost analysis Deciding whether to employ resources and the quantity of resources to employ for a project or program (for the production of a good or service) by comparing the benefit with the cost.

Benefit-loss rate The percentage of any increase in earned income by which subsidy benefits in a Negative income tax (*see*) plan are reduced.

Benefits-received principle The belief that those who receive the benefits of goods and services provided by government should pay the taxes required to finance them.

Bid rigging The illegal action of oligopolists who agree either that one or more will not bid on a request for bids or tenders or, alternatively, agree on what bids they will make, and forbidden under the Competition Act (*see*).

Big business A business Firm that either produces a large percentage of the total output of an industry, is large (in terms of number of employees or stockholders, sales, assets, or profits) compared with other Firms in the economy, or both.

Big trade-off (*See* Equality vs. efficiency trade-off).

Bilateral monopoly A market in which there is a single seller (Monopoly) and a single buyer (Monopsony).

Blacklisting The passing from one employer to another of the names of workers who favour the formation of labour unions and who ought not to be hired.

Board of Transport Commissioners The federal agency established by the Railway Act of 1903 to regulate freight rates; superseded by the Canadian Transport Commission (*see*) in 1967.

Boomerang effect The rise in average price caused by a publicly announced ceiling price in a market (such as rental accommodation) where previously a homogeneous price structure did not exist.

Bourgeois The capitalists; the capitalistic class; the owners of the machinery and equipment needed for production in an industrial society.

Break-even income (1) The level of Disposable income at which Households plan to consume (spend) all of their income (for consumer goods and services) and to save none of it.

Break-even income (2) The level of earned income at which Negative income tax (*see*) is reduced to zero and at which normal (positive) income tax applies on further increases in earned income.

Break-even point Any output that a (competitive) Firm might produce at which its Total cost and Total revenue would be equal; an output at which it has neither a profit nor a loss.

Bretton Woods system The international monetary system developed after World War II in which Adjustable pegs (*see*) were employed, the International Monetary Fund (*see*) helped to stabilize Foreign exchange rates, and gold and the Key currencies (*see*) were used as Official international reserves (*see*).

Budget deficit The amount by which the expenditures of the federal government exceed its revenues in any year.

Budget line A curve that shows the different combinations of two products a consumer can purchase with a given money income.

Budget restraint The limit imposed upon the ability of an individual consumer to obtain goods and services by the size of the consumer's income (and by the prices that must be paid for the goods and services).

Built-in stability The effect of Nondiscretionary fiscal policy (*see*) upon the economy; when Net taxes vary directly with the Gross domestic product the fall (rise) in Net taxes during a recession (inflation) helps to eliminate unemployment (inflationary pressures).

Business cycle Recurrent ups and downs over a period of years in the level of economic activity.

Business unionism The belief that the labour union should concern itself with such practical and short-run objectives as higher wages, shorter hours, and improved working conditions and should not concern itself with long-run and idealistic changes in the capitalistic system.

Canada Assistance Plan The federal Act under which the federal government makes funds available to the provinces for their programs of assistance to disabled, handicapped, unemployed (who are not entitled to unemployment insurance benefits), and other needy persons.

Canada Deposit Insurance Corporation Federal Crown Corporation that, for a fee payable by the chartered banks and federally-chartered trust companies, insures their customers' deposits up to a limit of $60,000 per customer per bank or trust company.

Canada Labour Code The federal law of 1970 that consolidated previous legislation regulating employment practices, labour standards, and so on, in the federal jurisdiction.

Canada Pension Plan The compulsory, contributory, earnings-related federal pension plan that covers most employed members of the labour force between the ages of 18 and 65, and payable at the latter age; it came into effect in 1965; there is transferability between the Plan and the Quebec Pension Plan, which applies to the people of that province.

Canadian Congress of Labour (CCL) The Federation of Industrial unions (*see*) formed in 1940 and affiliated with the Congress of Industrial Organizations (*see*); amalgamated into Canadian Labour Congress (*see*) in 1956.

Canadian International Development Agency (CIDA) The federal agency responsible for the operation and administration of Canada's international development assistance programs of approximately $2.5 billion a year.

Canadian Labour Congress (CLC) The largest federation of Labour unions (*see*) in Canada, with 3 million members in international and national unions; founded in 1956 on the amalgamation of the Canadian Congress of Labour (*see*) and the Trades and Labour Congress of Canada (*see*).

Canadian Payments Association The federal agency set up in 1982 to provide for Cheque clearing (*see*).

Canadian Transport Commission The federal agency set up in 1967 to prevent abuse of monopoly power in the telecommunications and land, water,

and air transport industries; on its creation, it took over the Board of Transport Commissioners (*see*), the Air Transport Board, and the Maritime Commission.

Canadian Wheat Board Federal Crown Corporation established in 1935, which does not own or operate grain-handling facilities but has complete control over the way western wheat is marketed and the price at which it is sold. The Board also acquired complete control of the supplies of all Prairie coarse grains in 1949.

Capacity-creating aspect of investment The effect of investment spending on the productive capacity (the ability to produce goods and services) of an economy.

Capital Man-made resources used to produce goods and services; goods that do not directly satisfy human wants; capital goods.

Capital account That part of the Balance of payments (*see*) that records the net inflows and outflows of liquid capital (money) for direct and portfolio investments at home and abroad, and includes the balance in Official international reserves (*see*).

Capital account deficit A negative Balance on the capital account (*see*).

Capital account surplus A positive Balance on the capital account (*see*).

Capital consumption allowances Estimate of the amount of Capital worn out or used up (consumed or depreciated) in producing the Gross Domestic Product.

Capital gain The gain realized when securities or properties are sold for a price greater than the price paid for them.

Capital goods (*See* Capital.)

Capital inflow The expenditures made by the residents of foreign nations to purchase equity, shares, and bonds from the residents of a nation.

Capital-intensive commodity A product in the production of which a relatively large amount of Capital is employed.

Capital outflow The expenditures made by the residents of a nation to purchase equity, shares, and bonds from the residents of foreign nations.

Capital-output ratio The ratio of the stock of Capital to the productive (output) capacity of the economy; and the ratio of a change in the stock of Capital (net investment) to the resulting change in productive capacity.

Capital-saving technological advance An improvement in technology that permits a greater quantity of a product to be produced with a given amount of Capital (or the same amount of the product to be produced with a smaller amount of Capital).

Capital-using technological advance An improvement in technology that requires the use of a greater amount of Capital to produce a given quantity of a product.

Cartel A formal written or oral agreement among Firms to set the price of the product and the outputs of the individual firms or to divide the market for the product geographically.

Cash (primary) reserve The weighted average of the 10% of their demand (current and personal chequing) account deposits and the 3% of their notice account deposits that the Chartered banks (*see*) must hold as Vault cash (*see*) or on deposit with the Bank of Canada. In August 1986 the average required cash reserve ratio was 3.86%.

Causation A cause-and-effect relationship; one or several events bring about or result in another event.

Ceiling price (*See* Price ceiling.)

Central bank The bank whose chief function is the control of the nation's money supply: the Bank of Canada.

Central economic planning Determination of the objectives of the economy and the direction of its resources to the attainment of these objectives by the national government.

Ceteris paribus assumption (*See* "other things equal" assumption.)

Change in amount consumed Increase or decrease in consumption spending that results from an increase or decrease in Disposable income, the Consumption schedule (curve) remaining unchanged; movement from one line (point) to another on the same Consumption schedule (curve).

Change in amount saved Increase or decrease in Saving that results from an increase or decrease in Disposable income, the Saving schedule (curve) remaining unchanged; movement from one line (point) to another on the same Saving schedule (curve).

Change in the consumption schedule An increase or decrease in consumption at each level of Disposable income caused by changes in the Non-income determinants of consumption and saving (*see*); an upward or downward movement of the Consumption schedule.

Change in the saving schedule An increase or decrease in Saving at each level of Disposable income caused by changes in the Non-income determinants of consumption and saving (*see*); an upward or downward movement of the Saving schedule.

Chartered bank One of the 63 multibranched, privately owned, commercial, financial intermediaries that have received charters by Act of Parliament and that alone, with Quebec Savings Banks, may call themselves "banks"; and which accept Demand deposits (*see*).

Chartered banking system All chartered banks as a group.

Checkoff The deduction by an employer of union dues from the pay of workers and the transfer of the amount deducted to a labour union.

Chequable deposit Any deposit in a Chartered bank or other financial intermediary (trust company, credit union, etc.) against which a cheque may be written and which deposit, if it is in a bank, is thus part of the M1 or M1A (*see*) money supply.

Cheque clearing The process by which funds are transferred from the chequing accounts of the writers of cheques to the chequing accounts of the recipients of the cheques; also called the "collection" of cheques.

Circuit velocity of money (*See* Income velocity of money.)

Circular flow of income The flow of resources from Households to Firms and of products from Firms to Households accompanied in an economy using money by flows of money from Households to Firms and from Firms to Households.

Civilian labour force Persons fifteen years of age and older who are not residents of the Yukon or the Northwest Territories, who are not in institutions or the armed forces, and who are employed for a wage or salary, seeking such employment, or self-employed for gain.

Classical range The vertical segment of the Aggregate-supply curve along which the economy is at Full employment.

Classical theory The Classical theory of employment (*see*).

Classical theory of employment The Neoclassical theory of employment (*see*).

Class struggle The struggle for the output of the economy between the Proletariat (*see*) and the Bourgeois (*see*) in a capitalistic society.

Closed economy An economy that neither exports nor imports goods and services.

(The) close-down case The circumstances that would result in a loss greater than its Total fixed cost if a (competitive) Firm were to produce any output greater than zero and which would induce it to cease (close down) production (the plant); when the price at which the Firm can sell its product is less than Average variable cost.

Closed shop A place of employment at which only workers who are already members of a labour union may be hired.

Club of Rome An international group of scientists, business executives, and academicians that contends that future economic growth in the world is impossible; that bases its predictions on a Doomsday model (*see*); and that advocates ZEG (*see*) and ZPG (*see*).

Coincidence of wants The item (good or service) that one trader wishes to obtain is the same item another trader desires to give up and the item the second trader wishes to acquire is the same item the first trader desires to surrender.

COLA (*See* Cost-of-living adjustment.)

Collection of cheques (*See* Cheque clearing.)

Collective bargaining The negotiation of work agreements between Labour unions (*see*) and their employers.

Collusive oligopoly An Oligopoly (*see*) in which the Firms act together and in agreement (collude) to set the price of the product and the output each firm will produce or to determine the geographic area in which each firm will sell.

Combination The creation of a new Firm from two or more existing Firms or the purchase by one Firm of the stock or Assets of one or more other Firms.

Combined tax-transfer system The percentage of income collected as taxes less the percentage of income received as transfer payments in different income classes.

Combines Investigation Act The federal Act, first passed in 1910, whose avowed aim is to prevent agreements to lessen competition unduly; amended and renamed the Competition Act in June 1986.

Command economy An economic system (method of organization) in which property resources are publicly owned and Central economic planning (*see*) is used to direct and co-ordinate economic activities.

Commercial bank (*See* Chartered bank.)

Communism (*See* Command economy.)

Company union An organization of employees that is dominated by the employer (the company) and does not engage in genuine collective bargaining with the employer.

Comparable worth doctrine The belief that women should receive the same salaries (wages) as men when the levels of skill, effort, and responsibility in their different jobs are comparable (the same).

Comparative advantage A lower Comparative cost (*see*) than another producer.

Comparative cost The amount the production of one product must be reduced to increase the production of another product; (*see* Opportunity cost.)

Competing goods (*See* Substitute goods.)

Competition The presence in a market of a large number of independent buyers and sellers and the freedom of buyers and sellers to enter and to leave the market.

Competition Act The Act that amended the Combines Investigation Act (*see*) in June 1986 and, in so doing, renamed it the Competition Act.

(The) competitive industry's short-run supply curve The horizontal summation of the short-run supply curves of the Firms in purely competitive industry (*see* Pure competition); a curve that shows the total quantities that will be offered for sale at various prices by the Firms in an industry in the Short run (*see*).

(The) competitive industry's short-run supply schedule The summation of the short-run supply schedules of the Firms in a purely competitive industry (*see* Pure competition); a schedule that shows the total quantities that will be offered for sale at various prices by the Firms in an industry in the Short run (*see*).

Competitive labour market   A market in which a large number of (non-colluding) firms demand a particular type of labour from a large number of non-unionized workers.

Complementary goods   Goods or services such that there is an inverse relationship between the price of one and the demand for the other; when the price of one falls (rises) the demand for the other increases (decreases).

Complex multiplier   The Multiplier (*see*) when changes in the Gross domestic product not only change Saving but also change Net taxes and Imports.

Concentration ratio   The percentage of the total sales of an industry made by the four (or some other number) largest sellers (Firms) in the industry.

Conditional grant   A transfer to a province by the federal government for a Shared-cost program whereby the federal government undertakes to pay part of the costs (usually half) of programs run by the provinces in accordance with federally set standards; such grants are mostly for health, post-secondary education, and general welfare [mostly under the Canada Assistance Plan (*see*)].

Confederation of National Trade Unions (CNTU)   The Labour union (*see*) federation that represents approximately 20% of Quebec's union members; established in 1921 as the Federation of Catholic Workers of Canada, it was later renamed the Canadian and Catholic Confederation of Labour; it adopted its present name and became non-confessional in 1956.

Conglomerate combination   A group of Plants (*see*) owned by a single Firm and engaged at one or more stages in the production of different products (of products that do not compete with each other).

Conglomerate merger   The merger of a Firm in one Industry with a Firm in another Industry (with a Firm that is neither supplier, customer, nor competitor).

Congress of Industrial Organizations (CIO)   The organization of affiliated Industrial unions formed in the United States in 1936.

Constant-cost industry   An Industry in which the expansion of the Industry by the entry of new Firms has no effect upon the prices the Firms in the industry pay for resources and no effect, therefore, upon their cost schedules (curves).

Consumer goods   Goods and services that satisfy human wants directly.

Consumer sovereignty   Determination by consumers of the types and quantities of goods and services that are produced from the scarce resources of the economy.

Consumption schedule   Schedule that shows the amounts Households plan to spend for Consumer goods at different levels of Disposable income.

Contractionary fiscal policy   A decrease in Aggregate demand brought about by a decrease in Government expenditures for goods and services, an increase in Net taxes, or some combination of the two.

"Control by the ruble"   The requirement in the USSR that each plant's receipts and expenditures be completed through the use of cheques drawn on *Gosbank* (*see*) which enables *Gosbank* to record the performance and progress of each plant toward the fulfilment of the production targets assigned it by *Gosplan* (*see*).

Corporation   A legal entity ("person") chartered by the federal or a provincial government, and distinct and separate from the individuals who own it.

Corporation income tax   A tax levied on the net income (profit) of Corporations.

Correlation   Systematic and dependable association between two sets of data (two kinds of events).

Cost-of-living adjustment (COLA)   An increase in the incomes (wages) of workers that is automatically received by them when there is inflation in the economy and guaranteed by a clause in their labour contracts with their employer.

Cost overrun   The amount by which the final cost of a project exceeds its initially estimated cost.

Cost-plus contract   A contract that provides that the supplier of a product be paid an amount equal to the cost of producing the product plus an additional amount for profit.

Cost-plus pricing   A procedure used by (oligopolistic) firms to determine the price they will charge for a product and in which a percentage markup is added to the estimated average cost of producing the product.

Cost-push inflation   Inflation that results from a decrease in Aggregate supply (from higher wage rates and raw material prices) and which is accompanied by decreases in real output and employment (by increases in the Unemployment rate).

Cost ratio   The ratio of the decrease in the production of one product to the increase in the production of another product when resources are shifted from the production of the first to the production of the second product; the amount the production of one product decreases when the production of a second product increases by one unit.

Council of Economic Advisers (U.S.)   A group of three persons that advises and assists the President of the United States on economic matters (including the preparation of the economic report of the President to Congress).

Countervailing power   The power that (John Kenneth Galbraith believes) arises on the buyers' side of a market to check or restrain the power of a Monopoly or Oligopoly to control price and arises on the sellers' side to limit the power of Monopsony or Oligopsony over price.

Craft union   A labour union that limits its membership to workers with a particular skill (craft).

Credit   An accounting notation that the value of an asset (such as the foreign money owned by the residents of a nation) has increased.

Credit union   An association of persons who often have a common tie (such as being employees of the same Firm or members of the same Labour union) that sells shares to (accepts deposits from) its members and makes loans to them.

Creeping inflation   A slow rate of inflation; a 2 to 4% annual rise in the price level.

Criminal-conspiracy doctrine   The (now outdated) Common Law doctrine that combinations of workers (Labour unions) to raise wages were criminal conspiracies and, therefore, illegal.

Crop restriction   A method of increasing farm revenue when demand for the product is inelastic. Usually done through a Farm products marketing board (*see*) allotting quotas.

Crowding model of occupational discrimination   A model of labour markets that assumes Occupational discrimination (*see*) against women and minorities has kept them out of many occupations and forced them into a limited number of other occupations in which the large Supply of labour (relative to the Demand) results in lower wages and incomes.

Crowding-out effect   The rise in interest rates and the resulting decrease in planned investment spending in the economy caused by increased borrowing in the money market by the federal government.

Currency   Coins and Paper money.

Currency appreciation   (*See* Exchange rate appreciation.)

Currency depreciation   (*See* Exchange rate depreciation.)

Current account   That part of the Balance of payments (*see*) that records the total current receipts for merchandise exports, services, investment income to non-residents, and transfers and the total current payments for merchandise imports, services, investment income to non-residents, and transfers.

Current account deficit   A negative Balance on current account (*see*).

Current account surplus   A positive Balance on current account (*see*).

Customary economy   (*See* Traditional economy.)

Cyclically-adjusted budget   What the budget balance would be for the total government sector if the economy were operating at an average or cyclically-adjusted level of activity.

Cyclically balanced budget   The equality of Government expenditures for goods and services and Net taxes collections over the course of a Business cycle; deficits incurred during periods of recession are offset by surpluses obtained during periods of prosperity (inflation).

Cyclical unemployment   Unemployment caused by insufficient Aggregate expenditures.

Debit   An accounting notation that the value of an asset (such as the foreign money owned by the residents of a nation) has decreased.

Declining economy   An economy in which Net investment (*see*) is less than zero (Gross investment is less than Depreciation).

Declining industry   An industry in which Economic profits are negative (losses are incurred) and which will, therefore, decrease its output as Firms leave the industry.

Decrease in demand   A decrease in the Quantity demanded of a good or service at every price; a shift of the Demand curve to the left.

Decrease in supply   A decrease in the Quantity supplied of a good or service at every price; a shift of the Supply curve to the left.

Deduction   Reasoning from assumptions to conclusions; a method of reasoning that tests a hypothesis (an assumption) by comparing the conclusions to which it leads with economic facts.

Deficiency payments   A method of Price support (*see*) whereby the government pays a subsidy to producers when the market price is below the minimum price deemed suitable by the government.

Deflating   Finding the Real gross domestic product (*see*) by decreasing the dollar value of the Gross domestic product produced in a year in which prices were higher than in the Base year (*see*).

Deflation   A fall in the general (average) level of prices in the economy.

Deglomerative forces   Increases in the cost of producing and marketing that result from the growth of cities and the concentration of firms and industries within a geographic area.

Demand   A demand schedule or a Demand curve (*see* both).

Demand curve   A curve that shows the amounts of a good or service buyers wish to purchase at various prices during some period of time.

Demand deposit   A deposit in a Chartered bank against which cheques may be written for immediate payment; bank-created money.

Demand factor   The increase in the level of Aggregate expenditures that brings about the Economic growth made possible by an increase in the productive potential of the economy.

Demand management   The use of Fiscal policy (*see*) and Monetary policy (*see*) to increase or decrease Aggregate expenditures.

Demand-pull inflation   Inflation that is the result of an increase in Aggregate demand.

Demand schedule   A schedule that shows the amounts of a good or service buyers wish to purchase at various prices during some period of time.

Deposit multiplier   (*See* Monetary multiplier.)

Depository institution   A Firm that accepts the deposits of Money of the public (businesses and persons); Chartered banks and other Financial intermediaries (*see*).

Depreciation (1)   (*See* Capital consumption allowances.)

Depreciation (2)   A decrease in the international price of a currency caused by market forces; not caused by the central bank; the opposite of Appreciation.

Derived demand   The demand for a good or service that is dependent upon or related to the demand for some other good or service; the demand for a resource that depends upon the demand for the products it can be used to produce.

Descriptive economics   The gathering or collection of relevant economic facts (data).

Devaluation   A decrease in the defined value of a currency brought about by the central bank; the opposite of Revaluation.

DI   (*See* Disposable income.)

Dictatorship of the proletariat   The rule by the working class that is to follow the revolution overthrowing capitalism and the introduction of socialism in the Marxian vision of the future.

Differentiated product   A product that differs physically or in some other way from the similar products produced by other Firms; a product that is similar to but not identical with and, therefore, not a perfect substitute for other products; a product such that buyers are not indifferent to the seller from whom they purchase it so long as the price charged by all sellers is the same.

Differentiated oligopoly   An Oligopoly in which the firms produce a Differentiated product (*see*).

Dilemma of regulation   When a Regulatory agency (*see*) must establish the maximum price a monopolist may charge, it finds that if it sets the price at the Socially optimum price (*see*), this price is below Average cost (and either bankrupts the Firm or requires that it be subsidized); and if it sets the price at the Fair-return price (*see*), it has failed to eliminate the underallocation of resources that is the consequence of unregulated monopoly.

Direct investment   Investment by non-residents in a firm they thereby establish or control or come to control through the investment. (*See also* Portfolio investment.)

Directing function of prices   (*See* Guiding function of prices.)

Directly related   Two sets of economic data that change in the same direction; when one variable increases (decreases) the other increases (decreases).

Discount rate   The interest rate the United States Federal Reserve Banks charge on the loans they make to Member banks; equivalent to Bank Rate (*see*) in Canada.

Discouraged workers   Workers who have left the Civilian labour force (*see*) because they have not been able to find employment.

Discretionary fiscal policy   Deliberate changes in taxes (tax rates) and government spending (spending for goods and services and transfer payment programs) by Parliament for the purpose of achieving a full-employment, non-inflationary Gross domestic product and economic growth.

Discriminatory discharge   The firing of workers who favour the formation of Labour unions.

Diseconomies of scale   The forces that increase the Average cost of producing a product as the Firm expands the size of its Plant (its output) in the Long run (*see*).

Disposable income   Personal income (*see*) less Personal taxes (*see*); income available for Personal consumption expenditures (*see*) and Personal saving (*see*).

Dissaving   Spending for consumer goods and services in excess of Disposable income; the amount by which Personal consumption expenditures (*see*) exceed Disposable income.

Dividend tax credit   A federal government method of reducing the Double taxation (*see*) of corporation income.

Division of labour   Dividing the work required to produce a product into a number of different tasks that are performed by different workers; Specialization (*see*) of workers.

Dollar votes   The "votes" consumers and entrepreneurs in effect cast for the production of the different kinds of consumer and capital goods, respectively, when they purchase them in the markets of the economy.

Domestic income   (*See* Net domestic income.)

Domestic output   Gross domestic product (*see*).

Doomsday model   An economic model that predicts that within the next one hundred years there will be a sudden collapse in the world's food and industrial output and its population.

Double counting   Including the value of Intermediate goods (*see*) in the Gross domestic product; counting the same good or service more than once.

Double taxation   Taxation of both corporation net income (profits) and the dividends paid from this net income when they become the Personal income of households.

Dual labour market   A labour market divided into two distinct types of submarkets: a primary labour market, in which workers fare well and a secondary labour market, in which they fare poorly.

Duopoly   A market in which there are only two sellers; an Industry in which there are two firms.

Durable good   A consumer good with an expected life (use) of one year or more.

Dynamic progress   The development over time of more efficient (less costly) techniques of producing existing products and of improved products; technological progress.

Earnings   The money income received by a worker; equal to the Wage (rate) multiplied by the quantity of labour supplied (the amount of time worked) by the worker.

Easy money policy   Central bank expanding the Money supply with a view to decreasing interest rates.

Economic analysis   Deriving Economic principles (*see*) from relevant economic facts.

Economic cost   A payment that must be made to obtain and retain the services of a resource; the income a Firm must provide to a resource supplier to attract the resource away from an alternative use; equal to the quantity of other products that cannot be produced when resources are employed to produce a particular product.

Economic Council of Canada   A federally instituted and funded research and advisory body, mandated to study and publish reports on economic matters, including an *Annual Review*.

Economic efficiency   The relationship between the input of scarce resources and the resulting output of a good or service; production of an output with a given dollar-and-cents value with the smallest total expenditure for resources; obtaining the largest total production of a good or service with resources of a given dollar-and-cents value.

Economic flexibility Ability of an economy to respond to changes in consumer tastes, in supplies of resources, and in technology to achieve the maximum satisfaction of wants.

Economic growth (1) An increase in the Production possibilities schedule or curve that results from an increase in resource supplies or an improvement in Technology; (2) an increase either in real output (Gross domestic product) or in real output per capita.

Economic integration Co-operation among and the complete or partial unification of the economies of different nations; the elimination of the barriers to trade among these nations; the bringing together of the markets in each of the separate economies to form one large (a common) market.

Economic law (*See* Economic principle.)

Economic model A simplified picture of reality; an abstract generalization.

Economic policy Course of action that will correct or avoid a problem.

Economic principle Generalization of the economic behaviour of individuals and institutions.

Economic profit The total receipts (revenue) of a firm less all its Economic costs; also called "pure profit" and "above normal profit."

Economic regulation (*See* Industrial regulation.)

Economic rent The price paid for the use of land and other natural resources, the supply of which is fixed (perfectly inelastic).

Economics Social science concerned with using scarce resources to obtain the maximum satisfaction of the unlimited human wants of society.

Economic theory Deriving Economic principles (*see*) from relevant economic facts; an Economic principle (*see*).

Economies of agglomeration The reduction in the cost of producing or marketing that results from the location of Firms relatively close to each other.

(The) economies of being established Advantages that Firms already producing a product have over potential producers of the product.

Economies of scale The forces that reduce the Average cost of producing a product as the Firm expands the size of its Plant (its output) in the Long run (*see*); the economies of mass production.

EEC European Economic Community; (*see* European Common Market).

Efficient allocation of resources The allocation of the resources of an economy among the production of different products that leads to the maximum satisfaction of the wants of consumers.

Elastic demand The Elasticity coefficient (*see*) is greater than one; the percentage change in Quantity demanded is greater than the percentage change in price.

Elasticity coefficient The number obtained when the percentage change in quantity demanded (or supplied) is divided by the percentage change in the price of the commodity.

Elasticity formula The price elasticity of demand (supply) is equal to

$$\frac{\text{Percentage change in quantity demanded (supplied)}}{\text{percentage change in price}}$$

which is equal to

$$\frac{\text{change in quantity demanded (supplied)}}{\text{original quantity demanded (supplied)}}$$

$$\text{divided by} \frac{\text{change in price}}{\text{original price}}$$

Elastic supply The Elasticity coefficient (*see*) is greater than one; the percentage change in Quantity supplied is greater than the percentage change in price.

Emission fees Special fees that might be levied against those who discharge pollutants into the environment.

Employment rate The percentage of the Civilian labour force (*see*) employed at any time.

End products Finished commodities that have attained their final degree of processing, such as commodities used directly for consumption, and machinery.

Entrepreneurial ability The human resource that combines the other resources to produce a product, makes non-routine decisions, innovates, and bears risks.

Equality vs. efficiency trade-off The decrease in Economic efficiency (*see*) that appears to accompany a decrease in Income inequality (*see*); the presumption that an increase in Income inequality is required to increase Economic efficiency.

Equalization payment An Unconditional grant (*see*) made by the federal government to the seven less wealthy provinces in an attempt to equalize incomes and opportunities across Canada.

Equalizing differences The differences in the Wages received by workers in different jobs that compensate for non-monetary differences in the jobs.

Equation of exchange $MV = PQ$; in which M is the Money supply (*see*), V is the Income velocity of money (*see*), P is the Price level, and Q is the physical volume of final goods and services produced.

Equilibrium domestic output The real domestic output at which the Aggregate-demand curve intersects the Aggregate-supply curve.

Equilibrium GDP The Gross domestic product at which the total quantity of final goods and services produced (the domestic output) is equal to the total quantity of final goods and services purchased (Aggregate expenditures); and at which Leakages (*see*) and Injections (*see*) are equal.

Equilibrium position The point at which the Budget line (*see*) is tangent to an Indifference curve (*see*) in the indifference curve approach to the theory of consumer behaviour.

Equilibrium price The price in a competitive market at which the Quantity demanded (*see*) and the Quantity supplied (*see*) are equal; at which there is neither a shortage nor a surplus; and at which there is no tendency for price to rise or fall.

Equilibrium price level The Price level at which the Aggregate-demand curve intersects the Aggregate-supply curve.

Equilibrium quantity The Quantity demanded (*see*) and Quantity supplied (*see*) at the Equilibrium price (*see*) in a competitive market.

European Common Market The association of now twelve Western European nations (with Turkey as an associate member) initiated in 1958 to abolish gradually the Tariffs and Import quotas among them, to establish common Tariffs for goods imported from outside the member nations, to allow the eventual free movement of labour and capital among them, and to create other common economic policies.

European Economic Community (*See* European Common Market.)

Excess reserve The amount by which a Chartered bank's Actual reserve (*see*) exceeds its Required reserve (*see*); Actual reserve minus Required reserve.

Exchange control (*See* Foreign exchange control.)

Exchange Fund Account The account operated by the Bank of Canada on the government's behalf wherein are held Canada's Official international reserves (*see*).

Exchange rate The Rate of exchange (*see*).

Exchange rate appreciation An increase in the value of a nation's money in foreign exchange markets caused by free market forces; a decrease in the Rates of exchange for foreign monies.

Exchange rate depreciation A decrease in the value of a nation's money in foreign exchange markets caused by free market forces; an increase in the Rates of exchange for foreign monies.

Exchange rate determinant Any factor other than the Rate of exchange (*see*) that determines the demand for and the supply of a currency in the Foreign exchange market (*see*).

Excise tax A tax levied on the expenditure for a specific product or on the quantity of the product purchased.

Exclusion principle The exclusion of those who do not pay for a product from the benefits of the product.

Exclusive dealing and tied selling The illegal action whereby a supplier sells a product only on condition that the buyer acquire other products from the same seller and not from competitors; and forbidden under the Competition Act (*see*).

Exclusive unionism The policies employed by a Labour union to restrict the supply of labour by excluding potential members in order to increase the Wages received by its members; the policies typically employed by a Craft union (*see*).

Exhaustive expenditure An expenditure by government that results directly in the employment of economic resources and in the absorption by government of the goods and services these resources produce; Government purchase (*see*).

Exit mechanism Leaving a job and searching for another one in order to improve the conditions under which a worker is employed.

Expanding economy An economy in which Net

investment (*see*) is greater than zero (Gross investment is greater than Depreciation).

Expanding industry An industry in which Economic profits are obtained by the firms in the industry and which will, therefore, increase its output as new firms enter the industry.

Expansionary fiscal policy An increase in Aggregate demand brought about by an increase in Government expenditures for goods and services, a decrease in Net taxes, or some combination of the two.

Expectations What consumers, business Firms, and others believe will happen or what conditions will be in the future.

Expected rate of net profits Annual profits a firm anticipates it will obtain by purchasing Capital (by investing) expressed as a percentage of the price (cost) of the Capital.

Expenditure approach The method that adds all the expenditures made for Final goods and services to measure the Gross domestic product.

Expenditures-output approach (See Aggregate-expenditures–domestic-output approach.)

Explicit cost The monetary payment a Firm must make to an outsider to obtain a resource.

Exploitation Paying a worker a Wage that is less than the value of the output produced by the worker; obtaining Surplus value (*see*) or unearned income.

Exports Spending for the goods and services produced in an economy by foreign individuals, firms, and governments.

Export transaction A sale of a good or service that increases the amount of foreign money (or of their own money) held by the citizens, firms, and governments of a nation.

External benefit (*See* Spillover benefit.)

External cost (*See* Spillover cost.)

External economies of scale The reduction in a Firm's cost of producing and marketing that results from the expansion of (the output of and the number of Firms in) the Industry of which the Firm is a member.

Externality (*See* Spillover.)

Externally held public debt Public debt (*see*) owed to (Canadian government securities owned by) foreign citizens, firms, and institutions.

Face value The dollar or cents value stamped on a coin.

Factors of production Economic resources: Land, Capital, Labour, and Entrepreneurial ability.

Fair-return price The price of a product that enables its producer to obtain a Normal profit (*see*), and which is equal to the Average cost of producing it.

Fallacy of composition Incorrectly reasoning that what is true for the individual (or part) is therefore necessarily true for the group (or whole).

Family Allowance A monthly allowance paid by the federal government, normally to the mother, on behalf of each dependent child less than 18 years of age who is resident in Canada and is maintained by a Canadian citizen or landed immigrant resident in Canada.

Farm problem The relatively low income of farmers (compared with incomes in the non-agricultural sectors of the economy) and the tendency for the prices farmers receive and their incomes to fluctuate sharply from year to year.

Farm products marketing boards The federal and provincial boards, numbering more than 100, that set marketing regulations for commodities ranging from asparagus to turkeys. The boards have the power to allocate quotas, set prices, issue licences, collect fees, and require that the commodity be marketed through them.

Featherbedding Payment by an employer to a worker for work not actually performed.

Feedback effects The effects a change in the money supply will have (because it affects the interest rate, planned investment, and the equilibrium GDP) on the demand for money, which is itself directly related to the GDP.

Feedback mechanism A change in human behaviour that is the result of an actual or predicted undesirable event, and which has the effect of preventing the recurrence or occurrence of the event.

Female participation rate The percentage of the female population of working age in the Civilian labour force (*see*).

Fewness A relatively small number of sellers (or buyers) of a good or service.

Fiat money Anything that is Money because government has decreed it to be Money.

Final goods Goods that have been purchased for final use and not for resale or further processing or manufacturing (during the year).

Financial capital (*See* Money capital.)

Financial intermediary A Chartered bank or other financial institution (savings and loan association, trust or mortgage loan company, credit union, *caisse populaire*), which uses the funds (savings) deposited with it to make loans (for consumption or investment).

Financing exports and imports The use of Foreign exchange markets by exporters and importers to receive and make payments for goods and services they sell and buy in foreign nations.

Firm An organization that employs resources to produce a good or service for profit and owns and operates one or more Plants (*see*).

(The) firm's short-run supply curve A curve that shows the quantities of a product a Firm in a purely competitive industry (*see* Pure competition) will offer to sell at various prices in the Short-run (*see*); the portion of the Firm's short-run Marginal cost (*see*) curve that lies above its Average variable cost curve.

(The) firm's short-run supply schedule A schedule which shows the quantities of product a Firm in a purely competitive industry (*see* Pure competition) will offer to sell at various prices in the Short run (*see*); the portion of the firm's short-run Marginal cost (*see*) schedule in which Marginal cost is equal to or greater than Average variable cost.

Fiscal drag The difficulty encountered in reaching and maintaining Full employment when the revenues from Net taxes vary directly with the Gross domestic product.

Fiscal policy Changes in government spending and tax collections for the purpose of achieving a full-employment and non-inflationary Gross domestic product.

Five fundamental economic questions The five questions every economy must answer: what to produce, how to produce, how to divide the total output, how to maintain Full employment, and how to assure Economic flexibility (*see*).

Five-Year Plan A statement of the basic strategy for economic development and resource allocation that is prepared by *Gosplan* (*see*) and which includes target rates of growth for the Soviet economy and its major sectors and the general composition of the national output for a five-year period.

Fixed cost Any cost that in total does not change when the Firm changes its output; the cost of Fixed resources (*see*).

Fixed exchange rate A Rate of exchange that is prevented from rising or falling by the intervention of government.

Fixed resource Any resource employed by a Firm the quantity of which the firm cannot change.

Flat-rate income tax A tax that taxes all incomes at the same rate.

Flexible exchange rate A Rate of exchange that is determined by the demand for and supply of the foreign money and is free to rise or fall without government interference.

Floating exchange rate (*See* Flexible exchange rate.)

Food and Drugs Act The federal law enacted in 1920 as outgrowth of legislation dating back to 1875; subsequently amended, the Act and its Regulations now provide for controls over all foods, drugs, cosmetics, and medical devices sold in Canada.

Foreign exchange (*See* Official international reserves.)

Foreign exchange control The control a government may exercise over the quantity of foreign money demanded by its citizens and business firms and over the Rates of exchange in order to limit its outpayments to its inpayments (to eliminate a Payments deficit). (*See*)

Foreign exchange market A market in which the money (currency) used by one nation is used to purchase (is exchanged for) the money used by another nation.

Foreign exchange rate (*See* Rate of exchange.)

Foreign-trade effect The inverse relationship between the Net exports (*see*) of an economy and its Price level (*see*) relative to foreign Price levels.

Foreign investment (*See* Direct investment and Portfolio investment.)

Foreign Investment Review Agency (FIRA) (*See* Investment Canada.)

45° line A curve along which the value of the GDP (measured horizontally) is equal to the value of Aggregate expenditures (measured vertically).

Fractional reserve A Reserve ratio (*see*) that is less than 100% of the deposit liabilities of a Chartered bank.

Freedom of choice Freedom of owners of property resources and money to employ or dispose of these resources as they see fit, of workers to enter any line of work for which they are qualified, and of consumers to spend their incomes in a manner they deem to be appropriate (best for them).

Freedom of enterprise Freedom of business Firms to employ economic resources, to use these resources to produce products of the firm's own choosing, and to sell these products in markets of their choice.

Freely floating exchange rates Rates of exchange (*see*) that are not controlled and that may, therefore, rise and fall; and that are determined by the demand for and the supply of foreign monies.

Free-rider problem The inability of those who might provide the economy with an economically desirable and indivisible good or service to obtain payment from those who benefit from the good or service because the Exclusion principle (*see*) cannot be applied to it.

Free trade The absence of artificial (government imposed) barriers to trade among individuals and firms in different nations.

Frictional unemployment Unemployment caused by workers voluntarily changing jobs and by temporary layoffs; unemployed workers between jobs.

Fringe benefits The rewards other than Wages that employees receive from their employers and which include pensions, medical and dental insurance, paid vacations, and sick leaves.

Full employment (1) Using all available economic resources to produce goods and services; (2) when the Unemployment rate is equal to the Full-employment unemployment rate and there is Frictional and Structural but no Cyclical unemployment (and the Real output of the economy is equal to its Potential real output).

Full-employment rate of growth The rate at which an economy is able to grow when it maintains Full employment; equal to the Average propensity to save (*see*) divided by the Capital-output ratio (*see*).

Full-employment–unemployment rate The Unemployment rate (*see*) at which there is no Cyclical unemployment (*see*) of the Civilian labour force (*see*) and, because some Frictional and Structural unemployment is unavoidable, equal to from 4% to 6%.

Full production The maximum amount of goods and services that can be produced from the employed resources of an economy; the absence of Underemployment (*see*).

Functional distribution of income The manner in which the economy's (the national) income is divided among those who perform different functions (provide the economy with different kinds of resources); the division of Net domestic income (*see*) into wages and salaries, corporation profits, farmers' income, unincorporated business income, interest, and rent.

Functional finance Use of Fiscal policy to achieve a full-employment, non-inflationary Gross domestic product without regard to the effect on the Public debt (*see*).

Galloping inflation (*See* Hyperinflation.)

GATT (*See* General Agreement on Tariffs and Trade.)

GDP (*See* Gross domestic product.)

GDP deflator The Price index (*see*) for all final goods and services used to adjust nominal GDP to derive real GDP.

GDP gap Potential Real gross domestic product less actual Real gross domestic product.

General Agreement on Tariffs and Trade The international agreement reached in 1947 by twenty-three nations (including Canada) in which each nation agreed to give equal and non-discriminatory treatment to the other nations, to reduce tariff rates by multinational negotiations, and to eliminate import quotas.

General equilibrium analysis A study of the Price system as a whole; of the interrelations among equilibrium prices, outputs, and employments in all the different markets of the economy.

Generalization Statistical or probability statement; statement of the nature of the relation between two or more sets of facts.

Gentlemen's agreement An informal understanding on the price to be charged among the firms in an Oligopoly (*see*).

Given year Any year other than the Base year (*see*) for which a Price index (*see*) is constructed.

GNP (*See* Gross national product.)

Gold export point The Rate of exchange for a foreign money above which—when nations participate in the International gold standard (*see*)—the foreign money will not be purchased and gold will be sent (exported) to the foreign country to make payments there.

Gold flow   The movement of gold into or out of a nation.

Gold import point   The Rate of exchange for a foreign money below which—when nations participate in the International gold standard (*see*)—a nation's own money will not be purchased and gold will be sent (imported) into that country by foreigners to make payments there.

Gold standard   (*See* International gold standard.)

Gosbank   The state-owned and operated (and the only) bank in the USSR.

Gosplan   The State Planning Commission in the USSR.

Government current purchases of goods and services   The expenditures of all governments in the economy for Final goods (*see*) and services, less investment goods.

Government purchase   Disbursement of money by government for which government receives a currently produced good or service in return.

Government transfer payment   Disbursement of money (or goods and services) by government for which government receives no currently produced good or service in return.

Green revolution   The major technological advance that created new strains of rice and wheat and increased the output per acre and per worker-hour of these crops.

Gross capital information   (*See* Gross investment.)

Gross domestic product   The total market value of all Final goods (*see*) and services produced in the economy during a year.

Gross investment   Expenditures by business *and by government* for newly produced Capital goods (*see*)—machinery, equipment, tools, and buildings—and for additions to inventories.

Gross national product   Gross domestic product (*see*) plus Net investment income from non-residents (*see*) (which is always negative in Canada).

Guaranteed annual income   The minimum income a family (or individual) would receive if a Negative income tax (*see*) were to be adopted.

Guaranteed Income Supplement   A 1966 amendment to the Old Age Security Act (*see*) provides for the payment of a full supplement to pensioners with no other income and a partial supplement to those with other, but still low, income.

Guiding function of prices   The ability of price changes to bring about changes in the quantities of products and resources demanded and supplied; (*See* Incentive function of price).

Homogeneous oligopoly   An Oligopoly (*see*) in which the firms produce a Standardized product (*see*).

Horizontal combination   A group of Plants (*see*) in the same stage of production and owned by a single Firm (*see*).

Horizontal merger   The merger of one or more Firms producing the same product into a single Firm.

Household   An economic unit (of one or more persons) that provides the economy with resources and uses the money paid to it for these resources to purchase goods and services that satisfy human wants.

Human capital investment   Any action taken to increase the productivity (by improving the skills and abilities) of workers; expenditures made to improve the education, health, or mobility of workers.

Hyperinflation   A very rapid rise in the price level.

IMF   (*See* International Monetary Fund.)

Immobility   The inability or unwillingness of a worker or another resource to move from one geographic area or occupation to another or from a lower-paying to a higher-paying job.

Imperfect competition   All markets except Pure competition (*see*); Monopoly, Monopsony, Monopolistic competition, Monopsonistic competition, Oligopoly, and Oligopsony (*see all*).

Imperialism   The Exploitation (*see*) of the less economically developed parts of the world by capitalists in the industrially advanced nations; and characterized by colonialism, the employment of the labour and raw materials of the less developed nations by the capitalistic nations, the sale of manufactured goods to them by the advanced nations, and investment by the developed nations in the underdeveloped ones.

Implicit cost   The monetary income a Firm sacrifices when it employs a resource it owns to produce a product rather than supplying the resource in the market; equal to what the resource could have earned in the best-paying alternative employment.

Import quota A limit imposed by a nation on the maximum quantity of a good that may be imported from abroad during some period of time.

Imports Spending by individuals, Firms, and governments of an economy for goods and services produced in foreign nations.

Import transaction The purchase of a good or service that decreases the amount of foreign money (or of their own money) held by the citizens, firms, and governments of a nation.

Incentive function The inducement that an increase (a decrease) in the price of a commodity offers to sellers of the commodity to make more (less) of it available; and the inducement an increase (decrease) in price offers to buyers to purchase smaller (larger) quantities; the Guiding function of prices (see).

Inclusive unionism The policies employed by a Labour union that does not limit the number of workers in the union in order to increase the Wage (rate); the policies of an Industrial union (see).

Income approach The method that adds all the incomes generated by the production of Final goods and services to measure the Gross domestic product.

Income-creating aspect of investment The effect of net investment spending upon Aggregate expenditures and the resulting effect upon the income (output) of an economy.

Income effect The effect a change in the price of a product has upon the Real income (purchasing power) of a consumer and the resulting effect upon the quantity of that product the consumer would purchase after the consequences of the Substitution effect (see) have been taken into account (eliminated).

Income inequality The unequal distribution of an economy's total income among persons or families in the economy.

Income-maintenance system The programs designed to eliminate poverty and to reduce the unequal distribution of income.

Incomes policy Government policy that affects the Money incomes individuals (the wages workers) receive and the prices they pay for goods and services and thereby affects their Real incomes (see Wage-price policy.)

Income velocity of money (*See* Velocity of money.)

Increase in demand An increase in the Quantity demanded of a good or service at every price; a shift in the Demand curve to the right.

Increase in supply An increase in the Quantity supplied of a good or service at every price; a shift in the Supply curve to the right.

Increasing-cost industry An industry in which the expansion of the Industry through the entry of new Firms increases the prices the Firms in the industry must pay for resources and, therefore, increases their cost schedules (moves their cost curves upward).

Increasing returns An increase in the Marginal product (*see*) of a resource as successive units of the resource are employed.

Independent goods Goods or services such that there is no relationship between the price of one and the demand for the other; when the price of one rises or falls the demand for the other remains constant.

Indifference curve A curve that shows the different combinations of two products that give a consumer the same satisfaction or Utility (*see*).

Indifference map A series of indifference curves (*see*), each of which represents a different level of Utility; and which together are the preferences of the consumer.

Indirect taxes Such taxes as Sales, Excise, and business Property taxes (*see all*), licence fees, and Tariffs (*see*), which Firms treat as costs of producing a product and pass on (in whole or in part) to buyers of the product by charging them higher prices.

Individual demand The Demand schedule (*see*) or Demand curve (*see*) of a single buyer of a good or service.

Individual supply The Supply schedule (*see*) or Supply curve (*see*) of a single seller of a good or service.

Induction A method of reasoning that proceeds from facts to Generalization (*see*).

Industrial Disputes Investigation Act The 1907 law that marked the beginning of federal labour legislation; it required disputes in the federal jurisdiction to be submitted to a Board of Conciliation and Investigation; replaced by Canada Labour Code (*see*).

Industrial policy Any policy in which government takes a direct and active role in shaping the structure and composition of industry to promote economic growth.

Industrial regulation The older and more traditional type of regulation in which government is concerned with the prices charged and the services provided the public in specific industries; in contrast to Social regulation (*see*).

Industrial reserve army A Marxian term; those workers who are unemployed as a result of the substitution of Capital for Labour, the growing capacity of the economy to produce goods and services, and the inadequate purchasing power of the working class.

Industrial union A Labour union that accepts as members all workers employed in a particular industry (or by a particular firm), and which contains largely unskilled or semiskilled workers.

Industry The group of (one or more) Firms that produces identical or similar products.

Inelastic demand The Elasticity coefficient (*see*) is less than one; the percentage change in price is greater than the percentage change in Quantity demanded.

Inelastic supply The Elasticity coefficient (*see*) is less than one; the percentage change in price is greater than the percentage change in Quantity supplied.

Inferior good A good or service of which consumers purchase less (more) at every price when their incomes increase (decrease).

Inflating Finding the Real gross domestic product (*see*) by increasing the dollar value of the Gross domestic product produced in a year in which prices are lower than they were in the Base year (*see*).

Inflation A rise in the general (average) level of prices in the economy.

Inflationary expectations The belief of workers, business Firms, and consumers that there will be substantial inflation in the future.

Inflationary gap The amount by which the Aggregate-expenditures schedule (curve) must decrease (shift downward) to decrease the nominal GDP to the full-employment non-inflationary level.

Inflationary psychosis Tendency of consumers and business Firms to increase their spending before an expected rise in the general level of prices occurs.

Inflationary recession (*See* Stagflation.)

Infrastructure For the economy, the capital goods usually provided by the Public sector for the use of its citizens and Firms (*e.g.*, highways, bridges, transit systems, waste-water treatment facilities, municipal water systems, and airports). For the Firm, the services and facilities it must have to produce its products, which would be too costly for it to provide for itself, and which are provided by governments or other Firms (*e.g.*, water, electricity, waste treatment, transportation, research, engineering, finance, and banking).

Injection An addition of spending to the income-expenditure stream: Investment, Government current purchases of goods and services, and Exports.

Injunction An order from a court of law that directs a person or organization not to perform a certain act because the act would do irreparable damage to some other person or persons; a restraining order.

In-kind investment Non-financial investment (*see*).

In-kind transfer The distribution by government of goods and services to individuals and for which the government receives no currently produced good or service in return; a Government transfer payment (*see*) made in goods or services rather than in money.

Innovation The introduction of a new product, the use of a new method of production, or the employment of a new form of business organization.

Inpayments The receipts of (its own or foreign) money that the individuals, Firms, and governments of one nation obtain from the sale of goods, services, and investment income, from remittances, government loans and grants, and (liquid) capital inflows from abroad.

Input-output analysis Using an Input-output table (*see*) to examine interdependencies among different parts (sectors and industries) of the economy and to make economic forecasts and plans.

Input-output table A table that lists (along the left side) the producing sectors and (along the top) the consuming or using sectors of the economy and that shows quantitatively in each of its rows how the output of a producing sector was distributed among consuming sectors and quantitatively in each of its columns the producing sectors from which a consuming sector obtained its inputs during some period of time (a year).

Insurable risk An event, the average occurrence of which can be estimated with considerable accuracy, that would result in a loss that can be avoided by purchasing insurance.

Interest The payment made for the use of money (of borrowed funds).

Interest income Income of those who supply the economy with Capital (*see*).

Interest rate The rate of Interest (*see*).

Interest-rate effect The tendency for increases (decreases) in the Price level to increase (decrease) the demand for money; raise (lower) interest rates; and, as a result, to reduce (expand) total spending in the economy.

Intergovernmental grant A transfer payment from the federal government to a provincial government or from a provincial to a local government. (*See* Conditional grant and Unconditional grant.)

Interindustry competition Competition or rivalry between the products produced by Firms in one industry (*see*) and the products produced by Firms in another Industry (or in other Industries).

Interlocking directorate A situation in which one or more of the members of the board of directors of one Corporation are also on the board of directors of another Corporation; and which is illegal in the United States—but not in Canada—when it tends to reduce competition among the Corporations.

Intermediate goods Goods that are purchased for resale or further processing or manufacturing during the year.

Intermediate range The upsloping segment of the Aggregate-supply curve that lies between the Keynesian range and the Classical range (*see both*).

Internal economies The reduction in the cost of producing or marketing a product that results from an increase in output of the Firm (*see* Economies of (large) scale).

Internal growth Increase in the size of a Firm accomplished by using the firm's earnings and by selling securities to obtain the funds to construct new Plants.

Internally held public debt Public debt (*see*) owed to (Government of Canada securities owned by) Canadian residents, Firms, and institutions.

International Bank for Reconstruction and Development (*See* World Bank.)

International gold standard An international monetary system employed in the nineteenth and early twentieth centuries in which each nation defined its money in terms of a quantity of gold, maintained a fixed relationship between its gold stock and money supply, and allowed the free importation and exportation of gold.

International Monetary Fund (IMF) The international association of nations that was formed after World War II to make loans of foreign monies to nations with temporary Payments deficits (*see*) and to administer the Adjustable pegs (*see*); and which today creates Special Drawing Rights (*see*).

International monetary reserves The foreign monies—in Canada practically entirely U.S. dollars—and such other assets as gold and Special Drawing Rights (*see*) that a nation may use to settle a Payments deficit (*see*).

International value of the dollar The price that must be paid in foreign currency (money) to obtain one Canadian dollar.

Intrinsic value The value in the market of the metal in a coin.

Inversely related Two sets of economic data that change in opposite directions; when one increases (decreases), the other decreases (increases).

Investment Spending for (the production and accumulation of) Capital goods (*see*) and additions to inventories.

Investment Canada (formerly Foreign Investment Review Agency—FIRA) The federal agency with the professed aim of screening, for benefit to Canada, the setting up in Canada of new firms by non-residents or the taking over of existing Canadian firms by non-residents.

Investment curve A curve that shows the amounts firms plan to invest (along the vertical axis) at different income (Gross domestic product) levels (along the horizontal axis).

Investment-demand curve A curve that shows real Rates of interest (along the vertical axis) and the amount of Investment (along the horizontal axis) at each Rate of interest.

Investment-demand schedule Schedule that shows real Rates of interest and the amount of Investment at each Rate of interest.

Investment in human capital (*See* Human capital investment.)

Investment schedule A schedule that shows the

amounts Firms plan to invest at different income (Gross domestic product) levels.

Invisible hand The tendency of Firms and resource suppliers seeking to further their self-interests in competitive markets to further the best interest of society as a whole (the maximum satisfaction of wants).

Jurisdictional strike Withholding from an employer the labour services of its members by a Labour union that is engaged in a dispute with another Labour union over which union is to perform a specific kind of work for the employer.

Key currencies The foreign monies that nations universally accept from foreigners in the payment of debts, can always use to make payments to foreigners, and utilize as Official international reserves (*see*); the American dollar and, in the immediate post–World War II period, the British pound.

Keynesian economics The macroeconomic generalizations that are today accepted by most (but not all) economists and which lead to the conclusion that a capitalistic economy does not tend to employ its resources fully and that Fiscal policy (*see*) and Monetary policy (*see*) can be used to promote Full employment (*see*).

Keynesianism The philosophical, ideological, and analytical views of the prevailing majority of western economists; and their employment theory and stabilization policies.

Keynesian range The horizontal segment of the Aggregate-supply curve along which the economy is in a depression or severe recession.

Keynesian theory Keynesian economics.

Kinked demand curve The demand curve a Noncollusive oligopolist (*see*) sees for its output, and which is based on the assumption that rivals will follow a price decrease and will not follow a price increase.

Labour The physical and mental talents (efforts) of people that can be used to produce goods and services.

Labour force (*See* Civilian labour force.)

Labour-intensive commodity A product in the production of which a relatively large amount of Labour is employed.

Labour-Management Relations Act (U.S.) (*See* Taft-Hartley Act.)

Labour productivity Total output divided by the quantity of labour employed to produce the output; the Average product (*see*) of labour or output per worker per hour or per year.

Labour theory of value The Marxian notion that the economic value of any commodity is determined solely by the amount of labour required to produce it.

Labour union A group of workers organized to advance the interests of the group (to increase wages, shorten the hours worked, improve working conditions, and so on).

Laffer curve A curve that shows the relationship between tax rates and the tax revenues of government and on which there is a tax rate (between 0 and 100%) at which tax revenues are at a maximum.

Laissez-faire capitalism (*See* Pure capitalism.)

Land Natural resources ("free gifts of nature"), which can be used to produce goods and services.

Land-intensive commodity A product in the production of which a relatively large amount of Land is employed.

Law of capitalist accumulation The tendency seen by Marx for capitalists to react to competition from other capitalists by investing profits (Surplus value) expropriated from workers in additional and technologically superior machinery and equipment (Capital goods).

Law of demand The inverse relationship between the price and the Quantity demanded (*see*) of a good or service during some period of time.

Law of diminishing marginal utility As a consumer increases the consumption of a good or service, the Marginal utility (*see*) obtained from each additional unit of the good or service decreases.

Law of diminishing returns When successive equal increments of a Variable resource (*see*) are added to the Fixed resources (*see*), beyond some level of employment, the Marginal product (*see*) of the Variable resource will decrease.

Law of increasing cost As the amount of a product produced is increased, the Opportunity cost (*see*)—the Marginal cost (*see*)—of producing an additional unit of the product increases.

Law of supply   The direct relationship between the price and the Quantity supplied (*see*) of a good or service during some period of time.

Leakage   (1) a withdrawal of potential spending from the income-expenditures stream: Saving (*see*), tax payment, and Imports (*see*); (2) a withdrawal that reduces the lending potential of the Chartered banking system.

Leakages-injections approach   Determination of the Equilibrium gross domestic product (*see*) by finding the Gross domestic product at which Leakages (*see*) are equal to Injections (*see*).

Least-cost combination rule (of resources)   The quantity of each resource a Firm must employ if it is to produce any output at the lowest total cost; the combination in which the ratio of the Marginal product (*see*) of a resource to its Marginal resource cost (*see*) (to its price if the resource is employed in a competitive market) is the same for all resources employed.

Legal cartel theory of regulation   The hypothesis that industries want to be regulated so that they may form legal Cartels (*see*) and that government officials (the government) provide the regulation in return for their political and financial support.

Legal tender   Anything that government has decreed must be accepted in payment of a debt.

(The) lending potential of an individual chartered bank   The amount by which a single Chartered bank can safely increase the Money supply by making new loans to (or buying securities from) the public; equal to the Chartered bank's Excess cash reserve (*see*).

(The) lending potential of the banking system   The amount by which the Chartered banking system (*see*) can increase the Money supply by making new loans to (or buying securities from) the public; equal to the Excess cash reserve (*see*) of the Chartered banking system multiplied by the Monetary multiplier (*see*).

Liability   A debt with a monetary value; an amount owed by a Firm or an individual.

Limited liability   Restriction of the maximum that may be lost to a predetermined amount; the maximum amount that may be lost by the owners (stockholders) of a Corporation is the amount they paid for their shares of stock.

Liquidity   Money or things that can be quickly and easily converted into Money with little or no loss of purchasing power.

Liquidity preference theory of interest   The theory in which the demand for Liquidity (the quantity of Money firms and households wish to possess) and the supply of Liquidity (the quantity of Money available) determine the equilibrium rate of interest in the economy.

Loaded terminology   Terms that arouse emotions and elicit approval or disapproval.

Lockout   The temporary closing of a place of employment and the halting of production by an employer in order to discourage the formation of a Labour union or to compel a Labour union to modify its demands.

Long run   A period of time long enough to enable producers of a product to change the quantities of all the resources they employ; in which all resources and costs are variable and no resources or costs are fixed.

Long-run competitive equilibrium   The price at which the Firms in Pure competition (*see*) neither obtain Economic profit nor suffer losses in the Long run and the total quantity demanded and supplied at that price are equal; a price equal to the minimum long-run average cost of producing the product.

Long-run farm problem   The tendency for the prices of agricultural products and the incomes of farmers to decline relative to prices and incomes in the rest of the economy.

Long-run supply   A schedule or curve that shows the prices at which a Purely competitive industry will make various quantities of the product available in the Long run.

Lorenz curve   A curve that can be used to show the distribution of income in an economy; and when used for this purpose, the cumulated percentage of families (income receivers) is measured along the horizontal axis and the cumulated percentage of income is measured along the vertical axis.

(The) loss-minimizing case   The circumstances that result in a loss which is less than its Total fixed cost when a competitive Firm produces the output at which total loss is a minimum: when the price at which the firm can sell its product is less than Average total but greater than Average variable cost.

Lump-sum tax   A tax that is a constant amount (the tax revenue of government is the same) at all levels of GDP.

M1 The narrowly defined Money supply; the Currency (coins and Paper money) and Demand deposits in chartered banks (*see*) not owned by the federal government or banks.

M1A Includes currency outside banks, demand deposits, chequable personal savings, and chequable non-personal notice Canadian dollar deposits at chartered banks.

M2 Includes, in addition to M1A, Canadian dollar non-chequable personal savings, fixed term personal savings, and non-chequable non-personal notice deposits at chartered banks.

M3 Includes, in addition to M2, Canadian dollar non-personal fixed term deposits and bearer term notes plus all foreign currency deposits of Canadian residents booked at chartered banks in Canada.

Macroeconomics The part of economics concerned with the economy as a whole; with such major aggregates as the households, business, international trade, and governmental sectors and with totals for the economy.

Managed floating exchange rate An Exchange rate that is allowed to change (float) to eliminate persistent Payments deficits and surpluses and is controlled (managed) to eliminate day-to-day fluctuations.

Managerial prerogatives The decisions, often enumerated in the contract between a Labour union and a business Firm, that the management of the Firm has the sole right to make.

Marginal cost The extra (additional) cost of producing one more unit of output; equal to the change in Total cost divided by the change in output (and in the short run to the change in total Variable cost divided by the change in output).

Marginal labour cost The amount by which the total cost of employing Labour increases when a Firm employs one additional unit of Labour (the quantity of other resources employed remaining constant); equal to the change in the total cost of Labour divided by the change in the quantity of Labour employed.

Marginal product The additional output produced when one additional unit of a resource is employed (the quantity of all other resources employed remaining constant); equal to the change in total product divided by the change in the quantity of a resource employed; Marginal physical product.

Marginal productivity theory of income distribution The contention that the distribution of income is equitable when each unit of each resource receives a money payment equal to its marginal contribution to the firm's revenue (its Marginal revenue product).

Marginal propensity to consume Fraction of any change in Disposable income spent for Consumer goods; equal to the change in consumption divided by the change in Disposable income.

Marginal propensity to import The fraction of any change in income (Gross domestic product) spent for imported goods and services; equal to the change in Imports (*see*) divided by the change in income.

Marginal propensity to save Fraction of any change in Disposable income that households save; equal to change in Saving (*see*) divided by the change in Disposable income.

Marginal rate of substitution The rate (at the margin) at which a consumer is prepared to substitute one good or service for another and remain equally satisfied (have the same total Utility); and equal to the slope of an Indifference curve (*see*).

Marginal resource cost The amount by which the total cost of employing a resource increases when a Firm employs one additional unit of the resource (the quantity of all other resources employed remaining constant); equal to the change in the total cost of the resource divided by the change in the quantity of the resource employed.

Marginal revenue The change in the Total revenue of the Firm that results from the sale of one additional unit of its product; equal to the change in Total revenue divided by the change in the quantity of the product sold (demanded).

Marginal-revenue–marginal-cost approach The method that finds the total output at which Economic profit (*see*) is a maximum (or losses a minimum) by comparing the Marginal revenue (*see*) and the Marginal cost (*see*) of additional units of output.

Marginal revenue product The change in the Total revenue of the Firm when it employs one additional unit of a resource (the quantity of all other resources employed remaining constant); equal to the change in Total revenue divided by the change in the quantity of the resource employed.

Marginal tax rate The fraction of additional (taxable) income that must be paid in taxes.

Marginal utility The extra Utility (*see*) a consumer obtains from the consumption of one additional unit of a good or service; equal to the change in total Utility divided by the change in the quantity consumed.

Margin requirement The minimum percentage down payment purchasers of shares of stock must make.

Market Any institution or mechanism that brings together the buyers (demanders) and sellers (suppliers) of a particular good or service.

Market demand (*See* Total demand.)

Market economy An economy in which only the private decisions of consumers, resource suppliers, and business Firms determine how resources are allocated; the Price system (*see*).

Market failure The failure of a market to bring about the allocation of resources that best satisfies the wants of society (that maximizes the satisfaction of wants). In particular, the over- or underallocation of resources to the production of a particular good or service (because of Spillovers) and no allocation of resources to the production of Public (social) goods (*see*).

Market for pollution rights A market in which the Perfectly inelastic supply (*see*) of the right to pollute the environment and the demand for the right to pollute would determine the price a polluter would have to pay for the right.

Market period A period of time in which producers of a product are unable to change the quantity produced in response to a change in its price; in which there is Perfect inelasticity of supply (*see*); and in which all resources are Fixed resources (*see*).

Market policies Government policies designed to reduce the market power of labour unions and large business firms and to reduce or eliminate imbalances and bottlenecks in labour markets.

Market socialism An economic system (method of organization) in which property resources are publicly owned and markets and prices are used to direct and co-ordinate economic activities.

Marxian economics The Economic theories and perceptions of Karl Marx (and his followers); an explanation of the forces and contradictions that would cause the breakdown of a capitalistic economy.

"Material balance" Preparation of the Five- and One-Year Plans (*see each*) by *Gosplan* (*see*) so that the planned requirements and the available supplies of each input and commodity are equal.

Materials balance approach A method of dealing with pollution problems that compares the production of waste materials with the capacity of the environment to absorb these materials.

Medium of exchange Money (*see*); a convenient means of exchanging goods and services without engaging in Barter (*see*); what sellers generally accept and buyers generally use to pay for a good or service.

Microeconomics The part of economics concerned with such individual units within the economy as Industries, Firms, and Households, and with individual markets, particular prices, and specific goods and services.

Miniature replicas A Canadian phenomenon created by the Canadian tariff, which induced foreign Direct investment (*see*) and allowed non-resident-owned corporations (mostly U.S.) to set up their subsidiaries in Canada to produce their full line of products at one-tenth the parents' scales; the basic reason for the inefficiency (high cost) of Canadian manufacturing industry.

Minimum wage The lowest Wage (rate) employers may legally pay for an hour of Labour.

Mixed capitalism An economy in which both government and private decisions determine how resources are allocated.

Monetarism An alternative to Keynesianism (*see*); the philosophical, ideological, and analytical views of a minority of North American economists; and their employment theory and stabilization policy, which stress the role of money.

Monetary control instruments Techniques the Bank of Canada employs to change the size of the nation's Money supply (*see*); Open-market operations (*see*), a change in the Bank Rate (*see*), and Switching Government of Canada deposits (*see*).

Monetary multiplier The multiple of its Excess reserve (*see*) by which the Chartered banking system (*see*) can expand deposits and the Money supply by making new loans (or buying securities); equal to one divided by the Cash reserve ratio (*see*).

Monetary policy Changing the Money supply (*see*) in order to assist the economy to achieve a full-employment, non-inflationary level of total output.

Monetary rule The rule suggested by the monetarists (*see*): the Money supply should be expanded each year at the same annual rate as the potential rate of growth of the Real gross domestic product;

the supply of money should be increased steadily at from 3 to 5% per year.

Money   Any item that is generally acceptable to sellers in exchange for goods and services.

Money capital   Money available to purchase Capital goods (*see*).

Money income   (*See* Nominal income.)

Money interest rate   The Nominal interest rate (*see*).

Money market   The market in which the demand for and the supply of money determine the interest rate (or the level of interest rates) in the economy.

Money supply   Narrowly defined: M1 (*see*); more broadly defined: M1A, M2, and M3 (*see*).

Money wage   The amount of money received by a worker per unit of time (hour, day, and so on).

Money wage rate   (*See* Money wage.)

Monopolistic competition   A market in which many Firms sell a Differentiated product (*see*), into which entry is relatively easy, in which the Firm has some control over the price at which the product it produces is sold, and in which there is considerable Non-price competition (*see*).

Monopoly   (1) A market in which the number of sellers is so few that each seller is able to influence the total supply and the price of the good or service; (2) a major industry in which a small number of Firms control all or a large portion of its output. (*See also* Pure Monopoly.)

Monopoly capitalism   A Marxian term; the ownership and control of the economy's Capital (machinery and equipment) by a small number of capitalists.

Monopsonistic competition   A market in which there is a fairly large number of buyers.

Monopsony   A market in which there is only one buyer of the good or service.

Moral suasion   The statements, pronouncements, and appeals made by the Bank of Canada that are intended to influence the lending policies of Chartered banks.

Most favoured nation clause   A clause in a trade agreement between Canada and another nation which provides that the other nation's Imports into Canada will be subjected to the lowest tariff rates levied then or later on any other nation's Imports into Canada.

MR = MC rule   A Firm will maximize its Economic profit (or minimize its losses) by producing the output at which Marginal revenue (*see*) and Marginal cost (*see*) are equal—provided the price at which it can sell its product is equal to or greater than Average variable cost (*see*).

MRP = MRC rule   To maximize Economic profit (or minimize losses), a Firm should employ the quantity of a resource at which its Marginal revenue product (*see*) is equal to its Marginal resource cost (*see*).

Multinational corporation   A business Firm chartered as a Corporation in one nation that employs resources and sells its products (often through subsidiary corporations) in other nations of the world.

Multiplier   The ratio of the change in the Equilibrium GDP to the change in Investment (*see*), or to the change in any other component in the Aggregate-expenditures schedule or to the change in Net taxes; the number by which a change in any component in the Aggregate-expenditures schedule or in Net taxes must be multiplied to find the resulting change in the Equilibrium GDP.

Multiplier effect   The effect upon the Equilibrium gross domestic product of a change in the Aggregate-expenditures schedule (caused by a change in the Consumption schedule, Investment, Net taxes, Government current purchases of goods and services, or Exports).

Mutual interdependence   Situation in which a change in price (or in some other policy) by one Firm will affect the sales and profits of another Firm (or other Firms) and any Firm that makes such a change can expect the other Firm(s) to react in an unpredictable (uncertain) way.

Mutually exclusive goals   Goals that conflict and cannot be achieved simultaneously.

National income   Total income earned by resource suppliers for their contributions to the production of the Gross national product (*see*); equal to the Gross national product minus the Non-income charges (*see*).

National income accounting   The techniques employed to measure (estimate) the overall production of the economy and other related totals for the nation as a whole.

National Policy   Sir John A. Macdonald's 1879 policy of high tariff protection for Canadian (Ontario and Quebec) secondary manufacturers; still Canada's basic industrial policy.

National unionism (labour) The concept that Canadian Labour unions (see) should be independent of the international (American, continental) unions.

Natural monopoly An industry in which the Economies of scale (see) are so great that the product can be produced by one Firm at an average cost that is lower than it would be if it were produced by more than one Firm.

Natural rate of unemployment (See Full-employment unemployment rate.)

Near-money Financial assets, the most important of which are savings, term, and notice deposits in Chartered banks, trust companies, credit unions, and other savings institutions, that can be readily converted into Money.

Negative income tax The proposal to subsidize families and individuals with money payments when their incomes fall below a Guaranteed (annual) income (see); the negative tax would decrease as earned income increases (see Benefit-loss rate).

Neoclassical theory of employment The Macro-economic generalizations that were accepted by most economists prior to the 1930s and that led to the conclusion that a capitalistic economy would tend to employ its resources fully.

Neoclassical synthesis The Post-Keynesian (see) term for mainstream Keynesianism.

Neocolonialism Domination and exploitation (see) of the economies in the Third World by private business Firms and governments in the United States and the industrially developed nations of Europe.

Net capital movement The difference between the real and financial investments and loans made by individuals and Firms of one nation in the other nations of the world and the investments and loans made by individuals and Firms from other nations in a nation.

Net domestic income The sum of the incomes earned through the production of the Gross domestic product (see).

Net exports Exports (see) minus Imports (see).

Net investment Gross investment (see) less Capital consumption allowances (see); the addition to the nation's stock of Capital during a year.

Net investment income The interest and dividend income received by the residents of a nation from residents of other nations less the interest and divi-dend payments made by the residents of that nation to the residents of other nations. In Canada, always a negative quantity.

Net national income National income (see).

Net national product Gross national product (see) less that part of the output needed to replace the Capital goods worn out in producing the output (Capital consumption allowances [see]).

Net taxes The taxes collected by government less Government transfer payments (see).

Net transfers The personal and government transfer payments made to residents of foreign nations less the personal and government transfer payments received from residents of foreign nations.

Net Worth The total Assets (see) less the total Liabilities (see) of a Firm or an individual; the claims of the owners of a firm against its total Assets.

New International Economic Order A series of proposals made by the Third World (see) for basic changes in its relationships with the advanced industrialized nations that would accelerate the growth of and redistribute world income to the Third World.

New Left The radical economists; those who hold the views called Radical economics (see); the present-day followers of Marx and proponents of Marxian economics (see).

NIEO New International Economic Order (see).

NIT (See Negative income tax.)

NNP (See Net national product.)

Nominal domestic output (GDP) The GDP (see) measured in terms of the price level at the time of measurement (unadjusted for changes in the price level).

Nominal income The number of dollars received by an individual or group during some period of time; the money income.

Nominal interest rate The rate of interest expressed in dollars of current value (not adjusted for inflation).

Nominal wage rate The Money wage (see).

Non-collusive oligopoly An Oligopoly (see) in which the Firms do not act together and in agreement to determine the price of the product and the output each Firm will produce or to determine the geographic area in which each Firm will sell.

Non-competing groups Groups of workers in the economy that do not compete with each other for employment because the skill and training of the workers in one group are substantially different from those of the workers in other groups.

Non-discretionary fiscal policy The increases (decreases) in Net taxes (*see*) that occur without Parliamentary action when the Gross domestic product rises (falls) and that tend to stabilize the economy.

Non-durable good A Consumer good (*see*) such as food, beverages, and tobacco.

Non-exhaustive expenditure An expenditure by government that does not result directly in the employment of economic resources or the production of goods and services; *see* Government transfer payment.

Non-financial investment An investment that does not require households to save a part of their money incomes; but that uses surplus (unproductive) labour to build Capital goods.

Non-income charges Capital consumption allowances (*see*) and Indirect taxes (*see*).

Non-income determinants of consumption and saving All influences on consumption spending and saving other than the level of Disposable income.

Non-interest determinants of investment All influences on the level of investment spending other than the rate of interest.

Non-investment transaction An expenditure for stocks, bonds, or second-hand Capital goods.

Non-market transactions The production of goods and services not included in the measurement of the Gross domestic product because the goods and services are not bought and sold.

Non-merchandise balance The addition of the balances on services, investment income, and transfers in the Current account (*see*) of the Balance of payments (*see*).

Non-price competition The means other than decreasing the prices of their products that Firms employ to attempt to increase the sale of their products; and that includes Quality competition (*see*), advertising, and sales promotion activities.

Non-price determinant of demand Factors other than its price that determine the quantities demanded of a good or service.

Non-price determinant of supply Factors other than its price that determine the quantities supplied of a good or service.

Non-productive transaction The purchase and sale of any item that is not a currently produced good or service.

Non-resident investment Foreign investment (*see* Direct investment and Portfolio investment.)

Non-tariff barriers (NTBs) All barriers other than Tariffs (*see*) that nations erect to impede trade among nations: Import quotas (*see*), licensing requirements, unreasonable product-quality standards, unnecessary red tape in customs procedures, and so on.

Non-union shop A place of employment at which none of the employees are members of a Labour union (and at which the employer attempts to hire only workers who are not apt to join a union).

Normal good A good or service of which consumers will purchase more (less) at every price when their incomes increase (decrease).

Normal profit Payment that must be made by a Firm to obtain and retain Entrepreneurial ability (*see*); the minimum payment (income) Entrepreneurial ability must (expect to) receive to induce it to perform the entrepreneurial functions for a Firm; an Implicit cost (*see*).

Norris-LaGuardia Act (U.S.) The federal Act of 1932 that made it more difficult for employers to obtain Injunctions (*see*) against Labour unions in federal courts and which declared that Yellow-dog contracts (*see*) were unenforceable.

Notice, term, and savings deposit A deposit in a Chartered bank against which cheques may or may not be written but for which the bank has the right to demand notice of withdrawal.

NTBs (*See* Non-tariff barriers.)

Occupational discrimination The form of discrimination that excludes women from certain occupations and the higher wages paid workers in these occupations.

Occupational licensing The laws of provincial governments that require a worker to obtain a license from a provincial board (by satisfying certain specified requirements) before engaging in a particular occupation.

Offers to purchase A method of Price support (*see*) whereby the government buys the surplus created when it sets the minimum price above the equilibrium price (*see*).

Official international reserves The International monetary assets (*see*) owned by the federal government and held in its behalf by the Bank of Canada in the Exchange Fund Account.

Official reserves Official international reserves (*see*).

Okun's law The generalization that any one percentage point rise in the Unemployment rate above the Full-employment unemployment rate will increase the GDP gap by 2.5% of the Potential output (GDP) of the economy.

Old Age Security Act The 1951 federal Act, as subsequently amended, by which a Pension is payable to every person aged 65 and older provided the person has resided in Canada for ten years immediately preceding the approval of an application for pension; in addition a Guaranteed Income Supplement (*see*) may be paid; the Pension is payable in addition to the Canada Pension (*see*).

Old Left Karl Marx and his followers during the latter part of the nineteenth and the early part of the twentieth century.

Oligopoly A market in which a few Firms sell either a Standardized or Differentiated product, into which entry is difficult, in which the Firm's control over the price at which it sells its product is limited by Mutual interdependence (*see*) (except when there is collusion among firms), and in which there is typically a great deal of Non-price competition (*see*).

Oligopsony A market in which there are a few buyers.

One-Year Plan A detailed operational plan that is prepared by *Gosplan* (*see*) and which specifies the inputs and outputs of each enterprise in the U.S.S.R. for a one-year period.

OPEC An acronym for the Organization of Petroleum Exporting Countries (*see*).

Open economy An economy that both exports and imports goods and services.

Open-economy multiplier The Multiplier (*see*) in an economy in which some part of any increase in the income (Gross domestic product) of the economy is used to purchase additional goods and services from abroad; and which is equal to the reciprocal of the sum of the Marginal propensity to save (*see*) and the Marginal propensity to import (*see*).

Open-market operations The buying and selling of Government of Canada securities by the Bank of Canada.

Open shop A place of employment at which the employer may hire either Labour union members or workers who are not (and need not become) members of the union.

Opportunity cost The amount of other products that must be forgone or sacrificed to produce a unit of a product.

Optimal distribution of income The distribution of income that would result in the greatest possible (maximum) satisfaction of consumer wants (Utility) in the economy.

Optimum population The population size at which the real output per person (real output per worker or Average product, *see*) is a maximum.

Organization of Petroleum Exporting Countries The cartel formed in 1960 by thirteen oil-producing countries to control the price at which they sell crude oil to foreign importers and the quantity of oil exported by its members.

"Other things (being) equal" assumption Assuming that the factors other than those being considered are constant.

Outpayments The expenditures of (its own or foreign) money that the individuals, Firms, and governments of one nation make to purchase goods, services, and investment income, for Remittances, for government loans and grants, and (liquid) capital outflows abroad.

Output effect The impact a change in the price of a resource has upon the output a Firm finds it most profitable to produce and the resulting effect upon the quantity of the resource (and the quantities of other resources) employed by the Firm after the consequences of the Substitution effect (*see*) have been taken into account (eliminated).

Paper money Pieces of paper used as a Medium of exchange (*see*); in Canada, Bank of Canada notes.

Paradox of thrift The attempt of society to save more results in the same amount or less Saving.

Partial equilibrium analysis The study of equilibrium prices and equilibrium outputs or employments in a particular market that assumes prices, outputs, and employments in the other markets of the economy remain unchanged.

Participatory socialism A form of socialism in which individuals would take part in the process by which the decisions that affect them are made and would be able to control their own lives and activities.

Partnership An unincorporated business Firm owned and operated by two or more persons.

Patent laws The federal laws that grant to inventors and innovators the exclusive right to produce and sell a new product or machine for a period of seventeen years.

Payments deficit (*See* Balance of payments deficit.)

Payments surplus (*See* Balance of payments surplus.)

Peak pricing Setting the price charged for the use of a facility (the User charge [*see*]) or for a good or service at a higher level when the demand for the use of the facility or for the good or service is greater and at a lower level when the demand for it is less.

Perfect elasticity of demand A change in the Quantity demanded requires no change in the price of the commodity; buyers will purchase as much of a commodity as is available at a constant price.

Perfect elasticity of supply A change in the Quantity supplied requires no change in the price of the commodity; sellers will make available as much of the commodity as buyers will purchase at a constant price.

Perfect inelasticity of demand A change in price results in no change in the Quantity demanded of a commodity; the Quantity demanded is the same at all prices.

Perfect inelasticity of supply A change in price results in no change in the Quantity supplied of a commodity; the Quantity supplied is the same at all prices.

Personal consumption expenditures The expenditures of Households for Durable, semidurable, and nondurable consumer goods and for services.

Personal distribution of income The manner in which the economy's Personal or Disposable income is divided among different income classes or different households.

Personal income The income, part of which is earned and the remainder of which is unearned, available to resource suppliers and others before the payment of Personal taxes (*see*).

Personal income tax A tax levied on the taxable income of individuals (households and unincorporated firms).

Personal saving The Personal income of households less Personal taxes (*see*) and Personal consumption expenditures (*see*); Disposable income less Personal consumption expenditures; that part of Disposable income not spent for Consumer goods (*see*).

Phillips curve A curve that shows the relationship between the Unemployment rate (*see*) (on the horizontal axis) and the annual rate of increase in the price level (on the vertical axis).

Planned economy An economy in which only government determines how resources are allocated.

Planned investment The amount that business firms plan or intend to invest.

Plant A physical establishment (Land and Capital) that performs one or more of the functions in the production (fabrication and distribution) of goods and services.

P = MC rule A Firm in Pure competition (*see*) will maximize its Economic profit (*see*) or minimize its losses by producing the output at which the price of the product is equal to Marginal cost (*see*), provided that price is equal to or greater than Average variable cost (*see*) in the short run and equal to or greater than Average (total) cost (*see*) in the long run.

Policy economics The formulation of courses of action to bring about desired results or to prevent undesired occurrences (to control economic events).

Political business cycle The tendency of Parliament to destabilize the economy by reducing taxes and increasing government expenditures before elections and to raise taxes and lower expenditures after the elections.

Political fragmentation The existence within the larger urban (metropolitan) areas of a number of separate political entities (counties, townships, cities, suburbs, and so on) that have their own governments.

Portfolio investment The buying of bonds and shares by non-residents, the number of shares bought being insufficient to attain control of the firm. (*See also* Direct Investment.)

Post hoc, ergo propter hoc **fallacy** Incorrectly reasoning that when one event precedes another, the first event is the cause of the second.

Post-Keynesians Economists who believe mainstream Keynesianism is more correctly labelled the Neoclassical synthesis.

Potential output The real output (GDP) an economy is able to produce when it fully employs its available resources.

Poverty An existence in which the basic needs of an individual or family exceed the means available to satisfy them.

Predatory pricing A general, illegal policy of selling at prices unreasonably low with a view to eliminating competition; forbidden under the Competition Act (*see*).

Preferential hiring A practice (often required by the provisions of a contract between a Labour union and an employer) that requires the employer to hire union members so long as they are available and to hire non-union workers only when union members are not available.

Premature inflation Inflation (*see*) that occurs before the economy has reached Full employment (*see*).

Price The quantity of money (or of other goods and services) paid and received for a unit of a good or service.

Price ceiling A government-fixed maximum price for a good or service.

Price-decreasing effect The effect in a competitive market of a decrease in Demand or an Increase in Supply upon the Equilibrium price (*see*).

Price discrimination The selling of a product (at a given time) to different buyers at different prices when the price differences are not justified by differences in the cost of producing the product for the different buyers; an illegal trade practice under the Competition Act (*see*) when it consists in giving a trade purchaser an unfair advantage over its competitors by selling to it at a lower price.

Price elasticity of demand The ratio of the percentage change in Quantity demanded of a commodity to the percentage change in its price; the responsiveness or sensitivity of the quantity of a commodity buyers demand to a change in the price of the commodity.

Price elasticity of supply The ratio of the percentage change in the Quantity supplied of a commodity to the percentage change in its price; the responsiveness or sensitivity of the quantity sellers of a commodity supply to a change in the price of the commodity.

Price guidepost The price charged by an Industry for its product should increase by no more than the increase in the Unit labour cost (*see*) of producing the product.

Price-increasing effect The effect in a competitive market of an increase in Demand or a decrease in Supply upon the Equilibrium price (*see*).

Price index A ratio (expressed as a percentage) of prices in a Given year (*see*) to prices in the Base year (*see*).

Price leadership An informal method that the Firms in an Oligopoly (*see*) may employ to set the price of the product they produce: one firm (the leader) is the first to announce a change in price and the other firms (the followers) quickly announce identical (or similar) changes in price.

Price level The weighted average of the Prices paid for the final goods and services produced in the economy.

Price-maker A seller (or buyer) of a commodity that is able to affect the price at which the commodity sells by changing the amount it sells (buys).

Price support The minimum price government allows sellers to receive for a good or service; a price that is the established or maintained minimum price.

Price system All the product and resource markets of the economy and the relationships among them; a method that allows the prices determined in these markets to allocate the economy's Scarce resources and to communicate and co-ordinate the decisions made by consumers, business firms, and resource suppliers.

Price-taker A seller (or buyer) of a commodity that is unable to affect the price at which a commodity sells by changing the amount it sells (or buys).

Price-wage flexibility Changes in the prices of products and in the Wages paid to workers; the ability of prices and Wages to rise or to fall.

Price war Successive and continued decreases in the prices charged by the firms in an oligopolistic industry by which each firm hopes to increase its sales and revenues and from which firms seldom benefit.

Primary reserve   (*See* Cash reserve.)

Prime rate   The interest rate the Chartered banks (*see*) charge on demand note loans to their best corporate customers.

Priority principle   The assignment of priorities to the planned outputs of the various sectors and industries in the economy of the USSR and the shifting of resources, when bottlenecks develop, from low- to high-priority sectors and industries to assure the fulfilment of the production targets of the latter sectors and industries.

Private good   A good or service to which the Exclusion principle (*see*) is applicable; and which is provided by privately owned firms to those who are willing to pay for it.

Private property   The right of private persons and Firms to obtain, own, control, employ, dispose of, and bequeath Land, Capital, and other Assets.

Private sector   The Households and business Firms of the economy.

Product differentiation   Physical or other differences between the products produced by different Firms that result in individual buyers preferring (so long as the price charged by all sellers is the same) the product of one Firm to the products of the other Firms.

Production possibilities curve (frontier)   A curve that shows the different combinations of two goods or services that can be produced in a Full-employment (*see*), Full-production (*see*) economy in which the available supplies of resources and technology are constant.

Production possibilities table   A table that shows the different combinations of two goods or services that can be produced in a Full-employment (*see*), Full-production (*see*) economy in which the available supplies of resources and technology are constant.

Productive efficiency   The production of a good in the least-costly way: employing the minimum quantity of resources needed to produce a given output and producing the output at which Average total cost is a minimum.

Productivity   The production per input in a given time period (usually per hour or per year and related to labour).

Productivity slowdown   The recent decline in the rate at which Labour productivity (*see*) in Canada has increased.

Product market   A market in which Households buy and Firms sell the products they have produced.

Profit   (*See*) Economic profit and Normal profit; without an adjective preceding it, the income of those who supply the economy with Entrepreneurial ability (*see*) or Normal profit.

(The) profit-maximizing case   The circumstances that result in an Economic profit (*see*) for a (competitive) Firm when it produces the output at which Economic profit is a maximum: when the price at which the Firm can sell its product is greater than the Average (total) cost of producing it.

Profit-maximizing rule (combination of resources)   The quantity of each resource a Firm must employ if its Economic profit (*see*) is to be a maximum or its losses a minimum; the combination in which the Marginal revenue product (*see*) of each resource is equal to its Marginal resource cost (*see*) (to its price if the resource is employed in a competitive market).

Profit-push inflation   The inflation that results when Firms with market power increase the prices they charge in order to increase their Economic profits (*see*).

Program for the Advancement of Industrial Technology   A federal program of providing financial assistance, normally 50%, for the development of new or improved products and processes incorporating advanced technology.

Progressive tax   A tax such that the tax rate increases as the taxpayer's income increases and decreases as income decreases.

Proletariat   The workers; the working class; those without the machinery and equipment needed to produce goods and services in an industrial society.

Property tax   A tax on the value of property (Capital, Land, stocks and bonds, and other Assets) owned by Firms and Households.

Proportional tax   A tax such that the tax rate remains constant as the taxpayer's income increases and decreases.

Proposition 13   A proposal approved by the voters of California to limit the level and growth of property taxes within the state.

Proprietors' income The net income of the owners of unincorporated Firms (proprietorships and partnerships); the sum of the accrued net income of farm operators from farm production plus the net income of nonfarm unincorporated business, including rent.

Prosperous industry (*See* Expanding industry.)

Protective tariff A Tariff (*see*) designed to protect domestic producers of a good from the competition of foreign producers.

Public assistance programs Programs that pay benefits to those who are unable to earn income (because of permanent handicaps or because they are dependent children), which are financed by general tax revenues, and which are viewed as public charity (rather than earned rights).

Public choice theory Generalizations that describe how government (the Public sector) makes decisions for the use of economic resources.

Public debt The amount owed by the Government of Canada to the owners of its securities and equal to the sum of its past Budget deficits (less its Budget surpluses).

Public good A good or service to which the Exclusion principle (*see*) is not applicable; and which is provided by government if it yields substantial benefits to society.

Public interest theory of regulation The presumption that the purpose of the regulation of an Industry is to protect the public (consumers) from the abuse of the power possessed by Natural monopolies (*see*).

Public sector The part of the economy that contains all its governments; government.

Public-sector failure The failure of the Public sector (government) to resolve socio-economic problems because it performs its functions in an economically inefficient fashion.

Public utility A Firm that produces an essential good or service, that has obtained from a government the right to be the sole supplier of the good or service in an area, and that is regulated by that government to prevent the abuse of its monopoly power.

Pure capitalism An economic system (method or organization) in which property resources are privately owned and markets and prices are used to direct and co-ordinate economic activities.

Pure competition (1) A market in which a very large number of Firms sells a Standardized product (*see*), into which entry is very easy, in which the individual seller has no control over the price at which the product sells, and in which there is no Non-price competition (*see*); (2) a market in which there is a very large number of buyers.

Pure monopoly A market in which one Firm sells a unique product (one for which there are no close substitutes), into which entry is blocked, in which the Firm has considerable control over the price at which the product sells, and in which Non-price competition (*see*) may or may not be found.

Pure profit (*See* Economic profit.)

(The) *pure rate of interest* (*See The* rate of interest.)

Pursuit and escape theory An explanation of the stability of labour's relative share of the National income (*see*) in which Labour tries to obtain (pursues) higher money wages by decreasing the Economic profits of capitalists and capitalists avoid (escape) a reduction in their profits by increasing the productivity of labour or the prices they charge for products.

Quality competition A change in the characteristics (quality) of the product produced by a Firm that is intended to change the quantity of the product the firm can sell.

Quantity-decreasing effect The effect in a competitive market of a decrease in Demand or a decrease in Supply upon the Equilibrium quantity (*see*).

Quantity demanded The amount of a good or service buyers wish (or a buyer wishes) to purchase at a particular price during some period of time.

Quantity-increasing effect The effect in a competitive market of an increase in Demand or an increase in Supply upon the Equilibrium quantity (*see*).

Quantity supplied The amount of a good or service sellers offer (or a seller offers) to sell at a particular price during some period of time.

Quasi-public good A good or service to which the Exclusion principle (*see*) could be applied, but which has such a large Spillover benefit (*see*) that government sponsors its production to prevent an underallocation of resources.

Radical economics The modern version of Marxian economics (*see*), which criticizes the methods of orthodox economists, contends that large monopolistic Corporations dominate modern capitalism and government, argues that the expansion of capitalism produces society's major problems, and advocates some form of socialism.

R&D Research and development; activities undertaken to bring about Technological progress.

Rand Formula A modified Union shop (*see*); all employees must pay union dues but are not obliged to join the union; part of an arbitration award of Mr. Justice Ivan Rand in 1945.

Random shock An event that has a significant effect on an economy but which was unexpected and is not likely to occur again.

Ratchet effect The tendency for the Price level to decline by less when Aggregate demand decreases than an equal increase in Aggregate demand increased the Price level; the Reversibility problem.

Rate of exchange The price paid in one's own money to acquire one unit of a foreign money; the rate at which the money of one nation is exchanged for the money of another nation.

Rate of interest Price paid for the use of Money or for the use of Capital; interest rate.

Rational An adjective that describes the behaviour of an individual who consistently does those things that will enable the achievement of the declared objective of the individual; and that describes the behaviour of a consumer who uses money income to buy the collection of goods and services that yields the maximum amount of Utility (*see*).

Rational expectations theory The hypothesis that business firms and households expect monetary and fiscal policies to have certain effects upon the economy and, in pursuit of their own self-interests, take actions that make these policies ineffective.

Rationing function of price The ability of price in a competitive market to equalize Quantity demanded and Quantity supplied and to eliminate shortages and surpluses by rising or falling.

Reaganomics The policies of the United States Reagan Administration based on Supply-side economics (*see*) and intended to reduce inflation and the Unemployment rate (Stagflation).

Real-balances effect The tendency for increases (decreases) in the price level to lower (raise) the real value (or purchasing power) of financial assets with fixed money values; and, as a result, to reduce (expand) total spending in the economy.

Real capital (*See* Capital.)

Real gross domestic product Gross domestic product (*see*) adjusted for changes in the price level; Gross domestic product in a year divided by the GDP deflator (*see*) for that year.

Real income The amount of goods and services an individual or group can purchase with his, her, or its Nominal income during some period of time; Nominal income adjusted for changes in the Price level.

Real interest rate The rate of interest expressed in dollars of constant value (adjusted for inflation); and equal to the Nominal interest rate (*see*) less the rate of inflation.

Real domestic output (GDP) The GDP (*see*) measured in terms of a constant price level (adjusted for changes in the price level).

Real rate of interest The Real interest rate (*see*).

Real wage The amount of goods and services a worker can purchase with his or her Money wage (*see*); the purchasing power of the Money wage; the Money wage adjusted for changes in changes in the Price level.

Real wage rate (*See* Real wage.)

Recessionary gap The amount by which the Aggregate-expenditures schedule (curve) must increase (shift upward) to increase the GDP to the full-employment non-inflationary level.

Reciprocal selling The practice in which one Firm agrees to buy a product from a second Firm, and the second Firm agrees, in return, to buy another product from the first Firm.

Reciprocal Trade Agreements Act of 1934 (U.S.) The federal Act that gave the U.S. President the authority to negotiate agreements with other nations and lower American tariff rates by up to 50% if the other nations would reduce tariff rates on American goods, and which incorporated Most favoured nation clauses (*see*) in the agreements reached with these nations.

Refinancing the public debt Paying owners of maturing Government of Canada securities with money obtained by selling new securities or with new securities.

Regional Development Incentives Act The federal Act of 1970 designed to create jobs in Canada's slow growth, or "designated" areas.

Regressive tax A tax such that the tax rate decreases (increases) as the taxpayer's income increases (decreases).

Regulatory agency An agency (commission or board) established by the federal or a provincial government to control for the benefit of the public the prices charged and the services offered (output produced) by a Natural monopoly (*see*).

Remittance A gift or grant; a payment for which no good or service is received in return.

Rental income Income received by those who supply the economy with Land (*see*).

Reopening clause A clause in an agreement between an employer and a Labour union that requires each to give the other sixty days' notice of its intent to modify or terminate the agreement.

Required reserve [*See* Cash (primary) reserve and Secondary reserve.]

Reserve ratio [*See* Cash (primary) reserve and Secondary reserve.]

Reserves [*See* (1) Official international reserves; (2) Cash (primary) reserves and Secondary reserves.]

Resource market A market in which Households sell and Firms buy the services of resources.

Retiring the public debt Reducing the size of the Public debt (*see*) by paying money to owners of maturing Government of Canada securities.

Revaluation An increase in the defined value of a currency brought about by the central bank; the opposite of Devaluation.

Revenue sharing The distribution by the federal government of some of its tax revenues to provincial governments.

Revenue tariff A Tariff (*see*) designed to produce income for the (federal) government.

Reversibility problem The failure of the Price level to decrease when Aggregate demand decreases (because prices are inflexible downward) and an increase in the Unemployment rate that is greater than the fall in the Unemployment rate which would have resulted from an equal increase in Aggregate demand; the Ratchet effect.

Right-to-work law (U.S.) A law that has been enacted in twenty states which makes it illegal in those states to require a worker to join a Labour union in order to retain his or her job with an employer.

Roundabout production The construction and use of Capital (*see*) to aid in the production of Consumer goods (*see*).

Rule of 70 A method by which the number of years it will take for the price level (the increasing variable) to double can be calculated; divide 70 by the annual rate of inflation (the rate of increase).

Sales tax A tax levied on expenditures for a broad group of products.

Saving Disposable income not spent for Consumer goods (*see*); not spending for consumption; equal to Disposable income minus Personal consumption expenditures (*see*).

Savings account A deposit in a financial institution (*see*) that is interest-earning and that can normally be withdrawn by the depositor at any time (though the institution may legally require notice for withdrawal).

Saving schedule Schedule that shows the amounts Households plan to save (plan not to spend for Consumer goods, *see*) at different levels of Disposable income.

Say's Law The (discredited) macroeconomic generalization that the production of goods and services (supply) creates an equal demand for these goods and services.

Scarce resources The fixed (limited) quantities of Land, Capital, Labour, and Entrepreneurial ability (*see all*), which are never sufficient to satisfy the wants of human beings because their wants are unlimited.

Schumpeter-Galbraith view (of oligopoly) The belief shared by these two economists that large oligopolistic firms are necessary if there is to be a rapid rate of technological progress (because only this kind of firm has both the means and the incentive to introduce technological changes).

SDRs (*See* Special Drawing Rights.)

Seasonal variation An increase or decrease during a single year in the level of economic activity caused by a change in the season.

Secondary boycott The refusal of a Labour union to buy or to work with the products produced by another union or a group of nonunion workers.

"Second economy" The semilegal and illegal markets and activities that exist side by side with the legal and official markets and activities in the USSR.

Secondary reserve   The Chartered bank cash in excess of cash reserve requirements, Government of Canada Treasury bills of one year or less, and day-to-day loans to investment dealers who have lines of credit with the Bank of Canada; the maximum imposable ratio of secondary reserves to Canadian dollar deposits is 12%.

Secular trend   The expansion or contraction in the level of economic activity over a long period of years.

Selective controls   The minor techniques used by the Bank of Canada to change the availability of credit: changing the Secondary reserve ratio and Moral suasion (*see both*).

Self-interest   What each Firm, property owner, worker, and consumer believes is best for itself and seeks to obtain.

Self-limiting adjustment   A change that eliminates the reason or motive for the change as the change occurs.

Semidurable goods   A consumer good (*see*), other than a nondurable (*see*), with a life expectancy of less than a year, for example, clothing.

Seniority   The length of time a worker has been employed by an employer relative to the lengths of time the employer's other workers have been employed; the principle that is used to determine which workers will be laid off when there is insufficient work for them all, and which will be rehired when more work becomes available.

Separation of ownership and control   Difference between the group that owns the Corporation (the stockholders) and the group that manages it (the directors and officers) and between the interests (goals) of the two groups.

Service   That which is intangible (invisible) and for which a consumer, firm, or government is willing to exchange something of value.

Shared-cost programs   (*See* Conditional grant.)

Sherman Act (U.S.)   The federal antitrust Act of 1890, which made monopoly, restraint of trade, and attempts, combinations, and conspiracies to monopolize or to restrain trade criminal offences; and allowed the federal government or injured parties to take legal action against those committing these offences.

Shortage   The result of a price ceiling: a maximum price set by government below the Equilibrium price (*see*).

Short run   A period of time in which producers of a product are able to change the quantity of some but not all of the resources they employ; in which some resources—the Plant (*see*)—are Fixed resources (*see*) and some are Variable resources (*see*); in which some costs are Fixed costs (*see*) and some are Variable costs (*see*); a period of time too brief to allow a Firm (*see*) to vary its plant capacity but long enough to permit it to change the level at which the plant capacity is utilized; a period of time not long enough to enable Firms to enter or to leave an Industry (*see*).

Short-run competitive equilibrium   The price at which the total quantity of a product supplied in the Short run (*see*) by a purely competitive industry and the total quantity of the product demanded are equal and which is equal to or greater than the Average variable cost (*see*) of producing the product; and the quantity of the product demanded and supplied at this price.

Short-run farm problem   The sharp year-to-year changes in the prices of agricultural products and in the incomes of farmers.

Simple multiplier   The Multiplier (*see*) in an economy in which government collects no Net taxes (*see*), there are no Imports (*see*), and Investment (*see*) is independent of the level of income (Gross domestic product); equal to one divided by the Marginal propensity to save (*see*).

Single-tax movement   The attempt of a group that followed the teachings of Henry George to eliminate all taxes except one which would tax all Rental income (*see*) at a rate of 100%.

Social accounting   (*See* National income accounting.)

Social good   (*See* Public good.)

Socially optimum price   The price of a product that results in the most efficient allocation of an economy's resources and which is equal to the Marginal cost (*see*) of the last unit of the product produced.

Social regulation   The newer and different type of regulation in which government is concerned with the conditions under which goods and services are produced, their physical characteristics, and the impact of their production upon society; in contrast to Industrial regulation (*see*).

Social insurance programs   The programs that replace the earnings lost when people retire or are temporarily unemployed, which are financed by pay deductions, and which are viewed as earned rights (rather than charity).

Soil bank program (U.S.) A program in which the federal government made payments to farmers who took land away from the production of crops that were sold for cash, and used the land either to grow cover crops or for timber.

Sole proprietorship An unincorporated business firm owned and operated by a single person.

Special Drawing Rights Credit created by the International Monetary Fund (*see*), which a member of the IMF may borrow to finance a Payments deficit (*see*) or to increase its Official international reserves (*see*); "paper gold."

Special-interest effect Effect on public decision-making and the allocation of resources in the economy when government promotes the interests (goals) of small groups to the detriment of society as a whole.

Specialization The use of the resources of an individual, a Firm, a region, or a nation to produce one or a few goods and services.

Speculative motive Keynes' term for the Asset demand for money (*see*).

Spillover A benefit or cost associated with the consumption or production of a good or service that is obtained by or inflicted without compensation upon a party other than the buyer or seller of the good or service; (*see* Spillover benefit and Spillover cost).

Spillover benefit The benefit obtained neither by producers nor by consumers of a product but without compensation by a third party (society as a whole).

Spillover cost The cost of producing a product borne neither by producers nor by consumers of the product but without compensation by a third party (society as a whole).

Stabilization funds International monetary reserves (*see*) and domestic monies used to augment the supply of, or demand for, any currency required to avoid or restrict fluctuations in the rate of exchange; in Canada held in the Exchange Fund Account by the Bank of Canada on behalf of the government.

Stabilization policy dilemma The use of monetary and fiscal policy to decrease the Unemployment rate increases the rate of inflation and the use of monetary and fiscal policy to decrease the rate of inflation increases the Unemployment rate; *see* the Phillips curve.

Stagflation Inflation accompanied by stagnation in the rate of growth of output and a high un-employment rate in the economy; simultaneous increases in both the price level and the Unemployment rate (*see*).

Standard of value A means of measuring the relative worth (of stating the prices) of goods and services.

Standardized product A product such that buyers are indifferent to the seller from whom they purchase it so long as the price charged by all sellers is the same; a product such that all units of the product are perfect substitutes for each other (are identical).

Staple An exported raw material.

Staple trap The result of increasing the export of a staple in inelastic foreign demand: the higher the exports the *less* the revenue received.

State ownership The ownership of property (Land and Capital) by government (the state); in the USSR by the central government (the nation).

Static economy (1) An economy in which Net investment (*see*) is equal to zero—Gross investment (*see*) is equal to the Capital consumption allowances (*see*); (2) an economy in which the supplies of resources, technology, and the tastes of consumers do not change and in which, therefore, the economic future is perfectly predictable and there is no uncertainty.

Store of value Any Asset (*see*) or wealth set aside for future use.

Strike The withholding of their labour services by an organized group of workers (a Labour union).

Strikebreaker A person employed by a Firm when its employees are engaged in a strike against the firm.

Structural unemployment Unemployment caused by changes in the structure of demand for Consumer goods and in technology; workers who are unemployed either because their skills are not demanded by employers or because they lack sufficient skills to obtain employment.

Subsidy A payment of funds (or goods and services) by a government, business firm, or household for which it receives no good or service in return. When made by a government, it is a Government transfer payment (*see*) or the reverse of a tax.

Substitutability The ability of consumers to use one good or service instead of another to satisfy their wants and of Firms to use one resource instead of another to produce products.

Substitute goods Goods or services such that there is a direct relationship between the price of one and the Demand for the other; when the price of one falls (rises) the Demand for the other decreases (increases).

Substitution effect (1) The effect a change in the price of a Consumer good would have upon the relative expensiveness of that good and the resulting effect upon the quantity of the good a consumer would purchase if the consumer's Real income (*see*) remained constant; (2) the effect a change in the price of a resource would have upon the quantity of the resource employed by a firm if the firm did not change its output.

Superior good (*See* Normal good.)

Supermultiplier The Multiplier (*see*) when Investment is directly related to the level of income (Gross domestic product); when the Investment curve (*see*) is positively sloped.

Supplementary labour income The payments by employers into unemployment insurance, worker's compensation, and a variety of private and public pension and welfare funds for workers: "fringe benefits."

Supply A Supply schedule or a Supply curve (*see both*).

Supply curve A curve that shows the amounts of a good or service sellers (a seller) will offer to sell at various prices during some period of time.

Supply factor An increase in the available quantity of a resource, an improvement in its quality, or an expansion of technological knowledge, which makes it possible for an economy to produce a greater output of goods and services.

Supply schedule A schedule that shows the amounts of a good or service sellers (a seller) will offer to sell at various prices during some period of time.

Supply-side economics The part of modern Macroeconomics that emphasizes the role of costs and aggregate supply in its explanation of Inflation and unemployed labour.

Supply-side shock One of several events of the 1970s and early 1980s that increased production costs, decreased Aggregate supply, and helped generate Stagflation in Canada.

Supply-side view The view of fiscal policy held by the advocates of Supply-side economics that emphasizes increasing Aggregate supply (*see*) as a means of reducing the Unemployment rate and Inflation and encouraging Economic Growth.

Support price (*See* Price support.)

Surplus The result of a price floor or price support: a minimum price set by government above the Equilibrium price (*see*).

Surplus value A Marxian term; the amount by which the value of a worker's daily output exceeds his daily Wage; the output of workers appropriated by Capitalists as profit.

Switching Government of Canada deposits Action of Bank of Canada to increase (decrease) backing for Money supply (*see*) by switching government deposits from (to) itself to (from) the Chartered banks (*see*).

Sympathy strike Withholding from an employer the labour services of its members by a Labour union that does not have a disagreement with the employer but wishes to assist another Labour union that does have a disagreement with the employer.

Tacit collusion Any method utilized in a Collusive oligopoly (*see*) to set prices and outputs or the market area of each firm that does not involve outright (or overt) collusion (formal agreements or secret meetings); and of which Price leadership (*see*) is a frequent example.

Taft-Hartley Act (U.S.) The federal Act of 1947 that marked the shift from government sponsorship to government regulation of Labour unions.

Tariff A tax imposed (only by the federal government in Canada) on an imported good.

Tax A non-voluntary payment of money (or goods and services) to a government by a Household or Firm for which the Household or Firm receives no good or service directly in return and which is not a fine imposed by a court for an illegal act.

Tax-based incomes policies (TIP) An Incomes policy (*see*) that would include special tax penalties for those who do not comply and tax rebates for those who do comply with the Wage-price guideposts (*see*).

Tax incidence The income or purchasing power that different persons and groups lose as a result of the imposition of a tax after Tax shifting (*see*) has occurred.

Taxpayers' revolt A movement in the United States during the late 1970s to impose ceilings on government expenditures and taxes.

Tax shifting   The transfer to others of all or part of a tax by charging them a higher price or by paying them a lower price for a good or service.

Tax-transfer disincentives   Decreases in the incentives to work, save, invest, innovate, and take risks that allegedly result from high Marginal tax rates and Transfer payment programs.

Tax "wedge"   Such taxes as Indirect taxes (*see*) and pay deductions for Social insurance programs (*see*), which are treated as a cost by business firms and reflected in the prices of the products produced by them; equal to the price of the product less the cost of the resources required to produce it.

Technical and Vocational Training Act   The Act of 1960 that launched the first major federal initiative in this area. Most of the funds went to capital projects involving vocational high schools. Replaced by Adult Occupational Training Act, 1967 (*see*).

Technology   The body of knowledge that can be used to produce goods and services from Economic resources.

Term deposit   A deposit in a Chartered bank or other Financial intermediary against which cheques may not be written; a form of savings account; part of M2 and M3 (*see both*).

Terms of trade   The rate at which units of one product can be exchanged for units of another product; the Price (*see*) of a good or service; the amount of one good or service that must be given up to obtain one unit of another good or service.

The economizing problem   Society's human wants are unlimited but the resources available to produce the goods and services that satisfy wants are limited (scarce); the inability of any economy to produce unlimited quantities of goods and services.

Theory of human capital   Generalization that Wage differentials (*see*) are the result of differences in the amount of Human capital investment (*see*); and that the incomes of lower-paid workers are increased by increasing the amount of such investment.

Theory of public choice   Generalizations that describe how government (the Public sector) makes decisions for the use of economic resources.

The **rate of interest**   The Rate of Interest (*see*) that is paid solely for the use of Money over an extended period of time and which excludes the charges made for the riskiness of the loan and its administrative costs; and which is approximately equal to the rate of interest paid on the long-term and virtually riskless bonds of the Government of Canada.

Third World   The semideveloped and underdeveloped nations; nations other than the industrially advanced market economies and the centrally planned economies.

Tied selling   (*See* Exclusive dealing.)

Tight money policy   Increasing the Rate of interest (*see*) by contracting the nation's Money supply (*see*).

Till money   (*See* Vault cash.)

TIP   (*See* Tax-based incomes policies.)

Token money   Coins that have a Face value (*see*) greater than their Intrinsic value (*see*).

Total cost   The sum of Fixed cost (*see*) and Variable cost (*see*).

Total demand   The Demand schedule (*see*) or the Demand curve (*see*) of all buyers of a good or service.

Total demand for money   The sum of the Transactions demand for money (*see*) and Asset demand for money (*see*); the relationship between the total amount of money demanded and nominal GDP and the Rate of Interest.

Total product   The total output of a particular good or service produced by a firm, a group of firms or the entire economy.

Total-receipts–total-cost approach   The method that finds the output at which Economic profit (*see*) is a maximum or losses a minimum by comparing the total receipts (revenue) and the total costs of a Firm at different outputs.

Total revenue   The total number of dollars received by a Firm (or Firms) from the sale of a product; equal to the total expenditures for the product produced by the Firm (or Firms); equal to the quantity sold (demanded) multiplied by the price at which it is sold—by the Average revenue (*see*) from its sale.

Total-revenue test   A test to determine whether Demand is Elastic (*see*), Inelastic (*see*), or of Unitary elasticity (*see*) between any two prices: demand is elastic (inelastic, unit elastic) if the Total revenue (*see*) of sellers of the commodity increases (decreases, remains constant) when the price of the commodity falls; or Total revenue decreases (increases, remains constant) when its price rises.

Total spending   The total amount buyers of goods and services spend or plan to spend.

Total supply The Supply schedule (*see*) or the Supply curve (*see*) of all sellers of a good or service.

Trade balance Balance of trade (*see*).

Trade controls Tariffs (*see*), export subsidies, Import quotas (*see*), and other means a nation may employ to reduce Imports (*see*) and expand Exports (*see*) in order to eliminate a Balance of payments deficit (*see*).

Trade deficit The amount by which a nation's imports of merchandise (goods) and services exceed its exports of merchandise (goods) and services.

Trade surplus The amount by which a nation's exports of merchandise (goods) and services exceed its imports of merchandise (goods) and services.

Trades and Labour Congress of Canada (TLC) The federation of Craft unions (*see*) formed in 1886 and affiliated with the American Federation of Labor (*see*); amalgamated into the Canadian Labour Congress (*see*) in 1956.

Trading possibilities line A line that shows the different combinations of two products an economy is able to obtain (consume) when it specializes in the production of one product and trades (exports) this product to obtain the other product.

Traditional economy An economic system (method of organization) in which traditions and customs determine how the economy will use its scarce resources.

Traditional view (of oligopoly) The belief that oligopoly (because it is similar to Monopoly) will result in smaller outputs, higher prices and profits, and slower technological progress.

Transactions demand for money The amount of money people want to hold to use as a Medium of exchange (to make payments); and which varies directly with the nominal GDP.

Transfer burden (effect) The outflow of interest and dividends abroad resulting from foreign investment.

Transfer payment A payment of money (or goods and services) by a government or a Firm to a Household or Firm for which the payer receives no good or service directly in return.

Turnover tax The tax added to the accounting price of a good in the USSR to determine the price at which the quantity of the good demanded will equal the quantity of the good it has been decided to produce, the rate of taxation being higher on relatively scarce and lower on relatively abundant goods.

Tying agreement A promise made by a buyer when allowed to purchase a patented product from a seller that it will make all of its purchases of certain other (unpatented) products from the same seller.

Unanticipated inflation Inflation (*see*) at a rate which was greater than the rate expected in that period of time.

Unconditional grant A transfer to a province by the federal government that goes into the general revenues of the province to be used as it sees fit; such grants are made for two reasons: (1) as an Equalization payment (*see*) and (2) to make up for the general inadequacy of provincial revenues in relation to provincial responsibilities.

Underdeveloped nation A nation in which per capita Real income (output) is low; a less developed country (LDC).

Underemployment Failure to produce the maximum amount of goods and services that can be produced from the resources employed; failure to achieve Full production (*see*).

Undistributed corporation profits The after-tax profits of corporations not distributed as dividends to stockholders; corporate or business saving.

Unemployment Failure to use all available Economic resources to produce goods and services; failure of the economy to employ fully its Civilian labour force (*see*).

Unemployment insurance The insurance program that in Canada is financed by compulsory contributions from employers and employees and from the general tax revenues of the federal government with benefits (income) made available to insured workers who are unable to find jobs.

Unemployment rate The percentage of the Civilian labour force (*see*) unemployed at any time.

Unfair competition Any practice that is employed by a Firm either to eliminate a rival or to block the entry of a new Firm into an Industry and that society (or a rival) believes to be an unacceptable method of achieving these ends.

Uninsurable risk An event, the occurrence of which is uncontrollable and unpredictable, that would result in a loss that cannot be avoided by purchasing insurance and must be assumed by an entrepreneur (*see* Entrepreneurial ability); sometimes called "uncertainty."

Union shop A place of employment at which the employer may hire either Labour union members or workers who are not members of the union but who must become members within a specified period of time or lose their jobs.

Unitary elasticity The Elasticity coefficient (*see*) is equal to one; the percentage change in the quantity (demanded or supplied) is equal to the percentage change in price.

Unit labour cost Labour costs per unit of output; equal to the Money wage rate (*see*) divided by the Average product (*see*) of labour.

Unlimited liability Absence of any limit on the maximum amount that may be lost by an individual and that the individual may become legally required to pay; the maximum amount that may be lost and that a sole proprietor or partner may be required to pay.

Unlimited wants The insatiable desire of consumers (people) for goods and services that will give them pleasure or satisfaction.

Unplanned investment Actual investment less Planned investment; increases or decreases in the inventories of business firms that result from production greater than or less than sales.

Unprosperous industry (*See* Declining industry.)

Urban sprawl The movement of people and firms from the inner city and into the suburbs of a metropolitan area and the resulting expansion of the geographic area of the metropolitan area.

User charge A price paid by those who use a facility that covers the full cost of using the facility.

Utility The want-satisfying power of a good or service; the satisfaction or pleasure a consumer obtains from the consumption of a good or service (or from the consumption of a collection of goods and services).

Utility-maximizing rule To obtain the greatest Utility (*see*) the consumer should allocate Money income so that the last dollar spent on each good or service yields the same Marginal utility (*see*); so that the Marginal utility of each good or service divided by its price is the same for all goods and services.

Value added The value of the product sold by a Firm less the value of the goods (materials) purchased and used by the Firm to produce the product; and equal to the revenue which can be used for Wages, rent, interest, and profits.

Value-added tax A tax imposed upon the difference between the value of the goods sold by a firm and the value of the goods purchased by the firm from other firms.

Value judgment Opinion of what is desirable or undesirable; belief regarding what ought or ought not to be (regarding what is right or just and wrong or unjust).

Value of money The quantity of goods and services for which a unit of money (a dollar) can be exchanged; the purchasing power of a unit of money; the reciprocal of the Price level.

Variable cost A cost that, in total, increases (decreases) when the firm increases (decreases) its output; the cost of Variable resources (*see*).

Variable resource Any resource employed by a firm the quantity of which can be increased or decreased (varied).

VAT Value-added tax (*see*).

Vault cash The Currency (*see*) a bank has in its safe (vault) and cash drawers; till money.

Velocity of money The number of times per year the average dollar in the Money supply (*see*) is spent for Final goods and services (*see*).

VERs (*See* Voluntary export restrictions.)

Voluntary export restrictions The limitation by firms of their exports to particular foreign nations in order to avoid the erection of other trade barriers by the foreign nations.

Vertical combination A group of Plants (*see*) engaged in different stages of the production of a final product and owned by a single Firm (*see*).

Vertical merger The merger of one or more Firms engaged in different stages of the production of a final product into a single Firm (*see*).

Wage The price paid for Labour [for the use or services of Labour (*see*)] per unit of time (per hour, per day, and so on).

Wage differential The difference between the Wage (*see*) received by one worker or group of workers and that received by another worker or group of workers.

Wage discrimination The payment to women (or minority groups) of a wage lower than that paid to men (or established groups) for doing the same work.

Wage guidepost Wages (*see*) in all industries in the economy should increase at an annual rate equal to the rate of increase in the Average product (*see*) of Labour in the economy.

Wage-price controls A Wage-price policy (*see*) that legally fixes the maximum amounts by which Wages (*see*) and prices may be increased in any period of time.

Wage-price guideposts A Wage-price policy (*see*) that depends upon the voluntary co-operation of Labour unions and business firms.

Wage-price inflationary spiral Increases in wages rates that bring about increases in prices, which in turn result in further increases in wage rates and in prices.

Wage-price policy Government policy that attempts to alter the behaviour of Labour unions and business firms in order to make their Wage and price decisions more nearly compatible with the goals of Full employment and stable prices.

Wage-push inflation The inflation that results when Labour unions demand and business firms grant higher Wages to workers in excess of the rate of Productivity (*see*) increase.

Wage rate (*See* Wages.)

Wages The income of those who supply the economy with Labour (*see*).

Wagner Act (U.S.) The federal Act of 1935 that established the National Labor Relations Board, guaranteed the rights of Labour unions to organize and to bargain collectively with employers, and listed and prohibited a number of unfair labour practices by employers.

Wastes of monopolistic competition The waste of economic resources that is the result of producing an output at which price is greater than marginal cost and average cost is greater than the minimum average cost.

Welfare programs (*See* Public assistance programs.)

(The) "will to develop" Wanting economic growth strongly enough to change from old to new ways of doing things.

World Bank A bank supported by 135 nations, which lends (and guarantees loans) to underdeveloped nations to assist them to grow; formally, the International Bank for Reconstruction and Development.

X-inefficiency Failure to produce any given output at the lowest average (and total) cost possible.

Yellow-dog contract The (now illegal) contract in which an employee agrees when he or she accepts employment with a firm that he or she will not become a member of a Labour union while employed by the Firm.

ZEG Zero economic growth; no Economic growth (*see*).

ZPG Zero population growth; no increase in the population of an economy (in the population of the world).